Rank and Gravity

THE LIFE
of
General John Armstrong
of
CARLISLE

William W. Betts, Jr.

HERITAGE BOOKS
2011

HERITAGE BOOKS
AN IMPRINT OF HERITAGE BOOKS, INC.

Books, CDs, and more—Worldwide

For our listing of thousands of titles see our website
at
www.HeritageBooks.com

Published 2011 by
HERITAGE BOOKS, INC.
Publishing Division
100 Railroad Ave. #104
Westminster, Maryland 21157

Copyright © 2011 William W. Betts, Jr.

Other Heritage Books by the author:
Bombardier John Harris and the Rivers of the Revolution

All rights reserved. No part of this book may be reproduced or transmitted in any form or by any means, electronic or mechanical, including photocopying, recording or by any information storage and retrieval system without written permission from the author, except for the inclusion of brief quotations in a review.

International Standard Book Numbers
Paperbound: 978-0-7884-5273-4
Clothbound: 978-0-7884-8600-5

*for Tom,
without whom* . . . .

Contents

A Prefatory Note v
Acknowledgments vii
Order of Events xi

PART ONE: THE PIONEER xvii

Chapter I: The Scotch-Irish 1
Chapter II: The Armstrongs 7
Chapter III: The Cumberland Valley 15
Chapter IV: Carlisle 21
Chapter V: A Road for Braddock 31
Chapter VI: Defending the Frontier 43
Chapter VII: Fort Granville 63
Chapter VIII: The Kittanning Expedition 77
Chapter IX: Fort Loudoun 111
Chapter X: The Forbes Expedition 133
Chapter XI: Bouquet and the Roads West 203
Chapter XII: Pontiac's War 231
Chapter XIII: The Susquehanna Expedition 253
Chapter XIV: The Conestoga Massacre 263
Chapter XV: The Black Boys 279
Chapter XVI: The Frederick Stump Murders 287
Chapter XVII: The Surveyor 311
Chapter XVIIII: The Presbyterian Church 327
Chapter XIX: Rebeckah 339

PART TWO: THE PATRIOT 349

Chapter XX: The Siege of Charleston 351
Chapter XXI: The Brandywine 385
Chapter XXII: Germantown 411
Chapter XXIII: Whitemarsh 425
Chapter XXIV: Valley Forge Winter 435
Chapter XXV: The Continental Congress 459
Chapter XXVI: Dickinson College 487
Chapter XXVII: Last Days 521

Afterword	531
Appendix: Letter of General John Armstrong to his son James	541
Image Credits	543
Works Consulted	545
Notes	563
Index	621

A Prefatory Note

Best known as the "first citizen of Carlisle" and as the "hero of Kittanning," General John Armstrong played a prominent role in the colonial settlement of Pennsylvania and in the birth of the nation. He enjoyed significant and consequential associations with the Provincial proprietors John Penn and Thomas Penn, and with Governors Robert Hunter Morris, William Denny, James Hamilton, Thomas Wharton, Jr., and Joseph Reed. His productive relationships included also Benjamin Franklin, Provincial Secretary Richard Peters, Dr. Benjamin Rush, John Dickinson, John Hancock, Henry Bouquet, and the Generals John Forbes, Horatio Gates, Charles Lee, Hugh Mercer, William Irvine, and Richard Butler. He was a warm and close friend of George Washington for almost forty years, and was a principal influence in the decision made by Washington to accept the Presidency of the United States.

His life is distinguished by his Scotch-Irish ancestry, by his devotion to the Presbyterian Church, by his military commands in the Pennsylvania militia forces and in the Continental Army, by his service to Pennsylvania as Assemblyman, surveyor and magistrate. And, as an energetic and committed member of the Second Continental Congress, he helped much to forward through its infancy the United States of America.

Because he suffered great personal loss at the hands of the Delawares and the Shawnee Indians, and was witness to unspeakable atrocities, he was never quite able to adopt the Quaker attitude toward the native American Indians. Instead Armstrong played a major role in the defense of the Pennsylvania frontier and in opening a gateway to the west.

A familiar figure on the streets of Carlisle, on the farms of Cumberland County, in the church, and in the halls of Congress, "the old General," while in trouble from time to time, as the earnestly active always are, was dearly loved by those who knew him well. When death came to him, on March 9, 1795, it came to a man whose entire life had been one of service—to his family, to his community, to his Pennsylvania, to his country, and to his Presbyterian God.

Acknowledgments

The author's childhood years were enjoyed along Little Clearfield Creek and on the banks of the West Branch of the Susquehanna River in a community that had appeared at the site of a series of Indian villages, the most recent and best known of which was the Delaware town of Chinklacamoose. But in all that time this youngster never heard the name John Armstrong, nor was ever made aware that a man by that name had marched an anti-Indian army through the Pennsylvania wilderness just a little south of Chinklacamoose.

When at the most welcome close of World War II, I enrolled in the college of my choice, Dickinson College, in Carlisle, Pennsylvania, I was, like all veterans, in such a hurry to get past my education, to make up for "lost time," I learned little of the history of Carlisle or of the College. Indeed, I saw very little of the community, my trips "downtown" always terminating at a favorite watering place, like the Jimmy Wilson Hotel, or the Molly Pitcher, or the Chocolate Shop. I never got to the Courthouse, or to the First Presbyterian Church, or even to the "Old Graveyard," presided over by the Molly Pitcher monument. Certainly I never heard the name of one of the principal founders of the College, John Armstrong.

In the 1960s and '70s, as I rummaged through the farm fields of the Great Island, near Lock Haven on the West Branch of the Susquehanna, in search of artifacts, the sense of a long-ago Indian civilization washed warmly over me. On one afternoon in one of those glorious summer days, as I plucked a beautiful red jasper projectile from the glistening rain-wet soil, a vivid image of the village's flintknapper, an ancient warrior plying his art, appeared in my mind's eye. But I did not know then that a pioneer by the name of John Armstrong, some two hundred years ago, had frightened the Delaware Indians from this very ground.

For nearly forty years I taught the English language and literature in college classroom buildings reposing precisely on the trail that the Armstrong force had followed on its way to the Delaware town known as Kittanning, on the Allegheny River, twenty-five miles to my west. As I traveled "the road to Kittanning" on my way to and from Pittsburgh, of course I crossed many times the Allegheny River at the site of the famous battle, having perceived along the way historical markers designating "Armstrong County" and "Blanket Hill" and "Kittanning, site of . . . ." After all these years, and approaching "retirement," I was finally beginning to learn of General John Armstrong. With my interest piqued at last, I resolved an old man's resolve to discover all I could about this shadow who had traveled in and out with me. And, though with an old man's natural anxiety about a "project," I ventured on still a bigger resolve—to put it all together in one place. I knew that I would need help. Happily, help was close at hand.

    I found myself a captive of the Pennsylvania Room (Special Collections) at the Stapleton Library on the campus of Indiana University of Pennsylvania, and was enthusiastically supplied by the staff (notably Dr. Theresa McDevitt, Jean Popovich, Michelle Corcoran, and Daniel Shively) with all of the available resources that led to an understanding of the life of General John Armstrong. For genealogy and pioneer life in Carlisle and Armstrong's will and family records I am much indebted to Ms. Debbie Miller and the Cumberland County Historical Society. And I owe a great deal to the enthusiasm and instincts of the indefatigable Jack Mullen, my Carlisle tour guide, and to Bill King and Armstrong County Commissioner James Scahill, my Kittanning tour guides, to Kelly Linn, my Pittsburgh researcher, as well as to many members of the large Armstrong family, like Arthur Brockie of Melbourne Florida, and genealogists Raymond Bell, of Washington, Pa., and John Armstrong Herman of Harrisburg. A big boost to my research was provided by my fellow Dickinsonian, the late Dr. Robert Crist, whose dissertation produced for The Pennsylvania State University, *John Armstrong, Proprietary Man*, cut the highway and paved it well. I am very grateful, too, to Thomas Betts of Home, Pa., for along-the-way graphics and formatting. And I acknowledge gratefully the earlier work of those historians whose accounts of Armstrong in one event or another have contributed so much to the impression I have come to, like George Donehoo, William Albert Hunter, Wayland Dunaway, Frederic Godcharles, Dennis McIlnay, Israel Daniel Rupp, Sylvester Stevens, Paul Wallace, and Conway Phelps Wing.

And finally to the Dickinson College Archivist, James Gerencser, without whose encouragement and very real help with materials this life of Armstrong never would have appeared. Ms. Deborah Ege and Ms. Malinda Triller of his staff were able to produce not only many of the surveying records and business papers left by Armstrong, but also the voluminous and well organized notes taken by Dr. Crist in the course of his research and left to the College.

To all of these, and to many other very helpful librarians and earlier commentators, the present writer expresses his gratitude and urges the hope that what follows is an accurate and faithful portrait of a life that meant a great deal to Carlisle, to Pennsylvania, and to the United States.

Order of Events

Birth of John Armstrong	October 13, 1717
Birth of Rebeckah Armstrong	May 2, 1719
Walking Purchase	September 19, 1737
John Armstrong marries Rebeckah Armstrong	November, 1746
Birth of son James	August 29, 1748
Armstrong family to Carlisle	Summer, 1750
Armstrong made Deputy Surveyor for the Province	October 8, 1750
Carlisle laid out by Nicholas Scull	Summer, 1751
Carlisle made County Seat	1751
Construction of Fort Lowther, at Carlisle	May, 1753 - fall, 1756
Carlisle Indian conference	October 1-3, 1753
Armstrong missions to Connecticut	March, 1754; November-December, 1754
French build Fort Duquesne	April, 1754
Armstrong surveys Braddock supply road	March-July, 1755
Braddock Expedition	Summer, 1755
Defeat of General Braddock on the Monongahela	July 9, 1755
Tragedy at the Great Cove	November 1, 1755
Construction of Fort Lyttleton	1755-56

Carlisle Indian conference	January 15-22, 1756
Construction of Fort Shirley	1756
Armstrong commissioned Lt. Colonel, Pa. Militia	May 11, 1756
Fall of Fort Granville	July 30, 1756
William Denny becomes Lt. Governor of Pennsylvania	August, 1756
Kittanning Expedition	August 30 - September 8, 1756
Grand Council at Easton	November 8-17, 1756
Construction of Fort Loudon (by Armstrong)	Winter, 1756
Armstrong receives hero's welcome in Philadelphia; "Kittanning Destroyed" Medal struck	January 5, 1757
Forbes Expedition	March 1, 1758 - February 1, 1759
Armstrong commissioned Colonel, appointed Commanding Officer of Pennsylvania's First Battalion in the Forbes Army	May 27, 1758
Construction of Fort Bedford	June, 1758
Battle of Grant's Hill	September 14, 1758
Fort Ligonier assaulted	October 12, 1758
Fort Duquesne abandoned by French	November 24-26, 1758

Birth of John Armstrong, Jr.	November 25, 1758
Bouquet Expedition to Presque Isle	June-July, 1760
Armstrong re-surveys town of Carlisle	1762
Armstrong's office destroyed by fire	1763
Pontiac's War	1763-1766
Bouquet Expedition to the relief of Fort Pitt	Summer 1763
Battle of Bushy Run (Edge Hill)	August 5-6, 1763
Siege of Fort Pitt lifted	August 10, 1763
Armstrong Expedition against the Indian towns of the West Branch of the Susquehanna	Sept. 30, 1763
Paxtang (Conestoga) massacres	December 13, 27, 1763
Enoch Brown and his pupils murdered	July 26, 1764
Bouquet's Expedition to the Ohio Indians	August 5 - October 10, 1764
Black Boys' Rebellion	Summer, 1765
Frederick Stump murders	January 10, 1768
Meeting in Carlisle to express sympathy for the citizens of Boston	July 12, 1774

Congress declares war on Great Britain	May 10, 1775
Armstrong commissioned Brigadier General in the Continental Army	March 1, 1776
Armstrong arrives in Charleston, S.C.	May 3, 1776
Siege of Charleston	May 31- July 1, 1776
Armstrong resigns commission in the Continental Army	April 2, 1777
Armstrong appointed Brigadier General of Pennsylvania militia	April 4, 1777
Armstrong appointed Major General of Pennsylvania militia forces	May 4, 1777
Armstrong commands Pennsylvania militia at Brandywine	September 11, 1777
Armstrong commands Pennsylvania militia at the Battle of Germantown	October 4, 1777
Armstrong at Whitemarsh	December 4-8, 1777
Armstrong at Council at Valley Forge	May 8, 1778
Sinking Spring Valley Conspiracy	April 11, 1778
Raid on Cherry Valley	November 11, 1778

Armstrong elected to Continental Congress	November 20, 1778
Fort Armstrong built near Kittanning	June, 1779
General John Sullivan campaign against the Senecas	July 31 - October 7, 1779
Armstrong re-elected to Continental Congress	November 12, 1779
British capture Charleston, S. C.	May 12, 1780
Articles of Confederation adopted	March 2, 1781
Carlisle incorporated	April 13, 1782
The Treaty of Paris	September 3, 1783
Dickinson College chartered	September 9, 1783
George Washington accepts Presidency	April 14, 1789
General Josiah Harmar defeated by the Miami war-chief Little Turtle and the Ohio Indians in the Maumee Valley	October 20-22, 1790
General Arthur St. Clair defeated by Little Turtle on the Wabash River	November 4, 1791
Battle of Fallen Timbers	August 20, 1794
Death of John Armstrong (age 77)	March 9, 1795
Treaty of Greenville	August 7, 1795
Death of Rebeckah Armstrong (age 77)	November 16, 1797

Armstrong County created, named for John Armstrong	March 12, 1800
Death of Dr. James Armstrong (age 79)	May 6, 1828
Death of John Armstrong, Jr. (age 84)	April 1, 1843

PART ONE

THE PIONEER

I

THE SCOTCH-IRISH

Among the most beautiful bowers of the whole world is the Emerald Isle, by some known as Ireland, and by the poets as Erin. With the gently flowing river Shannon, the Liffey and the Lee, and the enchanting Killarney lakes, and the embracing highlands known as Donegal, and Antrim, Connemara, and Kerry; and with its lovely seascapes and its plains of brilliant green grass, the island delivers a constant charm to all who there reside.

One of the most awesome sections of this lovely country is the region known as Ulster, in the extreme north, celebrated, rightly, for its idyllic, pastoral beauty. Why, ask the bewildered, would anyone ever elect to depart this fairyland?

Why, indeed, was the young man known as John Armstrong, in 1746, standing on the frontier edge of civilization, in a totally strange world, contemplating a vast and forbidding wilderness? Perhaps he was deranged?

But he could hardly be mad, for he was but one of a momentous, steady emigration from Ulster during the most of the 18th century. Indeed, Armstrong and his Scotch-Irish fellows had four very good reasons for departing their homeland. The movement has been well chronicled.[1]

The historian Wayland Dunaway cites the principal reasons for the massive emigration. He regards as the most "potent," as well as the most "constant" cause, as one might suppose, economics. The biggest blow to economic security was felt when there was passed, in 1699, an act that forbade the exportation of Irish wool products except to England itself and to Wales. As the wool industry was the chief source of revenue for the Irish, this action delivered an insufferable hurt.

Another cause that is economic was the unconscionable raise in rents, which were as much as tripled. Exacted by the English landlords when the original leases on the farmlands began to expire, about the year 1717, the practice was called, derisively, "absentee landlordism." The effect was to render farming no longer profitable.

Besides all this, the Irish in 1727 and again in 1740 suffered exhausting periods of famine. And when later in the century the linen industry simply collapsed, a great swelling in emigration occurred.

But the causes were not all economic. The Established Church of Ireland was the Church of England. The Ulster Scots were almost 100% Presbyterian. Trouble. The intolerance took the form of persecution and oppression. The Presbyterian Ulster Scots left Ireland in droves.

On top of all this, there was, according to Dunaway, from early in the century a very real political cause. It had its most severe expression in the Test Act of 1704, which disqualified the Ulster Scots from holding any political office or commission in the army. A young Scotch-Irishman, like a John Armstrong, who aspired for a military career or office as a magistrate or judge, was simply being told to forget it.

Still another cause for the almost wholesale emigration of the Ulster Scotch-Irish, especially during the middle years of the eighteenth century, though surely a lesser one, was the "indentured servant" system. In return for service for an agreed upon number of years, shipmasters would provide transportation to the New World at no other fee to the passenger. Well advertised by merchants and ship captains, it became a popular program and accounts for some numbers in the exodus. Indeed, it has been calculated that in the early years of the 18th century "not one in ten Ulster immigrants" had the means to pay the passage fare.[2]

Dunaway cites James Anthony Froude's very telling capsule account. It well explains the presence of John Armstrong in the New World:

Men of spirit and energy refused to remain in a country where they were held unfit to receive the rights of citizens.... Flights of Protestant settlers had been driven out earlier in the century by the idiocy of the bishops... bigotry, commercial jealousy, and modern landlordism had combined to do their worst against the Ulster settlement.... Vexed with suits in ecclesiastical courts, forbidden to educate their children in their own faith, treated as dangerous in a state which but for them would have had no existence, and associated with Papists in an Act of Parliament which deprived them of their civil rights, the most earnest of them at length abandoned the unthankful service. They saw at last the liberties for which their fathers had fought were not to be theirs in Ireland.... During the first half of the eighteenth century, Down, Antrim, Armagh, and Derry were emptied of their Protestant families ....[3]

Scotch-Irish (or Scots-Irish) is the term used for those peoples of Scotch ancestry who had been born or were living in Northern Ireland at the time of the great 18th-century emigration to America. Annual departures of these people for the years 1717-1775 averaged 3000-4000.[4] It has been estimated that during these years "about a quarter of a million people . . . left Ulster in Northern Ireland."[5] One of these was the young John Armstrong.

And just what sort of haven were these people seeking? Of course they were en route to the New World, to colonial America. Some made their new homes in South Carolina, some in Maryland, some in New Jersey, and just a very few (for the colony was far from cordial) in Massachusetts. But most settled in Pennsylvania, and the reasons were many.

What the first Scotch-Irish settlers were reporting to their families back home was that they had found a "paradise." They had discovered precisely what they had been denied in Ulster: absolute freedom to practice the Presbyterian religious beliefs that were so important to them, and a climate that favored earnest education. These first immigrants assured their friends and family members also that the political arena was unrestricted and open. Besides, the fertile land and the abundant springs meant a rewarding farm life, for which most of the Scotch-Irish hungered. And then there was the land itself! Land was readily available. Some immigrants were even reporting that the land was "free." Certainly it was true that the Penns were encouraging settlement with promises of easy land and a prosperous future.

The Scotch-Irish were ready to oblige. And the Quaker James Logan, who had arrived in Philadelphia with William Penn on his second visit, and had become Secretary to the Provincial Council, was very quick to welcome them. He regarded them as natural frontiersmen, used to wrestling with the land. But so many appeared that by 1729 he experienced a change of heart and began to wonder whether Ireland were not sending "all of its inhabitants thither." He declared fearfully that "If they continue to come they will make themselves proprietors of the Province." [6]

Just exactly what kind of person was this Scotch-Irishman or woman who was coming to Pennsylvania? Many, it is well documented, provided some trouble for the Land Office and for the tax collectors, as they tended to "squat" upon the land and assume rights for which they had no deed or warrant, Logan declaring that they seemed to feel that "it was against the law of God and nature that so much land should be idle, while so many Christians wanted it to labor on, and to raise their bread." [7] And, clearly, the Scotch-Irish, men and women alike, could be exasperatingly stubborn and unyielding.

But except for the additional complaint that they were sometimes "unruly" (Logan insisting that "five Scotch-Irish families in a settlement give me more trouble than fifty of any other people") and that they were "rough" with the Indians, characterizations are extremely complimentary. The terms that one hears today for the Scotch-Irish are precisely those that have been employed in accounting for the early settlers of Pennsylvania. The most prevalent epithet in any profile is "hardy." And, indeed, they were a hardy people, so long accustomed to difficult times that they could not only endure trial and deprivation but do so impressively. They were self-sufficient and very industrious. Always they have relished politics, and always the Scotch-Irish have been very high on education. For their social habits they enjoyed an enviable reputation, considered, as they were, to be genuinely "cordial" and "hospitable."

Although one might find a Baptist here and there among them, or even an Episcopalian, or a Quaker, they are almost universally Presbyterian, and devout in their faith. Historically, they have felt a close kinship to the soil, preferring farming as an occupation. These settlers were plain-living and God-fearing. They did not want for courage, and the proof of that is everywhere in their ancestry, in their frontier trials with the Indians and the French, and in their heroism in the battles of the Revolution. They have always, because of their Scots blood, been a frugal people, and it may be the Scotch in them, too, which makes them a consciously moral and scrupulous people, inclined to the sober and serious manner of life. They expected their ministers to be stern in the pulpit, and they relished the "fire and brimstone" sermons that promised not only damnation but "eternal" damnation. Some analysts of their character credit their Irish blood for the habit of turning their fields of grain into rye whiskey; these same analysts insist that it is their Scots blood which discourages the flow of whiskey on the Sabbath.

About the Indians. There is no question that the Scotch-Irish settlers of Pennsylvania, frontier people that they were, did not like Indians. Hard put as they were to defend their farms and their homes and their families, and suffering unspeakable barbarities from raiding parties, they cherished no illusions about the Shawnee and the Delaware, whom they preferred to label "savages." Dunaway, while noting that "while others might seek to invest the Indian with romance and to descant at length upon the primal virtues of the 'noble savage,' to the Scotch-Irishman he seemed bloodthirsty, cruel and treacherous." [8] And B. J. Witherow has presented the Scotch-Irish view of the native American Indians thus: "The Indian has a dislike, well-nigh unconquerable, to all labor; he can with difficulty be confined within limits . . . . His method of making war is never open and manly. He skulks in ravines, behind rocks and trees; he creeps out in the night and sets fire to houses and barns; he shoots down, from behind a fence, the ploughman in his furrow; he scalps the woman at the spring, and the children by the roadside, with their little hands full of berries. He lounges about, idle and dirty, and forces the women of his tribe to do all the work. He is proud as Lucifer, and yet will beg like the lazzaroni." [9]

And at least one historian credits the Scotch-Irish for the insistence that "The only good Indian is a dead Indian."[10]

The attitude of the Scotch-Irish is clearly antithetical to that of the Quakers. It must be remembered that the Quakers lived in Philadelphia, and in the city regions of New Jersey. They did not experience the frontier ravages, indeed were rarely witness to anything like what is described above. Certainly the Quakers and the Moravians deserve great credit for the peaceful co-existence which characterized colonial Pennsylvania for so long a time. That they sent representatives to the treaty sessions to make certain that the Indians were being treated fairly is commendable. During the time the Quakers controlled the Pennsylvania Assembly the settlers were held in check. But when the Quakers lost control of the Assembly, everything changed.

This profile of the Scotch-Irish who settled southeastern Pennsylvania is presented here for the reason that the subject of this narrative is first and foremost a Scotch-Irishman. John Armstrong is a Scotch-Irishman true-blue and through and through.

II

THE ARMSTRONGS

When the young John Armstrong set foot on the Delaware River shore, he delivered to the New World a most impressive ancestry. The history of the Armstrong family tree with its many branches reaching out across the centuries and with its roots reaching deeply into the soils of Scotland and Denmark is a rich and storied one. It includes heroic episodes and dramatic events, moving tragedy and high adventure. The history is made entertaining by scores of popular ballads which attend the narrative, many featuring Johnny (or Johnie) Armstrong. The family tree has at its heart the gentle King Duncan of the 11th century, him who was murdered by Macbeth. And there is Siward, too, the Norseman, who, called "The Armstrong," descended from the Royal House of Denmark.

One of the most celebrated members of the Armstrong clan is the young surveyor John Armstrong who showed up in the American wilderness of Pennsylvania in the eighteenth century. He was born in Brookeborough (often Brookborough or Brookboro) Parish, County Fermanagh, in the northernmost and most prosperous and industrious area of Ireland, Ulster. He came into the world on October 13, 1717.[1]

He was born to James Armstrong of Terwinney, who had been born ca.1684 and was to die at Terwinney in 1745, and to Mary Campbell, who had been married to James, April 26, 1704.[2] Both of John's parents could boast a rich Scotch ancestry.

John's father's father was Edward Armstrong of Terwinney, and it was his father, William, known as "Christie's Will," who in 1630 fled from Scotland, crossing the border into the Fermanagh County of Ireland. William was the grandson of John (of Gilnockie) Armstrong, the highly celebrated "Johnie Armstrong," whose exploits as a border outlaw and whose tragic death produced the touching folk ballad which exists in so many versions.

John of Gilnockie was the son of Thomas Armstrong, of the 15th century, the Lord of Maingertoun (Mangerton). And the ancestry retreats eagerly all the way back through King Duncan of the 11th century Scotland to his father-in-law, Siward the Norseman,[3] who died in 1055.

According to *Chronicles of the Armstrongs*, the John Armstrong who arrived in Pennsylvania in the fourth or fifth decade of the 18th century had at least one sister and four brothers. But according to Raymond Bell, who produced a genealogy for the Cumberland County Historical Society, the brothers and sisters numbered ten: Edward of Terwinney, the oldest, who did not come to America; James, who died by drowning in Juniata County in 1774; George, who served in the militia forces with brother John, and who lived in the Bedford region until his death; William, who lived for a time in Carlisle, but eventually on a farm near Fort Granville, and also served in the militia and became a surveyor in what is today Mifflin County; Andrew, who remained in Ireland (but whose son James came to America under John Armstrong's patronage);[4] Margaret, who came to Pennsylvania in 1763 as the wife of John Lyon;[5] Ann, who was married to a William Graham and lived in what is today Juniata County, and there had a child killed by the Indians; Rebecca, who married James Turner on November 1, 1759, and lived in Chester County; Andro, a sister who married Lieutenant Graydon and stayed on in Ireland; and another sister, who is mentioned in the Cumberland County Deed Book (16-397) as the wife of Thomas McCord, of present Mifflin

~ *The Armstrongs* ~

County.[6]

But the genealogy for the Armstrongs in colonial Pennsylvania is difficult to work out. By 1750, when almost all of the settler families of Lancaster and York and the new Cumberland County were Scotch-Irish, the name Armstrong was everywhere. By 1768, in the Cumberland Valley alone (!), there could be counted five by the name of William, four by the name of James, three named John, two named Thomas, two named George, and also an Alexander, Andrew, Joseph, and Robert.[7]

Those Armstrongs who left Ulster with Pennsylvania on their mind at one of the principal ports of the Island booked passage for the long trip across the big water to the Delaware River. In Benjamin Franklin's *Pennsylvania Gazette* for November 20, 1729, there appeared portions of a letter printed in a London newspaper noting that "There is gone and to go this Summer from this port [Londonderry] Twenty-five Sail of Ships, who carry each, from One Hundred and twenty to One Hundred and forty Passengers to America." The *Gazette* also reported that "last year" (1728) there arrived in New Castle 4500 persons, "chiefly from Ireland." At some ports in America during these years sailing ships were arriving every two or three days for weeks at a time.

The immigrants would disembark each with a modest bedroll which included a change of clothes (but not a second hat or pair of shoes), a Bible and such other personal necessities as could be accommodated. The bundle served as a pillow for its owner as he or she lay on the open deck or in the crowded quarters below. As the voyage was a very long one, the family of four which had left Ulster sometimes arrived on the Delaware as a family of five.

It is not known by what route John Armstrong came to the shores of America, nor indeed is it known exactly on what date he arrived, or how many of his family were in his company. The Ulster emigrant ports were (besides Londonderry), Newry, Larne, Portrush, and Belfast. It may be presumed that he boarded ship at Belfast, as it had by 1745 become the chief port of embarkation for those Ulster Scots bound for the New World. It may be presumed also, for his family was fairly well-to-do, that he did not make the passage as an indentured person. The voyage would require as long as seven weeks, depending upon winds, and was likely to be extremely perilous. Armstrong, together with probably one hundred fellow passengers, most likely came ashore at New Castle or Lewes on the Delaware.

Just exactly when this was may never be determined. Early commentators had his arrival as early as 1737, when he would be nineteen or twenty years old. *Chronicles of the Armstrongs* is quite specific. It has John Armstrong coming to Pennsylvania with his brother William and settling on 200 acres of land "west of the Susquehanna on Feb. 13, 1737." And, indeed, earliest warrant for land to a John Armstrong in any of the first five Pennsylvania counties as recorded in the Land Records is Warrant # A-46, which is dated April 26, 1738, and awarded said Armstrong 250 acres in Paxtang Twp., Lancaster County. This warrant was directed to Benjamin Eastburn, Surveyor General.[8]

But partly because there is no colonial mention of *the* John Armstrong for the years 1737-1744, and largely because of the biographical sketches produced by the General's grandson, it is not thought that these acres were his. It may very well be that the John Armstrong to whom this land was warranted is the John Armstrong who was murdered by the Indian Musmeelin at Jack's Narrows on the Juniata in 1744 in a dispute over pelts and a horse.[9]

The popular opinion now is that the surveyor John Armstrong arrived at some time during the years 1744-46, most likely shortly after the death of his father James (May, 1745), and perhaps even because of it.[10]

It is to be regretted also that there is no record of Armstrong's first impression of the American soil. But he likely regarded the land just as a surveyor would take it in. In his mind's eye the vast forests vanished. In their place he envisioned sprawling farms, each with a large central house, a barn and outbuildings, and fields of grain, and orchards. He perceived tidy settlements, composed of quaint homes of all descriptions, neatly ordered on their well defined lots.

What is known definitely is the date and site of his marriage. As a Pennsylvania license discloses, John Armstrong was married to Rebecca (spelled variously) Lyon in November of 1746 at New Castle, in the Lower Counties. For a long time it was thought that because she carried the name Lyon, she was the daughter of William Lyon, a prosperous landowner in the Ulster region of Ireland. But Rebecca was actually an Armstrong, the daughter of Archibald Armstrong, who had come to America, to New Castle (in present Delaware) at some time in 1745 (when it is known he paid taxes), or earlier, from Aghalurgher Parish, in Fermanagh, only thirteen miles from John Armstrong's childhood home.[11] She was, supposedly, the widow of a Lyon, but nothing is known of him; and her maiden name was definitely Armstrong. As Raymond Bell points out, "Proof of her birth name is to be found in the will of Archibald Armstrong, of Christiana Hundred, New Castle County, Delaware, written 21 August 1767, where he names as a beneficiary 'my beloved Daughter, wife to my beloved son in law Coll: John Armstrong.'"[12] Further substantiation of her birth name comes in a deed, 23 May 1775, which names "Rebecca, wife of Colonel John Armstrong, one of the heirs of her brother Edward Armstrong."[13] And there is the marriage license itself, dated November 1746.[14] And, if further proof were needed, a 1773 letter of Armstrong to his son James provides it. In this letter Armstrong reminds James that his mother "in about a week" will be setting out "to your grandfather's."[15] The "grandfather" here is certainly seventy-seven-year-old Archibald Armstrong, who was then living in New Castle.

Archibald Armstrong had four other children: William, the first born, who lived on White Clay Creek; John, who was married to Mary Springer, and had three children (Archibald, James, and William), and died on Christmas Day, 1806; the third-born, Margaret, who on March 5, 1759, married the Reverend George Duffield of Carlisle; and the unmarried Edward, who was killed in the defense of Fort Granville.

It is not known *exactly* when the wedding occurred, as the *Pennsylvania Archives* provide only "November, 1746" as the date of the marriage of John Armstrong to Rebecca Armstrong.[16] It may be presumed that Armstrong had been visiting his relatives (the family of Archibald Armstrong, which included his widowed daughter Rebeckah Lyon) in New Castle off and on from his nearby farm. The bride was twenty-seven years old, the groom twenty-nine, and likely they are close cousins.

It is not known either where Armstrong was living at the

time of the marriage, but apparently he was already an industrious and prosperous farmer-surveyor. In any case, in a time not long after the wedding, the couple were settled into housekeeping on a farm in the Marsh Creek settlement of that portion of Lancaster County which would become York County and then Adams County, not far from the home of the Mary Jemison family, near present Gettysburg, and in the shadows of South Mountain.[17] And it was on the farm here, on August 29, 1748, that their first son, James, was born.

At this time Rebeckah had in southeastern Pennsylvania, besides her father and her mother, Ann, in New Castle, her brothers Edward and William and John, and her sister Margaret, four members of her first husband's family, William (who was the same age as Rebeckah), Samuel, John, and James. The Lyons too were close, William living near Fort Granville, and James near Patterson's. Seven of John Armstrong's brothers and sisters, with their families would eventually be living in southeastern Pennsylvania. Some cousins from both the Lyons and the Armstrongs rounded out the clan.

It was not long after the birth to Rebeckah of little James Armstrong, just when York County was formed out of Lancaster, that Armstrong was named to the Provincial Assembly, which meant, as required, that he either owned fifty acres or could show fifty pounds.[18] On October 14, together with John Wright, he appeared in the State House in Philadelphia to represent the new county. Longtime Clerk of the House, Benjamin Franklin was elected Clerk "for the ensuing year," and James Hamilton was "Deputy Governor of His Majesty's Province."

As Assemblyman, Armstrong apparently was given no heavy assignment, serving on such committees as those to address the killing of deer out of season, and to inspect the Flour Act, and to amend the Shooting of Squirrels Act.

But he was not to represent York County long, for in the next year, Richard Peters, the Provincial Secretary, noting that the surveyor John Armstrong was "the most proper person to manage the Proprietary Affairs in and about Carlisle," persuaded him to leave Marsh Creek for Cumberland County. Though most reluctant to make the move, he did agree, because of "expectations . . . advantageous to him." [19]

And so the little family moved on to the just formed Cumberland County. And on October 8, 1750, John Armstrong was made Deputy Surveyor for the region. His immediate future would lie in service to the Proprietors in land management. The Land Office would open on February 3 (or 5), 1755, and Armstrong would before long operate out of his own office in Carlisle. Through his surveying and land management he steadily built a reputation for business and organization, and again he was called on, this time by the settlers of Cumberland County, to represent his people in the Assembly.[20]

III

THE CUMBERLAND VALLEY

By the Indians, to whom it was very dear, it was known as M'chewamisipu, "the river on which lie extensive flats." This is the North (or East) Branch of the Susquehanna. It flows west a little on its way out of the Iroquois country of New York, and then (except when angry) simply wanders east and south in a most leisurely manner. Its twin sister, known as the West Branch, flows east from its source at "Canoe Place" in western Pennsylvania some 150 miles, then abruptly turns south. Both branches for untold centuries have provided for the activity of Indian villages. At the site of the historic Indian town of Shamokin[1] the sisters clasp hands before striking out for the Chesapeake. The big river now embraces from the east the region which by the settlers was first called North Valley and was soon to be called the Cumberland Valley, and would be known affectionately as "Mother Cumberland."

And far to the west, just beyond the Tuscarora Mountain range, flows all the while the lovely blue Juniata (Tyunayate, "projecting rock").[2] The limpid waters of the Juniata carry the

Indian canoes north and then east and then for a little while south until they enter the larger stream, the Susquehanna. The Juniata thus provides a cradling arm for the other side of the Cumberland Valley.

The valley, so long and so justly celebrated for its many charms, lies between two great mountain ridges. The North Mountain was by the Indians given the reverent name *Kau-ta-tinchunk* (endless mountains). The South Mountain, with its serrated skyline, has always been even more beautiful than the North, especially in the fall of the year, when its maples, poplars, hickory, chestnut, elm and many kinds of oak radiate in a great panoply of vivid color.

It was to this region that the newly married John Armstrong came in the summer of 1750. He knew little of the land's first inhabitants. It would have startled him to learn that for hundreds and hundreds of years a people had traveled this valley, and that in fairly recent times temporary villages had been occupied.[3]

In fact, Armstrong and the early settlers knew little of the history of this land. But they did surely appreciate that William Penn the Founder of the province given his father by the King had to deal with a people already occupying the land. And they knew that William Penn and his heirs were determined to purchase from the Indians the land they had been given. And they had the impression that there had been little trouble with the Indians in Pennsylvania. From the time of Penn's first purchase of the land that would include Philadelphia and its environs, everybody understood that the land belonged to the Indians until purchased. The relationship of the Indians to the Quakers and the Quaker-controlled Assembly was a most amiable one, the Assembly lavishing upon the Indians all kinds of generous gifts. The sense of "brotherhood," for which the Quakers genuinely aspired, governed the colony.[4]

At the time the Armstrongs arrived in the Cumberland Valley, in 1750, except for a few small groups of Delawares in the region at the head of the Delaware Bay to the "Forks," where the Lehigh River flows in from the Blue Mountains, there were almost no Indians to be seen. The Indian presence in this region had ceased some thirty or forty years ago. The Susquehannocks, who had made their home near the broad water of the Delaware and had hunted the forests and fished the streams of the land between the rivers Susquehanna and Potomac, were vanished, dominated as they were by the aggressive tribes to be known as the Iroquois Federation. And the very few Delawares and Shawnees whom the settlers encountered were found to be most friendly.

Shortly before Armstrong's arrival in 1750 these lands of the North Valley had been purchased by the Penns, and, indeed, by as early as 1736 all Indian claims to the land in this area of Pennsylvania had been extinguished.[5]

Although no "official" licenses could be granted white settlers in the valley before purchase from the Indians, people did take up land much earlier. It is difficult to identify the first to make his home in the valley, but it may have been the trader James LeTort. Reputedly a great friend of the Shawnee Indians, LeTort, a French Hugenot, had, as early as 1713, been granted a license to trade. At that time he was living at Conestoga. At some time after that, but before 1719, he moved to Bonny Brook (Great Beaver Pond). He built his cabin precisely at the head of what has come to be known as LeTort's Spring, not far from the present site of Carlisle. From there, for some years, he conducted his trade, journeying well into the country west beyond the mountains.[6]

LeTort of course had no deed to the land he occupied. It was not for many years, sometime in 1733, that the heirs of William Penn, hoping to lure settlers and to compete successfully with the province of Maryland, commissioned Samuel Blunston, a member of the Assembly, to act as their agent, and provided him the authority to issue licenses to settlers arriving at the Delaware from Europe.

Other very early white settlers who assumed property without any deed or license, have been identified: Richard Parker, who located "two miles west of the present town of Carlisle in 1725"; James Macfarlane, one year later and some five miles farther to the west; Andrew Ralston, who built a home at the Big Spring that same year; and Tobias Hendricks in the succeeding year, three miles from the Susquehanna. Historians of the valley have determined that by the year 1731 some four hundred families had built homes in the North Valley, on land that still belonged to the Indians.⁷ And from this time on, great waves of immigrants, most from Ireland, began to settle in this valley, which by now had acquired a well-deserved reputation for scenic beauty, for fertile land, and for spring-fed waters. Water, of course, was a most attractive feature, and, not surprisingly, the first settlements (small clusters of homes) were to be found close to the truly lovely streams and springs known today as the Conodoguinet, the Yellow Breeches (called by the Indians "Minnimingo," or "Callapatscink" or "Callaptsing"), Big Spring, Middle Spring, Falling Spring (now Chambersburg), and the Conococheague, which in a very winding way wanders into the Potomac at Williamsport, Maryland, and which the Delaware Indians called the "Long Way, Indeed" stream.⁸

The first "official" settler, according to the Blunston License Book, was Robert Miller, who, on January 24, 1733, acquired a deed to 200 acres "at the head of Letorts Spring." ⁹ And a most notable early settler was George Croghan, the "Prince of Indian traders," who assumed property and settled near the present Silvers Spring, where he was to remain for almost ten years.¹⁰ By 1750, after some other great waves of immigration, one of which flooded the Juniata Valley, the Cumberland Valley could boast a very substantial population, almost exclusively Scotch-Irish. Indeed, it has been estimated that in 1751, "when there were about five thousand people in the Valley, all except fifty families were either Scotch or Scotch-Irish, principally the latter." ¹¹

Although John Armstrong had not at first been happy with the move he had been requested to make, he must have been much impressed by his view of the North Valley when he led his wife with infant James into this region. Surely he thrilled to the purple mountain ridges awash in the swirling mists of the early morning. Surely he took *some* delight in the beautiful white limestone which here and there and everywhere emerged from the soil.¹² And as the little family moved deeper into the valley, he may even have approached rapture at the sight of the cold, clear, alkaline, spring-fed streams; and what must he have felt at the view of the springs themselves! That it was a fertile land he was quick to discern. That the valley would provide his home for a long time to come he did not doubt. But he was not a romantic, and though he would march all his life long toward the pearly gates of Paradise, he was not about to use that term for any region he might come upon in this life. He was not a poet, and was not keeping a journal, and it is not likely that even if he were recording his sensations, he would have confided to his diary, "Ah, how charming!" Still . . . .

IV

CARLISLE

When William Penn organized the Province of Pennsylvania in 1682, and laid out the city of Philadelphia, only three counties were designated. These original counties were Philadelphia; Bucks, which was named for the Penn family home in England, Buckinghamshire; and Chester. By 1752 five more counties had been defined and established Lancaster, which was carved from parts of Chester County, was the first of these, in 1729; twenty years later York County was formed from parts of Lancaster County; in 1750 Cumberland County was organized; and in 1752 both Northampton, which was taken from Bucks County, and Berks, which was named for the English county of Berkshire and was by this time accommodating great numbers of German immigrants, were named counties in the Province of Pennsylvania.

By the time of Lexington and Concord the vast territory awarded to William Penn by King Charles II was still composed of only eleven counties. Bedford, a large region removed from Cumberland County, was defined on March 9, 1771; Northumberland, which was even more expansive, formed as it was from parts of Lancaster, Berks, Cumberland, Northampton, and

Bedford, was organized in 1772; and Westmoreland, the westernmost county, was erected in 1773. In later years Cumberland County lost even more of its territory, to Franklin County in 1784, Mifflin in 1789, and Perry in 1820. Thus thousands of the early settlers were transplanted without moving.

Cumberland County, as defined by the new organization, included the Provincial land that lay west of the Susquehanna, a territory almost as large as Scotland and by far the largest county yet formed. By an act of legislature, January 27, 1750, the new county was carved principally out of Lancaster County: "All and singular the lands lying within the province of Pennsylvania, to the westward of the Susquehanna, and northward and westward of the county of York, and is hereby erected into a county, named and hereafter to be called Cumberland, bounded northward and westward with the lines of the Province, eastward partly with the river Susquehanna, and partly with the county of York, and partly with the line dividing the said province from Maryland." [1]

The Cumberland Valley, which was at its heart, and which until this time had been known as North Valley, accommodated at this time "a population of about 3000." [2] By the end of the Revolution many of these residents of the Valley would find themselves paying taxes to the counties of Northumberland and Franklin.

Cumberland County and of course the valley as well were named for Cumberland County of England, which lies in the extreme north of the country. The Irish Sea washes its shores on the west, and Scotland provides its border on the north, where the Caldew, Petteril, and Eden Rivers run together. As Ulster is to Ireland, so the Cumberland is to England. Long a peacefully prosperous section of Old England, the land supports dairy farming and the grazing of sheep and cattle. Like its namesake in Pennsylvania it provides a soil rich in limestone and slate. This serenely pastoral land has always been among the most beautiful and most celebrated regions of the British Isles. Its 1500 square miles include part of that much renowned region called the Lake District, which, with its fifteen lakes and its lovely waterfalls and two of England's highest mountain peaks, and its flower-strewn meadows, inspired the immortal lyrics of the poets Wordsworth,

Coleridge, Southey, Keats, Shelley, and Tennyson.

One wonders whether those responsible for the naming of Cumberland County in the Province of Pennsylvania were aware just how much the regions were alike. Very likely they were, as Carlisle, which is the county borough of Cumberland England, lent its name as well to the county town of Cumberland County in the colony founded by the Penns. Yet, while the names Cumberland and Carlisle are quite appropriate for lots of reasons, doubtless Armstrong and his fellow Scotch-Irish must have wondered whether names celebrating features of Ireland (or Scotland) might not have been even more natural.

In the waning winter of 1749, the then Lieutenant Governor James Hamilton directed the Deputy Surveyor of Lancaster County, Thomas Cookson, to study the whole area of Cumberland in order to determine the most fitting place for a county town. Before long, March 1, Cookson filed his recommendation. He thought the ideal spot to be the neighborhood of LeTort's Spring. This site, he declared, would enjoy a bountiful water supply, as well as a rich and productive soil. It was just about equidistant between the parallel ridges of the beautiful Blue Mountains; and it was hardly twenty miles from the Harris Ferry on the Susquehanna, at the crossing of two much traveled Indian trails. Besides, it was in a neighborhood of spring-fed streams; and the town would be sure to bask in the warm winds which swept upward from the south from the Valley of Virginia into Cumberland.[3]

Although it was more than a year before Governor Hamilton was able to choose among the many sites that had been suggested, eventually he approved Cookson's recommendation. On April 1, 1751, he ordered the Surveyor General of the Province to lay out the town. In order to do this the Province had to buy back land from farmers who were already settled within the limits of the site.[4]

The work required the whole summer and all of September and October, but the job was done. Carlisle historian William Ames has described the lay-out of the community, which now numbered some 700 inhabitants:

The town at first extended no further than the present

North, South, East, and West Streets, all the other part now within the borough being known as commons. A center square was staked off, 440 by 489 feet, and sites marked thereon for a court house, a market house, and the Church of England, one corner being left vacant. 312 lots were laid out, traversed by [five] *broad streets* [like those of the town's namesake], *rectangular and sixty feet wide, except High and Hanover, which were eighty feet in width.*[5]

Nicholas Scull, at the time Surveyor-General of the Province, responding to instructions received from the Provincial Governor James Hamilton on April 1, 1751, laid out Carlisle, some eighteen miles west southwest of the Harris Ferry crossing.[6] On the land which the early settlers had cleared, he defined the limits of the borough, taking full advantage of the beautiful streams which were fed by the ages-old limestone springs and by the freestone tributaries. He located the community along the limestone stream then known as Letort Spring Run, at the very spot where two Indian trails came together. Not far away flowed the serene and lovely Yellow Breeches Creek (the Indians' Minnimingo) on its course to the Susquehanna River. As it passed through the broad valley, picking up the sparkling clean water of the many springs, including Mount Holly Springs and Boiling Springs,[7] it produced a spell for the Cumberland that the Scotch-Irish settlers had found irresistible. Indeed, one historian declares that "there are few more beautiful spots in Pennsylvania than the lake at Boiling Springs, with the surrounding willow trees, set in the sweeping hills and valleys . . . at the foothills of the South Mountain." [8]

At mid-summer 1750, John Armstrong, Deputy Surveyor General for all of the County had been given warrants by the Land Office in Philadelphia to conduct the surveying of "certain lots" in the burgeoning town of Carlisle.[9] And, with his assistant, nephew William Lyon,[10] whose lot would one day actually adjoin that of Armstrong on East High Street, he laid out the town of Carlisle in 1750-51, as ordered by the Proprietors. For this service, he was awarded, typically, a warrant good for the purchase of 3,030 acres.[11]

As Scull's plan for the town of Carlisle did not accord

sufficiently with what he had had in mind, Proprietor Thomas Penn had proposed one of his own. When neither Scull nor Governor Hamilton took any notice, John Armstrong somehow got into the confused authority. As Robert Crist has noted, Armstrong was asked by Penn (1) to enforce the ruling that a house must appear on the purchased lot within one year; and (2) "to survey and supervise the awarding of 'outlots' to the persons who built dwellings."

At Armstrong's urging, Thomas Penn agreed to selling the outlots, rather than awarding them free, but insisted they be no larger than ten acres (Armstrong had been thinking two to three hundred acres, big enough for modest farms rather than vegetable gardens.).[12] In the succeeding year the community was made the county seat of Cumberland County, taking over the government from Shippensburg, and thus became officially the government center of the ever-growing Scotch-Irish community. The borough was finally incorporated in 1782, on April 13, some six years beyond the time it had come into the "United States of America," and just a little over a year before the end of the Revolution.

After the town of Carlisle was laid out in 1751, the community steadily became a busy, busy, ever-bustling place. It was a market town. Here traders came and went, and farmers appeared for repairs and purchases. Situated as it was in a kind of gateway to the west, it rapidly became the most energetic and the most important frontier settlement in the Provinces. Though it was a lively and prosperous community and half-conscious of its place, nobody, not John Armstrong nor any of his most visionary fellow settlers, could have guessed, in 1751, how much history the frontier community of Carlisle would write. Indeed, one historian has declared that "All of the historic events which are associated with the early history of the Square in Carlisle would fill a large book. It is one of the most historic Public Squares in any city or town in America."[13]

Early in the history of the community Indians came into the picture. Although most of the Delaware and Shawnee Indians had long since withdrawn westward, a substantial number remained in the general vicinity of Carlisle. And, naturally, land problems occurred. A letter of John O'Neal to Governor Hamilton, dated Carlisle, May 27, 1753, is ominous: "The Irish immigrants have acted with inconsiderate rashness, in entering upon Indian lands not purchased. It is a matter of regret that they do not conciliate and cultivate the good will of the Redman." In noting that "The garrison here consists only of twelve men," he adds that "I have directed several block houses to be erected agreeably to your desire."[14] By late summer, the Indians were insisting on a hearing for their grievances.

The Delaware Indians not only saw their lands gobbled up by fair and rightful purchase, but from time to time, as with the infamous Walking Purchase of 1737, had the strong impression that they were being cheated out of their lands. Most ironically, Penn's policy, which required purchase, had so cemented in their minds their implicit right to the land that now there festered in them a sense of deprivation. Not surprisingly, they became increasingly hostile. "Incidents" occurred. And with each Indian raid and with every atrocity the situation on the frontier was exacerbated. The sons of William Penn, following the death of their mother in 1727, were quite unable, and perhaps unwilling, to extend or even to enforce their father's "Quaker" policy.

As the tensions mounted, councils which brought the Indians together with the Pennsylvania officials were convened. One such was scheduled for Carlisle on September 25, 1753, and was conducted October 1-3. The conference was held very near to the home of John Armstrong, which was in dead center of the community. Representing the settlers were Commissioners Richard Peters, Isaac Norris (Speaker of the House), and forty-seven-year-old Benjamin Franklin, appointed by Governor James Hamilton. Members of the Assembly, including John Armstrong,[15] were present.

The Six Nations and a number of other tribes were represented by a large number of chiefs, and very nearly 100 Indians showed up. The chief sachem of the Delawares, Shingas, who would become the scourge of the frontier and a fierce adversary to Armstrong, was in attendance. So were his brother, Pisquetomen, and Delaware George. Rendering the Iroquois into English and the English into Iroquois-Delaware were the familiar German-born mediator Conrad Weiser and the half-breed go-between Andrew Montour.

The council was convened in the courthouse, a stone's throw from Armstrong's home. During the entire session the chiefs and warriors sat cross-legged on the floor, leisurely smoking their pipes, as was their wont. The Indians had requested the conference in order that they might air their many complaints. Grievances were discussed and some satisfaction was realized, but not very much that could be considered momentous occurred. The familiar complaint was lodged by the Indians, that they had been given nothing for their lands, nothing, that is, but rum. And by the third day the negotiations, according to some reports, collapsed into a "drunken brawl," which pointed up one of the big problems, which, ironically, was rum. The Indians, while constantly protesting the traffic in rum, seemed always happy to have it.[16] And for the Indians it generally meant trouble. The *Colonial Records* include the note that "drunken Indian emissaries to Philadelphia caused so much disturbance that liquor in any form was eventually denied them in the city."[17] And the Carlisle Conference concluded with the rather naive promise from the treaty Commissioners: "We grant your Women and Young Men their Request for Rum, on Condition it shall not be delivered to them until You shall have passed the Mountains."[18]

    The agreement that was reached cost the colony, counting gifts to the Indians, £1400. Franklin published on November 1, 1753, a complete account of the proceedings, which is most interesting.[19] And later, in his *Autobiography,* he provided a less than flattering impression of the early Americans:

As these people are extreamly apt to get drunk, and, when so, are very quarrelsome and disorderly, we strictly forbad the selling any liquor to them; and when they complain'd of this restriction, we told them that if they would continue sober during the treaty, we would give them plenty of rum when business was over. They promis'd this, and they kept their promise, because they could get no liquor, and the treaty was conducted very orderly, and concluded to mutual satisfaction. They then claim'd and receiv'd the rum; this was in the afternoon: they were near one hundred men, women, and children, and were lodg'd in temporary cabins, built in the form of a square, just within the town. In the evening, hearing a great noise among them, the commissioners walk'd out to see what was the matter. We found they had made a great bonfire in the middle of the square; they were all drunk, men and women, quarreling and fighting. Their dark-colour'd bodies, half naked, seen only by the gloomy light of the bonfire, running after and beating one another with fire-brands, accompanied by their horrid yellings, form'd a scene the most resembling our ideas of hell that could well be imagin'd; there was no appeasing the tumult, and we retired to our lodging. At midnight a number of them came thundering at our door, demanding more rum, of which we took no notice.

Franklin, whose judgment of Indians was rarely complimentary, notes that they were sheepish in their leave-taking:

The next day, sensible they had misbehav'd in giving us that disturbance, they sent three of their old counselors to make their apology. The orator acknowledg'd the fault, but laid it upon the rum; and then endeavored to excuse the rum by saying, "The Great Spirit, who made all things, made every thing for some use, and whatever use he design'd any thing for, that use it should always be put to. Now, when he made rum, he said, 'Let this be for the Indians to get drunk with,' and it must be so." And, indeed, if it be the design of Providence to extirpate these savages in order to make room for cultivators of the earth, it seems not improbable that rum may be the appointed means. It has already annihilated all the tribes who formerly inhabited the sea-coast.[20]

Another of the big problems at this time concerned that section of Pennsylvania on the North Branch of the Susquehanna that included Wyoming,[21] the region that had been settled by both Pennsylvania people and by farmers from Connecticut. Claims to the land were hotly contested and trouble was inevitable. By 1754 the dispute had become so heated that Governor Hamilton felt obliged to take action. He prepared letters for Connecticut Governor Roger Wolcott and his Deputy Thomas Fitch. These he entrusted to the surveyor John Armstrong as the man most likely to accomplish an understanding. He explained to Wolcott that Armstrong carried the authority of Pennsylvania, that he was "a Gentleman whose Relations may be received with the utmost Confidence in whatever he desires to give an account of." [22]

Fighting through some very rough weather, Armstrong on March 6 by horseback reached Windsor and enjoyed a conference with Governor Wolcott. Although the session was amiable, Wolcott, pleading ignorance on the question of rights, and providing only promises, it did not provide a satisfactory solution to the problem.

After some continued squabbling through the summer, which involved the Iroquois nation and included a conference at Albany, the Pennsylvania Governor, now Robert Hunter Morris (who had succeeded Hamilton on October 3), decided to dispatch Armstrong once again to Connecticut, where Thomas Fitch was now the Governor.

In November John Armstrong was commissioned by Morris to make this second trip to New Haven, to lodge letters of complaint with Governor Fitch, and "to make Discoveries of an illegal Purchase of Lands within the Province of Pennsylvania by a Number of persons in the Colony of Connecticut." Armstrong, armed with the letters, promptly launched his mission, conducting along the way an investigation with such notables as James Alexander (Lord Stirling). On December 11, Armstrong returned his report to Morris.

He advised the Governor that on November 28 he had delivered the letters of complaint to the Governor of Connecticut at New Haven, and that he had been informed by a number of officials that "the Purchase was intirely of a Private nature, contrary to their Own as well as Our Laws, that the Government (as such) had nothing to do with it."

Having been informed of the boundaries of the purchase made from the Indians by the Susquehanna Company, Armstrong reported the precise measurements, noting that there were now 800 subscribers, at first at seven dollars each and lately nine dollars. His investigation yielded this impression: "The Generality of the more knowing People despise the Scheme as wild & preposterous, but some others mightily cry up the Antiquity and extent of their Charter whereon their claims are chiefly built." Then for Morris he detailed four strong arguments challenging the claim of the Company, and expressed the hope that Morris's letters would discourage "any

Considerable Number coming in the Spring to Settle on the Susquehannah Lands." [23]

Governor Fitch had already replied (November 29) to Morris. He professed ignorance of the scheme, and declared a confidence that when Morris's letters were "laid before our Assembly for their Consideration," the difficulty would vacate. "If any Thing worthy of Notice occurs [I] shall further advise You." [24]

Of course, the matter was not at an end, big trouble erupting in 1778 and continuing for some time after the close of the Revolution. Armstrong's own son would one day be involved, much to the discomfort and embarrassment of his father.

V

A ROAD FOR BRADDOCK

By the early summer of 1754 the rival colonizing empires of England and France had entered into a shooting war for the territory in the new world already settled by peoples of both nations. Although war had not been formally declared, the French, as early as April 16 had reached the junction of the Allegheny and Ohio Rivers. Taking advantage of the heavy spring rains, a thousand men, with eighteen cannon, rode the floodwaters south from their forts, and under their commander, Monsieur de Contrecoeur, began the building of a fort at the forks, clearly the most strategic military site in the region.

The fighting begins with the victory of a young Virginian, George Washington, over the French forces of Ensign Joseph Coulon de Jumonville near present-day Uniontown, and with Washington's subsequent defeat at Fort Necessity. It continued in the ill-fated Braddock Expedition in the summer of 1755.

Carlisle's John Armstrong played but a modest role in the Braddock assault on Fort Duquesne. Yet the experience equipped him well for three later expeditions against the French and Indians in which he was a principal figure.

Edward Braddock

Edward Braddock, who had arrived in Virginia in February of 1755, expected substantial reinforcements from the colonies. He had requested 3000 men from Pennsylvania, which was the colony being invaded by the French. But he had been promptly greeted by the Governor of Virginia with the astonishing news that he could expect no support at all from Pennsylvania, and, indeed, had no reason to expect any from Maryland either.[1]

Pennsylvania's Governor Robert Hunter Morris, though well-intentioned, had been unable even to supply maps of the frontier country. Supplies had not been assembled, and the necessary wagons had not appeared. Morris was more than disappointed. He was beside himself. He referred to the Pennsylvania Assembly as my "Quaking Assembly" and charged it with dalliance. Very close to uncontrollable anger, he registered his disgust: "Such is the infatuation and obstinacy of the people I have to deal with, or at least their representatives, that even though their country is invaded, yet I could not persuade them to act with vigor at this juncture, or even grant the supply expected by the Crown." And shortly thereafter, he again lamented Pennsylvania's failure to supply any aid for the defense of the colony, "either by establishing a militia or furnishing men, money or provisions."[2]

Braddock complained that he had so far met only one man who seemed to know anything about the wilderness. That man was a twenty-three-year-old Virginian named George Washington. And it was from Washington that he learned that he had not fifteen miles of wilderness to traverse to reach Fort Duquesne, but perhaps six times that many, and that these miles would present formidable mountains and extremely rough terrain.[3]

Naturally the first problem to be dealt with was the route. Braddock had declared, "A General must have a road that can facilitate the transport of Provisions and also provide security for any necessary retreat." [4] The Virginians were particularly eager to see the expedition launched from its province; and the Pennsylvanians, though unwilling to provide much real help either in soldiers or supplies, were equally hopeful that the Braddock Expedition might organize at Carlisle and set out from there. In the end, not surprisingly, Braddock elected to march from the post at Will's Creek, not the most expeditious route or most direct route.

Meanwhile, Quartermaster-General Sir John St. Clair had requested of Governor Morris the building of a supply road that would reach across the Province of Pennsylvania and facilitate the passage of supply wagons for the support of the Braddock army. Actually, two roads were to be built, one westward to the forks of the Youghiogheny, and one southward from Raystown to Braddock's Camp at Will's Creek (Fort Cumberland) in Maryland. Morris, who had received the request on February 24, promptly proceeded to the Assembly of Pennsylvania, who, though in control of a fund of 5,000 pounds, declined to finance the work. But when the head of the Delaware Assembly agreed to meet the expenses, Morris was quick to commission a survey team. On March 12, he appointed for the survey the five best men he knew for the job. These were John Armstrong, whose reputation for surveying was by this time an exalted one, known as he was as the "best surveyor on the frontier"; James Burd,[5] a courageous soldier and road builder par excellence; William Buchanan, of Carlisle; the shrewd and resourceful frontiersman and Indian trader George Croghan; and Adam Hoops (spelled also Hoop and Hoopes) of Antrim, who had worked closely with

James Burd

Armstrong. Croghan was a vital figure, as he was friendly with the Indians and as he knew the country they would be traversing far better than anyone else.[6]

The work was to be done in secret. The Commission's instructions were "to reconnoitre, explore and view the country west and north of the Kittochtinny or Blue Hill, and of the great Virginia road leading from Harris's Ferry through Carlisle and Shippensburg," and "as carefully and as secret as may be to survey and lay out such roads as shall be most direct and commodious to answer as well for the carriage of provisions from the settled parts of the province to a branch of the Monongahela, called Yohiogin [Youghiogheny], and also to the camp at the mouth of Wills' creek." [7]

On this same day, March 12, Morris notified Braddock that "I have ordered the Country from a place called Carlisle near Sasquehanna Westwards towards the Turkey's Foot [the meeting of the branches of the Youghiogheny] to be reconnoitered by Persons best acquainted with those Parts, with whom I sent a Draughts man, and if it be possible to make a Road that Way I will recommend it to the Assembly to enable me to do it." [8]

On the 15th Secretary Richard Peters dispatched to Armstrong his Commission, "which you may perceive by its Tenor requires Prudence, Secrecy where necessary, and the utmost Expedition." The commissioner was urged to convene the others, and "prevail with them to go upon the Service without any Loss of Time, and to continue thereon till all be finished." Needlessly, he added that the General cannot march until the roads are opened.[9]

But it was March 29 by the time Armstrong had the commissioners organized. Having had earlier a meeting at Francis Campbell's store in Shippensburg, on that day they set out from Carlisle,[10] determined, though they knew the dangers, to blaze a trail to the Ohio. They were accompanied by two scouts, four packhorsemen, three blazers, two chain-carriers and the few Indians they found willing to help in the scouting. It was the opinion of Croghan that if they meant to take the shortest route to the Ohio they should begin from just south of Shippensburg, to cross the mountains and to pick up Raystown Creek. Thus they began on an old Indian path, and, blazing the trail as they went, proceeded with commendable dispatch to a site some eighteen miles from the Turkey

Foot. The date was April 11. By this time they had lost all but one of their Indians, so frightened were they of the French, whom they knew to be prowling the wilderness. And, indeed, no sooner had the party begun to savor their achievement than they were compelled by the approach of a French and Indian company to turn back and return to Fort Cumberland by way of the trail they had blazed.[11] The road they had surveyed, from McDowell's Mill, near Chambersburg, to where they left off on the Youghiogheny, was sixty-nine miles long.

In their report later to Governor Morris, the commissioners described the extremely ungrateful and rude reception they received from General John St. Clair on April 16 at the camp at Will's Creek. Because they had risked their lives to do the work, and because they felt that they had blazed the very best trail that could be expected, they were shocked by the treatment they were accorded. Armstrong and the others filed this report with Governor Morris:

We waited for Sir John's coming to camp . . . [he] treated Us in a very disagreeable manner; he is extremely warm and angry at our Province; he would not look at our Draughts nor suffer any Representations to be made to him in regard of the province, but stormed like a Lyon Rampant. He said our Commission to lay out the Road should have been issued in January last upon his first Letter, that doing it now it is doing of nothing, that the Troops must march on the first of May, that the want of this Road and the provisions promised by Pennsylvanians has retarded the Expedition, which may cost them their Lives . . . ; That instead of marching to the Ohio he would in nine days march his Army into Cumberland County to cut the Roads, press Horses, Wagons, etc.; that he would not suffer a Soldier to handle an Axe, but by Fire and Sword oblige the Inhabitants to do it . . . ; that he would kill all kind of Cattle and carry away the Horses, burn the Houses, etc. . . . That he would tomorrow write to England by a Man-of-War, shake Mr. Penn's Proprietaryship, and represent Pennsylvania as a disaffected Province . . . and told Us to go to the General if We pleased, who would give Us ten bad words for one that he had given.[12]

This torrent of wrath and abuse the commissioners suffered was clearly owing to the disappointment the English officers felt in the failure of Pennsylvania to support better the expedition. At least the Province was grateful enough to make good in its payment, each commissioner receiving seven pounds, ten shillings, and all expenses, for twenty-five days of service.[13]

But now the roads had to be cut. Of course the project would cost money, probably a lot of money. Governor Morris continued to experience trouble with a less than enthusiastic Assembly. In the last week of April he could secure no more than a grudging promise of 200 pounds "for the cutting of a road westward to the forks of the Youghiogheny on which supplies might eventually be carried to Braddock's army." [14] At this time, at the recommendation of Morris, the Secretary to the Province, Richard Peters, was made "intermediary" between Sir John St. Clair and "a project of road building." Peters was gung ho on the expedition and very much determined to see that adequate roads were cleared. He meant to do all he could to forward the mission. On April 25, he dispatched an urgent communication to the commissioners, who, as we have seen, had been surveying the possible routes. In the Governor's name he now urged them "to clear the roads a sufficient breadth which should be thought by them necessary to be opened, to make causeways and lay bridges, and to set about it with the utmost expedition." They were to assemble the necessary workers "immediately," and "further the work by all possible methods." [15]

In May, Secretary Peters was in Shippensburg to make arrangements for the opening of the road westward from Carlisle to Youghiogheny. From Shippensburg on the 18th of the month he directed a letter to Governor Morris: "Sir—I desired to John Armstrong to write to you; and as he is perfectly acquainted with the whole affair of the roads, his information and sentiments will be sufficient for you to proceed upon. Perhaps a new commission will not be necessary, and may breed contention." He notes also that "Mr. John St. Clair went to discover a new road, but finding none, returned to the General [Braddock, at Fort Cumberland]; they concluded to take the old road to the Meadows." [16]

As Morris could dispatch to Armstrong the 200 pounds that had been initially promised by the Assembly, the commissioners got to work. They advertised for workmen in the counties of York, Cumberland, and Lancaster. And Armstrong was able to report to

Morris the most welcome news that "We have Spades and Pick-axes a-making, Crow-Bars We think to borrow, Kettles to boil Provisions must be bought, and some Blankets, &c; if a sufficient Number of Hands come, two or three Wagons would be necessary to attend them." He added that two merchants had agreed to provide abundant flour, and that a third one would stand for the bacon.[17] Sufficient grass for the packhorses had been promised. The road-building work party was ready to go.

Morris was getting edgy about expense. Of Armstrong he requested an estimate. The Commissioner provided one. His best guess was 800 pounds. Shortly after, he revised it upwards, to 1500 pounds. And on May 18 he provided still a third: "We [the House] have also in our hands another letter from the same Commissioner [Armstrong], dated fifteen days after the former, wherein, after more Experience in the Work, he makes a *third Estimate*, judging that the 'Expence of opening both Roads will be little under Two Thousand Pounds.'"[18] Armstrong had appended to his report that Cresap's son would be "receiving contributions from Pennsylvania," and he spoke in disgust at the "knavery of that family."[19] But Morris was not staggered. He was confident that the Assembly, which was controlled by the Quakers at this time, could eventually be persuaded to its obligation.

But the road-building in the early going did not proceed all that well. In the first place, Burd was left to superintend the work on his own. Croghan had a new assignment, as he had been placed in charge of the Indians who were to augment Braddock's forces. Armstrong, because of the Purchase of 1754, was overwhelmed with surveying activities for the Province; and both Buchanan and Hoops were engaged in private affairs.[20]

At some time in the second week of May, Secretary Peters, in a meeting with Commissioner Armstrong, learned that there were but sixty men at work upon the road, and that Mr. Burd had the responsibility for the entire party. Burd, though a very good man, and very conscientious, could, as Armstrong reported, hardly be supposed equal to such a task. Peters was informed by Armstrong that in the ten days the gang had been at work they had cut hardly seven miles. At this rate, the Commissioner did not need to point out, six months would be required to reach the Turkey Foot of the

Youghiogheny.

What was to be done? Peters considered replacing Burd. He considered the appointment of an engineer. Naturally additional workers were needed. A number of changes were ordered. At the outset, two roads had been planned, one from Raystown south to Will's Creek and one from Carlisle-Shippensburg to the Turkey Foot on the Youghiogheny; and courses for both had been studied by the commissioners. Now Peters, with the approval of both General Braddock and Sir John St. Clair, decided to give up the road to Will's Creek. For the sake of time, all road-building would be concentrated on the main road.

And there was a second change, one which would expedite the work dramatically. The commissioners had been ordered to lay out and build roads sufficient for the progress of the supply wagons. They had elected to go with a width of thirty feet (and had done so for about ten miles). Commissioner Burd had reduced the width to twenty feet; but now Peters had this reduced to twelve. And in those regions where a good deal of digging or quarrying was required, the workers went with ten feet.[21]

A third, and very necessary improvement was made simply by enlarging the work force. By May 15, Burd had seventy men at work, and by the end of the month he had 120. Besides, an engineer named William Smith was appointed to assist Commissioner Burd, and by the 28th he had shown up.[22]

Peters, concerned for the safety of the workers and fearful that, without protection, they would desert, urged, further, an additional number of men to serve as an escort. Although this proposal, as well as the suggestion that additional scouts were needed to warn of the presence of Indians, was met at first with scorn, Braddock (with reports of Indian ravages on the work parties) did finally send out from Fort Cumberland a military escort to provide protection for the road-builders of Commissioner Burd. This protection, a company of 100 Virginians under Captain Peter Hogg, was most welcome, and discouraged desertions which had been occurring.[23]

Ground had been broken, and actual work begun, on May 6. On this morning ten men reported to Commissioner Burd for work. The road, which was but following an old Indian trail, proceeded from McDowell's Mill (present-day Markes in Franklin County) to Parnell's and Jordan's Knobs, and from thence into what has always been known as the Path Valley and into Cowan's Gap. From there it proceeded to Burnt Cabins, to Sugar Cabins, to Anthony Thompson's, and to Sideling Hill. The road was then cut through to the point at which the Indian trail crossed the Juniata, and then, never far from the river, to Raystown, up and across the Allegheny Mountain range and on to the Youghiogheny, some three miles from the intended Turkey Foot forks.[24] The work was terminated on July 5.

For the most part the road had been constructed at the rate of about one mile per day, the work beginning May 6 and terminating on July 5. Seventy days to provide a wagon road through the wilderness some seventy miles. During the time of the work the road was known as the Burd Road. It has been since known as the Braddock Road. It reached from McDowell's Mill, twenty miles west of Chambersburg, across the mountains to Raystown (now Bedford), to the forks of the Youghiogheny, and was intended to meet the Virginia road, "somewhere on the Monongahela."

On June 8, and now amply provisioned, as he thought, and with the road being cut ahead of him, General Edward Braddock at the head of a column of 2300 troops and supply vessels that would extend for four miles, set out from Fort Cumberland. He was marching into a wilderness, a wilderness strange and unfriendly. It was a fateful day in the history of Pennsylvania. He had a company of Indians with him, thanks to George Croghan, but they proved to be less than devoted. By the time the expedition reached the Monongahela, only eight (!) Indians remained, and these were courtesy of George Washington.

By June 24 the army had made the Great Crossings, still some three miles from the Turkey Foot. On July 2, the soldiers marched six miles to the Indian camp known as "Jacobs' Cabin," which belonged to the notorious Delaware chieftain known as Captain Jacobs, with whom Armstrong would one day soon have some dealings. The camp was located at the headwaters of Jacobs Creek, some one or two miles southeast of present-day Mt. Pleasant. It was July 8 when the Braddock regiments reached Turtle Creek. The army had negotiated 110 miles in thirty days. It had made twenty encampments.

The frightful disaster occurred next day on the banks of the Monongahela.

The bad news flew on swift wings to the east. By noon of July 10, a full report had reached Fort Cumberland. It required only a week to reach Carlisle, where a disbelieving Governor Morris received it, and by the 18th of July Benjamin Franklin, the Pennsylvania Assembly, and all of Philadelphia knew that the expedition of General Braddock had experienced a calamitous defeat in the shadows of the French fort. Arrangements for a glorious celebration had been made in Philadelphia. Hardly a soul could at first believe the report. But when the truth was realized a heavy gloom fell over the entire province. Not a lot of wisdom was required to understand what was likely the prospect for the frontier.

Indeed, the instant the terrible news arrived a great change came over the people of Pennsylvania. Governor Morris, in Carlisle when he had the news, immediately set out for Philadelphia to begin organizing against what everybody sensed was coming. On the 17th of July, before he left Carlisle, he reported to the Secretary of the Province, Richard Peters, on the mood of the settlers:

The People here are under great apprehension of being disturbed by the Indians and many have been with me from Juniata and Connegogee to know whether it was not best they should quit their Plantations but I have encouraged them to form themselves into bodys for their common defence and to make them a little regular I have Issued some commissions but doubt whether this will have any effect... there is a genl complaint of the want of arms and ammunition I have already distributed what I bought at Harris's ferry and wish I had it in my power to furnish these people with the means of defending themselves for they seem very well disposed and under proper regulation would be an Excellent barrier to the rest of the Province—I shall leave this Place in about two hours and return to Philada by way of Lancaster....

Even preparations for fortifying the town of Carlisle were undertaken, Morris noting for Peters that he has "laid out a place in the middle of this town which the inhabitants intend to fortify withlogs as a retreat for their women and Children in case they should be attacked." [25] And the same advice for defense he directed to the people of Shippensburg.

At a mini-council held in the Council Hall in Philadelphia on Wednesday, July 23, Deputy Governor Morris laid before those present (John Penn, Joseph Turner, Robert Stretell, Richard Peters, and Lynford Lardner) all that Secretary Peters had acquired on the tragedy. Next day the Governor addressed the Speaker and the Gentlemen of the Assembly: "It is with the greatest Concern I now lay before you the melancholy Account of the Defeat of the Forces under the immediate command of General Braddock, which you will find is attended with very shocking Circumstances, the General killed and most of the Officers that were in the Action are either killed or wounded, the Bulk of the Men cut off, His whole Train of Artillery taken, and Colonel [Thomas] Dunbar is now retreating with the Remains of the Army to Fort Cumberland." [26]

On the very day that Braddock's body was secretly interred at the Orchard Camp near the Great Meadows, Commissioner John Armstrong had dispatched to the General a letter from Carlisle, in which he noted that the new road would "soon be completed."

VI

DEFENDING THE FRONTIER

From the time of his arrival in his province, on October 27, 1682, until the illness of his last years, William Penn insisted on a Quaker policy toward the Delaware Indians of land purchase by treaty. Penn could not have known that this land had been inhabited by the native peoples for hundreds, nay, thousands of years. But he could perceive that they were living on it now. He had found the native people, who continued to be called "Indians," to be a simple and friendly people. Thus, although his father had been given the land by the King of England, he installed and practiced a policy that required the provincial authorities to purchase from the Delawares the land they meant to settle upon.

At the same time, however, unhappily for the native peoples, he was constantly and vigorously encouraging settlement within the province. He did this by proclaiming to the people of the British Isles, particularly to the unhappy in Scotland and Ireland, that here in Pennsylvania were to be found available land, civil liberties, and freedoms limited only by conscience. As these features of the province proved to be true, great numbers of would-be settlers appeared in ever increasing numbers, and before long, by mid-century, Penn's province, although the twelfth to be established, was third largest in population.[1]

But Penn's province was ill prepared for the great waves of immigration from the Old World. By the time of the Braddock expedition, thirty-seven years after the death of William Penn, the Quaker policy had proved quite incapable of accommodating the situation. Indeed there had never been any real hope that the administrators of the province could purchase land from the Indians at a rate equal to the rate of settlement, never any real hope that William Penn's policy, grounded in friendship and honorable relations, could be perpetuated to the lasting satisfaction of the native peoples. By the time of Braddock, the Indians, who had been pushed steadily and inexorably westward, clear to the Ohio, and northward into the Wyoming Valley, had become steadily less friendly and accommodating.

The Delaware Indians, in all of their time, had never established in the region now called Pennsylvania a town that could be considered permanent. Consequently, resistance to white settlement they found quite impossible. Three kinds of settlers were appearing: (1) the settler who acquired his property on land purchased by the province from the Indians (For this homestead, secured by warrant through the Land Office, he would pay five pounds per hundred acres, and by 1732 three times as much.); (2) the settler who secured his land in the same way but on property that in the confused surveying process actually still belonged to the Indians; (3) the settler who simply blazed the trees embracing a plot of land without payment to anybody, thus establishing a "claim" that more often than not went unchallenged (Such a settler was called a "squatter," and there were lots of them.).

The consequences of the disaster which had occurred to the British army of General Edward Braddock on the banks of the Monongahela were immediate and dire for the English colonies in America, especially as the French dreams of empire were greatly vitalized. But for the people of Pennsylvania the consequences were much more immediate, and terrifying. Beyond the imaginings of the most apprehensive of the settlers were the events of the succeeding three years. Depredations and atrocities too horrible to describe were carried out all along the frontier, and even as far east as Carlisle and Shippensburg.

To quiet the fears of the settlers, the Province arranged for another peace conference. On January 15-22, 1756, it was convened in Carlisle. Present on this occasion, besides ex-Governor Hamilton and Secretary Peters, were Deputy Governor Robert Morris, William Logan, Joseph Fox, and George Croghan, who served as interpreter. The conference concluded in a declaration of war against those Delaware Indians who had allied with the French.[2]

Not surprisingly, thirty-eight-year-old John Armstrong was right in the middle of it all. Indeed, the soon-to-be Lieutenant Colonel now assumed a military role. Before long he would find himself in charge of the defense of the frontier in Pennsylvania south and west of the Susquehanna. Happily he had the support of the present Governor, Robert Morris, and the energetic help of James Burd, William Buchanan, and Edward Shippen.

The company that Armstrong raised was stationed at Carlisle when, on May 11, 1756, he was commissioned Lieutenant Colonel. Carlisle became headquarters for the Armstrong battalion, the 2nd Battalion of the Pennsylvania Regiment. This organization installed the companies of John Potter, the Reverend John Steel (pastor of the Presbyterian Church at present Church Hill), Hanse Hamilton, Hugh Mercer, James Burd, and James Patterson, as well as that of Armstrong himself into the battalion. Historian William Hunter notes that "the establishment of Armstrong's company at Carlisle marked a second step in the formation of an inner Provincial defense line, of which the placing of the garrison at McDowell's had marked the beginning."[3]

The rout of the Braddock forces had occurred in the middle of the summer of 1755. The Provincial Government did not at first appreciate sufficiently what the defeat of Braddock would mean to the frontier. It had no idea in what a terrible and ruthless ferocity the Shawnee and Delaware Indians would be unleashed. Consequently, nothing much was done to provide protection for the settlers; and in no time at all the region of Carlisle and Shippensburg and all the wilderness to the west was alive with bands of hostile Indians, often led or accompanied by French soldiers. Philadelphia, where the Assembly held its sessions, was besieged with demonstrations and threats even. Pennsylvania historian Frederic Godcharles tells of how "troops of frontiersmen rode through the city streets threateningly brandishing their weapons," and of a party of German settlers who "laid the corpses of their countrymen, scalped within sixty-five miles of the capital, at the door of the State House." It was obvious to most that the Quaker peace policy needed to be overhauled, and at once.[4]

By early autumn, the massacres carried out by the Indians were so numerous that even the people living in Carlisle feared for their lives. The ruthless Delaware chief Shingas, still smarting from Braddock's insulting declaration that "no savage should inherit the land" that the British army would liberate from the French, and though suspicious of Britain's enemy, made the fateful decision to ally with the French, as the Shawnee were determined to do. But to the settlers it seemed as though the Indians were only dimly aware that they had been pushed ever more and more westward and that they were conducting raids not so much in the hope of recovering their lands, and not even to steal cattle or horses, but simply for the sheer delight of killing. They killed women and children as well as men, and they destroyed stock and grain and orchards. And they did this all with the greatest impunity.

In the last week of September, in the year of Braddock's defeat, the Provincial Government seated in Philadelphia was warned that an army of Indians was moving on Shamokin, at the forks of the Susquehanna. Even their route had been defined: They were approaching by way of the West Branch of the Susquehanna, coming down the river, past the old Delaware village of Chinklacamoose and Bald Eagle Creek and the Great Island.

By the time it was realized what was actually happening it was too late. One of the earliest, and definitely among the most horrible of all the attacks that alerted the people of the frontier to their very real danger, was the massacre that occurred at Penn's Creek, just where it joins the Susquehanna, on October 16, 1755. On this day the Delaware raiding party under the command of Shingas fell without warning upon the settlement a few miles south of Shamokin, near present-day Selinsgrove. The warriors in a frenzy ruthlessly murdered and scalped thirteen men and women, and an infant. Eleven young men and children were carried away.[5]

One man, who was terribly wounded, was able to reach the people at Gabriel's settlement at Mahanoy Creek, on the west side of the Susquehanna, five miles downriver from the forks at Shamokin, with the terrible news. Members of the burial party that returned to the scene were horrified to discover the mutilated bodies of thirteen men and elderly women, and one child two weeks old. Completely burned to the ground was the house of Jacob Le Roy, and the body of the farmer was lying next the ashes, two tomahawks buried in his forehead.[6]

Le Roy's daughter Mary had been carried off. She would live to escape captivity and to tell of the horrors of October 16, 1755. One hundred and sixty years later the memorial which had been erected at the site was unveiled. A beautiful boulder with a bronze tablet on which was inscribed "It marks the scene of one of the most horrible of the Indian massacres in Pennsylvania" commemorated the event.[7]

At the very same time that the Shingas warriors carried out their assault, a smaller party of Delaware warriors, having been dispatched by the Chief, appeared at the Delaware town of Shamokin, just up the Susquehanna. Their faces were painted black. They had come to advise the Susquehanna Delawares that their brothers on the Ohio were now allied with the French and were at war against the English. They were bringing an invitation from Shingas to join him "in ridding the land of the English." [8]

The Susquehanna Delawares were unmoved, and determined to remain neutral. A disappointed Shingas in November repeated his determination in the strongest terms: "We, the Delawares of Ohio do proclaim War against the English. We have been their Friends many years, but now we have taken up the Hatchet against them, & we will never make it up with them whilst there is an English man alive." [9]

At this time it was the range of mountains known as the Blue Mountains which marked the distinction between "Indian country" and the white settlements. But the distinction was fast being blurred; and, actually, one of the most awful of the massacres occurred in Cumberland County, not all that far away from the County Seat at Carlisle, in the region that would later be taken in by Fulton County. This was the tragedy of the Big Cove, or Great Cove, as it was popularly called. Known today as Morrison's, or Morrison's Cove, the valley reaches north from Yellow Creek along both the west and east sides of Tussey Mountain to present-day Williamsburg. It is a beautiful, very fertile, limestone valley.

The settlement was composed of Scotch-Irish who had crossed over the Cove Mountain in the decade 1730-40. The cluster of houses was near the present-day site of McConnellsburg. The farms and homes were protected by Fort McDowell, a "private" fort, which was located at "the most important pass, most exposed to danger," on the east bank of the West Branch of the Conococheague Creek. It was just about midway between Reverend Steel's Fort at Church Hill on the south and the later site of Fort Loudoun on the north, about ten miles from each. Until Loudoun was built it was a principal base of supplies, and had served as Braddock's starting point on the Burd Road.

But at the time of the Indian assault, Saturday, November 1, 1755 (Some accounts give the time of the attack as Friday, Oct. 31.), the tiny village at the Cove, just about the farthest west of all settlements in the Province of Pennsylvania,[10] was ill-prepared for war parties.

Early reports had identified the Indians, in number approaching one hundred, as the Delaware and Shawnee warriors of the two most notorious Delaware chiefs, Shingas and Captain Jacobs (Tewea). It is known now that the war party was sent out by the French Commander at Fort DuQuesne, and that Frenchmen were members of the party.

Shingas, the most prominent of the Indians ravaging the frontier in these years, was known as "King of the Delawares." Called by his people Shingask (Bog-meadow), he was far and away the most influential, the most powerful, and the most to be feared of the Delaware warriors. He was well known to George Washington, who had visited with him at his home near present-day McKee's Rocks, in 1753. According to the Moravian missionary John Heckewelder, Shingas was "a bloody warrior, cruel his treatment, relentless his fury, small in person, but in activity, courage and savage prowess unexcelled."[11] Shingas was intimately familiar with all of the Indian trails, and it was Shingas who was regularly at the head of the marauding raiding parties. He had to his credit a long catalog of the most horrible and cruel murders. Settlements everywhere along the frontier—Conococheague, Big Cove, Sherman's Valley—knew his name. And it was a name that never failed to inspire terror in all who heard it. From time to time through these bloody years, even as early as 1753, Shingas was in residence with Captain Jacobs at Kittanning, though while there he was normally on the side of the river opposite to Jacobs' house.

The force divided into two parties. One, under the command of Captain Jacobs, assaulted the Conolloway settlement; the other, under Shingas and his two lieutenants, the Delaware Chiefs Captain John Peter and Captain Will, fell upon the Great Cove.

And the first news had not only the settlement at Big Cove, but the settlement south, at Tonoloway Creek, completely "wiped out." Refugees were showing up at Reverend Steel's fortified meetinghouse, and at McDowell's, with the most gruesome stories to relate. Sheriff John Potter had the news at three o'clock in the afternoon of Saturday. He promptly sent out the word that a reprisal party would be assembling at Fort McDowell. "I was not there six minutes," he reported later, before he perceived that the new home and barn of Matthew Patton was in flames. By this time he had 150 men assembled. But only forty were willing to accompany him to the farm![12] And of course it would have been most unwise to pursue the Indians with forty men. Potter had to content himself with scathing remarks about the "cowards" he had to deal with. Disgusted and disappointed, he declared from his home that night that he would "not guard a man who will not fight when called in so imminent a manner."[13]

By Sunday afternoon the news of the massacre had reached John Armstrong in Carlisle. A conference with others, notably John Smith and William Buchanan, promptly produced the decision to dispatch the companies of Hanse Hamilton and James Burd (who had had the news Saturday night) for relief and pursuit of the Indians. It was not until Thursday, however, that a sufficient force had been assembled at McDowell's; and by that time the Indians had vanished.[14]

Much of what is known of the Indian attack on the settlements at the Cove derives largely from the account provided by Charles Stuart, who was captured, together with his wife and their two children, William and Mary. According to Stuart, the raiding party which attacked the settlement was unusually large, composed as it was of some ninety Delaware, Mingo and Shawnee. The Indians burned the Stuart house, the barn, the haystacks, and the fodder house. They slaughtered the calves and hogs that were in the pasture, stole what horses they could, and shot the others. At the Stuart farm they murdered two men.

The Indians lingered in the settlement until Monday morning, butchering everything that lived, including every settler who had not escaped (excepting those they preferred to hold as captive), and destroying everything of value. They set out, then, that morning from Licking Creek for the Sideling Hill Gap. At Raystown, according to Stuart, the party was joined by the infamous Delaware Chieftain Captain Jacobs, who, it is now thought, had just returned from a raid into the German settlements in Berks County. As was their custom, the warriors now deliberated in council, to determine what was best to do with the prisoners. The judgment that was reached called for Stuart and a second prisoner, John Condon, to be put to death. Stuart's account of the ordeal is graphic and testifies to the limitless reach of the Indian imagination:

The deaths we were to suffer were as Follows: First our fingers were to be cut off and we were to be forced to eat them, then our eyes pulled out which we were also to eat, after which we were to be put on a scaffold and Burnt, the manner of Scaffolding is first to tie them to a post or tree with so much length of rope as to allow them about three foot to move about the tree, then they raise them a little from the ground on a Logg or what else happens to be most convenient to set them on and then puts wood about them and burns them up — .

Although the council had come to this judgment, it needed yet the consent of the Chief Judge, who was Shingas. Apparently because he enjoyed fond recollections of Stuart and his family, Stuart was spared. He was taken, together with the other prisoners who had not been doomed, to Shingas's home, which was at that time a little less than a mile downriver from Kittanning on the west side of the Allegheny. Here, however, Shingas's fond remembrances of Stuart dimmed a little. With a number of the other prisoners Stuart was obliged to run the gauntlet, to the great glee of the Indian women and children, who, with the warriors, reached the number of 100 on each side! [15] Stuart was kept a prisoner for two years.[16]

Sheriff John Potter, who, together with Reverend John Steel, had been determined to pursue the Indians, until he found most of the available men faint of heart, eventually produced a tally of the casualties. He claimed that of the ninety-three families at risk, forty-seven had been lost, and that the fires that the fleeing settlers had seen burning behind them had destroyed twenty-seven plantations.[17]

From Conocoheague, on November 3, Adam Hoops reported to Governor Morris. No stranger to the bloody business of the frontier, he writes in pained lamentation, of the fires, of the butchery, of "horses standing bleeding with Indian arrows in them," of a husband required to watch his wife's head cut off, of "Children's blood drank like Water." [18]

Settlers were now fleeing in droves from the frontier settlements. Armstrong was dismayed, and, with James Burd at Shippensburg, very much feared what the Indians might move on to next. Both wrote promptly to Governor Morris. Both letters throbbed with urgency. Armstrong, signing his letter "your honor's disconsolate humble servant," wrote from Carlisle:

At four o'Clock this afternoon [Nov. 2], *by Expresses from Conocoheague, we are informed that Yesterday about 100 Indians were seen in the Great Cove, among whom was Shingas, the Delaware King; that immediately after the discovery, as many* [settlers] *as had notice fled, & looking back upon an high Hill they beheld their Houses on Fire; heard several Guns fired, and the last shrieks of their dying neighbors; 'tis said the Enemy divided and one part moved towards the Canallowais* [Conolloways]. *Mr. [Hanse] Hamilton was here with 60 men from York county when the Express came, and is to march early to-morrow to the upper part of the County. We have sent out expresses every where, and intend to collect the Forces of this Lower part; expecting the Enemy at Sheerman's Valley, if not nearer hand.*

And then he makes his second mention of the plan he is to urge hereafter every chance he gets (a strategy which the young George Washington was quick to borrow for his defense of the

Virginia frontier). To Morris he repeated the proposal he had set forth on November 2: "I'm of opinion that no other means than a Chain of Block Houses along or near the South side of the Kittatinny Mountain, from Susquehannah to the Temporary Line, can secure the Lives and Properties even of the old Inhabitants of this County; the new Settlement being all fled, except [those of] Sheerman's Valley, whom (if God do not preserve) we fear, will suffer very soon." [19]

He wrote also to Peters that very night, which was a Sunday, referring the Secretary to the letter he had just written Morris, and repeating his great concern, and appealing for protection. He even fears for his own wife and child and for Carlisle: "You will see our melancholy circumstances by the governor's letter and my opinion of the method of keeping the inhabitants in this country, which will require all possible despatch. If we had immediate assurance of relief a great number would stay; and the inhabitants should be advertised [advised] not to drive off, nor waste their beef cattle, &c. I have not so much as sent off my wife fearing an ill precedent, but must do it now, I believe, together with the public papers and your own." And he continues with an update for the Secretary: "There are no inhabitants on Juniata, nor on Tuscarora by this time, my brother William being just come in. [Andrew] Montour and Monaghatootha are going to the Governor. The former is greatly suspected of being an enemy in his heart—'tis hard to tell—you can compare what they say to the Governor with what I have wrote. I have no notion of a large army, but of great danger from scouting parties." [20]

Burd, who had had the news a little earlier than Armstrong, reports refugees in Shippensburg, and great panic and confusion. Work on Fort Morris, which he had begun, is proceeding apace, but he appeals for help from Philadelphia ("a few great guns, small arms and ammunition"). We have, he concludes, "one hundred men working . . . with heart and head every day." [21]

On learning that Sheriff Potter had arrived in Philadelphia, some two weeks after the tragedy, Governor Morris sent for him and requested an account. According to Potter, at least twenty-seven plantations had been burnt, "and a great quantity of Cattle killed." He reported also that "a Woman of 93 years of age was found lying killed with her Breast tore off and a stake run thro' her Body," and that in all, "of the ninety-three families which were settled in the two

Coves... 47 were either killed or taken and the rest deserted."[22]

In consequence of this terrible massacre, and partly because of the size of the Indian raiding party, the Provincial Assembly in short order had before it two petitions, one from the inhabitants of Cumberland County, and another from those of Paxton-Narrows in Lancaster County. Both insisted in strong terms on protection from forts. Another immediate consequence was the increased energy put into the establishment of private forts, the best known of which was that of John McDowell's Mill, which, lying due west from Chambersburg, had been fortified in that November by the people of Peters Township as supervised by Captain William Maxwell of the local militia.[23]

But the assault on the settlement at Great Cove was but one of a great number of vicious attacks that occurred in the region. A number of raids were made on the settlements near Shamokin at the Susquehanna forks; another was carried out by a war party which had come east of the Great Cove clear into the Path Valley.[24]

For the most part the depredations were the work of very small raiding parties (sometimes including Frenchmen), composed of as few as three warriors to perhaps ten or twenty. The tactics were to scout out the target, a farm or some kind of stockade or fort, on the night before the intended attack, in order to determine the number of people on hand. Then a sufficient number of Indians would be assigned to that plantation. The idea was to attack the unsuspecting and unprepared. Surprise was the Indians' chief advantage, and they worked very hard to insure it. Mercy was never a consideration. And then, generally, though not always, the party would vanish as suddenly as it had appeared. It was difficult for the settlers to defend themselves.

As there was no organized defense against these raids, by the end of November "the Pennsylvania frontier from the Maryland border to the Delaware Water Gap was aflame—houses were set afire by howling warriors, barns destroyed, farms raided, livestock seized, and men, women, and children scalped or carried away into captivity."[25] Settlers were fleeing the frontier in droves, seeking refuge in towns like Carlisle and Shippensburg.

The Indians responsible for these incursions and depredations and ruthless butchery were Shawnee and Delaware.

Notorious among their leaders, besides Shingas and Captain Jacobs, were Captain Will, Captain John Peter, Killbuck, Shingas' brother, Pisquetomen, and Delaware George (Nenatcheehunt). They were unbridled and went unpunished.

It needs to be remembered too that the Indians who were carrying out these raids on the frontier were not the Indians of William Penn's first acquaintance. They still carried the bow and arrow, the tomahawk and the scalping knife and the war club, and some had muskets. But those who would understand war on the frontier have got to appreciate the way in which the rifle revolutionized for the Indian his methods of warfare. How abruptly and dramatically it transformed the life of the Delaware and the Shawnee, as well as that of all the other Indian tribes along the frontiers in the Northeast, can hardly be exaggerated.

As early as 1750, before the time of Braddock's expedition, the Delaware Indians were almost completely armed with rifles, and it is known that the Chickasaws, who became expert marksmen, had been hunting with the rifle as early as 1736.[26] Most Indians preferred the rifle to the musket. It required a little more time to load, but its advantages were many: it delivered a smaller ball, needed less powder, and could be held more steady. It was ever so much more accurate; in the hands of a skilled marksman it was deadly at 100 yards and still dangerous at four times that distance. And of course the rifle was *far* superior, every Indian understood, to the bow and arrow, both for accuracy and for range. He therefore never missed an opportunity to acquire one, no matter what its condition.

The Indian had four means by which to secure his rifle. He could kill a white settler, or a hostile Indian, for it; or he could steal it from a careless or sleeping owner; or he could trade for it; or he could pledge service to the French, or to the English, for it. Remarkable stories of exchanges have come down. A gun may have been purchased by an Indian from a trader, like George Croghan, with a stack of furs as high as the gun was long. How much this rifle was costing the Indian has been calculated by one interested accountant. Noting that beaver was the chief fur of the trading, and that some 200 pelts would be required for a stack three and one-half feet high, and that a beaver skin went in those days for about six shillings, he figured the cost to the Indian at 1200 shillings. The gun, in many cases not a high-quality piece, likely was actually worth 20 shillings.[27] And, in fact, more often than not, the Indian was receiving a fourth-rate firearm.

A trader like Croghan could regularly present to an Indian village a number of these weapons. But he could not carry many, and, doubtless, like all the traders who had long distances to negotiate, simply took orders. He would exhibit samples of his wares, and schedule a meeting for later, at a specifically designated spot and time, not necessarily close to the village. For the Indian this might mean a long journey with a heavy load of furs. To purchase one rifle with raw beaver pelts he would need to deliver about 300 pounds. For such trading trips he depended upon companions, often pressing the Indian women into service. Most of this trading took place on the waterways, on such rivers as the Susquehanna, the Juniata, and the Allegheny.

Of course the rifle did not replace the tomahawk or the war club or the scalping knife. And certainly the bow and arrow did not completely disappear. Where stealth and quiet were required the bow had its advantages. The bow could also deliver flaming arrows to buildings and grain fields, when the Indian desired a fire. Besides, a skilled Indian could launch as many as twelve arrows in the time it took an expert rifleman to fire once and reload. But the rifle was the thing. And the Indian eventually became so attached that he was virtually inseparable from it. He would place on its stock some distinctive signature, a mark of adornment or identification; and he rarely left it from his sight. For the last fifty years of the eighteenth century, nothing was more precious to the Indian brave than his rifle.

So it is well to understand that rifles had been in use on the Pennsylvania frontier much earlier than is generally supposed. From Edward Shippen at Lancaster, Governor Robert Morris had a letter dated April 24, 1756, which acknowledges this development:

... the Indians make use of rifled guns for the most part, and there is such a difference between these sort of Guns and Smooth bored, that if I was in an Engagement with the Savages, that I would rather Stand my chance with one of the former Sort, which might require a minute to clean, load and discharge, than be possessed with a Smooth bored gun which I could discharge three times in the same

space, for at 150 yards distance, with the one, I can put a ball within a foot or Six Inches of the mark, whereas with the other, I can Seldom or ever hit the board of two feet wide to Six feet long.[28]

The year 1756 was a year of great pain for the frontier people. It opened with a series of very damaging raids on the Cumberland Valley. Although rewards were being offered for the heads of Shingas and Jacobs,[29] the two fierce chiefs led their warriors on a campaign of terror all over central and eastern Pennsylvania. Indeed, the raiding parties assaulted settlements within seventy miles of Philadelphia, in a ceaseless orgy of plundering and butchery.

At the end of the year, when a tally was taken at Fort Duquesne, the French Commandant was able to count 500 scalps and 200 present prisoners, almost all of which and whom had come from Pennsylvania.[30] And at the council which was convened at Carlisle in the middle of January, and lasted for a week, the source of the trouble was early established.

In attendance were the Lieutenant Governor of Pennsylvania, Robert Hunter Morris, and Commissioners James Hamilton, William Logan, Richard Peters, and Joseph Fox. Among the Indians present were Chief Belt and Seneca George. George Croghan and Conrad Weiser served as interpreters. Croghan had a lot to report. He informed the council that he had sent a Delaware Indian, called Jo Hickman, or "Delaware Jo," to the Ohio for intelligence, and that just yesterday this brave had reported that he had been to Kittanning, "forty miles above Fort Du Quesne, the residence of Shingas and Capt. Jacobs, where he found 140 men, chiefly Delawares and Shawanees, who had there with them above *one hundred English prisoners*, big and little, taken from Virginia and Pennsylvania." [31]

Hickman had then gone on to Logstown, a French and Indian community located on both sides of the Ohio River, immediately below the present town of Economy, some eighteen miles downriver from present Pittsburgh, in present Beaver County,[32] where he discovered thirty English prisoners held captive by one hundred Indians. When he returned to Kittanning, which the Indians called Attigue, it was to learn that ten Delaware warriors had been dispatched to the Susquehanna to persuade (Hickman was assuming) the Indians of that region to take revenge on those settlers who may have been responsible for the "mischief lately done in Northampton." Croghan, in summarizing, assured the council that he had good reason to believe that the Delaware and Shawnee were acting in this hostile manner with the advice and consent of the Six Nations.[33] (Not good tidings, as was soon disclosed) The conference ended without much to feel good about. It was clear that Croghan was recommending aggressive reprisal, and it was the kind of information showing up here that by summer's end determined the assault on Kittanning.[34]

Meanwhile, the raids continued, with such an ever-increasing ferocity that fear and consternation gripped the settlements. Even Shippensburg was in terror. A letter written by William Trent from Carlisle on February 15 describes the effect of the raids: ". . . all of the People have left their Houses betwixt this [Carlisle] and the Mountain, some come to Town and others gathering into little Forts; they are moving their Effects from Shippensburg and every one thinks of flying . . . ."[35]

In the dead of winter, on February 29, an Indian raiding party attacked the David Davis Fort in the Little Cove. On the same day warriors wreaked havoc at McDowell's Mill on the Conococheague. Within a month they had led an assault on Patterson's Fort, which, originally a "private fort," had just been completed in December; next they captured the fort just west of Chambers Mill, in Conococheague, known as McCord's. McCord's was a private fort. The building had been fortified by John McCord to provide protection for the settlers in the neighborhood during the fall and winter of 1755-56. It was located at the foot of the mountains near the gap called "Nancy's Pack-saddle." The raiding party which appeared on April 1 was a large one, and likely the same as had been seen hovering around Fort Shirley and Fort Granville. The attack was a most fierce one. Here the Indians killed or captured twenty-seven persons. Among those who were murdered or carried off were Mary McCord, Mrs. John Thorn and baby, Mrs. Annie McCord, wife of John, and two daughters, Martha and a youngster.[36]

The fall of McCord's inspired a pursuit by Pennsylvania militia forces. Robert Robison, in his narrative, which provides his eye-witness accounts of many of the Indian depredations, describes the battle of Sideling Hill, which he calls, the "first fought battle after

Braddock's defeat." He reports that the Indians, on leaving McCord's "took their course near to Fort Littleton," and that Captain Hans [Hanse] Hamilton, who commanded the garrison there, immediately set out in pursuit with his company. Robison remembers that Hamilton's Indian guide was able to follow the tracks of the band to Sideling Hill, where they discovered the party with their prisoners. Hamilton's men had the benefit of the first fire, but did no damage. According to Robison, the Indians on their return of the fire "defeated our men, and killed a number of them." Robison's brother James was one of those slain. And he adds a gruesome detail: "The Indians had M'Cord's wife with them; they cut of[f] Mr. James Blair's head, and threw it in Mrs. M'Cord's lap, saying that was her husbands head; but she knew it to be Blair's." [37]

Another report has Captain Alexander Culbertson in pursuit of the Indians, with "about fifty men." In this account the Indians were overtaken just beyond Ray's Hill, "near Sideling Hill." In the fierce battle which followed, twenty-one soldiers, including Captain Culbertson and his Ensign, John Reynolds, were killed, and eleven were wounded.[38]

The disheartening news Captain Hamilton reported officially two days later, on April 4: "These are to Inform you of the Melancholy News that Occurd on the 2nd Instant . . . our men Engaged about 2 hours, being about 36 in Number & we Should have had the better had not thirty Indians Came to their Assistance. Some of our men fired 24 Rounds a piece, and when their Ammunition Faild were oblig'd to Fly." The effect of the assault and the following battle was described by the Reverend Captain John Steel in a communication of April 11. While lamenting the condition of the frontier forts, both private and provincial, Steel reports: "Since McCord's Fort has been taken, & ye men defeated that pursued, our Country is in the utmost confusion. Great Numbers have Left the Country & many are preparing to follow." [39]

Although forts were in place and were being garrisoned, the terrible massacres of the Big Cove and at the Connolloways and the destruction of Fort McCord in the winter and spring of 1755-56 cast a pall over the frontier. The provincial army was becoming a reality, because of the energy of Colonel Benjamin Franklin, who was raising troops in Philadelphia, and Conrad Weiser, who was doing the same among the German settlers, and John Armstrong, who was doing the same in the Cumberland Valley,[40] but it was still a long way from an effective fighting force. The confidence that the settlers had felt originally when the plan for the forts was announced was now much shaken.

Meanwhile Governor Morris, appalled by the raids and by stories of torture, and as yet unable to persuade the Assembly to provide protection, on April 14 issued a proclamation. He was officially declaring war on the Delaware Nation.[41] To the people of Pennsylvania he announced the reward of bounties for Indian prisoners or scalps. For every male prisoner over twelve years of age the captor was provided 150 Spanish dollars (pieces of eight),130 dollars for each scalp of such an Indian;130 dollars for every female and for every child under twelve brought in alive; fifty dollars for each scalp of a woman or child.[42] Matters had come a long way from the Quaker Penn Indian policy; and of course the Quaker dominated Assembly did not take kindly to the proclamation. Indeed, Morris was before long compelled to withdraw the bounty on scalps, and, even, on June 2, to declare a suspension of hostilities, to last for thirty days.[43] And, "To the credit of the hardy pioneers of Pennsylvania . . . no Indian was wantonly killed for the sake of the reward." [44]

Although the ring of forts was in place, and seemed to be having a deterrent effect upon Indian raids, just how confused and unprepared the colony was for a declaration of war is apparent from a letter sent by Secretary Richard Peters to Proprietor Thomas Penn. The letter is dated April 28, 1756, and notes a want of provisions, a lack of ammunition, and a deplorable "Cowardice and backwardness of the people."[45]

And *still* the depredations continued.

From Carlisle, Lt. Colonel Armstrong advised Captain Burd that he had heard from Captain Hugh Mercer "that on Wednesday last [May 26] John Watson about three miles from McDowels Mill was found kill'd & his body inhumanly mangled, and his wife's tracts [tracks] found going off with the Tract of an Indian on each Side & the House burn'd, a detachment from Capt [John] Steel's and [John] Potter's company are going in Quest of the Enemy." [46] And for the same region came report of another incident. Commissary

James Young is writing in great pain to Governor Morris from Carlisle on July 22: "By the Winchester Post we have Advice that the 20 Inst in the Morning a party of Indians Surprizd two of Captn Steels men as they were Guarding some Reapers 4 miles on this side M'ckdowels mill that went with two Women to the Spring for some water is missing the Women got in safe to the fort, and almost at the same time a man and a Woman were Scalp'd a few miles on the Other side the mill . . . ."[47]

Virginia joined Pennsylvania in placing bounties on the scalps of Jacobs and Shingas; and, though Shingas was nearly brought in, wounded as he was at Fort Cumberland on April 18, the two continued their ravages of the settlements. On June 11, the Fort known as Bigham's, a private fort near Patterson's Fort, which the Indians had assaulted in the spring, was captured. Apparently the French officer in charge of a raiding party of seven Frenchmen and twenty Indians, Ensign Niverville de Montizambert, had been ordered to "annoy George Croghan's fort," which was Fort Shirley. Disappointed there, he elected to assault Bigham's, in the Tuscarora Valley, less than fifteen miles south of Fort Granville. Here the party killed five and carried off the remaining eighteen of the occupants.[48]

The Provincial Commissioners in the middle of June added a great deal of fuel to George Croghan's implied recommendation that some aggressive action be taken. Aware that the Governor was very shortly to leave on a trip for Amboy, New Jersey, they penned a letter, apparently on June 13, 1756, to the Governor. The letter was signed by Commissioners Benjamin Franklin, Evan Morgan, John Mifflin, John Hughes, and Joseph Fox. Hoping for an immediate action, the Commissioners reviewed the situation for Governor Morris. Morris read this letter to the meeting of the Council, June 14, at which these five commissioners were present. The letter definitely helped to produce a climate which would make Armstrong's proposed expedition to Kittanning seem the thing to do: "When the Indians first began to Infest our Frontiers, the Commissioners were of Oppinion, that the best means of Securing our Inhabitants, was to Carry the warr into the Enemys Country, and hunt them in all their Fishing, Hunting, Planting and dwelling places." Then, having spoken of the failure of the forts, they noted the failure of the bounty proclamation. The letter closes with the recommendation of an aggressive offensive, one which even included the possibility of assaulting Fort DuQuesne.[49]

Although not yet mounting any kind of campaign into Indian country, Morris and the Council did take some action promptly. First, they ordered Armstrong to send Captain George Armstrong to organize and send a party to build Pomfret Castle[50] and to organize rangers to "Scour the woods Westward." Secondly, the provincial commissaries were ordered to supply Armstrong with all the ammunition and supplies he may be in need of. And the Commissary General of Musters, James Young, was ordered to inspect the forts and garrisons along the frontier, to see that they were properly garrisoned and provisioned.[51]

As it turned out, these actions were insufficient, and perhaps too tardy, to discourage the Indian depredations. A signal moment in the frontier wars occurred less than six weeks later, on July 22, when Shingas and Jacobs showed up at Fort Granville. Here they brazenly threw down the gauntlet, challenging the garrison to "come out and fight." [52] Jacobs was fond of declaring that if it's made of wood, it can burn.

And even though this summer season of 1756, according to both Armstrong and Adam Hoops, was the most abundant in "the Memory of Man," *still* the farmers fled their plantations, leaving the tall corn standing in the fields.[53]

By the time of the autumn harvest the raids had reached an all-time high in ferocity. Some had the impression that the Indians had achieved such a confidence that they envisioned the complete withdrawal of the English from what they regarded their land.

VII

Fort Granville

One of the most momentous events of the frontier wars of 1755-1758 occurred at mid-summer in 1756. One historian declares, "The total destruction of Fort Granville by the French and Indians on July 30, 1756, was the greatest disaster which had taken place on the frontiers since the defeat of the army of General Braddock a year before."[1]

Fort Granville was one of the forts built as one of Armstrong's "chain of forts" designed to provide protection for the people living in the settlements west of the Susquehanna in the Province of Pennsylvania. In December of 1755, George Croghan was ordered by Governor Morris to build Fort Granville, Fort Lyttleton, and Fort Pomfret Castle (Croghan's trading post, soon to be Fort Shirley, was already in place, on Aughwick Creek.). For Granville Croghan chose a virtually ideal site. He had the fort built at a most strategic spot, on the north bank of the Juniata River, a mile to the west of the mouth of Kishacoquillas Creek. Despite some problems with workers and pay, construction proceeded at a fair pace. By January 17, Morris thought the fort close enough to completion to accommodate a garrison. Accordingly, he appointed to the command of the fort Captain James Burd, Lieutenant Edward

Ward, and Ensign James Potter. These officers would command a company of seventy-five men "enlisted in the County of Cumberland &c. & some now doing Duty near the Mouth of Kishecoquillas." [2]

In the orders delivered to Burd were these directives: "You are as soon as possible to proceed with your Company to the Place called Kishecoquillas and to take upon You the Care and direction of the Fort now erecting there, which you are to cause to be built with all possible Dispatch, as near as may be in the Form herewith given You, and which I have named Fort Granville." And further, "As soon as the Fort is finished and the Ground about it cleared You are then to detach Partys from time to time to range & scour the Woods from Fort Granville towards Fort Shirley at Aughwick & Pomfret Castle near Manitango . . . ." [3]

But it is doubtful that Fort Granville was ever amply provisioned or fortified. As of February 1, Burd could report seventy-three guns, but only two pounds of powder (!), 176.75 pounds of lead, and no flour or meal. His orders to Lieutenant Ward, given when Burd was about to head up a detachment to Mahantango, reveal how unfinished and how unready was the fort:

As I shall march with 25 men of my Comp^y for Mahantango tomorrow I have left with you 41 men to Garison this Fort & Carry on the works here—You'l every day mount a Gaird of 1 Serg^t or Corporall & 12 men, as Usuall, & give the Serg^t or Corporall of the Gaird your orders in writing—You'l Endeavour to gett all the buildings finished first, & then gett the Fort Cleared of all the Chips & then you'l begin the trinch for the Stockade, you'l digg it 4 foott deep in the outside of the Stakes I have drove in the Ground & line your Trinch—you'l Cutt the loggs 16 foott long & lett them be quite Streight and of a good Size—When the party returns from Carlisle you'l immediately draught a New gaird of 12 men under Corporall [John] Donihow [Donaghew] & send them to Carlisle the Road that you find the party has Cutt & write to Mr Buchanan to send by them for the use of this Garison one whole Barrell of Gun poudder letting him know that we have not one ounce in store there . . . . [4]

During all of March of this year there occurred a great deal of hostile Indian activity in the region of Fort Granville. On his mission to deliver the soldiers' pay to Armstrong's garrisons west of the Susquehanna, Elisha Salter, Commissary General of the Musters for the Province, arrived at noon on April 4 in Carlisle. As he reported in a letter to the Governor, while at Carlisle he heard news of Fort Granville, which fort of course was on his schedule. According to the report that had come into Carlisle, just a few days ago, on March 31, "There was a party of Indians, 4 in number, within one mile of the fort, which fort is so Badly stor'd with Amunition, Not having three Rounds per man, they thought it not prudent to Venture after them. . . . I think it highly Necessary, & shall, if possible, get an Escort from Adam Hoop's, to go the Rounds with me as I am Verry Sencible Great part of the Souldiers have left their posts & Come to the inhabitants, particularly from fort Granville." [5]

Burd was experiencing great difficulty in recruiting his quota for the garrison at Granville. From Carlisle on April 19 he wrote to provide the Governor a progress report. Having indicated to Morris that he would be going from Carlisle to Granville and then back to Carlisle in his recruiting, he addressed the situation at the Fort: "I am inform'd that they are entirely out of all manner of Provisions at Fort Granville, which is a very bad Situation, as the Enemy are Constantly Visiting them, they have wounded two men within sight of ye Fort & one of ye mens lives are dispair'd off, they would have Carried off one of them had not Lew^t Ward rushed out of the Fort & Rescued him, Mr Ward sent a Detatchem^t under ye Com^d of Ensigne Clark after the Enemy but Could not Come up with them."

Later in the letter, Burd painfully reports want of a surgeon and medicines, and then, prophetically, identifies the big problem: "I am convinced that unless these garrisons are re-inforced to one hundred and fifty men each, and sufficient stores of ammunition and provisions [supplied], that this part of our province will be forced." [6]

By January 24, Governor Morris, having personally inspected the progress on the forts, was able to report to the Provincial Council that three of the forts were "already in hand." He predicted the completion of Fort Pomfret Castle "in about ten days," but in fact that fort, whose construction was turned over to James Burd, was never finished. [7]

Croghan's structure, it is known from the later French account of the battle there, took the form of a square, each side eighty-three paces in length (35,000 square feet, about an acre), with a bastion strengthening each corner. Upon its completion, Morris, as promised, had the fort named in honor of John Carteret, the Earl of Granville.[8]

James Burd had been the first to assume the command at Granville. But in the late spring of 1756, by which time hostile Indian activity was everywhere in the region, Burd, who on April 24 had been promoted to Major, was replaced by Edward Ward. Ward was on May 22 commissioned captain and given command of the company at Granville. At the same time Edward Armstrong, brother to John Armstrong's wife Rebeckah,[9] was assigned to Ward as his lieutenant. Ward was not immediately happy with the garrison. He promptly complained that he had "not One man at the Fort fit for a Serjeant." [10] Besides, he found the fort woefully short of supplies.

Lieutenant Colonel John Armstrong, responsible for the provisioning of the forts, was from the beginning much concerned. When he was advised of Ward's situation, he promptly dispatched a letter to Major Burd, then at Harris's Ferry. The letter, written at Carlisle, was delivered by John Donaghew the ten miles to Burd on May 29: "I have rec^d from Capt Ward the most mournfull letter that the Subject can admit, shewing his want of men and other necessarys at Fort Granville and begging particularly that Shepherd & Jo^n Donaghew may be continued there assuring me he has not One man at the fort fit for a Serjeant, or that can give him ye least assistance in teaching the new recruits . . . ." Armstrong then urges Burd to get the muster and other administrative records to Ward at once: "Capt Ward writes me that nothing can be Settled by the pay master nor himself with that Company for want of the Attestations and other necessary papers yet in your hands. These you'l please to Send Over with proper remarks on each that justice may be done both your selfe & the men."[11] Burd responded immediately with the roll of names for thirty-nine men whom he had enlisted for Fort Granville, "with an Amount of Money Advanced." [12]

There had been a settlement here at the site of Fort Granville (present-day Lewistown). It was called Old Town, and it was precisely at the site of a very important Indian town of years ago. Historian U. J. Jones, in his account of the Juniata Valley, invites a view of the scene: "It was the outlet of a large and fertile valley, through which ran a northwestern Indian path, and in which dwelt five or six tribes, who found this the natural outlet to the Juniata. The council-house stood upon the east side of the creek, near its mouth, and the line of wigwams stretched toward the north." [13]

It seemed an ideal spot for a fort. As the Juniata wends its way through the mountains it arrives here at a very narrow pass. A fort presiding over this pass is not only in a commanding position but is so well elevated as to enjoy a view for many miles, perhaps for as many as six, east and west.

The settlement has a strange history. The white settlers who first came to this lovely base of the valley were Scotch-Irish. It seems that they were members of four families. The little company was headed up by a man named Arthur Buchanan, who had two sons with him. It was Buchanan who first approached the Indians. He offered to purchase from them whatever land they were willing to sell. He talked chiefly to Tewea, an enormous Lenni Lenape brave, and obviously the chief. Because he so much resembled an equally gargantuan German whom Buchanan remembered from Cumberland County, he addressed the chief as Jacobs, adding "Captain" to appeal to his vanity. As the story goes, Tewea was at first not listening, but, having been mellowed by generous portions of rum, finally agreed to sell. The Indians were selling only that portion of the land that Buchanan coveted most, and it seemed that whites and Indians might live together here for some time. But Jacobs, inexplicably (although it may have been because settlers were appearing in ever increasing numbers) gathered up his people, directed them to lay waste to their wigwams, and pulled out.[14]

Naturally, the settlers feared for what might come next. But this all occurred in 1754, and for more than a year there was no sign of hostility from Indians in the immediate region. And in fact the village prospered. All of this changed abruptly in the spring of 1756, during the time the fort was constructed. Hostile Indians were showing up in the Kishicoquillas Valley in small parties, obviously bent on plunder. From time to time one party or another would approach the fort, but, uncertain of the garrison, never ventured an assault. Toward the middle of the summer these Indian parties became more brazen and began to threaten the farmers in the fields. On hearing of assaults on the farmers in the Tuscarora region, Lt.

Edward Armstrong sent out a detachment, under the command of Lieutenant Faulkner, to protect the farmers who were bringing in their grain. It was apparently at just this time, July 22, that a band of Indians, some sixty or seventy in number, appeared before the fort, hideous in war paint, and arrogant in posture. They challenged the garrison to "come out and fight." [15]

When Captain Ward, replied from the fort with contempt, the Indians fired a volley which slightly injured one man. Franklin's *Pennsylvania Gazette* on August 5 printed an account of this episode:

We have Advice from Cumberland County, that on the 22 . . . about 60 Indians appeared before Fort Granville, and challenged the Commander of it to come out and fight them; but that he being but weak-handed, did not think proper to accept of the Challenge; that they fired at, and wounded, one of the Men that belonged to the Fort in the Thigh, who happened to be a little Way from it, but not so badly but that he got safe in; that they lurked about the Place for some Time, expecting to catch some of our People, but that they being upon their Guard, were disappointed; and that then they went off, after shooting down all the Cattle they could find.[16]

The Indians now divided their numbers into the customary small raiding parties and set out to do mischief where they could. At the mouth of the Juniata, one party attacked the home of Robert Baskins, whom they promptly murdered. After burning down his cabin, they carried off his wife and children. Hugh Carroll and all of his family were made captive by another of the parties.[17] The settlers had the impression that the number of Indians lurking in the Juniata Valley was quite large, some estimates reaching 150. The force seemed to be composed largely of the Delaware and Shawnee from Kittanning, under Jacobs and Shingas, but perhaps a third of the whole party were French, including the commander.

It was about one week after this incursion, on July 30, that Ward elected to head up a detachment of soldiers to march to the protection of the harvesters north in Sherman's Valley. He turned over the command of the fort to Lieutenant Edward Armstrong, who had remaining to him only twenty-four men.

Not long after Ward had disappeared into the valley[18] a very large party of hostile Indians appeared out of nowhere. Estimates vary, some having the party's number at one hundred Indians and some fifty French soldiers. The French account of the siege gives a much lesser number. According to the report of the battle made by the French, the party consisted of thirty-two Shawnee, Delaware, and Illinois Indians, and twenty-three Frenchmen. In command of this company was Captain Louis (sometimes Francois) Coulon de Villiers, the French officer whose younger half-brother, Joseph, had been killed by Washington's forces, possibly by the Mingo Half King, in the confused fighting at Little Meadows. It was this very officer who compelled the surrender of George Washington at Fort Necessity. The French report has De Villiers departing Fort Duquesne on July 22 and attacking Granville on August 2 (July 30, according to Pennsylvania records).

It was learned later that the attack made upon Granville was made in mistake. Apparently the guide for the war party was supposed to be leading the force to Fort Shirley, which was the intended object. Somehow he got confused. It seems that, having taken the French and Indians properly over the Kittanning Trail, which opens at Frankstown (present-day Hollidaysburg), he then elected to follow "the path leading down the Juniata valley, instead of taking the path leading directly to Aughwick [Fort Shirley]." [19]

The assault was immediate and fierce. According to accounts exacted from prisoners who were later delivered, the siege continued throughout the afternoon and well into the night. As the damage done was but slight, the Indians, taking advantage of the darkness, skulked along beneath the bank of the river, and crept into the very ravine that was once thought to be a big advantage to the fort. From here it was only a matter of some twelve or fifteen yards to the walls of the fort. Thus it was an easy matter for the warriors to set fire to the timbers, and this they were quick to do. As the fire burned ever more and more eagerly, one of Armstrong's soldiers who could speak French requested leave of Armstrong to parley with the French commander. According to one report, the enraged lieutenant answered, "The first word of French you speak in this engagement, I'll blow your brains out." He then urged his men to fight the fire bravely, assuring them that the flames were failing and that soon the fire would be extinguished.[20]

However, by this time, early morning, a sizable hole had appeared in the logs, and as Lieutenant Armstrong was heading up the detail fighting the flames he was shot and killed. A private was killed at the same time and three other soldiers were wounded.

Noting the progress of the fire, and perhaps sensing that the fort's commander had been hurt, the French commander called for a cease-fire. He then ordered the garrison to surrender, and made the all-too familiar promise that if they did so, their lives would be spared. From the depositions that were later taken, what happened next was this: One of the occupants of the fort, a corporal by the name of John Turner, previously a resident of Buffalo Valley,[21] was persuaded. With no one superior in command, and apparently strictly on his own, he lifted the bar and opened the gate. The Indians came pouring in, two pausing to bind Turner securely.[22]

In all, twenty-two men, three women, and an unknown number of children (probably five or six) were made captive. (The French report of the battle provided a tally showing the return of twenty-seven prisoners and four scalps.) After the fort was plundered, and the long march to Kittanning was organized and in motion, Chief Jacobs gave the French commander a questioning look, and at his nod returned to the fort to set fire to its corners and prove to all that "I can burn down any fort. Forts are built of wood."

Then began the agonizing march to Kittanning. It was well known that these raids were being launched out of the Delaware nest at Kittanning, and most of the captives knew that the Allegheny River was a long, long distance away. Most understood also that, despite the pledge of the French commander, death could be waiting for them at the Allegheny. They would have a long time to think about that.

Indeed it was a terrible march, as all reports of the journey agree. All of the captives were most barbarously treated. Prisoners who showed the slightest sign of fatigue were dealt horrendous blows and cruelly whipped; soldiers were required to carry the plunder. One soldier, named Brandon, who had identified himself as a Roman Catholic, was, because he had been shot through one knee, naturally unable to keep up with the party. He was taken to the top of a high hill, scalped and tomahawked. Another, a man by the name of Barnhold, because he had been wounded in the fighting at the fort, was not bound at night. Happily, he was able to manage an escape. And it was he who brought the story to the *Pennsylvania Gazette*, which on August 19, printed an account of the tragedy.

After six agonizing days the journey finally came to an end. But the end was not all that welcome. All reports received from captives who escaped agree that at Kittanning the prisoners were most cruelly treated. The most terrible moment of all occurred when they were compelled to watch the torture death of John Turner. It has been inferred that the Indians chose Turner for their favorite torture because of their contempt for cowardice. That may very well be the case. Indians experience fear of course, and they can run like a deer when they are frightened, as when they hear the "thunder sticks," which is their term for the artillery. But they know how to die, and generally do so with great courage. Those who abhor torture are inclined to equate cruelty with cowardice. That is probably a mistake. Historians and anthropologists have tried, pretty much in vain, to explain the Indians' passion for torture. That they took an extreme delight in it there is no question. But that it is an expression of cowardice is rarely suggested.

It was with the familiar fiendish glee that the warriors of Captain Jacobs and Shingas here put to death in the cruellest way they could devise the man who had admitted them to the fort. How awful the scene must have been for those captives required to look on cannot be imagined. All accounts agree on the details.

Turner was bound securely to a pole which had been blackened and planted in front of the council-house. In the customary way a slow-burning fire was built at his ankles. Then for three hours gun-barrels which had been made red-hot in the coals were forced through his body. Eventually his scalp was ripped from his head, while all the while youngsters and the Indian women pierced his flesh with flaming splinters. At the last, an Indian boy who was held aloft over Turner's bloody head, dutifully split his skull with a hatchet.[23]

It is not known just how many of the captives taken from Fort Granville were tortured to death. It is known that many were never heard of again. There is the report of the settler George Woods. He had been held captive with Jane Gray, the daughter of John and Hannah Gray of the Juniata Valley, and recollected for those who had the stomach to listen a torture similar to that experienced by Turner. In Woods' account the hapless victim had holes cut in his cheeks, after which the Indians passed a rope through the holes and secured the rope to a tree. Then began the red-hot gun barrel treatment which had been Turner's fate. When the poor fellow tried to avoid the gun-barrel by moving round the tree, he was met by another brave with a ready gun-barrel. After some time in this exercise, the warriors pierced the victim's abdomen to free his intestines, which they secured to a tree, then continued to scorch him to force him to move. His movements of course served to extract his intestines. Finally, as Woods reported, he was killed when one pierced his heart with the gun barrel. According to Woods, it was a common practice of the Indians to plunge "sharp sticks through the wrists and ankles of captives," after which they would twist them "until their limbs were ripped off." [24]

    An escaped prisoner by name John Cox at the time of Armstrong's raid on Kittanning reported for the *Pennsylvania Journal* of September 9, 1756, an account of the torture death of one John Bradley at the village. According to Cox, Bradley was submitted to the "usual cruelty," the Indian men and women alike beating him for half an hour "with clubs, billets of wood and tomahawks." Then they secured him to a post, "cropped his ears close to his head, chopped off his fingers," and shot countless arrows into his body. All the while the men and women and children who were held captive in the village, "about fifty," were compelled to look upon this unspeakable cruelty.[25]

    Naturally explanations for the disaster were searched for, and scapegoats were fingered. It was Colonel William Clapham's opinion that the fall of the fort could be blamed on a scarcity of ammunition. He noted that he had received from Colonel Armstrong a letter some few days before, in which Armstrong had lamented that there were in the fort "only one Pound of Powder & fourteen Pounds of Lead." [26] But Benjamin Franklin printed in his *Gazette* a contradictory impression: "By Lieutenant Colonel Armstrong's Returns, it appears that there was on the 11th of last Month 57 effective Arms, 50 Pound of Powder, and 100 Weight of Lead, in Fort Granville." [27] And the French account of the battle reports the recovery of "two swivel guns, 100 kegs of powder, some [?]

ammunition, and six months' provisions for the garrison." [28]

Still others (Edward Shippen was one.) placed the blame on the ravine which provided the Indians access to the fort and made the fire possible. They faulted Captain Ward for leaving the "Gutt" (gully) that was left "just as Nature left it." And some pointed to the great distance that separated the forts in Armstrong's chain.[29] Granville was fifteen miles northeast of Fort Shirley; it was fifteen miles also from Fort Patterson (Fort George) at Mexico.

Barnhold, who escaped from the Indians on the way to Kittanning, was the first to report the details of the Fort's surrender. But others later on escaped. One of these, Peter Walker, was in Carlisle by August 20; Jonathan Rodmon was at Fort Augusta on August 31; John Hogan reached Carlisle almost a whole year later, June 1, 1757; John Street required a month more than Hogan, showing up at Fort Cumberland on July 10; and two unnamed soldiers managed their escape in the fall of 1757, arriving at Fort Lyttleton in September.[30] And of course additional prisoners were delivered to their families by John Armstrong in the raid on Kittanning. But many of the thirty-one who were taken from Fort Granville were never heard from again, and one can only guess at their fate.

Lieutenant Colonel John Armstrong took depositions from both Peter Walker and John Hogan, who had returned to Carlisle. From Walker, he learned that the Indians were designing "very soon" to attack Fort Shirley with 400 warriors. Armstrong of course promptly relayed this information to the Provincial Council, together with the warning that Fort Shirley could not stand up to a serious assault.[31] And, said Walker, Captain Jacobs had declared he would take the fort because it would burn. He had learned also that the war party assaulting Granville "had had two Indians killed." (Armstrong would later be informed by Captains George Armstrong[32] and Ward, whom he had directed to survey the ruins, that they found evidence suggesting that eight of the warriors had been killed and thereafter burnt in the fire.)

But the most impressive element of Walker's report had to do with the conduct of Lieutenant Edward Armstrong. John Armstrong must have been much moved when he heard of the courage and the inspiring leadership of his brother-in-law. Walker reported that he behaved with the greatest bravery to the very last, scorning all demands to surrender, even though he had been two days without water, was conscious of how short was the ammunition, the fort on fire, and the enemy prowling the ravine a few yards away.[33] And later Armstrong was to learn that his brother-in-law's soldiers were most devoted to their lieutenant, and that they had requested of Captain DeVillier permission to bury him. And how, even when they explained that it would require of them but a few minutes, as they meant to place the body in the hole they had dug to remove clay to drench the fire, the disdainful commander refused.[34]

On June 1, 1757, the deposition of John Hogan was taken by John Armstrong, who was at the time a justice of the peace[35] for His Majesty in the County of Cumberland:

... before me, John Armstrong ... came John Hogan, late a soldier belonging to Capt. Edward Ward's company of Foot in the pay of the Province of Pennsylvania ...and did declare that on or about the first day of August last past ... he ... with several others was taken prisoner at Fort Granville by a party of French and Indians—consisting of one hundred Indians and fifty French—who took him this Deponent and the rest of the prisoners to the Kittanning, where they were about three hours, at which time John Turner, one of the prisoners, was burnt. They were then taken down the river to Fort Duquesne where they staid but a few hours —the French and Indians not agreeing—they then proceeded to Logs Town, where this Deponent mostly continued until he made his escape. And this deponent further saith ... that the Indians having sold a prisoner to the French received a nine-gallon keg of brandy. This Deponent and George Hily, another prisoner thought that would be a good time for them to escape, as it was customary for the Indians on such occasions to make a frolick and get drunk, which they did, whereupon they set off and brought Martin Borrowelly, another prisoner, along with them and arrived at the south branch of the Potomack in three weeks from the time of their escape. Sworn at Carlisle the first day of June, 1757, before John Armstrong.[36]

Armstrong also learned from Hogan everything there was to know about Fort Duquesne, information that was to prove quite useful one day to General John Forbes.

But the fall of Fort Granville had delivered a shock to the settlers on the frontier. Granville was a provincial fort, garrisoned by soldiers. Its destruction declared to the settlers that they really had no protection at all from the relentless hostiles. Almost immediately, as the news reached out, the frontier was abandoned. Livestock and crops were deserted. Terror-stricken settlers, in "a great runaway," fled to the stable communities in the east, to Carlisle, and to Shippensburg, and even farther east to York and Lancaster. "Cumberland County," notes one historian, "was almost deserted by its defenders [and] whereas a year before it had 3,000 men capable of bearing arms, it [now] had less than one hundred, exclusive of the Provincial soldiers." [37]

Three weeks beyond the fall of Fort Granville, the Reverend Thomas Barton woefully declared in a communication penned at his home in Carlisle, "Such a Panick has seized the Hearts of People in general since the Reduction of Fort Granville, that this Country is almost relinquished, & Marsh Creek in York County is become a Frontier." [38]

It was a short and most dramatic history for Fort Granville. The stockade was never rebuilt. Captain Ward, who was absent on the fatal day, as well as those soldiers who were with him in Sherman's Valley, was reassigned to Fort Patterson and placed in the Company of Captain George Armstrong, the brother of John Armstrong.

VIII

THE KITTANNING EXPEDITION

T he fall of Fort Granville marked a dramatic change for Cumberland County and all of southeastern Pennsylvania. It was not long before Fort Shirley and Fort Patterson were evacuated and abandoned. The chain of forts, while clearly providing some protection for the settlers, and some sense of security, had proved to be inadequate for the effective defense of the frontier. Estimates suggested that for the Juniata Valley alone some 3,000 settlers had fallen victim to the hostile Indians during the eighteen months following Braddock's defeat; and countless numbers had fled to the east. Settlements from the Blue Mountains northward and westward to the West Branch of the Susquehanna were abandoned, the residents fleeing in terror. Some of the fugitives retreated to Fort Augusta; a great many refugees were showing up in Carlisle and in Shippensburg.

The idea of the forts seemed a good one, but it was not enough simply to build a structure here and there. The forts needed to be provisioned and staffed with a garrison equal to the enemy threat. Perhaps, as some suggested, the forts should have been built a little more closely together. While Armstrong and Morris and Burd and Clapham understood well enough that the forts were not prepared, somehow they never became prepared. Whose fault was this? Many blamed recruiting difficulties, which of course had something to do with pay provided and the harvest season.

So many blamed the Quaker government for the devastation of the frontier that by the end of 1756 it had fallen out of favor. In fact, in the 1756 elections anti-Quaker feeling was so strong that the Quaker representation in the General Assembly fell from twenty-six to twelve! Everything now was at sixes and sevens, but certainly stronger measures would now be taken for protection against the Indians. What was needed now was some event that promised hope. Happily that event was not far away.

Almost everybody who lives in western Pennsylvania, as well as those who read the colonial history, has heard of John Armstrong's 1756 raid on the Delaware village at Kittanning on the lower Allegheny River. Indeed, this attack on the Indians is one of the most celebrated events in the early history of Pennsylvania. It has fascinated historians for two hundred years, and accounts in the literature are so numerous as to defy an accurate tally. Of course all accounts derive first from Armstrong's own long and minutely detailed report of the expedition, which was dispatched from Fort Lyttleton to Governor Denny on September 14,[1] and from the accounts supplied by captives of the Indians: (1) *Narrative of Robert Robison* (sometimes Robinson), a member of the expedition;[2] (2) "An Account of the Captivity of Hugh Gibson,"[3] and (3) "The Narrative of Marie Le Roy and Barbara Leininger."[4]

It is surprising that no one kept a journal of the journey, no day-by-day account, in which the time required for a day's march might be noted, or perhaps the sighting of a den of rattlesnakes, or the intolerable harassment of the voracious mosquitoes. Of course, the Kittanning march was nothing in terms of time to compare to that of Sullivan's anti-Indian expedition up the Susquehanna thirteen years later, for which expedition virtually every one of the many officers kept a journal.[5]

By mid-summer of 1756 it was clear, at least to some, that some very new kind of action had to be taken. Indeed, Benjamin

~ The Kittanning Expedition ~

Franklin had proposed at the time of the very first Indian raids upon the settlements that an expedition should be sent into the Indian country. His recommendation had of course been put down by the Quaker Assembly (the "peace party"), which continued to insist on the policy laid down by William Penn at the first treaty. But the climate now was appreciably changed.

At some time in the late spring or early summer Armstrong had proposed to Governor Morris, or Morris to him, that an assault be made upon the source of the trouble. It was well known that most of the raiding parties were organized and launched from the Delaware Indian village known as Kittanning, the home of the principal war-chiefs, Shingas and Captain Jacobs.[6]

Even before the fall of Fort Granville, Armstrong and the Governor had worked out a plan, and had begun to execute it. The collapse of the fort only intensified their determination to punish the Indians and to put an end to the devastation suffered by the settlers on the frontier.

Armstrong had presented a map of Kittanning (*Kit-Han-Ne*), which Indian name means "place at the great stream," to Governor Morris. This map had been composed from information provided by nineteen-year-old John Baker, who had been an indentured servant of George Croghan before he was captured by Indians while he was wandering around Fort Shirley. He had escaped from Kittanning this past spring, after two months of captivity, and on his return to Fort Shirley was able to describe in great detail the make-up of the village at Kittanning.[7] William Peters, serving as Secretary to Governor Morris, was in attendance during the session Armstrong had with the Governor, and it was at this meeting that Peters inscribed on the map the request made by Armstrong: "I[f] it is the Pleasure of the Governor and the Commissioners, I desire to go personally upon this Servise." [8]

All of this organizing and planning was done in great secret. Morris, in informing the council on August 2 of the plans, insisted on *complete* secrecy. He did not provide an update for the Provincial Council until August 27, with Armstrong scheduled to set out on August 30.[9]

Armstrong, now thirty-eight years old, was placed in command of the expedition, which was composed of seven companies, the men drawn from the various fort garrisons. Armstrong himself headed one company, and the other six were commanded by Captains Hugh Mercer, in command at Fort Shirley; John Potter, and the Reverend John Steel, both at McDowell's Mill; Edward Ward, late of Fort Granville and now at Fort George; George Armstrong, also at Fort George; and Hanse Hamilton, in command at Fort Lyttleton. Some accounts have Armstrong's cousin Joseph in command of a company.

  Of these captains, the man with the most military experience was Hugh Mercer. Mercer had been born in Scotland and was at this time only thirty years old. Although he was a physician, earning his medical degree from the University of Aberdeen, he was a veteran of the wars. He had been an assistant surgeon in the army of Bonnie Prince Charlie (1745); and he was present (at age twenty) at the climactic Battle of Culloden, April 16, 1746, when the army of Charles was annihilated. As the survivors were ruthlessly hunted down and slain, Mercer was fortunate to have survived. He had come to America in 1747 as a fugitive. He still aspired to medicine, and did not think of himself as a professional soldier. He could not have known at this time what a future he was to have.

  The Reverend John Steel, already known as "the fighting parson," was a Presbyterian minister. He had been born in Londonderry, Ireland, and was eleven or twelve years older than Captain Mercer. He had a reputation for valor, and, despite his calling, for being anti-Indian. Captain Hanse Hamilton's military experience was highlighted by the distressing battle of Sideling Hill, which followed the assault on the fort at McCord's.

  The force was to be composed of 350 men, fifty per company, but not a single company achieved that quota. Captain Potter's company, made up of farmers from the Juniata Valley, was the largest, with forty-seven men. Captain Steel's soldiers, also from the Juniata Valley, may have numbered as few as thirty. The total number of men was probably 300, though some accounts indicate 307. The companies, except for an advanced troop which was to join at the Beaver Dams, were to travel from their respective forts by the most convenient route, to assemble on the scheduled August 30, at Fort Shirley.[10]

  Many of the men who made up this modest army had, like

their commander, been born in the Old World. Almost all were God-fearing Presbyterians of Scotch or Scotch-Irish ancestry. Most were farmers, and those who were not were tradesmen of some kind. Almost every single soldier of the army, like his commander, had lost to the Indian raids and depredations one or more members of his family. And, no question, their mission was inspired in part by the need for revenge. They thought of the expedition as one to punish the Indians. But the larger purpose of course was to discourage the Indian raids on the settlements; and Governors Morris and Denny, and the officers of the Province of Pennsylvania, were fervently hoping that it might do even more, that it might bring peaceful co-existence to the land.

And so 300 men set out for a village in the wilderness that only one or two of them had ever seen. Every "soldier" was equipped with a musket and a cartridge pouch. And almost every man had a scalping knife, all well honed on the whetstone a night or two ago. All understood that there would be rewards for scalps. Each man had a canteen (some quite rude), and a few carried a kind of tomahawk. Food and other provisions were borne by pack horses. But there were no tents. Armstrong had ordered tents, but when he heard that they would not be forthcoming, he rationalized that they would have been an unnecessary encumbrance anyway. And at least there were blankets. Those soldiers who thought much about the weather prayed to their Presbyterian God that it would not rain,

Armstrong had been warned by Baker, "our best assistant," that the journey to Kittanning would be treacherously difficult, and, as it happened, nobody, not even Baker, knew precisely the route to be followed. Armstrong had learned from Baker to expect about 100 warriors at the town, and the young man guessed that there could be that many prisoners as well.

And what of the commander of this expedition? With what credentials did John Armstrong of Carlisle assume the leadership of the first Pennsylvania attack on an Indian village? Well, Armstrong, so far as is known, had had no military training whatsoever. Not in his native Ireland, where he was educated in the art of surveying. Not in Pennsylvania, where he had been living since he came to America. Although he had played a role in the Braddock campaign of last year, it was not as a military man. He had been a surveyor only, responsible for blazing the trail to Fort Duquesne. His only military experience had been in the building of forts on the frontier in the Cumberland County region and in the administration of these forts. Although he understood well enough the strategies and wiles of the Indians, he had had no combat experience at all. But he had been commissioned Lieutenant Colonel on May 11, 1756, and placed in command of the 2nd Battalion of the Pennsylvania Regiment.

His credentials for command were in his character, which had courage way out front, and which was vitalized by resolution. He was known as "brave and prudent." [11] By one historian he has been described as "one of the most remarkable men of his time. To fearless intrepidity of the highest cast was united in his character a strong sense of religious responsibility, that rarely blends with military sentiment." [12] Besides being governed by this kind of character, Armstrong could relate to his men through a personality which inspired confidence and devotion.

And, though without combat experience, he was by this time rich in the experience of the Delaware and Shawnee raiding parties; and he had been educating the frontier families as best he could in the wiles of the warriors. Certainly he had seen enough of the fighting on the frontier to know what was responsible for the success of the warriors. In a word, it was Surprise. He very well understood that the Indians would almost never attack a settlement or a fort or even a party on the road unless they could do so with the great advantage of surprise. It helped also of course, as Armstrong knew well enough, to enjoy an advantage in numbers, but surprise was the big thing. Accordingly, in his consultations with Governor Morris, he strongly agreed that the campaign simply had to be carried out in secret.

Now how does a commander march a force of 300 men along the well traveled Indian trails over a period of nine days through Indian country without being observed? Impossible, of course. No, not so. As it happened, there is a happy irony here. The fall of Fort Granville, while a great victory for the Indians, cost them dearly. Because of their triumph at Granville they returned with their captives to their nest in Kittanning to celebrate, as was their custom. Although they already had their next target, Fort Shirley, in mind, they had but barely begun to execute that plan by the time Armstrong got underway. The only Indians Armstrong saw on his way west were a handful at Blanket Hill some six miles from Kittanning, and these he was able to skirt easily. The victory that was to be his at Kittanning was his because of surprise.

He had had to make a decision on the route to be followed. There were two Indian paths that he could travel. There was the trail through Raystown, which he had helped to blaze himself, but in the end he elected to go by the Frankstown Road (often called the Allegheny Path or the Ohio Path and now sometimes called the Kittanning Road), which was an old, old Indian trail, well traveled by Conrad Weiser and the Indian traders. He knew the trail to be somewhat longer than the Raystown Path, in its distance to the Allegheny, but he knew too that it was well traveled and that the grades were not so formidable.[13]

He had been corresponding with his officers, chiefly Hanse Hamilton, and with Commissary Adam Hoops, for almost a month; and he had made the necessary preparations. In a letter to Robert Morris, who had just been succeeded as Lieutenant-Governor by William Denny, who had just arrived in the province, August 20,[14] Armstrong reported his schedule and his arrangements. He was writing from Carlisle. He was ignorant of the action taken by the King just five days earlier, which had vetoed the militia act of 1755 and therefore rendered the provincial forces not only illegal but dissolved.

Governor Denny's first meeting with the Provincial Council occurred on August 27. At this meeting, ex-Governor Morris explained to Denny and to the Council that he had planned an expedition against Kittanning. He reported that the mission would be commanded by Colonel John Armstrong, who would have as officers Captains Hamilton, Mercer, Ward, and Potter. Then he proceeded to read the letter which Armstrong had written to him from Carlisle on August 20:

To-morrow, God willing, the men march from McDowell's for Fort Shirley, and this afternoon some part of my own company, with the provisions here, set out for Shearman's valley, there to halt until the residue come up. This night I expected to have been at Fort Shirley, but am much disappointed in getting in of the strays, for collecting whereof we shall not wait longer than this day. [Joseph] Hunter has got about half a score, and commissary Hoops about a dozen. *The commissioners (for which your Honor will please to make them my sincere compliments) have sent every thing necessary except the canteens wrote for by Mr. Buchanan, which I am persuaded they have forgot, and which we must supply by tin quarts. They were probably right in keeping back the tents, as they might have proved an incumbrance, and there is not one shilling laid out on this occasion that does not give me sensible uneasiness, but through the want of experience, and fewness of our numbers, the good end proposed should fail of being obtained.*

After some lament about ammunition he proceeds in his very long letter to an account of Granville, and reports that he has dispatched Captains George Armstrong and Edward Ward to Fort Shirley ahead of him, as he desires them to investigate on their way to Fort Shirley the ruins of Fort Granville and to supply a tally of all that remains. He concludes his letter with an expression of great concern for Fort Shirley, which he is very sure cannot withstand an attack. "Lyttleton, Shippensburg and Carlisle (the two last not finished) are the only forts now built that will, in my opinion, be serviceable to the public." [15]

The men from the various garrisons assembled at Fort Shirley, now Shirleysburg. Armstrong with his little army left Fort Shirley on the morning of August 30. It was precisely one month to the day that Fort Granville had fallen. He was headed now for the Beaver Dams, which were on the Frankstown Road, just a few miles west of Frankstown on the north branch (Beaver Dam Branch) of the Juniata, present-day Hollidaysburg. According to Charles Hanna, "Franks Town was a name given by the Traders to the old town of the Delaware and Shawnees . . . known in 1731 as Assunepachla [which signifies a meeting of the waters]. At that time its population consisted of twelve families and thirty-six men, all Delawares. It received its English name from Francis, or Frank, Stevens, a trader at Allegheny as early as 1734." [16] He notes also that "Contrary to the statements of local historians of Frankstown, the Indians had abandoned their settlements there a number of years before the time of Braddock's defeat," and then he adds that "when Conrad Weiser passed over the Path in 1748, he came to Frank's Town, but saw no houses or cabins." [17]

It was here that Armstrong hoped to catch up with the troops that had been sent out in advance. He arrived with the main force at the Beaver Dams on the evening of Friday, September 3.[18] The union of the forces occurred on the flats where the hamlet of Gaysport in later years would appear.

Some accounts of Armstrong's expedition report the preaching of the Reverend Charles Beatty to the troops at this site, but there is no real evidence that this ever occurred, and, in fact, lots of reason to doubt it.[19] It is known that Armstrong himself regularly led the troops, morning and evening, in prayer.[20]

From Frankstown to Kittanning Town was a distance of 80 miles. Because of the terrain and the poor quality of the path, the pace would be slow. Probably the best the army could hope for was something like two miles per hour. Counting their encampments and periods of rest, the trek might require most of a week. The men would be marching Indian style, single file. Discovery was the thing most to be feared.

At daybreak on the 4th the troops left the Beaver Dams. The way led first from the region of present-day Altoona to Burgoon's (Burgeon's) Pass (now called Kittanning Point, or Kittanning Gap, but best known as the Horseshoe Curve on the Pennsylvania Railroad). From this point the troops moved on up the eastern slope of the mountain to the region then known as the Clear Fields (present-day Ashville), which was on the summit, about twenty miles beyond Frankstown and a mile east of the present post office at Chest Springs (on present-day Route 36).

The going was slow, but, happily, the Indian path from time to time would reveal a mountain spring. What a joy it was for the weary troops to come upon a tiny pool of clear, cold water, with clean sand at its bottom, and sometimes embraced by a structure of stones fashioned by some Indian, or by some trader who had traveled the trail, with a large flat piece of slate provided for kneeling. More precious than his musket, or his boots, was the soldier's leather or wooden or tin canteen; and at such a spring he would fill it gratefully.

At some point near here, on the night of September 4, the army must have paused for a much needed rest. September 5 finds the column moving steadily forward along the narrow path. With the pilots out front and every man following the fellow ahead of him, the army plodded on. After twelve miles the soldiers found themselves at Hart's Log (Hart's Sleeping Place), some two or three miles north of present Carrolltown. There was nothing much here, nothing but legend really. The site had been named for the Indian trader John Hart. His famous log was a different kind of spring. It had been hollowed out so that it would contain water and could provide for Hart's packhorses. Some say the site got its name from a hollow tree which stood near. Legend has it that a tomahawk found stuck in the tree was intended as a warning to Hart that hostile Indians were near. "Sleep somewhere else." A monument today marks the spot where this tree is supposed to have stood.

All this time the army had been marching along an Indian path that was way south of the West Branch of the Susquehanna River. But they were all the time headed for the river, and, twelve miles from Hart's they would reach it at its headwaters. From Hart's hollow log the men marched north now to the site from which the West Branch originates, to the beautiful, secluded hollow called by the Indians Canoe Place (present Cherry Tree).[21] The site was known to the Indians as "Canoe Place" because it marked the limits of water transportation, as dugouts and canoes could not pass over the gravelly shallows waiting upstream. Here the Delawares, who had come up the West Branch from the Great Island, or perhaps even from Shamokin, would abandon their crafts to follow the Kittanning Trail over the mountains to "the place of the great river." [22]

The Indian path was very plain here, and clearly much traveled. It led from the waters of the Susquehanna up Cush Cushion Creek to a principal fork in the trail. Here, between the present villages of Beringer and Cookport (Indiana County), four miles beyond Canoe Place, the path divided. One branch led northwest to Venango, and the other southwest to the forks of the Kiskiminetas and Kittanning paths, about four miles from Owens' Camping Ground, which included several Indian cabins.[23]

Armstrong was now well into his march. Fewer than fifty miles remained to Kittanning. It was here that he elected to camp for the night. It was Sunday, September 5. The ground lay along Cush Cushion Creek. Some of Armstrong's soldiers knew that this site was called the "Forty Mile Lick" (meaning forty miles to Kittanning Town); but few, if any, knew that this was the spot on the Kittanning Trail "where the Indians trimmed the hair of their prisoners before reaching the Kiskiminetas." [24]

On either this day, Sunday, or the next, Colonel Armstrong sent out two old traders, who are identified by Robert Robison in his narrative as Thomas Burke and James Chalmers. With an officer and a guide, they were to determine "the true Situation" of Kittanning.

Camp was broken at dawn's first light on Monday. The army, now fairly well rested, made twenty miles this day. The force proceeded some twelve miles to the Shawnee (Shawana) Cabins, just a mile southwest from the present Cookport, near the forks of Two Lick Creek. Their course took the soldiers next across Ramsey's Run, a very tiny stream (running through the present borough of Indiana) which required of the troops only an extra long stride or a little jump to negotiate. From there the men marched over the ground which now accommodates the borough of Indiana, and in fact drew water from Shaver's Spring (Peter Shaver's Sleeping Place), which is now swallowed up by the campus of Indiana University of Pennsylvania.[25]

On the evening of the 6th the army camped in an area known as Two Licks or Salt Springs, pretty much within the limits of present White Township, which includes Indiana Borough. In years later, a majestic white oak was conspicuous here. It was known as "Armstrong's Oak." Kittanning Town lay to the west only a little over a day's march away. On this day, or the next, Armstrong ordered his men to stash their supplies, "everything that you cannot carry on your backs," high

up on scaffolds.

It was this point that Armstrong in his report mentioned as "thirty miles" from Kittanning. It was from here that he made his last day-and-night march on the 7th and 8th.

On the seventh day of the month the army proceeded west, never far off present Route 422 toward the great river. They came before long to the parting of the trails, to that site where the Kiskiminetas and Kittanning Paths intersect, just a mile or two to the south of what is now Shelocta Post Office. From here the Path to Kittanning led over the site of present Shelocta, passing an old Indian field and thence to the forks of two streams very important to the Indians.

The larger stream, and the one the soldiers would cross first, was called by the Indians Woak-hanne ("Crooked Stream"). This may have been the water that was called (because of its distance from Kittanning) Eighteen Mile Run. They had been just a little to the south of this stream for the last five miles of their march from Shaver 's Spring. The other stream was known to the Shawnee and the Delaware as Sipuas-hanne ("Plum Stream," meaning "plumb" or "straight"). This is present-day Plum Creek. It was close to the mouth of this stream that James LeTort in the decade 1730-40 operated a trading house, which was sometimes called Le Tort's Town, or Litart's Town. It was at this very site that from time to time, over hundreds of years, one Indian village or another had been active. The cabins that appeared here were called by the Iroquois Tohogases, their term for "Shawnee Cabins."

The waters that were formed by the union of Plum and Crooked Creeks, took the name of the larger Crooked Creek. The stream still flows today southwest to enter the Allegheny downriver from Kittanning.[26]

Armstrong's men on their march had nothing to tell them that this ground that they were crossing, here in this cleared region where the two meadow streams run together, had accommodated for untold years a succession of Indian camps and villages. The soldiers could not have known that a little scratching of the surface of the ground would reveal artifacts from long ago (spear points, axe heads, arrowheads, pottery shards, fire stones, and flint chips). They could not have known either that, because of the march they were now engaged in, this very ground would one day be named for their commander.

The Kiskiminetas, or Main Path, proceeded from here in a southwesterly direction, along the ridge west of the present villages of South Bend and West Lebanon, to the "Ten-Mile Lick." Armstrong left the Main Path at this point, to proceed west the last twenty miles to Kittanning Town. The Colonel, still a little nervous, but grateful for good luck, continued to keep scouts in the van of the expedition. They had been marching for the better part of a week. And as yet there had been no sign of Indians.

Throughout the day September 7, the force passed from Shaver's Spring to present Shelocta to Plum Creek and on west along the narrow trail.

The first sign of Indians came at about nine o'clock in the evening of September 7. The four men Armstrong had sent ahead to "reconnoiter" were now returned. Their report was a comforting "All clear," but Colonel Armstrong understood from the vagueness of their account that the party had not got all that close to the town. He still did not know exactly what his plan of attack might be. So the march was simply continued in the hope that Kittanning could be reached yet that night.

By about nine or ten o'clock that night, the army had proceeded some twenty miles to within about six miles from the river, when one of Armstrong's guides came hurrying back to the column to report the sighting of "two or three Indians" just ahead around a campfire. After he had made a second scout, the pilot returned with the information that there were "not above three or four Indians at the fire." He ventured the opinion that these Indians could be easily overpowered, and he urged his commander to surround them. Armstrong promptly rejected the proposal, fearing one or more of the party might escape and hurry off to alert the town to its danger. Instead, he ordered the pilots to lead the troops out and away from the Indians. When at a considerable distance, which was negotiated over a "very rough and incommodious" route, "on Account of the Stones and fallen Timber," [27] he had his men secure the packhorses, and all supplies, including the blankets, in a secluded hollow. He then placed Lieutenant James Hogg, of Captain George Armstrong's company, in command of thirteen men, including the scout who had made the discovery, and ordered Hogg to watch through the night. These men were ordered not to attack until the main force had reached the village, presumably daybreak.[28]

The many accounts of what thereafter transpired are roughly the same in the essential details, and accord closely with Armstrong's personal report to the Governor.[29]

It was in the wee hours of the morning of September 8 that the company (now some 290 strong) came into view of the River. This was the present-day Allegheny of course, although the Indians called it *Oh-he-hu* or *Ho-he-hu* (Ohio), meaning the handsome or beautiful river.[30]

Colonel Armstrong had never been this far west. He had been only as far as his trail blazing took him for the Braddock Road. He had never seen this river. Most of his men had never seen this river, and they were not at this moment able to make it out all that well. It was just a ribbon in the light of the setting moon. The Delaware town was nowhere to be seen. Armstrong was informed by his scouts that it was "upriver, not very far." In fact, it was probably no more than one-third of a mile (Armstrong later reported 100 "perches."). As the column now proceeded up the river, the men very soon began to hear the "Beating of a Drum and the Whooping of the Warriors at their Dance." A few more steps and a piercing whistle froze the column. Armstrong was alarmed, fearing discovery. But the young John Baker, who, though he belonged to Hugh Mercer's company, had kept close to the commander during this critical moment of the march, explained that, no, it was not an alarm but merely the call of a brave to his woman.

This same Indian "kindled a fire, cleaned his gun, and shot it off," before lying down to sleep in the cornfield, which occupied the space between the town and the banks of the river. Armstrong's force, much wearied by its long day's march of almost thirty miles, did the same. "We were obliged," reported the Colonel later, to halt here, "to lie quiet and lurk, till the moon was fairly set." As the soldiers sank into a welcome sleep, by and by, like fireflies, dots of light adorned the cornfield. Baker knew what this was all about. He explained to the officers that because of the heat the warriors had elected to sleep outside; the fires, he suggested, were built to keep away the tiny gnats, which the Indians called "ponkies." [31]

After allowing some time to elapse, Armstrong organized the attack, which he noted happily was going definitely to have the much desired advantage of surprise. As many of the warriors were sleeping in or about the cornfield, he made that the focus of the attack. But he ordered a number of the soldiers to make their way "quietly" along a kind of ridge from which they could assume a position commanding the upper part of the town, that cluster of huts farthest from the river. It was now close to four o'clock in the morning. After some twenty minutes allowed the detachment to advance along the ridge, and satisfied that all of the troops were in place, Colonel Armstrong, as Robert Robison vividly remembered, ordered the assault: "Every man do for himself!"

As the troops raced through the cornfield and into the village they plunged into the hoped for consternation. Robison reports:

We rushed down to the town, the Indian's dogs barked, and the first house we came to, the Indian came out, and held his hand, as shading the light from his eyes, looking towards us, until there was five guns fired at him; he then ran and with a loud voice, called shewanick, which signifies white men, there was in the house a young woman, a prisoner, who came out with both her hands raised up, but the guns were firing so fast she got frightened, and ran back to the house again, where she got a grain of swan shot through her arm; she then made out a second time and was received by us, the Indians being then alarmed, were running through the cornfield, the Indians fired on us, but to no purpose, we rushed into the town, and the Indians left it except Captain Jacobs, his squaw, son, and one called by the traders Pisquetum, and some others that were blown up with their magazine.[32]

A wild and chaotic firing followed. Those Indians who could reach their huts had done so as speedily as they could, and then began a musketry from the loopholes in the walls. Protected as they were, they were able to do some damage. Indeed, one "large" musket ball, apparently fired from the hut of Captain Jacobs, which was in the very center of the town,[33] the site of the tortures, lodged in the shoulder of Colonel Armstrong as he was directing his men. From that house now sounded the fiendish war whoop of Captain Jacobs.

He was encouraging his warriors, declaring that they would soon have scalps aplenty."

Armstrong, now aware that the advantage of surprise had been nullified by refuge and the protection of the log and bark walls, ordered the burning of the huts. "Is there none of you lads," he yelled, "that will set fire to these rascals that have wounded me, and killed so many of our men?" [34]

According to Robison, it was a private by the name of John Ferguson who responded to the challenge. Swearing that "by the Lord God" he would do it, he ripped from a house that was already aflame a burning piece of bark, and, then, at great risk to his own person, he rushed to the hut of Captain Jacobs. There he stood, an heroic figure, holding the burning bark firm against the bark of Jacobs' house until it was flaming too. Then amid a hail of musket balls he dashed for cover.

Other soldiers fired the remaining huts. House after house now began to burn, and it is noted in the reports of the action that from one house a warrior was heard to sing, while at the same time his woman began to cry. As Indians fled from the burning huts they were shot down. They were ordered to surrender, but those who understood were defiant. One warrior sang out that he was a man and that he would never be a prisoner. When he was told in his own language, "Then you will burn!" he replied that he did not fear death, and that he would enjoy taking four or five whites with him.[35]

There was some firing from the opposite shore, and some Indians were perceived to be swimming across the river. But nothing much came of that, those who got across the water content to round up some horses.

The house of Captain Jacobs was now being consumed in flames. Jacobs could understand English. Armstrong invited him again to surrender. The soldiers yelled that he would be burned alive. Jacobs replied in contempt and defiance. According to some accounts, he mocked the soldiers. "I eat fire." [36]

The reports of the death of Captain Jacobs vary some. Historian James Myers notes three very different versions. Certainly Colonel Armstrong in his report does not go out of his way to make the war-chief's death an heroic one: "It was thought Captain Jacobs tumbled himself out at a garret or cockloft window." Another version is a little different: "At the cockloft door of Captain Jacobs's house appeared the head and shoulders of an Indian. Quickly aimed, a bullet tumbled him forward out of the loft." [37] The account of Robert Robison, who is a member of the expedition, is different still. When the magazine in the Jacobs house blew up, "then Jacobs and those before mentioned sprung out, Jacob's squaw wielded a tomahawk round her head before she jumped the fence, Jacobs fell first, then his wife, and then his son, in proportion seven feet high." [38]

The account supplied by James Smith, who at age eighteen had been taken prisoner by the Delawares, accords generally:

When Colonel John Armstrong surrounded the Cattanyan [Kittanning] town, on the Allegheny river, Captain Jacobs, a Delaware Chief, with some warriors, took possession of a house, defended themselves for some time, and killed a number of our men. As Jacobs could speak English, our people called on him to surrender: he said that he and his men were warriors, and they would all fight while life remained. He was again told that they should be well used, if they would only surrender; and, if not, the house should be burned down over their heads;— Jacobs replied he could eat fire: and when the house was in a flame, he, and they that were with him, came out in a fighting position, and were all killed.[39]

Myers cites the account provided in a letter of the Reverend Thomas Barton, September 23, 1756, to the Reverend William Smith of Philadelphia: "I shall . . . observe to you, that the famous Captain Jacobs fought, & died, like a Soldier. He refus'd to surrender when the House was even on Fire over His Head; And when the Flame grew too violent for him, he rush'd out into the Body of our Men flourishing his Tomahawk, & told them he was born a Soldier & would not die a Slave." [40]

If Armstrong did indeed deliberately belittle the death of Captain Jacobs, it is well to remember that his brother-in-law was killed by Captain Jacobs, and that the Colonel was probably in no mood to glorify Indians in any way.

Although the death of Captain Jacobs had been reported twice before, earlier in this year, he was positively identified by prisoners who had been rescued.[41] It was well known that the war-chief had stolen the boots of Lieutenant Edward Armstrong at the surrender of Granville, and in exchange for those had received from a French officer the powder horn and pouch he was now wearing. Besides, he wore his hair in a very distinctive way. Some of the prisoners recognized him from that. And his wife was identified by an ornament she wore in her hair.[42]

A number of Indians were killed by the explosions of gunpowder that was stored in "virtually every hut." Robison learned in his captivity that the Indians felt they had enough in the way of firearms, ammunition, and gunpowder to wage war against the colonists for ten years at least.[43] Armstrong in his report noted that when the roof of the hut of Captain Jacobs blew off, the blast was so forceful as to hurl into the air the leg of a warrior and the body of a child. So high were they blown that they "appeared as nothing and [then] fell in the adjacent Corn Field."

According to Patterson's *History of the Backwoods* the explosion which leveled Captain Jacobs' house was so loud that it could be heard at Fort DuQuesne. [!] Fearing an attack on Kittanning, a party of French and Indians set out upriver, but did not apparently reach the burned out town until the next day, and were dismayed to discover the bodies of Captain Jacobs, his wife, and son.[44]

As the firing lessened, Armstrong learned from the wounded, who had been carried to an elevated position above the town, that many of the Indians instead of attempting to cross the river were taking to the hills. When it was suggested to the Colonel that the warriors may be organizing to cut off the withdrawal of his forces, he could not believe that to be the case. Nevertheless, he sent out scouts hither and yon to determine the enemy's intention.[45]

Armstrong had liberated eleven prisoners. From some of these he learned that two bateaux of French soldiers had been due in Kittanning that very day, that they were to join with Captain Jacobs in a march of 400 warriors and French against Fort Shirley. He learned, further, that a scouting party had been sent ahead to get a feeling for the defenses of Fort Shirley. With Lieutenant Hogg in mind, Armstrong found the information that this party was composed of twenty-four warriors most disturbing.

He was disappointed also to learn that Shingas was living

~ *The Kittanning Expedition* ~

on the other side of the river (the west side), and that many of the Indians' captives were there also. It was later learned that King Shingas may actually have been at Fort Duquesne at the time of the attack on Kittanning Town.[46]

In view of all this, and with nothing more to be done in Kittanning Town, the Colonel ordered the troops to prepare to march. It was now noon on the day of September 8. He learned to his dismay that the horses he had left behind had been found by the Indians and driven off; and he had to presume that the soldiers in charge of the horses had been killed or captured. The withdrawal from Kittanning was thus accomplished in considerable confusion. Although it was daytime, Armstrong's forces were disorganized, and some groups had no pilots to lead the way. They rounded up as many of the Indian horses as they could find, in order to transport the wounded. Many of the companies became lost. One group which was conveying prisoners lost four of these prisoners back to the Indians. They were constantly on the alert for ambush, and indeed from time to time were fired upon. One Andrew Douglas, who lived near Jericho, in Fermanagh Township, Juniata County, was shot through both ankles, but survived.

When east of the Allegheny Mountain, a soldier by name Samuel Chambers remembered that he had left his coat in the neighborhood of the Clear Fields, some fifteen miles northwest of Frankstown. He begged leave of Colonel Armstrong to break off here in order to retrieve the coat, as well as three fatigued horses the army had left at the Clear Fields. According to Robison, Armstrong "advised against it," but when Chambers persisted, the Colonel let him go. Information later acquired from Indians by Captain Patterson disclosed that Chambers was soon discovered by hostile Indians, who pursued him all the way to the Great Island, and "killed him in French Margaret's Island." [47]

The march homeward was painfully slow, what with the liberated seven prisoners, and the wounded (who were carried on what horses the soldiers could collect from the Indians' corral), and the need to guard against attack. Armstrong estimated that the company moved not more than "two miles an hour," but the troops kept pressing forward, and the main body was in Fort Lyttleton in a little over five days, arriving on Sunday night September 14. They were now only twenty miles from Fort Shirley.

But not all were back safely. There are two very distressing stories to relate. The first concerns Captain Hugh Mercer.

Mercer had been put out of action early when a musket ball shattered his right arm. What followed was not much to the credit of his company. Having been carried to the top of a hill, where the wounded were being cared for, Mercer was apparently persuaded by some of his men that the situation was so desperate there could be but little hope for their lives. The men indicated that they were going to head out, and they urged their company commander and his ensign, John Scott, to join them. Mercer, not aware that Armstrong had sent a detachment to recover his company, and sorely wounded, agreed to accompany the men.

As the story goes, not long into their flight, somewhere near Blanket Hill, the party was set upon by the same Indians who that morning had been engaged with Lieutenant Hogg's party. As the soldiers scattered, losing, according to Robison, "about twenty men," Mercer, who was on horseback, was joined by Thomas Burke (the old trader who was one of the men sent ahead to do the reconnoitering of Kittanning) and Ensign Scott. When Mercer had to pause to dress his wound, he became faint and may have fallen from his horse. It was at that moment that they were jumped by a solitary warrior. Scott and Burke leaped upon the horse that had been carrying the wounded captain and fled.[48] Robison, who presumably had the story later from Captain Mercer, in his narrative describes the rest: "Mercer lay down behind a log, it happening to be thick of weeds, the Indian came about six feet from him, and seeing Burke and Scott riding, he gave out a halloo and ran after, in a short time Mercer heard two guns go off: he then went down through a long plumb bottom, and lay there until night, when he made the best of his way."

As can be imagined, it would be a long and most arduous trip for Captain Mercer. Robison's account continues:

It was at the time of the plumbs being ripe, but that did not last long enough, for the captain had a month to struggle with, before he got home, all the food he got after the plumbs were done was one rattle snake, and to eat it raw. On the north side of the Allegany mountain, he saw one day what he thought to be an Indian, and the other saw him, both took trees and stood a long time; at last the captain thought he would go forward and meet his fate, but when he came near, he found it to be one of his own men: both rejoiced to meet, and both in that situation scarcely able to walk, they pushed over the mountain, and were not far from Franks town, when the soldier lay down unable to go any further, with an intention never more to rise. The captain went about seven miles when he also lay down giving up all hopes of ever getting home. At this time there was a company of Cherokee Indians in kings pay, and being at fort Littleton captain Hamilton sent some of them to search along the foot of the Allegany mountain to see if there was any signs of Indians on the route, and these Indians came upon captain Mercer, able to rise, they gave him food, and he told them of the other, they took the captains track and found him, and brought him to fort Littleton, carrying him on a bier of their own making.[49]

  The date was September 23, nine days behind the arrival of the main force. In all, Captain Hugh Mercer had required two weeks (not a month as Robison reported) to reach Fort Lyttleton. And the Pennsylvania colonists had come that close to losing one of the officers who would be most important to John Forbes and George Washington.[50]

  Most interesting is the report of Mercer's ordeal published in the *Pennsylvania Gazette* September 30: "We hear that Captain Mercer was 14 Days in getting to Fort Littleton. He had a miraculous Escape, living ten Days on two dried Clams and a Rattle Snake, with the assistance of a few Berries. The Snake kept sweet for several Days, and coming near Fort Shirley, he found a Piece of dry Beef, which our People had lost, and on Trial rejected it, because the Snake was better. His wounded Arm is in a good Way, tho' it could be but badly drest, and a Bone broken." [51]

  The second sad story concerns Lieutenant James Hogg, who had been left behind to account for the supposed four Indians discovered at their fire. There is some confusion in the various accounts of the incident at Blanket Hill, as it is now called. One account of the disgraceful affair Colonel Armstrong had from deserters. Upon their return to the area in which Hogg had been left, the Armstrong forces met up with a sergeant of Captain Mercer's company and two or three others who had fled from the battle in Kittanning. According to their account, they had discovered Lieutenant Hogg lying wounded by the side of the trail. Hogg had explained to them that he had lain concealed in a thicket when his men abandoned him. Mercer's sergeant, with his companions, then took up Hogg and proceeded along the trail until, after only a short distance, they were attacked by Indians. Although the sergeant spoke of "a large number"of Indians, there were apparently only four. Without the courage to stand and fight, as the wounded Lieutenant Hogg was urging, they fled, abandoning Hogg, who, though on horseback, was terribly wounded. As it happened, the Indians in pursuit killed one man and shot Hogg in the stomach, inflicting a wound from which he died in a few hours, having ridden with his wounds some seven miles.[52] It was obvious to Armstrong that these men were putting the best face on the affair that they could. The Colonel, properly it would seem, in his report of the whole expedition, blamed "that cowardly sergeant and his co-deserters" for the death of Hogg.

Robert Robison's account, which may be accurate in most of its other details, has the lieutenant killed in the first exchange. According to this story, Hogg had done the best he could to stay quiet on the watch. They had crawled close to the Indians, however, just before daybreak, and when one of the warriors wandered from the campfire, he came so close to Hogg's men that they became nervous and opened fire, prompting all the Indians to run from the fire, leaving their guns on the rack which they normally set up. Robison writes, "Our men standing, and not laying hold of the Indians guns, gave them time to return for their guns, and commence a battle. Out of which party the Indians killed the lieutenant, and five men, and wounded two others." [53] According to Robison, the engagement ended when the Indians heard the firing of guns at Kittanning Town.

And there is still a third only very slightly different version of Hogg's death. In this account, there is an hour-long exchange of fire, during which Lieutenant Hogg suffered two very serious wounds and had three of his men killed outright. As the battle heated up, a few of Hogg's men fled in fright. At a lull in the fighting Hogg's soldiers lifted the lieutenant to his feet and hoisted him upon a horse. When at this very moment they were surprised by four warriors, the soldiers abandoned their officer. Hogg took a third musket ball to the stomach and was soon dead.[54] In all accounts, however, Lieutenant Hogg is a tragic casualty of the Armstrong Expedition.

Few of the blankets and provisions which Armstrong had left at this site on the way to Kittanning were ever recovered. "Because of the cowardice of the said sergeant and other deserters," Armstrong reports, "we here sustained a considerable loss of our horses and baggage." Now known as "Blanket Hill," the spot is identified with an historical marker.[55]

Blanket Hill Marker

Armstrong's army suffered losses, according to the Colonel's report, of seventeen killed (one of whom was the Baker lad), thirteen wounded, and nineteen (some reports say eighteen) missing. One of those listed as "missing" was Captain Hugh Mercer.[56] Captain Hugh Mercer's company, "which consisted mainly of old civilian traders," lost the most men, seven killed, nine missing, and one wounded. According to one of the captives of the Indians, who was able to observe the fighting close up, Captain Jacobs alone killed fourteen men. This figure of course can hardly be accurate.[57] The company of Captain Joseph Armstrong, Colonel John's cousin,[58] also suffered losses. The wounded all survived, and seventeen of the reported nineteen missing men eventually made their way home.[59]

As for Indian casualties, there continues great confusion in the many accounts of the battle.[60] Armstrong acknowledged that he could provide only an estimate, especially as many must have died in the explosions of the huts. His best guess was that Captain Jacobs lost "thirty or forty killed." Armstrong may have been way off, as possibly twice that many Indians were killed at Kittanning. At some time after the raid the Indians allowed to the French that they had buried fifty of their people, and that even more were yet missing.[61] The cornfield was bathed in blood, and the river certainly consumed some bodies. As for warriors of distinction, besides Jacobs and his son, there may have been killed also a cousin, called "Young Jacob." In a congratulatory letter to Armstrong, Colonel Adam Stephen, citing the authority of a returned captive from Muskingum, notes that Young Jacob, who stood "about seven foot high," was among the slain. In declaring that "many of them were killed that we know nothing of," he suggests that the "noted warrior" known as The Sunfish may very well have been one.[62]

It is worth noting that not a single Indian was taken prisoner.

Thirty huts were burned to the ground. And of course lost to the Indians were great quantities of gunpowder, arms, and ammunition. And also, though Armstrong had not the time to cut down the corn, all of the huge store of provisions which the French had delivered just ten days earlier was consumed in the firing of the buildings.

At least four of the captives who were liberated by Armstrong were recaptured by the Indians during Armstrong's withdrawal. Those who made it home were Ann McCord, who had been captured at McCord's private fort, and who had been told by the war party at Sideling Hill that it was her husband's head being thrown into her lap; seven-year-old Martha Thorn, also captured at McCord's; Barbara Hicks, taken at Connolloways in what is now Fulton County; Catherine Smith, a German child captured near Shamokin; Margaret Hood, taken at Conococheague Creek; Thomas Girty, brother to Simon Girty, taken at Fort Granville; and Sarah Kelly, made a captive at Winchester, Virginia. An unidentified woman, a boy, and two girls, who had been with Captain Mercer and Ensign Scott, did not make it to Fort Lyttleton and nothing is known of their fate.[63]

As for the ninety or so captives who had been kept on the

other side of the river and even moved farther west,[64] conditions for them would naturally not improve. And as for those who had taken advantage of the raid to effect an escape and had failed, what agonies for them.

Among the horror stories to come out of the Kittanning raid is that of the wife of Alexander McAllister, who was taken captive in the raid of Tuscarora Valley. To the torture spot at the council house (Captain Jacobs' house) amid the charred ruins of Kittanning Town, the Delawares returned their captives. As an example to the rest, Mrs. McAllister was submitted to the cruellest suffering the Indians could devise. Because she had made an effort to escape, she was now led to the torture post, where she was scalped. Then burning slabs of wood which had survived Armstrong's fire were pressed against her body. Her ears were then sliced off, and then her fingers, and these she was compelled to swallow. An ugly white man, supposedly an English soldier who had escaped from prison at Lancaster to join the French in the war against the British, hacked from her body a portion of her flesh and ate of it. Somehow the poor woman was still living at the end of the day. Finally a French officer delivered her from her suffering. The Indians chopped her body into halves and turned these over to the camp dogs. The youngster Hugh Gibson, who had been a captive of the Indians since July, in describing all of this, says finally, "Of this shocking spectacle at which human nature shudders the prisoners were all brought to be spectators."[65]

Another narrative of this kind is that by Peter Williamson, who was kidnaped in his native Scotland at age eight or ten, sold into slavery "to one of my countrymen," acquired his own land at age seventeen, and was captured by the Indians on his farm on October 2, 1754. In the time of his captivity he was tortured, but, perhaps even worse, was required to look on as other prisoners were horribly brutalized and mutilated. He reports on the slaughter of the Jacob Snider family, and the John Adams family, as well as the families of Jacob Miller and George Folke. He describes the torture deaths of prisoners brought into camp. All of this in the fall of 1754 and the winter of 1754-55. One needs a *very* strong stomach to read his accounts.

The description of another horrible torture has survived in a number of documents. According to these, it was some three days after the torture of Mrs. McAllister that an unnamed male settler who likewise had tried to escape during the raid and was recaptured was brought to the same blackened stake. When efforts to burn him in the customary way failed because of a pouring rain, the resourceful Indians simply discharged gunpowder from their muskets into his body. As can be imagined his pain was unbearable and his screams were terrifying. "When he begged for a drink of water, the Indians poured a ladle of molten lead down his throat. He died instantly." [66]

Among the captives who were being held by the Indians at the time of Armstrong's assault were Marie Le Roy and Barbara Leininger, who had been taken by warriors at the time of the Penn's Creek massacre on October 16, 1755. Sometimes regarded as "the first captives taken by the Indians from the frontiers of Pennsylvania," these young women produced later an account of their captivity.[67] At Penn's Creek the girls lived one half-mile apart. The Indians plundered first the Le Roy homestead, murdering Marie's father and burning down the house. They next assaulted the Leininger home, murdering Barbara's father and brother. At the end of three days of pillaging and murder the small bands of Indians came together and began their march to Kittanning. They had fourteen stolen horses and ten prisoners (one man, one woman, five girls, and three boys).

Barbara Leininger, not far into the march, attempted to escape. She was promptly recaptured and condemned to be burned at the stake. The fire was already burning, and the poor girl was in tears, when a young Indian boy began to plead earnestly that her life be spared. When she promised not to try to escape again, and promised to stop her crying, she was pardoned.

The caravan did not arrive in Kittanning until December, but this town was to be their permanent abode, and, indeed, might have proved so had not Colonel Armstrong appeared.

In their narrative, the girls, having described a little the life they lived among the Delaware at Kittanning Town, report the arrival of Colonel Armstrong's army:

In the month of September Col. Armstrong arrived with his men, and attacked Kittanny Town. Both of us happened to be in that part of it which lies on the other side of the river. We were immediately conveyed ten miles farther into the interior, in order that we might have no chance of trying, on this occasion, to escape. The savages threatened to kill us. If the English had advanced, this might have happened, for at that time the Indians were greatly in dread of Col. Armstrong's corps. After the English had withdrawn, we were again brought back to Kittanny, which had been burned to the ground.

Then the girls describe in their narrative two of the gruesome torture deaths they were compelled to watch. One confirms in its details the account supplied by Hugh Gibson of the woman compelled to swallow her own fingers, and the other repeats Gibson's story of the man into whom the gunpowder was fired, and who was required to swallow molten lead.

The girls, who later in their captivity had the pleasure of meeting the Moravian missionary Christian Frederick Post, finally accomplished their freedom. On the sixteenth of March, 1759, with two Englishmen, Owen Gibson and David Breckenreach, the young women slipped away from Barbara's hut at Moschkingo, and made an incredibly difficult journey to the Muskingum, where they found an Indian raft by which they crossed the river. On the last day of March they miraculously reached the newly built Fort Pitt. Here their calls for help were answered, just as darkness descended, by Colonel Hugh Mercer, the fort's commandant. Dr. Mercer did everything he could to restore the party to good health, and eventually, on Sunday, the sixteenth of May, Barbara Leininger and Marie Le Roy arrived in Philadelphia.

Armstrong was lionized in Philadelphia. By one fell swoop the Colonel was catapulted into fame. By the victory at Kittanning he achieved lasting greatness, or by the people of Philadelphia he had greatness thrust upon him. In a long and public life, vigorously active and productive, this was to be his finest hour. Drama attended him everywhere throughout his long life, but the most notable event, his signal moment, was experienced that morning of September 8, 1756, on the Allegheny. He was exactly midway through the eventful life he was to lead.

Students of the Kittanning Expedition have wondered why Armstrong in his report to Governor Denny[68] did not note the heroism of certain individuals, like perhaps most especially Lieutenant Robert Callender. Although Robison recollects that a soldier by the name of Ferguson was the man to set fire to the Jacobs house, Myers calls attention to a letter written by Thomas Barton to Thomas Penn on Feb. 28, 1757, which reads in part:

One Mr. Callender, who at that Time bore only a Lieutenant's Commission, distinguish'd himself by the most uncommon Bravery & Resolution. It is asserted that when Jacobs took to a House, out of which he kill'd & wounded Many of our Men—Callender undertook to fire it, which he accomplish'd at the infinite Hazard of his Life;—And that when our People precipitately retreated upon a Report prevailing that the French were to be up that Day from Fort du Quesne, Callender not content to leave the Houses standing, went back with a small Body of Men, & set Fire to them all.[69]

Barton, who was not a member of the expedition, does not identify the source of his information ("It is asserted . . ."), but as Callender was one of his parishioners, mention of such an heroic act might well come out.

It was Callender, of course, to whom Armstrong dictated the report of his mission, and one has to wonder why, if indeed Callender did so distinguish himself, Armstrong would not, especially while dictating to the man himself, make it a point to mention it.

In his report he complained some of the confusion experienced by his pilots, and implied that they should have known better than they did the route they were to follow. But in fact, all problems considered, it was most remarkable, if not incredible, that the army made the trip in the time that it did, without detection.

And it is curious, too, that Armstrong did not express more than he did the terrible pain he must have felt at the loss of so many good men. The poor Baker lad, who had supplied the information necessary for the success of the mission, who had been a prisoner in Kittanning, and still volunteered to return, was killed; and at the time Armstrong dictated to Callender his letter to Governor Denny, nothing had been heard of Captain Hugh Mercer. It would be natural to assume him lost. And then there was the courageous Lieutenant James Hogg, who had been left to handle the party of Indians discovered at Blanket Hill, the terribly wounded Hogg, abandoned by his men and left to die in the unforgiving wilderness.

The likely reason for the strange tone of Armstrong's report is that while he was trying earnestly to put the best face on the raid, he knew deep down, that the mission had not accomplished all that he had hoped for. He would have liked to regard the raid as a "victory," as the kind of triumph that might justify the loss of good men by discouraging the Indian depredations, that might even put an end to the ruthless ravaging of the frontier that the Indians for so long had carried out with complete impunity. But at the close of his report to Governor Denny, he acknowledged it could have gone much better. He realized that he had enjoyed a lot of good fortune, but for the failure to do more he blamed confusion.

In any event, the raid on Kittanning was big for Philadelphia. Though the Colonel was not actually to possess it for a while, the Penns promptly made arrangements to award Armstrong choice bottom land at the very site of the Indian village.[70]

And the celebration continued with a follow-up by the *Pennsylvania Gazette* of its publication of Armstrong's report with a ten-stanza "Ode to the Inhabitants of Pennsylvania." And one week later, October 7, this high praise was published:

We hear that Colonel ARMSTRONG, and his Officers, have generously given their Part of the Money for the Scalps brought in from Kittanning, likewise for the released Prisoners, and what Plunder they got, to the private Men, as a Reward, for their good Behaviour in the late Expedition, and to encourage them to go out again against the Indians. An Instance of Generosity this, which shews that those Gentlemen did not go against the Enemy, from a mercenary Motive, but from a Regard for the Service of their King and bleeding Country.[71]

On October 5, the Corporation of the City of Philadelphia voted to commend Colonel Armstrong and his soldiers and to express the gratitude of the city for the great success of the expedition. The council minutes for that day read in part as follows:

It being proposed that this Board should give some public testimony of their regard and esteem for Col. John Armstrong, and the other officers concerned in the late expedition against the Indians at Kittanning, and the courage and conduct shown by them on that occasion, and also contribute to the relief of the widows and children of those who lost their lives in that expedition; Resolved, That this Board will give the sum of £150 out of their stock in the Treasurer's hands, to be paid out in pieces of plate, swords, and other things suitable for presents, to the said officers and toward the relief of the said widows and children.[72]

But it was three more months before the Corporation of Philadelphia had matters well enough organized that a "proper" commemoration of the "Victory at Kittanning" could be provided. It was on January 5 that the Corporation addressed to Colonel Armstrong a complimentary letter. It was signed by Atwood Shute, the Mayor of the city, and read much like the council minutes. Couched in the most laudatory terms, it expressed the gratitude of the city and the province. It commended the officers for their courage and for their professional conduct. Armstrong was presented by Thomas Penn a sword and belt, and was informed that he would be receiving a piece of plate and a silver medal. Each of his commissioned officers was to receive "a medal and a small sum of money, to be disposed of in a manner most agreeable to them."

The medal that was struck portrays an officer followed by two soldiers, with the officer pointing to a soldier firing from behind a tree, with an Indian prostrate before him. In the background can be perceived the huts of the Indians all aflame. The legend inscribed on the medal reads: "Kittanning destroyed by Col. Armstrong, September 8, 1756."[73] On the reverse side of the medal appears the arms of the Corporation, consisting of four images: a ship under full sail; a pair of scales equally balanced; above the ship, a wheat sheaf; and on the left, with the scales, two hands clasped. The legend accompanying it reads: "The gift of the corporation of the city of Philadelphia." A watchmaker of Philadelphia, Edward Duffield, did the engraving, and the medal was struck by the silversmith Joseph Richardson, also of Philadelphia. Historians have declared the Kittanning Medal (1756) to be the very first such award to be made to colonial soldiers. Silver medals were presented to Colonel Armstrong and to his commissioned officers, copper to the men.

On January 24, from Carlisle, John Armstrong penned a letter of appreciation. It was addressed to the Mayor, Recorder, Aldermen and Common Council of the Corporation of the city of Philadelphia: "GENTLEMEN: Your favor of the 5th instant, together with the medals and other genteel presents made to the officers of my battalion, by the corporation of the city of Philadelphia, I had the pleasure to receive by Capt. George Armstrong." The letter continues:

The officers employed in the Kittanning expedition have been made acquainted with the distinguished honor you have done them, and desire to join with me in acknowledging it in the most public manner. The kind acceptance of our past services by the corporation gives us the highest pleasure and furnishes a fresh motive for exerting ourselves on every future occasion for the benefit of His Majesty's service in general and in defense of the province in particular. In behalf of the officers of my battalion, I have the honor to be, gentlemen, your most obedient and obliged humble servant.

Unfortunately, not all was wine and roses for Armstrong in the months immediately following the victory at Kittanning. In an exchange of letters between Governor William Denny and the provincial commissioners, it is apparent that not only did Armstrong have a good many complaints to register against the commissaries, he actually accused Adam Hoops and William Buchanan, the agents, of profiteering. Armstrong, and some of his officers as well, complained bitterly about the quality of beef the troops were being supplied. Besides, Armstrong declared that Hoops and Buchanan were realizing exorbitant profits. Armstrong supplied the mathematics: He pointed out that each man in the battalion was provided for a week four pounds of beef, three pounds of pork, 10.5 pounds of flour, and 7/8 quart of hard liquor. For these provisions the commissioners paid them 5 shillings. For 400 men for one year, this totaled more than 5,000 pounds; yet the cost to the contractors was less than 3,000 pounds.[74]

Benjamin Franklin, who had already pointed out to Governor Denny that Armstrong's expedition had cost more than it should have, responded to the colonel's complaint: "It is very possible that the Beef may not be equal to what the Philadelphia Market affords; but of that prime Beef the Quantity in this Province is small, and too dear even for middling People to purchase, only the richer sort are able to buy it, and the whole Quantity of that Kind rais'd in the Province would in our opinion be insufficient to feed half Col. Armstrong's Battalion." [75]

But, needless to report, the commissioners had had their feathers ruffled. In a letter signed by Benjamin Franklin, John Mifflin, Joseph Fox, and William Masters (Jan. 25, 1757), they prepared an account of the provisions consumed by the Battalion, and declared, "We know not what Col. Armstrong means by the sundry Instances of our taking Umbrage at his Conduct, and shall enter into no Disputes with him, having on many Accounts a Respect for him and his Officers." [76]

That he was not getting along with the commissioners, Armstrong was quick to acknowledge. He was particularly puzzled by Ben Franklin. On the one hand he was active in establishing the chain of forts, and he was certainly of great assistance to Colonel Bouquet. On the other hand . . . . In a letter to James Burd, dated Feb. 22, 1757, Armstrong wrote: "The Commissioners and we are at great odds. It seems to me as if the devil has got possession of Bennie Franklin." [77] And Burd replied: "I don't know what can be the matter with B.F. cum multas dias, but I think there is some Infatuation somewhere Amongst us. God only knows how Affairs will terminate. I hope Lord Loudoun will be able to put us to rights." [78]

Many years later, when Armstrong formally was presented his grant of land on the Allegheny, 556.8 acres, which included the site of Kittanning Town, he gave (or accepted for) the tract the title "Victory." The patent for this tract, dated March 22, 1775, makes the grant "In testimony and Memorial of the Services of Colonel John Armstrong in his arduous and successful Expedition against the Indians at the Indian town and Settlement of Kittanning on the Allegheny which was the first instance of carrying the War into the Indian Country and gave a check to their Incursions into this Province." [79]

Historical markers today commemorate the expedition: One has been erected at the site of Armstrong's Carlisle home, the intersection of High & Bedford Streets. And in the area of Kittanning no fewer than seven memorial plaques and markers remember the 1756 mission.

Two re-enactments of Armstrong's trek have been conducted. The first was in the year 2000; and the second, staged as a part of the 250th anniversary celebration of the "victory at Ktttanning," took place on the weekend of September 7-10, 2006.[80]

As it turned out, the raid accomplished a lot, but it had not done all that it might have. Captain Jacobs was dead. That, declared the settlers, was good. And Shingas, who was not dead, had, according to reliable information, not only abandoned the French but had disappeared into the region west of Kittanning. Armstrong had recovered eleven captives, but four had been lost back, and the Baker boy had reported the presence of 100. Great quantities of stored ammunition and arms were destroyed. That was good. And some of the most fierce of the Delaware warriors were dead, but the number was unknown and might not be large.

Definitely the shock value was large. This was the first assault on the Indians in their own nest and it had ended as "the very first victory for the British in any conflict with the French and Indians beyond the mountains." [81] And it was accomplished not by professional soldiers but by rag-tag militia. The *Gazette* on September 23 proclaimed it "The greatest blow the Indians received since the war began." One historian insists that "It must be noted that the only successful offensive to be mounted in America in 1756 did occur in Pennsylvania." [82]

Although raids continued wherever settlements were vulnerable,[83] and the familiar atrocities occurred here and there, it was almost immediately apparent that the Delaware and Shawnee Indians had been made a great deal less bold and aggressive. And those Delaware and Shawnee who had had the terrible experience of Kittanning had apparently lost their feeling for the French and had determined to remove to the west of the Ohio. Shingas had not been brought to the peace table, but a "friendly" Susquehanna Delaware, who was known as Teedyuskung, was now proclaiming himself a "king" and was professing friendship with the English.

Another consequence of Armstrong's success was the action of the Assembly taken just one week after the news of the "Victory at Kittanning" had been published in Philadelphia. Loudoun on August 20 had insisted that the provincial government supply the necessary funds to raise troops for the regiment to be known as the Royal Americans. For the colonial war against France, Britain was now composing an army of 51,000 men, and half of these were to be provided by the colonies. The Pennsylvania Assembly had been squabbling for a month. Armstrong's victory definitely contributed to the compromise that was effected, the Assembly voting late in the month to provide thirty thousand pounds for recruiting Pennsylvania's share of the soldiers.[84]

IX

FORT LOUDOUN

The raid on Kittanning delivered a blow to the Indians, and discouraged a good bit their depredations into the settlements, but small parties continued to conduct raids and to commit barbarous crimes all along the Pennsylvania frontier through the remainder of 1756 and all of 1757. The settlers lived in constant fear.

Armstrong was disappointed. Naturally he felt a large responsibility. He had hoped for more out of Kittanning. And now it seemed that almost every day brought report of another atrocity.

At the time of the Braddock Expedition there was no armed frontier in Pennsylvania. Indeed there was no military establishment whatsoever, no army, no organized militia force. And of course with the defeat of Braddock, settlers fled in droves from the settlements west of Carlisle.

Finally, when, after Braddock's defeat, it became apparent that there would be absolutely no protection provided by the remnants of Braddock's army, or by British troops anywhere, the provincial Government, in early 1756, by vote of the General Assembly, authorized the chain of forts Armstrong had been urging. Governor Morris, persuaded by Armstrong and James Burd, ordered the forts built. The string was to run along the Blue Mountains, one side or the other, from the Susquehanna to the Maryland border (later extended to the Delaware). The forts were to be erected ten to fifteen miles apart, depending of course on the terrain. As patrols would regularly pass between them, the chain could be considered unbroken. The stockades were to be built of heavy planks, and were to include one to four blockhouses providing the necessary firing loopholes.

In the early planning, the forts designated were Fort Shirley, at Aughwick, near today's Shirleysburg in Huntingdon County; Fort Lyttleton, at the tiny village of Sugar Cabins, where apparently both Indians and, later, the settlers boiled down the maple sap, in what is today Fulton County; Fort Pomfret Castle, on the Mahantango Creek in present Juniata County; and Fort Granville at Old Town (present-day Lewistown) on the Juniata.[1]

Already of course there were in place modest stockades or buildings used for refuge (private forts); these were to be used as complements to the main line of defense. Most important among them were Forts Patterson, Bigham, and Robison.

The principal forts in the chain were to be garrisoned by provincial troops. It was the plan of the provincial government to make the standard complement a company of seventy-five men, these all members of the Second Battalion of the Pennsylvania Regiment. Placed in command of the Second Battalion was Lieutenant Colonel John Armstrong of Carlisle, who on May 11, 1756, had been commissioned by Governor Morris and the Provincial Council. Armstrong was thus responsible for the forts west and south of the Susquehanna. It became his job to see to the garrisons, to assign detachments to address Indian incursions, to provide protection for harvesters, to provision the forts, and to see that each was properly fortified with guns and ammunition. He had administered the building of the forts from Fort Carlisle (or Lowther), and he continued to conduct affairs from that site.

It was a very critical time for the people of Pennsylvania. The future stared darkly at them from beyond the Tuscaroras. But, chiefly because of the courage and the resolution of men like Governors Morris and Denny, and John Armstrong and James Burd, the province prepared to defend itself—with a chain of forts and an organized militia. By the time the resolve had been firmly formed, by the events of Penn's Valley and the Great Cove, the forts began to appear. By early 1758, twelve forts had been built and garrisoned in a cordon surrounding the settlements between the Susquehanna and the Delaware.[2]

Well before Braddock there had been a fort at Carlisle. Perhaps called Fort Lowther (although there is no good evidence that it carried that name), it apparently housed a garrison as early as May 27, 1753. It was located between present-day Hanover and Pitt Streets, on High Street. By the time of Braddock, however, it required restoration or replacement. Historian of the frontier forts William Hunter notes that the Carlisle Fort "has the distinction of having been the first fort undertaken on Provincial authority and the only one laid out by Governor Morris himself." [3] Though authorized in mid-July of 1755, upon the news of Braddock's defeat, work was much delayed and by November only a "small stockade" had been erected. And even by August of the succeeding year, the fort remained incomplete; its assigned garrison by late in 1757 was still being housed in the town. The battalion of Colonel William Clapham, which was assigned to the fort in April of 1756, was the first garrison, and Lt. Colonel John Armstrong's company took over the fort in May. From that time forward through the troubled times, Fort Carlisle remained the headquarters for John Armstrong's battalion of Provincials, which of course was responsible for manning the forts west of the Susquehanna.[4]

On July 23, 1756, as above noted, Armstrong reported to Governor Morris on the forts: "Lyttleton, Shippensburg [Fort Morris] and Carlisle (the two last not finished) are the only forts now built that will in my Opinion be Serviceable to the publick. McDowels or thereabouts is a necessary Post, but the present Fort not defencible. The Duties of the Harvest has not admitted me to finish Carlisle Fort with the soldiers, it should be done, and a Barrack erected within the Fort, otherwise the Soldiers cannot be so well governed, and may be absent or without the Gates at the time of the greatest necessity." [5] And, now, in the time after Kittanning, of course Fort Granville was no more; and Forts George and Shirley, no longer considered serviceable or defensible, had been abandoned.

And more than a year later work is still being done on the entrenchments at Carlisle, as is known from the communications from Colonel John Stanwix. Armstrong noted for Secretary Peters, June 30, 1757, "Colonel Stanwix has begun and continues his entrenchment on the northeast part of this town and just adjoining it." Armstrong actually borrowed stones from Stanwix's constructions to further the building of the long-scheduled Presbyterian meetinghouse. "To-morrow we begin to haul the Stones for the building of a Meeting House on the North Side of the Square, there was no Other convenient place; I have avoided the place you Once Pitch'd [on] for a Church. The Stones are rais'd out of Colol. Stanwixes entrenchment . . . ." [6] And on the same day, in a letter to an unnamed person, he reported that he is "raising stone out of Stanwix's entrenchment" for "the building of a meeting house." [7]

By the fall of the year 1756, four forts remained in the jurisdiction of Armstrong: Carlisle, Morris (in Shippensburg), McDowell's Mill (soon to be replaced by Fort Loudoun), and Lyttleton. The management of these forts (the garrison, provisions, ammunition) was Armstrong's responsibility. But he was busy, busy with all kinds of extraneous duties. He had been to Philadelphia on October 20 to accept 272 pounds for the prisoners recovered and for the scalps taken at Kittanning. As is known from a letter written much later to Governor Denny, on November 20, Armstrong on his way home "called in the small parties of soldiers who had been guarding the harvesters and assigned larger detachments to other duties." [8] This is the kind of thing he was doing, all the time.

Fort Morris, at Shippensburg, was begun in 1755, and completed in the winter of 1756-57, under the direction of Major James Burd, son-in-law of the town's proprietor Edward Shippen. Named of course for the governor, this bastion was built a short distance to the west of the settlement and high on a rocky bluff. It was known to the settlers by the affectionate term "The Bull's Eye."

A letter posted from Fort Morris by Armstrong on November 21, 1756, indicates that the fort has been designated "one of the forts which [are] to remain over the Susquehanna to be garrisoned by two of the eight companies of Colonel Armstrong's battalion, two in each fort, by whom patrols [can] be kept constantly marching between fort and fort." [9]

Fort Shirley had been built at the location of George Croghan's home and trading post on Aughwick Creek, the site of an old Indian village. Croghan himself had actually fashioned a stockade here in September of 1755, shortly after the defeat of Braddock. In January of 1756 it was named by Governor Robert Morris of Pennsylvania for the Governor of Massachusetts, General William Shirley, who for a brief time after the death of General Braddock served as Commander-in-Chief of the British Forces in North America. For a time the fort was garrisoned by soldiers from Pennsylvania, but it was inexplicably abandoned in September of 1756.[10]

There were lots of problems with the forts, both private and provincial, and Armstrong was generally the one to address them. But Governor William Denny, not long after he took office, was determined to see for himself just how well the frontier was protected. Accordingly, he arranged a tour of the forts, taking with him a British engineer, Lieutenant Elias Meyer. One of the conclusions reached was that there was need of a fort in the heart of the region where much of the Indian trouble was occurring, about fifteen miles south of Fort Lyttleton and twenty miles west of Chambersburg. The site that was fixed on was a spot called Barr's place, just where had stood the house of Thomas Barr before it was destroyed by Shingas and Captain Jacobs, March 1, 1756, when the settlements along the Conococheague were raided. Armstrong was ordered to build the fort "right here." On November 8, after Kittanning, the Colonel dutifully informed Governor Denny that "This Week, God willing, we begin the Fort at Barr's."[11]

However, because of a need to escort supplies to Fort Lyttleton, he did not get started as expected. And, indeed, when he had a chance to study more closely the ground at Barr's, he recommended instead a site not far away, and, assuming the Governor's approval, actually began the excavation on November 19 or 20. His letter to Denny is the letter of a surveyor:

> *According to y' Honour's Orders I have carefully examined Barr's place, and could not find it in a proper Situation for a Fort, the Soil being too Strong to admit the Ditch and the Spot itself, Overlook'd by an adjoining Hill, but has fixed on a Place in that*

> neighborhood near to *Parnel's Knab* [Parnell's Knob] *where one Patton* [This is the Matthew Patton who saw his new home and barn burned by the Indians in the raid on the Big Cove, noted above.] *lived, the Spot I hope will be very agreeable to your Honour & to Mr. Myer, and as its* [sic] *near the New Road, will make the distance from Shippensburgh to Fort Lyttleton two Miles Shorter than by McDowel's. I'm makeing the best preparation in my power to forward this new Fort, as well as to prepare by Barracks, &c., all the others for the approaching Winter. Yesterday the Escort of one hundred men returned from Lyttleton who left the Chattle, &c., safe there, and to-day we begin to Digg a Cellar in the New Fort; the Loggs & Roof of a New House having there been Erected by* [Matthew] *Patton before the Indians burn'd his Old One. We shall first apprise this House, by which means the provisions may the sooner be remov'd from this place, which at present divided our Strength.*[12]

    Patton had begun a new house on the site of the one that had been destroyed, but it was not far along. He had so far put up the logs and constructed the roof. While he built his fort, Colonel Armstrong used this house as a depository for the stores he had removed from McDowell's Mill. The cellar was promptly excavated, but the erection of the stockade was long delayed because of the heavy snows. Armstrong turned the actual building over to Captain John Potter, the Sheriff of Cumberland County, and to his cousin Captain Joseph Armstrong, and the companies they commanded. And later, men were furnished, in detachments of twenty, from various other garrisons.[13] Wagoners to haul in the logs and a steward to provide the foodstuff were the only civilians employed. The workmen had been constantly complaining about the poor and insufficient food; and it was plain that the commissary with whom Armstrong had contracted (Hoaks and Buchanan by name) was not living up to its agreement. Armstrong used a favorite phrase for the contract, "the most mistaken thing I ever knew."[14]

    But work moved along, and by December 22, Armstrong was able to report, "The Public Stores are safely removed from Mcdowell's Mill to Fort Loudon, the barracks for the soldiers are built, and some proficiency made in the stockade, the finishing of which will be doubtless retarded by the inclemency of the weather, the snow with us being upward of a foot deep." [15]

Armstrong had been concerned for a name, and wondered whether the name Governor Morris had proposed for the fort that was never built, Pomfret Castle, might be okay. Apparently it did not suit Denny, because by December 22 the name Fort Loudoun was being used. It seemed a proper name, as it honored John Campbell, the 4th Earl of Loudoun, who was at that time Commander-in-Chief of the British Forces in America.[16]

And so Fort Loudoun, which, in a most strategic spot, commanded the "entrance to the Ohio by way of the gateway to Path Valley at Parnell's Knob," assumed a prominence akin to that of Fort Augusta at the forks of the Susquehanna.[17] It was to enjoy quite a history, figuring critically in both the campaign against Fort DuQuesne and in the later expedition of Colonel Bouquet to the relief of Fort Pitt. It would play host to very important personages.[18] According to Hunter, the fort was the latest active of all these frontier forts in the Cumberland County region, serving a British detachment "until November, 1765." [19]

One awkward and unfortunate affair in this business of the forts concerned the two four-pound swivel guns which had been supplied to the private fort known as Chambers' Mill (at present-day Chambersburg), not all that far from Barr's Place, the site of Fort Loudoun. The cannon had been provided by the Province on November 25, 1755, and were still in place in October of the next year, when Provincial Commissary James Young, together with Engineer Elias Meyer, visited the fort. Upon his return, Young wrote to Governor Denny from Harris's Ferry to express his concern. It was his feeling that the fort, like McDowell's, was indefensible, and, if captured (which was likely) would surrender the guns to an enemy who would bring them to bear upon nearby Shippensburg and Carlisle.

Governor Denny promptly ordered Armstrong to confiscate the cannon. Armstrong notified Benjamin Chambers of the order. Chambers's reply (that he meant to go to the Governor himself if he had to in order to keep the guns) Armstrong relayed to the Governor on November 30. Over two months later the swivel guns were still in place. The Governor, now impatient and not a little offended, renewed his order to Armstrong "to cause the said two Cannon to be removed from the dwelling House of the said Benjamin Chambers to Shippensburg or some other Fort under [your] Command." Armstrong, accordingly, dispatched Lieutenant Thomas Smallman, of Captain Mercer's company, which was at Fort Morris, to confiscate the guns. When his detachment was met by Chambers at the head of "divers other Persons unknown armed with Swords, Guns, and other Warlike weapons," Smallman naturally backed off. When the Governor now ordered Chambers placed under arrest by Sheriff William Parker,[20] the county justices resigned! These officials were apparently expressing their resentment of the Governor's treatment of Ben Chambers, who was extremely popular with the populace. Armstrong, never bashful about registering an opinion of someone who has annoyed him, said of Chambers that he "has the Brass [Is this a pun?] & Malice of the Devil." Chambers, it was rumored, was preparing to bring suit against Armstrong—just as soon as new justices could be put in place! Armstrong, so far as is known, had the last word in this teapot tempest, for when he advised the Governor to suggest to Colonel Stanwix that the Royal Americans seize the guns, the case disappears from the public records.[21]

By March of 1757, the system of frontier forts appeared to be firmly in place. Lord Loudoun, Commander of the British Forces in North America, convened a conference to effect an appraisal. He met in Philadelphia with the Governors of Pennsylvania, North Carolina, Virginia, and Maryland to discuss not only the forts but the total defense against the French and Indians. When the size of the garrisons and the distribution of the forces in Pennsylvania were considered in discussions with Clapham, Weiser, and Armstrong, the fort in Paxton Township known as Fort Hunter became a casualty. It was determined that because it was not a finished fort, and not all that strategically located, it should be abandoned. And, to the dismay of the citizens, the magazine was removed and the stockade demolished.[22]

Armstrong had promised Governor Denny a plan for the protection of the frontier people at the time of harvest. In July of 1757 he explained his scheme:

For the Security of the Inhabitants in the Harvest, I have strenuously recommended the people's working together in partys as large as possible; and have from William Maxwell's, near the Temporary line, to John McCormick's near Sasquehannah, placed about Twenty Guards, altering and Changing the Station, as well as the number of Each guard . . . . Where a Number of Women and Children happen to be in any Fort, the guard Stays with them, by which Means all the Men belonging to such Garrison are enabled to labour; but where Women and Children are not with the party, then the Soldiers are station'd with the Reapers, keeping Centry around the field; whereby some of the Sculking Enemy have been discover'd & repuls'd; but such is the infatuation of a Number of the people, that they can't be prevail'd on to convene in proper partys for their Own Safety, in consequence whereof the following Melancholy accidents have happen'd, please to Read the list.[23]

The list appears at the end of the very long letter, which provides information chiefly about the strange illness at Fort Loudoun. The situation was bad news that Armstrong did not need. But he would address it. The mysterious sickness the Colonel, who was constantly complaining about inadequate provisions, was quick to attribute to improper food. To Governor Denny from Carlisle, on July 25, he got off a plaintive report: ". . . last Week Learning from Fort Loudon, that Twelve of their Men had the Flux, and not One pound of Meat in Garrison . . . . I was again Oblig'd to apply to Colonel Stanwix . . . . The Colonel Order'd Mr Hoops to Provide Cattle, Salt, Pork, and a little Rice for the Sick Men, which I immediately Sent off . . . . Doctor [Thomas] Blair is return'd from Loudon, and reports that only Six of the Men were bad of the disorder . . ." [24]

At this time the sixty-seven-year-old Colonel John Stanwix[25] was serving as Colonel Commandant of the 1st Battalion of the 60th Royal Americans Regiment, having been appointed January 1, 1756. Upon his arrival in America he was given command of the Southern District, which included Pennsylvania. During the year 1757 his headquarters was at Carlisle, and he was appointed to the rank of Brigadier General on December 27 of that year.

As Colonel Stanwix, with his British commission, outranked Colonel Armstrong, it might be supposed that Armstrong would be resentful. But that certainly does not seem to have been the case. Indeed, Armstrong's letters to the Colonel over the next several months radiate a genuine respect. And, as historian William Hunter points out, it was Stamwix, because of his far-reaching influence, who was able to get done some things that Armstrong could not have achieved. "It was Stanwix," notes Hunter, "who oversaw the negotiations with the Cherokees," and who "enabled Armstrong to send two hundred Provincials to Raystown in June to guard against a threatened enemy attack, who ordered tainted beef buried and commanded Hoops to furnish fresh provisions," and who "issued ammunition for which he billed the Provincial Commissioners," and "who criticized these commissioners' instructions for Armstrong to send three companies to Wyoming with men who were to build a town for Teedyuscung." [26]

Indeed, from the very beginning Colonels Armstrong and John Stanwix got along very well together. Upon the arrival of the British officer, Armstrong declared in a letter to the governor that "All is well," and, noting that Colonel Stanwix "treats me with much civility," he insisted that he would, "according to your Honor's orders, assist him in every thing I can." [27]

And letters dispatched to Governor Denny by Colonel Stanwix on June 12, 13, and 19, and July 18 and 25, are most interesting for what they reveal of the Stanwix-Armstrong relationship, which naturally the Governor had been apprehensive about. It is plain from these communications that Stanwix enjoys the respect of Armstrong and that he is being acknowledged as the superior officer. At the same time, it is just as clear that Stanwix not only appreciates how well Armstrong knows the frontier and of how well he understands the Indians, but realizes how vital that is to him, as he himself is a "stranger to the Indian matters."

During this time no really significant change was urged for the four principal forts on the west of the Susquehanna: Lyttleton, Loudoun, Shippensburg (Morris), and Carlisle. These were to continue to be garrisoned by Colonel John Armstrong's Battalion, which, composed as it was of eight companies, could afford two companies (100 men) to each fort.

Fort Lyttleton was clearly the post of most concern. It was not what might be regarded as formidable. In fact, it was hardly more than a stockade erected to surround some buildings. Some say it was laid out by Daniel Boone. Located some thirty miles south of Fort Shirley (in present-day Dublin Township of Fulton County), it was named by Governor Morris for the then Chancellor of the Exchequer, Sir George Lyttleton. Though not an impressive structure, it was in a hot spot; and it would play a role in the Forbes expedition.

During the fall and early winter following the raid on Kittanning a lot of trouble occurred in the region of Fort Lyttleton, for of all the Provincial forts it was the farthest west and also the farthest south. It was in a most vulnerable location. Now at home in Carlisle, and before the building of Fort Loudoun, Armstrong had his concern for the fort renewed. He determined to beef up the garrison, and to see that it was amply provisioned.

Not long after these steps had been taken, Armstrong's fears for the fort were excited by the report that "a party of French and Indians had encamped [Dec. 23] at Raystown." [28] But all remained fairly quiet thereafter until June 1, when Armstrong had a report from an escaped prisoner, the John Hogan referred to above, that (1) the French fort at Duquesne was expecting "a large Reinforcement of French and Indians from Canada and Mississippi," and (2) that thus reinforced the garrison at Duquesne would then "endeavour to cutt off the back inhabitants." [29] To Armstrong, this suggested an attack on Lyttleton. But the next incident occurred near Fort Loudoun, when a detachment of provincial troops from the fort was attacked by Indians and lost seven men.

It was just a little earlier than these events that a number of Cherokee warriors arrived in Maryland from the South. Traditionally hostile to the Iroquois and the Delaware, they had been invited by the English, who very much desired their help in combating the French and their Indian allies. To Governor Denny, Armstrong, who had been ordered by the Governor to win these Indians over to Pennsylvania, addressed a letter, on May 4:

Honored Sir: A list of what was thought most desired by the

> Cherokee Indians, I sent down with their speeches to your Honor, and would beg leave to alledge that a considerable part of the present ought to be wampum, with some Beads, and next to these an assortment of some silver trinkets, with three laced hats, as it is probable that three captains will be there—two or three coats with tinsel lace might be very well.... I have ordered my brother [Captain George Armstrong], who yesterday returned, to write your Honor the several sorts of goods given by the governor of Maryland, that yours may have a convenient variation. That province has given about £280 in value; and, though I should be glad Pennsylvania would a little exceed it; yet am fully of opinion that a number of Indians will actually assist us this summer, and more of their nation come to these provinces, which will require some future rewards, as from time to time prudence may direct.[30]

Armstrong then led a delegation to Fort Frederick, which was located on a hill overlooking the Potomac, near present-day Big Pool. It was here that the Cherokees had stopped to receive gifts from the Governor of Maryland, Horatio Sharpe. On May 18-19, with his brother arriving a bit later, Armstrong hob-nobbed with the Cherokees. He promised them that upon their going to Fort Loudoun, they would receive even more presents.[31] Unfortunately, by the time Armstrong got back to Fort Loudoun, June 10, the Cherokees were factionalized, greedy as they were for gifts. In a very long letter to Governor Denny, June 19, Armstrong reported information that "thirty-three Cherokees had Stole away towards Pennsylvania." [32]

In this same letter, Armstrong reported to Denny the startling news that "a large enemy force" had left Duquesne to assault Pennsylvania. His interest in the Cherokees now on the back burner, he hurried back to Carlisle to ready his troops.[33] In his letter to Governor Denny he was quite specific about the French threat. He fears for Fort Cumberland:

> This Day Colonel Stanwix is to write your Honour of his preparations to March immediately from this place [Carlisle], having receiv'd Intelligence from Capt[n] [John] Dagworthy, at Fort Cumberland, that six Cherokees that staid to view the situation of

Duquesne, observ'd the French hurrying greatly and making preparation, as they thought, to March out an Army; accordingly, the Indians watched their motions, until on the Tenth Inst., they saw a large Body cross the Monongahela, near the place where Genl Braddock was defeated, with wheel'd Carriages and Guns larger than any at Fort Cumberland, and Men, as the Indians phrase it, that cou'd not be counted. Captn Dagworthy [thinks] *they are coming against that place* [Cumberland] *(which indeed is most probable) where they have but 180 Men, raw troops from Maryland. Col^l Washington told me, if he came without Erecting something by the way, that it was not in his power to be early enough to assist the Garrison, nor wou'd all his men be more than a Breakfast to the French & their Indians.*[34]

Much concerned, Armstrong, as he reported to Denny, at once ordered scouts from Fort Lyttleton to the Allegheny Hills, "least [lest] the whole, or any part of [the enemy force] shou'd be Destin'd to this province." He then advised that "Colonel Stanwix has ordered me to join him with at least 250 men, his first object is Winchester, except [unless] future intelligence prevent or alter his Rout [route]. He has allow'd us two Waggons, we have but little Baggage, having but few Tents and not enough of Kettles, Blankets, nor Arms." He continued in his letter to inveigh bitterly against the failure of the Commissary to provide sufficient provisions, and again declared the beef to be rotten.[35]

But apparently Stanwix, before he could march with his five companies of Royal Americans, heard that the French force had left the Braddock Road and were going cross-country to the road that had been built by James Burd. According to a letter written by Joseph Shippen, Jr., to William Shippen,[36] Stanwix elected to remain in Carlisle but dispatched two companies of Armstrong's Battalion to Fort Lyttleton with orders to destroy the fort and "bring away all the provisions & Stores to Fort Loudoun." As the fort was not then, or even later, destroyed, Hunter suggests that these orders were countermanded by provincial authorities.

What happened to this large force of French and Indians remains a mystery. Some incidents (a daughter of Gerrard Pendergrass killed and scalped within sight of the Fort; and some attacks by small parties of Indians near the Maryland line) did occur, but there was no further report of a large enemy force. Lieutenant Colonel Armstrong reported to Secretary Peters on June 30 from Carlisle what he understood of it all:

> *Tis now said that the First Party of those Indians who brought Capt Dagworthy the Intelligence of the Enemy's March with Artillery, was not rightly understood for want of a proper Interpreter and that a party later from Duquesne than they and who had been nearer that Fort, say there was no great Guns nor wheel'd Carriages with the Enemy, but that a large Number, consisting of French and Indians with Baggage Horses did actually leave Fort Duquesne about the 9th Inst, bending their Course by the old Aleghenny Path which leads from that place towards Reas Town, on the Departure of which Detachment the French fir'd their Cannon.*

Apparently the new and more accurate report meant a revision in the plans. It may have been at Armstrong's suggestion that the march of Colonel Stanwix be aborted and that Armstrong's troops make whatever response might be necessary. In any case,

This later and Surer Intelligence put a Stop to Colonel Stanwix's March to Winchester . . . . But least [lest] Loudoun or Lyttleton shou'd be attack'd he allowed me to send all I cou'd from this Battalion as far as Lyttleton and as much farther as I might think requisite, not to exceed three Days March from the Inhabitants, but oblig'd me to stay with him [in Carlisle] least [lest] he shou'd be suddenly call'd to take some Rout[e] which he, being a Stranger might not understand—Capt Hamilton therefore commands the party consisting of 200 private Men and a sufficient Number of officers—They have the best general Orders I cou'd give them, but in this Service much must be left to the Commanding officer. They are now encamp'd some where near Reas Town, and Nothing yet heard from them, save that one of our Spies had discover'd some Indian Tracks and saw two Indians fishing in Juniata . . . .[37]

And nothing whatever happened in this curious business, Dagworthy's scouts, in the neighborhood of Fort Cumberland, having even less to report.

Of all the forts that were built by Pennsylvania during the French and Indian wars, it was Fort Augusta, named for the Princess of Wales (mother of the soon-to-be King George III) that was the most impressive. Not only did it sustain the longest uninterrupted garrison, but it was the last to serve a strictly military purpose.

As early as the fall of 1755, Governor Morris had had in mind a fort for the site of the old Indian village of Shamokin, where the two branches of the Susquehanna join. In the aftermath of Braddock, the unsettling report that an army from the French forts would be coming down the West Branch of the river "to fortify Shamokin" had spurred him to action. Although he understood that the Shamokin site still belonged to the Iroquois, he determined to go ahead with his plans. His decision was made the easier by a letter from Armstrong, November 2, which included the welcome information that he (Armstrong) had been advised by Scarroyady (head of the Iroquois in Pennsylvania) "that a Fort should immediately be Errected at Shamokin." [38]

Not a Cumberland County fort, and never under the command of Armstrong, it was constructed in the summer of 1756 by, first, Colonel William Clapham and then by Major James Burd. The fort was kept active by a garrison of Pennsylvania troops until June 13, 1765.[39]

Of course, in the wake of the raid on Kittanning, some rearranging of the garrisons of the forts became necessary. William Denny had succeeded Morris as Governor on August 20, 1756. He saw the situation at first through rose-colored glasses. In the spring he sent an appraisal of conditions to the Proprietaries: "After Col. Armstrong's successful expedition against the Kittanning and the conclusion of peace at Easton, the back inhabitants enjoyed rest from their incursions of the savages and the poor people who were driven from their plantations generally returned to them. Since the affair of Kittanning the Indians on this side of the Ohio have mostly retired with their wives and children under the French forts on that river." It was not long, however, before the new Governor would find himself addressing countless Indian problems, not that he would prove unable. Indeed, many historians credit Denny with the arrival of a "relative peace" in the Province. One, while describing him as a "pompous, arrogant army officer," and while acknowledging that he regularly exhibited many of Morris's faults ("insufficient tact and patience without [Morris's] energy"), declared that the war situation "steadily improved" during his term as Governor.[40]

One problem was the militia. Denny, disturbed by the reports of depredations and disheartened by increasing numbers of requests for protection, appealed to the Provincial Assembly for a more substantial militia. The Assembly, on September 28, 1757, declaring militia next to worthless, replied curtly, asking, "What Service has been done by those Troops? What Protection has the Province received from them? Have they relieved the Frontier Inhabitants from the insupportable Burthens of keeping watch Night and Day at their own Expence? Or has a single Indian been killed or taken Prisoner by them, tho' our enemies have been continually committing Depredations on the Frontier, and constantly murdering the People?"[41]

John Armstrong, as much dismayed as anyone else by the atrocities occurring on the frontier plantations, was not made happy by the impression of the militia registered by the Assembly. He was in fact quite proud of the militia forces, and in a letter to the *Pennsylvania Gazette*, which appeared October 13, 1757, commended them for the protection they were providing the frontier against a ruthless and barbarous enemy:

. . . such of the provincial Forces as his Honour the Governor has been pleased to station to the Westward of the Susquehanna, have been this Summer, active against the Enemy, by scouring the Woods, as often as the Soldiers were capable of that Duty; by sending out Parties to Ray's Town; by keeping out Spies so far as the Allegheny Hills, and sometimes even to the Waters of

Yohiogane; and by being particularly diligent in covering the People on this Frontier during the whole of their Harvest; for which Purpose, near twenty different Parties were detached from the four Garrisons in this County; and Divine Providence was pleased so far to favour their endeavours, that no Inhabitant, on this Frontier, has fallen into the Enemies Hands where Soldiers were stationed; whereby it is highly probable that a great Number of Lives have been saved, which, without the Benefit of the Guards, and great Care of the Centinels, would no Doubt, have fallen an easy Prey to a skulking Enemy; as did the two unfortunate Parties in Cessny's and Steenson's Fields, who refused to join in Partnership with their Neighbours, where they might have had the Benefit of the common Guards. These several Services, among many others, tho' not the most considerable among military Operations, will, we hope, appear so necessary to the Eyes of all unprejudiced Persons, as to acquit the Second Battalion of being a useless Burthen to the Publick.[42]

    Of course, in consequence of the Indian trouble, the prospect of martial law had to be considered real. The forces at this time were composed of twenty-five companies, some 1400 men. Eight of the companies had been placed under the command of James Burd, and because they were stationed at Fort Augusta, they were known as the Augusta Regiment. Responsible for the west side of the Susquehanna were eight additional companies. Labeled the Second Battalion of the Pennsylvania Regiment, they were commanded by Lieutenant Colonel John Armstrong. He had them stationed thus: two companies at Fort Lyttleton; two companies on Conococheague Creek, two companies at Fort Morris in Shippensburg, and two companies at Carlisle.

    It was not long after this that Governor Denny implemented a slight change in the organization of the Pennsylvania forces. It was Denny's idea to form the province's three battalions (one at Augusta, and the two battalions of the Pennsylvania Regiment) into two battalions of one regiment. After the plan was approved by Colonel Stanwix, on October 24, and after Weiser resigned his commission, John Armstrong was commissioned Lieutenant Colonel of the First Battalion (effective December 2), and James

Burd, who had been Major at Augusta, was commissioned Lieutenant Colonel of the Second Battalion, effective January 2, 1758.[43]

As the province readied itself for the Forbes campaign, however, a third battalion appeared to be necessary. This was organized and delivered to the command of Hugh Mercer. In May, all three lieutenant colonels were promoted to the rank of Colonel. In order to realize the number of men requested by Forbes from the province, the Assembly authorized the recruiting of twenty-three new companies. Three of these new companies were assigned to Armstrong's battalion; four were turned over to Colonel Burd; and the other sixteen composed the Third Battalion, under the command of Colonel Hugh Mercer. Each battalion was composed of sixteen companies. Armstrong and Burd and Mercer are now at the rank of Colonel. The other field officers of the Pennsylvania Regiment were Lt. Colonel Hanse Hamilton, Major Jacob Orndt, Lt. Colonel Thomas Lloyd, Major David Jameson, Lt. Colonel Patrick Work, and Major George Armstrong. In all, the Province would be contributing 2700 men to the army of General Forbes.

This organization would remain in effect until the conclusion of the Forbes Campaign, at which time the 3rd Battalion disappeared. Colonel Armstrong remained in command of the First Battalion.[44]

But this period, from Armstrong's return from Kittanning to the time of the Forbes Expedition, troubled as it was, was a time for talk too. A succession of councils, which brought the officials of the province together with the leaders of the Delaware Indians, had brought at least a semblance of peace to the much harassed frontiers.

During these sessions, and including the Grand Council held at Easton on November 8, 1756, and lasting nine days, the big bone of contention was the purchase made by Pennsylvania twenty years earlier. This was the famous, infamous, "Walking Purchase" of September 19, 1737. In the councils that were now occurring, the Indians regularly maintained that all the trouble on the frontier was the result of the loss of these lands, which they insisted was accomplished through deceit and treachery. Declared Chief Lappawinsoe: "The [white men] should have walkt along by the

River Delaware or the next Indian path to it . . . should have walkt for a few Miles and then have sat down and smoakt a Pipe, and now and then have shot a Squirrel, and not have kept up the Run, Run all day."

The Grand Council, held at Easton, at the junction of the Lehigh and the Delaware Rivers, on November 8, 1756, brought together Governor Denny and the Delaware King Teedyuscung, who, some infer, was in a mood to talk because his people were losing their second consecutive harvest. The conference, which had in attendance a great many Delaware chiefs and warriors, and included Benjamin Franklin, lasted nine days. Teedyuskung, whose reputation as an eloquent and persuasive speaker preceded his attendance, did most of the talking for the Indians. The Walking Purchase was discussed, but in the end the Indians accepted the agreement that had been reached by Lappawinsoe in 1737. The result of the conference was satisfaction on both sides. Teedyuskung signed for the Delawares, and, insisting that he had the authority so to do, signed as well in the name of ten (!) other Indian nations, including those of the Five Nations.[45] With this treaty a time of relative peace seemed assured. Indeed, while some settlers adopted a wait and see attitude, many promptly returned to their frontier homes.

After the reconciliation in November, Teedyuskung, in another session at Easton, July 30, 1757, made a request. "As we intend to make a Settlement at Wyoming, and to build different Houses from what we have done heretofore . . . we desire you will assist us . . . in building Houses." The Pennsylvania commissioners promptly acceded to this request, and ordered Armstrong to send three companies from the Pennsylvania regiment to Wyoming to assist in the building of a town for Teedyuskung. It never did happen, however, as Colonel Stanwix (as before noted) just as promptly countermanded the order.[46]

Another conference, perhaps the most notable of all, was held in October of 1758, again at Easton. With the purchase of the lands extending as far as the western limits of present-day Bedford and Blair Counties, it did a lot to quiet the Delaware at the critical time of the Forbes Expedition.

But the veracity of the Walking Purchase would continue to

be questioned. Almost three years after the Grand Council, Benjamin Franklin laid the issue before the Privy Council in London. When Sir William Johnson was asked to investigate Teedyuskung's claim that wrongdoing had occurred, a great exchange of letters took place, and a number of hearings were scheduled. Finally, Teedyuskung backed away from any concern, and in consequence was awarded by Governor Denny a "handsome present." [47]

Teedyuskung's life closed out in horribly tragic fashion, however. In the spring of 1763, during which time the Chief was pressuring Pennsylvania to grant his people lands in the Wyoming Valley, the Connecticut settlers were moving into those very lands. Naturally there was trouble. Indians, Pennsylvania settlers, Connecticut settlers. Tragedy occurred on the night of April 19, 1763. As he lay asleep, perhaps, as some say, in a stupor caused by rum, Teedyuskung was burned to death by a fire that consumed the whole of the log house. Investigation produced evidence sufficient to suggest strongly that the fire had its beginnings outside the house.[48]

. There remained great concern over the "other" Delawares, those who had always been the more hostile, those who had moved west instead of north. Armstrong learned that there had occurred significant changes in the leadership. Contrary to rumors, Jacobs was dead of course. And possibly because of the rewards which both Virginia and Pennsylvania had posted for his scalp, Shingas had removed to the sidelines. He had been replaced by his brother, King Beaver. From Colonel Adam Stephen, Armstrong learned something of Shingas's whereabouts following Kittanning. In a letter dated November 14, 1756, Stephen wrote to Armstrong from Fort Cumberland: "By a woman who once belonged to John Fraser (his wife or mistress) and has now, after being prisoner with Shingas, &c., thirteen months, made her escape from Muskingum, we learn that Shingas and some Delawares live near the head of that River, within three days march of Lake Erie, where there is a town of Wiandots; and about five days travel from the Lower Shanoe [Shawnee] Town, on a branch of Scioto." [49]

Armstrong promptly forwarded Stephen's report to Governor Denny, and some months later supplied some additional information. According to what the Cherokees had learned from their examination of a Delaware warrior whom they had taken captive, there were "At Cuscuskas and Shenango . . . about two hundred warriors." The largest body of the Shawnee, this prisoner revealed, is "at the mouth of Siotha [Scioto], 300 men." [50]

During the late summer and into the fall of 1757 Armstrong was very busy protecting the harvesters. He dispersed the major part of the three easternmost garrisons of his battalion among the people, scattering small parties of his men in such a way as to "cover and assist . . . in Sowing their Winter Corn, bringing in of Grain from deserted places, &c." [51] And he explained to Governor Denny, in a letter of October 24, that he would be unable to satisfy the request for three companies "to carry on the works at Wioming," as he needs the men for protecting the harvesters. He may be able to provide one company, but he notes the occurrence of recent attacks, and declares that "we are at least equally Lyable to incursions from the Enemy." [52]

And in this uneasiness and apprehension the year of 1757 closed out. Something very big was about to happen in Pennsylvania. Carlisle would be the launching pad. And Colonel John Armstrong, now a military man of considerable stature, would be right in the middle of it all.

X

THE FORBES EXPEDITION

The colonial period lasting from 1688 through 1763 is regarded by historians as the time of the French and Indian Wars. It features a struggle for empire in the New World. It includes the horrors of border warfare carried on by the Indians and the settlers on the frontier; and it includes King William's War (1688-1697), Queen Anne's War (1701-1713), and King George's War (1745-1748). The first battle fought in what is called in Europe the Seven Years' War and in the colonies the French and Indian War (1754-1760) resulted in the surrender of Fort Necessity by Washington to the French, in July of 1754. A signal moment in the conflict occurred with the building of Fort Duquesne by the French in that year in the English colony of Pennsylvania. This occasioned in the next year, first, a British declaration of war against France (May 17), and the response of a formal declaration of war by France against England on June 9; and, second, the British mission against Fort Duquesne by General Edward Braddock, which resulted in the disaster on the Monongahela. Through all of this time the two super powers of western Europe, France and England, while suppressing the interests of the Dutch and the Spanish, sought to extend their empires through North America. The British had designs on New France. The French envisioned a New France that reached south to the Ohio and westward to the Mississippi.

With the shocking defeat of Braddock, it began to seem as though the English had almost lost interest in the New World. It looked as though King George II was not going to contest for territory. It looked as though the settlers in Pennsylvania would be on their own in defending their homes against the French and their Indian allies. The lull lasted roughly two years. Then all began to change.

William Pitt

The change in British policy occurred with the appearance of a new Prime Minister. His name was William Pitt, the first Earl of Chatham.[1] Pitt was inheriting a policy in foreign affairs that had been so weak (at least with regard to the American colonies) as to seem altogether indifferent. Pitt was a horse of a different color. Indeed, it is quite proper to think of him as an imperialist. He was very intent on Canada and the West Indies. Called by the people the Great Commoner, he excelled as an orator and as a politician. He was a most eloquent speaker. With a flair for the dramatic he was not bashful about his pride in his country. Although he never got along well with King George II, and was not to be all that close to George III, he assumed to speak for all the British. When he came into power in 1756, he promptly revitalized foreign policy. And it was not long before he began most aggressively to address the problem of the American colonies. It was good news for the settlers. It seemed to them that when the mighty hand of the new Minister of State took hold of the helm, "the heavens began to brighten and the storm to lose its power."[2]

In the summer of 1757 Pitt commissioned his military minds to draw up a plan for repelling the French from what he regarded as British territory. The plan in its final draft took the form of a three-pronged campaign. It had the British forces directed at three of the principal French strongholds, Carillon (later Ticonderoga), Louisburg, and Fort Duquesne. These forts were not only most strategically located, they enjoyed a huge symbolic value. They proclaimed the French presence in North America. Most obnoxious was Fort Duquesne, as it was regarded an encroachment on territory that the Penns had long been assuming belonged to the British colony of Pennsylvania. Pitt, who was to prove a most able war minister, was quick to fix on the officers to carry the war to the French in America. Very much disappointed in John Campbell, Lord Loudoun, who, on March 17, 1756, had been appointed Commander-in-Chief of British Forces in America, and who had been received in America by Benjamin Franklin,[3] he determined to recall him. His plan called for Generals Jeffrey Amherst and James Wolfe to support the ships of Admiral Edward Boscawen and recapture Louisbourg. General James Abercromby, who had embarked at the head of six transport vessels carrying 1,040 British troops on April 15, 1756 (arriving in New York June 16), together with Lord Richard Howe, would command the expedition attacking Fort Carillon. Succeeding John Campbell as Commander-in-Chief in March of 1758 was Abercromby.

To America Pitt also dispatched the Scotsman John Forbes, who was at this time, like Pitt, fifty years old.[4] Born in Dumferline, Scotland, Forbes, having given up on a career in medicine, entered the military service at age twenty-eight and served with distinction in the War of the Austrian Succession (1740-48, called King George's War in North America), winning commendation and promotion. He served also with the Scots Greys under the Duke of Cumberland as acting Quartermaster-General in the bloody battle of Culloden, April 16, 1746.

The battle of Culloden, one of the most grisly of all military engagements in recorded history, pitted the King's troops under the Duke of Cumberland, the King's younger son, against the Scots, who were supporting the claim of Bonnie Prince Charlie to the English throne, lost by his Stuart grandfather. The Duke's army boasted 8800 men. It was well equipped with cannon. The Jacobites could marshal at best some 5400 men. The battle was engaged for one hour in a marshy moorland terrain. The Scots

John Forbes

Highlanders, fighting with swords, spears and axes, lost 1250 dead and as many more wounded. Almost 600 more were taken prisoner. In all, the Jacobites lost half their force. The army of Cumberland, behind their cannon, which were taking a terrible toll of the enemy with grapeshot, lost fifty-two dead and 259 wounded. But the most horrifying is what followed the battle.

For the rest of the day and throughout the day following the Duke continued the slaughter with patrols searching out the fugitives. At least seventy more of the Prince's supporters were killed. Besides, the Duke had many of the prisoners and the wounded executed; many of the high-ranking officers were given mock trials and summarily executed at Inverness. For all of this the Duke of Cumberland was hereafter known as "The Butcher." Bonnie Prince Charlie, with a price on his head of 30,000 pounds, escaped the round-up, and was later able, disguised as a lady's maid, to make his way to France.

The Battle of Culloden is mentioned here, not only because John Forbes was involved, but because two additional principal figures in the Forbes expedition against Fort Duquesne were miraculous survivors of the massacre.[5] John Forbes himself, who was fighting on the side of the Duke, was saved, so the story goes, by a small coin in his pocket, which stopped the shot. Another survivor was the nineteen-year-old Hugh Mercer, who was Assistant Surgeon-in-Arms in the Jacobite army of Bonnie Prince Charlie. Mercer, who would become Forbes's Colonel in charge of the Pennsylvania Third Battalion, lived in hiding for almost a year before he was able to buy his way onto a ship (March, 1747) and make his way safely to Philadelphia. A third survivor of the battle and the aftermath was James Burd, at the time of Culloden just a youngster of fourteen or fifteen. Burd, who, like Mercer, was fighting in the army of the Jacobites, would be, as road builder and as Colonel of the Second Pennsylvania Battalion, extremely important to General Forbes.

Colonel Forbes, who was known to be most thorough and resourceful in his quartermaster responsibilities, had also a well deserved reputation for courage in the field. To the military he was known as "The Iron-Headed." Pitt dispatched him to America with the 17th Regiment of Foot from Portsmouth, England on March 13,

1757. His first assignment concerned the French fortress of Louisburg in what is now called Nova Scotia. Forbes was ordered to bolster the British forces laying siege to that bastion, and he contributed to the final success of the assault. On December 30 of that year (although he was not to learn of it until the succeeding March) he was promoted to Brigadier General by the King, placed in command of the Southern District, and ordered to take Fort Duquesne. The Southern district consisted of the colonies of Pennsylvania, Maryland, Virginia, and the Carolinas. Troops were to be raised from these colonies.[6]

A month before he learned of his promotion and of his assignment to take Duquesne, Forbes was aware that General Loudoun was planning an attack on the French fort. To Loudoun on February 4 he expressed encouragement: "If in case you design any attack upon the Ohio—which indeed has the flattering Air of Success, as you may send two thousand regulars, besides the provincial troops which I am assured will be readily granted for this Expedition, and Mr. Bird [William Byrd, III] assures me that he could easily bring 500 Cherokees but there is not time for those— But as it is, our force would be greatly superior to Braddocks, who had scarce 2000 men." [7]

Forbes had the news of his promotion at his Adjutant-General Headquarters in New York City. He was fortunate to have at hand the detailed plans for the expedition that had been submitted to Loudoun. He promptly began to organize his campaign. As he began to work out the details for troops and provisions, and to think about the route to be followed, he could have no idea that he would be responsible for one of the most momentous, and most historically significant, events in the annals of Pennsylvania. Happily, because of the incredible number of letters that passed among the officers of the expedition, many of which have been preserved, and with the General's Orderly Book, we can join the mission and make the march from Carlisle to Fort Duquesne. We can march with General Forbes, Colonel Henry Bouquet, Sir John St. Clair, Archibald Montgomerie, Colonels John Armstrong, James Burd, Hugh Mercer, and George Washington.

On March 20 Forbes wrote to Governor William Denny from New York, to give the Governor instructions on the raising of troops in Pennsylvania. And on March 23 Governor Denny sent orders to Armstrong "to hold in readiness the first Battalion of the Pennsylvania Regiment for Offensive Duty by the first of May." [8] The Governor found Armstrong, who was destined to play a major role, chomping at the bit. The Colonel, with a great deal of feeling, promptly replied:

This Opportunity is Embrac'd with much Alacrity . . . . The Vigorous efforts determined by his Majesty thro' the ensuing Campaign must greatly animate every British Soul, and indeed every true Protestant; may Heaven Vouchsafe to assume the Supreame Command both by Land and Sea. As I Doubt not your Hon'rs care & Vigilance in furnishing the Battalion with necessaries for the Campaign, permit me to assure you Sir, that not only the above Orders, but also the Orders of the Officers set over us by his Majesty (so far as in our Power) shall be punctually & Cheerfully obey'd, as well by every officer of this Battalion . . . . [9]

To Governor Horatio Sharpe of Maryland Forbes got off pretty much the same letter as that he had sent to Governor Denny. As he was hoping to rendezvous all elements of the army "at Conegochie [Conococheague] about the 20th of April," he directed Denny to "give orders for all Manner of Diligence to be used in raising the Numbers that your Province is to send [2700]."

General Forbes had heard of Armstrong and the Kittanning raid, and he had heard of the Indian attacks on the settlements and the frontiersmen's response. He had some idea of what sort of soldiers he would prefer: "I am informed that the Inhabitants upon the Frontiers of your Province being much used to hunting in the Woods, would consequently make good Rangers, In which case I am to beg you will give your direction for the forming some of your properest Men into Companies of Rangers with good officers, who are well acquainted with the Country, to Command them." [10]

But even as the province prepared for an assault on the French bastion on the Ohio, atrocities continued to occur on the frontier, some of them very close to Carlisle. Most of these, of course involved Armstrong. One occurred in April, near what was known as the Marsh Creek region, Armstrong's former home.

Colonel Armstrong was saddened, as he always was, by the murders and the taking of captives, and was disturbed by the failure of the settlers close to Fort Morris to seek aid from the fort. It bothered him not a little, too, that the Indians, as they regularly did, had accomplished their barbarities with total impunity. He dispatched a report of the whole incident to Governor Denny, from Carlisle on April 11.[11]

At about the same time, April 5, and in the very same general region, there occurred the murder of the Jemison family and the capture of young Mary by a raiding party of Shawnee warriors and French soldiers. On the forced march west, all the captives, including Mary's mother, were murdered, except for Mary herself and a neighbor boy.[12]

Forbes, not oblivious to these atrocities, continued hopeful that the French would be without a significant force of Indian allies at Duquesne.

At the suggestion of Quartermaster Sir John St. Clair, who was much concerned about a base for supplies, the place of rendezvous was later changed from the Conococheague to Raystown. But, as Pennsylvania historian George Donehoo notes, no matter where they were assembled, it was abundantly evident that for the Pennsylvania troops that were raised, "nearly all of the commanding officers and subordinate ones, as well, [would be] taken from the lists of these frontiersmen, all of whom were greatly experienced woodsmen and Indian fighters."[13] Indeed, as it happened, the "thirty-five best men of each Pennsylvania company" were those drafted for the campaign.

For a month Forbes remained in New York City; then at the middle of April he was ordered to Philadelphia by General James Abercromby, who had succeeded Lord Loudoun as Commander-in-Chief on the same date that the King had commissioned Forbes. Now in Pennsylvania, where he would live out his life, he assaulted problems that would have overwhelmed and discouraged a lesser man.

First, of course, he had to assemble an army. As he could depend on the British regulars for only a fraction of the necessary force, he naturally turned to the influential provincial officers. Most important to him in the composing of the army were Colonels

George Washington and William Byrd III[14] of the Virginia Troops; and Colonels John Armstrong, James Burd, and Hugh Mercer of the Pennsylvania militia forces.

And fortunately General John Forbes, who was very ill from the time of his appointment, had as his Chief of Staff one of the most able and accomplished military men of the time, Colonel Henry Bouquet. He had been commissioned Lt. Colonel in the British Army January 3, 1756, and promoted to full Colonel January 16, 1758 (in America only); and he had embarked for America from England with Frederick Haldimand on May 4, 1756.[15] He would one day be acclaimed by Pennsylvania historian Sylvester Stevens "the shrewdest commander ever to serve under the British flag in the colonies," and the "first great military figure in the history of Pennsylvania." [16]

Because of General Forbes's illness, Bouquet's responsibilities in the campaign were greatly increased over what would normally be his case. He directed the building of the road over the mountains; he arranged for the wagons and for the provisions and for the ammunition, dealing with recalcitrant provincials. He

James Abercromby

Henry Bouquet

oversaw the building of the forts and the lesser fortifications. And he did the scheduling all along the line of communications from Carlisle to the Ohio. He smoothed the relationships among the officers of the diverse elements of the army. All of this required of course hundreds of letters, written with a quill pen, by candle light, and delivered by couriers up and down the line of communications. Bouquet in June had fixed September 11 as the date for the British occupation of Fort Duquesne, but he could not have foreseen the damage which would be done to the march by the incessant rains.

Forbes had available to him the soldiers who had been under the command of General Loudoun, some 3000 British regulars, soldiers who had been raised and trained in the British Isles and who were paid by the crown. These troops included a few colonials who had enlisted in the regulars and the First Highland Battalion, Highlanders under the 32-year-old Scotsman, Colonel Archibald Montgomerie.[17]

Montgomerie had arrived in Philadelphia in June. He came with a reputation for great military ability and a ferociously hot temper.

Archibald Montgomerie

The Regulars included also 400 soldiers of the Royal American regiment (60th Regiment of Foot), as well as forty artillery men and officers, a regiment of Royal Welsh volunteers, and the 42nd Royal Highland Regiment of Foot (Black Watch).

Besides, Forbes was quite happy to use Indians. Indeed, even though he was hoping they could be of help to his mission, his overtures of friendship were clearly sincere. Working with Edmund Atkin, a member of the Provincial Council of South Carolina, whom the King had appointed to the position of Superintendent of Indian Affairs for the Southern Provinces (May 13, 1757), he very early invited the Southern Indians, the Catawba and the Cherokee, to join the mission, and they began to show up in significant numbers (perhaps as many as 700) at Fort Cumberland, at Carlisle, and at Fort Lyttleton. As he had been warned, however, these Indians were not all that dependable, and, without a lot to do early in the campaign, many before long went home. Forbes understood, too, very well, that it would be *very* important to dissuade the Delaware and Shawnee Indians from alliance with the French. He was hoping to confer with them, and win them to peace.

But the largest element of the Forbes Expeditionary Force was supplied by the Provincial governments, 4650 frontiersmen militia, mostly from the two colonies of Pennsylvania (2200) and Virginia (1600), but 100 from Delaware, and 250 from Maryland. Colonel George Washington had been placed in command of the Virginia troops, whom he preferred to have attired in the Indian style hunting shirt and leggings, and Colonel John Armstrong, who had been promoted to rank of Colonel Commandant, on May 28, 1758,[18] had assumed command of the Pennsylvanians, the most substantial unit of Forbes's army, including a number who had been with him on the Kittanning expedition. In addition, a few companies of men from North Carolina proved willing recruits. The wagoners and laborers essential to the expedition numbered at least 1000. In all, there may have been as many as 7200 men serving the expedition. The provincials of course were all volunteers who had enlisted for varying periods of time and who were paid by their respective colonial governments.

Of course one of the General's immediate problems was the question of rank. He was made to understand by Minister Pitt (in a letter to Governor Denny) that such well qualified Provincial officers as he knew Colonels Armstrong, Mercer and Burd to be were to have the authority and position of equality which their rank entitled them to, when they were superior in rank to the officers of the British regular service who might be assigned to their commands.[19]

Over-all command of the Provincial forces was given to Brigadier General John Stanwix, who had been in Carlisle with his First Battalion of Royal Americans since May 30, 1757,[20] and had received the Second Battalion (under the command of Colonel Frederick Haldimand)[21] in September of that year.

Through April and May General Forbes was steadily writing letters, to Governors Denny and Sharpe, and the acting Governor of Virginia, John Blair. From Philadelphia on April 20 he wrote to Abercromby: "I arrived here Tuesday evening and Immediately waited upon Governor Denny, who I found disposed to do every thing in his power for the good of the service."[22] This same day he appealed to Denny for a "serviceable army." On May 1 he reported to Pitt on the provinces, noting that Pennsylvania "has just now begun to raise their Men by naming their officers &c." He expects zealous recruiting to follow. And a number of his letters had to do with the southern Indians. A letter of Forbes to Abercromby on May 7 discloses the first indication that he is settled on the northern route, for he speaks of the need for "200 tents for the Pennsylvanians that must now march up to Cover the Convoys of Provisions, clear the roads, and build a pallisaded Deposit for the same at Raystown."[23]

The Pennsylvania forces, taken together, composed a regiment. At this time the regiment, newly reorganized, was made up of three battalions, totaling 2192 men, including 136 of officer rank. The First Battalion (755 men) was under the command of Colonel John Armstrong, who had as his chief officers Lieutenant-Colonel Hanse Hamilton of York (who had been a captain in Armstrong's Second Battalion, and whose present commission dated from May 31, 1758);[24] Jacob Orndt, Archibald Blane, the pious and very zealous Presbyterian preacher Reverend Charles Beatty (who had been appointed Chaplain to Armstrong's battalion, June 9), Adjutants John Philip de Haas and Robert Anderson, Quartermaster Thomas Smallman, and Surgeon John Blair.

The battalion included sixteen companies, each of which was under a captain, two of whom were Armstrong's brothers George and William.[25] Other captains were Edward Ward, formerly of Fort Granville and a veteran of the Kittanning expedition and previously in Armstrong's Second Battalion; and Robert Callender, of Carlisle, also on the Kittanning raid and soon to be Forbes's wagonmaster general.

Armstrong's nephew William Lyon[26] was a lieutenant in Captain William Thompson's company in this First Battalion. Carlisle's William Thompson,[27] who had been commissioned Captain on May 1, 1758, had been put in command of a troop of light horse.

The Second Battalion (666 men) was under the command of thirty-two-year-old Colonel James Burd, by now an experienced frontiersman and fort builder and road builder,[28] and an enemy soldier to John Forbes at Culloden. Second in command was a physician, Lt. Colonel Thomas Lloyd.

The Third Battalion (771 men) was commanded by Colonel Hugh Mercer, who had been with Armstrong at Kittanning, and who had also been an enemy to Forbes at Culloden. Second in command was Lt. Colonel Patrick Work.[29] For the Forbes campaign, the three battalions were combined into two, these to be commanded by Armstrong and Burd.

Armstrong, Burd and Mercer were, of course hardened frontiersmen, and, indeed, many of the company captains, as Forbes had requested, had had lots of beneficial experience in fighting the French and Indian raiding parties. The Pennsylvania officers were "to chuse in their Regiments or amongst the Country People the most fit men for [the] Expedition, and to give a List of their Rangers & marks men. They will fix upon proper People to be employ'd as Guides and Spies." [30] Probably about half of the men in the Pennsylvania Regiment, 1200 at least, could be counted "good woodsmen."

Bouquet, who at this time held rank as Lieutenant-Colonel was in command of the Royal Americans,[31] but actually, because of General Forbes's severe illness, assumed large duties for the whole expedition. Sir John St. Clair, a Scotsman who had served the Braddock Expedition as Deputy Quartermaster-General (and had been wounded) continued in that post for General Forbes. St. Clair, who had proved a difficult man for Armstrong and for James Burd in their surveying for Braddock, was not all that popular with General Forbes either. The General was most impatient with him, and was not bashful about admitting it: "He is a very odd man and I am sorry it has been my fate to have any concern with him." And he complained about St. Clair's indifference to his duties: "No Sergeant or Quartermaster of a Regiment is obliged to look into small detail more than I am." [32] Still he would play for Forbes an important role. He helped in the planning of the Forbes Road and supervised its construction; and it was St. Clair, too, who would choose the site for the building of Fort Ligonier. And it is worth noting that the Quartermaster, who had been so insufferable for Armstrong and Burd at the time of Braddock, here, on June 5, just as the expedition was getting underway, wrote from Winchester to Bouquet to pay compliments to both of the commissioners.

Heavy recruiting had been carried on in York, Lancaster and Cumberland counties. George Stevenson, of York County, had, on the recommendation of Armstrong, been appointed, in May, the recruiting officer for the Pennsylvania Regiment. He was doing a good job, and was told so by Colonel Bouquet: "Sir, it is with great Satisfaction that I see by your letter of the 31st that you answer the Character Col. Armstrong had given me of you, as a man of Publick Spirit, and Zealous for the Good of the Service and the Prosperity of his Country." He urged Stevenson to promote enthusiasm and support for the expedition: "I depend, therefore, on your Assistance, to spirit up the People of York County, where, I know, you have a great influence, and make them Sensible of the necessity of exerting themselves for the Success of this Expedition upon which, the very being of this Province depends." [33]

Actually, troop organization had been moving rather fast since the last week of May. The troops recruited from Maryland and Virginia, as well as those from the so-called Lower Counties of Pennsylvania (Delaware) were assembled at Winchester. The principal forwarding point for troops and supplies was Carlisle, and for the first week of June Bouquet was in Carlisle directing operations. The full Pennsylvania Regiment organized its force at Raystown,[34] where they awaited the arrival of the provincial troops under Washington. General Forbes had hoped to march his regulars to a union with Bouquet at Raystown, but was much delayed by his illness and compelled to linger at Carlisle. It was already early summer, and although his troops were way behind schedule, Forbes had a good feeling about the organization of the army and about its numbers. He was, finally, in command of an army that, despite its diversity, could be regarded as formidable. The muster showed the number of troops at 7200.

The second major decision to be made concerned the route to be followed west of Raystown. This decision of course had to be made by General Forbes, and the sooner the better. He had two clear options for the road west of Raystown. He could drop south from Raystown to Fort Cumberland, to pick up the Braddock Road, which could then be followed west to the Ohio, or he could cut a new road (that is, widen the Indian trail known as the Raystown Path)[35] and proceed more directly west to Fort Duquesne.

He had been well briefed on the Braddock expedition, and he sensed the value of any change that would reduce identification with that disaster. He also had secured an update on the old Fort Cumberland road. He had, as was his wont, been very careful and very thorough in his investigation of possible routes. He had dispatched scouts to produce highly detailed accounts of distance and terrain. With those reports in hand, to William Pitt he dispatched a letter from Carlisle, in which he expressed the hope that he might find a better way over the Allegheny Mountain than that taken by General Braddock. "If so," he wrote, "I should shorten both my march, and my labor . . . about 40 miles over Mr. Braddock's route." That road, he noted, is "now a brushwood, by the sprouts from the old stumps." [36]

Colonel Bouquet, who had been out as far as Raystown, was from the beginning inclined for a new route. But he was having difficulty in persuading the Virginia and Maryland provincial officers of the advantages. Washington, whom Forbes knew he had to rely on heavily for an understanding of the country, was chief among those arguing for the old road. He was very strongly for the Braddock route all the way, which of course meant a corridor to the Ohio country for settlers from Virginia. In a conference with Bouquet he pointed out that work had already been underway on the Braddock trail, that the old Indian path had been much widened, and that in fact it was complete to within six miles of Fort Duquesne. He noted also that the distance saved by the proposed new road could not be more than nineteen miles. Bouquet was not convinced. He urged a new trail, doing what was necessary to open the road from Carlisle to Raystown, and cutting the trail directly after that to the Monongahela.

Colonel Armstrong, of course, as well as James Burd and the Pennsylvania people, were just as strongly for the most direct route from Carlisle. They had convincing arguments for the Raystown route. They pointed out to the General that it was at least a few miles shorter than the southern route, that there were no major waterways to accomplish, that forage for the packhorses, the bullocks, the swine and the sheep was much more readily discovered, and that all in all there would be fewer difficult moments in the terrain. They were particularly insistent on a direct route from Raystown to Loyal-hanna, which would mean a march of no more than forty-five miles.

Forbes did not require a lot of persuasion. From the beginning he had assumed a course different from that of Braddock. He was determined to rid the mission of everything that smacked of the Braddock catastrophe. When he understood that he had the support of his chief officer, Henry Bouquet, it was enough. On July 31, Bouquet reported an interview with Washington, complaining that he had "learned nothing satisfactory from them." He declared that ". . . the majority of these gentlemen [Washington and those favoring the southern route] do not know the difference between a party and an army, and, overlooking all difficulties, they believe everything which flatters their ideas."[37]

In the end, Forbes opted for the new road,[38] and commissioned Bouquet to open it. This expedition was to be an exclusively Pennsylvania mission. Forbes had in mind to leapfrog the army across the province to the Ohio, establishing forts and supply depots at convenient spots along the way. It was European strategy, known as "protected advance." Carlisle would provide the launching pad, and the garrisoned Forts Loudoun and Lyttleton, and the forts to be built at Raystown and Loyal-hanna would be principal stepping stones to the west.

It must be remembered that there are no settlements west of Shippensburg. There could be found a house or two at Loudoun and at Lyttleton, nothing at Raystown, nothing at all. There was no habitation, not even a wagon trail. Forbes was cutting his way through a wilderness. This was Indian country, familiar to only a few white traders.

As the road was finally mapped out, it ran in its first section from Carlisle to Fort Loudoun, at which all troops assembled, except those from the southern colonies. Loudoun, the fort which Armstrong had built in 1756 as one of his "ring of forts," could be considered the assembly point. This structure, as Armstrong had placed it, was located on the east side of the west branch of the Conococheague, not far from the present site of the community of Fort Loudon, at the foot of the steeply ascending Tuscarora Mountain range. The road proceeds north and west from Fort Loudoun to Fort Lyttleton, thence to Sideling Hill, and on to the crossing of the Raystown Branch of the Juniata through what is present-day Everett to Raystown.

The next section of the road ran almost due west (and a wee bit south) over the Laurel Hills to Loyal-hanna (now Ligonier). Loyal-hanna was in a particularly strategic position on the route, and Forbes understood that it was vital to have a substantial fort and base of operations located here. Loyal-hanna, a corruption of the Delaware Indian name, *Lawel* (meaning "middle") and *hanna* (meaning "stream"), refers to the small stream which flows here, midway between the waters of the Juniata and the waters of the Ohio.[39] And from Loyal-hanna west to the Forks of the Ohio was a distance of fifty miles.

With the road now determined, the General could turn his full attention to the problem that had tormented him from the time he assumed command. It was the problem that had plagued General Braddock three years earlier. Somehow he had to round up wagons and drivers and teams of horses; and he needed to acquire supplies sufficient to provide for an army of 7000 men for perhaps as long as seven months! He needed ammunition and ammunition wagons. One would think that with the French threatening their province and with all of the Indian troubles, the people of Pennsylvania would welcome the chance to support an army. But the fifteen shillings per day that Forbes was offering for a team-of-four and a wagoner proved quite unattractive. And Forbes's military authority counted for nothing with the civil servants. Bouquet and Forbes were beginning to appreciate all that General Braddock had gone through.

On May 11, Forbes had run in the *Pennsylvania Gazette* an advertisement for wagons. That he knows wagons is abundantly clear. One would swear that he has been a wagonmaster for twenty years. He spells out *exactly* the specifications, for both the provision wagons and the ammunition wagons. Everything is to be outfitted in Carlisle.[40]

At the height of this organizing, the General had an alarming communication from Bouquet. In a long letter, composed in French, the Colonel reported, "Colonel Armstrong believes that we shall soon be attacked." He says, "The French have now gathered all their Indians together; and for lack of food and presents to give them, they could not keep them inactive very long, and would be obliged to march against us, if we do not advance upon them." And Bouquet had more: Noting that Armstrong and Burd will march for Forts Loudoun and Lyttleton in four days, he complains about the muskets, which are "too heavy" and "burst when fired." (!) He concludes with the good news that he has had from Armstrong, who "tells me that you have given Captain Callender the contract for pack horses because of his knowledge of the country." The provincial soldiers, he assures the General, who have been in the service of Indian traders "will be well suited to load and conduct the horses." In a letter to General John Stanwix, dated May 29, 1758, Forbes had "complained bitterly" about his difficulties with the provincials and particularly the commissioners. Sounding very like General Braddock, he described the Pennsylvanians as "the most perverse generation of mortalls that ever breathed Air." He went on to report that "I meet with rubbs and hindrances in every thing depending on the Commissioners, and they meddle, and give orders in the meerest trifles." [41]

But Benjamin Franklin, in summarizing the session of the Assembly that ended early in May, expressed a very different view: He is writing for his *Pennsylvania Gazette*. He notes that the men have been raised "with astonishing Expedition," that the people have shown a great spirit and a determination to defend their country, that Colonel Armstrong's Battalion is in motion, and that "a very good Understanding" subsists between Forbes and the commissioners. He declares that "tho he hath requested many things of us we cou'd not grant, everything has been done by this

Province that cou'd be expected of it." [42]

Of course the Forbes expedition would not enjoy a big chance for success if the Delaware and the Shawnee Indians took up the hatchet on the side of the French. No one appreciated this fact better than John Forbes. Accordingly, Christian Frederick Post was dispatched on a peace mission to the Indians of the Ohio region, many of whom were refugees from Armstrong's Kittanning raid. He made the difficult, and very dangerous, trip by way of the Shamokin Path, beginning at Fort Augusta, and "then over the trail up the West Branch and across to Venango, and thence to Kuskuski on the Beaver (where many who had escaped Armstrong were now living), at the junction of the Mahoning and Shenango Rivers." At great risk he would meet with Indians in the various villages and make peace overtures, talking with the most prominent chiefs. He would meet with Shingas at Kuskuski for ten days, August 28-September 7.

Naturally, Shingas was not crazy about either the French or the English. He declared to Post that both were fighting for the Indian lands, "the Land that God has given us." He did not care to assist anybody to take his land. He insisted that if his people sided with the English against the French, the English, if indeed they conquered, would take the land from the Indians.[43]

But now, finally, the expedition is in motion. It was to be very different from the modest expedition of Colonel Armstrong to Kittanning. Surprise was not essential to success in this case. Indeed, just the opposite was to be desired. Forbes had every reason to believe that a show of great force might have a discouraging effect, if not on the French, at least on their Indian allies. As early as May he had had the most welcome report of frontiersman Christopher Gist and his Indians who had scouted Fort Duquesne. Gist had reported the fort "weakly defended."

In this early going Armstrong is back and forth among Fort Lyttleton, Lancaster, and Carlisle. From Lancaster, on June 6, he dispatched a most interesting communication to Colonel Washington, whom he is just getting to know. It has largely to do with recruiting, but provides a good impression of the problems and confusions which attend the organization of an army such as this. Addressing Washington, who by date of commission outranks the three colonels of the Pennsylvania battalions, as "Honoured Sir," he reports his orders from Bouquet, apologizes for "not writing yesterday," and then complains about the raw and undisciplined nature of the troops from the Lower Counties, before advising that he expects to march his battalion within the week. The very long letter is signed: "I am Honoured Sir with Greatest Respect, your Most Obedt. Servt. John Armstrong" [44]

It must be remembered that all through this organizing General Forbes was suffering a most severe and painful illness. A letter to his superior, General James Abercromby, dated, June 7, includes the complaint, "I have been much out of order by a kind of Cholera Morbus, which prevented my writing to you, and giving you the detail of our proceedings." [45]

On that same day, while he was yet in Philadelphia, Forbes had a letter from Colonel Bouquet, then in Carlisle. Bouquet was explaining his delay in marching, noting that tents and ammunition have not yet arrived, but insisted that the Second Battalion would be marching "tomorrow to join Armstrong at Littleton."

He then appended the first of what would be many complaints about the rain: "In spite of all the repairs made on the roads, they are almost impassable beyond Shippensburg because of the continued rains on the clay soil. Several wagons have stuck in the mud, and several have been three days in going from Shippensburg to Fort Loudoun. I am having them [the roads] worked on continually, but they must be given time to become hard. This is an obstacle that cannot be overcome." [46]

And even the boundless energy with which he was endowed was not sufficient to ward off the discouragement that was visited upon him by his association with the provincials. To Forbes on June 11 he addressed a weary lamentation that could not have much pleased the General: "You are not to overlook the fact that no one in this country can be relied on. At all times, private interests outweigh the general welfare . . . . The farther I go away from the settlements, the more I see that this expedition, which is believed so easy, is full of almost insurmountable difficulties. For want of stores prepared in advance, we shall consume daily almost as much provisions as can be transported over such roads."

He warned Forbes that he should not expect the army to

move at much pace, and that there was not much to be expected of packhorses. "If obliged to open all the roads, we shall be obliged to march like tortoises, very slowly, and carrying everything on our backs." He remembers that Braddock's army for three days could discover no grass for the horses, and "he would have likely to die of hunger, [even] if he had beaten the enemy." Moreover, "No reliance can be made in the reports of the people who claim to know the country, after passing Reas Town. All whom I have questioned contradict each other, and we should only learn the truth about it by exploring the country ourselves." [47]

But by the middle of June organization was complete, and all units were given marching orders. Colonel Armstrong's First Battalion (800 men) had been ordered to march from Carlisle to Fort Lyttleton, and, as is known by a letter from Sir Allan MacLean to Bouquet, date Lancaster, June 9, measures had been taken to complete his battalion as well as that of Burd; and there were now upon the roads tents and several other necessities for the Provincials.

Armstrong was to proceed at a good rate along the wagon road ahead of the other bodies of troops. It was his job to build depot stations at sites one or two days' marching distance from each other. Forbes's plan called for Washington with his Virginians to follow and widen the road. Colonel Montgomerie with his Highlanders would then follow, both to provide reinforcement for the troops of Armstrong and Washington and to supply a vanguard to the British Regulars, the main part of the army, and the artillery. Armstrong was made to understand that if he completed a redoubt before Washington came up, he was to work back, clearing the road as he went.[48]

Forbes continued from Philadelphia all through the month of June to direct the army, delivering a steady fusillade of letters to Bouquet and to other officers. Many of his letters end with this kind of lament: "I am quite tired and so bid you farewell." [49]

As he often defers to the judgment of Bouquet, for "you are on the spott," late in June he agreed to go with Bouquet's plan to use pack horses rather than wagons for the transport of provisions, for the advanced part of the army. This Bouquet had urged because of the terrible condition of the roads. Forbes noted that Sir John St.

Clair and Colonel Armstrong were presently employing as many pack horses as 200, and they "may engage more."[50]

But the month of June was a trying one for Armstrong and his men, as they were still short on tents and blankets. And it continued to rain!

On the matter of roads Bouquet received at the end of the month a long letter from Colonel Armstrong, who had been shown by Sir John St. Clair a report of a proposal for a new road of sixty miles from Fort Frederick to Fort Cumberland. Citing needless fatigue and waste of precious time, the Colonel is obviously most unhappy with such proposals: "I'm Sorry to Say, that so many New experiments of Roads at this advanc'd Season, doesn't Seem to me calculated to fervour [favor] Our expedition.... I have told him [Sir John] I thought you were now got thro' the greatest difficulties upon Reas Town Road & Sundry things to that import, but he says the More Roads the better, I don't desire it shou'd be known I wrote you on this Subject...."[51]

Forbes departed Philadelphia, with the Highland Battalion of Montgomerie and the train of artillery, on June 30, reaching Carlisle on July 4. On the 10th he dispatched another communication to Pitt, in which he described the trip from Philadelphia to Carlisle as an arduous one ("120 miles in excessive hot weather") and noted the prospect of an "immense Forest of 240 miles of Extent." Here in Carlisle the illness that was to kill him hit hard. Here he remained for all of July and the first week of August. He had hoped to join Bouquet at Bedford in July, but he did not leave Carlisle until August 12! And he did not get far. At Shippensburg, just a few miles to the southwest of Carlisle, he remained for three more weeks.[52]

Construction of a fort at Bedford had been urged by Armstrong as early as the fall of 1756, but work was not begun until June 24, 1758. The fort was located on the Raystown Branch of the Juniata. "It embraced 7000 square yards and besides its five bastions and swivel guns it had a Gallery with loop holes extending from the central bastion on its north front to the water's edge."[53] Forbes, not arriving until the first week of September, did not catch up to Bouquet, who had gone on to Loyal-Hanna. But here the main body of the army was joined by the troops under Colonel

Washington, who had marched from Fort Cumberland. And here the road pulled away from the road cut by Burd and Armstrong for Braddock in the summer of 1755.

The course would take the army from Raystown pretty much due west through present-day Wolfsburg, Schellsburg, Edmunds Swamp, Stoystown, and Jennerstown, to Ligonier. At Ligonier the road crossed the Loyalhanna Creek, and proceeded over the most formidable Chestnut Ridge at present-day Youngstown, and then north and west a little to Old Hannastown, near Greensburg, across the headwaters of Brush Creek and on to present Murrysville. In its final stages it proceeded along the Monongahela to the fort.[54]

For one hundred miles the road was built, wide enough for the Conestoga wagons, over a series of steep mountain ridges, made formidable by large rock outcroppings, swamps, and steep grades. Toughest was the fifty-mile distance of dense forest between Raystown and Loyal-hanna. But as late as July, Bouquet remained concerned about the course to be taken through the wilderness west of Raystown. Indeed he seemed to be in a mood to complain. On July 11, from the camp near Raystown, he declared in a letter to Forbes that it may be "impossible" to find a passage through Laurel Hill, which was the next-to-last ridge of the Appalachians. He even suggested, with Virginia and Pennsylvania in mind, that the choice of roads may be determined by politics. At this time, too, he complained about a disturbing number of desertions, and about the quality of the arms supplied the troops. The sabers which had been delivered to the light cavalry he termed "a joke." These, he insisted, "could not kill a chicken." [55]

From Carlisle, Forbes on July 14 had advised Bouquet that "I have sent up Major [George] Armstrong with one Dunning [probably James Dunning, for whom Dunning's Creek is named] ane old Indian trader who has been many a time upon the Road from Raes town to Fort Duquesne, and he says there is no Difficulty in the road across Laurell Hill to Fort Duquesne along the top of Chestnut ridge." He also at this time lodges a complaint about the "infernal" wagons, declaring, "The Waggons have been the plague of my life, as I found them here [Carlisle] in the greatest degree of Confusion." [56]

Although most of his battalion is long gone, commander Armstrong is himself *still* in Carlisle. On the 8th of July to an unnamed party (but apparently a minister) he had provided a long update on the situation for his battalion. In the letter he noted that peace had been made with the Reverend Barton (with whom the Colonel had had a difference)[57] and also that Sir John St. Clair "is now very polite." And he expressed the confidence that General Forbes would be leaving Carlisle in "three days." By the 20th he was himself ready to go. To Governor Denny he wrote: "This day I March from this place with the last of the Provincials, being part of the three Companys, Consisting of about thirty-five Each, but without a Single Kettle or Canteen . . . . There are before us at Fort Loudon upward of One hundred Canteens, but no Kettles, so that we Shall have some difficulty in Cooking untill these Kettles are Sent."

He expressed confidence, too, in the new recruits, finding them "equal to what cou'd be expected." And he reported that General Forbes "has Sent my Brother George to Reas' Town, with Orders to take with him a hundred Men, in Order to find Out and Mark a Road from Reas' Town as near to Fort Duquesne as he can possibly go, leaving General Braddock's Road & the Yohiogaine entirely to the left, and afterward to attempt a Scalp or Prisoner." Armstrong, however, feared for the safety of the road-cutters as they approached nearer and nearer to the Fort, "as the Enemy doubtless will View them every Step from Reas' Town." [58]

By this time there were some 300 Conestoga wagons on the line of communication. Called "Conestoga" wagons because they first began to appear in the region of the Conestoga valley in southeastern Pennsylvania (south of Lancaster and north of the Susquehanna River, the wagons were heavy farm wagons designed to carry large quantities of produce or freight. As loads were large, the wagons were ingeniously designed to keep the weight from shifting.

Builders shaped the floor of the wagon so that it would rise at both ends. This worked effectively in going uphill (or downhill) in that the weight could not pressure the tail gate or the headboard. It was very important, too, of course, that the load be protected from the weather. Most distinctive was the covering, made of hempen homespun and later of canvas, but white, and adorning the carriage with a lady's bonnet effect. So "pretty" were the wagons as they moved singly or in a train along the woodland trail or through a clearing that they were accorded the appellation "ships of inland commerce," and later in the migration of settlers westward, "prairie schooners."

Each wagon could accommodate eight tons of provisions for Forbes's army, and each was pulled by a team of horses, normally six. The driver, who for the Forbes campaign had a loaded musket close to hand, was perched over the left wheelhorse, sometimes on a specially prepared "lazy board." [59]

Conestoga Wagon

The wagons carried, besides the provisions necessary to the feeding of an army, and hospital supplies, also the tools essential to the cutting of the road (shovels, picks, sledges, and axes). And everything required by the coopers, the shoemakers, the wheel-wrights, the saddlers and blacksmiths.

Of course also on the road were as many pack horses and most of the time a good many more. And there were the smaller ammunition wagons as well. And conveyed in the train of the army somewhere were bullocks, the swine, and sheep.

Concerned about alienating the friendly Indians, Forbes ordered Bouquet to notify the soldiers, and especially those of George Armstrong, who were out front, of the "marks of distinction" (yellow bands and Union flags) which he is dispatching to those Ohio Indians known to be friendly. "This method for distinguishing friendly Indians," Forbes insisted to Bouquet, "must be published at Fort Cumberland & if you can to the parties sent up the Ohio. And if Major Armstrong be gone out [already], pray let the knowledge of this signal be sent after him."

Determined as he is to keep the Delaware and Shawnee Indians "out of it," he hopes no costly mistake will be made. "So you will make [George] Armstrong proceed with great caution, and to observe the yellow band about the head or Arms of all those who want to come in a friendly manner from the Enemy, I having sent them word of that mark of Distinction, and I sent some union Flags [the British Union Jack] and some yellow Shalloon up to Fort Augusta to be given to the Messengers who might go from thence to the Ohio." [60]

As late as the last week of July, with Forbes yet in Carlisle and Colonel Armstrong now at Fort Loudoun, decisions are *still* being made on the route to be followed, or at least the Virginians think so. Indeed, bribery is at work now. Forbes writes to Bouquet on the subject of the formidable Laurel Hill: "Col. Byrd in a paragraph of his letter from Fort Cumberland . . . writes that he has upwards of Sixty Indians waiting my arrival and ready to accompany me, but they will not follow me unless I go by Fort Cumberland. This is a new System of Military Discipline truly; and shows that my good friend Byrd is either made the Cats Foot off [of] himself, or he little knows me, if he imagines that Sixty Scoundrells are to direct me in my measures." [61]

But General Forbes was having a very tough time of it. During the last two weeks of July and the first week of August, his illness was so severe that he could hardly manage; he even considered giving up his command. Although he improved steadily, albeit very slowly, through all of August and into the first week of September, he was so ill during this time that he was quite unable to write, and in fact hardly able to dictate. How acute and painful and disabling was the illness can be understood from the letters that the General's aide, Major Francis Halkett (the son of Sir Peter Halkett, the mortally wounded regimental commander under Braddock), dispatched to Bouquet and others. To Bouquet on the 23rd of July Halkett wrote that "General Forbes is so extreamly Reduc'd & low in Spirits with the Flux, and other afflictions, that he is not able to write you." On the 31st, he sorrowfully informed Bouquet that "The General is so indispos'd this day by taking Phisick, that he is not able to acknowledge the Receipt of your letter himselfe, and as he thinks that no time should be lost in makeing of the new Road, he has directed me to inform you . . . ." And on the 3rd of August, still in Carlisle, Halkett, having requested of Bouquet a surgeon, writes for Forbes: "I have been tormented day and night these 14 Days with what they call a Flux, and what I call a Violent Constipation. I hope I shall now get the better of it altho I neither eat nor sleep." This is a General in command of 7000 men hacking their way through a wilderness to capture a Fort that is defended he knows not how.

To General Abercromby on the very next day he had Major Halkett inscribe a letter: "I have been very much out of order by what Dr. Bassett [one of the surgeons attached to the medical force of the British army] will call the flux, which is a most violent constipation attended with Inflamation in the Rectum, violent pain & total suppression of the Urine. In short I have been most miserable nor am I yet much better, but [because of] this I can not move these 4 days . . . ."

Better news by August 7, Halkett to Bouquet: "I have the pleasure to inform you that the General recovers daily, but from the length of the Indisposition, & eating nothing, he was greatly reduc'd & still very weak, he goes out in his Chariot every evening which does him great good, & I think will soon set him on his legs again."[62]

But progress is terribly slow, both with the illness and the march westward. By August 16 Forbes has proceeded only as far as Shippensburg. Here he directed Halkett to pen a letter to Governor Horatio Sharpe of Maryland: "I can not paint the misery and distress that I have been in since I had the pleasure of seeing you, by that damnd Flux, which I hope has now made its last effort by knocking me up some days ago, at this blessed habitation, I now begin to mend a little, and hope in a day or two to gitt forward . . . ." And ten days later, still in Shippensburg, Halkett reported to Bouquet that while the General goes out to take the air daily, he still "recovers but slowly."[63]

By the end of August the General was feeling the need for "a few prunes," by way of a laxative, but was obliged to settle for raisins. On September 4, from Shippensburg, he thanked General Abercromby for expressing concern about his health, and on this date confessed that in his worst moments has considered resigning his command. He advised Abercromby that he has "been in such a condition this [past] month . . . from a most violent flux, with most excruciating pain in my Bowells, and rendered so low and weak that I had oftener than once or twice firmly resolved to have wrote you, to appoint some other person to take this Command, as I absolutely found myself incapable to proceed—But now thank God I am a great deal better, and [grateful] that my sickness has never retarded my operation one single moment . . . ."

He closed out this long letter with a P.S.: "You may guess my condition when I tell you I have not Strength to ride on Horseback, nor indeed in my Body able to bear the roughness of a Waggon, and [my] Backside (with Pardon) has been so pestered with Glisters and Stools, that I must Sally forth in a kind of Horse litter actually made by Doctor Russell and my Servants." [64]

Meanwhile, with most of the soldiers ignorant of their General's condition, and very few even of the officers aware of how serious the illness is, the army marches on.

On August 9 the General reminded Bouquet that he had hoped Major Armstrong "should have gone on from Laurell Hill, to try his fortune in getting Intelligence or a prisoner, and to have nothing to do with making the road, as I thought he knew nothing of making of roads." [65]

Bouquet received this letter at his encampment near Raystown. He reported promptly that he means to dispatch Major George Armstrong with a working party of 100 volunteers, "day after tomorrow" to mark the road through the Laurel Hill region. And he is asking Armstrong to send in regular reports, "every day (or two days)."

Before all of this, toward the end of June, shortly after he had set out from Raystown, George Armstrong, who has the benefit of three guides (Neal McConnell, James Brown, and Ralph Sterett), as well as the luxury of three Indian scouts, and ten Maryland Rangers, advised Bouquet that there was Indian activity in the neighborhood. (And indeed all through July skirmishes occurred along the roads.) But he means to go forward. In a later letter he reported from Edmund's Swamp (or Swamp Creek, now known as Miller's Run): "Sir, I arrived here last Night very late. There are about two miles of the Allegheny Hill, that is Stony, but the Stones can be removed without much Difficulty, and in these two Miles are two Hills, where all the Hardship in crossing the Allegheny lays

[sic], and even there, where the Road is cut to Advantage, [William] White is of Opinion that he can bring 200 W^t up in his own Waggon, So that it is without Doubt practicable to find a Waggon Road thro' this Mountain."

He is much encouraged. "There is a small Pinch above where we now lay [sic], and I can not learn that there is anymore in this Mountain, therefore am inclin'd to think the Road Cutters may be employ'd as soon as you please."

Faithful to Bouquet's request, he reported on the very next day, this time from Kickenapauling's: [66] He is much impressed with the locale, and finds it the "best situation" for a repository for supplies: "When I return from Loyalhanning, and after the Works are finished, I intend to employ myself in Surveying a very good Plantation or two that Lays [sic] upon this Creek." [67]

Next day he reported that he had found the Loyalhanning "a pretty place," with an abundance of water and grass for the stock. He declared that the officers from Washington's Virginia troops feel the same way. "The prospects for a wagon road are very good."

But that the route is not definitely determined *even yet* is clear from Bouquet's letter to Forbes (cited earlier), written from Raystown before he has had George Armstrong's letter about Laurel Hill. Washington's feeling for the Braddock Road he reports:

Colonel Washington has had the beginning of Braddock's Road cut which I have fixed at ten miles from Fort Cumberland. From the guides I have sent you, you will have learned the advantages of this route, which is open and requires few repairs, and its inconveniences, which are the lack of forage, its length, its narrow passes, and the river crossings. Colonel Washington who is animated by a sincere zeal to contribute to the success of this expedition, and ready to march from whatever direction you may determine with the same eagerness, writes me that, from all he has heard and been able to gather from reports, our route is impracticable even for pack horses, so bad are the mountains; and that Braddock's Road is absolutely the only one to take, etc.[68]

But Bouquet, who has been mulling over the choice of roads, is finally persuaded, by George Armstrong's reports, and by those of James Burd, whom he has sent out for confirmation, that the Braddock Road is not the way to go. In that long letter to Forbes from Raystown, which he composed the last day of July (cited above), he had reported the "nothing satisfactory" interview with Colonel Washington. And in this same letter he reported something to be dreaded whichever route is chosen—smallpox.[69]

Washington, apparently sensing that he has not persuaded Bouquet, addressed a letter to him from Fort Cumberland, on August 2. He continues *very* strong for the southern route, and he wants Bouquet to appreciate that if they elect the new road, the mission will have to be suspended, and renewed in the spring. There is just not the time. So he makes one more stab at it. At great length he assaults each argument for the northern route, coming finally to one of the strongest:

The shortness of the Road from Rays Town to Fort Duquesne by Loyal hanny, is us'd as an argument in disfavor of this Road [Braddock's], *and bears some thing in it unaccountable to me, for I must beg leave to ask here, if it requires more time, or is it more difficult and expensive, to go 145 miles in a good Road already made to our hands, or to cut 100 miles in length, great part of which over almost inaccessible Mountains, and, to say, or think, we can do nothing more this Fall than to fortify some Post on the other side of the Mountains and prepare against another Compaigne I must pray Heaven, most fervently, to avert!* [70]

And Washington, although he had strong political reasons for arguing for the southern route, seems really to have believed what all along he has been insisting to Bouquet. He thought that if the army cut and proceeded to march on the new road, it would be a failed mission. At the same time he wrote to Bouquet he got off a letter to Major Francis Halkett, whose father Washington had known well.

Now thoroughly convinced that Bouquet is not to be won over to the old road, he became distraught. He expressed his view disdainfully and with great vehemence: "My dear Halkett.... If

Colo. Bouquet succeeds in this point with the General, all is lost! All is lost by Heavens! Our Enterprise Ruin'd; and we stop'd at the Laurel Hill this Winter; not to gather Laurels, except the kind that covers the mountains." [71]

Meanwhile George Armstrong, from Drownding Creek (Kickenapauling), has now much to lament. He has finished the breastworks, but there are signs of Indian activity ("their tracks going to the westward"), and a pervasive illness ("some men dying") afflicts the workers; there is a great need for "more axes," and on top of all there is the incessant rain.

And Bouquet's August 3rd report to Forbes from the camp near Reas Town, while conveying the good news (1) that progress is in accord with the plan, and (2) that his Cherokee scouts have found little activity at Fort Duquesne (no tents or troops around the fort, the French not venturing out, and only a woman washing in the river, "too close to the fort for us to kill her"), is not brimming with good cheer. "The artillery," he reports, "will not arrive for two days. If they always march at that rate, the season will be over. Most of the pack horses are in terrible condition. The North Carolina troops are in pitiable condition, and lack health, uniforms and everything." He declares, "I have never seen such misery. I believe they are good only for guarding a fort. The Maryland men are of more value. I have given them tents, and it will be necessary to have the 48 tents and 74 canteens sent back from Fort Frederic [Maryland], which were sent to Governor Sharpe by Colonel Armstrong, after he . . . supplied his garrison." [72]

The army is marching forward, in short hops and with constant communication, but the men, both soldiers and axe men, are in want of practically everything. There are not sufficient axes, not enough canteens to go around, and never enough tents. Besides, Indians in small parties have been sighted in the forests, and, indeed, there have been skirmishes in the regions of Fort Lyttleton, Sideling Hill, and Fort Cumberland. Colonel Bouquet, partly because of the absence of Forbes, and partly because he attends to absolutely every detail, is much overtaxed. Progress is being made, but the summer is wearing on. Armstrong is at Edmund's Swamp. Bouquet is writing from the camp at Raystown to General Forbes on August 11: "Sir John [St. Clair] is returning to the road today to hurry the work. All the Virginians marched with the two companies of workmen, and as soon as the accounts of Armstrong's battalion are settled, I shall send them to Kickeny Pawlins [Kickenapauling's Old Town], where I am beginning a small provisions' depot today." [73]

     Sir John St. Clair has been doing the work of road-building supervision and the quartermaster work of provisioning the troops and caring for the animals. At the middle of August, from the very top of the Allegheny Mountain, he filed an update to Colonel Bouquet. Noting that he expects Colonel Armstrong "this day" to bring a number of horses, and advising that "I shall send Col. Armstrong to Camp on the 2nd rising at the spring and [to] work backwards," he then provides a map of the depots. "I cannot fix on any Day for having the Waggons at Edmunds Swamp," which he much prefers over the Shades of Death as a redoubt, but "If Col Armstrong will work I think we can get them to that place by Sunday. . . . The Enemy are all around us in partys of 6 and 10, how long they will continue so I cannot tell, I shall take all the care I can." [74]

     And before the week was out St. Clair was writing again to Bouquet from Allegheny Hill. Though the rains continue to come down, he has been working: "Tell me who I am to leave at the Redou[b]t [Sir Allan MacLean's encampment] between the two risings of Allegheny, and who are to be at Edmunds Swamp [Col. Adam Stephen's camp]. I shall go near to finish this rising this day and shall be able to join Sr Allan tomorrow. 'Tho the rain has hindred [Col.] Armstrong from marching it did not stop my party from working." [75]

     With the rains letting up just a little, Armstrong did get his troops moving the next day, Friday, August 18. And on that day Bouquet, who is impatient to get on to Loyal-hanna to establish a post, reported to Forbes, in French, on the "abominable" road forward from Lyttleton: "The rains have delayed them [the workers] a little, but tomorrow or Sunday the wagons can go to Edmund's Swamp. The parties have cut in four different places, eight miles apart from each other, which advances the work rapidly. I have sent two hundred men of the regular troops to Kickeny Pawlins, to protect the front of our workmen, and Armstrong's battalion has gone out to reinforce them."

He reported also on the presence of the hostile Indians, who are deathly afraid of the artillery, which they call "thunder sticks," and seem determined to know its number: "The enemy has discovered us, as one of their parties took a prisoner [not identified] Saturday [a week ago] near the Shawnee Cabins [on the Juniata], who escaped after being with them for two days. He said that the six Indians who captured him spoke English as well as he could, which makes me fear that they are some of our friends the Delawares. They went along about 150 paces from our workmen, and asked him several pertinent questions about the artillery. When he did not give a correct answer, they told him that he lied, that we had only so many cannon. The rascals have doubtless been following the convoy for several days." [76]

And that is not all that is irksome to him. On August 20 he complains bitterly (again!) to Forbes about the state of the wagons and about the farmers who simply will not supply provisions. "To count on the good will of the inhabitants of Pennsylvania or on the press warrants [by which the army could legally seize (impress) civilians' wagons] of the magistrates would be folly, and we should die of hunger." [77]

General Forbes received from Bouquet, just a few days later, a letter written in French. In this letter Bouquet reported the road open as far as Edmund's Swamp, and he assured the General that the post at Loyal-hanna will be built and occupied by the time he shows up. "While they are working at this post," Bouquet writes, "Colonel Armstrong with 400 men of his battalion, and two companies of workmen from Va. and one company from the Lower Counties will improve the road, build a redoubt at Edmunds Swamp, and cut the road from Kickeny Pawlins, in order to go and join them [at Loyal-hanna], leaving detachments at the redoubt which is at the head of the gap [probably Fort Dewart], on the Allegheny Mountain, at Edmund's Swamp, and at Kickeny Pawlins."

Armstrong on his march to Kittanning had his soldiers following the Indian path in the Indian way, that is, single file. Forbes's idea, with widened roads is different. Bouquet, now very conscious of the Indian presence and keenly aware that as they draw ever closer to Duquesne, the chances for ambush or assault grow steadily, here informs his General that his plan of marching has been installed, and that the troops march accordingly, that is, in double file: "In all encounters in the field or in the woods, I notice that the enemy—especially the Indians—attack our flanks first, and try to surround us. This will be impossible for them through this plan; we should outflank them every time, and if they detach parties to turn our position, they must encounter our light troops advanced at least 200 paces; but more about it at meeting."

Bouquet is also conscious of another problem, the coordination of the regular troops with the provincial forces, matters of command and of jealousy and respect. (Major James Grant, for example, dislikes taking orders from provincial officers.) On this subject he determines to quiet the General's anxieties. The date is August 23: "I can assure you that, whatever our fate, you will never experience the indignities suffered by General Abercromby through the laxness of his provincialls. I have established harmony between the different corps which will prevent any accident of that nature, and by holding of the balance, even, encouraging these, and restraining the overbearing spirit of the others, chiefly of your countrymen [the British Regulars], I can truly assure you that you will find no fault other than ignorance and inexperience, which I cannot remedy—but they are loyal and will not abandon you." [78]

As the army approaches Loyal-hanna, where a fort is to be constructed, Bouquet, via St. Clair, provides very specific orders governing all units of the army. Colonel Armstrong "is to command at Kickeny Pawlins and along the Communication from the Gap of the Allegheny to the fort at Lawrell Hill." And his battalion is "to polish and repair the Road" and to garrison Castle Duart,[79] Edmunds Swamp, and Kickeny Pawlins.[80]

It happened at this time that Colonel Armstrong was felled by a debilitating influenza, which had been afflicting soldiers of his battalion. He had in camp at Coal Run, near Fort Dewart, at this time only 100 men, and a number, perhaps as many as twenty-five, were too sick to do much of anything. Besides, as Armstrong urged Burd to report, his whole battalion was "out of provisions."

St. Clair made a same-day response to Bouquet, in which he

described these distressing conditions, and in letters on each of the next two days he reported that he had to leave Armstrong's Battalion at the Swamp in order to protect the magazine. When he arrived at Kickenapauling's Old Town on the 25th, he reported to Bouquet that Colonel Armstrong was still sick at Fort Dewart. Bouquet's letter sent out that day to Armstrong first gave orders for the disposition of road-cutting parties, and, second, gave Armstrong permission to return to Raystown to recover.

Colonel Burd was having his troubles too. He desperately needed horses. Happily, he found Armstrong, who had only nine he could spare, willing to surrender them. Then, unhappily, he found Armstrong reneging on the deal. In his letter to Bouquet, Burd did not refer to Armstrong's illness. And, indeed, the Colonel, though not fully recovered, was back in harness by the 27th or 28th, just in time to straighten out some confusion. Bouquet had informed St. Clair that he never intended that Armstrong's entire battalion be assigned to the redoubts ("25 men in Each are Sufficient for this time"). Instead, he ordered St. Clair to have the battalion "push that Road [to Loyal-hanna] with all possible dispatch." St. Clair is to build no more fortifications, but to muster all his strength for the opening of the road.

To make certain the work would proceed promptly, Bouquet now himself got in touch with Armstrong. Colonel Armstrong replied on the 28th from the fortifications at Dewart to report that, in accord with Bouquet's orders, he has dispatched Lt. Colonel Hanse Hamilton, who had briefly assumed command of the battalion, and Major David Jameson, whose redoubt was three miles west of Edmund's Swamp, on Oven Run, to march "immediately" to join St. Clair for the cutting of the road, "with every effective man they have." He indicated that he means to take the residue of the detachment up to Edmund's Swamp, "to Crawl up as well as I can to the Swamp," which he fears may be "another House of Bondage." He lamented that so many of the posts are upon low ground, "where the Air is Confin'd."

But feeling a little better, and perhaps sensible of the example of General Forbes, Armstrong decided not to take leave of the expedition: "I'm extreamly Oblidg'd to you for your friendly Concern for the recovery of my Health, & the liberty you propose to me of going back to Reas Town but rather chuse to wait a few Events . . . to see what may become of the detachment to the Ohio & whether the Batt may be got together again, as many inconveniences arises from a divided State. I have been in a low & distress'd condition with a flux Since I left Reas' Town, am yet very weak the disorder not remov'd, but in some Measure Abated." He closed out his letter with an apology for the failure of Captain Lieutenant Samuel Allen to supply an account of the sick, the absent, and those fit for duty. As always, he registered a great impatience with such incompetence.[81]

On the last day of the month Bouquet, in his regular report to Forbes on the progress and disposition of the troops, expressed a view of the provincial forces much less flattering than that of two weeks ago. Now very much disappointed in the Pennsylvania battalions, he delivered a diatribe on Armstrong in particular, though the precise reason for his anger is not clear: "I am incumbered with Col. Armstrong, and all these P--------- off------ [Provincial officers] without knowledge & Experiences since I would not trust a Serjeant's Guard. I recall [am recalling] that Col here [to Reas Town], under pretence, of your wanting to speak to him. They are all a cruel Incumbrance upon us, and Mr. Denny [Governor Denny], could have spared his Reafusel of Ranks." [82]

He is so exasperated by the illness and the idling of the provincial troops that he can hardly contain himself: "I draughted the first Batt of Pensilvanians as Soon as you gave me the order, and from that time they have been constantly employ'd in Escort, but the greatest number of them are Sick, and I was never able to relieve the Garrisons at Loudoun or Littleton; I see no body to do it unless you recall the 3 or 400 men Idling in the Forts at the East of Susq. And leaving besides all the N. Car. upon the Road."

This disgust and impatience Bouquet fortified with the particular example of John Armstrong's brother, Major George Armstrong, who on August 3 (date sometimes given as June 4), had been promoted from Captain to Major in the Third Battalion. Armstrong had been pleading for a chance to scout Fort Duquesne. Bouquet narrated for Forbes the story of Armstrong's "surveillance" of August 28: "After so many repeated Importunitys of Major Armstrong I permitted him to take a Party of 100 men besides Capt. [Evan] Shelby's Volunteers and 10 Rangers of Maryland which was the Strongest Party marched from this Camp: I ordered him to take provisions enough concealed in the Woods to be able to stay 6, or 7 days about the Forts pushing small Partys forwards and above all not to return without Intelligences, as I was tired of So many Partys doing nothing, in the time that the Enemys insulted us on all sides." The story he continued with great pain, making no effort to conceal his disgust or his disappointment:

He went at about 17 miles from the Fort [Duquesne] and detached two Small Partys to go forward with orders to join him [at 6 miles] again. Those Partys lost themselves, did not See the Fort and joined him next day, he being then at 6 miles from the Fort. One officer of the Maryland with a Single man went out again to see the Fort, and endeavour to bring a Party out, desiring the Major to wait there till one o'Clock P. M. for him: another officer was Sent along the Monongahela, and the Major himself with 14 men went to cross it, but at the Same time without waiting for the Poor officer, sent to the fort, he ordered [Captain Robert] *Callender[83] to march Immediately all his Party back, and himself joined them soon after not being able Said he to cross the Monongahela. The Maryland officer went to the fort had a good View of it, but Se[e]ing no body on this Side of the River returned where he had left the Party, and not finding them, and having not a morsel of Provisions he ran 25 miles before he could overtake them So diligent had they been to go back.*

He continued his extremely harsh criticism of Major Armstrong in a letter later dispatched from his camp at Raystown to Colonel Burd. Bouquet is remembering how not long ago he had had only high praise for the provincial troops. Now he is embarrassed: "The behaviour of Major A___ [George Armstrong] is so Extraordinary that he has cast a Cloud over all the Provincial Troops. If the picked officers and men act in that Scandalous manner, what can I expect of the Rest. This makes me very uneasy as I have answered to the General that they would give him satisfaction." [84]

Later, in his report to Forbes, he singled out Captain Evan

Shelby of the Maryland troops for the little praise he could allow the mission, noting that the officer refused to return without doing *something* and that he had marched on with his men to cross the river twenty miles upstream. He closed out his sorry story with incredulity and in heavy sarcasm: "The others are come back after that noble [exploit] and the Major void of all Shame came to my Tent with a free and disengaged air to tell me that he had had no Success: I examined him Step by Step, and having convinced him by his own account that he had behaved infamously, I handled him as he deserves. Such are the Gentl [men] that you have to command your troops." [85]

Bouquet had informed Forbes on August 31 that because he himself needed to talk to Colonel John Armstrong he would be notifying Armstrong that the General wanted to speak with him. Accordingly, on September 1 he ordered the Colonel to meet with them at Raystown, "as soon as you are able to make the trip." Armstrong at some time before he received these orders had written to Bouquet from the fortifications erected some eighty rods west of Stoney Creek, between present-day Kantner and Stoystown in Somerset County. Armstrong loved to write letters. He was a compulsive letter writer, in a day when the goose quill pen was the instrument of writing and only the sun or a candle provided light, when the page was simply folded over and sealed with wax from the candle. He wrote in a beautifully flourishing hand, albeit in a somewhat awkward style sometimes, and sometimes in detail ad nauseam. He desired to give full reports of his activities, and many of his letters are extremely long. He was never bashful about requesting ammunition or provisions, nor was he slow to express his political opinion. Besides he had counsel to provide. His letters were posted with a courier of course, often by "express." [86]

Because he is almost completely recovered from his illness, he means to catch up on his letter writing. After expressing some concern about General Forbes's determination to continue to man the smaller redoubts, he brings Colonel Bouquet up to date on the First Pennsylvania Battalion. In a *very* long letter he reports the illness of the troops, the terrible want of provisions, and the great need for more axes and road-building tools. Having been responsible for the escort through much of the march, he admits to an uneasiness about ambush. On the matter of garrisoning the redoubts he had more to say: "Sir John [St. Clair] Wrote Coll: [Hanse] Hamilton a Coppy whereof was Sent me, that he had your Orders, to leave Sixty of my Batt'n at every Post betwixt the Hills. I did not reply, but has not done it, because your late Orders to me were explicitly against it."

His missile closes with an apology for its length: "I am thro' Divine fervour [favor] getting rid of my disorder, and beginning to gather Som[e] Strength, the Men I hear are in good Spirits except a few Sick. Please to forgive the unreasonable length of this Letter as I find I have forgot my Self...." [87]

Now, on September 3, in possession of Bouquet's orders to meet with him and General Forbes at Raystown, Armstrong responded from Belle Air, the redoubt erected by Major David Jameson some three miles from Edmund's Swamp, on the north side of Oven Run. It is five o'clock in the afternoon: "Sir, this Moment I've received yours of the 1st Ins^t and shall in Obedience to the Generals desire & your Orders Set Out for Your Camp as Soon as I can attempt the Ride which (God willing) may be on Wednesday or at farthest on Thursday when One or two Doses of Physick are wrought off."

He has heard of Major Armstrong's Fort Duquesne fiasco and of Bouquet's displeasure: "I'm much Concern'd that my Brother has deviated from his Orders, and think he return'd too Soon, but of this more at Meeting."

He admits to some confusion, noting that a detachment from his battalion has returned as far as the Clear-Fields,[88] to erect a redoubt and desires orders for the disposition of his men.[89]

The report filed by Forbes with William Pitt on September 6 is neither cheerful nor optimistic. But it is a progress report, of course, and the General does have progress to report. He advised the Minister that his advanced troops, "consisting of 1500 Men, are now in possession of a strong post [Loyal-hanna] 9 Miles on the other side of Laurell Hill and about 40 from Fort Du Quesne, nor had the Enemy ever suspected my attempting such a road till very lately, they having been all along securing the strong passes, and fords of the rivers, upon General Braddock's route."

Not surprisingly, he reminded Pitt of the "small trust" he

can repose in the Pennsylvanians "in assisting me with any one necessary." And a very great distress, accordingly, is provisions. Moreover he is much disappointed in the conduct of the officers and the troops generally that have been supplied by Virginia and Pennsylvania. "With but few exceptions," he writes, "all are an extream bad Collection of broken Innkeepers, Horse Jockeys, & Indian traders." And, besides, he is obliged to report the almost total defection of the southern Indians, as only eighty remain.

Still he is confident of success, and he is already wondering what to do with the fort when he captures it. He closes, as always, with a reference to his "precarious health." [90]

It was at this time that the most momentous episode of the entire campaign occurred.

Although the mission of General Forbes would end in great success with the capture of Fort Duquesne, the first real engagement, as well as the biggest battle of the whole campaign, proved to be a most embarrassing defeat. Indeed, it may be called a debacle, or a fiasco, although neither term sufficiently accounts for the terror and the blood and tragedy of the fighting. This is the battle of Grant's Hill. A monumental blunder. And a slaughter second to very few. The battle was fought on the 14th day of September.

By mid-September Bouquet had pushed some ten miles beyond Loyal-hanna to erect the fortification which came to be known as Breastwork Hill, on Nine Mile Run. It was at this time, as the army neared the forks of the Ohio, that somehow, in a rare indiscretion, a detachment of thirty-seven officers and 805 enlisted men, under the command of Major James Grant, a British Regular,[91] was dispatched "on a reconnaissance mission" to Fort Duquesne. Just exactly what Grant was being permitted to do has never been clarified, but apparently he was chiefly to observe, to burn Indian camps and scout out Fort Duquesne. Certainly he had not been authorized, by Archibald Montgomerie or by Colonel Bouquet, to launch a full assault on the fort itself. In any case, Grant marched from the fort at Loyal-hanna on September 9 with a select detachment of Royal Americans, Highlanders, Virginians, and 100 Pennsylvanians, and by nightfall on the 13th had his forces occupying the hill just east a little of Fort Duquesne, in what is now downtown Pittsburgh, in fact exactly at the site of the present Allegheny County Courthouse.[92]

At daybreak, in full view of the fort, the soldiers announced their presence to "hundreds of painted warriors." These were not the Delaware, nor the Shawnee, but warriors from the Ohio tribes known as the Ottawa, the Potawatamie, the Ojibway,and the Wyandot. They had been sleeping soundly.

But the Indians, always quick to awake and appraise the situation, promptly surrounded the entire body of men, and proceeded, from concealment behind trees, to wreak havoc. Only a very few of the soldiers escaped the slaughter. Six hundred, perhaps seven, were killed on the spot; and some few were taken prisoner, among them Major Grant.[93]

One vivid impression of the battle is that discovered in the narrative of James Smith,[94] who at the time was a prisoner in Detroit: "Some time in May [1758] we heard that General Forbes, with seven thousand men was preparing to carry on a campaign against Fort Duquesne . . . . Upon receiving this news a number of runners were sent off by the French commander at Detroit, to urge the different tribes of Indian warriors to repair to Fort Duquesne."

He tells then how at mid-summer warriors from the Ojibway, Potawatamie, Ottawa, and tribes assembled at Detroit, had promptly marched off to Duquesne, in order to assist the French in the defense of the fort. The Indians were made to understand that they would serve Forbes as Braddock had been served, and much plunder was promised.

From this time [July] *until fall, we* [in Detroit] *had frequent accounts of Forbes's army, by Indian runners that were sent out to watch their motion. They spied them frequently from the mountains ever after they left Fort Loudon. Notwithstanding their vigilance, Colonel* [Major] *Grant with his Highlanders stole a march upon them, and in the night took possession of a hill about eighty rod from Fort DuQuesne:—this hill is on that account called Grant's Hill to this day. The French and Indian knew not that Grant and his men were there until they beat the drum and played upon the bag-pipes, just at day-light. They then flew to arms, and the Indians ran up under covert from the banks of Allegheny and*

Monongahela, for some distance, and then sallied out from the banks of the rivers, and took possession of [a] *hill above Grant; and as he was on the point of it in sight of the fort, they immediately surrounded him, and as he had his Highlanders in ranks, and very close order, and the Indians scattered, and concealed behind trees, they defeated him with the loss only of a few warriors:—most of the Highlanders were killed or taken prisoner.*[95]

Immediately after the battle, Major Grant (with the permission of his French captors) penned a long and highly detailed report of his defeat to his General. He is providing the best account "I can give you of our unlucky affair." He places a great deal of the blame on Major Andrew Lewis, whose readings of the situation in no way accorded with Grant's own. Once surrounded, he insists, I "did all in my power to keep things in order, but to no purpose." He complains that the Pennsylvanians, "who were posted on the right at the greatest distance from the enemy, went off without orders, without firing a shot." After that all was panic and confusion, "every soldier taking the road he liked best." Finally, "Surrounded on all sides by the Indians, and when I expected every instant to be cut to pieces . . . a body of the French with a number of their officers came up and offered me quarters, which I accepted of." This was at eleven o'clock in the morning, within a league of the fort. "What our loss is, you best know, but it must be considerable."

He concludes, "I endeavoured to execute the orders which I had received to the best of my power; as I have been unfortunate, the world may possibly find fault in my conduct. I flatter myself that you will not." And, then, incredibly (hopeful of prompt prisoner exchange), to General Forbes he writes, "I am willing to flatter myself that my being a prisoner will be no detriment to my promotion in case vacancies should happen in the army . . . ."[96]

The Indian Tecaughretanego, who had adopted James Smith, had his own notion of the battle. As Smith reported, he said that he could not easily account for the extraordinary and contradictory behavior of Major Grant, and that "the art of war consists in ambushing and surprising our enemies, and in preventing them from ambushing and surprising us, Grant, in the first place, acted like a wise and experienced officer, in artfully approaching in the night without being discovered." However, as Tecaughretanego noted, "when he came to the place where the Indians were lying asleep outside of the fort, between him and the Allegheny river, in place of slipping up quietly and falling upon them with their broad swords, they beat the drums and played upon the bag-pipes." He said that he "could account for this inconsistent conduct no other way than by supposing that he had made too free with spiritous liquors during the night, and became intoxicated about daylight." [97]

Some accounts have Grant, when confronted by the Indians, ordering his Highlanders to throw off their coats and to march forward with fixed bayonets and swords. This had the effect of causing the warriors to vanish into the forest, but only to reappear in awesome numbers on all sides. The Indians, as is their wont after a victory, retired in great glee to the neighborhood of the fort. Here they held a council to determine what was likely next. Many, according to the narrative of James Smith, felt that now Forbes would turn back, just as Braddock's officers had done; but some were very confident he would come on. Of course the French were urging the Indians to remain. In the end, perhaps half of the warriors stayed on. The others lingered only for the customary torture of the prisoners and the celebration before returning to their villages to contend with the winter.

It was about a week after Grant's defeat that Bouquet's report reached Forbes, who was just now arriving at Raystown. The Colonel is writing from Loyal-hanna, and is apparently ignorant of the fact that Grant is among the captured. He notes a "considerable" loss in officers and at least 270 men missing.

Forbes, is, not surprisingly, extremely critical of Grant and "his inconsiderate and rash proceeding." From Raystown, on the 23rd, he reported that "the two wounded Highland officers just now arriv'd, have given so lame an account of how matters proceeded, or any kind of description of the ground, that we can draw nothing from them." One thing was certain: "My friend Grant had most certainly lost the *tra mon tane*, and by his thirst of fame, brought on his own perdition, and run a great risque of ours, which was far wide of the promises he made me at Carlisle, when soliciting to command a party, which I would not agree to." [98]

Colonel Washington had learned details of the disaster

from wounded survivors. In a letter to his brother John Augustine, composed at Raystown at about the same time that Forbes was writing Bouquet, he lamented the misfortune.

Almost one month after Grant's defeat, Forbes, now much more fully informed on the affair, got off a letter to General Abercromby from Raystown. He thinks now that Grant had the impression that the French were very weak at Fort DuQuesne, and it was because of this confidence that the Major "run headlong to grasp at a name, and publick applause, forgetting the inevitable mischief he was bringing upon me, and the rest of us. However, it is now over and I am glad to tell you, that Grant is a prisoner and untouched, and is sent to Montreal with Major [Andrew] Lewis[99] of the Virginians and some other officers . . . ."[100]

Popularly remembered as "Grant's Blunder," the action was conceived in ignorance and carried out in unbridled arrogance. So calamitous was the engagement that it could not fail to remind of Braddock. Indeed, in its cost it could have been enough to encourage the Indians to prolonged support of the French; and it could even have been enough, when taken together with the illness of the expedition's commander, the steady rains and the approach of winter, to discourage General Forbes. But it did not play out that way.

In the meanwhile Armstrong had orders from Bouquet, who is ahead at Loyal-hanna, to repair bridges and roads, so that they may be negotiated by the wagons, and to secure supplies from Raystown. His response, written at Stoney Creek, September 15, is in the form of a report to Bouquet on these assignments.

He launched into great detail on the sad state of provisions, grumbled a little about the lack of orders, and then, sensing that he is in the doghouse, expressed great apprehension over the scheduled meeting with the General, even fearing the loss of his command. Although he appears to have no idea that it is chiefly Bouquet who is unhappy with him, he feels much put upon: "I'm extreamly uneasy, having of late reason to believe that by some means or Other, unknown to me, the General, with many Others & indeed even the Inhabitants of the Province, have conceiv'd of me, and the Battalion I Once [!] had the honor to Command, in a very unfavourable light."

He is not even all that happy about being asked to provide his name for this latest redoubt: "I thank you for your Compliment in regard to the name of this Fort, but beg to be escus'd, not chusing to have anything to do with these appelations. The Redout will be finish'd this night, and much more done about it. The men in my Opinion have done their duty. I hope it will please you, which as well as the good of the Servise, has been the Studdy of your Most Ob^t Servt John Armstrong." [101]

Forbes had paused for ten days at Fort Loudoun, September 6-15, resting at the Summer House on the River Side. It must be remembered that from the time the illness struck him in Philadelphia, it continued very strange and very serious. To General Loudoun on February 3 he had written from New York: "My Infirmitys are really no joke, nor are they to be played the fool with, Both legs and thighs being ane absolute sight, and the soals of my feet Blistered, so it was impossible for me to gett abroad——." And two days later, again to Loudoun, he complained: "My damn'd legs have fallen down to my toes and soles of my feet, so hope by tomorrow it will fly off—but at present can not walk." [102] Almost every letter that he wrote during this long summer concluded with some lament about his illness, which can only be described as a most severe and unrelenting attack of the bloody flux, today called dysentery. For most of the campaign, both on the way to the Ohio and on the return to Philadelphia, the General had to be transported on a litter carried between two horses. One historian has declared, "There are few more heroic cases of success in the face of adversity than that of General Forbes in his expedition of 1758." [103]

He reached Raystown at the middle of September, and would direct the army from this post for the next six weeks, not arriving at Loyal-hanna until the first week of November, by which time the fort had been constructed. Just exactly what transpired in his meeting with Armstrong is not known, as the letters which were after that exchanged among the officers Bouquet, Forbes and Armstrong make no mention of it. It would seem, if one judges by the tone of Armstrong's later communications, that somehow the Colonel worked his way out of the doghouse and back into the favor of his superiors.

While encamped on a hill half a mile southwest of present-day Hannastown, which is some three miles north of Greensburg, Forbes continued his complaint about the provincials: ". . . I have seen with regret for this some time past a Jealousy and suspicion subsisting on the part of the Virginians which they can have no reason for, as I believe neither you nor I values one farthing where we get provisions from, provided we are supplyed, or Interest ourselves either with Virginia or Pennsylvania, which last I hope will be damn'd for their treatment of us with the Waggons, and every other thing where they could profit by us from their impositions, Altho' at the risque of our perdition." [104]

On September 18 or 19, Armstrong received from Bouquet, who is at Loyal-hanna still, the news of Grant's defeat. At about this same time Bouquet heard from Forbes about Armstrong's proposal to take a detachment up the Allegheny to assault the French at their Fort Machault. Forbes, who is without good information on the strength of the fort, and now painfully conscious of the defeat of Grant, is interested but wary: "Col. Armstrong wrote me desiring he might have a party of 300 men of his own Regiment [precisely the number he took to Kittanning] to go against Venango [the French Fort Machault, located on French Creek, just at the point where it flows into the Allegheny]. I assure you I have had that long in view, but do not know at this time how proper it would be, as a repulse to any of our partys may be of bad consequence. I beg therefore you will examine into the practicability of such an attempt, as likewise into the difficulties that may attend it the succeeding in such a thing would be as lucky to us as the landing at Louisbourg was to them." [105]

Armstrong, still encamped at Stoney Creek, and *still* contending with a lot of sickness in the troops, at this same time responded to Bouquet's particular orders: "Sir, On looking Over Coll: [Hanse] Hamilton's Instructions [Bouquet to Hamilton, ca. Sept. 13] & finding there are Strong partys of the Enemy Out & your Orders to Evacuate the Forts Dudgeon & Dewart in Order to Strengthen the Escorts, it is done in this manner." He proceeds to detail, then, the assignments he has made to Captain James Patterson, Colonel Hamilton, his brother Captain William Armstrong, and to Captain John Wetterholt, with respect to provisions and wagons, and the sick. He reports that he has been unable to provide the necessary bridges but is building a cover for the stores. He is still intent on the mission to Machault: "I hope to be favour'd with an Answer to my request in my last . . . ." [106]

The letter that Forbes wrote to Bouquet September 23 on the Grant episode includes quite a passage on the decision made on the route to take. Forbes is here a little impatient with Colonels Adam Stephen and Washington and Byrd of the Virginia persuasion, who are *still* complaining about the road taken. The General, while acknowledging the need for repairs, hopes that he will never hear anything again on the topic! This long letter closes on a note of great impatience. He wants to get going: "When you have settled things to your mind, I beg you will write me, and as soon as you conveniently can, come down here [Raystown] for a day, and if Col. Armstrong could be spared, should be glad he came along, in order to settle our further proceedings, and to seize the first favourable opportunity of marching directly forwards."

And he closes, not with a direct reference to his wretched condition, but with "Pray make up a Hovell or hutt for me at L. Hannon or any other of the posts with a fire place if possible." [107]

As it turned out, Armstrong was extremely busy at this time and could not be spared immediately. He had received from Captain Harry Gordon the sledges and crowbars that he was in want of and was improving the road to Loyal-hanna. In a letter to Bouquet from Stoney Creek, he reflected on the pain that both Bouquet and Forbes must be feeling because of the Grant disaster, and expressed the hope that that misfortune will not adversely affect the progress of the expedition. He hopes the General is "getting over the shock," and advises Bouquet that Forbes has asked him to build for him a small hut at "this place" (Stoney Creek). He reports that the damage done by the heavy rains has been mended, and offers the opinion that "only this Post shou'd be kept up betwixt the Mountains." He is astonished that his men have not as yet been molested, but remains firm in the opinion that the garrisons and the escorts should be but little divided. He reports that the other two posts [Belle Air (Jameson's redoubt) and Kickenapaulings] "are now abandon'd, and were the Men even return'd I would not replace those Posts without further Orders." Though still just a little concerned about his standing with Bouquet and with Forbes, he writes in this letter as if he were definitely emerged from ill favor.[108]

But he has problems. The aforementioned Thomas Barton, an Anglican priest, had petitioned Forbes (through Sir John St. Clair) for the office of Chaplain to the Third Battalion of the Pennsylvania forces. When thirty-three Presbyterian officers complained, Forbes appointed the Presbyterian Andrew Bay, and accepted Barton as a "volunteer." Naturally, Barton[109] was offended and blamed his disappointment, properly it would seem, on Armstrong. Early in July, Armstrong had written to Secretary Peters, who of course was himself a minister: "I doubt not parson Barton will write you some very high Charge against me like Sacrilege, &c. I have neither time nor inclination to trouble you with a detail of his Conduct, only that it is Still very extraordinary; for the Publicks and your Sake, I have not Open'd his conduct nor Character to the General—he is at present quiet & I don't trouble my head with him . . . ."[110]

To Secretary Peters, Barton protested that he and his church had been insulted. He wrote that "The old [Side] Presbyterian Ministers & Congregations . . . have highly resented the treatment I have met and have drawn up a handsome paper in my favor." He continued with a plain reference to the culprit, Armstrong, declaring he was sorry that the assignment awarded him by Forbes would "subject me to the power of a Man who has already shewn himself an enemy to that Cause which I am bound by every Tye of Conscience, Duty & Inclination to support."[111]

Although, by all accounts, Reverend Barton acquitted himself very well in his ministry to the soldiers of the expedition, Armstrong had little time for him and no regard. Early in October, the Colonel, now back at Raystown to meet with the General, who is just arrived, shot off a letter to Secretary Richard Peters, who until a letter of September 25, has been strangely silent lately. Now much concerned about the seeming distance that has appeared between him and Secretary Peters, and always sensitive to slights, real or fancied, Armstrong wonders why he has not been hearing from him. He infers that the difference between him and Barton is responsible:

It never enter'd my head to Suspect your friendship, nor reproach you for your Silence, but should have imagin'd, had it not been a time of War, that Matrimony, or something of that Sort, had possess'd your thoughts. If any person has inform'd you that I have had any religious dispute, more or less, they have injur'd themselves & imposed upon you, for upon the strictest truth, tho' there has been a great deal of reason for Such Altercation yet have I had none, nor any body else that I know of; as for Mr. B....n, I have not had the least Communication with him since I saw you, nor ever intend to have. I have never been mistaken of that Gentleman, but shall Leave his Character to Persons of his own Community.[112]

But enough of that. Colonel Armstrong now provides for Peters a long summary of the campaign up to this point. Very obvious in his account is the unwavering respect he has for both General Forbes and Colonel Bouquet. The letter concludes: "About the last of this month will be the Critical hour. Every thing is Vastly dear with us, & the money goes like Old Boots; the Enemy are beginning to Kill & Carry off Horses, and every now and then Scalps a wandering person. I leave this place [Raystown] to-day [Oct. 3], as does Coll. Bouquet, and Some pieces of the Artillary.[113]

Armstrong's fears were realized when about one month after the massacre of Grant's troops, the Commander of Fort DuQuesne, Captain De Lignery, launched a fierce assault, with the Indians who had remained after the Grant defeat, on the newly built stockade at Loyal-hanna.[114] The site of the fort, as selected by Sir John St. Clair, was the north side of the Loyal-hanna Creek. It was a most strategic spot, and only fifty miles from Fort Duquesne. Construction had been begun by Colonel James Burd on September 3. When his assistant, Engineer Charles Rohr, was killed in the battle on Grant's Hill, the work was continued by Engineer Harry Gordon, a Captain in the Royal Americans, who had engineered the building of the fort at Raystown.

As it turned out, the fort proved to be a stout one, probably the strongest in structure of all forts along the line of communication. But it had not been erected long before it was sorely tested.

The date was October 12. Bouquet was at Stoney Creek with some 700 foot soldiers and a detachment of artillery. Armstrong would not arrive here at Loyal-hanna for two weeks yet. In command of the fort was Colonel James Burd, chief officer of the Second Battalion of Pennsylvania Provincial troops.

The attack commenced at eleven o'clock in the morning with some skirmishing involving the fort's sentries a little to the southwest of the fortifications. The Indians and French-Canadians, under the command of Monsieur Vetri, then crossed over the Loyal-hanna Creek in order to assault the stockade from the east, and the main battle took place in that quarter. The fighting continued, without great effect, for some two hours, until early afternoon. It was renewed with an increased vigor at three o'clock. But Burd's gallant frontiersmen defended the fort with great courage, presenting a very well disciplined and accurate musket fire. Although the French force, as reported in the account provided by a captured French grenadier, was composed of 1200 French and 200 Indians,[115] the provincial forces rudely repulsed the attack and sent the enemy packing. Burd lost twelve men killed, eighteen wounded, and thirty-one missing.

According to James Smith's narrative, the Indians, and the French too, were much impressed by the provincial force. They observed that the American riflemen were beginning to learn the Indian style of wilderness warfare, as they were scattered and firing from behind trees. Besides, they proved to be excellent marksmen. Turned away, and embarrassed, the force returned to Fort DuQuesne, where most of the Indians who had stayed on after Grant's Hill now decided that they had had enough, and went home. According to Smith, the Indians were declaring that if they had only the red-coats to deal with they could manage very well, but they could not fight effectively against *Ashalecoa*, or the Great Knife, which was the name they had given the Virginians.[116] Only six weeks later did Forbes learn that this attack on Fort Loyal-hanna was but a ploy, a ruse designed to make him think that the French were strong.[117] On October 16, from Raysown, he provided a full report of the affair to General Abercromby.[118]

As the unrelenting rains had delayed the opening of the road, Bouquet did not reach Loyal-hanna until October 18, a week after the successful defense of the fort. Armstrong, who was providing a 400-man escort for the artillery was not far behind him, having left Stoney Creek on October 20, and Bouquet, because Indians had been detected in the area, sent 350 men under Major Hugh Waddell of the North Carolina militia to reinforce Armstrong. On October 28, shortly after Armstrong's arrival at Loyal-hanna, Bouquet in some alarm reported to Forbes that "A rather large party of Indians has this moment been discovered." Because the army was now on the doorstep of Fort Duquesne, it was becoming (1) increasingly wary, and (2) obliged to draw up a plan of assault.

Concern for the Indian presence had never been far from Forbes's feeling for the total campaign. He had monitored the situation with the Delaware as best he could. Fortunately, over the past two years a number of treaty sessions with the Delaware and the Shawnee had been convened, including the council at Easton in November of 1756,[119] the sessions at Lancaster April 1-May 22, 1757, another at Easton July 21, 1757, a conference held in Philadelphia by Governor Denny with Teedyuskung and his deputies on March 15, 1758, and another convened by Bouquet at Fort Loudoun on June 14, 1758. But the session which came to be known as the Grand Council was the big one. It was convened at Easton on October 6, 1758, as the Forbes expedition drew close to the Ohio. It was presided over by Governor Denny and arbitrated by Conrad Weiser, who was a Mohawk by adoption and very close to the Delaware and Shawnee, and it continued for three weeks. Forbes did not have the news of the outcome of the conference until the first week of November. But it was happy news. And he had it from Christian Frederick Post, who was possibly more important to Indian affairs than the many councils.[120]

Post's second journey into the Indian country, made at an extremely hazardous time, was just being completed as the Forbes army approached Duquesne. On November 7, with the celebrated Shingas and a party of warriors, Post reached the newly erected fort at Loyal-hanna, where they were "gladly received" by General Forbes and his soldiers. On the next day Forbes assembled all of the Indians, and most graciously and warmly welcomed them to Loyal-hanna. He asked them to join him in drinking the King's health, and the health of Chiefs Shingas, and Beaver, and all the warriors and "friends of the English." After this gathering, which was public and out in the open air, Post and his party were escorted to a hut in which a private council was held with the General. Presumably Forbes said the proper things. As before noted, all evidence is that, unlike some of his officers, the General was genuinely respectful of Indians, and seemed to sense better than most with what pain they were seeing their lands vanish.[121]

Even though Forbes had enjoyed amiable sessions here with Shingas, and though he felt confident that the agreement arrived at in the treaty sessions at Easton would keep the Delaware and Shawnee Indians peaceful for the time of his campaign, yet he felt it a good idea to put a cap on it. To the Shawnee and Delaware people of the Ohio River region, on November 9, from Loyalhanna, he dispatched a letter to cement the peace: "Brethren, I embrace the opportunity by our brother, Pisquetomen [King Beaver, a strong-willed and very influential Delaware chief, brother to Shingas] who is Now on his Return home with some of your Uncles, the Six Nations, from the Treaty of Easton, of giving you Joy of the happy Conclusion of that great Council, which is perfectly agreeable to me, as it is for the mutual advantage of Your Brothers, the Indians, as well as the English nation."

He reminded them of what had been agreed to, and discreetly included a warning:

I am glad to find that all past Disputes and Animosities are now finally settled, & amicably adjusted; & I hope they will be forever buried in Oblivion, and that you will now again be firmly united in the Interest of your brethren, the English. As I am now advancing, at the Head of a large Army, against his Majesty's Enemies, the French, on the Ohio, I must strongly recommend to you to send immediate Notice to any of your People, who may be at the French fort, to return forthwith to your Towns; where you may sit by your Fires, with your Wives and Children, quiet and undisturbed, and smoke your Pipes in safety. Let the French fight their own Battles, as they were the first Cause of the War, and occasion of the long difference, which hath subsisted between you & your Brethren, the English; but I must entreat you to restrain your young Men from Crossing the Ohio, as it will be impossible for me to distinguish them from our Enemies; which I expect you will comply with, without Delay lest, by your neglect thereof, I should be the innocent Cause of some of your Brethren's Death. This Advice take and keep in your own Breasts, and suffer it not to reach the Ears of the French.

And as testimony to his sincerity he included "this String of Wampum."

A second letter, this addressed directly to King Beaver and Shingas and their fellow warriors, is much the same. Forbes refers to the Treaty of Peace recently concluded. He prays that the Friendship thus cemented "May . . . be lasting [and as] unmoveable as the Mountains . . . that there shall be an everlasting Peace with all the Indians, established as sure as the Mountains." [122]

Most impressive to Beaver and to Shingas and to the warriors in the council they had had with Forbes was the *tone* of the General's remarks. Here, they felt, is a man who respects us and really seems to care genuinely for us as a people. In this letter that same tone came through.

While reminding the Indians that he was the General of a very large army, Forbes concluded in the same engaging manner: "I sincerely wish it, for their good; for it will fill me with Concern, to find any of you join'd with the French, as in that Case you must be sensible I must treat them as Enemies; however, I once more repeat, that there is not time to be lost, for I intend to march with the Army very soon; and I hope to enjoy the pleasure of thanking you for your Zeal; & of entertaining you in the Fort [!] ere long. In the mean time I wish Happiness and Prosperity to you, your Women and children. I write to you as a Warrior should, . . . with Candour and Love, and I recommend Secrecy and Dispatch." [123]

Satisfied that the Indians were not going to be a problem, two days after he dispatched his letters, in camp at Loyal-hanna, General Forbes brought his principal officers together. The date was November 11. Colonel Bouquet afterwards filed a report: "The Army being encamped at Loyal-hanna, the General called a Council of War. . . . It was composed of Colonels Bouquet, Montgomerie, Sir John St. Clair, Washington, Byrd, Armstrong, Burd, and Mercer. After explaining the situation as regards to troops and provisions, his instructions and the news about the enemy's forces, he asked us to weigh each point carefully and, after discussing it thoroughly, to give him our opinion as to what would be the best course to pursue." Obviously, Forbes, partly because of the massacre of Grant's force, and partly because the assault on Fort Loyal-hanna disclosed that there were still some Indians among the French forces, but mostly because of the impending winter weather, was inclined to retire into winter quarters and make his attack in the spring. Indeed, his impression was pretty much what the French General Louis Montcalm expected he would come to. When he had the great news of Grant's defeat, and the report of the attack on Loyal-hanna, which while not successful, was at least an aggressive stratagem, he was most pleased. Writing to Marshal De Belle Isle, at just the time of Forbes's council, Montcalm declared, "I think that Fort Duquesne is safe for this autumn and winter, and that the enemy will also think of going into winter quarters, and content themselves with preserving their new establishment." [124]

The arguments that were heard for advancing were three: (1) The need to drive the enemy from the Ohio, not eventually but now; (2) the hope that a successful advance would remove the Indian presence; (3) the expense of the expedition needed to be justified. [!] The arguments for delaying an assault were five: (1) the great want of clothing and provisions; (2) possible reduction of the army to half its strength; (3) risk of losing artillery; (4) the difficulty of maintaining the fort; and (5) the fear of defeat and the concern for the consequences. Bouquet summed up the Council in this way: "The risks being so obviously greater than the advantages, there is no doubt as to the sole course that prudence dictates." [125] This after nine months of preparation, road-building, and marching. Many historians find the decision to abort the mission "astounding." You would expect that officers like Montgomerie, and Mercer, and Burd, and Washington, would be spoiling for a fight. Had Forbes thought much about how a delay might strengthen the French and their Indian allies? Had he considered the effect of the winter on a four months' encampment? Had he envisioned the humiliation his army would suffer in Philadelphia?

Just where Colonel Armstrong stood in these deliberations is not a matter of record. When it is remembered that, without any good information on the status of the French Fort Machault, he was recommending a separate assault, it can reasonably be assumed that he would be unhappy with delay.

The decision to put off an attack on the fort having been made, Forbes began to make plans for a winter encampment. At that moment, two events abruptly changed everything. One was the report of the Cherokee and Catawba scouts (now perhaps only fifty in number) that the Indians who had accomplished the slaughter of Grant's forces and had participated in the assault on Loyal-hanna, were now "completely vanished."

The second good bit of news emerged from a most unhappy episode of war. On the very day after the Council of War was convened, November 12, there took place what would turn out to be the last real military engagement of the Forbes campaign. The incident occurred while the chief elements of Forbes's army were yet in camp at Loyal-hanna, and very close to the post itself. It is an episode of incredibly wild confusion, involving "friendly fire" between two Virginia detachments resulting from a gathering darkness, and making for great danger to Washington.

Lieutenant Colonel George Mercer, long Washington's "best friend," had been ordered by Forbes to repel a French and Indian party that he understood to be approaching the post at Loyal Hanna. When Forbes later learned that Mercer was experiencing great trouble, he urged reinforcement under Washington. By the time Washington arrived, dusk had descended over the engagement.

Historians have two accounts to rely on for the details. One is the report published in Franklin's *Pennsylvania Gazette* for November 30, 1758. And the other is Washington's own version, which was reproduced for *Scribner's Magazine* in May of 1893, portions of which are on exhibit at Fort Ligonier.

The story as readers had it from the *Gazette* is somewhat confused:

Since our last we have had imperfect Accounts of a Skirmish between a Party of our Army, and another of the French, near Loyalhanning, from which the best Account we can at present give, is as follows, viz. "That on the 12th Instant, Colonel Washington being out with a Scouting Party, fell in with a Number of the

Enemy, about three Miles from our Camp, whom he attacked, killed one took three Prisoners, an Indian Man and Woman, and one Johnson, an Englishman (who, it is said, was carried off by the Indians some time ago from Lancaster County) and obliged the rest to fly: That on hearing the Firing at Loyalhanning, Colonel Mercer, with a Party of Virginians, was sent out to the Assistance of Colonel Washington, who, coming in Sight of our People in the Dusk of the Evening, and seeing them about a Fire the Enemy had been Drove from, and the two Indians with them, imagined them to be French; and Colonel Washington being under the same Mistake, unhappily a few Shot were exchanged, by which a Lieutenant, and thirteen or fourteen Virginians, were killed: That Johnson being examined, was told, he had forfeited his Life by being found in Arms against his King and County; and the only Way left to save it, and make Attonement, was, to give as full an Information of the Condition of Fort Duquesne, and of the Enemy, as he could.[126]

    Washington, who had experienced already four very close brushes with the Grim Reaper, and would in his time experience several more, always regarded this affair as his "closest call."

    The story as reproduced in *Scribner's Magazine* is as Washington himself told it in his "notes for a biographer." Just how *very* close Washington, at this time twenty-eight years old, was to early death is here apparent. Indeed it was he, who, in order to restore order, had to ride into the melee to brush aside the muskets leveled at him and to command the soldiers to "cease fire." The article reads in part:

The enemy sent out a large detachment to reconnoitre our camp, and to ascertain our strength; in consequence of intelligence that they were within two miles of the camp a party commanded by Lieut. Col. Mercer, of the Virginia Line (a gallant and good officer) was sent to dislodge them, between whom, a severe conflict and hot firing ensued, which lasting some time and appearing to approach the camp, it was conceived that our party was yielding the ground, upon which G. W. [Washington throughout refers to himself as G.W, rather than as "I" or "me."] *with permission of the Genl. called . . . for volunteers and immediately marched at their head, to sustain, as was conjectured, the retiring troops. Led on by the firing till he came within less than half a mile and it ceasing, he detached scouts to investigate the cause, and to communicate his approach to his friend Colo. Mercer, advancing slowly in the meantime. But it being near dusk, and the intelligence not having been fully disseminated among Col. Mercer's corps, and they taking us for the enemy who had retreated approaching in another direction, commenced a heavy fire upon the relieving party which drew fire in return in spite of all the exertions of the officers, one of whom, and several privates were killed and many wounded before a stop could be put to it, to accomplish which G. W. never was in more imminent danger, by being between two fires, knocking up with his sword the presented pieces.*[127]

Forbes, in reporting the distressing affair to Abercromby on the 17th, noted this as one of frequent recent "skirmishes and allarms." On this occasion, he explained, "Two hundred of the enemy came to attack our live Cattle and horses on the 12th —I sent 500 men to give them chace with as many more to Surround them, there were some killed on both sides, but unfortunately our partys fired upon each other in the dark by which we lost two officers and 38 private[s] kill'd or missing." [128]

But good news came out of all this. It was the information wrested from the Englishman Johnson, who was taken in the melee, to the effect that Fort Duquesne was but weakly defended. He had four disclosures to report: First, he revealed that those Canadians who had participated in Monsieur Vetri's assault on Fort Loyalhanna had "all gone home." Second, he reported that the Ohio Indians had all returned to their villages for the winter (which corresponded to the report of Forbes's Cherokee scouts). Third, he provided the happy news that the French garrison was very short of provisions, and much undermanned. That indeed the French were in want of provisions was borne out by the news that on their return march from Loyal-hanna they were obliged to kill and eat several of the stolen horses. And, fourth, he revealed that "the Attempt made by Vetri at Loyalhanning, was only to make [you] apprehend their Strength at Fort Duquesne to be very great." He summed this all up with the assurance that the British army would "certainly succeed."

When all of this was confirmed by the captured Indian, Forbes promptly made the decision to advance.[129]

Of course he was still much concerned about the weather, but he was confident now that a long siege would not be required. He was sure that an effective assault could be mounted before the weather turned bad. Accordingly, he decided not only to act, but to act promptly, to push forward with all possible expedition and launch an attack with "a selected body of men."

According to Washington biographer Douglas Southall Freeman, Forbes, concerned for mobility, had planned for the assault on the fort to divide his command into three attacking forces. One of these would be under the command of Colonel Bouquet; a second would be the 77th Highlanders under Montgomerie; and the third, "the only one entrusted to a provincial officer," would be that of George Washington. Besides his own Virginia troops, Washington would have two companies of artificers, the soldiers of the Maryland, North Carolina, and Lower Counties (Delaware) forces. Of course before any attack could be launched there was some road-cutting to do.[130] Axes before muskets.

From the encampment at Loyal-hanna, on Nov. 16th, four days after the Washington-Mercer confusion, Bouquet, who would be marching forward on the morrow, relayed to Washington the road-cutting instructions of Forbes for the last little distance: "Dear Sir, I am directed by the General to inform you that he had receiv'd your Letter, and Sends you 42 falling axes which could not be collected Sooner."

Armstrong had been ordered forward from Loyal-hanna on November 13 to join Colonel Washington in opening the road. But he is apparently somewhat confused, and Forbes, much concerned about the distances between encampments, means to speed up the work. He advised Washington that "Col. Armstrong is not upon the good Road," and he urged Washington to join him and march together and "mark out an Incampment at about 20, or 22 miles from here . . . . You will then take the necessary tools and march with a Sufficient force to the heads of Turtle Creek where you [may] Camp."[131]

Under his command Armstrong had 1000 handpicked

frontiersmen and a portion of the artillery train. At some time the Armstrong force actually moved ahead of Washington, for Washington from the Camp at Chestnut Ridge on the 17th advised Forbes that "A junction with Colo. Armstrong this morning would have prevented the good effects of a fortified Camp to night and retarded our operations a day at least: for which reason I desired him to march forwards this morning, at 2 o'clock to such place as Captn. Shelby should point out . . . and there secure himself, as you have directed. If he accomplishes that work before night he is, in that event, to begin opening the Road towards me. I shall struggle hard to be up with him to night, being but 2 and one-half miles from his last camp." [132]

By the 18th Armstrong considered he was within seventeen miles of the Fort, and on that day, Washington, as ordered by Bouquet, set out for Armstrong's encampment promptly at daybreak. He was able to reach Armstrong by eleven o'clock that morning. On the next morning, now in advance of Armstrong, he set out with some 1000 men for the headwaters of Turtle Creek, leaving Armstrong with 500 men. He was not sure of the distance yet to Fort Duquesne, and reported that the woodsmen he has conversed with feel it "still thirty miles." But, certain that he was closer, he here intensified vigilance, and apparently waited for the other elements of the attacking party to come up.[133]

Forbes, who had hoped to set out the day after Armstrong, was simply unable to get going. Terribly ill and fatigued, and suffering from exposure as well, but as determined as ever, he finally departed Loyal-hanna four days after Armstrong, on the 17th. According to the *Gazette*, "The General marched from Loyalhanning 4300 effective Men, all well, and in good Spirits, besides Indians, and left a strong Garrison there, and at Rays-Town, &c." The *Gazette* further reported that the sickness and desertion their readers had been hearing so much about was "not near so great as has been represented," and that "there is the greatest Harmony among the Troops, who, we hear, love their Officers, and obey them cheerfully." [134] In spite of heavy rains, Forbes was able to march the twenty miles from Loyal-hanna to Armstrong's camp at a good pace.

Washington and Armstrong had opened the road to within a

day's march of the fort. At that point, near Turtle Creek, some twelve miles from the fort, Colonel Bouquet established his camp. The entire advance army, the complete attacking force, now assembled and able to move rapidly, pressed forward. When close to the Fort, at Bouquet's encampment, on the evening of the 24th, the troops camped for the night. The army of General John Forbes, which had expected to be in this spot by September 11, was here at last, snuggled in the hills just a wee bit west of Turtle Creek. The wagons and all the artillery, except for a few light pieces, were left behind. In fact, there were no tents or baggage. Soldiers carried knapsacks and blankets only. The normal precautions were taken, of course, with scouts out constantly. But some very special precautions were taken as well. Orders were for perfect quiet. Any man firing his musket without an officer's order was to suffer 200 lashes "on the spot." [135]

All firearms were inspected on the evening of the 24th; to the soldiers it was explained how to recognize a friendly Indian; barking dogs were hanged. The General's orders explained that on the morrow the army would proceed, advancing in three columns. "It is to be hoped," the General announced to his officers, "that as our honor, interest, and in fine our all, depends on the happy issue of the service we are just going on, . . . the officers will in a particular manner exert themselves in getting everything in the best order and not be sparing of their pains at this critical juncture, and in case of action it is particularly recommended to each officer to keep their men calm and prevent their throwing away their fire, which they are apt to do when in a hurry." [136]

Although Washington's manuscript account has his brigade out front, according to the *Pennsylvania Gazette* for November 30, it was actually Colonel John Armstrong who led the advance. Clearly, the two provincial colonels were in the van, marching forward 2000-2500 very carefully selected troops of frontiersmen, the very best riflemen among the provincials. [137]

And so it had come to this. No one knew, of course, what tomorrow would bring, how fierce a battle might ensue, or, indeed, whether there would be any battle at all. But every soldier was experiencing the "night before" apprehension. For more than six months they had been marching through the wilderness, felling trees, and crushing stones, building bridges, and erecting earthworks and fortifications. And now they were ten miles from destiny.

And then, suddenly, all suspense dissolved. Here returned the Indians who had been sent ahead to scout out the Fort. The first to come into camp had only smoke to report, as he had not been quite to the fort itself; but the second scout came dashing in wildly gesticulating and in a state of great excitement. He had really great news. He had made it to the fort, and he had found it . . . vanished!

Scouts were dispatched immediately to secure confirmation of this astounding news. Upon their return, with the report that indeed it was so, General Forbes dispatched a detachment under Captain John Haslett, who had orders to extinguish the fire and to save as much as possible of the buildings and supplies.

It was next morning before the troops set out, the strong advance guard at the head. General Forbes, now *very* ill and carried in a litter, was next. Following their General, whose courage was deeply moving to them, came the troops in three parallel columns. On the right marched the Royal Americans, on the left the Provincial forces, and in the center the Highlanders under Montgomerie.[138] It was an all-day march. Indeed, it was six o'clock in the evening of one of the shortest days of the year before they could negotiate the distance. But just enough light remained to afford them a view of an eerie and strangely thrilling scene. On the little spit of land, where the high banks of the Monongahela surrender her waters to her sister, the Allegheny, to form the great Ohio, the weary soldiers stared in disbelief. Historian Douglas Freeman accounts for the scene:

Stark above the charred debris of walls and floors and roofs stood thirty chimneys in the fields and in the forts, as if to mock the half-frozen Englishmen who looked for shelter. One magazine of the fort had been exploded; the other contained sixteen barrels of powder, a great pile of rusted iron, some worthless gun barrels and, significantly, a large store of scalping knives. In the gathering darkness, this was a poor reward for so much of sickness and shivering, of muddy marches and long nights' misery—an ugly, disappointing scene to men who doubtless had pictured a frowning fort, its bastions crowded with stubborn French. No fort, no food, no booty the British found, but almost beneath them, full of movement, full of mystery, was the Ohio, . . . the mighty stream that watered a valley of fabulous riches as it swept to the vast Mississippi.[139]

It was Colonel John Armstrong, the senior officer of the Pennsylvania Provincial troops, who on the morrow was given the honor of raising the British Union Jack over the broken walls of the abandoned fort.[140] He could not have known, of course, but at this moment, perhaps at this very moment, Mrs. Rebeckah Armstrong, far away in Carlisle, was giving birth to their second child!

Here for a little while had flown the flag of France, and here for a much shorter time than General Forbes or Colonel Bouquet could imagine would fly the British flag, and here after that would fly the Stars and Stripes of a nation not yet born. It was a glorious moment in the history of nations.

For his *History of the United States* the eminent historian George Bancroft provided a memorable image of the scene:

As the banners of England floated over the waters, the place, at the suggestion of Forbes, was with one voice called Pittsburg. It is the most enduring monument to William Pitt. America raised to his name statues that have been wrongfully broken, and granite piles of which not one stone remains upon another; but, long as the Monongahela and the Allegheny shall flow to form the Ohio, long as the English tongue shall be the language of freedom in the boundless valley which their waters traverse, his name shall stand inscribed in the gateway of the West.[141]

And the later historian of Pennsylvania, George Donehoo, has declared that "the names of Washington, Braddock, Forbes, Bouquet, Armstrong, Mercer, Burd, Post,---should all be inscribed upon the foundation of the pillars of this "Gateway to the West." [142]

Casting a terrible pall over the triumphal capture of the fort was the news supplied by a twelve-year-old boy who for two years had been a prisoner and had just now escaped. He informed General Forbes that the French had carried a great quantity of wood into the fort in order to burn to death on the parade ground five of the prisoners taken on Grant's Hill. According to the youngster's report, the remaining prisoners were turned over to the Indians, who promptly tomahawked them on the spot.[143] Mute confirmation of the lad's tale could be read outside the charred ruins of the fort, where lay the bodies of the soldiers of Grant, and the bones of the soldiers of Braddock. Severed heads had been placed on stakes by the Indians. Forbes was appalled. No doubt the General felt pretty much as did Shakespeare's King Henry V at Agincourt upon learning of the savage and brutal slaughter of his camp boys by the cowardly French. The poet has the king exclaiming in uncontrollable grief and anger. Certainly Forbes was angry enough to pursue the French up the Allegheny River to Fort Machault, and, indeed, he considered doing just that. Wasn't Colonel Armstrong going to take Fort Machault with 300 men? Only the winter season and the want of provisions, as he explained to Secretary Pitt in his report, held him back. Doubtless his illness and the fatigue of the soldiers after six months on the wilderness road figured in his decision too.

Certainly the tragedy that had befallen the men of Grant and the inhumane execution of the prisoners did much to chill the first sense of triumph. The French fort had been reduced to smouldering ruins, but only at great cost to the Crown and the English provinces. Still the mission had ended with the object gained. And this day, the 26th day of November, General John Forbes proclaimed "A Day of Public Thanksgiving to Almighty God." Colonel Armstrong's close friend the Reverend Charles Beatty, chaplain to Colonel Clapham's Pennsylvania regiment, preached a moving sermon, which one historian has judged "probably the first Protestant sermon preached west of the mountains."[144]

The day after, the troops enjoyed a grand *feu de Joye*, and on Tuesday the 28th Colonel Bouquet sent out a detachment to the site of the Braddock defeat to bury the bones of Grant's men, as well as the bones of Braddock's men! An anonymous correspondent, who could summon up no love for the French, in a dispatch to the *Pennsylvania Gazette* remarked: "To-day a great Detachment goes to Braddock's Field of Battle, to bury the Bones of our slaughtered Countrymen, many of whom were butchered in cold Blood by (those crueller than Savages) the French, who, to the eternal Shame and Infamy of their Country, have left them lying above Ground ever since. The unburied Bodies of those killed since, and strewed round this Fort, equally reproach them, and proclaim loudly, to all civilized Nations, their Barbarity." [145]

Colonel Bouquet was quick to praise his General for the success of the mission. He credited the General, first, with discouraging the Delaware Indians from assisting the French. In a personal letter, composed some two weeks after the event, the Colonel wrote that the General had "procured a peace with those inveterate enemies more necessary and beneficial to the colonies than driving out the French." [146] And to Chief Justice William Allen, in a long report of the expedition, he declared the highest praise for John Forbes:

After God, the success of this expedition is intirely due to the General, who by bringing about the treaty with the Indians at Easton, has struck the blow, which has knocked the French in the head; in temporizing wisely to expect the effects of the treaty; in securing all his posts, and giving nothing to chance; and not yielding to the urging instances for taking Braddock's Road, which would have been our destruction; In all these measures I say that he has shown the greatest prudence, firmness and ability; Nobody is better informed of the Numberless difficulties he had to surmount than I am, who had an opportunity to see every step that was taken from the beginning and every obstruction that was thrown in his way. I wish the Nation may be as sensible of his service as he really deserved and give him the only reward that can flatter him; The pleasure of seeing them pleased and satisfied. [147]

And all of this without a word about the terrible illness from which the General suffered throughout.

Forbes had now of course to secure the ground, rebuild the fort and garrison it, and sustain peace with the Indians. To Governor Denny and to Generals Amherst and Abercromby he wrote on November 26 to advise them of the "signal success of his Majesty's Arms over all His Enemies on the Ohio." To Governor

Denny he reported the capture of the fort, and a reconciliation with the Indians, with whom he had already scheduled conferences. In his letter, which was read before the Council on December 11, he noted also his determination to repair the barracks and to garrison the fort against the winter with 200 men of the Pennsylvania Provincials, together with a proportion of the Maryland and Virginia troops. He remarked the need for Pennsylvania to accommodate Colonel Montgomerie's Battalion of 1300 men in "Comfortable Winter Quarters." He expressed the hope that he could summon enough strength to make the return journey to Philadelphia. Very poignant was his concern for his health: "I kiss all your Hands, and flatter myself that if I get to Philadelphia, under your Cares and Good Companys, I shall yet run a good Chance of re-establishing a Health that I run the risque of ruining to give your Province all the Satisfaction in the Power of my weak abilities." For the Province of Pennsylvania he declared it was a great moment. "I hope, " he wrote, "the provinces will be so sensible of the great benefit of this new Acquisition, as to enable me to fix this noble, fine Country, to all Perpetuity, under the Dominion of Great Britain." [148]

On the very next day the General commenced a letter to William Pitt, but he was unable to complete it until January 21, after he had arrived in Philadelphia. In this letter he reported the capture of the abandoned fort, and the expulsion of the French "from this prodigious tract of Country," which he attributed in large part to the desertion of the Indian allies, "whom I had previously engaged to leave them." As above noted, he regrets that because of the season of the year and the want of provisions he was unable to press "up the River" to Lake Erie and destroy the French forts at Venango and Presque Isle. After advising that his physicians were insisting he return to England directly if he would save his life, he reports that "I have used the freedom of giving your name to Fort DuQuesne,[149] as I hope it was in some measure the being actuated by your spirits that now makes us Masters of the place." [150]

Obliged to leave Pittsburgh because of his illness, Forbes turned over the command to Colonel Bouquet. One of Bouquet's first functions was to take up the conferences with the Indians that Forbes was now unable to call or to attend. Early in December these conferences were convened. Both the English and the Indians professed a desire for peace, and both were eager to see a resumption of healthy trade. But the English desired to erect a fort "right here," at the forks of the Ohio; and the Indians were unshakably determined "to see the English soldiers return over the mountains." When Christian Post, who was still hard at work among the Indians, finally got across the river to the Fort (December 4), he found himself one day too late to speak to Forbes. But he learned that Bouquet was much displeased with the Indians' "order" to Forbes. Bouquet had held a conference with the Indians. Present were several officers, including Armstrong, and George Croghan, Deputy Agent to Sir William Johnson, and Captain Henry Montour, serving as interpreter. Bouquet was urging peace. He asked the Delawares to reject the French, "as they are a restless & mischievous People and the Disturbers of your Peace." He went farther. He urged them to persuade the Indians of the West to peace. He invited deputies from each nation to "come with you" to Philadelphia, to meet Forbes and the Governors of the Several Provinces this winter.[151]

When Post insisted that the Indians would "no way" ever grant permission to build a fort, Bouquet urged him to persuade them otherwise. And he promptly called Croghan and Colonel Armstrong to an afternoon tent conference on the matter.

Informed that the Indians had changed their minds, Post determined to find out for himself. He brought King Beaver, Kekeuscund and Shingas together to ask them if they would change their answer. He found that nothing had changed. He was told by the Indians that "Mr. Croghan and Henry Montour had not spoke and acted honestly and uprightly . . . . We have told them three times to leave and go back, but they insist upon staying here; if, therefore, they will be destroyed by the French and the Indians, we cannot help them." [152]

General Forbes had left Pittsburgh on December 3 for Fort Loyal-hanna, which he was now naming Fort Ligonier, in honor of Sir John Ligonier, Commander-in-Chief of land forces in Great Britain. He remained at the fort here for almost the entire month of December, in a vain attempt to recover his strength. When he finally set out for the east, he was still extremely ill. He reached

Carlisle on January 7, and was in Lancaster on the 13th. To General Amherst he here dispatched a report. In his closing, he remarked despairingly on his health: "Major Halkett will be at New York in two or three Days to receive your commands—I hope you was so good as to send Doctor Huck altho by the time I reach Philadelphia I don't know whether he will be of any service to me or not As I am weaker than a child and recover no Strength . . . ."[153]

On the 17th he reached Philadelphia, where he was welcomed with a clamoring enthusiasm and accorded great honor by the people of the city and by the administrators of the Province. Not surprisingly, he continued in great concern for the lasting success of the mission. He was astute enough to appreciate that difficulties with the Indians were not only possible but extremely likely. The letter he wrote to Amherst on the 18th closes with a postscript: "As to the Indians and Indian affairs I did everything that lay in my power to settle them as well as time & circumstances would admit off [of] But they will require a thorough search and a just and equitable settlement to fix them our friends as long as we please to keep them—"[154]

The General, now very conscious of how close he was to his end, composed his last will and testament on February 13. A week later, in one of his last official acts, he directed that a Gold medal be struck to commemorate the campaign. Colonel Bouquet had his General's impression: "The Medal has on one side the representation of a Road cut thro an immense Forrest, over Rocks, and mountains. The motto Per tot Discrimina—on the other side are represented the confluences of the Ohio and Monongahela rivers, a Fort in Flames in the forks of the Rivers at the approach of General Forbes carried in a Litter, followed with the Army marching in Columns with Cannon. The motto Ohio Brittanica Consilio manaque. This is to be wore round the neck with a dark blew ribbon—by the General's command."[155]

This most courageous and noble officer of the King and Minister William Pitt now had but little time left. He died on Sunday, March 11, and was buried in the Episcopal Christ Church, in the chancel. Somewhat ironically, General Forbes at Christ Church is in close company with seven signers of the Declaration of Independence. Five of these are Pennsylvanians: Dr. Benjamin

Franklin, Dr. Benjamin Rush, George Ross, Robert Morris, and Carlisle's James Wilson. Also interred at the Church are Francis Hopkinson of New Jersey and Joseph Hewes of North Carolina. And for a time there lay not far from John Forbes the body of John Penn, grandson of William Penn and Governor of Pennsylvania.

On Thursday the 15th, there appeared in the *Pennsylvania Gazette* a very touching and very reverent obituary. A Memorial Tablet to "Brigadier General Forbes" is in place to this day on the north wall of Christ Church, on North American Street in Philadelphia.

The name Forbes appears everywhere in the Pittsburgh area too. He is remembered in Forbes Avenue, one of the city's principal and longest streets; in the Forbes Oakland Building; in Forbes Elementary School in Verona; in Forbes Elementary School in the Penn Hills School District of the city; in Forbes Tower, and Forbes Hall at the University of Pittsburgh; and of course in the beautiful baseball stadium known as Forbes Field, which opened in June of 1909 and closed in June of 1970. And Forbes Field, appropriately, had Bouquet Street in its supporting cast. And there is always the Forbes Road across the state. Although the highway's principal route now goes by different names, many still prefer to remember it as "The Forbes Road." And travelers have little trouble recollecting the expedition, as some three dozen historical markers adorn the highway, each marked "Forbes Road," and including information on a particular feature.

That the Forbes Expedition ended in spectacular success is indisputable. Its object was won completely, and, as the years would prove, with finality. The French presence in colonial Pennsylvania was removed. Credit for the success of the mission goes first of all to its commanding officer, General John Forbes, who, while suffering unspeakable anguish and pain from beginning to end, remained steady at the helm, to direct the operation with impressive military acumen and heroic resolve.

And incalculable credit goes to his chief lieutenant, Colonel Henry Bouquet, who, while a stranger to the formidable wilderness, executed the orders of his General with a zeal and persistence that could have been provided by no one else.

Plaudits go also to the officers of the British Regulars and the colonial militia, to the battalion commanders, Archibald Montgomerie, Colonels John Armstrong, James Burd, Hugh Mercer, George Washington, and William Byrd. And to the indefatigable Quartermaster General, Sir John St. Clair.

There should not be forgotten the post riders, the courageous couriers, like Lieutenant Johnny Piper, who kept open the fragile lines of communication, racing night and day up and down the line of march to convey the incessant stream of letters, which included orders, information, and requests. And the wagonmasters, and the scouts and pilots, including the handful of Cherokee and Catawba Indians who remained faithful to Forbes and served him well.

Most important too were the missionaries, most notably Christian Post,[156] whose considerable influence kept the Shawnee and the Delaware and the Ohio Indians out of it. George Donehoo, the eminent historian of Pennsylvania, in composing a beautiful tribute to the energetic and courageous missionary,[157] urges us to consider what might have been, and why it did not happen.

Mention must be made of Benjamin Franklin and Governor William Denny and the Pennsylvania Assembly and the Commissioners, who provided the wagons, the teamsters, and the provisions necessary to the support of an army of 7200 men.

And, finally, of course the great credit goes to the army itself, the British regulars and the colonial militia, who hacked their way through a torturous wilderness 200 miles from Carlisle to the Ohio, enduring relentless rain and debilitating illness. For seven months they stayed the course, clearing a broad avenue through the dense forests, building redoubts and forts, and relay stations, and all the while marching forward over the mountains, through swamps and laurel thickets bristling with hostile Indians to who knows what kind of terrible combat.

Certainly a fierce battle to climax the expedition would have attached a greater glory to the cause. That no such battle occurred does not, however, belittle the mission. Indeed, the campaign ended with the kind of battle every general surely prefers, in victory without the loss of a man.

And General John Forbes certainly did right when he named the captured fort as he did and etched into history forever a beautiful tribute to William Pitt.

XI

BOUQUET AND THE ROADS WEST

Colonel Bouquet left for the East a few days after his General. Colonel Hugh Mercer was left in command of a garrison of 200, with his first obligation the rebuilding of the fort, and his second obligation the maintenance of peace with the Indians.

Captain de Lignery, who had commanded Fort Duquesne and who had made the decision to burn it down and abandon it, went up the Allegheny River to Fort Machault, where, under orders from the Governor General of Canada, he would remain throughout the winter.

For the withdrawal of the army, the homeward trek, Colonel Armstrong was given Fort Bedford. It was there that the discursive elements of Forbes's force were to assemble for assignment or severance. As it turned out, it was a big, big job.

On December 16, from Raystown, Colonel Armstrong directed a letter to Colonel Bouquet, who was still back with Forbes at Fort Ligonier. Armstrong has a lot of confusion and real trouble to report. He is much disturbed by the apparent dissolution of his authority, especially with respect to the British Regulars and Highlanders, and also feels the need for specific orders having to do with troop dispersal. Most irksome is the impression that "Provincial Rank is now at an end," and that he should not exert any authority over the King's troops.[1]

With letters composed on both December 23 and 24, Colonel Bouquet responded to Armstrong's request for orders, directing him, in part, to specify troops for the garrisons of the lower forts. Armstrong, as he reported to Bouquet from Raystown on the 27th, executed the orders promptly and marched the troops out of Fort Bedford for Carlisle. But he continued to feel insufficiently appreciated, and found lots to complain of:

This day I got the Garrison of this Post [Fort Bedford] *Consisting of 200 Men under Cover, and has* [have had] *a report made of all the Houses or Hutts here, and what Number of Men they May Contain, but has yet turn'd Out no person, the*[y] *being in the Old & part of the New Hospital. Had the General Known how Often my face & Stomach has been heated with the Culpable Conduct of this place, and how many different Measures have been taken to prevent every Scandalous practice, he wou'd rather have pitied, than Charg'd me with defect . . . my Men have not travel'd Less than One hundred & Twenty Miles, to detect & bring back Villians* [sic] *. . .*

It is not known just exactly when Armstrong had news of the birth of his second son, but one can imagine how eager he was to get home when he did have the news. He concluded his report with an air of finality ("The greatest part of what I can do, is now finish'd.") and in the fervent hope that he now could be returned to Carlisle.[2]

Apparently Bouquet's letter composed the day after Christmas, which countermanded the orders laid down in the letters of the 23rd and 24th, did not reach Armstrong in time. Only in a letter dated January 1, did Armstrong acknowledge receipt of the change. The mis-communication turned out to be unfortunate. Major Halkett is accompanying General Forbes on the return march. They are not yet to Raystown. From his encampment at the foot of the east side of the Allegheny Mountain, the Major in a letter of the 29th, as ordered by Forbes, described to Colonel Bouquet the General's exasperation: "The inclos'd letter [Armstrong's letter to Bouquet, Dec. 27] was met upon the Road this day, and as the General saw it was upon His Majesty's service, and from Colonel Armstrong he open'd it, when he was extreamly supris'd to find that all the Regular troops were march'd from Reas Town so contrary to his inclination, but this mistake he will Remidy." Forbes is much upset: "The steps taken by Colonel Armstrong, are very different from what the General and you [Bouquet] settl'd at Fort Ligonier, but it will all be put to Rights upon the Generals getting down to Fort Bedford, when he will write you what he has done." [3]

Inscribed on the back of the letter was a note: "Mr. Sinclair [likely Captain James Sinclair of the 22nd Regiment] got to Reas Town yesterday and immediately Colonel Armstrong sent off orders [never found] to stop the Highlanders, the first Division had past [sic] Littleton and the Second to Juniata." [4]

In a letter of apology and explanation, dated January 1, Armstrong from Fort Bedford apprised Colonel Bouquet of the corrected deployments, making it very plain that he has been careful in following orders as received, and reporting that he has "Stop'd the Troops on their March," and has met the General "at his Chimney," the luxurious lodging provided for Forbes at the foot of the east side of the Allegheny Mountain, seven miles from Fort Bedford. He is pleased that "integrity & Politeness wou'd not Suffer him to throw blame on any particular person."

And then in great detail Armstrong accounted for his conduct in the hours since, noting once again his great desire to be released from these duties. He closed out the letter politely: "In Case you send forward the hundred Pennsylvanians, give me leave to recommend that Eight or Ten of my Battalion, who may have the greatest reason of Complaint, be Chang'd for an equal Number of those at Ligonier. There are some young boys among them, but those you need not fear, as they will undoubtedly Stand all weathers." On another matter, "There is a quantity of the Kings Liqour at Stoney-Creek, you'd please to think how it's to be dispos'd of . . . forgive this piece of freedom, and believe me to be,

Dear Sir, Yours Affectionately, John Armstrong."[5]

On this very day, the first day of the new year, General Forbes, with Bouquet still at Ligonier, departed Fort Bedford on his way to Philadelphia. Consequently, Bouquet would hear again from Armstrong. The Colonel had more problems, and, because, as often seemed to be the case, he was incapable of simple decisions, he solicited orders. By express, in the person of Charles Boyle, he got off one more impatient letter to Bouquet. This time the problem has to do with providing warm underjackets and shoes and stockings for eighty Highlanders, with 170 additional troops to show up. What Armstrong needs is a directive and authority.[6]

The Colonel is very hopeful for the arrival of Bouquet "every hour." He continues most impatient to see his wife, who has experienced a difficult pregnancy, and his son John, whom he has never seen. He sees no need to stay on at Bedford, and, indeed, hopes that his service will not be required in any other capacity, as "it is not easy to proceed to Philadelphia," and he has obligations to his family. Happily, Bouquet did show up at Fort Bedford the evening of that very day, the 6th, not long after Armstrong's express had been dispatched; and, happier still, the Colonel was promptly given leave to go home to Carlisle.

Some more, most interesting, light is cast on the strange business of clothing for the Highlanders by the letter of Captain Alexander McKenzie sent to Bouquet at the same time as Armstrong's letter, on the 6th. He notes the distress of the Highlanders and the Royal Americans, who he insists are in great want of shoes and clothing. Then, though he is a captain writing of a colonel, he launches into a very sharp criticism of Armstrong: "Therefore I aplyed to the General [Forbes] to have blankets from the Kings Stores here [Bedford] to Suply the party with Jackets. But not having this order in Writing was Refused by Col. Armstrong the Commandant of that place which puzled me very much and [I] did not know how to Carry on the party without them. Luckily the General Adverted to Col. Armstrongs Puzzelanimity [!] and Directed Major Halket to writ me giving me Authority to take from the Kings Stores as many blankets as I might find Nesessary for making under Jackets for each Soger [soldier] . . . ."

And Captain McKenzie is not through: "Our Commandant

Armstrong is so timorous & Confused that probably he may attempt to baffle thus my best Endeavours, therefore it will be proper to write me Explictly in the Management of our men here present and those coming up [from Carlisle] so as to be out of his reach." [7]

Armstrong stayed on two more days with Colonel Bouquet at Bedford, but when he was relieved of his duties there, he was headed home. By the 10th of January he was at Fort Loudoun. On the next day, leaving his men at the fort, at long last he set out for Carlisle. He arrived on the 16th to look upon for the first time his newborn son, John, Jr., and to "renew acquaintance" with his beloved Rebeckah, who, the nurse reported, had been doing poorly, sapped of all energy and strength. In spite of Rebeckah's condition, it was a happy homecoming, made all the more so by its long delay.

Colonel Armstrong continued his friendship with Colonel Bouquet during the months immediately following the close of the campaign. He was sorry to hear, toward the end of January, that he would not have the pleasure of the officer's company "for the two days at least," which had been expected. Apparently Bouquet had taken the "other road" from Fort Loudoun to his quarters in York (arriving February 8), rather than to go by way of Carlisle. But Armstrong in his letter to the Colonel (Jan. 27) had some good news, and some anxiety, to report: "At coming here I found Mrs. Armstrong much recover'd and a promising Babe[8] in the Nurses Lap which gave me great joy, and in my imperfect thanks was rank'd among the favours of the Year. The childe was Healthful untill Yesterday Morning but since that time has been dangerously Ill, yet rather easier this afternoon than last Night, so that there is hopes it may recover." [9]

Armstrong having promised Bouquet that he would help to find him a comfortable home in the York-Lancaster region, had recruited Major David Jameson,[10] who lived in York, and Mr. George Stevenson, who had been appointed to manage the wagons for Forbes, to provide assistance.

The Colonel had hoped to go on to Philadelphia with

Major Jameson, but because of the illness of the infant John, Jr., he now thought that he might be tied up for "eight or ten days." He thus urged Bouquet to order Jameson to proceed without him "unless you should have other commands for him." As for the other instructions received from Bouquet, "I have wrote to Lt. Col. [Patrick] Work [of the Third Pennsylvania Battalion] without fail to repair to Bedford at the time you appointed, and in Case anything extraordinary shou'd happen to Work, shall write Lt Col [Hanse] Hamilton to hold himself in readiness for that duty."

He was still much concerned about the condition and provisioning of the Forbes Expedition troops, many of whom are "feeble and sick." And he reports that "some person is wanted here [in Carlisle] to take Charge of the Kings Stores."

Bouquet had asked Armstrong to see to it that his personal articles got to York safely, and Armstrong reported that, "I shall Send your Sword & Coat by Mr Philips [Lt. Ralph Phillips, a provincial, but commissioned Dec. 5, 1756, in the Royal Americans] if he can Carry them; your Other Articles are already gone in a Waggon before I came down [to Carlisle]. I hope to see you at York, or in Philad^a . . . ." [11]

As if Colonel Bouquet did not have enough to worry about, there came from Fort Ligonier another critical comment on Colonel John Armstrong. The letter, dated March 10, 1759, is in the hand of an important officer. This was Lieutenant Colonel Thomas Lloyd, a physician and great-grandson of the former Lieutenant-Governor, who had been commissioned Captain and aide to the Third Battalion of the Pennsylvania Regiment on April 2, 1756, and had been promoted to Major on February 22, 1758, and for the Forbes campaign further promoted to Lieutenant Colonel (May 30) in the Second Battalion, commanded by James Burd. Such a letter Bouquet was getting used to. Colonel Lloyd reports the arrival at Ligonier of Ensigns James Hughes and John Baird of the Pennsylvania Regiment, whose only orders are "to relieve who shoud please to be relieved by them." No written orders "or one line from the Commanding officer" (Armstrong). Lloyd closes by noting that the two "have been an Age on their March & were detached it seems by Col. Armstrong with whom 'tis not my Business to differ or to censure his Conduct." [12]

But by this time Bouquet had much bigger problems to address. The Forbes expedition, while a success in its mission, had not quieted the frontier, and had not completely removed the threat from the French. Parleys with the Indians at Fort Pitt had not been very satisfying. Concerns for the forts of Ligonier, Bedford and certainly Pitt were huge. Minister Pitt had confirmed the earlier decision to fortify Fort Pitt permanently, and Bouquet was aware how dangerously slowly the building of the fort was progressing. Indeed, Mercer had had reports as early as February 16 that French forces were assembling at Fort Le Boeuf, some fifteen miles south of Lake Erie in the French Creek Valley, presumably for an attack on Pittsburgh.

A most responsible and resourceful officer was Hugh Mercer,[13] but he had been left with a modest force of 250 men in a remote spot in the wilderness, the forks of the Ohio. Between him and the "civilization" of Carlisle and Shippensburg to the east only two tiny outposts were occupied by white men, Ligonier and Bedford. To his north lay the French posts of Machault, Le Boeuf, and Presque Isle. Changes were occurring in the British command. Abercromby had been called back to England and had sailed January 23rd; General Amherst, who did not like America, had been made Commander-in-Chief of His Majesty's Forces. Brigadier General John Stanwix, who seemed to Mercer to be a "good man," had been put in charge of everything having to do with Indian affairs. It was a good choice, thought Mercer, as Stanwix, like Forbes, by exhibiting respect and insisting on fairness, was able to achieve the good will of the Indians.

Certainly Mercer's situation was a perilous one. He feared the new generation of Delaware Indians. And he remained apprehensive about the French, from whom an attack was not only possible but probable. To ease tensions, councils with the Indians were scheduled. The first was held at Buckaloons, an Indian village at the mouth of Brokenstraw Creek on the Allegheny River, on January 4. The second was convened on January 25 at King Beaver's village of Kuskuski, near present New Castle. The third council, July 5, was held at Fort Pitt. Present were King Beaver, Delaware George, Shingas, Killbuck, and The Pipe. George Croghan served as mediator, and Mercer was present with his officers. At all of these councils rum flowed freely and promises were made, both ways. Colonel Mercer remained "nervous."

Work on the fort had been underway from late February, and the ditch and glacis were completed by March 18. It had been a dark and dreary, dismal winter, and Mercer with his handful of soldiers has been living in a kind of remote exile, but now has come the spring, and he is not unhappy. Colonel Bouquet, in a letter of April 13, has noted the probability of relief, and indeed Mercer has surmised that Bouquet himself may be placed in command of Fort Pitt. He could applaud that choice. Bouquet, he insists, would provide a "proper balance" between the Provincial Corps and the British Regulars, as he is "a Gentleman whom every Man must esteem."

But he is not impatient for relief. Though now well removed from his medical practice, he is actually enjoying his command at Fort Pitt. This is readily apparent from a most interesting letter to Colonel James Burd. The letter is dated Pgh., April 23. The soldiers have survived the depressing gloom of winter, with their duties and the "frequent perusal of the History of the four Kings [!]," and now at last are most "happily arrived, among shadie Groves, purling Streams, and verdant Fields. This place becomes now very agreeable to most of us, and excepting the Sick & the Lazy, 'tis my Opinion that a few of the Soldiers & Not One Officer of a Grain of Sense or Spirit would take it of Choice to go down the Country; For what Purpose are we to be relieved now? To have the additional fatigue of marching some hundred miles, starving all the Way . . . ?"

He does appreciate of course the possibility of an assault on the fort, and very much fears the consequence: "In the Event of An Attack on this Post, a scene of horrors must have ensued, too shocking for the Imagination." But with every day that passes he feels more secure, and his pride in his men and in their work steadily grows. He has some advice for his fellow battalion commanders, not only for Burd, but for Armstrong as well: "I propose writing on this subject to Col Armstrong And hope you will agree, not to harass your People, after what they have already suffered. The Subject might become too serious, was I to describe to you the Miseries of the Pennsylvania Troops, here, & much more so at Ligonier, for want of Surgeons; Your Battalions have lost immensely this Way . . . ."

As both Burd and Armstrong have been working hard to secure some augmentation of pay for the soldiers, Mercer is quick to congratulate them: "We are extremely oblidged to your endeavours & Col. Armstrongs, before the Assembly," but a caution: "I tell you a Word in Your Ear, Your Battalion and Col. Armstrongs will never be in Character, till half a Dozen Officers are broke down from the service in utter Disgrace."

Mercer has been happy enough with the location of Fort Pitt, naturally, as it commanded the forks of the river; but he has been authorized to select an alternative site for the fort, and, dutifully, in April, has been considering the possibility of a second fort: "To day I make an excursion to Chartier old Town [on the west bank of the Allegheny, at the mouth of Bull Creek, near the site of present-day Tarentum, well up the river from Fort Pitt], One of the finest places for a Strong Post to be found perhaps in America, besides a View infinitely superior to Any about Pittsburgh & the River equally commanded." [14]

Armstrong was at home in Carlisle the most of April, and still in close touch with Colonel Bouquet. On April 24 of this year (1759), Colonel John Armstrong, himself a justice of the Cumberland County Court,[15] wrote Provincial Secretary Richard Peters[16] that the Crown Prosecutor had ordered the presiding judge of Cumberland County to bring three indictments against himself and his soldiers for rioting. Noting that one of the indictments still remained, Armstrong, pleading a paucity of evidence and faulty legal procedure, objected strenuously.[17] But the indictment was to hover over his head throughout the summer, before it was eventually brought to court. When it was finally dropped, Armstrong had his loyal friend Colonel Bouquet to thank. Bouquet, in writing to Peters from Fort Bedford on August 8, added a postscript to his official letter: "Col. Armstrong informs me this moment that the Prosecution is renew'd against him, by new Bills found by an irregular Jury your friend Mr Chew[18] Should remove that [fop?] . . . and appoint an honest man to represent him, you will Serve your friends, & I hope your friends will Serve you." [19]

On the 26th Armstrong addressed a long update letter to

Bouquet. He expressed concern for the Indian threat to families returning over the mountains to their plantations, and he continued in great concern for the condition of the troops returned from the Expedition: "Mr. Blain [Lt. Archibald Blane] will advise you of the miserable State of Our people at Ligonier, and how Scarce, as well as bad the provisions are along the communication, except the Salt pork that is here [at Carlisle] & at Bedford." He insists that "Our Men here are very little better like [off], than when they left the Campaign." He was pleased to report that his brother, Major George Armstrong, "goes to command at Bedford." [20] And he is pleased also to be able to inform Bouquet that he has located the Colonel's special bed, and that he will have it sent to his own house. In response to Bouquet's expressed concern for Mrs. Armstrong, he advised that his wife and the children (ten-year-old James and the infant John, Jr.) are very well, and that she "gratefully accepts" your compliments and returns the same.[21]

At about this time also, May 2, Armstrong reminded General Stanwix that Lt. Colonel Adam Stephen, "with about three hundred Men [Virginians]" is to march from Bedford to Ligonier, though there are "too few Men for the Convoys on this side Ligonier." Armstrong was hoping that the General had "not lost sight of the great necessity of fresh Provisions for those poor fellows along the Communication who are living all the Winter & Spring upon Salt Pork without vegetables." [22]

It was plain enough through the first months following the close of the Forbes campaign that the Indians had to be considered hostile. It was plain enough that the line of forts had to be maintained in garrison. Consequently, in order to keep open the line of communication from Carlisle to Fort Pitt, each of the forts, at Shippensburg (Morris), Loudoun, Lyttleton, Bedford, and Ligonier, was provided a force of 100-300 men. And of course actual communities, because of support services, began to grow up at these forts.[23] At this time, toward the end of May, the forts were reporting dangerous supply shortages. Pittsburgh, which on the 25th of May advised it had only one week's food supply left, and Fort Ligonier were particularly desperate. When, because General Stanwix (who had returned to Pennsylvania from New York State) installed a schedule of very low payments for the wagon contracts, the wagonmasters of Cumberland County refused to cooperate, Colonel Armstrong authorized seizure of the wagons. And Edward Shippen, Sr., in a tour of the Lancaster area farms, tried to revive cooperation. When that was not forthcoming, because the army prices were simply too low for the farmers, Shippen seized fifty bushels of oats from recalcitrant farmers, and Bouquet drafted orders to impress the needed wagons.

While Bouquet and Stanwix supervised the provisioning of the troops in the counties of York, Berks, and Cumberland, Armstrong, commanding at Carlisle, was arranging for contracts with providers of forage, grain, wagons, wagonmasters, horses, and flour, particularly in Cumberland County. He also received parcels of letters to relay to the various commanders at Bedford, Ligonier, and Pittsburgh.[24] Just how *very* much involved is Armstrong in every affair involving funds or provisions is apparent from the incredibly long letter directed to Colonel Bouquet on May 28. After apologizing for his failure to respond to Bouquet's recent communications, and lamenting the missed opportunity of getting together with him in York, he addressed the current business.

He acknowledged receipt of the advertisements for provisions, supplied by Captain Lieutenant Lewis Ourry, recommended Captain John Byers as the person most fit to contract for wagons, as well as to take charge of the King's Store, and reported the appointment of a "proper person for Director of the Meadows near Carlisle." He noted also that he has people in mind for Director of the Meadows at both Shippensburg and Loudon. He urged the appointment of William Lyon "to reside here for a Certain Servise of Moment, in consequence of an Order from the General." He is sending Archibald Crawford, "who knows the Woods," to collect the stray horses at Bedford, and he is ordering two officers with fifty men to the service of Lt. Col. Adam Stephen.

Moreover, "I have wrote Coll: Burd to forward a Company of New Levys Said to be at Lancaster,"and "yesterday I made a demand of the Majestrates for about 20 Waggons in Order hastily to throw up Flour, as Sundry Posts, especially Pittsburgh are in want, they issu'd Summonses which I have sent to the Constables to bring the people and their Teams, if that measure won't do, I will be under a necessity of Using force."

He closed with concern about the prospect of war with the Indians, and noted the Indian attack on the convoy of Captain Thomas Bullitt, May 23, just three miles from Fort Ligonier. "Things," he feels, "have a disagreeable Aspect, and neither Our manner of making War, nor Our Politicks Seem to have with those Savages the proper Effect. Is it possible to avoid attacking the Indian towns, or renewing the War, with the Delawares? The few Pennsylvanians with [Captain Jacob] Morgan have done well. Please excuse this incorrect letter."[25]

Captain Lieutenant Lewis Ourry is at this time in the Carlisle home of John Armstrong. He is in Carlisle to employ wagons for the transport of workman's tools, and to direct the locating of warehouses. Writing on Armstrong's dining room table, he also composed a letter (in French) to Bouquet. He reported in some detail the misfortune of the Bullitt convoy. Ourry's letter was carried with Armstrong's to Bouquet by the courier Lt. John (Johnny) Piper, who was already en route for Philadelphia.

On this same day Colonel Burd, who is at Lancaster and has just received a letter from Armstrong, also wrote to Bouquet. In some exasperation he complained about the difficulty in securing the wagons necessary for transporting forage to Bedford: "I shall leave no stone unturn'd, nor no Methods untryed, to procure the Wagons of this County, but if it was possible the People could be paid it would facilitate the Business much."

The distressing details of the Bullitt affair, which he had from Johnny Piper, he now repeated for Bouquet. According to the Piper-Burd account, Captain Bullitt's convoy of 105 men was assaulted on the road not far from Fort Ligonier. Bullitt lost forty men murdered by the Indians. And the warriors carried off five wagons and fifty horses. On hearing all of this, Colonel Burd enjoined Piper to mention nothing of the affair anywhere in the country, "as it may have a bad Effect at this time."

In a postscript Burd reported that he has properly relayed the £500 meant for Colonel Armstrong.[26] In a letter to Bouquet from Lancaster two days later, Edward Shippen confirmed the £500 to Armstrong, and then went on to explain that the difficulty in procuring wagons vanishes with reasonable pay for the service.[27]

Armstrong's letter of May 28 was answered by Bouquet on

June 1. He is responding from Philadelphia, and is obviously (and characteristically) on top of everything. He thanked Armstrong for the pains he has taken in his Department, and proceeded to address the Colonel's concerns, noting that General Stanwix "approves all the measures you have taken."

Bouquet so far has fairly well disguised his impatience with Armstrong's need for very specific instruction. But he has provided some subtle intimation that the Colonel should himself make decisions on matters that approach routine. One benefit would be the better use of time. "The General leaves it to you to take the measures you think proper." [28]

Throughout the summer and fall of 1759 and during the year 1760, the provincial forces of Pennsylvania continued to work hand-in-hand with the British regular troops under General John Stanwix and Colonel Henry Bouquet to solidify their military installation in the province. After the building of Fort Pitt, a number of lesser fortifications were erected in the neighborhood of Pittsburgh, both north and south along the rivers. Henry Bouquet, depending heavily on Armstrong and Burd, served as Deputy Adjutant General answering to Generals Stanwix and Robert Monckton. It was his job to see that the various frontier posts were properly garrisoned and provisioned.

At the end of June and all through the first two weeks of July, 1759, reports of French and Indian forces assembling in the Presque Isle-Venango region came steadily into Pittsburgh and to Carlisle. With fears for the safety of Pittsburgh, Colonel Hugh Mercer stepped up defense preparations. He wrote that "the young Villains who have swilled so much of our Blood, and grown rich by the plunder of the Frontiers, have still some French poison lurking in their Veines that might perhaps break out at a Convenient Opportunity." [29]

On August 1, Bouquet arrived at Fort Bedford, where six Royal American companies were garrisoned. On the 13th, just as General Stanwix was showing up at Bedford, the Colonel had the very good news that the French had destroyed their forts at Venango and Presque Isle and Le Boeuf. With this news the General proceeded to Ligonier, arriving the 22nd, and journeyed on to Pittsburgh, arriving the 29th. Once in Pittsburgh Stanwix was quick to get on with the building of Fort Pitt, and real construction actually got underway on September 3.

Throughout the whole summer of 1759 Inspector General Bouquet, though headquartered in Philadelphia, had been scurrying from fort to fort, and from Philadelphia to York, constantly seeing to the garrisoning and provisioning of the various outposts, to the disposition of the King's troops, and to the repair and maintenance of the roads. During all of this time he was depending upon his close friend and chief Provincial resource person, Colonel John Armstrong, for all that was needed. Late in the summer Armstrong, continuing apprehensive, himself traveled the roads and scheduled the provisions.

September finds Colonel Bouquet at Bedford, where he has been since August 1. Armstrong at this time is at Castle Dewart, the redoubt built on the Forbes Road at the very peak of Allegheny Hill. Appalled by how very close he is to Heaven when at the height of the mountain, he writes to Bouquet, who is impatiently awaiting the arrival of General Stanwix. It is Monday, the 10th, 2:30 in the afternoon: "Dear Sir, Thru the Poverty & weakness of our horses Our utmost invention has been put to the Rack, to surmount the Aerial Heights of Allegheny with our utmost Endeavours from Six this morning I have but just reached this place. . . how we shall go on to Ligonier, 'tis impossible to say, but . . . as we shall of necessity be much longer on the Road . . . than I expected, I have ordered two Baggs of flour to be left at Stoney Creek."

He included a letter from Colonel Adam Stephen denoting charges against Ensign Alexander (or George) McDowell, who is delivering Armstrong's communication to Bouquet. Armstrong does not really know the young McDowell, but the person bringing the charges he knows as a "Sutler," and he thinks the charges false and "ridiculous," and expects McDowell "can exculpate himself." [30]

Bouquet responded promptly from Fort Bedford. Armstrong, he is sure, has the right impression of McDowell. "Dear Sir," writes the Colonel, "Your officers must need be very Idle at Ligonier to pick up Such nice quarrels as the one you was pleased to communicate me: If walking with a Sutler was unbecoming the character of an officer, I deserved [a] hundred times, myself to be broken: I have permitted McDowell, to go to the Settlements to collect the proofs of his Justification."

But the Inspector General has a big assignment for Armstrong, and a new route to follow: "I shall Send you immediately every Man of your Battalion, fit for Duty, as by the letters I had yesterday from the General [Stanwix], you are to repair the Roads from Ligonier to Pittsburgh [fifty miles], but he notes that Captain [Evan] Shelby is "reconnoitering a new Road which must be a great deal Shorter, and you will have less work to open it than to repair the old one."

He requests then an accounting of all the men, women, and stores at Ligonier, and stresses the need for such a report "by every opportunity." He is aware that there is no meat at Ligonier, and implores Armstrong to find some bullocks for the post.[31]

On Sept. 11, with Armstrong not yet at Ligonier and himself still at Bedford, Colonel Bouquet cheerfully informed General Stanwix that at Bedford there can be found an abundance of everything (forage, corn, oats, flour, salt, and, not least, liquor). He reported also that he is sending supplies on to Fort Ligonier, and while noting that Armstrong has the general's orders, he advised he is requesting tools for Armstrong "sufficient to open and Repair the Road." [32]

Bouquet also had instruction for Colonel Adam Stephen, who waits at Fort Ligonier for Armstrong. Having advised the Colonel that Armstrong will be sending him (or bringing to him) the Bullocks he has requested, he penned his orders: "You are to march to Pittsburgh with the rest of your Regiment as Soon as Col. Armstrong arrives," and you are to send from Pittsburgh tools sufficient "to open & repair the Roads from Ligonier to that Post which is to be done by Col. Armstrong's Battalion." [33]

Finally, on the morning of September 14, Armstrong reached Fort Ligonier. He was quick to inform Bouquet of conditions and of his response to several orders: "Dear Colonel," he wrote, "This day in the fore Noon we got to this place without the loss of a Bullock or any Other Article, we were much beholden to the fair weather & had the Assistance of three of the officers Horses the greater part of the Road. I received your Sundry favours on the March & am persuaded that you & mr. Ourry both gave us all the Assistance your Circumstances wou'd admit. I took a great deal of pains to find some of the Kings Horses, or Other Strays but did not get One that cou'd move from the Spot. [!] I shall write Mr. Ourry respecting the Waggoner you sent after me."

Apparently the supplies Bouquet has intended for Ligonier have not yet appeared, for Armstrong complained about the paucity of flour and other provisions. In the same letter he reported that Colonel Adam Stephen will be delayed in his march, "the Waggon horses that [George] Morton[34] is to send up requiring . . . rest."

Colonel Adam Stephen, unable to contain his considerable disgust, has been complaining to Bouquet about the exorbitant number of camp followers who attend the workers, and Bouquet, readily persuaded to the same impression, has ordered Armstrong to "do something" about them. Stephen, on September 16, reported to Bouquet that he has seen "your directions to Col Armstrong [letter not found] about the fair, I may Say, the foul Sex, I informd Him that I would advise you of his Conduct, who would have thought it?" He is not happy. Armstrong, he says, "has brought up a mere Seraglio with him, and among the Rest, three of our Cast offs, Sent down some time ago. If a person of his Rank and Gravity, a person whose example is so much respected, Connive at those things I fancy the thing will soon gain ground." He complains bitterly: "All of the women I wanted to get rid off [of], claim his patronage, and I have been obliged to Confine a Groupe of them, for pretending to go down [return east], and then fetching a Compass, and Returning in the night to the Suburbs of Ligonier again . . . ."[35]

Armstrong, in his letter of the 14th assured Bouquet that "I have produc'd your Orders relative to the weomen to Coll: Stevens, we shall endeavour to reduce their number as fast as possible."

The orders for opening the new road, which Bouquet has from Stanwix, Armstrong is perfectly content with. He agreed with Bouquet that opening the new road on the route recommended is as easily done as to repair the old one, so long as the numbers of workers and escorts is not diminished. He promised to "take the first good day to examin[e] the Road for eight or Ten Miles West of this Post," and expressed a willingness to join the workers, as his presence "might hasten the Work."

In a postscript he noted that he is enclosing the General's

letter which has to do with his brother Will: "I beg you'd be so good as to Send him [Captain William Armstrong] the necessary Orders to take the Command at Carlisle." He also speaks of the "Other Gent^n," presumably Captain James Armstrong, Colonel John's brother,[36] of the new levies, who "may come up" [to Bedford], and whom "I may need for duty in my Battalion during the Stay of the New Levies." Stanwix, writing from the post at Pittsburgh, assured both Armstrong and Bouquet that whatever they agreed on with William and James Armstrong would be okay with him.[37]

Now, although Armstrong was sending the letter "express," he did not get it off that night, and before it was dispatched, the Colonel was apparently shown a letter which Colonel Stephen had just received from General Stanwix. As it included Orders for the Virginia Company of Artificers to "repair the Road from this Place [Ligonier] until they meet Capt. Shelby who with the Artificers and his Own people are to open the New Road," Armstrong, who already understood that some troops from Pittsburgh were to help out, was given the impression that he was being relieved of the duty to open the new road, and he so informed Colonel Bouquet.[38]

But Colonel Armstrong has misunderstood. He is not being relieved of his obligations to the new road, far from it. The very next day he received from Bouquet a letter to set him straight:

The General's orders concerning the Rouds are that you Send an Officer & 50 Men of the Pennsylvanians to Assist the Virginia Artificers in Repairing the Road as far as the three Redouts, and that you please to forward all the Tools that may be left at Ligonier after Supplying your Men working on the Roads: and as you will probably have orders to cut the new road blazed by Shelby from the 3 Redouts you must keep falling Axes for that use: Shelby will in that Case Send you a Man Acquainted with his blazes, and so Cutting at both Ends you would soon meet. But for this new Road I refer you to the General's orders.

After relieving Armstrong of his apprehensions about provisions (by advising that he has forwarded 51,148 pounds of flour, with 70,000 more pounds to come), and after noting that he has made the requested arrangements for Captain William Armstrong, he made, in a postscript, very certain that the Colonel understood about the new road: "The General recommends in a particular manner that the Road be well repaired forward, you will please to Supply the Men with Provisions and Liquor."[39] Bouquet, who is still at Bedford, then promptly reported the details of his instructions to General Stanwix.

George Morton, Supervisor of Wagons for the Southern Department of the British Army, is in command at Fort Ligonier. But he has been ill, and during that time Armstrong apparently has had the command. Stanwix, who is at Fort Pitt, has expressed to Bouquet his approval of the directions given to Armstrong on the roads; and he is very confident that Armstrong will comply with them. On September 19, 1759, from Ligonier, Armstrong wrote to Colonel Bouquet. After thanking him for supplying the "particulars from Quebec [Montcalm and Wolfe]," he provides a much detailed account of the shipping of flour and salt, etc., and notes the prospect of a "Brigade of Waggons from you this Night," as well as a parcel of wagons coming from Pittsburg. And he reports that "According to your Orders I sent three officers & 50 Rank & Files to Assist as far as the three Redoubts." He means to repair the guard houses, which are "all out of Order."[40]

Three days later found Armstrong again writing to Bouquet. Not a whole lot has happened since his last communication. All is quiet at the Fort, and on the roads. He has been busy repairing guard houses and hospitals. But he does here again express some anxiety over Indians. He knows that the Indians yet have time for mischief before they return to their villages from the fall hunt. And he is aware that as an assault on Fort Pitt is unthinkable Ligonier must come to mind. Accordingly, he is posting sentries and sending out small reconnoitering parties. There is to be no surprise.

In this same letter he reported that he has not had any progress report from Captain Edward Hubbard, of the Virginia forces, whom he knows to be about sixteen miles out front, and supposes the Captain is reporting to Colonel Stephen. He is also curious to know whether the people on the road ever proceed farther than the three redoubts. He is most unhappy with the women, the "Females," as he calls them. Orders, he insists, whether issued by me or somebody else, simply do not apply to that element. "As no Orders are Obey'd by the Females I'm beginning to Duck & Drum Out, but nothing less than force will persuade them to Visit their Old friend Capt Ourry, by which he will naturally Suspect they have neither true hearts nor Sound Bottoms they are in short the Bane of any Army, the Devil & two Sticks."

Theft is a constant problem, and theft of rum or wine is a real problem. The Colonel complains: "I have had the misfortune either at Bedford or here [Ligonier] from under the Centry [sentry] to have One Kegg of Wine Stole, and have now but a few Gallons left of half a Pipe [A pipe would normally contain about 126 gallons.]; if without injuring your Self you can Spare me Twelve or Fifteen Gallons of your Madeira, and Order it up by the first Waggons, you will thereby lay me under the greatest Obligations, as at this Post it is very dear & very bad."

After some comment on deserters and on soldiers who fail to comply with orders, he reported a letter from Colonel Hugh Mercer, which has given him the impression that he will not be moved forward from Ligonier for some weeks.[41]

During the last week of September, while Stanwix is at Fort Pitt and Bouquet is at Bedford, a steady stream of letters is exchanged. Many have to do with provisions, especially flour, and the bullocks. Armstrong reports that he has fenced the garden and the bullock pen and is concerned now chiefly with twenty sick Virginians who have been left with him. "What's to be done with them?" He found all the redoubts, Guard Houses & Hospital "Out of Repair and full of Dirt," but "these have been repaired." He acknowledges orders from Stanwix to send 100 of his strongest men, besides those who are in the company of Captain Hubbard and his escorts, to Fort Pitt.

And he concludes the letter by providing the precious information that "Captain Hubbard has had two Barrels of Rum, and this day Sent for two more." [42]

For Stanwix, on the 29th, Armstrong filed a report. He has sufficient flour, but is taking great pains to preserve it: "The weather being Yet warm & the Flour in Bulk, I'm somewhat doubtful [fearful] of it's [sic] heating, or Souring, tho' at present there is not time for any appearance of that Sort, and where the

Situation of any flour Store is Low, I have Order'd Drains to be Cut, that . . . damps may be prevented as much as possible, we shall also very soon be without Store-rooms of any Sort without Building, or detaining the Baggs which hitherto has not been done." As Morton's wagons are not of condition to convey the flour to Pittsburgh, and the wagons that are being purchased by Captain John Hambright are going to be very tardy, Armstrong proposed to ship the flour by pack horses. But he must have orders, either from the General or from Bouquet!

He continued to worry about the twenty sick Virginians, and would like orders on that subject too. He expressed to the General the hope that the 100 men he has sent up for work are pleasing to him, as they were the very strongest he had. Of Captain Hubbard he reminded the General that "his demands for Rum are pretty Quick."[43]

General Stanwix was in fact pleased with Armstrong's 100 men, but, as he explained to Bouquet on October 3, he is ordering 100 more. And he expects them, as that will leave Armstrong still 240 "well and Sick," at Ligonier.[44]

As it turned out, Armstrong was able to get wagons on the road, but in the October of this fall came the rains that Bouquet and Armstrong remembered from the dismal September of the Forbes Expedition. Colonel Bouquet got letters off to Armstrong on both the 4th and the 19th, having to do with provisioning Fort Pitt. He is now urging Armstrong's Plan B:

Dear Sir, The Heavy Rains we have had for two days, and threatening to continue, I am obliged to Stop upon the Road our Brigade of Waggons, to prevent their Ruin in such a Weather, But being apprehensive that they may want flour at Pittsburgh; I beg you will order all the Pack Horses or such Part of them as you will think necessary from the knowledge you may perhaps have of their provisions to make a Trip there with flour & some forrage if they want it: As I have had no return [report] of their Provisions I do not know if they want or not; I am Sorry to be obliged to Send the Pack Horses further than Ligonier, as this Part of the Communication will sooner be [more?] impracticable for want of grass than the West of the Mountains.

Declaring that he can leave nothing to chance, he apologizes for the trouble, and closes with regret: "I expected to have the Pleasure to see you to-morrow, But there is no travelling till this storm is over." [45]

On the British victory at Quebec and the tragic death of General James Wolfe (Sept. 13) Armstrong remarks in a letter to Bouquet, October 19: "I have wrote the General two lines, inclosing a pitiful piece of paper [on the capture of Quebec], but if true (as I hope it is) embelish'd with the most Interesting Contents. We are left in the midst of triumph to condole the loss of the Noble Wolfe, who in the moment of dischargeing the last demands of Nature, has not forgot to do his Country the most important Service!"

He then agreed to send on to Captain John Wetterholt the men Bouquet has requested (Bouquet to Armstrong, Sept. 16). He is resisting complaint, and declares that "we shall do as well as we can without grumbling." But "I assure you I shall be much difficulted . . . as we Shall have about Seventy [left] for all kind of duty here."

Armstrong is *still* at Ligonier at the end of October. He pens at this time a most interesting letter to his Colonel Bouquet. He explains at the outset that "as I was Out a hunting when the last express went up, I Order'd Mr Dehaas [Adjutant John Philip de Haas, an immigrant from Holland, at this time twenty-four years old][46] to write you two lines and enclose the Provision & Forrage returns, which I find he has done."

Perhaps Colonel Armstrong has been harboring a grudge against Colonel Adam Stephen (whose name he only sometimes spells properly), for Stephen's remarks about him on the business of the camp followers, or perhaps without any real resentment he is simply angry. In any case, he here lashes out at Stephen with the kind of petulance he is often capable of:

You will see in [Captain Robert] *McPhersons return 477 W^t of Flour Sent to Coll: Stephens, which was done in my absence, and Loaded on the Horses without the knowledge of any officer here; upon Sending for McPherson to answer his Conduct of sending any thing Out of the Kings Stores as private property without my* *knowledge, he says Coll: Stephens requested him at leaving, this place to give it Storeage until he cou'd send for it: I find it has been mingled with the Common Stock, and the fellow cannot tell me whether it has been included in his returns or not, nor never before mention'd it either to you, or me. I have given him a Severe rebuke, and did I know what to do with the Stores, he shou'd pay in another manner for his impudence, ignorance, or both. Coll: Stevens Conduct I think is very extraordinary in sending here a parcel of Horses to be loaded Out of the Publick Store without any Authority, or even a line to me that might explain the matter. If the thing were even less than it is, I'm Oblig'd to write you so much in Order to explain the N: B: in the return, and have done it with more sofiness, than the conduct deserves.*

After some information on wagons and supplies, he returned to the matter that has so excited him: "I am daily cautioning Mr. Morton in regard to this Article, & have you may depend on't a watchful eye on Mcpherson. De Haas is as Careful on this point as I have ever known him about anything." And then, probably with Stephen still in mind, he reported on the old problem of the women: "I have sent down a parcel of Superfluous women and Other unnecessary people, perhaps some who have been discharged this place may make application to the General or you, for further Stay, such as Bakers &c which shou'd not be granted: as I plainly discover the smaller the Garrison & it's [sic] attendants, the better for this Service, this being no more than a Post of passage."

The closing is on another matter: " . . . inclos'd you have a Counterfeit pass or discharge produc'd here by a Deserter from Capt Gordons Company, which cost Six of my people a Case [chase] of Eighteen Miles before they took him. He shall go up by the first Opportunity."

And still the heavens gush: "We have at present a very great rain, the Road from Stoney-Creek to the Alleghany will doubtless be knee-deep. I thought to have mix'd this heavy letter, with some other Subject, but must refer to it at this time . . . ."[47]

Wagonmaster George Morton had full responsibility for the wagons and wagoners between Bedford and Pittsburgh. Apparently

Armstrong, who is commanding officer at Ligonier at this time, is aware of some question about his distribution of the provisions. On November 6, 1759, hoping to persuade Bouquet that he has been conscientious, Morton reported on provisions and the wagon schedule: "I have been informed By Coll Armstrong of your Writing to Him that the Forrage was wasted at this Fort, I Hope you'll Please, to Believe such Insinuations false as I Have always taken the greatest Care in my Power to Be frugal of any of his majesty's Stores yet come under my Care & Distribute it to the Best Advantage for the Publick Interest, Using no Partiality Between King & Continental teams, as it Can Be made appear By their Receipt Both By Allowing them equall for the trip & also meeting them on the Road. I'll Be a[l]ways Willing and Ready to Obey your orders in any Particular." [48]

Bouquet did not have the letter for some days, but he replied promptly when he did receive it, and he assured Morton that "your method of Supplying the Brigade with forrage is very proper." [49]

A momentous event occurred on December 7. The Pennsylvania Assembly passed a resolution to disband the provincial troops, except for 150 men, who were expected to serve through the winter. And despite the earnest pleading of Governor Hamilton that they reconsider, the members of the Assembly stood firm; by January 2 the last detachment of the Pennsylvania provincial force had reached Bedford, on its way to being discharged.

On the 27th of December, from Lancaster, Bouquet had got off a letter to Captain William Armstrong, who was in command at Carlisle: "As the new Levies are to be discharged in This Town, I beg you will order them here as soon as they come to Carlisle: They are to receive four days Provisions from the King's Stores for their March, after which time they will be supplied here on account of the Province. The old troops are to be discharged at Carlisle, Therefore you will please to keep them there, till the Paymaster can go up." [50]

As the Pennsylvania Regiment was broken up, many of the men who had served on the Forbes Expedition were required to consider their future. Typical was Ensign Frederick Van Hamback, who had been commissioned on April 2, 1758, and who had thereafter served in Colonel Armstrong's First Battalion. Hamback in reporting to Bouquet that he has been "discouraged from seeking my fortune in the army," requests assistance from the Colonel. He is hoping to marry and to enter into the plantation life, perhaps in Path Valley. Path Valley, which was that part of the Tuscarora Path that consisted of the valleys of the West Branch of Conococheagaue Creek and Tuscarora Creek, was at this time most attractive to settlers. Colonel John Armstrong, "who knows these people," declared the ensign, has been "most helpful." [51]

Bouquet, at home in Lancaster for the winter, in an extremely long letter on sundry matters to Richard Peters, Secretary of the Province and Clerk of the Provincial Council, reproached the Secretary gently for his handling of commissions, long a troublesome matter: "I thought that in some other occasions you had slighted my recommendations concerning Rank, and Commissions for your Troops, whenever they happened to fall in competition with those of Col. Armstrong, which I took at that time the more in Dudgeon that I had chosen to have those things done by you, tho' being of military nature and intended for the Good of the Service, I could have transacted them without difficulty with the Governor." [52]

As is known from a March 6, 1760, letter of Lt. Ourry from Fort Bedford to Bouquet at Lancaster, Colonel Armstrong remained quite active in the provisioning of the forts. Ourry reported that, thanks to Colonel Armstrong, he has sent on to Pittsburgh some fruit trees (250 apple trees, fifty peach trees, twelve cherry trees, nine plum and two pear trees), which have been "forwarded from Conegochee [Conococheague, present-day Williamsport, Md.]. [53]

Armstrong had pledged, as noted above, to find Bouquet a comfortable home somewhere in the region of Lancaster. But his failure to come through inspired an expression of disappointment from the trader George Croghan. To Bouquet Croghan lamented: "I am sorry that Colonel John Armstrong has not returned ye Tracts [of land] run out for you last Fall, with ye Tract of ye Spring on Vinord Creek, which are all done. I have wrote him to return them as soon as possible. As to ye Tracts on Vinord Creek, you may depend upon it, I will have them run out next month when I shall be at Bedford." [54]

Indeed, Bouquet's efforts to acquire land from the Penn proprietary holdings had failed totally. On November 10, 1759, Thomas Penn, at that time Proprietor of Pennsylvania, penned a letter on the matter to Secretary Peters:

We resolve to keep Ross's plantation, tho' the price offered is very great . . . pray tell Col. Bouquet this with my compliments, and assure him I would sooner have obliged him with it than any other Person. I cannot think they [retiring British officers] *have any reason to expect we should give them Land, if the back part of the Country had been secured to us, and we had not been taxed we proposed to give Land to encourage the raising Men, but as we are taxed, we do not think ourselves obliged to grant any. You have not sent me a Copy of Col. Armstrong's letter in favour of Col. Bouquet nor said what kind of favour Armstrong thinks he would expect. He is an honest worthy Man, was Governor to a nephew of my Lord Essex's, whose Family are among our most intimate Friends, and was by them recommended to me. As to foreign officers they are well paid and I suppose the King will give them Lands on the common terms in some of his provinces—I wish Bouquet may settle in Pennsylvania—he and Col.* [James] *Prevost have bought a large plantation and Negros in Carolina.*[55]

But by June of 1760, Bouquet was finally most comfortably settled at Long Meadow, a 4000-acre estate in Frederick (now Washington) County, Maryland, in the vicinity of present-day Hagerstown, which he had been granted by Governor Horatio Sharpe.[56]

It was in this summer that the British conceived a big job for Bouquet. They were hoping to install a fort at the site abandoned by the French on Presque Isle in Lake Erie. Armstrong by Bouquet was offered command of one of the two provincial battalions that were being organized. But Armstrong found himself unable to participate in the campaign. He did, however, with two companies pledge to defend the frontier should Bouquet's absence require it. And he continued very high in the regard of Bouquet, who was grateful for whatever Armstrong could do. To Armstrong, from Philadelphia, on May 15, in anticipation of the expedition,

Bouquet penned a note to his old friend, then at Carlisle: "I am sorry that we are deprived of the Pleasure of your Campaign, but I hope that you will be so good to assist us." He has a particular favor to ask. He is hoping that Armstrong can appraise the King's horses which are now at Fort Loudoun, to determine which are fit for the wagons and which should be employed as pack horses. "But if your affairs don't permit you to go; Will you please to appoint your brother Capt William Armstrong, who I hear is at Fort Loudoun to be one of the appraisers on behalf of the crown. Mr [Captain John] Byers is to be the other; These Gentlemen will have a Consideration for their Trouble and Expences: I hope to be soon in Carlisle . . . ."[57]

In June of 1760 Bouquet assumed command of the expedition whose object was to erect a fort that would command the southern shore of Lake Erie, and thus provide a link to the Detroit-Niagara chain. He arrived at Fort Pitt on June 16, and on July 7 he marched from the Fort with 500 men. Two days later Mercer set out for the same place with a similar force. Bouquet, discovering the 120 miles to be more like 140, arrived at Presque Isle at 10:00 in the morning of July 17, and proceeded to erect a British fort.[58]

By the end of the year, "the peace that had been made with the Delaware and Shawnee at Easton and which had been ratified with the Ohio Indians through the efforts of Christian F. Post at Kuskuskie, etc., and then continued again with Gen. Forbes, seemed a real and enduring friendship . . . ."[59]

But Pennsylvania continued edgy, and with the chances for a sustained peace steadily improving, the Assembly was extremely sensitive to anything apt to rock the boat. One disturbing event actually occurred within the community of Carlisle in the winter of 1760. It was a most barbarous massacre of Indians. A Delaware known as "Doctor John," together with his wife and two small children, was brutally murdered in the family home along the Conodoguinet Creek very near the town. As it was well known that Doctor John enjoyed boasting about having killed "sixty" whites, and was constantly expressing his contempt for soldiers, the motivation for the murders seemed obvious, and several suspects were arrested. However, all were promptly released. The indignant Assembly immediately offered a reward of 100 pounds, and sent a messenger to the Indians at Wyoming, to inform them of the crimes and of the methods that were being employed "to bring the Offenders to Justice." But for these murders those responsible were never identified or apprehended, and no one was ever prosecuted.[60]

An event very different occurred in the Carlisle-Lancaster region in the summer of 1762. On July 10 Frederick Post left Pittsburgh for the big council scheduled for Lancaster. He had in tow the most influential chiefs of the Ohio River region, King Beaver and White Eyes, and a number of prisoners to be returned. On the 18th, at Fort Littleton, he hooked up with George Croghan, now Deputy Commissioner for Indian Affairs. By the 24th the company had reached Shippensburg, and next day Carlisle, where Post found "The people . . . were most all gathered to see the prisoners and the Indians; although we did whatever we could to prevent Liquor among the Indians, they got some."

It is not known whether Armstrong was present for the preliminary council held in Carlisle on the 25th, but there it was decided to proceed to Harris's Ferry to wait for four days for any Indians who might be coming from the north on their way to the Council at Lancaster. That night the Indians "had a frolick by dancing, singing, and drinking all night long." One of the captives was stolen away from the Indians by some of the Carlisle people, "which displeased the Beaver greatly." The Indians left Harris's Ferry on August 8, which was a Sunday, and because the Irish wagon drivers did not work on Sunday, they walked to Lancaster. Here for the council were now assembled 557 Indians of many tribes. Discussed, naturally, were the problems over land and trade relations. But the big thing was the return of many captives.[61]

For the four-year period between the capture of Fort Duquesne in November of 1758 and the harvest season of 1762 the Pennsylvania frontier was relatively quiet. For Colonel John Armstrong it was a busy, busy time, as he had his hands full with the roads west and with the various forts and with garrisoning and provisioning both the British troops and the provincial militia. But such problems as he was required to address were more a nuisance than a matter of life and death. All of that was about to change.

XII

PONTIAC'S WAR

From the time of Braddock's defeat until the first years of Washington's Presidency, the Pennsylvania frontier was a sea of blood. Except for the lull immediately following the fall of Fort Duquesne, Indian depredations and the settlers' response produced an unceasing reign of terror. Forbes's capture of Duquesne and the peace concluded between England and France in 1763 should have brought quiet to the settlements, but they did not. While the period 1755-1795 was almost never free of atrocity and barbarity, of panic and flight, the most terrible of these years were those of 1763-1766. This is the period known as the time of Pontiac's Conspiracy, or Pontiac's Rebellion. The uprising was inspired by the British activity in the West, and the consequent threat to the Indian lands "beyond the mountains." The war, for it was that, was ignited at a council on the Ecorse River in the early spring of 1763. At this council, the forty-three-year-old Ottawa chief Pontiac (Obwandiyag), who had led the Ottawa faction at Braddock's defeat, assumed the leadership of the Indian tribes known as the Wyandot, the Potawatamie, the Ojibwa, and the Senecas, which were readily incensed. And brought into the war in Pennsylvania were the Delaware and the

Shawnee as well.

The cunning and resourceful Ottawa chief had in mind to unite all the Indian tribes into one great onslaught against the settlers. Under Pontiac the various Ohio tribes enjoyed more organization than perhaps at any other time in their history. And they had a plan. Pontiac was sternly determined to cut off all communications among the frontier posts and to destroy crops and livestock. He was looking forward especially to the harvest time, when the settlers would be particularly vulnerable. His vision included the province of Pennsylvania, and he was depending upon the Seneca war-chief Kayahsotha (Guyasuta) to ravage that frontier and most especially the upper part of the Cumberland Valley, northward of the Blue Mountains.

But at the top of the list for Pontiac was Fort Detroit, and he was relying on a cunning duplicity to gain entrance. When that plot was foiled, and a frontal assault of the fort on May 10, 1763, was turned back, he laid siege to Detroit that lasted until November! One of the major battles that were fought was that at Bloody Run, in which British Captain James Delzel suffered great losses to Pontiac. That was July 31.

Although Detroit never fell to the Indians, a great many other forts were overrun, some by the same duplicity that Pontiac had planned for Detroit. Among these forts were Venango, Le Boeuf, Presque Isle, Sandusky, and Michilimackinac (Mackinac). At all of these engagements horrible massacres occurred. Both Fort Pitt and Fort Ligonier would withstand assault and siege, but Pontiac's War had come to Pennsylvania with a vengeance.

Indeed, in Pennsylvania conditions actually heated up very shortly after Pontiac's initial assault on Detroit. And Carlisle naturally became the hub of the anti-Indian activity. It was from Carlisle that protection for the settlers was dispatched. It was in Carlisle that the fleeing settlers sought refuge. It was in Carlisle that General Stanwix had his headquarters and from which he directed the British military.

To Secretary Richard Peters, Stanwix regularly filed reports. One of these lamented that Colonel Armstrong "has so few men here that I could only get six of them to each piquet by way of guides." He noted that "In spite of our blood, the Indians will do us mischief, but the last effect does really proceed from both obstinacy and carelessness of which Col. Armstrong will give the governor a particular account as he has it from Shippensburg." The "skulking Indians still hover about us." [1]

That spring (1763), on June 13, from Carlisle, Armstrong responded to Bouquet, who, now in Philadelphia, had requested information on the Indian activity:

Dear Colonel, Having been over the Mountain for these few Weeks past, I could not sooner acknowledge the receipt [of your] very friendly Letter, which on my return I found [illegible phrase] with regard to the Indians Depredations first of the Alleghanys Capt Trents Letter to his Wife and the Indian Speech to Calhoon, is all I have yet seen in writing and should have sent you a Copy of the latter had [I not] been persuaded you have some time ago been furnish'd with [this] piece of Intelligence . . . all things will yet work together for good tho' another bloody Scene may now be at the Door, which doubtless will retard your proceeding down the River [the Ohio], but at length, put that design on more Safe and respectable footing.I am distress'd for the State of our Frontier, scatter'd and already thrown into great confusion and difficulty as the people already are thro' Pannick infatuation and lyes. I have wrote the Governor a few lines on this matter, and am this morning a Setting out for the North Side of the Hills, in order if possible to prevent such a ruinous and Shamefull flight. Ammunition is greatly wanted throughout this County.

Although he fears a general war and another great runaway of the settlers, to Bouquet he here commends the farmers: "I can say nothing more than the Spirit and diligence of those people ought to meet with some kind of reward." Some thoughts about revitalizing the militia and a repeated concern about ammunition conclude his letter.[2]

On the very day after Armstrong penned this letter, there arrived at the fort at Hunter's Mill, near Harris's Ferry on the Susquehanna, a messenger from Fort Augusta, bearing a belt and a string of wampum. He reported that a Cayuga had delivered this message to the Indians on the Susquehanna, and that it was to be interpreted as follows: "This String of Wampum comes to let you know that the French that was killed is come alive again, and that there is seven of your out Posts taken and all the people killed by the French, and a number of wild Indians that have tails like Bears & live a great way from hence, they cant say how far & that the same Speech was sent to Sir William Johnson, as likewise up the River to the Delaware & Munsies, and was to be returned to the Commanding Officer at Fort Augusta." [3]

A week later, Governor James Hamilton, who had succeeded William Denny on November 18, 1759, found in his hands an alarming letter which had been written by Colonel John Armstrong and Thomas Wilson to Colonel Joseph Shippen, Jr., dated Carlisle, June 20. It expressed their highly valued opinion that "a general War with the Indians is now fully evident, & their depredations already begun in the Murder of Sundry Families near Bedford." Armstrong and Wilson proceeded, then, to request of Shippen powder and lead for the "use of the frontier inhabitants." [4]

On the same day that he had Armstrong's letter the Governor received another forwarded communication which had been written by Doctor William Plunket to Colonel Joseph Shippen, Jr., in which was provided dire news about Fort Pitt. According to the letter, Lieutenant Archibald Blane, in command at Fort Ligonier, had informed Colonel George Armstrong, in command at Fort Bedford, that he had heard nothing in some time from Pittsburgh, which, he said, with other things that have happened, "gives Mr. Blaine [Blane], with many others, Reason to Conjecture that Pittsburgh is invested and the Communication cut off." [5]

The Governor at once brought these two letters to the attention of the Council. Colonel Joseph Shippen, Jr., in command at Hunter's Mill, on this very day had some news of Fort Pitt, but it was not good. He wrote to Colonel James Burd, in command at Fort Augusta:

Since you were here, one Express from Fort Pitt & two from Bedford have passed by Harris', but as I had no Letter by them I cannot know what particulars they brought. Inclosed is a Copy of Capt. Ourray's [Ourry's] *Letter to Colo. Armstrong, which was sent open to me. The Express from Pittsburgh acquainted me that the*

Indians keep about the Fort, in the Woods, & have killed one man on Grant's Hill & that Eight Expresses have been sent from thence to Venango, four of whom were killed, two wounded & two returned. The late Mischiefs done near Bedford, I am told, have so alarmed the Frontier Inhabitants, as to occasion the whole of those settled on Juniata & in the Path Valley to remove to the interior parts of the Country.[6]

On June 23, David Hall dispatched to Benjamin Franklin a letter in the same tone. He reported "very bad Accounts . . . relating to the Indians," and declared that "there is not the least Reason to doubt that the Indians design us all the Mischief in their Power." As proof he cited John Armstrong's June 20 letter to Adam Hoops, Commissary of Provisions, part of which letter Hall had printed in the *Pennsylvania Gazette*. Armstrong had written to Hoops about an Indian whom he knows well, who is married to a white woman, and who had come into Shippensburg from Potomac with information about the Indian intentions: "That a great many Tribes are joined in the Affair; That they are to carry the War to as great an Extent as they can: That they are to attack the Inhabitants in the Season of the Harvest: That they design to burn and destroy all Kinds of Provisions; and are determined to make no Prisoners, but to kill all that fall into their Hands. This Account, the Colonel says he had from several People who had seen the Indian. He adds, that the People are leaving their Places fast, and that the Distress and Confusion the Country is in, is more easy to imagine than to express."

In this same letter, Hall reported distressing incidents, and informed Franklin that "At Shippensburgh they are in great Confusion, expecting to be attacked, where they have neither Arms nor Ammunition. In the Path Valley they expected the Indians every Moment. . . . Pittsburgh is certainly invested, and the Communication cut off, as there are no Accounts from thence since the Second of this Month."[7]

Path Valley and the Juniata had become almost totally deserted. While Hamilton and Bouquet "were attempting to persuade General Amherst to the gravity of the situation," even the region of Cumberland, except for the large towns, was following suit. Carlisle, insists one historian, presented such a grievous picture that words could not account for it. Yet he made a try:

> *The little town was filled with settlers who had fled in terror from their log cabins, the Scotch Highlanders of the famous "Black Watch," and the 77th Regiment, with the no less famous soldiers of the Royal Americans . . . were gathering about the historic Square in the evenings to listen to the wild tales which came from the dark, forest-covered mountains, from the far distant ridges where stood Fort Ligonier, guarded by their comrades in arms. Sometimes an "express" from Fort Bedford would ride into the town, throw his messages to one of the officers and then hasten on to Harris's Ferry, while the terror-stricken people of the crowded town would wait with wide-open eyes and ears to hear . . . the news . . . from beyond the mountains.*[8]

On July 3 of this summer such an express arrived in Carlisle. As the courier from Fort Bedford rode into town, he stopped to water his horse. He was promptly "surrounded by an anxious crowd, to whom he told a sad tale of woe, and as he hurriedly mounted his horse to ride to Colonel Bouquet's tent, he shouted, 'The Indians will soon be here.'"[9]

Here is historian George Donehoo on the Cumberland Valley of John Armstrong in July of 1763:

> *It is difficult for anyone who is familiar with the beautiful, fertile and populous Cumberland County of today [1926], with its sweeping corn and wheat fields, its far-flung orchards of apple and peach trees, its wealth of cattle and its chain of Prosperous towns, to picture what this valley was in July, 1763, when terror brooded over every home, and when panic-stricken men and women came trooping into Carlisle over all of the roads and trails from the mountains. One must read the hundreds of letters written in these frontier towns during that summer, in order to grasp the situation . . . .*[10]

More bad news reached the Governor on July 7. And it was very bad news for Fort Pitt. Colonel Bouquet from Carlisle was reporting the fall of the three forts north of Fort Pitt: "I am sorry to acquaint you that our Posts at Presque-Isle, Le Beuf, and Venango are cut off, and the Garrisons massacred by the Savages, except one Officer & Seven men, who have escaped from Le Beuf." [11]

Accounts of the massacre at Venango are all bloodcurdling, but vary in some details. In the popular version, printed in the William Johnson Papers, the Indians "put the garrison to death, except 2 officers whom they made prisoners and the Sentinel at the gate, who while they were murdering the garrison, got into one of the Indian canoes and made his escape down the River." In this version the two officers were killed in the woods by the Indians, who beat them and abused them unmercifully as they marched along.[12]

Bouquet's report continues: "Fort Pitt was briskly attacked on the 22nd [of June]; had only a few Men killed & wounded, & dispersed the Enemy. Fort Ligonier has likewise stood a vigorous attack, by means of some Men who reinforced that small Garrison from the Militia at Bedford. The Indians expect a strong Reinforcement to make new attempts on these two Posts." [13]

Governor Hamilton was moved to action. On July 11, from his office in Philadelphia, he issued orders to Colonel John Armstrong:

It having been agreed upon between me and the assembly, that Seven hundred men should be forthwith raised for the defence of the Frontier against the incursions of the Indians . . . I have thought it necessary that Companies should be rais'd in your County, each to consist of a Capt, Lieutenant & Ensign, two Serjeants, 2 Corporals & 43 Privates, to be immediately employed in protecting such part of your Frontier as may stand in need of it. And to the end that there may be some person of Prudence & Judgment near the spot & at hand to direct the Operations of the said Companies . . . I have . . . appointed you to the Command of the said Companies, & desire you will give all the Encouragement in your power for the speedy raising of them, and when raised that you will station them in such places, & in such numbers, and direct such Services to be performed as shall appear to you to be most to the general Benefit of the Inhabitants.

Armstrong is to be paid twenty shillings per day, and "if any of the people should be so unreasonable as to demand a Bounty for inlisting," you are to let them know that if they will not serve without a bounty they must take the consequence. They "can have nobody to blame but themselves in case any Misfortune befall them." The letter included pay instructions (eighteen pence a day for privates) and recruiting instructions, Armstrong to provide each officer a copy.

On the deployment of the troops the Governor had given thought: "As the Western Frontier is at present in the greatest danger of being attacked by the Enemy, I have thought it advisable to station four hundred of the Men to be raised on the West side of the Susquehanna for protecting the counties of Cumberland & York, and to each of the 3 of Lancaster, Berks and Northampton, I have appointed one hundred men to be reinforced from the others as occasion may from time to time require." He closed by stressing the urgency.[14]

With all of this alarming news one would expect the British response to be prompt and vigorous and in the form of a sufficient army. Not so. The arrogant General Jeffrey Amherst had nothing but contempt for the "savages," whom he regarded as the "vilest of beings that ever infested the earth."[15] He could not be moved to concern. To Bouquet, who had informed him of the great danger to Fort Pitt, he wrote: "The post of Fort Pitt, or any of the others commanded by officers can certainly never be in danger from such a wretched enemy."[16] American history, for this unfettered arrogance, and for many other reasons as well, has not accorded General Jeffrey Amherst a lofty place in its

Jeffrey Amherst

pages. But history is mistaken if it supposes that this contempt, which sees the Indians as animals merely, is peculiar to Amherst. Washington's epithet for the Indians was "wolves," and Franklin concurred in the popular frontier attitude that the Indians should be hunted down by dogs. Bouquet, who knew the Indians just about as well as any white man, was not above using Amherst's smallpox idea.

Now where is General John Armstrong in all of this? His attitude toward the Indians is close to that of Benjamin Franklin: outraged by atrocities but not determined, as some were, on the annihilation of the Indians as a people. Certainly he had more personal reason than Bouquet, or Amherst, or even Washington, to despise Indians. Yet his inclination to rage is mitigated by sorrow.

Very few of the frontier people had more to say about Indians than did John Armstrong, who in hundreds of letters reported atrocities of all kinds. Occasionally, he would employ the term "savages" for those who assaulted the settlements, and on at least one occasion he referred to them as "Barbarians"; yet his normal term for the Indians was "Enemy," a term that allowed at least a modicum of respect. Armstrong's was certainly not the Quaker position, but it was not the extreme position of Amherst either, nor even that of Washington. It is better to think of Armstrong as an Indian fighter, rather than an Indian hater. He lived the most of his life on the Pennsylvania frontier, a frontier whose soils and streams ran red; and it was natural for him to feel that the Indians should be punished for their barbarities. But he seemed to sense deep down that a great injustice was occurring here. As a surveyor he understood better than most the feeling of the Indians for the land, and he was quite conscious of "squatting" and of the acquisition of land without purchase. He was constantly dispossessing the settlers who had taken to the Indian land beyond North Mountain, and he regularly applauded the Penns' purchase of land from the Indians.

He had come to Pennsylvania at a time before the terrible clash of cultures. It was a time when a peaceful co-existence for whites and Indians seemed possible, with trade bringing the peoples together. But of course John Armstrong was not a philosopher. His considerations were confined by the practical. While supporting his church and the efforts of the missionaries, he did not himself search deeply into matters of human rights. He was a surveyor nudged by circumstance into the military. While embroiled in the frontier wars, he defended the frontier. He defended the Scotch-Irish settlers, who were his people. He built forts, and protected farmers with rangers. He resorted to aggression when it seemed necessary to protection. But, like Franklin, he allowed for "good" Indians, and he was hurt by reports of cruelty to the innocent and the helpless.

But back to Amherst, who had Fort Pitt to answer for. While scalping parties ravaged the settlements, an army of Indians had surrounded Fort Pitt and cut it off totally from the outside world. Of course the Indians had no artillery, but they had bravado and they had patience. They understood that the Fort could last only so long without provisioning. So they stationed themselves along the banks of the Monongahela and the banks of the Allegheny, and poured an unceasing rain of fire arrows and musket balls into the stockade. As the fort was very far from any point of relief, it was a grim situation.

Happily, the garrison had been bolstered by the few settlers of the region and by traders there at the time. Repairs had been made to the fortifications and some artillery could be brought into play. In command of the fort at this time was Captain Simeon Ecuyer, a very able officer. The fort was not about to surrender. Every single defender knew very well what would be his fate in that event.

As the reports of one outrage after another came pouring into Amherst, the General finally began to see the need for action. Even his disdain for the use of provincial troops had weakened. By the middle of the summer he was urging Governor Hamilton to raise an army to address "the Indian problem." Pennsylvania, despite continued Quaker reluctance, was ready. On July 4, the Assembly convened in Philadelphia. Two days of vigorous debate produced a resolution. The Province would raise 700 troops and provision them. Lt. Colonel John Armstrong, as noted above, was appointed to command them.[17]

But Amherst's satisfaction was much muted when he

learned (1) that the Assembly was thinking of these troops as militia only, men who would protect the farmers in the fields and the settlers in their homes, and (2) that they were not to march with the British Regulars against an organized enemy. They were volunteers and only limited funds would be forthcoming for pay or for provisions. Hamilton apologized to Amherst, but both the General and Bouquet, whom Amherst was ordering to lead the expedition to the relief of Fort Pitt, were made furious by the Pennsylvania Assembly. Amherst called the legislators timid and stubborn. Bouquet wondered about saving a people who would not save themselves. "I meet everywhere," he wrote to Amherst, "with the same backwardness, even among the most exposed of the inhabitants, which makes everything move on heavily and is disgusting to the last degree." [18]

Meanwhile the incursions continued. One particularly gruesome series of events occurred in the middle of July, while Bouquet was in Carlisle endeavoring to get his Fort Pitt expedition organized. One Shawnee raiding party ravaged the whole of the Juniata Valley, murdering four settlers at the home of William White, slaying two more, and seriously wounding four at the home of Robert Campbell on Tuscarora Creek, ambushing the militia force which had been dispatched in pursuit, and killing six. In the Sherman Valley, where so many atrocities regularly occurred, they tomahawked to death four more settlers. [19]

Finally, after a torrent of gloomy news, the General ordered two companies of the 42nd and 77th Regiments to join Bouquet, to march to the relief of Fort Pitt. And to his orders he added, "No prisoners." [20]

At the time of the orders Bouquet was in Philadelphia, and there had been not a word from Fort Pitt in a long, long time. Though orders had been delivered through channels to prepare provisions for the time when Bouquet might reach Carlisle, almost nothing had so far been done.

In Carlisle to make arrangements for the expedition, Bouquet was appalled by the number of refugees who had appeared from the land beyond the mountains, and was even more distressed by their reports of the atrocities committed by the raiding parties, some actually very close to Carlisle. Naturally apprehensive about the situation, he addressed a letter on July 13 to Governor Hamilton. It closed with "I march the Day after toMorrow to the Relief of Fort Pitt, & hope to draw the Attention of the Enemy upon me, & by that Means to be of more Service to this People." [21]

From his headquarters in Carlisle, the Colonel organized his army. But in Carlisle confusion reigned, as indeed it did throughout the whole of the Cumberland Valley. Carlisle teemed with refugees, a condition which stressed to Bouquet the urgency of his mission. And it did not slow him down much to learn (on July 3) that the British forts of Presque Isle, Venango and Le Boeuf, had not only fallen to the Indians, but had had their garrisons massacred. He was most impatient to get going. But two weeks were required to amass the provisions necessary for the expedition. One of the problems was that the refugees in Carlisle actually needed help, and expected help, from the stores of Bouquet. Another was that the wagoners, in the midst of fleeing settlers, were not eager to serve the mission. Indeed, so disgusted was Bouquet by the lack of support that he complained to Amherst, "I find myself utterly abandoned by the very people I have been ordered to protect." At length the mood of the people clearly began to change, but only when they came around, and the Colonel felt sufficiently provided—with wagons, drivers, packhorses, and oxen—did he feel ready to begin the march.

The Colonel was in command of the "shattered remainder" of two Scottish Regiments, the 42nd (known as "the Black Watch") and the 77th Highlanders, lately returned from the siege of Havana in the West Indies. These (347 in all) were fine and tested soldiers, but they were in a "dismal condition," many actually quite ill, so ill in fact that some had to be carried in the wagons. With some companies of the Royal Americans, and some Rangers, they numbered fewer than 500 soldiers in all. Bouquet sent ahead thirty men to help out at Ligonier, where Lieutenant Archibald Blane had so far held off the Indians.[22] Though his force was almost ridiculously small, when compared to the troops assembled by Braddock and by Forbes, at least the commander had five years of American wilderness experience to draw upon. He was a hardened Indian fighter.

On July18 (with Colonel John Armstrong's "May God be

with you") this little army marched resolutely down the streets of Carlisle, and "soon disappeared into the brooding shadows of the forests in the mountains beyond." [23] The march, especially in its early hours, would prove most distressing to the soldiers, as in Cumberland County they would be passing through deserted farmland; and on the roads would be giving way to "distressed families, flying their settlements, & destitute of all the necessaries of life." [24]

With no trail to cut, the soldiers were able in two days to reach Fort Bedford, where Captain Lewis Ourry was in command. There they found the region quite deserted. Settlers huddled in the fort. As the Indians had been harassing the fort and the Bedford region for months, all had tales of terror to recount, of brutal murders and scalpings. One tale was of an incident just three weeks ago, when a party of mowers in the field was attacked. Not only were three of the mowers murdered, but three of the soldiers Ourry sent out in pursuit of the Indians were slain. Ourry had earlier described to Bouquet a "hornets' nest of warriors buzzing around Fort Bedford" at this time.[25]

But, happily, here at Bedford, Bouquet was able to augment his little army by thirty experienced frontiersmen (in their butternut brown), many of whom had lost members of their families in the Indian raids.

The Colonel left one company of men here, to help out with Fort Lyttleton, which was not garrisoned. Two days of rest considered sufficient, the troops were on the move again. They set out for Fort Ligonier, which they knew to be threatened. Following the Forbes Road, which nobody knew better than Bouquet himself, the soldiers left Bedford on the 28th, Bouquet, confident that he is being tracked by Indians, positioning woodsmen scouts both front and rear.

The army reached Fort Ligonier at noon on August 2. Under the command of Lieutenant Archibald Blane, the fort had been under siege for a good two months, and had scarcely escaped annihilation on June 21, when the Indians practiced artfully their favorite stratagem of feigned retreat.[26] But these warriors who had been harassing the fort for so long promptly disappeared when Bouquet got close. Thus easily was the siege at Fort Ligonier lifted.

Here the Colonel, who learned of Fort Pitt nothing helpful from the Ligonier garrison, and more than ever determined to reach the Fort quickly, left his wagons, and his oxen.[27] He continued the march with some 340 packhorses loaded with flour, that he had transferred from barrels to sacks. Those who knew the mind of Bouquet even supposed that he could foresee a novel use for sacks of flour.

    The little army left Fort Ligonier on the morning of the 5th. Without resistance, but supposing they are watched, the soldiers marched ahead on the trail Bouquet remembered well. He had secured little information about the enemy while at Ligonier, as scouts either failed to return or returned ignorant. He had left the somewhat deteriorated Forbes Road in order to follow the more recently opened South Fork Road leading to the supply depot at Bushy Run. But he was now very wary of the defile at Turtle Creek, which he considered dangerous because of its great length and because it provided ideal ambush conditions, bordered as it was by very high, steep hills. But on August 5, even before he could reach that defile, trouble appeared, at just an hour beyond noon in the region of Bushy Run, precisely at Edge Hill (near present-day Jeannette).

    Here, like a clap of thunder, a horde of the most fierce warriors of the Ohio Valley (Delaware, Shawnee, Mingo, Wyandot, Mohikan, Miami, Ottawa, and Hurons) fell upon the English soldiers and Pennsylvania backwoodsmen. Nobody knows just how many Indians composed the war party. Long afterwards the Delawares claimed there were ninety-nine. Bouquet had the impression there were "400." Likely there were present most, if not all of the warriors who had laid siege to Fort Pitt, a big number. It is not known for certain, either, who of the many war-chiefs present was in command. It is likely that Shingas and the Beaver were there, and possibly Custaloga. It is thought by some that the leader was Kayahsotha, who was Pontiac's lieutenant for Pennsylvania, and who, it is fairly certain, was responsible for the great cunning and deceit and treachery which led to the massacre at Venango. Such was his reputation that he was given credit for a lot of raids, like the much later burning of Hannastown, for which he was not responsible. Kayahsotha was a Seneca,[28] come to the Ohio River country from the finger lakes of western New York. He was the uncle of the half-breed Cornplanter, who, though born in New York, would become the most celebrated of all Pennsylvania Indians. Both, ironically, would, twelve years down the road, be allied with the British against the rebel colonists.

The ferocity of the battle can hardly be accounted for in words. It raged through all of the afternoon and into the gathering darkness. Fortunately Bouquet's soldiers had enjoyed just enough time to throw up a kind of barricade of flour sacks atop a little rise, and from behind this protection were able to do enough damage to discourage the attack. But by nightfall Bouquet found himself in an almost impossible situation; and the fact that his troops were in desperate need of water made it all the more grave. To General Sir Jeffrey Amherst he penned a message by candlelight from his encampment, "26 Miles from Fort Pitt." In his account of the predicament he reported that "we were attacked from every side, & the savages exerted themselves with uncommon resolution." Noting that "we expect to begin at daybreak," he is quite dismal about the prospect for the morrow. "Whatever may be our lot I believe it to be my duty to transmit this information to your Excellency .... in case that, after a second fight, I shall find myself unable to protect and transport our provisions. By the loss today of men and horses I am much weakened...."

He closed his letter in praise for his men in the first day of fighting, for the "devoted service" of Major Campbell, and for "the courage and resolution of the soldiers, who have not fired a shot without orders," and who have been so effective with the bayonet.[29]

It was hardly light enough to see your neighbor when the Indians rose up out of the ravines on all sides, shrieking the war whoop and striking up a frenzy. Somehow, Colonel Bouquet, by means of a feigned retreat, "invited" the warriors into the midst of his troops in such a way that they found the tables turned and themselves surrounded. The Colonel had two companies "retreat" to deep within the surrounded circle, thus opening a gap, through which, naturally, the Indians poured. When the companies reappeared, now on the outer edge of the fighting area, the Indians were so shocked and confused that they fled pell-mell into the forest. What had seemed a rout of the English all of a sudden turned into such a scattering of the enemy that all they could do was withdraw.

What happened at the battle of Edge Hill has been called a miracle by almost every historian who attempts a description. And one declares it "one of the most historic battles ever fought on American soil." [30]

Bouquet collected and put into order his beleagured troops and marched off a distance of about a mile. Secure in his new encampment and very proud of his soldiers, the Colonel composed a report: "The behavior of the troops on this occasion, speaks for itself so strongly, that for me to attempt their eulogism would not detract from their merits."

The two days of fighting cost the forces of Bouquet fifty men killed (including three officers), sixty wounded and five missing. The Indians lost about the same number, including their war-chief Kittiuskung and his son Wolf.

Historians, while regarding the victory a "miracle," have nothing but great praise for Bouquet. Says one, "The battle of Bushy Run was the most brilliant and effective battle ever fought between the whites and Indians." [31]

The significance of the battle of Edge Hill, often referred to as Bushy Run, can hardly be exaggerated. It was the kind of defeat from which the Indian does not easily recover. And so it was. Colonel Bouquet marched forward from this place all the twenty-five miles to Fort Pitt without resistance. The little army arrived at the Fort on August 10. A very happy Captain Simeon Ecuyer (like Colonel Bouquet a native of Switzerland) and garrison provided an enthusiastic welcome. Fort Pitt had been under siege by the Indians from the 27th of May until the warriors departed August 1 to meet Bouquet at Edge Hill.

Bouquet and his soldiers learned a little of what had happened at the Fort while it was under siege. They learned of Ecuyer's great courage. The commander had weathered a number of skirmishes, and had lost some men, but he had been heard to say of the Indians, "I wish they would take a notion to make an assault, even should there be 5,000, for the more they have, the more we shall kill." [32] That great confidence may have been subdued a little just a few days later when Ecuyer learned from the Delaware Chief Kitchi that Forts Presque Isle, Venango, and Le Boeuf had been overrun and their garrisons massacred. Although he did not altogether trust Kitchi, this news was confirmed on June 26, when survivors of Le Boeuf appeared at the Fort, and hours later was reconfirmed when Privates David Smart and Benjamin Grey, the only soldiers to escape, reported the same for Presque Isle.[33]

Bouquet was not surprised to learn that even smallpox had been employed in defense of the Fort, Ecuyer presenting to Kitchi blankets which had covered the bodies of two soldiers just dead of the disease.[34] Bouquet himself in July had responded to Amherst's proposal "to send the smallpox" among the Indians by agreeing wholeheartedly, writing that he would "try to innoculate the bastards with some blankets that may fall in their hands, and take care not to get the disease myself." [35]

Bouquet and his men learned that just a few days ago the Delaware and Shawnee chiefs had requested a parlay and how, on being admitted to the fort, they had accused the English of provoking the war by refusing to leave the Indian country. When Ecuyer insisted that the Fort had been taken from the French and that he meant to defend it to the last drop of British blood, the chiefs left in a huff. Bouquet's soldiers heard how on the next afternoon the warriors, some 1500 of them, poured a deadly fire into the fort. Captain Ecuyer himself was pierced in the leg by an arrow. The assault continued in unabated fury for most of the afternoon, the Indians, protected by the banks as they were, coming very close to the stockade. Fortunately they were finally discouraged by muskets and cannon and by explosives lofted into the ditches in which they were concealed. The intensity, however, continued for four more days, until August 1, when the Indians abruptly moved off, to ambush, Ecuyer supposed, whatever relief was approaching from the east.[36]

But now this tedious and terrifying siege was lifted. Armstrong, at home in Carlisle, was among the many who heard the news with great joy. Addressing his letter to Bouquet at Fort Pitt, and as yet without all the details on the battle at Edge Hill, he promptly dispatched his most fervent congratulations. But he did so only while reminding the Colonel that the Lord was on his side:

I heartily embrace the first opportunity of congratulating you and the brave troops under your command on your safe and very reputable arrival at Fort Pitt; and as heartily join you in paying due Honor to the great author of all true Heroism, conduct and success, who has at once crowned you with merit and made you the happy instruments of so much peace and joy to a large part of our American world. These Barbarians don't in action stand so close together as the Philistines of old who fell by the hands of the Hebrew hero, however they may consist of as many different tribes. May the same Almighty hand fight against those modern Infidels and extend his Sons heritage from Sea to Sea and from Pole to Pole.

At the same time he informed Bouquet that an expedition, very like his own of a few years ago, has gone up the West Branch of the Susquehanna toward the Great Island to strike a blow at the marauding Indians. These men, a party of volunteers, are from the other side (the east) of the river, and number one to two hundred. He thinks the men "good," but fears they may miscarry. "Our people," he reports, "have discovered a few single Indians but have been quiet since you marched except the taking of one prisoner who made his escape about the time you left Bedford."

He reported, too, that the "Number of Inhabitants killed within this country and eastward of the Allegheny hills were Forty eight or forty nine, as far as I have been able to learn." And he says, "We may expect to receive a few visits." He also informs that the Governor "has wrote for the Indians that were in this jail in a very pressing manner whom I have been obliged to send off under the protection of the Soldiers, as the Sheriff could raise no guard for that purpose." [37]

It was a great victory, at a critical time and a grateful Province by an official act of the Assembly made Colonel Bouquet "an honorary citizen of Pennsylvania." [38] But peace was not achieved by Bushy Run and the rescue of Fort Pitt. Although the Indians had withdrawn from all of their villages along the upper Ohio, and required some time to lick their wounds, they were eventually regrouped at the Muskingum and at Tuscarawas and Scioto; and from here they continued to raid the frontier settlements. In the summer succeeding the relief of Fort Pitt,

Pontiac's war heated up in the east. From Carlisle, on the 5th and again on the 6th of June, 1764, Armstrong reported to the Governor in great distress:

> But yesterday I wrote y' Hon' of the sundry mischiefs very lately Committed in this County, and have this moment received a Letter from Cap' Murray, of the Royal Highlanders, that yesterday Morning thirteen persons are Kill'd and several Houses Burn'd to the ground about four Miles South of Fort Loudon. Cap' Murray has not mention'd the number of the Enemy, nor who the persons are who are Kill'd, he sent out a Party who are already returned; a sufficient number of the Inhabitants are attempting to make out the Tracks of the Enemy, and are yet in pursuit, but at this season of the year have but a small Chance of Success; the ground Hard, the Cover Close, and the Enemy may well Lodge without Fire, which otherwise would tend to discover them. The Indians now appear to bend their force ags' the Frontier, & by burning the Houses intend to lay as much of the Country waste as they can. The summer opens with a dismal aspect to us. I shall be oblig'd to bring the Troops entirely on this side of the Mountains, and for some time give up those Settlements on the other side, as we are not able to Cover one half of the people; and how this country will make a stand, or their Crops be Sav'd, is not easy to devise; they are running upon me from every Quarter for what they call help, that is for a few Men to every three or four Families living the most convenient. I hope there is Ammunition on ye Road; no doubt Cap' Murray has wrote to Coll. Bouquet.[39]

Just a few weeks later one of the most heinous crimes of the Indian reign of terror occurred not far south of Carlisle, some three miles north of present-day Greencastle. It was July 26 when a small party of warriors burst in upon schoolmaster Enoch Brown and his pupils. In the horrible slaughter which followed, the teacher and ten of his eleven pupils lay murdered.[40] Bouquet, who, now at Fort Loudoun organizing his Ohio expedition, had just heard that Colonel John Bradstreet, who had led a force of 1400 to reinforce Fort Detroit, had made peace with the Indians, was horrified by this news. To General Jeffrey Amherst he wrote: "Had Col. Bradstreet been so well informed as I am, of the horrid Perfidies of the Delawares and Shawnees, whose parties as late as the 22nd instant killed six men and have taken four prisoners on this frontier (not to recall the shocking and recent murder of the schoolmaster and children) he never could have compromised the honor of the nation by such disgraceful conditions." It was while he was in camp at Fort Loudoun that he decided to "take no notice" of Colonel Bradstreet's peace and to proceed to the Ohio to punish the Indians.[41]

General Thomas Gage, who had been with Braddock on the Monongahela (and had been wounded), had succeeded Jeffrey Amherst as Commander of the British Forces in North America. For this summer of 1764, to put an end to the unbridled murdering and plundering, he had designed and mounted two separate anti-Indian campaigns. One army was early dispatched to the Great Lakes region under the command of Colonel John Bradstreet; the other, under Colonel Bouquet, was to march south from Fort Pitt to deal with the Delaware, the Shawnee, the Mingo, and the Mohickan.

So Bouquet had more to do. After staying out the winter at Fort Pitt, he had begun in the spring, even before orders from Gage, to organize an expedition to reach into the heart of the Indian country (now the Muskingum region) to destroy villages and cornfields and whatever served to support the tribes. He was experiencing again great difficulty in raising troops and provisions from the provinces. No matter the settlers were being murdered in their homes, Pennsylvania and Virginia remained unwilling to support a campaign. Besides, even from the troops he already commanded, desertions (despite executions) were occurring with alarming frequency.

Finally, he was able to assemble a sufficient army. On May 30, 1764, the Pennsylvania Assembly voted to provide 300 men to serve as home guards, and 1000 to join Bouquet. To this force were added some veterans of Bushy Run and 200 Virginians. But these numbers could not be realized until August. Not until August 5 was the army assembled in Carlisle, but on the 9th Bouquet at the head of a column of nearly 1500 men, departed for the "Indian country." He would be marching once again across the province through the wilderness; but this time, of course, he would have no road to cut.

Armstrong, still in command of the home force, at just this time (August 15) appealed to Governor John Penn for a company, or at least "half a company," to be sent from the east side of the Susquehanna to the west. And he expressed the need for blankets, kettles, and flints, which "cannot come too soon." He needs physicians too, and notes that there is one "who lives here in Carlisle" (doubtless William Irvine, who had just this year settled in the community, and was Armstrong's neighbor).[42]

Meanwhile Bouquet's army, without incident, has reached Fort Loudoun. It is August 13. While at Loudoun Bouquet received express dispatches from Bradstreet reporting his success in making peace with the Shawnee and Delaware Indians. Bouquet continued unimpressed, and as those same tribes were continuing their "murders and depredations," he marched on—with Gage's approval, of course.

The march from there to Fort Pitt was also quite uneventful, except that desertions were occurring in staggering numbers. But, at Fort Pitt, at which they arrived September 17, the Virginia soldiers showed up, and Bouquet was back to his 1500 men. He marched from the fort and crossed the river on Wednesday, October 3. The army included two battalions of Pennsylvania volunteers. The First Battalion of Pennsylvanians marched on the left face of the column; the Second Battalion was in formation at the rear. The troops, marching in "profound silence," and "carrying everything," passed northwest through the region that is today Ambridge and Aliquippa, then west to just south of present Canton, and then southwest to present Coshocton.[43]

Without resistance, this force reached Muskingum in a week's time. Here Bouquet, near present Bolivar, Ohio, promptly arranged for a grand council, which brought his officers together with the chiefs. Most of these Indians at Muskingum were Senecas (Mingos), Delaware, and Shawnee. The head chief was Kayahsotha,, who may have been in command at Bushy Run. On the second day of the council a most exacting and inflexible Colonel Bouquet delivered his terms, in a twelve-day ultimatum. Here by force of will and no-nonsense treating he won from the Indians an unconditional "lasting" peace. Terms required the

Indians to surrender *all* captives, within twelve days; captives to be provided for and to have transport arranged to Fort Pitt; each tribe to send delegates to a conference called by Sir William Johnson.[44] It was a big moment in the history of Indian-White relations.

Upon his return from the Ohio Indian country, Bouquet was honored and feted everywhere, and was rewarded with the long overdue promotion to General.

With the conditions agreed to, peace seemed assured. Certainly many of the settlers thought so, and when the news reached the east they promptly began returning to their homes over the mountains. Armstrong, as one historian put it, had been a "tower of strength on the frontier during Pontiac's war,"[45] And surely the settlers in the west appreciated that.

But the Indians, after treaty sessions at Fort Pitt, complained bitterly about the settlement "west of the mountains," and delivered a steady stream of warnings to the administrations of Pennsylvania and Virginia. When settlers continued to ignore the King's Proclamation, the governors of these two provinces issued their own Proclamations. Pennsylvania's provided that those who settled west of the mountains, as well as those who refused to remove, "shall suffer Death without Benefit of Clergy." The Governor even appointed a Commission to visit the regions in which settlements were occurring, to post the Proclamation, and to insist settlers withdraw "at once." The members of the Commission, which included Reverend John Steel, did just that, and even filed reports (with names listed!).[46] The settlers remained. And the troubled frontier remained troubled.

But formal hostilities were at an end. The Pontiac Wars closed out in July of 1766, when Pontiac himself made peace with British Superintendent of Indian Affairs Sir William Johnson. Three years later the Ottawa Chief was treacherously assassinated by a Peoria warrior, a nephew of Chief Black Dog.

XIII

THE SUSQUEHANNA EXPEDITION

The Great Island is the largest of the many islands of the West Branch of the Susquehanna River. It was central to the Great Island Path, which the Indians followed along the north bank of the river from Shamokin to the Ohio. The Great Island is just a mile downriver from present-day Lock Haven and just a little upriver from present-day Jersey Shore and Avis. According to tradition, a settler named William Dunn purchased the island from the Indians "for a barrel of whiskey, a rifle and a hatchet."

Indians of many different tribes over the centuries have camped on the island, and from time to time have extended their camps into temporary settlements. A number of trails led to the island, from the Potomac River region in the south, from the Genesee and Finger Lakes region in the north, from the Delaware in the East, and from the Ohio in the west.

From the east, often from the forks of the Susquehanna, the

Canasorgu marker

Indians would cross over the hills and follow the trail through the ravine cut by the stream that today is called McElhattan Creek, which led to the river. A fording of the Susquehanna here put them on the Great Island. From the Great Island the Indians intent on the Ohio River could proceed by canoes upriver past the site of the old Lenni Lenape village at Canasorgu, and the junction with Bald Eagle Creek, on past the Delaware town of Chinklacamoose (present-day Clearfield) and west to Canoe Place, the source of the West Branch, at present-day Cherry Tree, and from thence overland. From Shamokin, by way of the Great Island is a distance of 230 miles to the Allegheny at Kittanning.

The Indians loved the region of the Great Island, and this reverence for the land was in great measure because the largest of the tributaries of the West Branch flows into the river right here. Known today as Pine Creek, it comes into the West Branch just downriver from the Great Island, between present Avis and Jersey Shore. Together the streams produce for the region a most beautiful valley, and a soil rich for corn and squash and fruit trees. It was the Iroquois chiefly who came from the north via Pine Creek. They had a name for the stream. To them it was "Tiadaghton" (River of Pines, or The Lost River, or The Bewildered River). It cuts in its early flowing a deep and entrancingly beautiful gorge, and runs clean and clear through the oak and the pine and hemlock forests, to the site of the famous Tiadaghton Elm,[1] on its west bank just before where at last it joins the larger stream.

For four centuries at least and possibly many more, the native Americans hunted and fished this region, and in the later years (the 17th and 18th centuries) established villages and entered into planting and community life. All of this is the testimony of the thousands of artifacts still to be found on the Great Island and at the mouth of Pine Creek and at Canasorgu and Castanea on Beech Creek just upriver from Great Island.[2]

Colonel Bouquet, on leaving Carlisle in mid-July of the fateful year of 1763 was right to express fears for the settlers in the region he was leaving. For indeed by late August and early September the Indian depredations had reached far into the east, into the plantations and clusters of homes near Shippensburg and Carlisle itself and York and Lancaster and north near Allentown and Bethlehem. In this spillover from the Pontiac War, it even seemed probable that Fort Augusta would be besieged. Bouquet's expressed hope that his march to the imperiled Fort Pitt would attract the Indians' interest and divert them from these raids was a vain one. In fact, the Indians who were assaulting the settlers in central-east Pennsylvania were very happy to see Bouquet pull out.

The source of the trouble seemed to be the Great Island. It was from this island and from Indian villages in the neighborhood that the Indian raiding parties set out, as in earlier days it had been Kittanning. Indeed, seven years earlier, in the autumn of 1756, William Clapham, in command at Fort Augusta at the time, and fearful of a siege by the French, ordered Captain John Hambright of Lancaster "To attack, burn, and destroy an Indian Town or Towns, with their Inhabitants, on the West Branch of Susquehanna, to which Monsieur Montour will direct you." [3] (Colonel Clapham had previously ordered out expeditions against an Indian town on the Juniata and against the Delaware town of Chinklacamoose.) This was the town on Great Island. When Hambright arrived with his troops on the island, he found it totally deserted. He returned to Augusta, "without finding any Enemy." [4]

These Indians, considered by Francis Parkman to be a "debauched rabble" from many tribes but mostly the Delaware,[5] were not the kind to treat with and, indeed, seemed to be under the command of no recognizable chief. Certainly there was no love lost between them and the Scotch-Irish refugees who had been driven into the settlements in the east. These refugees from beyond the mountains, given heart by Bouquet's march and determined on revenge, assembled 110 men and rode into the Muncy Valley, near the end of August. Near Muncy Hill they came upon a party of fifty warriors who were apparently intent on another raid. The settlers promptly attacked the Indians and succeeded in scattering them. On the next, day, however, when the fight was renewed it ended in a standoff. Casualties showed twelve Indians killed; the settlers lost four killed and four wounded.[6]

To put a stop to the Indian raids, to protect the settlements, Governor Hamilton, at the suggestion apparently of General Amherst, directed Colonel John Armstrong "to organize a battalion of frontiersmen for immediate service." He was hoping the Colonel could attack the Indians in their nest. In accord with the instructions, Armstrong, without difficulty, promptly raised a force of 300 volunteer frontiersmen, mostly from the regions of Bedford, Shippensburg, and Carlisle. By the last week of September, two months beyond the lifting of the siege at Fort Pitt, he had assembled a volunteer militia army. Composed chiefly of the best sharpshooting musketeers, the force was composed of the same kind of men and the same number of men Colonel Armstrong had taken to Kittanning. Armstrong's captains were the veteran riflemen Sharp, Bedford, Laughlin, Crawford, and William Patterson, Jr. Their object was simply the destruction of the Indian town on the Great Island, or, according to William Plumsted, in his letter to Bouquet, "to destroy every thing they meet with." [7] Armstrong was envisioning another Kittanning.

He ordered his captains to have their men at Fort Shirley on the Aughwick by the end of the month. Upon rendezvouz, with everybody on schedule, the army set out for the Great Island, seventy-five miles away. The Colonel rode at the head of the column, but, hopeful of the kind of surprise that was so important to success at Kittanning, had scouts out front from the beginning. Each musketeer or rifleman carried his own equipment (firing piece, flint pouch, canteen, and knapsack, perhaps a scalping knife or a tomahawk) and provisions for two weeks.

With the scouts reporting "no sign," the troops advanced steadily, reaching the ford to the Great Island on October 6. Here Armstrong did not enjoy quite the surprise he was hoping for. The Indians had had just sufficient warning to flee the coop, and had done so. There was to be no battle here. A disappointed Armstrong did what he could. He ordered the firing of the bark houses, the destruction of the cornfields, and the capture of the cattle and stolen horses. Leaving this work to the principal body of his troops, he then led a detachment of 150 men in pursuit of the fleeing Indians, who he felt could not be more than two or three days away. Indeed, Armstrong had information about a reportedly small village in the neighborhood to which the Great Island Indians may have retired. It was called Myonaghquia. The trail, which passed through a most difficult terrain, led his force some thirty miles to this town. Happily he did come upon this village in surprise. Informed by his scouts that the huts were teeming with Indians, the Colonel ordered an encirclement of the area. However, when ordered to assault the huts, the militiamen found, to their utter amazement, that once again the enemy had vacated. Indeed, such had been their haste that their meals were found hot upon their plates of bark.

Again Armstrong ordered a total destruction, and only after the huts had been leveled by fire did he withdraw and proceed to the return march. Upon reaching the Great Island, he proclaimed the end of the expedition, and set his sights on Fort Augusta. According to those at the fort who welcomed these troops on October 12, the men were received in a "wretched condition, fatigued, half famished, and quarreling among themselves." [8]

There exist no journal accounts of the expedition, but one of the frontiersmen serving on this mission was James Smith of Conococheague, who had been five years a prisoner of the Indians, and had returned home from Montreal to find his sweetheart married. He reported in his account of his captivity that "In the fall of 1763 I went on the Susquehannah campaign against the Indians, under the command of General [Colonel] Armstrong. In this route we burnt the Delaware and Monsey towns on the West Branch of the Susquehannah, and destroyed all their corn." [9]

It is difficult to assess the value of the mission. Certainly a battle, considering the quality of Armstrong's men, would have been more effectual in discouraging the Indian raids, for clearly the ignominious flight did not produce the desired effect. The settlers may have been given a greater sense of security but, as it turned out, it was mistaken. For still the raids did not cease.

The naturally vengeful Delaware responded with a great many assaults on settlements, especially in Northampton County,[10] destroying homes and killing eleven settlers. They moved into the beautiful Wyoming Valley, which was being contested by Connecticut and Pennsylvania settlers. At the settlement there the incensed Indians tortured and slaughtered ten (some reports say twenty) of the thirty-one settlers who remained, and took the rest captive.[11] A Pennsylvania force led by Major Asher Clayton,[12] sent to remove the Connecticut "squatters," found its job done, and were much sorrowed by the manner in which it happened.

For the expected trouble, the Cumberland Valley readied itself as best it could. And the trouble came. Colonel Armstrong reported to the Governor on November 21 from Carlisle: "On the 13th Inst. we have had at a place in this County called the Great Cove, five persons Kill'd & Six missing—whether taken prisoners or Kill'd is not known—two of the dead were soldiers; the enemy was follow'd by a party as far as Sideling Hill, where they had Killed a Childe not able to travel, which they had taken from the Cove." He also informs the Governor that all of the settlers on the north side of the mountain had fled to the more inhabited part of the then south side, leaving their crops stacked in the fields, and taking with them such articles as they could carry." [13]

The Indians were roaming far to the east in these days, coming very close to Carlisle itself, and Shippensburg. Early in November of this first year of the Pontiac wars, parties of warriors had been sighted just to the west of Carlisle, in the vicinity of North Mountain, Sherman's Valley, and Bedford. They were detected also in the region to the north near Allentown and Bethlehem. One report declared that the war party had "killed and scalped one Williamson, and his two youngest children, and carried the eldest, a girl, into captivity." It was reported also that this same band killed and scalped two farmers by the names of William Reed and David Glass.[14]

It was into all of this trouble that there appeared a new

governor for the province. Hamilton's term had run out on October 31, 1763. Succeeding him as "Lieutenant Governor" was the thirty-four-year-old John Penn,[15] grandson of William Penn and the eldest son of Richard Penn. Although he was well educated with four years at the university in Geneva, and had served as a member of Pennsylvania's Provincial Council, he was but little prepared for the awesome problems confronting his administration.

John Penn

There were countless matters crying out for the Governor's attention of course, but two were monsters. First was the problem of the Scotch-Irish frontiersman, who had developed a passionate hatred of Indians and felt that their families and property were receiving a most inadequate protection from the Province. Second was the powerful force, headed up by Benjamin Franklin and Joseph Galloway, working energetically for a dramatic change in the government, from proprietary to royal. He could not begin to appreciate the drama that would attend his office. And he could not know, at the time he accepted his duties, how very soon all would descend upon him.

In a series of letters Armstrong, who was always to get along very well with John Penn, apprised the new Governor of the situation he was getting into. In one of these, dated Carlisle, Nov. 12, 1763, the Colonel wrote to congratulate him and to welcome him to a terror-ridden Pennsylvania:

May it please your Honor, Congratulatory addresses, Laudible as they are, may justly become burthensome thro' their number or other attending circumstances, as well as carry in them an air of insincerity, especially at present when your introduction to the Government happens at a time of general disquiet amongst the Inhabitants thro' the cruel depredations of a Savage Enemy not easily Suppress'd. Permit me therefore, on the present occasion, only to assure Your Honor that I heartily wish the whole of your Administration may be such as will do Honor to the Proprietary Family, and much good to the people under your Government.[16]

Two days later, Armstrong wrote the Governor to advise him on recruiting practices, and to repeat his concern for ammunition: "... we are almost out of Ammunition, especially Lead, the Paroling partys being now serv'd only with Buck & Swan Shot; the Quantity given of late to Volunteers, our frequent heavy rains and dispers'd situation, proving of the Arms, &c., has wasted the Ammunition beyond my expectation.... With respect to Stationing the Troops this Winter—where, in what numbers together, & under what kind of Covers as mentioned in mine of the 4th Ins^t. I shou'd be glad to be soon favour'd with y^r Honor^s Instructions." [17]

One week later, complaining of some injustice he sensed, he is writing the Governor for permission to "transact some private business in Philadelphia." But before he can attend to that he has a letter from Colonel Bouquet, who is at Fort Pitt, and who now has responsibility for defending the Forbes Road and providing for the soldiers of the late Forbes campaign. It is addressed to Colonel John Armstrong and the Gentlemen of the communities of Cumberland County:

Having received orders from His Excellency the Commander in Chief to quarter the Troops for this Winter at the most convenient Places, for the support of this Communication, I have ordered three Companies of the Royal Highland Regiment to be Stationed at Carlisle, the service not permitting me to send them beyond the Susquehanna, where they could be of no use. I therefore require you Gentlemen to provide Quarters for these Three Companies &

their Officers in your Towns in the best manner that Circumstances will allow, that the brave Troops may recover of the Excessive fatigues they have undergone during the Campaign. I Shall think myself particularly obliged to you for any favour you will be pleased to shew them.[18]

But this accommodation was just one of the obligations that fell upon Colonel Armstrong at this time. On the 14th of December he shot off a very long letter to John Penn. After thanking the Governor for permission to absent himself from duties, he explained that he has no desire to do so now as he is needed for the "protection & encouragement of the Inhabitants." He declared that he will indeed observe the Governor's orders "with respect to ranging, &c." Noting that the Governor may not be acquainted with the duties of "this Department," he says that he'll mention only one, which turns out to be the protection of the harvesters.

He proceeds to stress the need for much improved accommodations for the ranging soldiers, repeats his need for ammunition and urges the Governor "to order up One hundred Blankets and Twenty five Kettles." He knows the Governor will be pleased about the recruiting, which, because of little success in York County has led his staff into Maryland and Virginia. "We have at present on an average about thirty Men a Company. After a few days I shall go along the Frontiers & fix the duty until your further Orders, but am at a loss whether the Company at Bedford shou'd be continu'd there or not. Three Companys of the Kings Troops are Order'd for Winter Quarters to this Town [Carlisle], & will be here in two or three days." [19]

As he attended to these duties, Colonel Armstrong could not have envisioned what lay ahead for Cumberland County and its magistrates. It was well that he could not.

XIV

The Conestoga Massacre

The first year of Pontiac's War meant incredible suffering for the Pennsylvania frontier. The trader George Croghan in a letter to the Board of Trade estimated the terrible toll. In speaking of the rampaging Indians, he wrote: "They can with great ease enter our colonies, and cut off our frontier settlements, and thereby lay waste a large tract of country, which indeed they have effected in the space of four months, in Virginia, Maryland, Pennsylvania, and the Jerseys, on whose frontiers they have killed and captivated not less than two thousand of his Majesty's subjects, and drove some thousands to beggary and the greatest distress, besides burning to the ground nine forts or blockhouses in the country, and killing a number of his Majesty's troops and traders." [1]

All along the Pennsylvania frontier, the plantations, with their harvest and their livestock, had been burned to the ground. The barbarities which the settlers suffered and were made witness to were unspeakable. The consequence was inevitable. Among the settlers who were now abandoning their plantations (many for the second time) and fleeing in great droves to the seemingly secure communities of the east, to Shippensburg and Carlisle and Lancaster, even to Philadelphia, great rage and an insatiable thirst for vengeance was plenty evident. And, as Francis Parkman quite rightly suggests, the settlers blamed the Quaker attitude toward the Indians. They even declared that they were being offered up as a sacrifice to the Quaker desire for peaceful co-existence, that they were given no protection, that Indian atrocities went unpunished. Perhaps no single event of the frontier wars so well dramatizes the attitude toward Indians that the Scotch-Irish were driven to as the murders carried out by the Paxton Boys.

One historian insists that not in the most fertile imagination can there be conceived "the perils with which the settlement of Paxton was surrounded." To portray each scene of horror would be impossible—the heart shrinks from the attempt." [2] But one of the leaders of the Paxton Boys, Captain Lazarus Stewart himself, expressed what it was the settlers had been experiencing during the Pontiac years:

Did we not brave the summer's heat and the winter's cold, and the savage tomahawk, while the Inhabitants of Philadelphia, Philadelphia county, Bucks, and Chester, "ate, drank, and were merry"? If a white man kill an Indian, it is a murder far exceeding any crime upon record; he must not be tried in the county where he lives, or where the offense was committed, but in Philadelphia, that he may be tried, convicted, sentenced and hung without delay, If an Indian kill a white man, it was the act of an ignorant Heathen, perhaps in liquor; alas, poor innocent! He is sent to the friendly Indians that he may be made a Christian.[3]

Because the Pennsylvania frontier Scotch-Irish were virtually unanimous in the opinion that "the only good Indian is a dead Indian," it was inevitable that the unthinkable would occur. And it all came to pass, naturally enough, where the two peoples were most closely associated. The tiny community of Scotch-Irish known as Paxton, just slightly east of the Harris Ferry had a grisly and tragic history to remember. In the year of the Braddock Expedition it had been wiped out by marauding Indians, who not only burned the buildings to the ground but barbarously murdered many of those living there. In the time since, the community had been restored, but an extreme hatred of Indians continued real among the citizens.[4]

South of Lancaster, and not far from the Susquehanna, though yet on the east side, lived a small number of Indians, perhaps as few as twenty. Their village was called the Manor of Conestoga. These Indians, though far from prosperous, had learned to live with and among the whites, and had been friendly and well behaved from the time of William Penn, who had treated with their fathers. They were all who remained from the tribe known as the Andastes, which had been virtually destroyed by the Iroquois members of the Five Nations.

The problem with the Conestoga Indians was that so many of the Indian atrocities were being traced to them. It was not so much that they were thought to be directly responsible; rather, settlers suspected that they were providing useful information to the marauding Delaware west of the Susquehanna. Scouts had many times returned intelligence that ravages on the frontier could be traced to Conestogue.

Both the Reverend John Elder and Colonel Timothy Green had urged Governor Hamilton to withdraw the Indians from Conestoga. John Harris wrote to Governor Penn, "I hope your Honor will be pleased to cause these Indians to be removed to some other place, as I don't like their company." And Penn responded: "The faith of this Government is pledged for their protection. I cannot remove them without adequate cause."[5]

Feelings had been running high for a long time. They exploded at mid-December, 1763, during the first winter of the Pontiac Wars. Accounts agree pretty well on the order of events, and most derive from the story told by the principal figure Matthew Smith.[6] On the 12th there came to the home of Smith in Paxton a frontiersman who had news to report. According to this man, one of the Indians who had been responsible for recent crimes in the vicinity of Paxton had been identified as one of the Conestoga Indians. Smith was quick to form a posse, and with these five men rode through the evening hours south past Lancaster to Conestoga. An assault upon the Indians was, however, aborted, when Smith, in the gathering darkness, got the impression that armed warriors were present in the cabins.

The men returned to Paxton that night, and throughout the

next day Smith and his lieutenants did some recruiting. They had little trouble rounding up a sizable force, as very little excuse was needed for venting their hatred. And of course not a great supply of courage was required for the murder of unarmed men and women and children. The posse, when finally assembled the next day, numbered some fifty men,[7] each with his own horse, and all well armed. Parkman, drawing upon Smith's own account, tells the story:

Led by Matthew Smith, they took the road to Conestoga, where they arrived a little before daybreak, on the morning of the fourteenth. As they drew near, they discerned the light of a fire in one of the cabins, gleaming across the snow. Leaving their horses in the forest, they separated into small parties, and advanced on several sides at once. Though they moved with some caution, the sound of their footsteps or their voices caught the ear of an Indian; and they saw him issue from one of the cabins, and walk forward in the direction of the noise. He came so near that one of the men fancied that he recognized him. "He is the one that killed my mother," he exclaimed with an oath; and, firing his rifle, brought the Indian down. With a general shout the furious ruffians burst into the cabins, and shot, stabbed and hacked to death all whom they found there. It happened that only six Indians were in the place; the rest, in accordance with their vagrant habits, being scattered about the neighborhood. Thus baulked of their complete vengeance, the murderers seized upon what little booty they could find, set the cabins on fire, and departed at dawn of day.[8]

Five of the six thus murdered were women and children. One was an old man, a chief, by name Shaheas, who, by all accounts, had always been very friendly with his white neighbors.[9]

The Reverend John Elder,[10] much respected by his Paxtonian parishioners, had pleaded with the vengeful mob not to go to Conestoga. When he heard of the murders (though still not knowing how many Indians had been killed), he wrote promptly to Governor John Penn. In the letter, which is dated December 16, he first explained how he had attempted mightily to persuade the posse to "drop the enterprise." And then he urged the Governor not to impute this action to the frontier settlements. "For I know not one person here of judgment or prudence," he wrote, "that has been any wise concerned in it: but it has been done by some hot-headed, ill-advised persons; and especially by such, I imagine, as suffered much in their relations, by the ravages committed in the late Indian war." [11]

The posse, on the way home that day, experienced encounters on the road. To a wayfarer named Thomas Wright they proudly reported the murders, insisting that they had done as the Scripture would have it, "an eye for an eye." In order to provide for their horses and to secure food for themselves they stopped at the house of Robert Barber, a prominent farmer of the region, who proved most accommodating. Barber, however, was much shaken when his boy reported that he had seen a bloody tomahawk "hanging from each man's saddle." Guessing the truth, Barber rounded up some neighbors, and with them hurried off to the Indian cabins. Horrified by the bodies which were but partially consumed by the flames, they began the burial of the Indians. At this point the Sheriff of Lancaster County, John Hay, came riding up. He was very quick to read the situation and to appreciate the need to get to the remaining Indians, if indeed there were any. These he found, terrified, and pleading for protection. There were fourteen of them. He had them promptly escorted to the nearby jail in Lancaster, which he felt could surely insure their safety, as it was a very strong, stone building.[12]

Governor John Penn, when he heard of the murders, promptly denounced the act and offered a reward for "discovery of the perpetrators." These notices had no effect whatsoever upon the Paxton Boys, as they were now known. With again the excuse that one of the surviving Indians was known to have been responsible for the slaying of one of their party, they regrouped, and although Matthew Smith was yet present, this time under the leadership of the thirty-year-old Lazarus Stewart, who had a reputation for fearlessness. Though it was thought, according to Francis Parkman, that Stewart was determined only to have that one accused Indian captured and placed in the jail at Carlisle, the truth, as Parkman notes, seems to be that most of the fifty men who were this time collected would be satisfied with nothing less than the slaughter of all the remaining Conestoga Indians.

Whatever the mood of the party, it set out from Paxton for Conestoga on December 27. They were accosted at once by Pastor John Elder, who had already pleaded with them not to do this horrible thing. Of course Elder, the popular minister of the Paxton Presbyterian Church, had himself organized, largely from the pulpit, a squadron of rangers which had built up a big reputation as the "terror of the red men." According to Elder's son, who later recounted the incident to Parkman, the minister, now in his 57th year, and a formidable presence, "drew up his horse across the narrow road in front, and charged them, on his authority as their pastor, to return." From his saddle the minister pleaded, "Pause, pause, before you proceed." After some interchange then about guilt and innocence, the Reverend Elder, in a burst of impatience, exclaimed, "As your pastor, I command you to relinquish your design." At this point, Matthew Smith rode forward, and, knowing how much Reverend Elder loved his horse, pointed his rifle at the animal and "threatened to fire" unless the pastor drew the horse aside.

It was three o'clock when the posse rode into Lancaster. Dismounting in the yard of the public house, the rioters sprinted to the jail, "burst open the door, and rushed tumultuously in." The massacre, and indeed it was that, has been described in his deposition by the keeper of the jail, Felix Donolly, and by Lazarus Stewart, for whom it had all got out of hand.[13] Parkman has the story:

The fourteen Indians were in a small yard adjacent to the building, surrounded by high stone walls. Hearing the shouts of the mob, and startled by the apparition of armed men in the doorway, two or three of them snatched up billets of wood in self defence. Whatever may have been the purpose of the Paxton men, this show of resistance banished every thought of forbearance; and the foremost, rushing forward, fired their rifles among the crowd of Indians. In a moment more, the yard was filled with ruffians, shouting, cursing, and firing upon the cowering wretches; holding the muzzles of their pieces, in some instances, so near their victims' heads that the brains were scattered by the explosion. The work was soon finished. *The bodies of men, women, and children, mangled with outrageous brutality, lay scattered about the yard; and the murderers were gone.*[14]

Great confusion characterized the aftermath. It was Christmas time, and the magistrates were attending the service at the time. When the service was interrupted by the frantic screams of a man come for the magistrates, chaos followed. Edward Shippen, chief magistrate of Lancaster County, later reported that "upwards of a hundred armed men from the Westward" were responsible. He also reported that Sheriff John Hay and the Coroner had done the best they could to stop the rioters; others insisted that the Sheriff and the Coroner "aided and abetted" the rioters. Captain Robertson (Robinson?), who commanded a company of Highland Rangers, on their way from Pittsburg and encamped near town, proclaimed himself ready to help if called upon; yet several citizens of Lancaster declared that when they asked Robertson to interpose his troops, he replied that his men had suffered so much from Indians already that he would do nothing to save them.[15]

One historian insists, "It is not possible to exculpate the magistrates of the town from the charge of criminal negligence." He notes that it was "in their power to have prevented the assassination, or to have arrested the perpetrators."[16]

The reaction was predictable. The Quakers were outraged. Governor Penn took the position his office required. When the news reached them, the people of the frontier communities, and towns like Carlisle and Shippensburg, which were swarming with refugees, while not perhaps applauding the act excused it as the understandable work of rash and vengeful men.

Penn was advised by the former secretary of the province, Richard Peters, and by the new secretary, Joseph Shippen, Jr., to write at once to Colonel Armstrong at Carlisle and to the Reverend Mr. Elder at Paxton. They insisted that the Governor strongly urge Armstrong and Elder, as the most influential persons of the turbulent region, to exercise all of their powers to (1) identify the perpetrators, and (2) suppress any suggestion of another such vengeful action. Penn had rewards posted for the arrest of the leaders, who of course were well enough known; and plans for the protection of the remaining friendly Indians in the neighborhood of Philadelphia were drawn up.[17]

Justice concentrated on Lazarus Stewart, whose real intent as leader of the mission can never be known for certain, though his responsibility is fixed. The Reverend John Elder hurried to his defense. Writing to Colonel James Burd, this man of the cloth whitewashes not only Stewart, but, amazingly, Matthew Smith and the rest of the murdering party:

Lazarus Stewart is still threatened by the Philadelphia party; he and his friends talk of leaving—if they do, the province will lose some of their truest friends, and that by the faults of others. Not their own; for if any cruelty was practiced on the Indians at Conestogue or at Lancaster it was not by his, or their hands. [!] *There is a great reason to believe that much injustice has been done to all concerned. In the contrariness of accounts, we must infer that much rests for support on the imagination or interest of the witness. The characters of Stewart and his friends were well established. Ruffians nor brutal they were not; humane, liberal and moral, nay religious.* [!] *It is evidently not the wish of the party to give Stewart a fair hearing. All he desires, is to be put on trial, at Lancaster, near the scenes of the horrible butcheries, committed by the Indians at Tulpehocken, &c., when he can have the testimony of the Scouts or Rangers, men whose services can never be sufficiently rewarded.*[18]

In a letter to the Governor, dated January 27, Elder blames the government for the tragedy: "The storm which had been so long gathering, has at length exploded. Had Government removed the Indians from Conestogue, which had frequently been urged, without success, this painful catastrophe might have been avoided. What could I do with men heated to madness? All that I could do was done; I expostulated; but life and reason were set at defiance. And yet the men in private life, are virtuous and respectable; not cruel, but mild and merciful."

"The time will arrive," he continues, "when each palliating circumstance will be calmly weighed. This deed magnified into the blackest of crimes, shall be considered as one of those youthful ebullitions of wrath caused by momentary excitement, to which human infirmity is subjected."[19]

Not long after this second massacre Benjamin Franklin penned a most impassioned account of the barbarity. It was published as *A Narrative of the Late Massacres, in Lancaster County*.[20] Horrified by what he has understood to have happened, he vigorously condemned the rioters, and with great feeling described the consummation of the deed: "When the poor wretches saw they had no protection nigh, nor could possibly escape, they divided into their little families, the children clinging to their parents; they fell on their knees, protested their innocence, declared their love to the English, and that, in their whole lives, they had never done them injury; and in this posture they all received the hatchet!"

Historians, notably Parkman, noting that the "only persons present were the jailer and the rioters themselves," regard this as "a pure embellishment of the fancy." According to the jailer and the murderers who cared to describe the scene "the Indians died with the stoicism which [those of] their race usually exhibit under such circumstances; and indeed, so sudden was the act that there was no time for enacting the scene described by Franklin." [21]

Yet, whatever the posture of the Indians at the time, that the murders were extremely brutal there can be no question. And at least two historians have the "miserable wretches" prostrating themselves and "protesting their innocence" and professing "their love to the English." [22] And William Henry, a distinguished citizen of Lancaster (just a lad at the time of the massacre) who is the most impartial witness that can be found, remembers the scene in a letter to a gentleman in Philadelphia:

> *There are few if any murders to be compared with the cruel murder committed on the Conestoga Indians, in the jail of Lancaster, in 1763, by the Paxton Boys, as they were then called. From fifteen to twenty Indians, as reports stated, were placed there for protection, a regiment of Highlanders were at that time quartered at the barracks in the town, and yet these murderers were permitted to break open the doors of the city jail, and commit the*

horrid deed. *The first notice I had of this affair was, that while at my father's store, near the court house, I saw a number of people running down street towards the jail, which enticed me and other lads to follow them. At about six or eight yards from the jail, we met from twenty-five to thirty men, well mounted on horses, and with rifles, tomahawks and scalping knives, equipped for murder. I ran into the prison yard, and there, what a horrid sight presented itself to my view! Near the back door of the prison lay an old Indian and his squaw, particularly well known and esteemed by the people of the town on account of his placid and friendly conduct. His name was Will Soc; across him and the squaw lay two children of about the age of three years, whose heads were split with the tomahawk, and their scalps taken off. Towards the middle of the jail yard, along the west side of the wall, lay a stout Indian, whom I particularly noticed to have been shot in his breast; his legs were chopped with the tomahawk, his hands cut off, and finally a rifle ball discharged in his mouth, so that his head was blown to atoms, and the brains were splashed against and yet hanging to the wall, for three or four feet around. This man's hands and feet had also been chopped off with a tomahawk. In this manner lay the whole of them, men, women, and children, spread about the prison yard; shot—scalped—hacked and cut to pieces.*[23]

  The Indians so savagely and brutally slain in the prison yard were fourteen in all: Captain John and his wife Betty, whose Indian names were *Ky-un-que-a-go-ah* and *Ko-wee-na-see*; their son *Quaa-a-chone*; Bill Soc (or Sauk), whose Indian name was *Ten-see-daa-qua*, and his wife Molly (*Ka-mi-an-guas*); John Smith (*Sa-qui-es-hat-tah*) and his wife Peggy (*Chee-na-wan*); a little boy known as Jacob (*Sha-ee-kah*); a little boy named *Ex-un-das*, and another lad known as Christley (*Ton-qu-as*), and another little boy called Little Peter (*Hy-ye-na-es*); and three little girls, one named Molly (*Ko-qua-e-un-quas*), one known only as *Ka-ren-do-u-ah*, and Peggy (*Ca-nu-ki-e-sung*).[24]

  Matthew Smith and his fellows boasted of the murders, and could do so with impunity, because the climate was one that looked upon dead Indians as "good" Indians. To note that nothing happened in the way of punishment to the perpetrators is to note the fact. It was eight years before Stewart was finally arrested on the charge of murdering the Conestoga Indians. As he was to be tried in Philadelphia, he expected to be condemned. He escaped from jail almost immediately, returned to the Wyoming Valley, from whence he had come, and was never punished for the murders.[25] Matthew Smith, far from being punished, one day became the vice president of the Commonwealth of Pennsylvania.

Meanwhile, authorities were remembering that the posse had been overheard at Lancaster to declare that they were going next to Province Island, just downriver from Philadelphia. It was to Province Island that the Moravian Indians, refugees from a succession of awful barbarities, at the hands of Indians as well as frontier people, had been brought. When the alarm was sounded, Philadelphia braced for the confrontation. The people of the city and the neighboring communities appeared in great numbers (estimates are in the "many hundreds") to support the regular troops. According to Henry Muhlenberg, "many of the Germans in the city held back because of their sympathies with the frontiersmen." But he had the impression that a great many prepared to help in the resistance; and even a meaningful number of Quakers took up arms.[26] And one historian has the city's defense composed of "six companies of foot, one of artillery, and two troops of horse." [27] And apparently hundreds of Philadelphians (including armed Quakers!) were ready to assist should they be needed.

On Sunday, February 5, by order of the Governor, carpenters began constructing a redoubt and "several small fortresses or ramparts; and cannon were stationed in effective positions of defense." It was that very night that the bells began ringing to announce "The Paxton Boys are coming!" Benjamin Franklin was startled but flattered to hear from the Governor, who was searching for a secure post. "He did me the Honour, on the Alarm," wrote Franklin later, "to run to my House at Midnight, with his Counsellors at his Heels, for Advice, and made it his Head Quarters for some time." [28]

And indeed the Paxton Boys were coming. The bridges over the Schuylkill had been removed in order to discourage any entrance to the City, but when it was learned that the ferry at

Swedes Ford, some fifteen miles upriver from Philadelphia, was still in place, the force, numbering some 250 (but declaring more were to follow)[29] succeeded in crossing the river there, and proceeded to march south through Chestnut Hill to Germantown. At Germantown, on Monday, the 6th of February, they were obliged to pause, as the Governor had dispatched a number of clergymen to persuade them out of their purpose. The Paxton men, under the command of Matthew Smith and James Gibson, were astonished to learn of the defense (including "three companies of Royal Americans") the City was putting up. They listened to the clergymen, then gave them a "declaration" of grievances, which the clergy then delivered to Governor Penn. Smith and Gibson did not yet abort their mission but agreed to wait at Germantown to hear the commission which was being sent on the next day by the Governor.

The delegates who addressed the Paxton men early Tuesday morning, February 7, were some of the most prominent figures in the government of the province. The meeting was held at Coleman's Tavern, near Germantown. Among the speakers were Benjamin Chew, at that time Attorney General, whose home was in Germantown; William Logan, of the Council; Benjamin Franklin and Joseph Galloway, the two most influential members of the Assembly; the Mayor of the City, Thomas Willing; and Daniel Roberdeau, a prosperous merchant and one-time Assemblyman. Representing the Paxton army were Matthew Smith and James Gibson, and, according to some sources, a man identified by no more than the name Brown. Was Colonel John Armstrong present? According to Muhlenberg, he was, and as "perhaps the chief agent of the frontier inhabitants," he rode out to meet the mob. Indeed, according to some accounts, Armstrong, who had been in Philadelphia at this time, was the mediator.[30]

The conference lasted for a good part of the day, the Paxton men insisting that they did not mean to kill the Indians, "but only to conduct them out of the province." They would even post a bond of 10,000 pounds. Of course, no one was taken in by this, and when assured by Franklin and the others that any further progress would be met by a very stout resistance (including three companies of the Royal Americans), and that much blood would be shed, the Paxton men agreed to disperse. But on one condition. They insisted on a formal hearing, and indicated they were prepared to leave with the Governor a "Remonstrance." The Governor's delegation promptly agreed to that arrangement.

Apparently a great deal of care was taken with the statement Smith and Gibson were preparing, for it was not until six days later that the paper was delivered to Governor John Penn and the Assembly. It is dated February 13. The Governor presented it to the Council the next day. It proceeded to the Assembly, to whom it was read on February 15. It is a formal statement of grievances. It is composed of nine articles, not all having to do with the Indian problem. It is entitled "Remonstrance of the Distressed and Bleeding Frontier Inhabitants of the Province," and is addressed to the Pennsylvania Assembly. As it defines the principal differences between the people of the outer settlements and the largely Quaker population of the east, it is an important document.

Article 1 appeals for equal rights with the citizens of the counties of Philadelphia, Chester, and Berks. Article 2 notes the injustice of trying a person charged with a crime in a county (Philadelphia) in which the accused does not live, and in which the "crime" was not committed.

Article 3 is the big one. Here Gibson and Smith, for the habitants of the frontier, protest the injustice they perceive in the tolerating of the Indian barbarities. "We cannot but observe with sorrow & indignation that some Persons in this Province are at pains to extenuate the barbarous Cruelties practised by these Savages on our murdered Brethren & Relatives, which are shocking to human Nature and must pierce every Heart but that of the hardened perpetrators or their Abettors . . . ."[31]

Article number nine (a grievance noting the absence of sufficient protection on the frontier) read simply "The garrison at Fort Augusta had given little assistance or protection to the nearby settlers." Smith and Gibson appended a note to this article, in which they said they intended no reflection on the commander at Fort Augusta, their friend [!] Colonel John Armstrong.[32]

The Governor requested a joint conference on the paper, and the Assembly appointed a committee of nine (including Franklin and Galloway) to review this "extraordinary Remonstrance," and advise the Governor. Meetings were held and proposals between the Governor and the Assembly were exchanged, but not a whole lot came of them; and after the committee's final report, September 20, the matter disappeared.[33]

The 140 Indians who were responsible for so much turmoil stayed on for sixteen months in the Barracks at Philadelphia, until March 20, 1765. By that time only 83 had survived the ravages of dysentery and smallpox. These were led away by the Moravian missionary David Zeisberger. After a most arduous march, which reduced their numbers even more, they came to their new home. Far to the north on the East (or North) Branch of the Susquehanna they established their village. Their Moravian friends gave it a hopeful name, Friedenshuetten (Tents of Peace).[34]

The Paxton Boys affair did a lot to dramatize the Indian problem. Not surprisingly, the frontier people "understood" and defended what the rioters were about. But the Quakers and the prominent members of the Proprietary party were very quick to condemn and eager to punish the "whole lot of them." Governor John Penn declared that there was absolutely nothing which could be put forward to "justify the madness of these people in flying in the face of government."[35] Franklin was particularly outraged, declaring that the frontiersmen showed themselves to be no more civilized than the savages themselves. And Justice William Allen, directing his remarks to the people of Cumberland County, said the same, noting that "as they were Christians they were worse than the Indians."[36]

Now where is Magistrate John Armstrong in all of this? Of course as his jurisdiction does not reach into Lancaster County, he is not immediately involved. But he does get involved, very much so. After he received from Governor Penn the Proclamation subsequent to the Conestoga murders, he wrote the Governor, using the term "Barbarities," to report dutiful attention to it:

Your Proclamation respecting the Barbarities committed on the Indians at Canastogo is yesterday come to hand, and set up in sundry parts of this Town [Carlisle], *such as have come directed to particular persons are also delivered—and as I am just setting out along the Frontier . . . shall carry Copys to make the Proclamation general thro' the County, & advise the Majestrates in these parts of your Letter to them on the same occasion, the Majestrates in the neighbourhood of this place shall be called together in order to form and issue the Warrants.*

He proceeded then to speak scornfully of those who have committed the heinous crimes at Conestoga and Lancaster. It is to be hoped that the Colonel, while he is not respectful of Indians generally, is honest and sincere in what he here writes to the Governor about the Smith and Stewart posses: "I have the pleasure to inform your Hon' that not one person of the County of Cumberland so far as I can learn, has either been consulted or concerned in that inhuman and scandalous piece of Butchery—and I should be very sorry that ever the people of this County should attempt avengeing their injuries on the heads of a few inoffensive superannuated Savages, whome nature had already devoted to the dust." [37]

Whether Armstrong gave much credence to the suspicion that the Conestoga Indians had alerted the Great Island Indians of his earlier mission against them is not known. He makes no suggestion of it. A number of historians see Armstrong as a hypocrite in the Paxton affair, noting that when he is corresponding with John Penn he condemns the lawlessness and the inhumanity of those responsible for the massacres, but that he takes quite a different view when conversing with his fellow frontiersmen.[38] But certainly in crisis moments he seems to be a quieting influence. During the confrontation at Germantown he was, according to reliable accounts, pretty much at one with Franklin and the other members of the Philadelphia delegation.[39] Although his language does not survive, Colonel Armstrong, celebrated frontiersman and magistrate of Cumberland County, proved in this bad moment an able go-between. Certainly he commanded the respect of the Paxton Boys. In whatever mediating he did for the two parties in the anxious confrontation he rendered a great service. It is frightful to imagine the consequence had this mission of vengeance proceeded into Philadelphia.

In the end, no one was punished for these ruthless murders. John Penn was learning an awful truth: that his Pennsylvania people who were settling ever westward were far, very far, from condemning any such act as what transpired with the Conestoga Indians. John Armstrong knew this very well, and, while far from condoning murders of the helpless and innocent, understood it. Possibly no other person had seen firsthand and had had reported to him so much misery as he. He was after all responsible for the frontier defense. He was the protector of his people, the Scotch-Irish pioneering folk. He was well acquainted with the uncontrollable rage that comes over the farmer who has come home from the fields to find his wife and children brutally hacked to pieces. For such a person, Armstrong understood, it was a rage mitigated not one whit by the great grief that consumed him.[40]

XV

THE BLACK BOYS

For Colonel John Armstrong, in his role as surveyor, road-builder, commander of militia, and magistrate, there was rarely a dull moment. Certainly it was difficult for him to attend the Presbyterian church services as much as he would have liked. It was one thing after another.

One episode that much concerned him and much involved him is remembered as the Black Boys Rebellion.

Although by 1765 the Pontiac wars were coming to an end, and conditions all along the frontier had become considerably less troubled, the Indian presence was still felt, and no farmer worked his fields and provided for his family without anxiety.

The great concern of the settlers was the position of the British with respect to the Indians. Despite the success of the expeditions led by Colonel Bouquet, it seemed to them that the King's soldiers were quite indifferent to the atrocities perpetrated by the Indians in what was called the back country. Moreover, they were outraged by the trading practices employed by the unscrupulous, greedy merchants and Indian traders (including George Croghan). Aware of the trading of guns and rum for pelts, strictly illegal of course, some of the more aggressive settlers resolved to do something about it. When it became known that the firm of Boynton, Wharton, and Morgan of Philadelphia was planning a shipment of goods to the Indians in the west, in the spring of the year 1765, they took action.

Learning that the wagon train would be proceeding toward Fort Pitt along the private roads south of Fort Loudoun, thirteen miles west of present Chambersburg, and that the goods would be transferred from wagons to pack horses at Henry Pollan's (Pallens, Pawlins, Pawling's) on the Conocoheague, near present Greencastle, the concerned farmers determined to stop it. Led by William Duffield, an armed party of some fifty frontiersmen accosted the train at the Pollan farm on March 1. All they were asking was that the goods be stored until they could be inspected. When the request was refused, Duffield backed off. But later, as the procession of pack horses entered the Great Cove (present-day McConnellsburg), the traders were stopped again; and this time the raiders were permitted to inspect the goods. On finding nothing to alarm them, the frontiersmen allowed the caravan to move forward.

It was at precisely this moment that the soon-to-be-famous Black Boys made their first appearance. Called "Black Boys" from this time on, because of their habit of blacking their faces for disguise and effect, they had been organized by and were under the leadership of "Captain" James ("Jimmy") Smith, the same James Smith who had been taken by the Indians in 1755 and only returned to the settlements and Conococheague after five years of captivity. As noted, he had served with Armstrong in his Susquehanna expedition and as a lieutenant with Bouquet during the Pontiac wars. Hearing in the region of the Cove well-founded rumors that traders were delivering arms and ammunition to the Indians, he had organized his own company of Indian fighters. Now he had his Black Boys in their first action.

Smith's party at this time was composed of ten to twenty men. It had been following the pack horses for several miles. At Sideling Hill Smith prepared an ambush. When the train appeared, he ordered a warning fire from his men posted behind the trees on either side of the trail. The traders who had before simply mocked Duffield, now submitted meekly. No one was injured, though a number of horses had been shot. The goods, which in fact did include tomahawks, lead, and scalping knives, were destroyed.

Responsible for the goods and horses since the caravan's leaving the Great Cove was a man by the name of Ralph Nailer. He rode immediately to Fort Loudoun, which was at that time garrisoned by the 42nd Highland Regiment (the Black Watch), which had served the Forbes expedition. In command at Fort Loudoun was Lieutenant Charles Grant. His response to the news of the attack was to dispatch twelve soldiers under Sergeant McGlashan to the scene to recover what they could. On the way the party captured two men of whom they were suspicious. But at Sideling Hill the soldiers suddenly found themselves surrounded by fifty amply armed frontiersmen. Although he had been ordered to release the two prisoners, McGlashan stubbornly refused, and when it became clear that he would not give up the prisoners without a fight, the Black Boys dispersed. This day was March 7.

Two days later there appeared at Fort Loudoun a formidable party of frontiersmen, perhaps as many as 300, heavily armed. Their leader was James Smith. Smith advised Lieutenant Grant that they were here to secure the release of the two prisoners captured earlier and the two more they knew to be taken later. He declared that if any effort were made to transfer the prisoners, say to the jail at Carlisle, the troops would be fired upon. Grant at first refused, but inasmuch as Smith was holding some of his own soldiers (two for every one of his), who had been taken outside the fort, he was forced to give in. But he did not return their weapons.

Although no shots were exchanged, the Black Boys were prepared to fire, and blood could have been spilled. The troubles at Fort Loudoun, like all of the agitation in Boston, with the response to the 1765 Stamp Act and the later Townshend Acts and the Boston Massacre, and the Boston tea parties, and the battle of Point Pleasant, Virginia (October 10, 1774), were signs of the considerable unrest that would climax at Lexington-Concord.

Armstrong "and a few Others of the proprietary Minions" were paid a visit by the Governor and his Attorney General; and three Presbyterian clergymen, together with the Sheriff, were dispatched to Conogocheague, presumably to apprehend the robbers, but all returned to Philadelphia without so much as issuing a Proclamation or offering a reward. The outcome was no surprise, the Cumberland County Grand Jury not finding a Bill of Indictment against any one of the bandits, though "plain and positive proofs" were presented.[1]

Writing to his nephew, on June 8, 1765, in answer to a letter of March 16, Thomas Penn advised the Governor that he thought the traders deserved their loss for so directly violating the Royal Proclamation and the provincial laws, but he directed the Governor to do what he could to bring the rioters to justice and to proceed against the sheriff if he did not "execute the legal warrants."[2] He was concerned about the failure of justice to appear. "In short, When We consider That almost every Man in the County, has presumed to express Himself most disrespectfully of a Kingly Government, It is not to be wondered at, If They should unite to save their relations, from the Halter. I call them relations, because you may be convinced, That most of the Grand Jurors, were Relatives to some of the Robbers."[3]

And from the papers of Benjamin Franklin came this lament: "As soon as the Court broke up, all was Jollity and Uproar and They returned huzzaing to the upper parts of the Country, rejoicing at their Victory Over Conscience and the Laws of their Country."[4]

The same kind of raid was being made on other trains of trading goods at this very time, and indeed it became abundantly clear that the illegal trade was not about to be tolerated by the settlers. Governor Penn was at first in close accord with the settlers and felt they were right to feel aggrieved, and, he understood too, that though of course they were overstepping the law in resorting to violence, they were yet calling attention to a very dangerous situation. On the 16th of March, he had written his uncle Thomas that "The whole affair is justly Chargeable to Messrs. John Boynton and Samuel Wharton, merchants in this town, and Mr. Croghan, agent for Indian Affairs in the Western Department under Mr. Johnston.[5] He noted, further, that the traders had not applied to him for the required license.

Most of the trouble was taking place in the neighborhood of Fort Loudoun. One of these episodes involved a trader by the name of Joseph Spears, whose horses while grazing just outside the fort on May 7 were driven off by a party of some thirty frontiersmen. When Lieutenant Grant ordered a company of Highlanders to pursue the offenders, shots were exchanged, the first shooting between settlers and the King's Men. Three days later, the fort found itself facing an angry party of "Black Boys," numbering perhaps 200. They demanded inspection of all goods stored within the fort. Grant indignantly refused.[6]

It was a little more than two weeks later that Grant found himself in big trouble. The Black Boys had never forgot that the lieutenant had refused to return the rifles of the captured men he was releasing. While the lieutenant was riding outside the fort he was captured by Smith and a small party of his men. They advised Grant that he would be riding south with them to the Carolinas unless he returned the rifles. It required Grant a whole night in the woods to recognize that the Black Boys meant business. Finally he agreed to return the guns as soon as he got back to the fort.

By June 6, Governor Penn had had enough. While insisting on the licensing, he had the Indian trade resumed and ordered an end to the raiding of shipments. In a letter to John Armstrong and his fellow magistrates of Cumberland County, June 27, he warned that he would if necessary call out the Royal forces to punish the raiders. Although the entire frontier community supported the Black Boys and their ilk, the raiding of the traders' trains abruptly ceased. But that is not the end of the story of the Black Boys.

By late summer Lieutenant Grant had *still* not returned the captured rifles as promised. Consequently the Black Boys made a third warlike appearance at Fort Loudoun. At the head of a company of at least 100 men, Smith once more demanded the return of the rifles. When Grant refused, Smith ordered his men to fire upon the stockade. Happily, because Grant had no ammunition, no battle here occurred. The lieutenant agreed to surrender to a justice of the peace the troublesome rifles, and on the very next day the Highlanders marched out of Fort Loudoun to take up quarters at Fort Bedford.[7]

Although Smith himself was not much involved in the episodes of this kind that occurred over the next three years, in the narrative that he penned of his adventurous time he reported the great distress that came over him when he learned that some of the men who had been involved in the raids upon the traders were now (summer of 1769) under guard at Fort Bedford. He had some misgivings about the conduct of the Black Boys since he had given up command, saying, "Though I did not altogether approve of the conduct of this new club of black boys, yet I concluded that they should not lie in irons in the guard-house." Accordingly, he collected "eighteen of my old black boys" and marched at night the public road from Juniata Crossing to Bedford. In the neighborhood of the fort he pretended to be camping for the night, but at "about eleven o'clock," he roused the men and at daylight surprised the sentinels at Bedford. Gaining entrance to the fort, through the help of a local named William Thompson, and with the advantage of surprise, they "captured" the fort. First compelling a blacksmith to remove the irons from the prisoners, they then withdrew with the freed men. On recollecting the incident, Smith remarked in his narrative that "This, I believe, was the first British fort in America that was taken by what they called American rebels." The date was September 12, 1769.

But even this episode did not provide an end to the story of the first captain of the Black Boys. Ten days later, while he was on a westward surveying mission, Smith and some companions were accosted on the road near Bedford by armed men on horseback, apparently a company out to get Smith for the outrage at Loudoun. In the ensuing confusion, one of Smith's fellow travelers, a stranger named John Johnston, was killed by a shot, but it was not known by whom. The armed men accused Smith, whose gun indeed had been fired; and Smith, while insisting it was not his gun that was responsible, was placed in irons in the Fort Bedford guardhouse. A jury that was promptly summoned found him "guilty of wilful murder." Fearing an attempt at rescue, the authorities at Bedford dispatched him secretly through the wilderness to the jail at Carlisle. The date was September 22, 1769.

At this point magistrate John Armstrong enters the story. Smith had not been in jail long before, not surprisingly, a mob appeared and threatened to tear down the jail if he were not immediately released. Colonel John Armstrong, together with the Reverend John Steel, and a number of the leading citizens of Carlisle, attempted earnestly to dissuade them from their purpose. During the animated discussions, the sheriff subtly increased the guard by which he meant to defend the jail. Smith in his narrative explains that as he knew his gun was not the one to fire the fatal shot and because he was certain that a jury would exonerate him, he did not desire to be rescued. He preferred to stand trial. He urged the sheriff to allow him to speak to the mob. And from his prison window he pleaded with the mob "to return home." At length, by appealing to them in the most solemn manner "to return, and to shed no innocent blood," he was able to persuade the would-be rescuers, by now numbering 300 (!) men, to retire in peace.

But justice did not move fast. Smith remained in prison for four long months. He was, however, finally exonerated, the jury persuaded to his guiltlessness by powder stains which made it clear that it could not possibly have been Smith's gun which killed Johnston.[8]

Thus ended the episode of the Black Boys.

XVI

The Frederick Stump Murders

One of the most dramatic moments in the long life of John Armstrong occurred not in a battle situation or during the march of an army, but at the jail in Carlisle. And it all begins on Great Island.

In the spring of 1767, some Indian families left their homes on Great Island to better themselves. They settled on Middle Creek, and built bark huts at a site some fifteen miles upstream from the mouth of the creek. These people, ten in all, for almost a year lived in close and happy association with the white settlers of the region, hunting, fishing, and planting small garden plots. They were well known to their neighbors. One (probably a half-breed) was called the White Mingo, and was also known by the name John Cook. The others went by the names of Cornelius, Jonas (or Jones), and John Campbell. There were, besides, three women, and three children.

Their brutal, senseless murder has to be regarded as one of the most awful of the many, many atrocities committed on the Pennsylvania frontier, by Indians and whites alike. Responsible for this massacre was a German by name Frederick Stump, by all accounts an ugly and repulsive man. Nothing that is known of Stump relieves the impression of a monster. A perennial squatter, he had been constantly in trouble. Two years before these murders he had been driven off the stolen Indian land in the region called Shamokin. John Penn, in fact, had a vivid recollection of that incident, and had at the time described Stump as "one of the greatest Villains in the Country." [1] He was well known for his contempt of Indians and his indifference to their rights.

On Sunday, January 10, 1768, six of these Indians visited at the house of their good friend William Blyth (or Blythe), whose home was downstream, at the mouth of Middle Creek, some fourteen miles from their own homes. Here they were received graciously, as always. From there they proceeded to the nearby home of Frederick Stump. What happened after that is well known, as we have Stump's own account, which can be trusted in its record of the event if not in the self-effacing reasons for the murders. On January 12, Blyth caught up with Stump at Gabriel's Mill, a watering place near the mouth of Penn's Creek. Here he had the story first-hand. He later confirmed it by dispatching four men to the burned cabins on Middle Creek.

A week later he was in Philadelphia to report the sordid affair to the Governor. According to the deposition sworn to by William Blyth in Philadelphia before Chief Justice William Allen on the 19th of January, this is what happened:

That hearing of the murder of some Indians by one Frederick Stump, a German, he [William Blyth] *went to the house of George Gabriel, where he understood Stump was, to enquire into the truth of the matter; that he there met with Stump and several others, on the 12th of the present month January; and was there informed by the said Stump himself, that on Sunday evening before, being the 10th of the month, six Indians, to wit, the White Mingo, an Indian named Cornelius, one other man named John Campbell, one other man named Jones, and two women came to his (Stump's) house, and being in drink, and disorderly, he endeavoured to persuade them to leave his house, which they were not inclined to do, and being fearful that they intended to do him some mischief, killed them all, and afterwards, in order to conceal them, dragged them down to a creek near his house, made a hole in the ice, and threw them in—And that the said Frederick Stump further informed this deponent, that fearing news of his killing the Indians might be carried to the other Indians, he went the next day to two cabbins about fourteen miles from thence up Middle Creek, where he found one woman, two girls and one child, which he killed in order to prevent their carrying intelligence of the death of the other Indians, killed as aforesaid, and afterwards put them into the cabbins and burnt them; that this deponent afterwards sent four men up the creek, to where the cabbins were, to know the truth of the matter, who upon their return, informed him that they had found the cabbins burnt, and discovered some remains of the limbs of some Indians who had been burned in them—And further saith not.*[2]

Assisting Stump in these murders was his apprentice, or servant, a German lad of about eighteen years of age, by name Eisenhauer, known everywhere as Ironcutter. It has been believed by some that Stump actually encouraged the drinking of rum so that he could do his bloody work the more easily. And it is possible, as well, that Stump himself was intoxicated.

One of the bodies was not recovered until six weeks after the murders. Governor John Penn was promptly informed by James Galbraith and Jonathan Hoge. In a letter dated East Pennsborough, Cumberland Co., Feb. 29, 1768, they wrote:

We take this opportunity to inform you that on the 27th inst., at Allen township, in the county of Cumberland, one James Thompson found an Indian man lying dead within the water mark of the river Susquehannah, who, without doubt, is one of the Indians Stump killed, and was brought down there by the water. As soon as we heard thereof, hearing at the same time that the Coroner was sick, we went down and held an inquest on the dead body. He was struck, as appeared to us, on his forehead, which broke his scull. There was also a large scalp taken off his head which took both of his ears. We held the inquest on the 28th inst., and interred him decently—cut small poles and made a pen about his grave. We have nothing material more to inform you of at present, but beg leave to subscribe ourselves Your obedient and humble servants.[3]

That the murders were brutal and carried out with great savagery is evidenced by the nature of the scalping which carried off both of the Indian's ears. There was evidence enough the murders were committed with an axe or tomahawk and without feeling and clearly without remorse, as Stump enjoyed boasting of them.

These senseless murders inspired a great excitement, not only in the Penn's Creek Valley, nor only in Cumberland County, nor only in Pennsylvania. News of the atrocity raced through all the colonies, and cries for the capture of the murderers rang throughout the settlements. What the effect upon the Indians would be the settlers feared to think.

A horrified Governor John Penn promptly ordered the magistrates of Cumberland County to give every assistance to the sheriff and "other officers of Justice" in executing the warrant issued by Chief Justice William Allen and to bring Stump to Philadelphia. The Governor was deeply moved. "I have this matter so much at heart," he said, "that I have determined to give a Reward of Two Hundred Pounds." He intended to add in the proclamation that he was promising to punish the murderers with death.

Although he did not immediately post a notice of the reward, for fear of alerting Stump to his danger, the governor did dispatch notices to those Indians living in the region and to the Indians being addressed by the missionaries, promising exacting and prompt punishment, and urging all to trust him and to keep the peace.[4] He reminded the Delaware Indians that "There are among you and us some Wild, Rash, hot-Headed People, who commit Actions of this sort. All that can be done is immediately to acquaint each other of them, and to bring the Offenders to Justice . . . . We are going to send off a Messenger immediately to the Relations of the deceased People, who, we hear, live near Chenasse [the Genesee, in western New York], to inform them and the Seneca Nation . . . and to bury their Bodies, and wipe their Tears from their Eyes, that it may not break the friendship . . . But that we may live together and love one another as we did before this melancholy Accident happened . . . ."[5] And Sir William Johnson, British Superintendent for Indian Affairs, met with the Iroquois and other tribes of the region, effectively keeping the situation cool.

But there occurred a prompt response. Taking the matter into his own hands, an outraged Captain William Patterson, who at the time was living on the Juniata, and who was extremely close to the Indians, organized a party of nineteen men, and, not without trouble, placed Stump and Ironcutter under arrest. On the 23rd he discharged the prisoners into the custody of Sheriff John Holmes at the Carlisle jail. To the Governor that same day, from Carlisle, he duly reported:

The 21st instant, I marched a party of nineteen men to George Gabriel's house, at Penn's creek mouth, and made prisoners of Frederick Stump and John Ironcutter, who were suspected to have murdered ten of our friend-Indians, near Fort Augusta; and I have this day [23rd] delivered them to Mr. Holmes at Carlisle jail. Myself and Party were exposed to great danger, by the desperate resistance made by Stump and his friends, who sided with him. The steps I have taken, I flatter myself, will not be disapproved of by the gentlemen in the government; my sole view being directed to the service of the frontiers, before I heard his Honor the governor's orders— [6]

Thus the arrest of Stump and Ironcutter was accomplished before the reward (which would have been in the amount of £200) got posted, and even before the Governor could issue orders to the sheriff.

Armstrong, who with Robert Miller had been appointed a magistrate or justice of the peace for Cumberland County in 1764,[7] on the day after Patterson delivered Stump and Ironcutter to Carlisle, prepared a message to Governor Penn, which, however, was not at once delivered. In it he explained how the victims should be interred, and reported: "We have not attempted any formal Examinations here, but the Fellows frankly acknowledge that they were the only perpetrators . . . Stump killing nine . . . and the Servant One." He noted, further, that Stump and Ironcutter had formed a story in which they allege that the Indians were drunk and disorderly, and seemed to threaten their very lives. "A story," Armstrong wrote, "which I take to be false." Some days later he completed the letter. He explained why it was the prisoners had not

been conducted to Philadelphia. He wrote that there was "an Alarm
... in the Minds of many, touching their Priviledges in this and in
any future case, which they alledge would be infringed [if] these
Men would not be remanded for Tryal in the County where the fact
was committed, but the whole process carried through at
Philadelphia." He promised the "Safety of the Prisoners here," and
declared his determination to see justice done.[8]

Naturally, Governor Penn was offended. And the
Governor's Assembly was insulted. United in outrage, that body
even proposed that this kind of defiance of the King's Writ justifies
the removal of the magistrates from office.[9] But none of this came
to Armstrong in time to avert disaster.

Patterson, who was keenly aware that the families and
friends of the murdered Indians, those who remained on Great
Island, would be much hurt, promptly addressed a letter to them. It
was carried to the Great Island by Gersham Hicks. Patterson
enclosed a copy of the letter in his letter to Governor Penn, writing,
"The message I have sent to the Indians I hope will not be deemed
assuming an authority of my own, as you are very sensible I am no
stranger to the Indians, and their customs." Addressing the Indians
on Great Island as "Brothers of the Six Nations, and other
inhabitants of the West Branch of the Susquehanna," he wrote
"with a heart swelled with grief." He reported that Frederick Stump
and John Ironcutter have "unadvisedly murdered ten of our friend-
Indians near Fort Augusta." He wanted his Indian friends to know
that the Province strongly disapproved of the deed, and "as proof
thereof, I have taken them prisoners, and will deliver them into the
custody of officers, that will keep them ironed in prison for trial."
He assured his Indian friends that the guilty "will be condemned,
and die for the offence."

Like the Governor and Johnson, Patterson appreciated how
easily the murders could lead to a blood bath: "Brothers, I being
truly sensible of the injury done you, I only add these few words,
with my heart's wish, that you may not rashly let go the fast hold of
our chain of friendship, for the ill conduct of one of our bad men.
Believe me, Brothers, we Englishmen continue the same love for
you that hath usually subsisted between our grand-fathers, and I
desire you to call at Fort Augusta, to trade with our people, for the

necessaries you stand in need of. I pledge you my word, that no white man here shall molest any of you, while you behave as friends. I shall not rest by night or day, until I receive your answer." [10]

Captain Patterson had his reply two weeks later. The very touching letter came from Shawana Ben, who was related to four of those murdered:

> *Loving Brother: I am glad to hear from you—I understand that you are very much grieved, and that the tears run from your eyes—With both my hands I now wipe away those tears: and, as I don't doubt but your heart is disturbed, I remove all the sorrow from it, and make it easy as it was before. I will now sit down and smoke my pipe. I have taken fast hold of the chain of friendship; and when I give it a pull, if I find my brothers, the English, have let it go, . . . it will then be time for me to let go too, and take care of my family—There are four of my relatives murdered by Stump; and all I desire is, that he may suffer for his wicked action; I shall then think that people have the same goodness in their hearts as formerly, and intend to keep it there. As it was the evil spirit who caused Stump to commit this bad action, I blame none of my brothers, the English, but him.*

He concluded with the hope that the settlers would sit still. They will know it, if trouble is coming, he said.[11]

When it was understood that Stump and Ironcutter were to be taken to Philadelphia to be "tried," a rescue party was formed, and, indeed, did effectively on Friday, January 29, accomplish the rescue of the prisoners. Colonel Armstrong, who for four years had been serving the County as magistrate, and had handled prisoners sent to him by Colonel Bouquet and others, was in the middle of all this. The matter is terribly confused, but when all depositions and accounts are taken together, Armstrong emerges both heroic and much at fault.

It is probably best to begin with Armstrong's own account of the freeing of the prisoners. To Governor John Penn, the most unhappy Colonel, immediately after the rescue, explained:

In this perturbation of mind, I cannot write; but in real distress, only inform your Honor, that we are deceived and disgraced at once; for about ten o'clock this morning, to the number of seventy or eighty men under arms surrounded our jail, when a number of them unknown to the magistrates, I must say, appear to have had too ready entrance into the dungeon, and in less than ten minutes time, they carried off Stump and his servant, in open triumph and violation of the law—The few magistrates that were present, Messrs. [Robert] *Miller and* [William] *Lyon and myself, have, I hope, obviously enough done our duty; but while we were engaged at the prison door, exerting ourselves both by force and argument, a party, utterly without our knowledge, was in the dungeon, of which we were not acquainted either by the jailer, or any other person, who, before we were aware of it, had the prisoners in the open street, when we were unable to make further oppositions, and they were gone in less than a second.*

He cites the jailer's report that a pistol was held at his breast, and then says he has been made to understand that the rioters' reasons for the rescue were (1) that they did not want the prisoners taken to Philadelphia for trial, and (2) that even though a number of white men have been killed since the "peace," no Indians have been brought to justice. He concludes with a request for instructions, and notes in a postscript that the bearer of the letter, the Lancaster County farmer James Cunningham, "is a prudent young man—knows the state of these things, and may be depended on in any questions your Honor, or the chief justice may think proper to ask." [12]

As it happened, a deposition was taken from Cunningham on Thursday next, February 4. Present were Governor John Penn, James Hamilton, William Logan, Judge Benjamin Chew, Richard Penn, and James Tilghman, Secretary of the Land Office. Cunningham's account, while consistent with Armstrong's, provides a few more details. According to his sworn deposition, on that Friday morning, at about ten o'clock, while having breakfast with Armstrong, he was astonished to perceive a company of armed men surrounding the Carlisle jail. As he and the Colonel recognized that these men meant to rescue Stump and Ironcutter, they rushed to the jail, determined to put a stop to such "a wicked and illegal design." When they got to the jail, according to Cunningham, Armstrong forced his way through "a number of armed men," and, together with Sheriff John Holmes, attempted to enter into the door of the jail, "but were several times pushed back and prevented."

Cunningham reported that Colonel Armstrong "used many arguments to persuade them to desist from their lawless undertaking, and told them, among other things, that they were about to do an act which would subject themselves and their country to misery." Cunningham saw a man take hold of the Colonel and drag him down the steps, saw Armstrong push the man back violently, and heard the Colonel, once he regained his place on the steps, declare that they "should take his life before they should rescue the prisoners."

The young farmer, who was side by side with Colonel Armstrong throughout, continues: " . . . while the said John Armstrong and Robert Miller, and Wm. Lyon, Esq., [all magistrates] and the Rev. J[ohn] Steel, who had joined the said Armstrong, were endeavoring to disperse the said company, several other armed men appeared [from] within . . . the said jail, to the very great surprise of every one, with the two prisoners above mentioned in their possession, whom they brought forward, and after pushing the said Armstrong, Miller, Lyon, Steel, Holmes, and this deponent, by violence and crowding from before the said jail door, carried them off with shouts of rejoicing, and immediately left the town."

Cunningham, not sure just how many men were in the company, supposes their number to be seventy or eighty.[13] Certainly, ever how many there were, all were armed with guns, and some with tomahawks as well. He recognized nobody! He remembered that the party, after leaving town, notified Reverend Steel that they were agreeable to a council, and suggested they come to the plantation of John Davis. Armstrong, Lyon, and Holmes promptly rode off, but told Cunningham upon their return that the company had apparently had a change of heart. In any case they had not waited for them.[14]

Cunningham repeated this account, under oath, for the

Governor and the Council, and Chief Justice William Allen. In the second version there occurs very little difference, but a great deal of amplification. The words spoken by Armstrong when he was pushed down the steps are here remembered more exactly: "Gentlemen, I am unarmed, and it is in your power to kill me, but I will die on the spot before you shall rescue the prisoners." In this account Stump is brought from the jail still handcuffed, Ironcutter not; and the rescuers call out to the mob which was now assembled, "Make way, here are the prisoners. We have them." Again Cunningham insists that he "had no personal Knowledge of any of the rescuers," but he does allow that in the confusion he heard names like James Morrow and John Morrow, Beard, Adams, Parker, Williams (or Williamson).

In his deposition he does remember that Armstrong, disappointed in the failure to consult with the rescuers at the Davis plantation, sent a messenger "with a few lines" after them to advise them of the danger they were in. He remembers, too, that after the rescue he overheard some young fellows talking about how the mob provided an escort for the prisoners and how they carried a blacksmith with them (a man named McGonegal) with "a pistol held to his breast." [15]

He told also how three citizens of Carlisle, Ephraim Blaine, Ralph Nailor, and Joseph Hunter, were able to follow the mob to the Ferguson plantation, at the foot of the North Mountain, some six or seven miles from Carlisle; and that on coming up with them were very nearly able to persuade them to return the prisoners, but because they could not promise that the prisoners would not be taken to Philadelphia, did not in the end have success.

Most significant was his report that on the day before the rescue an armed party had come to the edge of the town, and that John Davis and John McClure had come on into town from the mob, to inform the magistrates that if indeed it seemed the prisoners were headed for Philadelphia for trial, a rescue party would be coming to prevent it. When persuaded by the Sheriff that in Philadelphia Stump and Ironcutter were to be interrogated only, not put on trial, they seemed satisfied. When Davis and McClure returned to the company of armed men, some fired their muskets and all rode off. It may have been the end of it; certainly it was a warning. The magistrates, according to Cunningham, who insisted he heard this, advised the sheriff to place a guard and to take whatever measures were necessary to strengthen and secure the prison. He advised that he did not know that such measures were taken, and in his deposition he described how the jail was entered, first by two men, and by means of a girl accomplice (possibly the daughter of the jailer).

He recalled that when Stump and Ironcutter were first brought to Carlisle by Patterson, the jailer was most apprehensive, fearing that Stump's friends would oppose his being taken to Philadelphia. Indeed, the jailer had urged Cunningham to "use his influence with them to quiet their minds and discourage them from so rash an attempt." Once again Cunningham repeated his insistence that he did not know the members of the rescuing party, but said he was informed later that "the principal part of the rescuers were inhabitants of Schearman's Valley," which is twelve miles distant from Carlisle.

At this point in the deposition young Cunningham was asked if he knew just why it was that the sheriff did not immediately convey the prisoners to Philadelphia, as ordered by the writ of the Chief Justice. His answer is most interesting. What he said was that "Stump and his servant were brought into Carlisle late on Saturday night, when they were put into jail, and the next day the sheriff endeavored to procure a guard to set out with them on Monday morning for Philadelphia." Although Cunningham very much desired to go home to Lancaster, he was asked by the sheriff to secure arms and to join the escort party, which was ready to go as scheduled on that Monday morning. It was at just the moment the sheriff had removed the irons from the prisoners and as he was about to set off that magistrate Miller and Mr. John Pollock came by, on their way to Colonel Armstrong's. They insisted to the sheriff that it "would not be proper to set off with the prisoners that day." They gave as their reasons (1) bad weather, (2) the possibility that the Susquehanna, because of the ice flow, may be too dangerous for crossing, and would thus afford an opportunity for rescue of the prisoners. So a meeting was held at the home of Colonel Armstrong. Present were the sheriff, who had been sent for, and a number of townspeople, including magistrates Miller and

Lyon, attorneys William Sweeny and a Mr. Campbell, a Mr. Tea, and the aforementioned Mr. Pollock. A vigorous debate ensued. Sheriff John Holmes and Colonel Armstrong were for setting out that day, but Miller and Lyon objected (for the reasons named above) and Sweeny, with some others, thought it would be "illegal to remove the prisoners from the county." In the end, the sheriff did not set out.[16]

Following Cunningham's depositions, the Council suggested to the Governor, who they felt was not acting diligently enough in the prosecution of the affair, that he send Colonel Armstrong instructions for recovering the prisoners, and bringing the members of the rescue party to justice. The Governor of course had promised the Indians that the murderers would be punished, and he remained fearful that the murders could ignite an uprising. He was quick to write the letter. He suggested to Armstrong that he make it plain to the rescuers that Stump was not to be tried in Philadelphia. He advised that if they continued to refuse to turn the prisoners over, or if, indeed, they had already permitted their total escape, "you are to make every effort to retake the prisoners and to round up the rioters, many of whom you surely know." The whole thing, wrote the Governor, is a "most daring Insult upon the Laws of the Country." [17]

It can never be known, of course, whether the rescue of Stump would have been attempted had Sheriff Holmes set out for Philadelphia with him, but the fact is that he was freed by an unlicensed mob. And while there are many ironies to note, the letter of Sheriff John Holmes addressed to Governor John Penn on February 7 makes Colonel Armstrong the villain of the piece:

> *Please your Honor—Though I am very certain you will receive full intelligence of the affair of Frederick Stump before this can reach you; yet as my conduct and character are so much concerned, I pray your Honor to receive the following plain statement of the case, as all the vindication I can offer of my conduct. James Galbreath, Esq., brought to Carlisle, and delivered to me the chief justice's warrant on the 3d day of January. Immediately on the receipt thereof, I summoned a guard to attend me next day to go in quest of Stump; but that very evening, Captain*

Patterson brought him with his servant, and delivered them to me. Next day I summoned a guard to set off in obedience to the chief justice's warrant, having the same morning received a letter from the sheriff of Lancaster, who waited for me at John Harris'. Col. Armstrong sent for me, and told me they had concluded to keep Stump, and not send him down. I alleged to him, I was not obliged to obey any orders of any magistrate in Cumberland county, as I had the chief magistrate's warrant to the contrary. But he insisted I should not take him off, but discharge my guard, which I absolutely refused, whereupon the Col. went to jail and discharged my guard, brought up the prisoner, examined him and by mittimus [a writ for removing a suit or a record from one court to another] *committed him, and wrote to some other justices to attend in Carlisle on Wednesday. On Wednesday, while said justices were sitting in council, a large party under arms came very near Carlisle and sent in messengers to the magistrates and to me, claiming that they* [the prisoners] *should be well used, and not sent to Phila. Being satisfied that they were properly used, and having been told they were committed to our jail, they dispersed. The magistrate wrote a full account to the chief justice, and I made free to acquaint him that I was ready to execute his orders, if he thought proper to call for the prisoners, being persuaded that we should now meet with no further trouble from the country; but on the 29th January, another large body of armed men, thought to be mostly the former, joined with a party from Sherman's valley, on a sudden rushed into town, and marched up to the jail, having sent a few without arms, to appear before them, who went into the jail when the company came up, seized the prisoner, making the jailer and his family prisoners; we labored with the armed men to disperse, to offer no violence, not dreaming they had got into prison, when, unexpectedly, they brought out Stump and made off. Mr.* [Reverend John] *Steel, at my request, followed them to the creek, two miles from town, but labored in vain.*

That he has done all he could to honor the warrant of the Chief Justice he is determined to make clear. He reports in his letter that on Sunday he assembled a posse and that on Monday, together with "most of the principal inhabitants of Carlisle," set out for Sherman's Valley. But in vain did they search for Stump, and in vain did they ask that he be delivered up. He declares that he has in this letter provided "a plain and true account of the affair," and he very much hopes that he will not be thought in disobedience to the warrant of the Chief Justice. He declares also his intent to set out on the morrow again for Sherman's Valley, and "do what lies in my power to have the prisoners delivered up." He is, however, quite pessimistic: "I fear that infatuated people will pay very little regard to my endeavors." [18]

Vigorous (some say half-hearted) efforts were made through the rest of February to recover the prisoners and to punish those who accomplished or in any way abetted the rescue. The magistrates of Cumberland County, and Armstrong was one, issued warrants for the apprehension of those responsible for the rescue, but, though perhaps as many as twenty were identified, all had come to naught. On the last day of the month, distinguished citizens of Carlisle dispatched a letter to the Governor. It is a letter of interest, as Colonel Armstrong, and perhaps the sheriff as well, here takes a hit. The writers described their efforts to recover the prisoners, but were convinced that the "licentious people who rescued Stump would . . . never return to justice the perpetrators of the late murder on the Indians." Their position on the crime they made clear to the Governor: "With all wise and good men, we abhor the base insult on government, sensible of the direct tendency of such a crime, to the subversion of order, justice and propriety." They commend Captain Patterson for his "brave conduct" in the affair, but most interesting is this apology: "We are concerned your Honor's order and the chief justices warrant were not immediately complied with, which we conceived might have been done with safety before these licentious people had time to cabal and contrive their plan, this, we think, might have prevented such disagreeable consequences, nor can we conceive why it was not done. But your Honor no doubt has had reasons laid before you."

The letter is then signed by six citizens of Carlisle: Jonathan Hoge, James Galbreath, Andrew Calhoun, John Byers, John McKnight and Herms. Alricks.

To get to the bottom of this disgraceful and embarrassing affair a search for a scapegoat was unleashed. Obstruction of justice was the issue. As already noted, it cannot be known whether Stump would have been conveyed to Philadelphia without incident had the sheriff been permitted to go when he meant to, but the Chief Justice's order had not been honored, and mischief occurred. On the 26th of February Governor John Penn "invited" Colonel John Armstrong to make an appearance before the Board of the Provincial Council.[19] It is very probable that Armstrong was being asked to appear because of the February 7 explanatory letter sent by Sheriff John Holmes to the Governor.

Three weeks later the Governor notified the Board that both John Armstrong and John Holmes were in Philadelphia. When they did appear before the Council, each told his story. Because the accounts did not correspond, the Council decided to call also the magistrates Robert Miller and William Lyon, who had been closely involved. The hearing was scheduled for May 3, but because only two Council members could be present, it was rescheduled for Friday, the 6th of May. Together with Armstrong, the magistrates appeared on this day before the Governor and the members of the Council, William Logan, Benjamin Chew, Richard Penn, and James Tilghman. After the three were "severally examined with respect to their own Conduct in the Detention of Frederick Stump in the Gaol at Carlisle, as well as all that they knew in regard to his Rescue from the Hands of Justice," the Board shelved the matter for further consideration.[20] But within a week, on the 10th of May, the members met again with Armstrong, Miller and Lyon. Armstrong delivered to the Governor "A Narrative of the Case, relating to the Detention of Frederick Stump and John Ironcutter at Carlisle." This statement was publicly read, as, indeed, were the several depositions, and some other pertinent papers. The magistrates Miller and Lyon were then publicly examined. The session ended with the scheduling of a meeting for the 13th, to take the matter into "further consideration." [21] This meeting, which turned out to be the final session on the matter, actually occurred on Thursday, the 12th of May.

The Council had reached a conclusion. The Cumberland County magistrates Armstrong, Miller, and Lyon stood before the bench to hear the verdict read. The consequence was a reprimand, which included an admonition. Even the sheriff, who was not present, got a rap on the knuckles.

Here is the text that was prepared for Governor John Penn:

> *Col. Armstrong, Mr. Miller, and Mr. Lyon—Upon the rescue of Frederick Stump, and John Ironcutter, who had been arrested for the murder of ten Indians, I was informed that you, as magistrates of Cumberland county, had interposed to prevent their being brought to Philadelphia, in obedience to the Chief Justice's warrant, in the hands of the sheriff; and that in particular, Col. Armstrong, had himself discharged the sheriff's guard, after he [the sheriff] had refused to do it; and committed the prisoners to the county jail, which was in a great measure the occasion of the rescue, as it gave the persons who committed that bold and daring insult upon the laws of the Government, time to consult measures for the execution of it. The matter was of such consequence, and the reputation of the Government so much concerned in it, that I could not pass it by, without making an enquiry into it, and upon hearing you and the sheriff, and considering the several proofs, which both you and he have laid before me, I find, that on Monday the 25th day of January last, the sheriff was ready to set off with the prisoners from Carlisle, under a guard of eight or ten men, in order to bring them to Philadelphia, as the warrant required—that the people of Carlisle, thinking the rights and privileges of their county would be infringed, by the prisoners being brought to Philadelphia, grew uneasy under these apprehensions, and did apply to you, and press you to interpose in the affair, until they could have an opportunity of remonstrating upon the occasion, which was first warmly opposed by Col. Armstrong; but that at length, partly to quiet the minds of the people, and partly from an apprehension of danger of a rescue, in case the sheriff with the prisoners, should be detained on the banks of the Susquehanna, which was then hourly expected to break up, you were induced to cause the prisoners to be examined, and upon their examination, they were committed by Col. Armstrong and Mr. Miller to Carlisle jail; in order, that the Government, informed by express, which was determined to be sent on that occasion, should give further orders respecting them.*
>
> *Tho' the transaction has not been proved in the aggravated light in which it was represented to me, yet, it was undoubtedly*

officious and beside your duty to interpose at all in the affair, as it was unjustifiable in the sheriff to pay any regard to your interposition, and your conduct, upon the occasion, was in itself an obstruction of justice, and is not to be justified; however, it may in some measure be excused by the motives of it. But as I am satisfied from the evidence, that both you and the sheriff were far from having any intention either to favor the prisoners, or to offer the least contempt to the authority of the Chief Justice's warrant, and that you acted for the best, in a case of perplexity, not expecting, but rather intending to prevent the consequences which followed. I shall take no other notice of the matter, than to admonish you for the future, to be very careful, in confining yourselves with the bounds of your jurisdiction, and not to interfere again in matters which belong to superior authority.[22]

What John Armstrong and the others are hearing here is: "You did wrong. You impeded, in fact blocked, the course of justice. You should not have done what you did. But we understand why you did it, and we know that you thought you were doing what was right. Let it not happen again." Surely this was the right ruling in this complex affair.

The affairs of the Province, because of the Stump murders and other unpunished atrocities, were now "in the opinion of all good men . . . reduced to the most desperate Circumstances." The Provincial Government, the proprietorship, headed up at this time by Governor John Penn, was constantly under assault by the Assembly. Thomas Wharton, a prosperous merchant and rising statesman and politician,[23] saw in the Stump affair another instance of the "ineptitude of the government" and an opportunity to place a "Gentleman of Governor Franklin's Abilities and Spirit . . . at the Head of Government." Writing to Franklin on February 9, with the Indian-hating Scotch-Irish in mind, he said, "Indeed I have not Words to Convey fully to thee, the Prevalence of a Disposition in the Inhabitants of Cumberland County, to support All persons who kill Indians." [24]

Speaker of the Assembly, Joseph Galloway, had been agitating for a long time for royal government in Pennsylvania. He rarely missed a chance to embarrass the administration. In a very long letter enclosed in a packet of correspondence, dated March 10, to Benjamin Franklin, who at the time is in London, Galloway seized upon the Stump affair to renew his attack on the "inept" Proprietary Government. Genuinely incensed by the brutal murders and the absence of justice, he declared to Franklin, "The Consequence whereof in this Province is, We have the Name of a Government but no Safety or Protection under it. We have Laws without being executed, or even feared or respected. We have Offenders but no Punishment. We have a Majestracy but no Justice; And a Governor but no Government. And, you well know, we possess the Warmest Allegiance to our Sovereign and our Mother Country and yet our Persons and Estates are every hour liable to the Ravages of the Licentious and Lawless, without any hope of Defence against them."

Galloway, who is well informed, continued in unmitigated and very angry disgust: "You will perceive from the Messages &c. how many Murders have been committed within the Province without one Offender being brot to Justice. In Several of the Instances No more Notice has been taken of them, than if the unhappy Victims had been so many Dogs; not a Proclamation or a Warrant being issued on the Occasions. And in others the Government has acted as if they really concurred in Opinion with the Murderers, that the Indians being Hereticks, it was highly Meritorious and doing God Service to cut them off from the Face of the Earth." And for Galloway the Stump murders affair makes the whole situation plain.

It will be seen that he has no use for Armstrong and the Cumberland County magistrates. He even intimates that Armstrong may have facilitated the rescue! To Franklin he provides an account that is most unflattering to everybody involved, except Patterson of course:

In the last Murder at Middle Creek our Rulers Seem to have thrown off all Disguise. Stump tis true was apprehended, but by the Activity and Virtue of a private person [Patterson] *without any Warrant or Authority from it, by which his* [Patterson's] *Person and property is rendered very insecure and their Destruction have been repeatedly threatened. He delivered his Prisoners to the Sheriff of* the County who had the C. Justice's Warrant ordering him to bring them to Philadelphia. Armstrong and Miller two Inferiour Justices interpose their Authority and forbid him to Obey his Warrant. They discharge his Guard and commit the Offenders to the County Gaol. He is there Chain'd. But the Day before a Rescue was expected, the Justices having Notice of it, and not making the least preparation against it, his Chains are taken off, that it might be the more easily effected—the Rescue is made. The Government Truckles to the Lawless banditti, and, as good as promises to pass over the atrocious Offence, if they would deliver up the prisoners. They despised the Terms. The Murderers are Set at large, and are escaped to Parts unknown out of the Province. It is now near two Months since the rescue and not a Warrant is issued against the rescuers, tho all are well known to the Majestracy and Government, and might be easily apprehended.

The much distressed Galloway closed with a summary statement, "The Impunity with which Offenders escape is a perpetual Encouragment to the Licentious and Wicked to commit new Offences." He urges Franklin to acquaint his Majesty and Ministry with the state of the Province.[25]

Galloway's fellow Assemblymen on March 29 in a very long letter to Franklin included a similarly indignant paragraph on the Stump affair: "Thoul no doubt by this Opportunity receive the Chronicle, and therein thoul see a New Proclamation relative to Stump [This proclamation identified many of Stump's rescuers, but made no suggestion of apprehending or punishing them.], but it is observable that No manner of Notice is taken of his rescuers nor is there any probability of obtaining Him as there [is] no doubt of his being gone to the back parts of Carolina. Col. Armstrong is come down to Undergo an Examination relative to his Contravening the Kings Writ by which Stump obtained the opportunity of his rescue, its [sic] generally supposed that He will return More in favor than before."[26]

Although Penn posted a reward of £200 "current money of this Province," for Stump and £100 for Ironcutter, the two remained free to roam through Maryland, Virginia, and the region which would one day be Kentucky, Stump dying "at an advanced age."

But the movement for royal government picked up no momentum from the Stump murders and the lawlessness on the frontier. Indeed the Assembly throughout the spring of 1768 seemed steadily more responsive to the proposals of the Penn administration. It certainly was quick to honor the Governor's desire to appropriate public funds for the Indians hurt by the murders. Still, all parties were anxious about the peace. A conference seemed necessary, and arrangements were made to hold a session at Fort Pitt at some time in the spring. The Assembly appointed George Croghan to head up the conference, and the wily old trader, though fearing for his life, agreed to do it.

The conference was convened on April 26, with the Stump murders three months old, the murderers escaped, and the rescuers of the murderers as yet unpunished. The anxiety was subdued a little by Croghan's opening remarks. To the members of the many different tribes he spoke with the obvious sincerity of a "brother." He offered wampum: "With this string of Wampum I clear your Eyes, and wipe away your Tears that you may see and look on your Brethren the English with Pleasure." He then spoke promptly to the point of the conference. Reading a message from John Penn, who was unable to attend, he expressed the hope that the Middle Creek tragedy would not disturb the peace that the two peoples had come to. Some days later in the council, John Allen and Joseph Shippen, Jr., read from another letter from John Penn. The Governor said that he wished to take the Indians by the hand and "condole with you." He urged them to think of the Stump incident as the work of one despicable man, not an act condoned by the people of Pennsylvania. He offered gifts, and in his letter wrote, "I, with this String of Wampum, gather up the Bones of all our dead Friends, and bury them in the Earth that they may no more be seen."

As the conference entered its last week, the Indians while complaining about the "squatters" who were settling on Indian lands, "over the mountains," seemed appeased. Of the Middle Creek massacre, they assured Croghan and Penn's representatives that it would not threaten the peace. It was the work of a wicked man, they said, caused by the Evil Sprit working in him. They acknowledged, too, that many white settlers had been killed on the frontier. The chief who was speaking said of them: "I now gather the Bones of your deceased Friends, and bury them in the Ground, in the same Place with ours."[27] The conference adjourned amicably, on May 6, with the parties confident that peace and friendship were affirmed.

Frederick Stump and John Eisenhauer were never brought to justice. They were last seen "heading for Virginia." It is thought by some that indeed they lived out their lives in Virginia; others insist that they made their way south into the Carolinas. Those who abducted them from the Carlisle jail were never prosecuted. Although all were easily enough identified, and some were, indeed, very well known to Armstrong and the other magistrates, apparently the authorities sensed that the public sentiment actually approved of the rescue. It was easily perceived that it would be futile to bring charges against any member of the posse. So the Frederick Stump murders and what followed remain a black mark in the history of Pennsylvania. It is shameful that Stump and Ironcutter were never brought to the bars of justice. Even more shameful is the behavior of those Scotch-Irish settlers who, though suffering as they had at the hands of the Indians, could not only wink at the callous murder of innocent Indian men, women, and children but actually provide protection for the murderers. It is one of the most ugly events in the chronicle of the Quaker State, an incident not of war but of peace. It needs to be placed in the infamy that is the Paxtang massacre and the later-to-come Gnaddenhuetten massacre of the ninety innocent Moravian Indians.

Where the Indian woman, two girls, and a child were brutally murdered, where their cabins were burned to the ground, where their bones were discovered, a tiny stream innocently enters the creek at present-day Middleburg. To this day it goes by the name Stump's Run.

It was in this same summer that Armstrong got embroiled in a less serious but yet awkward situation. We'll call it the Wilkins affair. Fort Pitt was of course in constant need of provisions.

Armstrong, thought of as a kind of quartermaster for the military of Pennsylvania, was regularly making arrangements for transport. At the end of June he had a letter from British Lieutenant Colonel John Wilkins, then stationed in Lancaster. The letter, which was in the form of a formal request for nineteen wagons, drivers and teams, announced that the Colonel would be arriving shortly in Carlisle with seven companies. The letter was polite enough, but Armstrong, detecting no urgency, did not act promptly. When some 300 troops descended on him that weekend, he could supply for Colonel Wilkins only wood for their campfires and his own personal riding horse.

Worse, the Carlisle wagoners, fearing impressment and remembering tardy pay, were making themselves scarce. It was twenty-one days to Fort Pitt, they noted, and the harvest season is upon us. Armstrong was unable to convene the magistrates to secure an order, but, happily (according to Armstrong's July 5 report to Joseph Shippen, Jr.) the Lancaster wagoners "sought me out" and offered to provide transport as far as Loudoun (on the condition that Wilkins pledge to release them at that point). According to Armstrong, the arrangement was agreed to graciously, without "incivilities."

Wilkins apparently did not have that impression. In a letter to General Gage he complained bitterly: "At Carlisle Col° Armstrong amus'd me with fair Speeches till not a horse or Waggon cou'd be found . . . assur'd me that there was plenty of Carriages in Connakagigg [Conococheague], & that the Inhabitants (accustomed to carry for the Army) would be fond of being employed . . . ."[28]

He was most unhappy with the experience at Fort Loudoun, which required thirteen (!) days of him. He called his situation "wretched" and the country "inhospitable." He reported the theft of much of the provisions he was transporting, and he complained of "piratical" fees.

At some time after his much delayed arrival at Fort Pitt, Wilkins learned that "soon after Mr. Armstrong had preached me out of that Town with the Lancaster wagons, the Teams and Carriages of Carlisle came in and crowded the Town." And much later still, more complaint was registered, this by the Lancaster wagoners, who declared they had been "cheated" by the Colonel

[Wilkins], who compelled them to drive clear to Fort Pitt and who paid them hardly one-third of what was owed them.

The Wilkins affair has been declared one more "Unsavory incident . . . in which John Armstrong figured." [29]

XVII

THE SURVEYOR

What with the Braddock Expedition, and the Kittanning Expedition, and the Forbes Expedition, and the missions of Bouquet, and the Armstrong assault on the Great Island, and the incessant Indian raids upon the frontier settlements, one would expect that John Armstrong through the decade 1755-1765 would have little time to practice his profession, which was surveying. But in fact he was very busy. And indeed, besides the surveying he did, he was busy in the acquisition of property, the Land Office records for Cumberland County alone showing him as a warrantee in no fewer than seventeen transactions during the years 1754-1774. Of course the Colonel was rewarded by the Penns with a number of land concessions.[1] And of course naturally some felt that Colonel Armstrong was taking advantage of his position as Deputy Surveyor to acquire much of the choicest land. And indeed it may have been so. Many of his properties were in size 200 and 300 acres. His largest property was a tract of 1015 acres in the Kishacoquillas Valley, Cumberland County (now near present Belleville in Mifflin County), awarded to him on March 6, 1764, for his surveying work.

But he and Rebeckah had made Carlisle their home in June

of 1750, and it was in Carlisle that they would live out their lives. From tax lists it is known that the John Armstrongs "owned" in the borough in 1769 two lots, two horses, three cows, and two Negroes.

He had plotted the lay-out of the town of Carlisle in 1751, and from time to time after that he was occupied in the surveying of parcels and in the assignment of properties. A "ticket" typical of those issued by Armstrong at this time is this one: "Issued and signed by John Armstrong for Lot # 286 in the borough of Carlisle, July 20, 1759. 60 ft. front & 240 ft. deep, granted to David Ruysel on condition that he build thereon a house of at least twenty five feet square, etc." [2]

For nine years he served as a deputy surveyor under Nicholas Scull, II,[3] of the famous Scull dynasty of surveyors, and some idea of his problems may be learned from a long letter he wrote to Scull on June 17, 1761, when Scull was in the last year of his life. At this time Armstrong's wife, Rebeckah, is just emerging from a long and very serious illness, and the Colonel himself is ailing. Armstrong in this communication is attempting to clarify the dispute that had arisen between George Sanderson and Samuel Fisher over land in Sherman's Valley. Having done that, he notes that *most* of his time is spent in this way, working out differences that arise:

> *You may naturally blame me for not settling this dispute myself, which, by the by, I always do, where disputes are known before hand, and am persuaded that at home and abroad near eight-tenths of my time is spent in hearing, persuading a settleing of them; and if you'l please to recollect, I don't remember that their complaints have gone down respecting any injustice in my surveys these nine years past. . . . I beg you will lay this letter before Mr Wm Peters previous to any decision of the debate, to whom I also intended writing, but am at present utterly unable, having strong symptoms of some approaching Illness . . . .*[4]

He had been able to do some surveying through the war years, and was able to get back more fully to his chosen work in 1762, when he was reappointed Deputy-Surveyor for Cumberland County. Having opened an office in Carlisle, he had his instructions from Thomas Penn and Richard Penn, the "true & absolute Proprietaries and governors of the province of Pennsylvania and Counties of Newcastle, Kent & Sussex upon the Delaware." The appointment letter opens with the customary greetings, and then proceeds, "Whereas in pursuance of a commission under the hand of James Hamilton, Esquire, Lieutenant Governor of our said province bearing date the Twenty-Second day of April 1762, Our Surveyor General [John Lukens] with our Approbation hath by a Commission bearing even date herewith deputed you the said John Armstrong to be Surveyor of the County of Cumberland."

The letter continues with a parade of instructions and cautions, for "thy better Guidance and direction in the Execution of the said Commission." The first instruction that the Penns thought proper to enjoin was this: "You shall faithfully execute every such Warrant as shall be directed to you to the best of your Skill Knowledge and Understanding according to the Express words and order of such warrants & no[t] otherwise without special Leave first had from us for thy so doing."

The second: "You shall not Execute any Warrant upon any Surveyd Land Manor or Reputed Manor Lands or any other such Lands appropriated to our Use by any former Survey Unless such Lands be Expressly mentioned in thy Warrant."

Not surprisingly, there had occurred over the past decade a great deal of confusion in the deeded properties. The Penns, naturally, were hoping to reduce the amount of confusion, and certainly hoped to put an end to "squatting."

Very specific instructions follow. Number three: "You shall lay out all Lands as Regular and nearly Contiguous as the Places will bear or allow of unless Directed by Your warrant to the contrary." Number four: "You shall make Returns of Every warrant into the Surveyor Generals office [on Second Street] at Philadelphia with a protracted figure of the Land exactly performed and the field works annexed and that within six months after the receipt of such Warrants or Order of Survey but if any thing should happen that the Survey cannot be performed within that time you shall transmit an account in writing into the Surveyor General's office containing the Reasons of such Delay if Demanded." And in the fifth place, "You shall deliver unto no Person any Draught Plot figure or Field work of his Land before your return be made into the Surveyor General's Office and be there allowed of."

The Penns are not through: "You shall not make any use of any Chain Carriers but such as are of Known Honesty and of good fame or Repute among the neighbours which Chain Carriers shall take a solemn attestation before some Magistrate justly and exactly to execute their trust without favor Partiality or Affection." The seventh instruction would hardly seem to be necessary: "You shall not make returns of any survey but what hath been actually made by you on the Spot and you shall take care that all outlines & Bounds be fairly and Visibly markd before you quit the field." But the eighth had to be clearly expressed: "Out of all the fees you Receive for Surveying or Re-surveying of Lands or Lotts during the force of your Commission you shall Pay unto our Surveyor General the full third part thereof for the due performance of which Instructions you shall give Bond to us with Security in the sum of Two hundred Pounds & sign a Counterpart of these Presents by Indenture."[5]

The bond was made promptly by Armstrong, co-signed, sealed, and delivered by his partner William Henry:

Know all Men by these Presents that we John Armstrong of the County of Cumberland Surveyor and William Henry of the City of Philada. Merchant: are held and firmly bound unto the Honorable Thomas Penn and Richard Penn Esquires, Proprietaries and Governors of the Province of Pennsylvania and Counties of Newcastle, Kent and Sussex, upon Delaware in the sum of Two hundred pounds lawfull money of Pennsylvania to be paid to the said Proprietaries or to their certain attornies Executors, Administrators, or Assigns, to which Payment well and truly to be made. We bind ourselves, our Heirs, executors, and Administrators firmly by these Presents Sealed with our Seals dated the 22: day of April in the Second year of the Reign of his Majesty King George the Third Anno: Domini 1762.[6]

From a time somewhat before the date of this appointment, April 22, 1762, until September 30, 1782, Armstrong was active as a surveyor in Cumberland County. For the year 1762 Armstrong was chiefly on assignment for the Penn family, performing twenty-eight surveys of 6511 acres.[7]

One of his first assignments, as directed by the Proprietaries, was to re-survey the borough of Carlisle. Although many of his records were lost in the fire which in 1763 destroyed his Carlisle office, many of his business papers survive.[8] These include many long lists of returns sent in to the Surveyor General's Office in Philadelphia. One such list (no date) sent to John Lukens shows 304 names, alphabetically listed. The lots here defined range in size from 215 acres (to James Armstrong) to 623 acres (to Benjamin Chambers).

For the period January, 1762, through March 5, 1764, John Armstrong's Returns to the Surveyor General's Office show eighty-one names. For April 14, 1763, is listed a warrant to William Lyon for 209 acres, 142 perches; and accepted on August 31, 1763, are two warrants to John Armstrong, one for 449 acres and another for 405 acres, ninety-five perches.[9]

The business papers include a number of interesting notations. For October 1, 1762, for example, it is reported that Richard Tea of Philadelphia sells a tract of land (251 acres) on "the Northside of Juniata River about a Mile above the falls, known by the name of the Island Tract," in Cumberland County to George Armstrong, John's brother.[10] Earlier that year, on September 7, a James Potter complained to William Peters at the Land Office in Philadelphia that there is "a jugle in the deeds and surveys." He lamented the apparent loss of records which show him to be the owner of two plots of land, one of 253 acres and one of 114 acres. When notified of the trouble, Armstrong replied to Peters that he remembers nothing of it, and certainly had not been aware that there was confusion.[11]

Armstrong was not always on the best of terms with Surveyor-General John Lukens,[12] partly because he seemed always to owe the Office money, but in the early going the two apparently got along all right. On February 4, 1762, Armstrong wrote to Lukens to congratulate the Surveyor General on his appointment and to discuss the handling of surveying reports. On June 10, the day he opened his office, the Colonel wrote a special letter to Lukens to describe the conditions of his office and to express the pledge that lists of warrants will be sent to the Land Office in Philadelphia just as instructed.[13]

But by the succeeding January Lukens had become much disturbed by complaints his office had been receiving, complaints of "irregularities" in the Cumberland County Surveys. He wrote to inform Armstrong and to express his concern. For the remainder of the year he was constantly urging Armstrong to make good on his debt to the Land Office. On February 12, and again on October 3 (and surely at other times) he insisted that the surveyor come through with the fifty pounds that was due. Armstrong during all of this time felt that he was showing good faith by making partial payment along the way with loads of wood and wheat, delivered by his Negro servant Caesar (Ceazar).[14]

Some six years (!) later, on March 27, 1769, when everything seemed to be going well enough in the filing of reports and in the payment of fees, Armstrong wrote to congratulate Lukens on the "large field of business now opening in the new Purchase, as half the county seem to set their faces that way." But more welcome than the congratulations was the twenty pounds which was enclosed, a sum which was arriving just a little in arrears.[15]

Through the first three or four years, as noted, a number of complaints about Armstrong's work were lodged with the Surveyor General's Office in Philadelphia. Some of the correspondence was very angry. Most of the complaints, or at least a great many, were occasioned by the loss of records consumed in the fire which had ravaged the Carlisle office of Armstrong.[16] One of these was sent directly to Benjamin Franklin. The writer is the Indian trader and map-maker Joseph Greenwood, who while living in Philadelphia had somehow become well enough acquainted with Dr. Franklin to assume a friendship. The letter is dated, Philadelphia, 6th of April 1763. Greenwood is making a plaintive appeal to Franklin to intercede on his behalf:

> *Dear Sir, As I knowing of you to be a gentle-man that can doe a great deal to help a poor man to his Wrights and as I am much reduced and have a large family have made bold to Beg the Assistance of so good a Gentleman to see me rightified who has it not in my own power without applying for your Assistance in geting*

of me Justice don against Collo. John Armstrong who has taken an Improvement from me in the last purchase of Lands which I hope Mr. Franklin will take into Consideration and help me to my Wright as I am not able to help myself and have a Large family to maintain by my Labour which is but small as I never was brought up to it untill necessity brought me to it for an honest lively hood and I shall in Duty Bound to pray for your welfare. I am Sir your most Obedient humble Servant. Joseph Greenwood.[17]

    Typical of those complaints which were filed with the Land Office are the following: (1) On June 6, 1763, James Kyle charged Armstrong with the confusion that continued to exist between himself and a William White over lands on the Juniata which Armstrong had surveyed. (2) On June 20, 1764, a John Fitzgerald filed a dispute over the claim of Colonel John and his brother George Armstrong to Juniata lands on the Tuscarora Creek. (3) The Joseph Greenwood who had written to Franklin wrote also in the same poignant terms to Lukens (October 22, 1764) to accuse the surveyor of misdoing: "John Armstrong has wronged me out of as good a plantation as any in Cumberland County." (4) On November 6, 1764, in the letter of a man by the name of F. West of Carlisle to John Lukens can be found a complaint not directly about Armstrong but about one of his deputies. According to West, the surveys of lands for the sons of George Sanderson, Robert and John by name, done by Samuel Finley, were inaccurate. (5) Strangely, this same Samuel Finley, on March 20, 1765, himself filed a complaint with the Land Office against John Armstrong for a survey of his land which had been done by Adam Hoops on October 4, 1753. (7) Very touching is the letter of John Cunningham of Shippensburg to John Lukens, July 17, 1765. Cunningham is complaining of Armstrong's failure to survey his land:

I have applyed to Colnl John Armstronge Sevral tims to Survey my Small Improvement which I got a warrant for last December ... And Colnl John Armstrong promised to do it many times but Still put me off[f] of it with faire Spech—till now: and he Say that theres a cavit Intred against my warrant in the Land Office by William Young and William MacCune two of my nehjboours Joning Lins with me .... *P. S.* Sir if the Colnl and the above Sad [said] *men getes the pece of Land that they entend it will do me and my small famley a very grait Ingrey* [injury] *indeed* ....[18]

For the work he did for the Proprietaries in the neighborhood of Carlisle at some time in 1768 the Colonel submitted the following bill: "The Honourable the Proprietaries in Account with John Armstrong To Surveying One Hundred & forty Out Lots near the town of Carlisle in Cumberland County, Ploting said Lots & making a Plan thereof with the Town, Waters, Roads & Alleys, shewing their Size and situation, as appears by a Return made into the Secretary's Office, in pursuance of an Order from his Honor. The Governor [Denny] .... £60." [19]

George Washington did a lot of speculating in lands during the decade 1765-1775, a habit that was resumed during the years following the Revolution. He had employed his good friend and land agent William Crawford, to whom he had taught the art of surveying, "to investigate and survey for me various new locations." When he learned that Crawford himself had gone through with his determination to buy himself a farm along Braddock's Road, Washington urged him to find for him a good piece of the same. This Crawford promptly did, securing some 300 acres for him for thirty pistoles, roughly a dollar per acre, at the very spot on which he had suffered, by the French and Indians, his first military setback.

In a letter to Crawford, September 17, 1767, he recalled that in an earlier letter, hastily written, "I ... desird the favour of you ... to look me out a Tract of about 1500, 2000, or more acres somewhere in your Neighbourhood ...." Now he writes, "It will be easy for you to conceive that Ordinary, or even middling Land would never answer my purpose or expectation .... No: A tract to please me must be rich ... & if possible to be good an[d] level." He is very much aware of Pennsylvania laws designed to discourage speculation in land, which place limitations on the size of the parcel. But he has a plan. "I am told the Land, or Surveyors Office is kept at Carlyle, if so I am of Opinion that Colo. Armstrong (an Acquaintance of mine) has something to do in the management of it. & I am perswaded would readily serve me to him therefore at all events I will write by the first oppertunity." And then, noting that "It is possible (but I do not know that it really is the case) that Pennsylvania Customs will not admit so large a Quantity of Land as I require," he makes a suggestion (He himself calls it a "scheme."). "If so this may possibly be evaded by making several Entrys to the same amount if the expence of doing which is not too heavy but this I only drop as a hint leaving the whole to your discretion & good Management."

But there is a second problem. It is the 1763 Proclamation of King George, which, except for the grants made to British officers who had served the King during the French and Indian Wars, forbade settlement of the region west of the crest of the Appalachian range of mountains. He means to wink at that also. In this same letter to Crawford (whom Washington would visit at his home on the Youghiogheny for four days in 1770), he wrote: "The other matter just now hinted at and which I proposed in my last to join you in attempting to secure some of the most valuable Lands in the Kings part . . . notwithstanding the Proclamation that restrains it at present & prohibits the Settling of them at all for I can never look upon that Proclamation in any other light (but this I say between ourselves) than as a temporary expedient to quiet the minds of the Indians & must fall of course in a few years . . . .Any Person therefore who neglects the present oppertunity of hunting out good Lands . . . will never regain it."

At the close of his letter, Washington notes that he means to invite some of his friends into the "Scheme." To Crawford he advises, ". . . my Plan is to secure a good deal of Land." After some detailed instruction on which lands in the Monongahela, Youghiogheny, and Chartiers Creek region he prefers, fearful of censure for defying the King's Proclamation and hopeful that others will not learn of his "Plan" and practice the same, he advises, "I would recommend it to you to keep this whole matter a profound Secret." [20]

Crawford responded on the 29th, advising that he can get the lands Washington desires, describing the properties he has in mind, and declaring he will lose no time. Toward the end of the letter he suggests that Washington write directly to Armstrong, who, "I understand . . . is one of the Surveyors, and may have the office in

Carlyle for all I [k]now but I shall [k]now soon my self." Then, as Washington had hoped, he declares, "You may depend upon my Keeping the [w]hole as a profound secret and Trust the Searching out the Land to my own Care, which shall be done as soon as possible, and when I have completed the [w]hole I shall wait on you at your own house where I shall be able to give you a more satisfactory account of what I have Transacted." [21]

But Washington, on September 21, from Mount Vernon, had already directed a letter to Armstrong:

Dear Sir: Since I had the pleasure of seeing you at the Warm springs I have been informed that [for] much of the Land upon Yaughyaughgany and Monongahela which was formerly conceived to lye within the limits of Virginia . . . Grants may at any time be obtained from the Proprietary for Tracts on these Waters and being [informed], moreover, that the Office from whence these Rights are to Issue is kept at Carlyle it immediately occurred from what you were telling me [at the Springs] of the nature of your Office that I could apply to none so properly as yourself for the truth of these reports it appearing but probable that you were the very person with whom Entries were made.

Determined on purchase, Washington, himself a surveyor, and always respectful of Armstrong, who is nearly fifteen years his elder, then inquires into procedure:

I have therefore taken the liberty Sir of addressing this Letter to you on the subject of these enquiries, and to request the further favour of you to advise me of the mode of proceeding in order to take up ungranted Land in your Provence; What quantity of Acres will be admitted into a Survey; whether a Person is restricted in respect to the quantity of Land and number of Surveys. If the Surveys are required to be laid in any particular form or optional in the taker up to lay them as the nature and goodness of the Land and Water courses may point out to him. What the Expence of Patenting these Lands amount to per Thousand Acres. And what the annual Rents are fixed at afterwards. Together with any other useful hints which may occur to you for my Information and Government as I would most willingly possess some of those Lands which we have labord and Toild so hard to conquer.

And he then refers to their fellow surveyor in the West: "I have desired one Mr. William Crawford who lives upon Yaughyaughgany [at present-day Connellsville], a friend of mine, and I believe an Acquaintance of yours as he was an Officer in my Regiment and in General Forbes' Campaign to look me a Tract of about 2000 acres and endeavour to secure it till he can give me advice of it." He has a favor to ask of his friend: "I have likewise taken the liberty of saying to him that I was fully purswaded if the Land Office was kept in Carlyle and you had any share in the management of it that you would do me the favour of giving him any assistance in your power consistent with the Rules of Office. And for such assistance Sir after thankfully acknowledging myself your Debtor woud punctually [reimburse you] with any expence that might arise on my account so soon as I could be advised thereof."

And he concludes with "I heartily wish that Mrs. Armstrong and yourself may find all the good effects from the Waters of the Frederick Springs that you would desire. Mrs. Washington makes a tender of her Compliments to your Lady and self—" [22]

William Crawford Cabin

Armstrong did not reply until November 3 of this year, 1767. But when he did, he wrote an extremely long letter. He explains the land acquisition procedure in Pennsylvania, but then scolds Washington for desiring land that even the Governor himself cannot grant until it is first purchased from the Six Nations. He expects this may soon happen, but "at present Sir, you may firmly depend that nothing cou'd be farther attempted than a distant or conditional application to Governor [John] Penn for a tract or two on them Waters when the Purchase shall be confirm'd, which done in your Polit manner & under good pretentions too, I'm persuaded cou'd give no Offense nor easily fail of Success."

He proceeds then to offer his best service: "And if any Offices of mine either on the present or any other Occasion, may be of the least use I beg you wou'd freely command them, as they are now tendered and shall be chearfully employed as often as you shall give me leave." The letter continues with a long account of the "loose" procedure for acquiring land and the expense thereof. At the close of this long letter he risks offending his longtime friend by rapping him on the knuckles once again. He expresses the hope that Washington will "here permit a single remark flowing from Old friendship, and it shall be on the infatuating Game of card-playing," for which Armstrong has little regard. "That game," he declares, is "always unfriendly to Society, turns conversation out of Doors, and curtails our opportunities to mutual good. I can easily presume on your good nature to forgive this piece of unfashionable freedom, and Believe me to be with great respect—Dear Sir, Your Most Obed^t and humble Servt John Armstrong."

In a postscript he writes, "Mrs. Armstrong and myself beg you'll please to present our best respects to your Lady & also to your worthy Neighbours, Coll. Fairfax & Lady. We have both I hope been better'd by the Warm Springs, except some returns of the Rheumatism that attend Mrs. Armstrong, which I apprehend is so constitutional that we can scarcely expect a perfect cure."

By the time he got the letter into the hands of a courier, which was December 2, he felt obliged to append a woeful note: "We have just learned that Gen. Gage has wrote Gov. Penn that Sir Wm Johnson expects the Indians to break out this ensuing spring. May God avert such a Calamitous Scene, for shou'd it happen a third time so near together, Our Frontier People appear to be undone."[23]

Washington apparently did never journey to Carlisle to discuss tete-a-tete this business with Armstrong, but, according to historian Thomas Slaughter, Crawford did travel east to Carlisle, and there "sought out Colonel Armstrong," whom he found "amenable," and "who helped circumvent the colony's laws." [24] In any case, it is clear from a letter addressed to Armstrong by Washington on August 18, 1769, that the Deputy Surveyor has been a big help. The letter comes from the Frederick Springs (Warm Springs) in Virginia, now Berkeley (Bath), West Virginia, to whose warm baths Washington has returned Mrs. Washington and her fourteen-year-old son "Jackie," and her twelve-year-old daughter Martha ("Patsy," sometimes "Patcy"), who is "troubled with a complaint" (epilepsy). He has thought "the efficacy of these Waters" might provide some relief, but has "found little benefit as yet from the experiment." [25] Washington, who over the years was a frequent visitor to the springs (a four-day carriage drive from Mt. Vernon), and in August of 1767 had actually met Armstrong and wife Rebeckah at the waters,[26] is pleased to have learned that Armstrong stands "in no need of assistance from these Springs," and is saddened by the "many poor, miserable objects now attending here."

But he is writing chiefly to thank Colonel Armstrong for "the polite and friendly assistance you gave to the affair I took the liberty . . . of recommending to your notice." He is happy to report that Captain Crawford has advised him that the official letter which Armstrong provided him won him "a free and easy admission to the Land Office, and to such Indulgences as could be consistently granted" and that consequently his work had become "much less difficult, than otherwise it would have been." He asked that his best respects, "in which Mrs. Washington joins," attend Mrs. Armstrong.[27]

Washington's interest in lands in the Pittsburgh region and down the Ohio continued right up until the outbreak of the Revolution. In letters from Mt. Vernon to Crawford and to Armstrong in the fall of 1773, he inquired into the surveying activities of Carlisle's William Thompson in the Mingo-Shawnee country of the Scioto watershed (present-day Ohio) and the assignment of lands to Virginia officers and to Pennsylvania officers (one of whom was Armstrong himself),[28] and into the prospect of Franklin's new government replacing the Proprietary.[29]

On these subjects Armstrong wrote to Washington a

number of letters, especially during the fall and early winter of 1773, and he had replies from Annapolis and from Mt. Vernon. But another subject was much on his mind at this time. It was the situation of his first-born son, James, now twenty-four years old. The young man was presently serving as a physician near the Rappahannock, but he was not in good health and he was not happy. Father Armstrong had for a long while been much concerned about James, whom he always called "Jamey." The young man was having a tough time finding his niche, and indeed in the spring of 1772 was about to seek his fortune in the West Indies. Somewhat shaken by news of this idea, Armstrong addressed on April 30 a long letter to his son. The letter provides a lot of advice on how to write a letter and includes news of Dr. William Irvine (his upcoming marriage), and of Dr. Rush, and of Dr. John Morgan, with whom James had served his apprenticeship.

But James had a good bit of Scripture thrown at him in this letter too, and he could appreciate easily enough that his father was hoping he would continue in his profession and that he should give his present place more time, staying on at least until November, at which time he could visit his parents in Carlisle. Sounding a little like Polonius to Laertes, the Colonel has some fatherly advice:

Neither reason nor Religion requires a Man to throw away himself, his time nor his acquirements, nor on the other hand, should he be too ambitious. Restless is the mind of Man indeed, but let me tell you in One word that the whole universe would not satisfy the extensive and craving desires of One human mind nor can anything give solid rest but a Spiritual union to the lord Jesus by faith, whereby the Once Straying Soul is brought back to god the only Center of it's [sic] Rest . . . . Eat no Idle Bread if you have few calls to the Sick you have important Studies to pursue both for this world and that which is to come . . . and am dear Jamey Your very Affectionate Father.

In a postscript he reports the death of their fine grey colt, a favorite of James.[30]

In another letter to "Dear Jamey," a "terribly concerned and affectionate father" provided additional counsel:

> *In my last I have informed you that your mother is designed to set out on a visit in about a week hence to your grandfather's and thence to Philad[1] where your Uncle Duffield is removed some six months ago. I expect her return by the Tenth of June which I think will answer to the time that in your last you promised to be here, you say about the 20th of June, but perhaps you may as easily come about the 15th this must depend on your own circumstances. I can only say we are very anxious to see you and your not coming in the winter renders us both very uneasy, having lots but too much impatience look'd for you ever since until last week when your last by the way of Baltimore came to hand. I have begun to Build at my meadow under much diffidence the expedience of that meadow and waited many weeks to have seen you before determined I cannot but immagin that your stay has been owing to something out of the common course of things, perhaps want of Health, but if occasioned by any other matter of importance you must be sensible how natural it must be for your Parents to assist and advise your deliberation in any matter whatever—and if anything perplexing be on your mind and the advice of friends in that neighborhood fail of affording you present satisfactions. I think you should postpone a determination here, unless the duty, matter or thing [?] until you come appear clear and satisfactory, having first been weighed and examin'd under or by the opinion of some judicious friend, which I hope you would always find in Mr. Waddle or any immergency whatever— and in various matters I should prefer that Gentlemans opinion even to Dr. Mercers to desirous of knowing both. As the bearer [James McClintogue] can inform you of various occurrences in our neighborhood, I shall not add. But recommending you to the mercy and good providence of God thro the admirably efficacious mediation of Jesus Christ his Son, Subscribe myself, Dear Jamey your terribly concerned and affectionate father.*[31]

    James did get in the hoped for visit to his father and mother, and shortly after his return to Virginia, Armstrong wrote to Washington: "If weather & the River Potomach admit, I hope my Son, now returning from a Visit here, to his present station . . . will have the pleasure of delivering you this Scrawl of Mount vernon." Armstrong is hoping that Washington may be helpful. Of James he reports:

He has some thoughts of moving from that Place, and Some intimations of another vacancy perhaps more agreeable at a place of which I immagin you have some acquaintance—but this intention to remove for prudential reasons he does not chuse to be known where he now lives, until he can be better determin'd, and on this point I know I need not ask you to render him any assistance you may think of Service to him. As to his Character, altho' I believe you would forgive me, I rather leave that to other people, and so far as it may be a necessary foundation of your letter or advice, I beg leave to refer you to Doctor [Hugh] *Mercer or Some of the Gentlemen where he lives, One of whom being a Member of the Assembly for the County of Lancaster* [Virginia] *you undoubtedly know, but as I expect he will see you, or write you soon, I shall not further trespass.*[32]

Throughout these two decades leading up to the Revolution, Armstrong's professional activity as a surveyor was of course much limited by his military responsibilities. Before very much longer they would consume him.

XVIII

THE PRESBYTERIAN CHURCH

At the time the twenty-eight-year-old John Armstrong arrived in America, he would have found himself unwelcome in some of the English colonies—because he was a Presbyterian. He had booked passage to the Delaware River in large measure because he understood that in Pennsylvania he could practice his faith without suffering prejudice or persecution. He might have emigrated to New Jersey, or to Maryland, with almost equal opportunity, but in the New England colonies, and in New York and the Carolinas he would have found himself most uncomfortable and he might have been paying outrageous taxes to support the Church of England, which was not tolerant of dissent.

And, indeed, although he was not surprised, he found the entire region of the Cumberland Valley inhabited by Presbyterians. Scotch-Irish they were, and they were here, as he was himself, to improve their condition while continuing in a faith that was fervent and unshakable.

These settlers were heirs to a religion that by the eighteenth century had become deep-seated and so intense among the Scotch and the Irish as to be life-dominating. Although born in Ireland, John Armstrong was born into the Church of Scotland. It was the Church founded almost two centuries earlier by the energetic and inspired John Knox. In no time at all, by 1560, it had become the Church of Scotland, and was confirmed as such in 1688. Although Presbyterianism became popular in Ireland, and even in England, Scotland remains the only country in the world where Presbyterianism is established by law.

The Presbyterian Church is grounded in the doctrines of John Calvin of course, and this means, first of all, a devotion to the Bible as the rule of faith and of conduct.

In the colonies the first Presbytery, which assumed jurisdiction over the ministers of a specified area, ordaining them and confirming their call to a specific church, came about in this way: The Presbyterian Church of Philadelphia had been organized in 1698, and the first real meetinghouse for the church was built six years later at Market Street and White Horse Alley (now Bank Street). The church was most impressive, in large measure because it was embraced by stately sycamores, in those days called "buttonwoods." Naturally, before many years had passed, the Church was being referred to affectionately as Old Buttonwood. It is regarded historically as the Mother Church of Presbyterians.

Not long after this church was erected, the very Irish Reverend Francis Makemie, regarded by historians of the Church as the father of American Presbyterianism, showed up in the City of Brotherly Love. Makemie, who for some time had been serving five churches in the Maryland colony, convened a meeting of his fellow ministers, who were from widely varying backgrounds, in the First Presbyterian Church of Philadelphia. The year was 1706. In consequence of this meeting there emerged the first Presbytery in America. It promptly announced its purpose: "Our design is to . . . consult the most proper measures, for propagating Christianity and . . . the improvement of our ministerial ability."

At a truly remarkable speed the ministers of this Presbytery reached out to the hitherto isolated churches of the Province of Pennsylvania, and by hardly more than a decade later had accomplished sufficient organization and cooperation to divide into three separate presbyteries and form a synod. This synod naturally held its first meetings in Old Buttonwood.

According to Conway Wing and the historians of Cumberland County, the history of the First Presbyterian Church of Carlisle dates from 1734. Established by the Scotch-Irish of then Lancaster County, it "had its first place of meeting on the south bank of the Conodoguinet, at Meeting House Springs, about one and one-half to two miles northwest of the present town." [1] In the town of Carlisle as first laid out, in 1751, some two acres of ground had been enclosed by a stockade, with a blockhouse at each corner. It was close to this stockade (Armstrong's fort, as described earlier) that a modest meeting house was constructed. In his June 30, 1757, letter to Secretary Richard Peters, as noted above, Armstrong announced, "To-morrow we begin to haul stones for the building of a meeting-house on the north side of the Square; there was no other convenient place. I have avoided the place you once pitched for a church. The stones are raised out of Col. Stanwix's entrenchment. We will want help in this political, as well as religious work." [2]

For the years 1759-1772 two Presbyterian congregations were competing in Carlisle. One was served in its early years by the Reverend George Duffield, who is an important figure in the life of Armstrong, not only because he was the Colonel's pastor, but because of his second marriage. Duffield, who had been born in Pennsylvania, in October of 1732, was graduated at age twenty from Nassau Hall (Princeton). He was ordained by the New-Side Presbytery of Newcastle in March of 1756. He served at Fagg's Manor, at Hanover in Virginia, and later at Carlisle and Big Spring. In April of 1763 he was called to the Second Church of Philadelphia, but was opposed and did not serve. In 1765 he was sent to North Carolina. In the next year, as below described, he was sent with his intimate friend the Reverend Charles Beatty to preach for two months on the frontiers. His first wife, a daughter of Samuel Blair, died in Carlisle in September of 1757. It was on March 5, 1759, that he was married again, this time to the sister of John Armstrong's wife Rebeckah. For a time it was thought (by Webster and others) that his second wife, Margaret, was a daughter of John Armstrong, but of course Armstrong had no daughters. Other historians (Alfred Nevin for one) assumed that Margaret was

John Armstrong's sister. But Armstrong's sister Margaret was married to John Lyon. The truth is that the Margaret Armstrong whom Duffield married was a sister of Armstrong's wife Rebeckah, and therefore John Armstrong's sister-in-law. Both Margaret and Rebeckah, as above noted, were daughters of the Archibald Armstrong who had settled in New Castle County in the "lower country" (Delaware). The will of Archibald Armstrong, Rebeckah's father, names his daughter Margaret, "wife of Reverend George Duffield," a beneficiary.[3]

Duffield's congregation had been meeting for some time within the limits of the community, and were in the process of building a structure when it was learned that the congregation of the forty-four-year-old Reverend Mr. John Steel, who had become pastor here in 1759, was also considering the building of a church. Accordingly, the Duffield people asked for an opinion from the Synod. The question was whether there should be one or two churches built in Carlisle. Not surprisingly the Synod opted for one, and after a review of the situation, delivered its reply: "The Synod is grieved that there should be a spirit of animosity still subsisting amongst the people, and would be far from encouraging any steps that would tend to perpetuate a divided state; therefore they warmly recommend it to the people of both congregations to fall upon healing measures and lay a plan for the erection of one house only; and enjoin it upon Messrs. Steel and Duffield to unite their counsel and use their influence to bring about a cordial agreement."[4] This was good advice probably, but it went unheeded, both congregations going their own ways.

By the fall of the year the Presbytery had scheduled a meeting for "Mr. Steel's meetinghouse in Carlisle," which certainly suggests a church erected. And within the year the Duffield group, headed up by Armstrong, successfully petitioned Governor Hamilton to conduct a lottery (presumably a kind of bingo game) in order to raise the funds sufficient "to build a decent house for the worship of God." Great confusion continues to exist in the matter, however, for historian Israel Rupp notes that a short time after the Duffield church was built, "the congregation in the country then under the care of Rev. Mr. Steel, constructed a two-story house of worship in town." Wing conjectures that Rupp is supposing that the Duffield structure was the meetinghouse constructed of stone that Armstrong mentioned hauling stones for in his June 30, 1757, letter to Secretary Peters. In any case, both congregations apparently later on found sites different from these. It is known that the Duffield congregation met in a church located on the east side of Hanover Street, on the corner of Hanover and Pomfret Streets, opposite the present Second Presbyterian Church. By a deed given by the proprietors Thomas and Richard Penn, dated September 20, 1766, there was conveyed "a lot of ground 180 by 200 feet, at the northwest quarter of the centre square, to the Presbyterian congregation of Carlisle for the erection of a church edifice." This building was begun in 1769 and sufficiently completed for public worship in 1772.[5] Located as it was, it provided a kind of sentry post to serve the "fort"; and the garrison (only twelve men in the beginning) returned the favor by providing armed guard for the assemblies on the Sabbath. And of course, the stockade served as a place of refuge for any time it was needed.

And, though it is less certain, apparently the membership of Reverend Steel had its "two-storied meeting house" on the lot Armstrong had numbered 145, "which is close the northwest corner of present Hanover Street and Dickinson alley."[6]

During these years, of course the nearby settlements were constantly being terrorized by the Indians, and consequently the ministers of the churches were regularly captains of militia parties. Both the Reverend Mr. Steel and Mr. Duffield served in this way, and in nearby Lancaster County the Reverend John Elder was known as the "fighting Parson." The Reverend Steel, a commissioned captain in the militia, and sometimes himself known as the "fighting parson," was noted for preaching with a rifle at his side, and sometimes with a stack of muskets neatly adorning the front of the pulpit. It is said that the Reverend Steel would terminate a service with a hasty benediction if it had been interrupted by report of Indian activity nearby, and go in pursuit of the ravaging Indians.

Before his time in Carlisle, Steel operated out of "Steel's Fort," a rude stockade surrounding a meeting house on the south side of the east branch of the Conococheague Creek. It had been erected in the fall of 1755, after Braddock's defeat, when the frontier was gripped in fear. And he commanded a company at Carlisle with the outbreak of the Revolution.

The Reverend George Duffield was of this persuasion also. He enjoyed a reputation for an extraordinary eloquence when speaking of soldiers or addressing them. By all accounts Duffield was, like Steel, a most zealous patriot, "an early, decided, and uniform friend of his country." He was very popular with congregations, and those who heard him always remarked his great energy and enthusiasm, his warmth of personality and his sincere concern for his sheep. He had a great talent, many observed, for "touching the conscience and seizing the heart." [7] One biographer, while noting that he was "a man of slight frame and of small stature," declared he possessed a "firm constitution and was capable of much endurance." [8]

The two congregations continued separate in accord with the 1741-58 schism within the Presbyterian Church, which resulted in the "New Lights" ("New Side") and the "Old Lights" ("Old Side").[9] The "New Lights" were modern in their thinking, desiring, for one thing, to limit the duties of civil magistrates; and the "Old Lights," generally in the minority, held fast to tradition and the conservative way. The disaffected (New Lights) early in 1759 chose the Reverend George Duffield to be their pastor, the Old Lights being served by the Reverend John Steel. Duffield was giving one-third of his time to the church in Big Spring (now Newville), and one-third of his time to Monaghan (now Dillsburg), and was not actually ordained and installed at Carlisle until the third Wednesday of September, 1759. And by this time there had occurred a reconciliation between the New Lights and the Old. And the Reverend Duffield, who had been decidedly a New Light, responded warmly to the re-union within the Presbyterian Church, although, as he confessed, "I hardly expected much comfort in it for a while." [10]

John Armstrong had been caught up in the Great Awakening inspired by the influential and passionate Methodist-Calvinist Reverend George Whitefield, which was responsible for the rift in the First Presbyterian Church. He was quite comfortable in the church of Reverend Duffield, who was married to his wife's sister, and he was from the beginning a very active elder.

Reverend George Duffield

As the frontier moved west and settlements became steadily more populated there arose the need to erect additional meetinghouses within the Presbytery. To determine the sites for such houses of worship, committees from established churches were formed and dispatched to the settlements. From time to time John Armstrong served on this kind of mission. On one occasion he found himself a member of a committee that included also the ministers George Duffield and Robert Cooper, and elders John McKnight and Thomas Wilson. This committee had been asked to hear the report of commissioners representing the people of a valley in the vicinity of the Juniata River and Sherman Creek. This valley, they discovered, was thirty-six miles in length and accommodated 126 settlers. When it was ascertained that these people would subscribe to the support of a minister, the committee recommended the placing of meetinghouses at three points within the valley.[11] Before very long these three churches became busy centers of worship for three distinct congregations.[12] In this way the church moved west.

 Armstrong was extremely prominent in the Church throughout his time. He was frequently appointed a delegate to meetings of the Presbytery and of the Synod, and he very often played a significant role in the official proceedings. In 1786 he was made a trustee. On August 26 of that year the General Assembly of the State of Pennsylvania "duly elected and appointed" John Armstrong and eleven others, including William Lyon and John Montgomery, to be "made and constituted a corporation and body politic in law and in fact to have continuance forever by that name, style and title of the Trustees of the Presbyterian Church in the Borough of Carlisle."[13] And he was a member of the Assembly that convened in Philadelphia in 1791 and also a member of the Assembly that met in the next year.

 Of course, though dedicated and committed to the church, he would, because of his military service, be missing out on many of the Presbyterian Sabbath services. The Forbes expedition alone caused him to be absent from some forty Sunday sessions.

 As for his religious stance, he was by all accounts a committed Christian, quite orthodox in his views, and very Bible-conscious. George Chambers, who wrote much of the Scotch-Irish in Pennsylvania, had very good things to say of General Armstrong: "He was a man of intelligence, of integrity, and of high religious and moral character. He was resolute and brave, and though living habitually in the fear of the Lord, he feared not the face of man."

The Reverend George Duffield was called by the Church to Philadelphia, April, 1771.[14] He was being asked to assume the pulpit of the Pine Street (now Third) Presbyterian Church, which was attended by John Adams, who promptly became much impressed by the Duffield sermons. And in August of 1779 occurred the death of Reverend John Steel, of whom one historian remarks that he left a reputation "for stern integrity, zeal for what he deemed truth and righteousness, and a high sense of honour."[15] The two Carlisle congregations finally united, and in 1785, when Armstrong was sixty-eight years old, the new church chose Dr. Robert Davidson to be its pastor. Davidson served for the next twenty-seven years! And the Reverend George Duffield's grandson, also named George, would return the Duffield style of preaching to the Presbyterian pulpit in Carlisle, and continue in the pastorship for seventeen years.

At some time after the loss of Reverend Duffield the church in which he had preached was consumed by fire. According to the story which has come down, builders who were blasting stones in the streets thereabouts, somehow so mismanaged the fuses that one or more were propelled to the roof of the church and ignited the shingles. The fire then spread so rapidly the structure could not be saved. For a time after that the congregation held its services in a room of the nearby Courthouse. Conway Wing has a story about that: "The bell in this Court House was said to be the gift of a sister of William Penn who resided at Carlisle, England, and it is also said that she stood by it when it was cast and threw in a few silver coins under an impression that this would give it a better quality of sound. There being no steeple to the church it was hung on a cupola of the neighboring Court House, with the understanding that it should serve for the courts on week days and for the church in all religious services. Unfortunately it was melted down and lost when the Court House was burned many years since."[16]

Armstrong had another good Irish friend in the ministry during the critical years of the 1760s. That was the Reverend Charles Beatty,[17] a man of about his own age. Beatty was an impassioned minister and a most compelling orator. He regularly

Reverend Charles Beatty

preached to the militia troops of Pennsylvania, and served as Armstrong's chaplain during the Forbes Expedition. For a time it was thought that he had addressed the soldiers of Armstrong when they were assembling for the raid on Kittanning, but, as above noted, that does not seem to have been the case. In fact at that time Beatty was with Colonel Benjamin Franklin, who was heading up 500 men come from Philadelphia to help with the building of forts and to repulse those who had burned the Moravian Missions near Lehighton.

Franklin, in later years, in his autobiography, very well remembered the animated and conscientious clergyman: "We had for our chaplain a zealous Presbyterian minister, Mr. Beatty, who complained to me that the men did not generally attend his prayers and exhortations." Upon their enlistment it was the habit of the militia to provide a gill of rum a day to each soldier. This was punctually served out to them on the approved schedule, one half in the morning and the other half in the evening. The practical and ever resourceful Franklin had the solution to Reverend Beatty's problem. To the much discouraged chaplain he proposed: "Mr. Beatty, it is perhaps below the dignity of your profession to act as a steward of the rum; but if you were to distribute it out only just after prayers, you would have them all about you." [18]

On May 30, 1766, the Presbyterian Synod of New York and

Philadelphia appointed the Reverend Charles Beatty and the Reverend Mr. George Duffield of Carlisle to promote the gospel on the frontier.[19] They were to serve as missionaries for the Church for a period of two months. Beatty, accompanied by his interpreter Joseph Peepy, a Christian Indian, showed up at Carlisle on Friday, August 15. On the Sabbath he preached for Reverend Duffield in the evening. During this time he had his lodging at the home of his good friends Colonel John Armstrong and his wife Rebeckah, and he delighted in little John, Jr., who was not yet eight.

The two ministers set out, then, on Monday the 18th. Before long they separated, with Reverend Beatty proceeding along the Juniata, and Duffield passing through Path Valley and the Cove. Both preached at various settlements, and to the Indians as well, and did baptisms. They ministered at Fort Ligonier, at Fort Pitt, at Logstown, and at Great Beaver Creek. Eventually they arrived at the Delaware town on the Muskingum that had been visited by Colonel Bouquet. They were now 130 miles downriver from Fort Pitt, but were made most happy by an enthusiastic welcoming committee. It was a great delight to them both to spread the gospel among the Indians, and especially so when it appeared the native peoples were most grateful.

The long trip back was relatively uneventful. They returned to Carlisle on October 10, Beatty lodging again in the home of Colonel Armstrong. In all, their mission required almost exactly two months, and to accomplish it the two ministers had journeyed nearly 800 miles. Happily, Beatty kept a detailed journal, which provides a "graphic picture of the conditions on the frontier at this early period."[20] And, happily also, the Reverend George Duffield published an *Account of a Missionary Tour through Western Pennsylvania, in 1766.*

XIX

Rebeckah

Rebeckah Armstrong was born on May 2, 1719, probably in Aghalurgher Parish, near Brookeborough County, Fermanagh, Ireland, and may have come to America with her father as early as 1740. Nothing is known of her first marriage, except that her husband's name was Lyon. As noted above, she was married to John Armstrong at New Castle in November of 1746. Settling as they did in the Kittatinny Valley, then the frontier in Pennsylvania, they were abruptly made pioneers. As the settlers came steadily under more and more pressure from the hostile Indians, Rebeckah from her new home in Carlisle responded every bit as courageously and energetically as did her husband.[1]

As we have seen, Pennsylvania during these critical years experienced a number of great "runaways," when terrified farm families fled the frontiers and returned to "civilization," meaning the communities of Carlisle and Shippensburg, Lancaster and York. The first of these panicky flights occurred in 1755-56, as a result of the failed Braddock expedition; the second occurred at the instigation of Pontiac, who determined to unleash his warriors on the outlying settlements at harvest time in 1763. A third mass exodus from the frontier would occur in 1777-78, during the

Revolution, after the Iroquois had allied with the British, and the Senecas and the Mohawks laid waste to Wyoming and Cobleskill and Cherry Valley, and many settlements in the Susquehanna Valley. Estimates had eighty per cent of the population of the West Branch Valley in flight from the raiding warriors.

On each of these very critical occasions, Rebeckah Armstrong received the fleeing settlers in Carlisle with the utmost sympathy and concern. She made arrangements not only in Carlisle but in the other communities of the region for temporary habitation of the frightened families, many of which had lost one or more of their members, and had left behind their household goods and clothing.

And when the war of the Revolution came, and Carlisle became a hub of activity, it was Rebeckah Armstrong who organized the women into a soldiers' assistance society ("the first in Pennsylvania") to provide clothing and other essentials, notably boots, blankets, canteens and knapsacks.

She has been described as very strong-willed and as a "leader of the women of Carlisle" during the Revolution,[2] when of course Carlisle's Mary Ludwig Hays ("Molly Pitcher") became the most famous of these patriotic women.

So compassionate, conscientious and energetic was Rebeckah Armstrong in all of this that one historian of the time declared that "no other woman was more respected—nor was there one whose patriotism and patriotic services were more highly appreciated." [3]

Mrs. Armstrong was also a gracious and good hostess, entertaining in her home the frequent business associates, and military comrades of her husband, and men and women of the church. Her home was open to such dignitaries as the Reverend Charles Beatty, and of course her own pastor and brother-in-law the Reverend George Duffield, as well as to General Stanwix, Colonel Burd, and Colonel Bouquet. At the same time she entertained church groups and homeless families and her many brothers-in-law.

Of course John Armstrong was away from home a long time, on his many expeditions (the Forbes expedition alone costing him more than a year) and during his military service in the early years of the Revolution, and on his many required trips to

Philadelphia while serving in the Continental Congress and in the State Assembly, and because of his surveying duties in the hinterlands. His concern for Rebeckah at such times was great, and, indeed, he encouraged his correspondents to apprise her of his situation whenever they could. Governor Denny during the time of the Kittanning Expedition wrote constantly to Rebeckah, and his letters did a lot to keep her spirits up. When that expedition ended, in the fall of 1756, Armstrong was quick to thank the Governor: "My Wife presents her best respects to you, and will not forget your friendly letters at a time when my coming back was very uncertain."

Rebeckah was very family conscious and stayed in touch with her father, spending a whole month with him in New Castle in May of 1773, and going on after that to visit with her sister Margaret, wife of the Reverend George Duffield, who had removed from Carlisle to Philadelphia in 1772.[4]

But few of the many letters that passed between the devoted couple are extant. One of much interest was sent from Philadelphia on February 6, 1776, at the time the British were still occupying Boston, and before Armstrong's commission in the Continental Army. It reports a serious accident suffered by the Colonel:

My dear—I have already wrote you by Mr. John Harris in which you are inform'd of the dangerous Fall I had about Eighteen miles from this City, occasion'd by the mare I rode Sudenly Rearing at an accidental Object, by which means I'm yet confined to Mr. Henry's House [William Henry was Armstrong's surveying business partner.], *altho' entirely well only that the blackness under my eyes is not quite removed, but I think to go abroad in town tomorrow or next day. It is some consolation to have rec'd a number of friendly visits from different classes of mankind here, but more to have been preserved by the invisible hand of God in that critical moment. Before this time I suppose Jamey is come down to see you, If his inclination should be towards the Army, I yet see no opening so natural in this province as that of being appointed to the head of some Hospital, wherever the continental Army may be encamped, I mean some Southern Encampment which more probably may be in Virginia, but cannot yet with certainty be known where. To this purpose I intend talking with Some members of Congress, that an Opening may be left, in case it shou'd be thought expedient to embrace it, but can not make any full attempt until I hear explicitly from him. I may probably Soon be Spoke to concerning the important question formerly agitated* [a commission in the Continental Army], *but remain much at a loss what answer to make, and have yet had no right Opportunity of consulting with friends here, may the Lord prepare an answer. The New England vacancy is filled up with a certain Mr.* [Joseph] *Frye who has not before been in the Continental Servise at which appointment our friend Coll:* [William] *Thompson is much Chagrined and has resigned the Service at least in that part of the country. I am Sorry for the occasion of this warmth, as the tories are ready to catch up every occasion against new England in order to promote a division. however, Coll: Thompson I think, and Doctor Mercer will very Soon be appointed Brigadiers for the Southern or rather middle department, which probably may also be my destiny if at all to be concern'd. If Jamey Shou'd have any thought of coming down here, I am at present against it and See no use to be anfavor'd by it, but Settleing his affairs above coming down to Carlisle, may be the immediate Step he Shou'd take, which need not stand in the way of going into the publick Service, if a proper Opening Shou'd present, as in that case, no doubt he would be Oblig'd to be at Philad^d sometime in March. I can't yet say what stay I must make, but as Short as possible. There are troops very lately from Boston landed on an Island near New York—and General* [Charles] *Lee is also near that City at the head of 700 Militia, but is himself bad of the gout. The Regulars it was thought were going to Dunmore, and some think to yet, their number is not fully known but said to be 600. The* [illegible] *pamphlet entitled Common Sense which occasions so much speculation here is now reprinting with additions, when* [word *when* repeated] *it is out I shall Send you One, perhaps by Mr.* [William] *Blyth. My love to Mr. & Mrs.* [William] *Lyon, as I have nothing different to write you can Shew him this—I have yet heard nothing from princeton, but have forwarded the letters. I send you Needles, pins, & thread by Mr. Hershey—and Spoke to Mr. Chesnut on my way down, for Some Flatcheleld Hemp, which he was good enough to promise to get done & Send it to Carlisle for you. I have been told that I can't get* *even half a piece of linnen to buy in all this City, and if any by the Smalls I suppose exceeding dear, I must try farther or Soon wear another kind. Mrs. Henry has bought the Knives & Case for £3 which was long held at £3,10, but it must go upon Some Trunk. Friends here are generally well. I have not yet found where Johny* [seventeen-year-old John, Jr.] *has left the Gentlewomans Gown, but expect with Mrs. Duffield.*

I am, my dear Love Affectionately Yours, John Armstrong[5]

The Armstrongs had two sons. James was born August 29, 1748, and John, Jr., entered this world on the very same day, perhaps during the same hour, that his father raised the British flag over the abandoned Fort Duquesne, November 25, 1758. These two sons were not like two peas in a pod. They were different as a hickory nut and a black walnut, as brothers often are. It was more than the great difference in age. They were extremely different in temperament, in personality, and in interests.

Young James was quite precocious and was dispatched to the Academy in Philadelphia. At age twenty he became "one of the first graduates" of the school of medicine. Medicine had been his enthusiasm from a time when he was quite young, and after an apprenticeship with Dr. John Morgan, an eminent physician in Philadelphia, he went into practice in the region of Winchester, Virginia. Not happy there, and after serving as a medical officer during the war, he was (at age thirty-seven) on his way to London to further his training in medicine.

Upon his return, after three years of study, he was married to Mary Stevenson, of a prominent Carlisle family, and not long after, the couple moved from Carlisle to his father's large (1015 acres) tract of land in the Kishacoquillas Valley (near Belleville, present Mifflin County), and there they lived for eight years, until after the death of both of James's parents, when they returned to Carlisle. James, who was most likely named for his grandfather, James Armstrong of Brookeborough, Ireland, was the father of nine children. The first-born, named for his paternal grandfather, died at the age of four. He was followed by Hannah, Rebecca (named for James' mother of course), who died young, and a third daughter, also named Rebecca, then John Wilkins, who became a physician,[6]

Mary Ann, Alfred, Catherine, and George.[7]

Dr. James Armstrong, before he "retired" to the old family home in Carlisle, and though not very keen about politics or government, was persuaded to accept election to the Congress, in which he served as a Pro-Administration delegate from March 4, 1793, to March 3, 1795. When he returned to Carlisle to continue his practice, he was appointed an associate judge in the Cumberland County Court (He had been an associate judge in the Kishacoquillas Valley.), which office he held until his death, in Carlisle, May 6, 1828.

Rebeckah's son James, by all accounts was the most mild-mannered, selfless, and gracious man one could ever expect to meet. One who knew him well had this to say of him:

A higher toned man than Dr. James Armstrong the state of Pennsylvania never produced. He was one who had an utter scorn for everything and everybody that was low or mean. He could not stoop to secure any favour. He would sacrifice everything to his self-respect. He would and did without a murmur dispense with not only the comforts but some of the very necessities of life rather than even appear to cringe. And yet he never boasted of his wealth, or family, or position in society. Wealth he held in light esteem, office had no allurements for him, and so reserved was he in speaking of his family that his surviving children were left in almost entire ignorance of its history.[8]

Dr. James Armstrong was interred in the Old Cemetery in the town that he loved, Carlisle.

And then there was John, Jr. John, too, was most precocious, and like his brother James very much enjoyed horseback riding,[9] but there the likenesses end. And, indeed, John, according to his biographer, was much closer to his cousin James, who lived in Chambersburg, than he was to his older brother. But certainly both boys enjoyed nothing more than riding with their father's pack of fox-hunting hounds, and both became expert riders.[10]

John received his early schooling at the grammar school in Carlisle and at age sixteen was off to the College of New Jersey (now Princeton). But before he could graduate he accepted appointment to the staff of General Hugh Mercer in the early days of the Revolution and was serving with Mercer at the battle of Trenton, and at Princeton, when Mercer was mortally wounded. Young Armstrong was himself pinned beneath his horse, which had been shot, and just barely escaped. John then served until the end of the Revolution on the staff of General Horatio Gates.

His was the world of politics, diplomacy and government. And quite a career he enjoyed in that world. He served Pennsylvania as Secretary of State (1783-87), and then the new United States as Senator (a Democratic Republican, 1800-1804), as Ambassador to France, and as Secretary of War. But because of his abrasive personality and an undisguised impatience, he regularly ruffled feathers and was often in trouble. Terms that his biographer uses for him are "pugnacious," "aggressive," "haughty," "contemptuous," and "ambitious." [11] By these faults of character his great abilities were much damaged.

On January 19, 1789, he was married to Alida Livingston of the prominent and very influential, very wealthy New York family. They had seven children: Margaret, who married William B. Astor, the richest man in America; Horatio Robert Gates; Henry Beekman; Robert Livingston; John; James Kosciuszko; and the last-born, son Edward, who died eight days after birth.[12]

John was never so attentive to his parents, especially his mother, as was James. In letters to his father on February 26, 1781, and again on May 10 of that spring, he considered the prospects for peace, but expressed no concern at all for his mother, who was at the time in very poor health. In his many, many letters references to his mother very rarely appear. Even after his father's death, he rarely wrote to his mother and constantly reneged on promised visits. Indeed, "he had never shown any deep attachment to his mother." [13] His brother, in reporting the death of their mother, noted the long lapse in the correspondence between John, Jr., and his mother, and remarked on John's failure to keep promised visits.[14]

As Rebeckah left no will, it was up to the sons to see to the disposition of the estate, and John left the management entirely to James. That John, Jr., was not close to his brother either is apparent from a letter to General Gates, written after brother James had returned to Carlisle: "The death of my last respectable parent leaves me but few motives for revisiting my native place." [15]

Yet Rebeckah loved both of her sons, dearly, and was very proud of both. Fortunately, both she and the General lived long enough to see their two boys much distinguished and happily married.

And all of this was in spite of Rebeckah's very precarious health. From a time when she was in her forties until the very end of her days, Rebeckah suffered from chronic rheumatism. At times she was in terrific pain. From a particularly long and very scary illness she finally emerged in June of 1761. But the rheumatism persisted, and it was in hope of some relief that Armstrong took her to the Warm Springs in Virginia in August of 1767. That she did not want for courage was evident to anyone who knew the pain she suffered.

And besides the rheumatism, she suffered a number of speech- and mind-affecting mini-strokes.

One of her last surviving letters was addressed to her sister Margaret from Carlisle, on Dec. 19, 1795. The letter is all about women—their dress, deportment, etc.[16]

Death came for her on November 16, 1797, just a few days before son John's thirty-ninth birthday. The passing of "always one of the most respectable inhabitants"of Carlisle was described by the *Gazette* as "peaceful." And the long obituary printed on November 22 read in part:

This excellent woman in her very advanced age continued to enjoy the free exercise of a well cultivated understanding and of her every faculty with much liveliness and vigor . . . . If a disposition, benevolent in a very high degree and ever ready to sympathize with and relieve the suffering; if a heart framed to delight in all the characteristics of social life, all the various and important duties of the consort, the mother and the friend; if a constant attendant to the duties and the piety, and the ordinances of that Divine Redeemer in whom she trusted for salvation, in perfect concert with the pious partner of her cares for the long period of half a century, can give ground for the most pleasant hopes, her surviving friends may solace themselves with this most important of considerations, that death is to her invaluable and eternal gain.[17]

Rebeckah was laid to her eternal rest next her dear husband in the Old Cemetery in Carlisle.

PART TWO

THE PATRIOT

XX

The Siege of Charleston

As the sense of injustice grew closer and closer to the unbearable, and the storm clouds roiled over Boston, support in the form of funds, pronouncements of sympathy, and militant expression came pouring into New England from other communities, like Salem, New Jersey, where on October 3, 1774, the citizens held a meeting to declare their outrage at the treatment their fellow colonials were receiving; and went on to raise $700, which was promptly dispatched to Boston. But the people of Carlisle actually headed up the support that New England needed to launch rebellion. As early as the 12th of July of this year,1774, the vigilant Scotch-Irish convened a most enthusiastic public meeting. Several townships of Cumberland County delivered its tradesmen and farmers to the County Seat and into the leadership of John Armstrong's good friend John Montgomery.

With Montgomery presiding, the meeting was held in the meetinghouse of the First Presbyterian Church. Nine resolutions were readily agreed to. Inspired by the British closing of the port of Boston, the delegates recognized that the citizens of Boston were suffering in the name of all the colonies. They promptly resolved on redress of grievances, and the organization of a Congress of Deputies from all the colonies. They agreed to place an embargo on British merchandise, including tea. They agreed to support the people of Boston with relief, and, finally, they resolved to form a committee of this province, "to co-operate in every measure conducing to the general welfare of British America." This Committee of Correspondence was immediately appointed. Besides Armstrong, the thirteen named constituted a Who's Who of Cumberland County. All, except perhaps one, would become most conspicuous in the revolution to come. All are Scotch, or Irish, or both. Except for Armstrong, all are young or middle-aged, very spirited, energetic men of action. Armstrong is a close friend to each, and as at fifty-six he is the oldest by far, he assumes a kind of patriarchal role. He is much respected and looked to for counsel.

Appointed to the committee, besides Armstrong, were the following: (2) Robert Callender, a hunter and trapper of reputation and a celebrated Indian fighter. He is a survivor of both the Braddock and the Kittanning expeditions. It was to him that Armstrong dictated his report of the Kittanning affair. He had only recently become father-in-law to Dr. William Irvine, with whom he was serving on the committee. (3) William Thompson, thirty-eight years old, and Ireland-born. He lived near Carlisle, and, like Armstrong, was a surveyor. He served as one of Armstrong's captains during the Kittanning mission. In the succeeding June he will be commissioned Colonel and given command of the Rifle Battalion he has formed (450 men). With these men, he will join in the invasion of Quebec. Captured at Trois Rivieres, he will be effectively lost to the rebellion. He is buried in the Old Graveyard in Carlisle. (4) Dr. John Calhoon, one of the region's two physicians, and son-in-law to Colonel Benjamin Chambers of Chambersburg. (5) Jonathan Hoge, ten years younger than Armstrong, and like Armstrong a justice of the peace, very active in Cumberland County affairs. He will one day be elected to the Pennsylvania State Constitutional Convention. (6) Robert Magaw, an Ireland-born Carlisle attorney. He served many years in the militia forces. He would play an heroic role in the battle of Long Island until compelled to surrender Fort Washington. Like Irvine and Thompson, he too would become a prisoner-of-war.[1] (7)

Carlisle's thirty-three-year-old Ephraim Blaine, who had just retired after three terms as sheriff. As Commissary-General of the Northern Department during the last five years of the Revolution, he would be responsible for provisioning the rebel forces.[2] (8) John Allison, who, like Blaine, Wilson, and Thompson, was still in his thirties. Another of the county's justices, he was born near present-day Greencastle, near Carlisle. In October of 1765 he had been appointed one of the Committee of Observation for Cumberland County. He would shortly be serving as Colonel of the Second Battalion of Cumberland County militia and would be prominent in the New Jersey campaign of 1776-77. He was active in the Pennsylvania General Assembly, and in 1782 he would lay out and establish the community of Greencastle. (9) John Harris, of Carlisle, about whom little is known. (10) Robert Miller, a very active owner of land near Letort's Spring. He would play an important role in the Revolution and was a close friend to Washington. (11) Carlisle's "other" attorney, James Wilson, the youngest member of the Committee, who was born in Scotland and was a newcomer to Pennsylvania. Having debarked at Philadelphia only eight years before the date of this meeting, he had already served in the law offices of John Dickinson and had spent two years in Reading before he was "adopted" by John Armstrong. Armstrong, already impressed by what he had heard of young Wilson, had had a letter from the attorney on the advisability of opening a law office in Carlisle. The Colonel was ready with advice: "Ride here, without bidding the people of Reading a final farewell," and determine for yourself whether you might take to Carlisle with a sense of permanence. "As for such practice as we have here [Robert Magaw at this time was Carlisle's only attorney.] and my Interest to a share of it, you may firmly depend you shall not be at a loss."[3] Instantly and always a most ardent patriot, Wilson would become a member of the Continental Congress shortly after Lexington-Concord, and help to draft the Constitution. (12) John Montgomery, Ireland-born. Ten years younger than Armstrong, he had come to America as a teenager, and settled in Cumberland County. He was a Carlisle shopkeeper, a farmer, a lawyer, a judge, and a politician. On top of all that, he was, as a very young man, an heroic Indian fighter during the frontier wars.

He became Sheriff of Cumberland County. In the Battle of Long Island he would fight alongside Robert Magaw, and like Magaw would become a prisoner at the surrender of Fort Washington. Although without formal education and inclined to speak in a manner unsophisticated, he was respected for healthy common sense and unshakable integrity. (13) Dr. William Irvine, Ireland-born, thirty-two years old, and one of two physicians serving the Carlisle area. Just two years before this time he was married to Ann Callender, the fourteen-year-old daughter of Robert Callender. Irvine, like Thompson, would participate in the invasion of Quebec and would be captured. Unlike that of Thompson, his parole would end in time for him to serve at Monmouth. He would play a huge role in the Revolution, much of it as Commandant of the Western Department with headquarters at Fort Pitt.

Within a month three additional members were named: two justices of the peace, John Agnew and John Byers, and James Pollock, a tavern-keeper and the County's coroner. And in March necessary replacements were named in the figures of William Lyon, Armstrong's nephew, who had long ago become a prominent citizen of Carlisle, a prosperous shopkeeper and sometimes county government official; William Brown, Robert Whitehill, Hugh McCormick, and the two masters of the Latin School, Henry Makinly and John Creigh.

From this committee the meeting resolved to send Wilson, Magaw and Irvine as Deputies to meet the Deputies from other counties of this province at Philadelphia on Friday next, "in order to concert measures preparatory to the General Congress." [4]

What makes this a most remarkable meeting, according to Carlisle historian William Ames, is that "This was the *first* occasion on which a declaration advocating revolution was formally adopted in any of the American colonies and was eight days prior to the famous Mecklenberg Declaration." And it should be remembered also that when the Continental Congress Declaration of Independence was finally acted upon, "the vote of Pennsylvania was carried by the deciding ballot of James Wilson of Carlisle."

The function of the Committee, as the war drew ever closer, was to recruit and organize (selecting officers, etc.) companies of soldiers and to provide from Carlisle whatever military resources the Congress might require.

Armstrong, of course, was the natural choice to head up the militia force which was authorized, but was reluctant, because of his age, to do so. A letter to his son James, who is in medical practice in Virginia, is dated Shippensburg, May 11, 1775:

> *Dear Jamey, From my last letters you might naturally about this time have expectations of seeing me in Virginia, but the very alarming news of the late action near Boston of which I take for granted you must* [have] *had some acct. together with the intelligence of 14 Regiments, & 15 Frigates, beside*[s] *Horses & Marines having sail'd either for Boston or New York in order to enforce the submission of the Colonies to the late execrable Acts &c. These things and their natural attendants have for the present prevented me the pleasure of almost every private matter on Earth.*
>
> *Cumberland is very unanimous in the common cause but their movements not easily directed in any one uniform line. The Committee of the County however have resolved to pay five hundred Men for the protection of the Continental Congress if requisite, or any other immergency that the publick service may require. The whole county are now under a military association & beginning to assemble for exercise. The Committee have been so far wrong as to chuse me at this late day of my life to Command the Troops they may send. Callender, Lt. Col Thompson, Major, Messers Wilson, Magan* [Magaw]*, and Dr. Irwin* [Irvine] *have Companies. Dr. Franklin is lately arrived and chosen a Delegate by our Assembly for the Congress, as is our Mr. Wilson who set out yesterday. It's said Franklin brings accounts that only three thousand Men with some Marines, and two or three troops of Horse (the Horses to be purchased at New York) are at present coming. A second action has been daily expected at Boston of which we have yet no advice. These are the most solemn days America ever Saw! May it please God to hasten them.*

And then he advises James of his sixteen-year-old brother's late mishap:

Your Brother the other day by going in to the stable alone &

mounting as we suppose a young Mare then abreaking had like to have lost his life, he is mended much & the marks on his face will be but small, altho' he may be said to be fully recover'd yet he cannot remember how he came by the accident. He had mounted the Mare in the stable once or twice before, a boy holding her by its head, and now doing so alone must have been struck against a joice. Y'r Mare has got a Mare Colt, a sorril—somewhat curled, & scarcily think it by any well bred horse yet a pritty good Colt . . . . Anxious for your happinging, I am, Your Affectionate Father, John Armstrong[5]

On December 29, 1775, Colonel Armstrong, with others of the Committee, wrote to Dr. Benjamin Franklin, President of the Committee of Safety, to request permission to raise a Battalion in Cumberland County for the defense of Pennsylvania, and even recommended the officers: "Sir, As we understand Troops are to be Immediately raised in this province by order of Congress, we think we are able to raise a compleat Battalion in this County, Therefore hope the Committee of Safety will indulge us with one." And then Armstrong writes, " I beg leave to recommend the Gentlemen whose names are in the inclosed list for officers." He explains, "We are of opinion that Corps raised in confined districts where both officers and men are acquainted, is the best mode, as it may not only prevent discord (too often prevalent amongst promiscuous Crowds of men), but be more likely to be of real service to the Common Cause." The letter is signed by "Your Humble Servants," John Armstrong, John Byers, Robert Miller, John Agnew, and James Pollock. The officers designated for commissions were Colonel—William Irwin [Irvine]; Lt. Colonel—Ephraim Blaine; Major—James Dunlap; Captains—James Byers and S. Hay. For lieutenant and lesser ranks there were listed seventeen names, including those of James Wilson and John Montgomery.[6]

By the succeeding May 5 this County Committee had brought into its association some 3000 (!) men, and had voted five hundred men to be armed and disciplined, to serve with pay, and to be prepared to march on the first emergency. Carlisle was ready for the Revolution.[7]

Of course until this time the only position being adopted

was an expression of resentment and the colonists' insistence on rights and relief from oppression. The matter of independence, though hinted at here and there, was not on the table. Leave it to Carlisle, though, to spearhead the notion of independence. After the Declaration of War by the Second Continental Congress (May 10, 1775), but long before the signing of the Declaration of Independence, great interest in actual separation from Mother England appeared in Carlisle. A very lively meeting on the subject took place at the village square, the same public square that exists today, two blocks from Armstrong's home.

Historian William Ames has described how two attorneys formally debated the matter. One was strongly for severing all political ties with England; the other proclaimed such a thought "sheer madness." At the close of the arguments, Armstrong's nephew William Lyon arose to test the feeling of the crowd. He made a very short speech, in words that made his position quite clear. He then challenged the crowd to commit. He declared that all who favored independence should move to the north side of the square; those opposed, said he, may move to the south. The consequence, since all were Scotch-Irish, was hardly surprising. Standing at the north side were the great mass of people; standing to the south were none at all. Three or four, according to Ames, "moved neither way." [8]

And so the war came early to Carlisle. And the community was destined to play a major role. Not only was Carlisle made an important place of rendezvous for the American troops, but because of its location, at some distance from the principal actions, it became a post in which to confine British prisoners. Two of the most famous prisoners held here were Major John André and his friend Lt. Despard, who had been taken by Richard Montgomery near Lake Champlain and were first imprisoned in Lancaster. While here, in the summer and fall of 1776, they occupied the stone house on Armstrong's lot number 161, at the corner of South Hanover Street and Chapel (Locust) Alley, and were on parole of honor of six miles; but were prohibited going out of town except in military dress. Later, because of an infraction, they were confined to the town limits. While these two were under arrest in Carlisle, a man by the name of Thompson marched a party of soldiers to the house in which the prisoners were confined and swore that he would have their lives. Because Thompson had been an apprentice to her husband, the mistress of the house, a Mrs. Ramsey, was able to persuade him out of it.[9]

The Continental Congress also installed at Carlisle a munitions depot, an armory, where artillery training was provided and where "muskets, swords, and wrought iron cannon of great strength were made."[10]

The Second Continental Congress declared war on Great Britain on May 10, three weeks after Lexington-Concord. On June 15, it named George Washington Commander-in-Chief of the Continental Army. Through the summer of the first year of the war Washington labored to assemble an army, building on the New England militia men. He needed foot soldiers, and of course he needed officers. Happily, with the declaration of war Carlisle had promptly stepped up to the plate. Just a week after the battle of Breeds and Bunker Hills, Carlisle's William Thompson was commissioned Colonel (the first after Washington to be accorded that rank by the Continental Congress),[11] and given command of a company of riflemen he had himself rounded up. These troops in their butternut brown became the very first to reach Boston from the colonies beyond the Hudson; and on the first day of the year 1776 were made First Regiment of the Continental Army.

Carlisle's Dr. William Irvine, just thirty-five years old, likewise was commissioned Colonel and given command of the riflemen he had assembled. These two forces were among those serving General Richard Montgomery in the ill-fated invasion of Quebec. And, as noted, both Thompson and Irvine were captured and served long terms as prisoners-of-war.

For officers Washington looked to the men he knew and had cause to respect. To Congress, now convening in Philadelphia, he made on August 23 of the first summer of the war some recommendations:

As the filling up the place of vacant Brigadier-General will probably be of the first business of the honourable Congress, I flatter myself it will not be declared assuming to mention the names of two gentlemen whose former services, rank and age may be thought worthy of attention on this occasion. Of the one, I can speak from my own knowledge; of the other, only from character. The former is John Armstrong, of Pennsylvania: he served during the last war in most of the campaign to the southward, was honoured with the command of the Pennsylvania forces, and his general military conduct and spirit much approved by all who served with him; besides which, his character was distinguished by an enterprise against the Indians [Kittanning], *which he planned with great judgment, and executed with equal courage and success. It was not till lately that I had reason to believe he would enter again on publick service, and it is now wholly unsolicited and unknown on his part.*

He then comments on Colonel Joseph Frye of Massachusetts Bay, and concludes that "Either of the gentlemen . . . will be received by me with the utmost deference and respect." [12]

And John Adams is concerned in this matter too. A letter of his (November 15, 1775) to twenty-eight-year-old Samuel Osgood,[13] at that time an aide to General Artemus Ward, is most interesting. He has been campaigning for Colonel Joseph Frye (spelled variously): "As soon as I arrived in Philadelphia, I made it my Business to introduce General Fries Name and Character into Conversation in every private Company where it could be done with Propriety, and to make his long services and Experience known. But I found an Interest making in private Circles in Favour of Coll. Armstrong of Pensilvania, a Gentleman of Character and Experience in War, a Presbyterian in Religion, whose Name runs high for Piety, Virtue and Valour." [14]

The Frye versus Armstrong matter had been vigorously debated in Congress on Thursday, September 21, 1775: "The Congress proceeded to the election of a Brigadier General and the votes being brought in and the ballots examined, it was found that Col. [John] Armstrong and Col. [Joseph] Frye had equal votes. On motion, Resolved, that the appointment of a Brigadier General be deferred." [15]

Armstrong's letter to his wife Rebeckah, February 6, (cited earlier) had included remarks on the matter of appointments to brigadier general, involving Frye, William Thompson, Dr. Mercer, and himself; and the Colonel had been concerned about the effect a commission to Frye might have on Thompson.

On February 18, 1776, Joseph Reed, President of Pennsylvania's Supreme Executive Council, directed to Washington a letter in which he inquired into the Commander-in-Chief's feelings for the military men of the colony who were being considered for commissions and assignments. Washington, from Cambridge, having apparently already discussed these matters with the Congress, replied on March 7. His high regard for Armstrong, whom he considered a close friend and with whom he had served on the Forbes Expedition, is quite apparent: "I am of opinion that Colonel Armstrong, if he retains his health, spirits, and vigour, would be as fit a person as any they could send to Virginia, as he is senior officer to any now there, and I should think could give no offense."

But, always acutely conscious of jealousies and injured feelings, he had discouraged the "bringing of Colonel Armstrong into this Army as Major-General, however great his merit." It was Washington's feeling that such a commission "would introduce much confusion." (Washington's term for the consequence of affronts to vanity and excessive consciousness of rank is "confusion.") His concern was for General John Thomas, whom Washington believed to be a "good man," and who, Washington was certain, "would surely quit."

He had serious reservations about Carlisle's William Thompson. He was not high, and never ever came to be, on Thompson. To place Thompson in command in Virginia "would throw everything into the utmost confusion; for it is by mere chance that he became first Colonel in this Army. To take him, then, from another Colony [Pennsylvania], place him over the heads of several gentlemen under or with whom he has served in a subordinate character, would never answer any other purposes than that of introducing endless confusion."

Of course Washington knows, better than anyone else, the Virginia military. Such an appointment, he says, "cannot be in contemplation." But he does at least give Thompson some credit for a little common sense:

> *Knowing the mischiefs it would produce surely Colonel Thompson would have more sense and a greater regard for the cause he is engaged in, than to accept of it, unless some common abilities or exertions had given him a superior claim. He must know that nothing more than being a Captain of Horse in the year 1759 (I think it was)* [Actually it was 1758.] *did very extraordinarily give him the start he now has, when the rank was settled here. At the same time he must know another fact, that several officers now in the Virginia service are much his superiors in point of rank, and will not, I am sure, serve under him. He stands first Colonel here, and may, I presume, put in a very good and proper claim to the first brigade that falls vacant; but I hope more regard will be paid to the service than to send him to Virginia.*

Looking ahead, Washington muses, "If Thomas supplies [assumes] the place of Lee, there will be a vacancy for either Armstrong or Thompson [at the Major-General rank]; for I have heard of no other valiant son of New England waiting promotion since the advancement of [Joseph] Frye, who has not done, and I doubt will not do, much service to the cause." [16]

Before this correspondence, on Friday, March 1, 1776, the Congress had finally held an election to determine Brigadier Generals for the Continental Army. "The ballots being delivered in and examined . . . the following gentlemen were elected: John Armstrong, Esq., William Thompson, Esq., Andrew Lewis, Esq., James Moore, Esq., the Right Hon. William, Earl of Stirling, Robert Howe, Esq., four of whom [including Thompson and Armstrong] are to command under you [Charles Lee] in the Southern Department, and two in the middle." [17]

And so John Armstrong was thrown into the War of the Revolution. On the very next day, by John Hancock, President of the Congress, he was informed of his commission and given his marching orders: "Sir: The American Congress from a sense of your merit and zeal in the American cause, have been induced to appoint you a Brigadier-General in the Continental Army. I do myself the honour of enclosing your commission; and shall only add, that I have it in charge from Congress to direct that you repair as soon as possible to South-Carolina, there to take the command of the

Continental Troops till further orders." [18]

President Hancock had his reply from Armstrong the same day. The fifty-eight year-old surveyor, conscious of his years, and anxious about his military experience, is yet proud to accept:

> *Sir: Your favour of this day, covering the commission of a Brigadier-General of that venerable body where you preside, does me great honour. The importance of the station in which they are pleased to place me, as well as the trust and confidence implied in the appointment, fills me with concern. Conscious as I am of my small degree of military knowledge, and sensible, very sensible, of the decline of nature I had no right to expect an appointment of this sort, and beg leave to assure the Congress that I accept the commission from a sense of duty to this much-injured country, and shall, by divine aid, endeavour to execute it to the best of my ability. Permit me, sir, to request you may please to return my grateful thanks to that August body for this mark of confidence and to assure them of my readiness to comply with their future commands to the utmost of my power.* [19]

Four days later (March 6), with Congress preparing for British assaults, and sensitive to vulnerable targets, President Hancock got off an updating letter to the Commander-in-Chief, who is in Cambridge. To Washington he wrote: "As there is reason to think that the force of our enemies will be directed against the Colonies in the Southern Department, Major-General [Charles] Lee is appointed to that command. The Brigadier-Generals are, John Armstrong, William Thompson, Andrew Lewis, James Moore, Esq., Lord Stirling [William Alexander], and Robert Howe, Esq. Of those gentlemen, General Armstrong is directed to repair to South-Carolina; General Lewis and General Howe to Virginia; General Moore to North-Carolina; and General Thompson and Lord Stirling to New-York." [20]

As early as January of this year (1776), the British, confident of great Loyalist support in the southern colonies, and expecting an enthusiastic reception from the Royal Governor of South Carolina, Josiah Martin, had drawn up a design that included an assault on Charleston. The plan was to send Sir Henry Clinton south, there to await support from Admiral Sir Peter Parker and Lord Cornwallis. Clinton was placed in command of the army, and Parker had command of the naval forces. The large plan was delivered a setback when a Patriot force dealt a resounding defeat to Loyalist forces near Wilmington, but Clinton pushed ahead and joined Cornwallis off Cape Fear, North Carolina. The Continental Army, aware of these proceedings, had in the meanwhile dispatched its second in command, Major General Charles Lee, responsible for the Southern Department, to the defense of South Carolina's principal seaport. Lee, although not altogether certain of what the British had in mind, sensed the danger to Charleston, and sent Armstrong posthaste to the seaport.[21]

Peter Parker

Where there come together the two rivers known as the Ashley and the Cooper, to form a bay some seven miles long, there had grown up on the land between the streams a thriving and energetic community, a seaport city, known as Charleston. In 1776 the settlement was the capital of the colony of South Carolina. Among the most attractive features of the beautiful bay were the many islands, including Sullivan's Island, James Island, and Morris Island. In the spring and early summer of 1776, Charleston was going about the normal very busy commerce of a seaport town. But the Continental Congress, meeting in far away Philadelphia was much concerned about it. The people too had heard enough to become anxious. It was pretty well understood that with the outbreak of revolution this harbor would become a principal target of the British.

As it happened, the colony of South Carolina, although a very large number of its people had been born in the British Isles, was by this time on fire with the spirit of the revolution. On the 26th of March, without actually declaring independence, it had made a formal move in that direction. The "Committee of Eleven" on that day had drawn up a constitution for South Carolina, which in effect made South Carolina an independent state rather than a colony. This document placed the executive power in the office of a President. On the very next day a President was chosen. His name was John Rutledge. A thirty-seven-year-old attorney, he had studied law in London, and had commenced the practice of law in Charleston at the age of twenty-two. With a rich experience in government, he was a natural choice. His vice-president was the soon-to-be famous Henry Laurens; and William Henry Drayton was named Chief Justice.

These men were as passionate about the Cause as any in Massachusetts or Virginia. Rutledge, in his very long acceptance speech, though not employing the term "independence," spoke in that spirit: "The eyes of the whole world are on America; the eyes of every other colony are on this, a colony whose reputation for generosity and magnanimity is universally acknowledged. I trust there will be no civil discord here; and that the only strife amongst brethren will be, who shall do most to serve and to save an injured country." [22]

On April 23rd the courts of justice were opened in Charleston. Chief Justice Drayton made the ceremony a most memorable occasion. After prefatory remarks, he proclaimed in sonorous tones, more than two months before the Continental Congress was to declare independence:

The law of the land authorizes me to declare, and it is my duty to declare the law, that George III, king of Great Britain, has abdicated the government, that he has no authority over us, and we owe no obedience to him . . . . O Carolinians! Happy would you be under this new constitution, if you knew your happy state. True reconcilement never can exist between Great Britain and America, the latter being in subjection to the former. The Almighty created

America to be independent of Britain; to refuse our labors in this divine work, is to refuse to be a great, a free, a pious and a happy people.

For the historian George Bancroft this was a signal moment of the American Revolution. He declared that with this pronouncement South Carolina deserved high praise for her "virtuous and glorious example of instituting a complete government." [23] And it should be noted, too, that her neighbor, North Carolina, was the first of the thirteen colonies to declare formally a state of independence. This occurred on April 12, 1776, fifty-one weeks after Lexington-Concord.

Charleston in 1776 was ready for the war if it came. From the spring of the year, it had been making preparations to defend against a British threat. Her young President was an ardent patriot, and, happily, the military was in the very capable hands of a veteran Indian fighter and experienced military man named William Moultrie. A fort had been begun at the entrance to the bay, on Sullivan's Island; and militia units, including two companies of riflemen, had been organized in the surrounding country. Loyalists, and there were many (including Moultrie's own brother), were made uncomfortable. Bullets were being cast from all available lead, even from window weights, and earthworks were being constructed.

General Armstrong comes as a stranger to Charleston. He has never been to this settlement. Indeed, though he has spent a good bit of time in Washington's Virginia, he has never traveled south of that colony. Besides, this is a warfare new to him. This is not an Indian village on a wilderness river. Here is a seaport, likely to be invaded by warships. But he comes to the colony as a representative of the Continental Congress and as a high-ranking officer of the Continental Army.

And when the General arrived in Charleston on May 3, he was most hospitably received. As he reported to President Hancock, he found the military "established in a different way from that which is Continental . . . so that at present I have little more to do than to receive the civilities of the gentlemen here, equally hospitable and polite." He is much impressed by the ardor with which the city, and indeed the whole colony, is supporting the rebellion: ". . . such is the activity and publick spirit of the officers, the great merit and distinguished abilities of the President [Rutledge], procuring to him the common suffrage of this country, that I see no reason to apprehend the publick service should suffer in his hands."

This letter to Hancock was dated May 7, 1776. On the same day Armstrong wrote also to General Charles Lee to request further orders, half-expecting to be recalled to North Carolina, "in case the enemy should gain a footing there." In the remainder of his letter to Hancock, he updated the Congress on the situation in the deep South:

I should be unpardonable to omit the very friendly reception given me by the President, to which, in a gentlemanly style, he has added a series of good offices. The great loss of this country is its want of men, and the misfortune of so many malcontents, said to be about two thousand or upwards. A number of the better part sort of these are coming over; but the greater part of them are said to be of the canaille [rabble], *who probably want to avail themselves of a day of publick calamity, for the abject purposes of rapine and plunder. Four thousand men, I think, have been voted by this Government; of that number, about two thousand are now raised, and many officers out recruiting. Some accounts from Georgia speak of two thousand British troops being at St. Augustine; not generally believed. The Continental troops at Georgia are about four hundred; and when joined by the Militia, are, by the gentlemen here, estimated at one thousand. I shall, however, write to the Colonel of that battalion. For the North Government, we hope for considerable numbers, and a short time will probably bring one of the Carolinas into action, as appears by a late accession to the fleet at Cape-Fear. Happy for these Colonies (particularly South-Carolina and Georgia) should the Insurgents, the domesticks, and Indians, be restrained.*[24]

This letter was read before the assembled Continental Congress on June 17.

Moultrie in his recollections noted the appearance of Armstrong: "General Armstrong arrived from the northward . . . .

He was a brave man and a good officer, but not much acquainted with our manner of defence, which was principally forts and batteries. . . . We had at that time at least 100 pieces of cannon mounted in different parts of our harbor."[25]

Armstrong, for his part, was very much impressed by Moultrie. He knew him already, by reputation, and much respected him for his frontier fighting abilities. Happily, in Armstrong the Continental Army had dispatched to Charleston an officer far removed from arrogance, and not likely to get carried away by his authority. Although the Continental Congress had given Armstrong, until such time as Lee could arrive, the command of the defense of Charleston, the General was quite willing to defer for strategy to the much younger Colonel William Moultrie.

William Moultrie

On the 29th of May, Armstrong got off a letter of happy information to General Robert Howe, then probably in Virginia. It read in part: "Last Saturday a sloop arrived here from St. Eustasia with ten thousand pounds of powder, the master of which says that a large vessel had arrived there from Holland, deeply laden with arms and ammunition, and that some Philadelphia vessels were loading out of her. He also says that the French ports in the West-Indies are open to us, and that the French men-of-war have orders to protect our vessels in and out of their harbours; that the French are fortifying Dunkirk, which produced a remonstrance from the British Court, but without effect." [26]

The expected occurred, much to the alarm of the city, on the last day of May when a large fleet of British warships was sighted off Dewee's Island, some twenty miles to the north of the Charleston harbor. Next day these vessels, probably fifty, gunships and transports, appeared just outside Sullivan's Island. In the settlement the alarm was sounded. The result was something approaching panic, but in the confusion, on orders from Rutledge, great numbers of militia were able to assemble in the city, and under the direction of Colonel Moultrie assumed the positions thought most necessary to defense. Rutledge accompanied Armstrong in a close inspection of all fortifications, both on the mainland and on the islands. Moultrie was placing most confidence in the fort still being constructed on Sullivan's Island, at the entrance to the harbor, a bit to the north. A few months ago the island had been nothing but a wilderness, and it was not expansive. But it featured large numbers of live oaks, palmettos and myrtle; and it was certainly large enough to accommodate a fort. On March 2, Colonel Moultrie had been given command of its defense and had been ordered to build a fort "large enough to hold a garrison of a thousand men." [27] The work had been begun, and Moultrie had installed thirty-one guns on the perimeter. But the fort was as yet only partially constructed.

Moultrie reported the arrival of the British on June 3. From Sullivan's Island, where he has been very busy in the building of the fort, he advised President Rutledge: "We have seen this day two large ships—a top-sail schooner and a tender. The tender has been very busy in sounding from the inlet at our advance-guard, all along to Long Island. It seems as though they intended their descent somewhere hereabout. Our fort is now enclosed. It is the opinion of every one that we should have more men at this post; but as I know they cannot be spared from the capital, I must make the best defence I can with what I have got, and doubt not but that I shall give four or five hundred men a great deal of trouble before they can dislodge me from this post." [28]

On June 8 Henry Clinton, under a flag of truce delivered (with some difficulty, because the first delegation was mistakenly fired upon!) a proclamation to the city. Noting "a most unprovoked and wicked rebellion within South Carolina," and chastising the "infatuated and misguided multitude" with a "succession of crimes," he promised "free pardon to such as should lay down their arms and submit to the laws." [29] He had good reason to expect rebuke and he got it.

Shortly after the appearance of the British fleet, General Lee, who had been apprised of the threat, arrived from North Carolina, accompanied by General Robert Howe. Moultrie was glad to see him, noting that many regarded his coming as "equal to a reinforcement of 1000 men." [30] Reported the Colonel afterwards: "His presence gave us great spirits, as he was known to be an able, brave, and experienced officer, though hasty and rough in his manners, which the officers could not reconcile themselves to at first."

Lee took immediate command, meeting with Rutledge on the ninth, inspecting first what would be Armstrong's fortifications at Haddrell's Point, and then the unfinished fort on Sullivan's Island, and all boats and munitions. "Every hour of the day," according to Moultrie, he was on horseback making mighty preparation. However, he did not approve of Moultrie's reliance on Sullivan's Island. As only one side and the front of the fort had been completed, he

Charles Lee

was not impressed. He regarded the fort as a "slaughter pen," and urged the Colonel to give it up. When Rutledge absolutely refused to withdraw the garrison, Lee insisted on bridges and boats for retreat! [31]

And Lee, while at first applauding Moultrie's plan to attack whatever British troops had been carried to Long Island, very soon discouraged all thoughts of that. On June 10, at six o'clock in the evening, he composed a note expressing his concern: "Sir, I am just returned from an excursion into the country. As the large ships are now over the bar, and as your bridge must be finished, I would wish you would lay aside all thoughts of an expedition against Long-Island, unless your scouts bring such intelligence as almost to insure a successful stroke." And next day he repeated the advice, insisting that "the bridge of retreat . . . be finished this night" and "I would have you, by all means, lay aside all thoughts of the expedition against Long-Island, unless you receive assurances from your scouts that you may strike an important stroke." [32]

Communication back and forth from the officers defending Charleston was a little difficult, as the pony express could not operate. Messages had to be delivered by boats, powered by oars. Fortunately distances from mainland and back and forth from the various islands were short. In most cases the courier would wait for his answer. There were lots of messages to be conveyed during the month of June. Lee and Moultrie stayed in touch as best they could.

How very much Lee opposed Moultrie's decision to defend Sullivan's Island is apparent in his letter of June 11:

> *Sir: I was much surprised that this morning the Engineer should make a report to me that a bridge of retreat was impracticable, as I understand that a few days ago yourself and the other Field Officers gave it as your opinion that it might be effected. . . . . As I think your security will be much greater by posting a considerable body of Riflemen on the continent than on the Island, I must desire that you will immediately detach four hundred of them to the continent. They are to post themselves, or rather extend themselves, from the left of Point Haddrell towards Long-Island, by which means they will be able to prevent the enemy*

from erecting works to cut off your retreat. I would order the whole body off the Island, but apprehend it might make your garrison uneasy. [!] .... *I request that this order may be instantly obeyed.*

And then in a postscript he adds that the detachment should be made up to 500 rather than 400.[33]

On the 13th he asked for an additional detachment of 100 men. And from Haddrell's Point on the 15th, he advises Moultrie: "I have stationed Brigadier-General Armstrong at this place. You are to make all your reports to him, and in all respects to consider him as your commanding officer."[34] Fortunately, Armstrong understood a whole lot better than did General Lee, how little Moultrie needed in the way of orders, or even counsel.

And Moultrie here took advantage of this line of command to secure from Armstrong a return of some of the men Lee had "stolen" from him. In the company of William Thompson, whose name is spelled variously, he sat down to write:

Colonel Thompson [whom Moultrie has placed in command of the infantry forces on the island] *is now with me, and informs me that he has taken particular notice of the movement of the enemy. He observed about ten o'clock two hundred Grenadiers and a small battalion (which he imagines came from Dewee to cover the landing of the rest), where they posted themselves about one mile from our advanced guard, and waited until about seventeen hundred men were landed. They then marched off to Dewee's Island. He observed every six men carried something like a tent. They are still landing as fast as the boats can bring them. Colonel Thompson begs that he may have at least his own men which are over with you (one hundred) without whom he cannot undertake to prevent their landing on this Island, should they attempt it. We are all in high spirits, and will keep a good look-out to prevent a surprise. Colonel Thompson requests as a favour, if you have time, that you could come over and take a ride on the Island to observe what a length of ground we have to defend.*[35]

It is not known whether Armstrong accepted this invitation. But he replied promptly, by return boat, assuring Moultrie that he would, "if you send the boats," comply with the request for the return of the one hundred men. He is a little concerned about the first of Lee's bridges, which is still under construction, and hopes that the German engineer, John De Brahm, can "be early at work there." Anxious about the possibility of a British attack on his troops at Haddrell's, he speculates: "Does not the movement of the enemy toward Dewees's look like an intention to use one of the creeks towards Haddrell's, probably Bolton's landing?" And he urges vigilance. "Keep your troops alert." Although not giving orders, and clearly more in approval of Moultrie's defense than is Lee, he writes, "I see no reason why you may not also reinforce Colonel Thompson; nay, if they appear indeed to land on Sullivan's, it must be done, and the point at the Island where they may best land prudently and vigorously defended at all events. . . . May Heaven attend you all." [36]

Clinton and Cornwallis had agreed that an assault on Sullivan's Island was imperative. And they agreed that the best approach to the island was from Long Island, which (now known as the Isle of Palms) was little more than an extended stretch of sand, and separated from Sullivan's by but a narrow passage of water. On the very day on which Lee arrived at Haddrell's Point, Clinton had boated between 400 and 500 men to Long Island. Although Armstrong and Moultrie and Lee could not know definitely, the British were preparing to launch a two-pronged attack on Sullivan's, with Clinton's troops charging the beaches, and the big guns of the warships laying waste to the fort. Lee every hour expressed his concern. Moultrie proceeded with confidence in his work to complete the fort.

Lee continued to worry about the bridges. In a note to Moultrie, delivered on the 21st, he complained that the bridge constructed by the Engineer De Brahm was "so illy executed" that it would promptly fail; and he urged Moultrie to see to its improvement. He wonders whether the second bridge has been begun. He is also critical of Moultrie's island defense so far: "I must likewise express my concern when I am told that your gunners are suffered to fire at the enemy when it is almost impossible that their fire should have any effect. I must desire you, sir, that you must establish it as an eternal rule, that no piece of ordnance, great or small, should be fired at a greater distance than four hundred yards; but all orders will be vain unless you make an example of the first who disregards your orders." In a postscript, still thinking negatively, he adds: "Those two field-pieces at the very end of the Point [those which Thompson is so proud of] are so exposed that I desire you will draw them off to a more secure distance from the enemy; in their present situation, it appears to me they may be carried off whenever the enemy think proper." [37]

Shortly after Lee dispatched this letter, he began to feel uncomfortable about its tone. To Moultrie that very evening he got off a second letter: "I hope you will excuse the style of my last letter. I must once more repeat that it did not arise from any diffidence in your judgment, zeal, or spirit; but merely from an apprehension that your good nature and easy temper might, in some measure, counteract those good qualities which you are universally known to possess. . . .I cannot wish this important post in better hands than yours: once more, therefore, excuse my manner of writing." He then informs Moultrie of officer assignments he has recently made, including the information that he has ordered Captain Tuffts "to put himself under the command of General Armstrong" at Haddrell's Point. "I shall write to the General [Armstrong] to-night, to order him to station him in such a manner as to be of the greatest use to you." He informs Moultrie that he is expecting Colonel John Muhlenberg's Regiment, "and I flatter myself that we shall be able to devise some means of baffling the enemy, should your post be really their object." [38]

The British got in motion the next day when the *Bristol*, escorted by three score lesser vessels, managed to cross the bar and to anchor some three miles out from Sullivan's. But action was delayed by unfavorable winds and by British indecision. Moultrie worked away on the fort. It was a week before Clinton, though still wary of water depth between Long Island and Sullivan's, was satisfied with his troops on Long Island. He had now three thousand well equipped soldiers, supplied with some artillery, ready to be boated the distance to Sullivan's. He ordered the assault for the 23rd. But again unfavorable winds made a delay necessary.

In the meanwhile, on orders from Lee, the "fighting parson," thirty-year-old John Peter Gabriel Muhlenberg, who had left his church in Woodstock, Virginia, to serve the cause, arrived with his regiment of Lutheran Germans. And Lee, on the fifteenth, had installed Armstrong with South Carolina's Continental Army forces of 1500 men across the bay to the north, at Haddrell's Point, that little spit of land jutting out into the ocean. And a regular regiment of South Carolina volunteers, the First Carolina Regiment, was in garrison at Fort Johnson, on the northern tip of James Island, which was three miles out from Charleston. This regiment was under the command of the redoubtable Christopher Gadsden, who was only a bit younger than General Armstrong. Gadsden, a wealthy merchant and educated in England, was, nevertheless, as passionate about the cause as any South Carolinian. The city itself was defended by Colonel Charles Pinckney, in command of a regiment of Carolina volunteers.

At the extreme of Sullivan's Island, roughly three miles to the northeast of the fort, Colonel Moultrie had stationed a Pennsylvania Scotch-Irishman, whose family had removed to South Carolina during his childhood. This was the above mentioned William Thompson,[39] of Orangeburg, by all accounts as courageous and able as any military man to be found in the South. A veteran of the Indian wars and now forty-seven years old, Thompson had at his command 750 men, including 300 skilled riflemen raised in Orangeburg, 200 North Carolinians, under Colonel Thomas Clark, who had arrived on June 11, and 200 South Carolina regulars under Colonel Peter Horry. Besides there was the famous company of fifty militia who were known as the Raccoon Company of Riflemen. All of these men Thompson had skillfully posted at the spots most likely to receive a landing. The Raccoon Company he had at the very point of the island, "behind some hills and myrtle bushes." A formidable swamp on his left made a landing there unthinkable. On his right, from which he expected Clinton's soldiers, he posted his two guns, an eighteen-pounder and a six-pounder, "which entirely commanded the landing."[40] As the British would at the last be wading through fairly deep water, even at low tide, Thompson and Moultrie were both confident that no landing could be effected without great cost, conceivably the death of every man.

Moultrie at the fort had but 435 men.[41] However, these

included his second-in-command, a man in whom he placed great confidence, the resourceful Isaac Motte; and a forty-four-year-old officer named Francis Marion, who, already a much experienced Indian fighter, would hereafter be a scourge to the British, and would, because of his phantom-like appearances and disappearances become known as the Swamp Fox.

Colonel Moultrie had thirty-one guns, but no more than twenty-one could be employed at the same time. The fort, although still unfinished, and with walls only seven feet high on two sides, was embraced by a thick plank, and the cannon. The courageous officer continued confident he could withstand an assault against a far superior number of soldiers.

Work on the fort proceeded apace. Virtually every single laborer of every kind, including contractors and mechanics, was delivered to Sullivan's Island, and there worked frantically to complete the structure. Moultrie remembers a visit from the skeptical General Lee. Taking Moultrie apart from the workers, he asked, "Colonel, do you think you can maintain this post?" Moultrie had no trouble in recalling his confident reply: "Yes, sir, I think I can." On another occasion a much experienced seaman advised the Colonel that when the British ships passed alongside the fort, they would "knock it down in half an hour." Replied Moultrie, "Well then, we shall lie behind the ruins and prevent their men from landing."

The supremely confident Moultrie had given orders to Thompson that if his men could not stand up to the enemy they were "to throw themselves into the fort, by which I should have had upwards of 1000 men in a large, strong fort, and General Armstrong in my rear with 1500 men, not more than one mile and a half off, with a small arm of the sea between us, that he could have crossed a body of men in boots to my assistance. This was my situation. I therefore felt myself perfectly easy because I never calculated upon Sir Henry Clinton's numbers to be more than 3000 men. As to the men-of-war, we should have taken very little notice of them if the army had attacked us." [42]

One thing was certain—the long delay, almost an entire month, had provided South Carolina the necessary time to mount a formidable defense. The delay had been caused in large measure by

British disagreements and indecision. And Moultrie enjoyed a little luck too. Dame Fortune was smiling on the Carolinas during this month of June. The movements of His Majesty's vessels were much restricted by uncooperative winds. The problem was later described in his memoirs by one of the British surgeons: "All our motions were so languid and so innervate that it was the 9th of June before the *Bristol* and *Pigot* passed [over] the bar of Charlestown. The *Bristol* in passing struck, which alarmed us all exceedingly; but, as it wanted two hours of high water, she soon floated again. The *Prince of Piedmont*, a victualling ship, was totally lost on the north breakers of the bar. General Clinton and Lord Charles Cornwallis were both on board when she struck, but as the weather was very fine, they were not in the least danger."

The delay thus caused resulted in the opportunity Moultrie's men needed. The surgeon who is recalling the scene remembers how astonished those aboard his vessel were at the great industry they could perceive through their field glasses.[43]

The strength of the resistance had grown dramatically in these thirty days. In all, the port of Charleston was now protected by the forces of Gadsden, Thompson, Muhlenberg, Armstrong, Moultrie, Charles Pinckney's regiment in the city, and a number of other units of Carolina militia, in all probably a good six thousand armed men. And strategically placed earthworks and fortifications bristled on the islands and along the shoreline.

On the 25th *HMS Experiment* with its fifty (!) guns crossed over the bar. The gunships, while yet discreetly remaining beyond the reach of Moultrie's cannon, were moving closer to the position from which a massive bombardment could be launched at the fort. In all, the British fleet, besides the fifty guns of the *Bristol* and the fifty of the *Experiment*, boasted another 142 on the other nine gunships and smaller frigates.

As the battle loomed, Armstrong grew apprehensive. To Moultrie on this day, the 25th, aware of the movement of the ships, he boated a letter from Haddrell's Point to report big problems with the bridge: "This moment I was about to write you to learn the occasion and utility of the firing from the Point. I hope some of your officers have been up to see and give the necessary directions. The Baron's [Baron Massenbaugh, one of the Continental

Engineers] conjectures may be right, but their breastworks may as naturally be designed as a defence against any effort made upon our part." He was guessing right when he predicted to Moultrie that the British troops now on Long Island "will not attempt to land on Sullivan's Island until the armed vessels are first before your fort."

But Armstrong is still not certain of British intent, and fears that Clinton's troops may attempt an invasion of the mainland as well, possibly, of course, head-on at Haddrell's Point. And the bridge continues a great concern:

The state of the bridge and marsh is like to give me great trouble. Part of the last detachment I ordered to your Island has this morning absolutely refused, until the passage between the two places is safely passable. I am a little surprised that your Sergeant, agreeable to orders of yesterday, did not meet the men I sent to stake out the best path through the marsh on your side the bridge; nor could the men I sent find any boards laid down, as you remember was ordered on Saturday night. This is the third day that, for want of boats, I could not get this detachment over—now part have refused. I sent an express to General Lee, and, in the mean time desire to know whether any new amendments for the bridge are going on on your side the water, and further notice as the movements of the enemy may require. I am obliged to throw up works in a kind of chain, near four miles from this camp; the enemy constantly striving to find new landing places on the main.[44]

A number of communications over this and the next two days express Lee's continuing concern about the bridge. One letter, written on the 27th, which is the eve of the engagement, reveals that Lee is now convinced that the attack will be made on Sullivan's Island. He reports to Moultrie that "I have ordered General Armstrong to send a hundred volunteers to ease Colonel Thompson's Regiment of their heavy duty." He is sarcastically critical of Colonel Horry: "I find that a part of Colonel Horry's Regiment has most magnanimously refused to take this duty on them; we shall live I hope to thank them." And he is still on the bridge, but now it is a bridge that can provide support, rather than one that facilitates retreat: "I am in hopes your bridge will be finished this night; you can then be reinforced at pleasure." [45]

On the morning of June 28, at about 9:30, while Colonel Moultrie was checking with Colonel Thompson at the outward corner of the island, he perceived small boats "in motion back of Long Island," as if they intended an assault on the shores of Sullivan's Island, and at the same time noticed that the men-of-war were getting underway. By the time he had got back to the fort, eight of the vessels had come close enough to the island to evoke cannon fire from Moultrie's guns.

At noon, Clinton ordered the troops on Long Island to embark for Sullivan's. These troops, however, composed of light infantry, grenadiers, and the Royal Fifteenth Regiment, never got so close to Sullivan's as to leave their boats and attempt a landing. Indeed the wading of the last water, deeper than expected, they would have found a perilous and very short journey. According to one of the British soldiers, all of whom turned back, Thompson's men were far too much for them. "They would have killed half of us before we could make our landing good." [46] Fortunately for the British force, Clinton had enough savvy to appreciate the catastrophe that would have resulted from an attempt on the island. As he withdrew, he considered an attack on Armstrong and his 1500 troops at Haddrell's Point, but, even though Parker was pledging frigates for support, he promptly gave up on that too.

The British fleet fared hardly any better. The ships were firing from a distance of 400 yards, and not all that accurately. The shelling that was delivered by the *Thunder*, which was equipped with mortars, fell harmlessly into the morass which lay at the center of the fort. And when the fleet's flagship backed up to the island, she was received by a withering barrage from Moultrie's cannon. The Colonel remembered well how "Mind the Commodore" was passed down the firing line. "Mind the two fifty-gun ships."

Revolutionary War historian Richard Wheeler has described the scene aboard the flagship, the terrible damage that she suffered: "Sir Peter Parker himself," he reports, "narrowly escaped a grievous and somewhat embarrassing injury. As one of the fleet's sailors later explained, 'In the hottest of the action, a [cannon] ball passed so near Sir Peter's coat tail as to tear it off, together with his clothes, clear to the buff....'" [47]

Moultrie recollects that General Lee showed up at the fort at the height of the action, and finding everything going so well that his presence was superfluous, decided to go "up to town again." The Colonel insisted that he never saw men fight more bravely. He was very much impressed by how cool his soldiers were in the heat of action: "Several of the officers, as well as myself, were smoking our pipes and giving orders." The only concern seemed to be a want of powder. The fort, its walls sixteen feet thick, stood up to the shelling astonishingly well.

Though the besieged did not want for inspiration, they had plenty of it in the courage exhibited by the wounded. After the battle, in writing to his wife, one of Moultrie's officers, a Major Barnard Elliott, recalled a tragic and dramatic moment: "The expression of a Sergeant McDaniel, after a cannon ball had taken off his shoulder and scooped out his stomach, is worth recording in the annals of America: 'Fight on, my brave boys; don't let liberty expire with me today!'" [48]

At about one o'clock, the British hopes for a successful landing on Sullivan's were elevated by an abrupt cessation of firing from the island. The fleet took the silence to mean that the fort was being abandoned. In reality, Moultrie had ordered the guns to cease because he was running perilously close to the end of the powder. His request for additional powder had been denied by Lee, who had returned the reply, from Haddrell's Point, "If you should unfortunately expend your ammunition without beating off the enemy or driving them on ground, spike your guns and retreat." But by three o'clock, now much impressed by the conduct of Moultrie's force, he had managed to round up "more ammunition for you," and had also ordered "a large corps of Riflemen to reinforce Colonel Thompson." And then, there arrived on the island a wee slip of paper with the most welcome pencil-inscribed note from President Rutledge: "Dear Sir, I send you five hundred pounds of powder. . . . You know our collection is not very great. Honour and victory, my good sir, to you, and our worthy countrymen with you." And there was added a caution: "Do not make too free with your cannon. Cool and do mischief." [49]

Fortunately Rutledge did come through with 500 pounds of powder, and another 200 were gained from a Carolina schooner anchored near the inside shore of Sullivan's.⁵⁰ British hopes were dashed when at about five o'clock Moutrie resumed the firing of the cannon.

But it was not only the courage and endurance of Moultrie's men that turned the tide of battle. In the early movements of the ships, three of the British flotilla, hoping to get between Haddrell's Point and Sullivan's, in the unfamiliar waters actually got blown together. The result was that the frigate *Acteon* was driven aground, was abandoned by her crew, who set her afire, and later (after she had been ransacked by the Americans) blew up. The *Sphinx* lost her forward sail altogether, and the *Syren*, while not seriously damaged was discouraged from her course. Each of these three frigates boasted twenty-eight guns.⁵¹

Moultrie, long after, recalled how the men, on this very hot day, were served along the firing platform a curious mixture of liquor and water ("never a more agreeable draught") in the buckets used to douse fires. And he remembered fondly how the people of the city were fixed all day upon the action; and he learned later how their hearts had fallen when the fort's flag, the beautiful blue with the white crescent, inscribed "Liberty," disappeared, and how their spirits soared when the flag was restored through the bravery of one Sergeant William Jasper,⁵² who had been recruited by Captain Francis Marion to serve with the Second South Carolina Regiment. As it was later recalled by Sergeant Jasper's men, Jasper, when he saw the flag staff severed by a cannon ball, called out, "Colonel, don't let us fight without our flag!" Moultrie, they remembered, replied, "How can you help it? The staff is gone." And Jasper, shouting, "Then I shall restore it," leaped from the fort to retrieve the flag which had fallen outside.

With the threat of a heavy storm, and the falling of night upon the sea, the firing steadily diminished. And "at length," says Moultrie (It was 9:30 at night.), "the British gave up the conflict. The ships . . . dropped down with the tide and out of the reach of our guns . . . . the firing . . . ceased . . . [and] I sent up to town to acquaint them that . . . we were victorious." ⁵³

Indeed the battle seemed to be over. General Lee had that impression in the early morning of the 29ᵗʰ. Having left Sullivan's to attend to the other posts, he later dictated to his secretary Joseph

Nourse a letter to Moultrie: "Dear Colonel: "I should have thanked you and your brave garrison this morning, vis-a-vis, at the fort, but am prevented by a great deal of business. I do most heartily thank you all, and shall do you justice in my letters to Congress. I have applied for some rum for your men. They deserve every comfort that can be afforded them." And, in the event that the break in the battle was only at an interlude, he promised "more powder."

President Rutledge was not so sure the battle was over. In his long letter of the same day, while expressing gratitude for the day's brave work, he also pledged powder and ammunition. "I send you fifteen hundred pounds. . . . I beg and entreat you only to fire your heaviest guns very slowly, only now and then, and take good aim; if a brisk fire is kept up on your side, to attempt . . . to equal theirs, your ammunition will soon be expended, and what shall we do then?" [54]

Two days later, with the British fleet hanging around, Christopher Gadsden from Fort Johnson extended his congratulations to the Colony "for the drubbing you gave those fellows the other day." And he, too, remarked on the powder. "Only wish you had had powder enough, that it might have been complete." [55]

But the victory was complete.

The cost to the British was terrific. In this vain encounter with the rebels of the South, the King saw a number of his proud fleet severely damaged. And of course the *Acteon* and the *Prince of Piedmont* were lost altogether. And, according to the surgeon quoted earlier, both the *Bristol* and the badly damaged *Experiment* each lost "upwards of one hundred men killed and wounded." The loss to the British fleet, killed and wounded, was, at the very least, 205. The astounded surgeon confided to his memoirs: "This will not be believed when it is first reported in England. I can scarcely believe what I myself saw on that day—a day to me one of the most distressing of my life." [56]

Although tallies vary, Colonel Moultrie and the South Carolina troops lost ten to twelve men killed and twenty-two to twenty-four wounded. Not a single officer was even wounded.

It was a thrilling victory. A feisty young Colonel, with a beautifully orchestrated plan of defense, and a wee bit of help from an attentive Mother Nature, had turned away the mighty British armada. He had repulsed the proud army of General Henry Clinton and the finest of the Royal fleet.

While the British officers in turn blamed each other and licked their wounds for another three weeks before transporting the army back to New York City, where the brothers Howe were marshaling their assault, the people of South Carolina rejoiced and passed out compliments. Rutledge was high in his praise of the officers and men who had defended the harbor; and Gadsden and Armstrong, who had witnessed the action and chafed at the bit, were quick to commend those most responsible for the victory. Even General Lee had the greatest respect to acknowledge. "No men ever," he declared, did behave better, or ever could behave better." [57] The Continental Congress promptly, after hearing the great news, dispatched congratulations and expressed thanks to Lee, Moultrie, Thompson, and the other officers, including General Armstrong.

This victory in the South may not be regarded as a momentous one in the chronicle of the Revolution, but it doubtless contributed to the spirit necessary to declare independence from Great Britain, which was to happen formally in one more week. The fighting also occupied seven regiments of British soldiers for more than two months. It destroyed British faith in the Loyalist population of the South. And perhaps most important of all, as a victory for the patriots, it was something to be looked to in the terrible month of November, after the defeat of Washington's army in the defense of New York, and the consequent, almost fatal, depreciation in numbers of soldiers.

The battle of Sullivan's Island also had a value in the regard it promoted for the American artillery, which at this stage of the war was in its infancy. Although Lee had been critical both of the placement of the guns and of their firing, the unnamed British surgeon who is quoted above expressed in his memoirs considerable praise: " . . . their artillery was surprisingly well served, it is said, under the command of a Mr. Masson and DeBrahm; it was slow, but decisive indeed; they were very cool, and took great care not to fire except their guns were well directed." [58]

All credit goes to Colonel William Moultrie. General

Armstrong and Christopher Gadsden, and the militia forces on the mainland, who would doubtless have acquitted themselves heroically had they been called upon, contributed to the victory only by their presence, which clearly counted for much in the discouragement of the British force. Lee, though of course well intended, can be given but little credit for the outcome. Indeed, it would not be too much to say that the battle of Sullivan's Island was won in spite of General Lee. The best thing that can be said for Lee is that he allowed himself to be persuaded that a defense of the island was worth attempting.

It was most appropriate that President Rutledge should visit the garrison of the brave, battle-scarred fort on the Fourth of July and there conduct a ceremonious celebration of the astonishing victory over His Majesty's army and navy. And certainly it must be regarded as most fitting that the post on Sullivan's Island should be given the name of its defender, and be known "for all time" as Fort Moultrie—as so it was decreed by the South Carolina Assembly.

XXI

THE BRANDYWINE

With British ships departed about a week, General Armstrong, still in Charleston, penned a long letter to the President of the Congress, John Hancock. He had been ordered by Lee (August 2) "to collect the returns from different corps, to digest them into one, and return them immediately to the Congress." The principal purpose of the letter was, however, to "please get me out of here." Dated August 12, it first provides a reminder of what has been the General's situation for the past three and one-half months:

> *Dear Sir, In the beginning of May last I wrote the honourable the Continental Congress the state in which I found the troops here, as being entirely upon the establishment of this Colony, and in no other respect Continental than that of the uniformity of their purposes to cooperate in the great Continental design. In that situation, and being without Continental troops, I did not debate for a dubious command, which, had it even been offered me (as it was not), I could not with propriety accept, but begged to be favoured with the further orders of the Congress; and being candidly asked by the president and others to wait the event, I*

preferred the disagreeable situation of long suspense to a precipitate departure, for reasons I conceived to be prudential and rather tending to the publick tranquillity; determined at the same time to repair to any neighboring Colony where the enemy should make their first impressions; but have not yet been so happy as to know whether my letter was received.[1]

  The General then proceeds to an account of the siege of the harbor, stressing, naturally, his role: "In some weeks the English fleet appeared, when the town began to barricade such places as we supposed would most favour the enemy's landing. In these and various other cases I contributed any advice I could give to the President of the Colony for the defence, who joined me in urging the march of General Lee with Continental troops; to whom, when he came, the President resigned the command."

  He then explains how the enemy took possession of Long Island, and how he was ordered by Lee to encamp at Haddrell's Point, and noted that Clinton was, happily, not aware of the "paucity of our numbers." He speaks highly of the troops under his command, noting their patience in waiting near six weeks for anything much to happen. He expressed astonishment that Haddrell's was not attacked, as Sullivan's would by British success in that quarter inevitably fall. He waxes extremely poetic, so much so that Hancock must have wondered who had taken up the pen: "Sullivan must have fallen of course, without the risk of tarnish to the splendid walls of England, unequally arranged with indignant brow in battle's noisy line, against the feeble, the simple cabbage-stalk, but by secret and patriotic texture, the irrefragable palmetto."

  And that was not all. To explain why he did not engage the British, nor they him, he resorts to a dance metaphor: "General Clinton, probably misled by magnified reports of our numbers, cautiously declined the expected visit, and we, in the attitude of resistance, were too rigid to make the bow, and unwilling to expose the young dancers to some awkward scrape on his slippery parade. In short, he was so surrounded by shipping, water, and impassable marsh, that we had no practicable access to him without a great many boats, and as these were collecting, he thought proper to decamp, and the last division of the fleet is now sailed about a week."

He has now arrived at the point of the letter: "The enemy being now far removed, and their return uncertain, I hope the Honourable Congress will not consider me regardless of their service when I beg leave to express my wishes to be recalled, conscious as I am that my constitution is too far run down by time to answer in any tolerable degree the designs of that appointment with which they have honoured me, in this very warm climate. . . . Little, indeed, can I now promise my country in any situation, but still less here. On this consideration, General Lee has as good as promised my liberty from hence as soon as the season will admit me to travel; nor can there be any necessity of my stay at present." He concludes by insisting that he is easily replaced. The letter was read before the assembled Congress, one month beyond its writing, on September 13, on the very day that Washington had need of officers at Harlem Heights.[2]

News, and orders, traveled slowly in those days, a letter from Philadelphia to Charleston often requiring weeks to make the trip. But by the middle of September (by a resolution of the Congress) Brigadier General John Armstrong was on his way north. On October 7, to the President of Congress, still John Hancock, he provided an account of his journey to date: "Sir: Brigadier [Robert] Howe being now at Charleston, permit me to acquaint you I am this far on my way to the northward, having first obtained the consent of General Lee, and shall be happy to find my return may not be disagreeable to Congress; but still more so should my motives be found to be such as to meet the approbation of that honourable body."

He yet regards himself as an officer with responsibilities to the Southern Department. "As the military affairs of this State [North Carolina] are not in so much forwardness as could be wished, I shall stay one day here [Wilmington] and one in Halifax, in order to represent to the Council of Safety now sitting at that place, several matters of importance to the future defence of these States, particularly that of South-Carolina; and if health permits shall make but a short stay at Carlisle and wait your further commands at Philadelphia." And he reports the movement of the British: "The English shipping which lay at Cape Fear are entirely gone off, having first burnt three vessels unfit for service. A negro who deserted them says he heard they were bound to New-York."[3]

During the time the South Carolina forces were defending Charleston against the British armada, Washington was preparing his defense of New York. Shortly after the rebel victory, on August 22, New York was invaded by the Howe brothers, with troops landing at Long Island. For three months the battle for the city raged, with fighting on Long Island and Brooklyn, the siege of Manhattan and Harlem Heights, and the battle of White Plains. The capture of the city by the British was made complete with the surrender of Fort Washington on November 16 and the fall of Fort Lee on November 20. Victory was totally to the British. Despite the success at Charleston, the rebel forces were in disarray. Indeed, the war seemed at an end.

The troops of Washington's Continental Army not slain or captured, some 3000, fled southward through New Jersey. And as the badly defeated army lumbered south, it continued to lose men, perhaps as many as one out of three! Some soldiers simply deserted, some noted that their enlistments had expired. Militia forces were hurt as badly. By early December the troops of Washington numbered 2000 (at the most!), and these, to a man, were so poorly clothed and equipped as to count for little. So little hope seemed to attach to the cause, and so little was left of the army that only "an insignificant few" joined up.

Prospects for new recruits were very, very dim. The British prepared surrender documents, and consulted King George's list of patriots to be hanged. Washington, as every historian of the Revolution has noted, appreciated the need to restore hope. He knew that a victory was needed, and not just a shadowy sort of a small battle won, but something to excite confidence in the Continental army. But he very well knew also, that he had first to repair the army. Accordingly at the middle of December he made an impassioned plea to the Governors of Pennsylvania and New Jersey for militiamen, Very few showed up from New Jersey, but there did appear at Trenton a very substantial force, perhaps as many as 2000 from southeastern Pennsylvania. The Scotch-Irish had come through, and in no small measure these spirited recruits showed up to serve with Washington because of the popular

~ *The Brandywine* ~ 389

Brigadier General John Armstrong of Carlisle.

Armstrong, at this critical juncture of the American Revolution, rendered the Congress and the Continental Army two important services. The first was by way of the information he could supply, and, implied as well as stated, advice on policy. The second service was in his role as recruiter of Pennsylvania militia.[4]

The Scotch-Irish who live today in the United States, many of whom are direct descendants of the eighteenth-century Pennsylvania settlers, are quick to declare that the Scotch-Irish were the heart and soul of the Revolution. It is quite all right for them to say so, not only because they themselves believe it, but because it is unequivocally true and undisputed. It has many times been set down, by the most responsible historians, that the Scotch-Irish were whole-hearted in their universal support of the revolt against the King, and all for a declaration of independence. While there were some few Tories among the Scotch-Irish in Massachusetts and in New York, and in the southern states, it has been observed, rightly, that from the time of Lexington/Concord hardly a soul loyal to the King could be discovered among the Scotch-Irish of Pennsylvania.

They had fought for the King in the colonial wars, as was their duty, but "when the alarm of the revolution first rang through the land, it called no truer or more willing hearts than those of the Scotch-Irish Presbyterians."[5]

General Armstrong found it easy to recruit from among the Scotch-Irish of Cumberland and Lancaster Counties. Sometimes, almost the whole company of Pennsylvania militia, whether foot soldiers or artillerymen, would prove to be Ireland-born. And the same was true of the Continental Army. Indeed so many of the soldiers of the Pennsylvania Line were Scotch-Irish that Light-Horse Harry Lee dubbed the troops "the Line of Ireland." Moreover, it has been noted that a great many of the officers contributed to Washington by Pennsylvania were of Scotch-Irish stock. Promptly there come to mind the names of Generals Edward Hand, William Irvine, William Thompson, James Ewing, James Potter, Ephraim Blaine, Andrew Porter, Joseph Reed, and of course John Armstrong.[6]

As a matter of fact, so many of the Revolutionary fighting force were Ireland-born that King George is said to have called the rebellion "a Presbyterian war." And at the time of Valley Forge a Hessian officer wrote that the Revolution was not an "American rebellion" but "nothing more or less than a Scotch-Irish Presbyterian rebellion." [7] And many a British soldier, astonished by the audacity and vigorous fighting abilities of the Pennsylvania frontiersmen, was moved to call the war "an Irish uprising." Even in the seat of government in England the role of the Scotch-Irish was dramatically acknowledged. Horace Walpole stood up in the House of Commons to speak of the trouble in the colonies. "There is no use in crying about the matter," he declared. "America has run off with a Presbyterian parson, and that is the end of it." [8]

Perhaps it is too much to say, but it may very well be that when the proud Scotch-Irish were compelled to flee Ulster for America, the British lost the thirteen colonies.

Now, at this critical time, with Washington's army in disarray from the New York City disaster, Armstrong would be asking a super effort from his fellow Scotch-Irish.

In the darkest hour of the entire war, on December 10, he sent off a letter to the Board of War and Ordnance from Washington's Head Quarters at Trenton Falls, just on the Pennsylvania side of the river in the Trenton region. The letter provides for the Board not only valuable information, but also Armstrong's views of the present situation, and his speculation on the expected invasion of Pennsylvania: "Gentlemen," he writes,

Since my coming up to the Army, I have wrote two short letters to town [Philadelphia]; *the first rather gloomy, arising from a view of our Army. . . . The second, of this morning, somewhat more sanguine, was built on the flattering opinion that the numbers of the enemy had been exaggerated, and* [by] *the expectations of being joined by General Lee and a respectable body of Militia. These reinforcements we still hope for, and wish it may be soon; but with respect to the enemy's numbers, there is reason to apprehend they are rather above than below the first estimation, as I have lately seen an Ensign of ours, who, by the violation of his parole, has made his escape from York, where he saw General Howe's horses put into the boat for Elizabeth-Town, to which place the General came on Wednesday last, and that he is undoubtedly at the head of* his Army, consisting, according to this officer's information . . . of fifteen thousand men. But although they should not be so many, we cannot suppose on an errand of so much consequence that Howe will throw himself at the head of diminutive numbers. There are eight battalions consisting chiefly of English and Hessian Grenadiers and Light-Infantry, with a few pieces of artillery, at Penny-Town [Pennington]; whether with a design to pass above General Washington, or with a design to intercept the junction of General Lee, is yet uncertain. On the other hand, we have heard this afternoon that they have repaired a bridge the General [Washington] had torn down between Trenton and Bordentown, on the Jersey side, and that a body of Infantry have already passed over it; in short they are spread for many miles along the Delaware, perhaps to distract General Washington, that he may not know what point to attend to.*

Armstrong *always* speaks in great regard of Washington. Here he writes,

Your worthy General, however, maintains the full possession of himself; is indefatigable by day and night, taking every precaution, I think as well to prevent surprise as to discover the place they intend to cross, that he may derive every advantage from the river, which if once crossed, could not, with his comparatively small army, be expected at any other place. He has sent a party to reconnoiter the creeks on the Jersey side, lest the friends of tyranny [Tories] should have boats concealed in them to aid the common enemy; but thinks the [Pa.] Council of Safety would do well to send also some fit persons, lest such secreted boats might escape the Party he has sent; and who knows but Howe's design may be to march on the Jersey side, as far as Billingsport, and there meet some of his own shipping and small craft for purposes too obvious to mention; or by taking the Bordentown route, he may design to pass over below the mouth of Shamaney.[9]

Interestingly, in light of Washington's own surprise attack two weeks hence, what the General fears most is a mid-night crossing "A passage in the night is to us the most dangerous, and what he probably will attempt. I had, without consulting the General, wrote for Colonels [Thaddeus] Kosciusko and Romond; but as General [Israel] Putnam is sent down for purposes on their way near town, I suppose they can't be sent home."

And, finally, Armstrong urges the Board of War, after its reading of his letter, to send it on to the Council of Safety.[10] Washington, on the 13th, also from his headquarters at Trenton Falls, got off a letter to the Congress, in which he did himself some speculating on the designs of the British. In the last paragraph of this letter he advised Congress on what to do with General Armstrong. Understanding how very effective the popular and well known Armstrong can be in recruiting among the Scotch-Irish, and in desperate need of substantial militia additions to his troops, he has a big job for his friend: "As General Armstrong has a good deal of influence in this State, and our present force is small and inconsiderable, I think he cannot be better employed than to repair to the Counties where his interest lies, to animate the people, promote the recruiting service, and encourage the Militia to come in. He will also be able to form a proper judgment of the places suitable for magazines of provisions to be collected. I have requested him to wait upon Congress on this subject."

He has the same recommendation to make for General William Smallwood, who at this time is in Philadelphia: ". . . and if General Smallwood should go to Maryland on the same business, I think it would have a happy effect. He is popular and of great influence, and I am persuaded would contribute greatly to that State's furnishing her quota of men in a little time."[11]

Armstrong, now in Philadelphia, had hoped to appear before the Congress to explain his mission and to solicit its approval, "but as your late adjournment forbids me that pleasure, I can only by this letter inform you what these intended services are." This letter he composed on December 15, but it was not read in the Congress until the 21st.

To the President of the Congress (Hancock), he described the "sundry pieces of publick service" he has been ordered by Washington to perform:

The General, under the last necessity, not knowing how far a strong and elated enemy may design to avail themselves of your circumstances by a rapid winter campaign, has desired me, as far as weather and strength will admit, to traverse the sundry parts of the State of Pennsylvania, to inspirit the Militia . . . to turn out and to aid the recruiting service by prompting the younger men to inlist, and to appoint proper places for magazines of provisions . . . naming the quantities to be laid in at each place. I mean quantity in the first instance; and have accordingly ordered the Commissary, Mr. Wharton, to lay in at the gulph mills on the west side of the Schuylkill, eight days' provisions for ten thousand men; at Lancaster, three months' ditto for twelve thousand—and [upon] *further thought, would now rather direct half the last quantity at Right's Ferry, which yet may be easily corrected; at York-Town for five thousand, three months; with quantities of forage at each place.*

Armstrong, not only at the head of recruiting in Pennsylvania, is into the commissary business now. He has a special concern. It is salt. "Carlisle and Lebanon left to further consideration for the same purposes, and the above sent to the General for his inspection &c. I am of opinion, that too much cannot be got, and that three months' salt provisions for forty thousand men ought to be in reserve for next summer."

Speaking next for Washington, he continues his briefing of the Congress: "Give me leave to inform your Honour, I am charged by the General to signify to Congress his earnest wishes that an augmentation of the Continental Army at least to that of one hundred battalions on the whole, may early be thought of and concluded; as, considering the efforts of the enemy to bring more foreign troops, and the uncertainty of our Militia, the expediency of the measure appears beyond a doubt; nor can any man answer, from the present prevailing spirit in several of the middle States, that the arms of tyranny will not be augmented from this side of the water."

As for recruiting, Armstrong is confident that it could be accomplished at greater speed if two shortcomings were addressed. "Permit me to mention the article of small-arms, by which I mean at least the middle size musket and bayonet, and salt, as perhaps requiring the first attention. Please to forgive the notice taken of these last; it is not meant to offend the anxiety and vigilance of

Congress already exerted to procure them, but only to revive the idea, and show the pressing necessity of more, persuaded as I am that a number of men may be got, but without arms; and of those you have, many are insufficient, and the scarcity of salt like to discourage our people at large."

He notes that, in the event the Congress requires more of him, he can be found at Carlisle in about three weeks, from which place any letter can be carried to him. In a postscript he notes that General William Smallwood will be playing pretty much the same role, that is, recruiting, in Maryland.[12]

This long letter, as noted, was not read in Congress until the 21st. But the members of that august body, who were already in the happy habit of endorsing Washington's recommendations, in a Resolution promptly expressed their approval of Armstrong's assignment, and ordered that Armstrong's letter of the 15th be referred to the Board of War.

On the 23rd Hancock addressed a letter to Washington from Baltimore, which since December 20 had been the meeting place of the Congress, and therefore the capital. He expressed the great concern of Congress over the British capture of General Charles Lee, and stressed the hope that he can soon be returned. Then he notes for Washington that the Congress "approve of your sending General Armstrong to Pennsylvania and General Smallwood to Maryland, to stimulate the people to exert themselves .... I have the pleasure," he informs the General, "to acquaint you that the Militia in the upper parts of Maryland are in motion, and seem at last sensible of the danger which threatens them."[13]

Hugh Mercer

Armstrong missed out

on the battle of Trenton, fought on Christmas night of 1776, but he rejoiced in the news. And he was very happy to hear, too, of the subsequent victory at Princeton, but much saddened as well. For it was at Princeton that the valiant Hugh Mercer, who had served Armstrong on the Kittanning Expedition and on the Forbes Expedition, and whom he counted a true and trusted friend, was mortally wounded. And Armstrong's eighteen-year-old son John, Jr., who was serving under Mercer, was at the same time very nearly a casualty. When his horse was shot, the lad was pinned beneath it, and rescued only moments before the British came up.[14]

Horatio Gates

John Armstrong, Jr., hoping to find a position with General Horatio Gates and the Northern Army, immediately after the battle of Princeton, set out from Morristown. He had not been gone long before his father arrived with a letter by which the younger Armstrong might present himself to Gates. The young man hit it off with Gates all right, and accepted a position as aide-de-camp with the rank of major. It proved the beginning of a very long friendship.[15]

But even before Armstrong had the news of victory at Princeton and of Mercer's tragic death, he had composed a letter to the Pennsylvania Council of Safety, headed up at that time by Thomas Wharton. He laments the despair and the sense of doom that have followed hard upon the loss of New York and the ignominious flight of Washington's dismembered army: "I'm but a few hours got to this place [Carlisle], and hope it will give you some pleasure to know that I have not travelled in vain; for notwithstanding the culpable stupor & timidity which had seized the minds of many in this State & partly arising from that temporary cloud which the wisdom and goodness of God thought proper to throw over our troops on their passage thro' the Jerseys—and partly from the spurious doctrines of dasterdly and ill principled men, I think there is good reason to believe that a number of the Americans—the generality of the Irish, and part of the jermans will stand firm in the common cause."

He looks for a big boost to the army from the militia forces: "Coll. M'Coy's Batt[n] is now coming into Town, and not quite so destitute of cloathing as has been said.—Five or Six Companys of Militia now on their march & getting ready betwixt this place & Lancaster. If the whole I have seen & heard of were joined Gen[l] Washington, I should hope his Army will at least consist of twenty thousand exclusive of what we may now expect will joine him of the associators of the Jersey."

He means to proceed immediately to York and to several other parts of the county to do his recruiting, the snow being too deep to venture west very far. He suggests that General William Howe may be at work in Philadelphia with his spies and secret agents to lay the foundations for a Tory army, which would support his expected invasion of "this State." [16]

When Congress was convened on Friday, January 31, 1777, the first item of business ended in a resolution concerning General Armstrong: "Resolved, that the Board of War be directed to confer with Brigadier General Armstrong, who is come to town to lay some matters before Congress, and that they meet him this evening at their office."

On the succeeding Wednesday the Congress heard the preliminary report of the Board: "The Board of War, who were appointed to confer with General Armstrong, reported, that they have had a conference with him; that the conference turned upon various and important subjects, relative to the raising the new army, supplying them with arms, ammunition, cloathing, provisions and medicines." It was then indicated that the Board, after digesting the said conference, would bring in a proper report on the several matters. This report was received by the Congress on February 11. It contained a great many recommendations.

In response to Armstrong, the Board agreed to the following: (1) "That a Circular Letter be written to the several

States, setting forth the absolute Necessity of having a strong Army to take the Field at the Beginning of next campaign." (2) "That the States collect arms from the Inhabitants, and deliver these to Washington." (3) "That all Arms or Accoutrements . . . shall be stamped with the words United States." (4) "That those who do not turn over their arms be punished." (5) "That the States be empowered to borrow arms from the militia." (6) "That the Clothier General be empowered to provide for the clothing of the troops. (7) That a Commissary General of provisions be appointed." (8) "That a Director of Magazines be appointed." (9) "That all Troops and Armed Vessels and Cargoes or exportation be supplied from [the erected] Magazines at first Cost." (10) "That the Commissary and Director General be appointed by the Commander in Chief and [serve] under his Direction." (11) "That the Director General draw all Monies for the purchase of Provisions, and render an Account thereof to Congress." (12) "That Forage be put under similar Regulations under the Superintending of the Quarter Master General." [17]

From Carlisle, on Feb. 17, 1777, Armstrong advised the Council of Safety that it must put an end to the distilling of wheat and rye and other grains, else there will be no bread in Pennsylvania. We must cast out the "complicated Demon of avarice & infatuation, or bind it in chains." One thing is obvious: "The matter complained of is in present circumstances pregnant with many evils and if not speedily remedied must be fatal." [18]

Washington, from his headquarters at Morristown, on March 5, after updating Armstrong on developments, including the location of magazines in the Philadelphia area, expressed also the hope that Pennsylvania might soon follow the example of the Southern States in "prohibiting the distilling of unreasonable Quantities of Wheat and other grain into Whiskey." Concerned about the appointment of officers, he wrote, "I expected you would have appointed your Younger Son [John, Jr.] to the Command of one of the four Companies that are at your disposal, and if you have not already filled up all the Commissions, it will give me pleasure to see it yet done." As for Armstrong's older son, James, "The Doctor [who had been serving as a surgeon in the general hospital in Virginia through the last year] will undoubtedly find a place in the New Hospital, suitable to his merit and abilities." [19]

On April 28, 1777, Armstrong wrote again to the Council of Safety, this time insisting on the need for Militia Law, and declaring his determination to work for it.[20]

The war, which had so far been fought in New England, in Canada, in New York City, and in New Jersey, was moving into Pennsylvania. The rebel forces had expelled the British from Boston, and had enjoyed modest victories at Charleston, and at Trenton and Princeton, but they had been banished, for all time, from Canada, and had suffered a most devastating defeat in the battle for New York. Washington, by the middle of the summer was convinced that Sir William Howe would be marching his army, by one route or another, to Philadelphia. Surely Howe was thinking that the capture of the country's capital would mean the end of this ridiculous insurrection. The war, as everyone knew, was coming to Pennsylvania.

Through the remainder of the spring and into the summer Washington's forces were encamped at Morristown, New Jersey. The Commander-in-Chief was trying to determine the exact intentions of Howe, and at the same time build up his army. After the battle of New York, the patriotic fervor had lagged a good bit. But "by strenuous efforts the flagging energy of the people was renewed." And Washington had had some good news. In the previous autumn, on Oct. 16, 1776, Carlisle's William Lyon (who that day took his seat as a member of the Council of Safety) had proposed to the Board of War to continue a larger force in the State, to protect it both against British troops and the "growing party of disaffected persons which unhappily exists at this time," also to carry on the necessary works of defense. It was resolved to raise the four battalions of 500 men each (for the immediate defense of the State), as well as one battalion of militia from each of the counties of York, Cumberland, Lancaster, and Berks. Not surprisingly, the news from Trenton, Dec. 26, 1776, and from Princeton, January 3, 1777, was to encourage greatly the people, and recruiting was to become more lively.[21]

An act of Pennsylvania's Supreme Executive Council passed March 17, 1777, provided for the appointment of one or more lieutenants of militia in each city or county. John Armstrong and Ephraim Blaine were appointed for Cumberland County, but both declined for sufficient reasons.[22]

On May 31, General Washington wrote to Virginia's Governor Patrick Henry of the expected sailing of "a large fleet of the enemy—estimated at a hundred sail—from New York." The General wondered whether it meant to ascend the North River (the Hudson) or to assault Philadelphia by sailing up the Delaware. From this time on, the Commander-in-Chief scheduled councils and solicited advice from his officers on what to do about Philadelphia.[23] The officers consulted on this matter, clear up until December 4, were Nathanael Greene, Anthony Wayne, Joseph Reed, Henry Knox, John Sullivan, Lord Stirling, Thomas Conway, William Maxwell, Adam Stephen, the Marquis de Lafayette, James Varnum, James Irvine, and John Armstrong.

At this stage of the war, and ever since the battle of Princeton, Pennsylvania was beginning to note how very inefficient and confused was the militia organization. It was high time, authorities agreed, that a regular and permanent militia be established. Accordingly the Assembly drew up a bill, which promptly passed. It first divided the counties into districts. Each district was then required to enroll in its militia unit not fewer than 640 men, nor more than 680. Each county was to have an officer of lieutenant rank at the head, and officers of lesser rank for the men of each district. To command this organized force five Pennsylvania military notables were accorded the rank of Brigadier General. These men were John Armstrong, John Cadwalader, James Potter, James Irvine, and Samuel Meredith. But the State promptly went a step beyond that. Recognizing that in John Armstrong they had the very best man to take complete charge of the militia forces, the administration suggested the post to him. On April 2, Brigadier General John Armstrong, having served the Continental Army thirteen months, resigned his commission. It was promptly accepted by Congress and effected by the 4th. Immediately, by the State of Pennsylvania he was accorded the rank of Brigadier General and placed in command of all the militia forces of the State. And one month later he was promoted to Major General.

Armstrong was in the saddle at once, and, though advanced

in age (He was in his sixtieth year.), he entered most energetically into the work of protecting the State against the enemy, and promptly began to erect and maintain defensive works all along the Delaware River.

By a resolution of Congress, April 17, he was "requested to inspect into the state of the magazines of provisions under the care of Commissary Wharton, and make report to Congress of their kind, quantity, and condition: and that General Armstrong be authorized to call on Mr. Wharton for information necessary to enable him to perform this duty, and if the said magazines should be found in a perishing or neglected state, that he take proper steps for their regulation; and the said commissary and his deputies are hereby ordered to pay due obedience to his directions." [24]

Joseph Reed

All of this he did with dispatch; and, besides, in a very short time, though suffering some discouragement, he made substantial gains for the Pennsylvania militia.

From Philadelphia on June 18, Joseph Reed, in a long letter, reported to Washington the state of affairs in Pennsylvania with respect to the rebellion. Reed, who had served Washington as secretary and aide-de-camp through the first year of the war, and had more recently served as Adjutant-General of the American Army, was rapidly becoming the most powerful political figure in Pennsylvania.[25] Here he writes in a most complimentary way of General Armstrong:

Colonel Stephen Moylan[26] *writes, that he thinks my knowledge of the country and people would be of use in the quarter where he is, and presses me to come up, which I shall do immediately and pay my respects at head-quarters. . . . I have been employed, for some time, in laboring an accommodation with the contending parties in this State, which through General Armstrong's and* [Thomas] *Mifflin's*[27] *influence, is at last effected, so as to attend the fairest prospects of bringing forth the force of this State.... General Armstrong is indefatigable in his endeavours, and I hope will be more successful than at present he seems to expect.*[28]

Washington, still in Morristown on the first anniversary of the Declaration of Independence, responded to Armstrong's late letter with compliments for the Pennsylvania militia: "The Spirit with which the Militia of this State [New Jersey] and Pennsylvania turned out upon the late alarm [General William Howe's maneuver in New Jersey] far exceeded my most Sanguine expectations and I am persuaded must have chagrined Genl. Howe, who, I believe, rather expected support than opposition, from Pennsylvania in particular." Concerned about the harvest season, he suggests that Armstrong dismiss as many of the militia as possible for the time.

The letter closed with his compliments: "I am pleased at the honorable mark of distinction, which the State of Pennsylvania have conferred upon you, by appointing you to the command of their Colonial Troops, and am convinced that by your acceptance of it you will be enabled to render the State and your Country very essential Service, Should She herself be attacked or her assistance demanded by any of her Sister Colonies." And in a postscript he asked about son James: "I shall be glad to know whether your eldest Son is provided for in a way suitable to his wishes. If he is not I have a vacancy in One of the 16 Regiments that I think will be worth his acceptance."[29]

Through the early years of the rebellion as the division between patriots and loyalists steadily became more heated, those in high places naturally were subject to suspicion. On August 12 Judge Benjamin Chew and Governor John Penn were both arrested. Penn had followed a neutral course, but when he was asked to sign the Loyalty Oath, which required him to declare that he would do nothing to injure the rebel cause, he refused. He was therefore exiled to the Allen family estate in New Jersey. Armstrong did not approve of this action, and when New Jersey's Governor William Livingston (a good friend to Washington) ordered Penn removed to "somewhere in New England," he "interceded in Penn's behalf," requesting the President of the Executive Council, Thomas Wharton, to route the exile of Penn (if he had to be moved) south rather than north. Wharton replied that Penn "was going nowhere without orders from the Board of War." As it turned out, Penn remained on the Allen estate until the 15th of May, when, with his wife Anne (daughter of William Allen), he was released and returned to Philadelphia.[30]

General Armstrong was referred to very different matters when, on August 28, 1777, the Supreme Executive Council suggested to him that he discontinue the distribution of a gill of rum or whiskey to each militiaman. They gave as their reasons (1) "Many have, instead of thanks, rendered grumbling and clamour." And (2) a distribution in which all did not share equally was not good for the morale of the Continental Army. "Soldiers, it is supposed are tolerably easy whilst every thing is dealt alike to all, but are disgusted by partiality." [31] Armstrong, now in Chester, in a letter of the succeeding day indicated that, as he was busy, he would address the problem later. In this same letter of the 29th he informed the Council of the disposition of his militia at Wilmington and Billingsport, and lamented the "want of arms." [32]

Next day the Council responded with "I wait your further opinion concerning the Spirituous liquors." [33] On September 1, from his Head Quarters at Chester, Armstrong replied, "With Regard to Liquors for the Militia, I am of opinion, all Things Consider'd, that a Quantity should be provided, to be delivered out Occasionally; for as the Continental Troops will be allowed Rum when on Fatigue & in bad weather, should the Militia be without it, might occasion Disturbances, I shall however Speak to General Washington on the Subject, and endeavour to have the Militia supplied equally with the Continental Troops, but for fear of Scarcity think it best to have a Quantity laid in." He reported, too, the building of the Brigades "to every additional strength that lays [sic] in my Power," and noted that "Col Bull goes off this Morning to Billingsport and Fort Island to Examin what Militia remain there." [34]

From the time of his commission as Major General in charge of the Pennsylvania militia (May, 1777) until the time Washington marched out of Valley Forge (one whole year),

Armstrong was in constant close communication with first Governor John Penn and then with the Pennsylvania Supreme Executive Council and its President Thomas Wharton, Jr., who, as Governor, was of course the Commander-in-Chief of the Pennsylvania forces.

For the Council he supplied information on the number of Militia, their condition, and their deployment. He expressed opinions on the conduct of the war, proposed action, and accepted assignment. In all, it was a very good and mutually respectful relationship.

On September 5, from Wilmington, Armstrong directed a long letter to President Wharton, in which he described the recent action:

This day the whole of the Continental Troops at this place are to move forward far as Newport, as in Genl Potter's Brigade [of Pa. Militia], *General Irwin's* [James Irvine's] *Brigade remains upon the works at this place until further orders. At Newport we are to form, and perhaps throw*

Thomas Wharton, Jr.

up lines from Christiana on the Left, to White, or perhaps Red Clay Creek (I forget which is the name) on the right. The enemy, as far as we yet learn, appear to spread over some considerable space of Country, but in a detached way from Couches Mills to some part of Notingham. In the Scirmiss of Wednesday morning perhaps the loss on each side may be nearly equal, but ours think themselves the best off. Deserters are frequently coming in, wholly Jermans, they call the enemy larger than they can possibly be.[35]

In a letter of the 8th, from Newport, Armstrong reported to President Wharton, "This morning we expected the approach of the Enemy & yet continue to look for their movement. My private Opinion is, which last night I delivered to his Excellency [Washington], that if Mr. Howe do not come on very soon, his intention is to Re-embark on the Delaware, Cross over & land where he may think most convenient on the Jersey Shore" and march to a position from which he can bombard the city. This he took to mean that "the Jersey Militia shou'd immediately finish the Labour at Billings-port or rather take post on their own Shore. This I shall mention to the General..... The Army generally are in good Spirits & look for Action."[36]

The Brandywine is a very small stream. It can hardly even be counted a river. Most call it a creek. It rises from the marshes north of the tiny community of Lyndell, and is bolstered some by the Indian Run branch, Beaver Creek, Valley Run, and Taylor Run. Just north of the settlement known as Lenape, its West Branch joins the East. It is an idyllic, meandering stream, which only infrequently becomes enraged. With its quiet, mist-enshrouded waters it delivers a charm to that lovely valley of Pennsylvania in the region of Downingtown and West Chester, before flowing into the Christina River at Wilmington, and hurrying on to the Chesapeake. On September 11, 1777, it would assume a big place in American history.

On July 23, General William Howe, disappointed that the

capture of New York did not put an end to the war, targeted, as expected, the capital of the new United States, the meeting place of the Continental Congress. With Charles Cornwallis, he marched his troops (13,000 British and 5000 Hessians) aboard a fleet of British vessels, and by sea sailed south for the Chesapeake Bay. He might have elected to go up the Delaware River to Philadelphia, as Armstrong had fully expected, but he was discouraged from that by Armstrong's fortifications and impediments, and instead had chosen this route as the safest and most expeditious. Proceeding north through the Bay, he landed, August 24-25, at what was then known as Head of Elk (present-day Elkton, Maryland), fifty miles south of Philadelphia and just a day's march from Chadds Ford on the Brandywine.

Washington, monitoring the British movement, but not yet determined on a site for a stand, had set out for Wilmington in time to reach that region by August 25. At six o'clock that evening he dispatched to General Armstrong, Commander of the Pennsylvania Militia, orders throbbing with urgency:

I have just received information that the enemy began to land this morning about six miles below the Head of Elk, opposite Cecil Court-House. The informant says he saw two thousand men, but he may be mistaken as to the number. I desire you to send off every man of the militia under your command, that is properly armed as quick as possible. If they were to begin their march this night while it is cool, it would be better. They are to proceed to Wilmington where they will receive orders for their destination. I desire you will immediately send for General [James] Potter and give him directions to come to Wilmington with all possible expedition. You must supply his planning the best manner you can. The first attempt of the enemy will be to seize horses, carriages and cattle with light parties, and we must endeavor to check them at the outset. Whatever militia are at Philadelphia and equipment should be ordered down immediately.[37]

Washington was in time to fortify Wilmington well enough to discourage a British assault at that point. When he understood that the British would be proceeding to Philadelphia by way of the

Baltimore road, he elected, with the 11,000 troops he had assembled, and the expectation of another 1000 at least with Armstrong's arrival,[38] to intercept the army at the Brandywine. It was not enough of a stream to pose any difficulty to fording, but dense waterside thickets and trees made crossing an adventure, except at the fords. Washington thought the creek a good place to engage Howe, and he had chosen the Chadds Ford section at which to make a stand. It was Chadds Ford that provided the normal crossing for those traveling from Baltimore to Philadelphia, and Washington naturally assumed that Howe would be crossing here. The stream was about 150 feet wide at this point, and at this time, because of no rain, unusually shallow. On the morning of September 9, the American army arrived in the region of the ford.

Here, on the next day from his headquarters at the farmhouse of the Quaker miller Benjamin Ring, Washington, with his officers, worked out a strategy. There was high ground at the ford, and the General had Anthony Wayne's brigade of Pennsylvanians and Colonel Thomas Proctor's artillery stationed in a most advantageous way, posted as they were on a little hill above the water, on the east bank, from which they could make a crossing hazardous. This site was pretty much the center of the positions taken by the Continental Army. Proctor and Wayne had support from General William Maxwell's light infantry and were backed by the brigades of Generals Peter Muhlenberg and George Weedon.

The extreme left wing of the emplacements, under command of Armstrong, was stationed at the Pyle's Ford, a little more than a mile downstream from Chadds. Armstrong had something over 1,000 men, virtually all of the active Pennsylvania militia. He was to discourage any crossing here, of course, but his militia had the additional very big responsibility of guarding the American army's supplies of all kinds. Washington's General Orders issued on the eve of the battle directed Armstrong to supply 400 men daily as picquets. All the fords upstream from Chadds were covered by the divisions commanded by Generals Sullivan, Stirling, and Stephen. Washington thus had six miles of the Brandywine defended.

It was early morning of a rather foggy September 11 that promised an oppressive heat when Howe arrived at the Brandywine.

He posted the Hessian General Wilhelm Knyphausen at Chadds Ford. Knyphausen had been instrumental in the British occupation of New York, exhibiting great courage at the battle of White Plains and accepting the sword of Carlisle's Colonel Robert Magaw at the surrender of Fort Washington. The Hessian had 6000 troops, including substantial artillery. And an artillery exchange, though Knyphausen delayed firing until after nine o'clock, became the first order of business. Armstrong and his men, just downstream, could hear the booming of the guns, and braced themselves for the attack they were certain was coming. What the Americans did not realize, however, was that Knyphausen was here simply "amusing" the rebels. As Howe had planned, the Hessian was to provide a distraction while a wide flanking march was performed by the main body of the army. Knyphausen was obliging, of course, and firing enough cannon to give the impression that Chadds Ford was a focal point. And Proctor's artillery returned the fire "with spirit."

When in the afternoon the astonished Washington was informed by Squire Thomas Cheyney, a local and a very fervent patriot, exactly what the position of Howe's main army actually was, he promptly reorganized his divisions, sending the most unwelcome news to Chadds Ford and to Armstrong at Pyles, that no relief troops would be coming. Besides placing the Chadds Ford command with Wayne, he ordered Greene to reinforce Sullivan upstream. Then, with a local farmer named Joseph Brown to guide them, Washington with his men raced posthaste to the real action.

When Knyphausen detected the unmistakable firing of Howe's troops, off to the north and west, he determined to take his artillery across the stream. In spite of the intense fire of Proctor's artillery, he was able to effect a crossing at the ford, and to engage Wayne's men in hand-to-hand combat.

While the action involving Knyphausen and Wayne was so heated that it almost seemed the principal action, it certainly was not. Howe had meant from the beginning to take the forces of Cornwallis, together with his own, against the right flank of the Continental troops, which he did not expect could offer resistance. This was the element of the army, the right wing, commanded by General John Sullivan, the 3rd Division (1st and 2nd Maryland Brigade), which Washington had positioned at Brinton's Ford, about a mile upstream from Chadds Ford.

Sullivan's forces were completely routed by the Redcoats and were in full flight by the time the troops of Nathanael Greene came up for support. Only the heroic stand of Greene's men who held firm once they arrived, and the equally valiant resistance provided by the troops under the immediate command of Washington, saved the rebel forces from total disaster. As the forces of Wayne fell back toward Chester, Armstrong, whose men had not seen any action at all, withdrew from Pyle's Ford. Darkness ended all. But Washington had been forced to remove his entire force to the community of Chester. It was a stunning victory for the British.

As the army retreated, carrying the wounded, which included the nineteen-year-old Marquis de Lafayette, who here had fought his first battle in the Patriot cause, Armstrong was busy. Again, as at Charleston, the action evaded him; but his men had had a role to play, and they played it well. Somehow, in the confusion of retreat and darkness, they were able to protect the American stores and to remove them completely from the danger zone.

All in all, it was a very bad day for the Continental Army. The only benefit that could be allowed the Americans was that the fighting did delay, if only for a little, the eventual British occupation of Philadelphia. In the time that he had gained, Washington had ordered removed from the city the materials most useful to the military. Whatever food and clothing could be transported out, as well as munitions and essential military supplies, was loaded into wagons and placed out of reach of the British. Even the Independence Bell (later known as Liberty Bell) was carried off to hiding in Allentown. And, besides, by the time Howe arrived, Philadelphia would no longer be the capital of the country. Howe never did capture the capital. It was very easy to move the capital. It required only that meetings of the Congress be scheduled for a different place.[39]

At midnight, from Chester, Washington, "in the first leisure moment I have had since the action," reported to John Hancock: "I am sorry to inform you, that in this day's engagement, we have been obliged to leave the enemy masters of the field." He blames the defeat on the mistaken intelligence received, which "prevented my making a disposition, adequate to the force with which the Enemy attacked us on the right." He describes the action, noting Knyphausen's crossing at Chadds, which forced the retirement of Wayne, and how the Militia, "under the command of Major Genl. Armstrong, being posted at a ford two miles below Chad's, had no opportunity of engaging." He laments the loss of "seven or eight pieces of cannon," but feels the loss of men not severe (though indeed he had lost upwards of 1000 men), and fewer than that of the enemy. He reports the wounding of Lafayette and General William Woodford, but is "happy to find the troops in good spirits."[40]

In his narrative account of the battle, General Arthur St. Clair, having noted that Washington "rarely missed any advantage that could be taken of the enemy," remembers that the General had asked him "to attend him to General Armstrong's quarters (about two miles from Chad's Ford, where the body of the enemy was posted) who, with the Pennsylvania militia, which he commanded, was to have had a share in it; but the Pennsylvania militia were not in readiness, and he was obliged to abandon the project." He recalled, too, that Washington's strategy at one point called for Greene's division "to descend the river to General Armstrong's quarters," that movement being concealed from Knyphausen "by the thick woods on the river's bank." The idea, according to St. Clair, was for the combined divisions of Greene and Armstrong to cross at Pyle's Ford and fall on the rear of Knyphausen, while Washington would himself cross at Chadds, and "attack him in front, which would infallibly oblige Sir William to retrace his steps."[41]

Following the disaster at Brandywine, Washington remained concerned about the Delaware River defenses, but he did not feel that he could deploy regular troops for that purpose. And of course defenses on the river might not be necessary. To the Congress he indicated his plans, which included orders to Armstrong: "A part of the Militia under Genl. Armstrong will be posted along the Schuylkill, to throw up Redoubts at the different Fords, which will be occasionally occupied, whilst I move to the other side with the Main Body of the Army."[42]

The next day, Sunday, September 14, at seven o'clock in the morning, the Commander-in-Chief got off very specific instructions to Armstrong:

> *Sir: I last night wrote to the Officer commanding at the Bridge, ordering him to have it moved immediately . . . . I have therefore to request that you will have it executed directly, as the Enemy (being now advanced near Chester) will probably detach a party of light Troops to take possession of it, particularly when they come to understand that we have taken the Route which is determined on. You will also pay due attention to the Fords up the Schuylkill, and have any Works you see necessary thrown up for their defence. Colo.* [Louis Lebègue] *Du Portail*[43] *and his Officers will attend you for this purpose.* [Washington on this day ordered Duportail to report to Armstrong "and take his orders about throwing up some small works along the Schuylkill."] . . . . *Guards should be kept at all the Ferries to take care of the Boats . . . .*[44]

Louis Lebègue Duportail

With the British moving on the capital, it clearly became necessary to remove from the communities in their path everything that might be of value to Howe and Cornwallis. Typical of the duties assigned Armstrong was the order from Congress, September 18, that "Major General John Armstrong be directed, forthwith, to cause all the printing presses and types in this city [Philadelphia] and Germantown, forthwith to be removed to secure places in the country." [45] But within two weeks Armstrong was back with the main army, or almost.

XXII

Germantown

As the British army continued its march on Philadelphia, Washington seemed content to retire "to the northern section of Chester County, where he apparently wandered without purpose along the Schuylkill for days." [1] But General Wayne, feeling that the British, now encamped at Tredyffrin in the Chester Valley (a region that the General knew well) were extremely vulnerable, urged an assault. When Washington did not take kindly to this idea, Wayne resorted to harassment and asked for support.

On September 20, nine days after the Brandywine, with his 1500 troops of the Pennsylvania Line, and hopeful of help from General William Maxwell coming from the north, but not waiting for it, Wayne moved into a position only three miles from the British encampment at Paoli. He had assumed all along that he was undetected, that the British were unaware of his presence. But, as a matter of fact, Wayne's movements had been monitored very closely.

That night the British Major General Charles Grey (who had led a ruthless bayonet charge at the battle of Culloden), under orders from Howe, launched a very carefully planned attack on Wayne's encampment. With stern orders that no muskets be fired, on the excessively dark night, rainy and "wretched," of September 20-21, Grey's soldiers massacred with bayonets all those of the sleeping troops who had no time to flee. Thomas Sullivan, of the British Forty-Ninth Regiment of Foot, later recalled that Grey's men set fire to the tents, and that the astonished soldiers would not even then come out, preferring death in the flames to the bayonet. The survivors were driven two miles, arriving at White Horse in the wee hours of the morning. It was a total rout of Wayne's force and one of the most bloody and terrifying episodes of the entire war.

Shortly after this disaster, Washington's main army, which had been encamped at Pottsgrove (Pottstown), and had been suffering a most inhospitable rain, prepared to move again. The General was expecting Wayne this very night, the 25th, and General William Smallwood on the morrow. He had sent orders, too, to Lord Stirling and to Armstrong, who somehow had never received the orders countermanding his march to Trappe.[2]

Breaking camp at nine o'clock in the morning of September 26, the soldiers marched on to Pennebecker's Mill (Schwenksville), between the Perkiomen and Skippack Creeks, where they established camp later that day. The British were on the move, too, or at least some of them. September 26 was in fact a big day for King George the Third. The command of General Cornwallis, which included two British Regular battalions and two Hessian grenadier battalions, and two squadrons of the 16th Dragoons, together with artillery field pieces, marched triumphantly into Philadelphia to the acclamation of the mostly Loyalist population who remained.

Of course Philadelphia was no longer the capital of the United States. All members of the Continental Congress had fled west to the new capital, Lancaster, Pennsylvania, eight days earlier.

The major part of the British army, under General Howe, who had been proceeding very cautiously, halted outside the city, at Germantown. At this time only thirty miles separated the armies of Washington and William Howe.

Armstrong's militia, in their tents at Trappe, broke camp on this same day, the 26th. A letter of information and speculation the

General addressed on this day to President Wharton:

I can't think of leaving this place without giving you a line . . . . Two points I shall touch in the laconic way; How the Enemy has passed the army to Philad^t without impediment, and what we think of doing next . . .the Enemy, in rapidly moving a part of their body up the Scuilkill, by French Creek, led the General [Washington] *to apprehend they designed to cross above us, & turn our right wing; to prevent this he marched high on this side on the Swamp road when the same night, next morning they passed at Fatland fort, and proceeded on to Sweeds ford, also by another road, I think, called the Manontany, so that before full intelligence of their crossing came to head quarters, or rather before it gained credit, they were thought, in Council, to be at too great a distance to be harrassed on the rear by fatigued troops. . . . We expect several reinforcements tho' Mr Douglas* [Alexander McDougall's] *and Waynes already joined the latter thro' a late misfortune* [Paoli] *is much smaller than we expected—we now draw nearer to the Enemy whom we hear are encamped on Chestnut Hill—two or three days rest are thought necessary for our Troops, as I'm persuaded the General designs to attack as early as he reasonably can—the Event will probably be great either way! Of the Militia I choose to be silent, and see what another tryal may produce.*[3]

At Pennebecker's Mill, Washington, having collected as much information as he could from the locals, paused to consider. As he reported to the Board of War, he had the impression that though "a part of the enemy had marched into Philadelphia, the main part of the army lay near Germantown." He felt that these troops numbered "about 8000 men"; and, noting that his force had been bountifully augmented by troops showing up under Generals McDougall, Smallwood, and David Forman, as well as by the Pennsylvania militia under Armstrong, he calculated his numbers at "about 8000 Continental Troops rank and file, and 3000 Militia." Accordingly, as he reported to the Board of War, he was convening a council "to consult and resolve on the most advisable measures to be pursued; but more especially to learn from them, whether with this Force it was prudent to make a general and vigorous attack upon the Enemy, or to wait further reinforcements."

And so there at his headquarters, which was the home of Samuel Pennebecker, Washington brought his officers, fifteen generals, together. The date was September 28. The question which came to the table was whether to assault immediately the British force at Germantown or to wait for a more opportune time. Smallwood, sensing what Washington preferred to do, urged an attack on the British at Germantown. Anthony Wayne, not surprisingly, provided an energetic second to that view, and Generals James Irvine, Charles Scott[4] and James Potter[5] were quick to join in. The very Scotch-Irish Potter was a Cumberland County man and had served under Armstrong on the Kittanning expedition.

However, when it was noted that in a little time perhaps they might enjoy some reinforcement from the army of Gates, at that time contesting Burgoyne in the north, the remaining generals (Henry Knox, Francis Nash, Nathanael Greene, John Sullivan, Alexander McDougall, Peter Muhlenberg, Thomas Conway, Lord Stirling, Adam Stephen, and John Armstrong) voted for a delay. It was a 2-1 majority. Washington was not impressed by the majority. Happily for him, it was shortly learned that Howe had sent a substantial portion of his army to capture those works on the Delaware which were making passage difficult, if not impossible, for the British fleet. And shortly thereafter he learned, also, from captured letters, that Howe had sent a strong detachment to New Jersey. With his confidence buoyed even more by this news, he took another tally, and this time he found all of his generals agreed on an assault.

The British were now occupying the region close to the small community some six or seven miles northwest of Philadelphia known as Germantown. Washington had had his impression of numbers confirmed, and was certain that Howe's troops could not number more than 9,000 men. He felt confident that with his slightly superior force (much bolstered by the militia recruiting efforts of Smallwood and Armstrong) and possibly artillery advantages, and perhaps the advantage of surprise, as at Trenton, he could launch an effective assault. The troops were fully recovered from Brandywine and seemed in a fighting spirit. But success could come, as he very well understood, only through a very strategically designed plan of attack. Accordingly, in consultation with his officers, Armstrong among them, the Commander-in-Chief drew up a very complex battle plan.

With the army now at Skippack, Washington on October 1 proclaimed General Orders: "The whole army are to strike their tents to morrow morning at 8 o'clock and get ready to march. At nine the march is to begin." Washington's orders defined the order of march: Sullivan's division would lead, with Lincoln's, McDougall's, and Greene's following to form the first line. Next came the artillery, and then the second line in this order: Stirling, Nash, Stephen. And all to encamp on the new ground in precisely the marching order. "General Armstrong is at the same time to move by the shortest route to the right of the first line, on the ground the [Quartermaster General] will point out."[6]

The plan as drawn up called for the assault to be made by four separate forces. It required almost perfect coordination and was designed not only for surprise but also for a total envelopment of the British forces. General Sullivan, with one body of the regular army, including Wayne's division, would command the right wing and strike from the west at the very center of the British position; at the same time forces under General Nathanael Greene, also regulars, and including Adam Stephen, would, as Washington's left wing, come from their position in the north to assail the British right flank. Detachments of militia would provide the pincer movements from both sides. These longer marches around the flanks would be performed by the Pennsylvania militia (1000 troops) on the right, nearest the Schuylkill; and by the Maryland and New Jersey militia (1600 men) under William Smallwood and David Forman, far to the left.

Sullivan was to advance down the Skippack Road. He would be followed by Lord Stirling and a reserve unit composed of William Maxwell's Pennsylvania riflemen, who had fought so courageously at Chadds Ford. General Francis Nash, in command of a fresh regiment of North Carolina troops, was in this force also.

Greene, whom Washington placed in command of two-thirds of the attacking army, was to enter the community by way of the Limekiln Road, to attack Howe head-on. With him were Generals Adam Stephen and Alexander McDougall.[7]

The particular assignment given to Armstrong was somehow to get past the Redcoats on the Schuylkill side and assume such positions as would effectively block any retreat by the British toward Philadelphia. From the journal of Timothy Pickering comes this impression of his orders. Noting that all assaults were to begin at once, he writes, "General Armstrong, with his division of Pennsylvania militia, was to move down the old Egypt or Schuylkill road, and take off a Hessian picket posted there, and attack the enemy's left wing and rear. The attack was to begin upon every quarter at five in the morning." [8]

An entry in the Orderly Book kept by General George Weedon through the fall of 1777 and the Valley Forge winter of 1777-78, shows the orders to Armstrong thus: "General Armstrong to pass down the Ridge Road by Levering's Tavern and take guides to cross Wissahickon creek about the head of John Vandeering's mill dam so as to fall in about [Joseph] Warner's new house. [The pickets on the left of Vandeering's Mill were to be "taken off" by Armstrong.] Smallwood and Forman to pass down by a mill formerly David Morriss' and Jacob Edge's mill into the White Marsh road at the Sandy Run—to Jenkins' Tavern on the old York road, then keep down the old York road below Armitage's beyond the seven mile stone; half a mile from which a road turns off short to the right fenc'd on both sides, which leads through enemy's encampment at Germantown Market House." [9] It was Washington's plan that Smallwood and Forman, in taking the old York Road, could get out around the other end of the British line.

Thus four assault forces would be advancing upon the British, two at the center, left and right, and two way outside in an encircling movement. All elements were to reach positions on their routes some two miles from the British sentries by two o'clock a. m. They were to halt, then, and begin advancing at such time as would bring them to the sentries precisely at five o'clock. They were to take the pickets with bayonets. Hopefully the firing on all four fronts would not begin before five o'clock. Washington, in laying out the operation, used the word "surprise" a good many times. All of this looked on paper like an excellent plan. And so it was. But it did not work.

In the first place, this four-pronged assault was scheduled

for a time when it was still very dark, which was good for surprise, but not so good for soldiers fighting on an unfamiliar terrain. Besides that, it was going to be very cold (forty or fifty degrees below the temperatures experienced at the Brandywine), hardly above freezing; and to make matters even worse, there would settle into the area by early morning a very heavy fog, much more dense than that experienced in the early hours of the Brandywine engagement.

But the American march was underway at the appointed time, seven o'clock on the evening of October 3. It proved a very long march (some fourteen miles), over very difficult, rough roads, from Metuchen Hill on the Skippack Road all the way to Chestnut Hill. Washington chose to march with Sullivan. The order of march for these troops, as dictated by the General, had General Thomas Conway (not his favorite officer, but courageous) at the head of the column with his advance brigade, followed by Sullivan, Maxwell and General Francis Nash. Just as the sun produced its faint, rosy glow in the Philadelphia east ahead of them, these troops reached Chestnut Hill.

The first fighting, at Mount Airy, was extremely hot and spirited. The engagement featured the troops of Sullivan and Conway, who of course were in the van, against those of Colonel Thomas Musgrave, by all accounts a most resourceful and courageous officer. It was Musgrave who had been put in command of the forces which at Paoli had been employed by Grey to prevent the escape of Wayne's men to the north, and though this detachment saw no action at Paoli, it had done its job. Musgrave was a hardened veteran, a favorite with Howe, whom he had accompanied to the colonies. He had been wounded in the battle of Pelham Manor on the King's Highway just about a year ago, on October 18.

Now Sullivan, in trouble, called for support from Wayne, and as these troops came forward Sullivan launched them in a bayonet charge against Musgrave. At this point there occurred one of those inglorious moments that all wars include.

Wayne's division was composed, in part, of the survivors of the Paoli surprise nighttime attack by the Redcoats under Charles Grey. These men, who were remembering the bayoneting of the sleeping soldiers and the burning of the occupied tents, fought with fury in the back-and-forth bayonet charges, and when the British fell back they "took ample Vengeance for that Night's work," cruelly doing their bloody business on the Redcoats, even those who were surrendering, bayoneting "many of the poor wretches who were Crying for Mercy, in spite of their officer's exertions to restrain them." [10] At last, a British bugle, mercifully, sounded retreat.

Still offering some resistance, the Redcoats fell back toward the little village of Germantown itself, and a number of the troops, six companies of the 40th British Regiment (some 125 men) under the resourceful Musgrave, took refuge inside the mansion of Judge Benjamin Chew, a close acquaintance of Armstrong, but a Loyalist.

Washington might have elected to bypass this "fortress," but, on the recommendation of Henry Knox, decided instead to storm it. Two guns of the 4th Continental Artillery (Proctor's regiment), were called to action, but because of the fog, which disguised the fact that it was a stone structure, the artillery men employed grape rather than cannon balls and the barrage was totally ineffective. The Redcoats were not dislodged. And, though in the course of the fighting at the Chew Mansion, Lt. Colonel John Laurens of South Carolina, son of the soon-to-be President of the Continental Congress, constantly risking his life, made a number of valiant efforts to burn the building down, these too were unsuccessful. Confusion reigned over the last hours of the battle. For a while it looked as though Washington's ingenious plan was going to work, because those troops under his personal command who had not been left at the Chew Mansion, were threatening to cut their way through the British lines, and Greene, though late to the fray, was doing well. Indeed, by late morning, the two wings of the main army, Sullivan's and Greene's had advanced so far as to view their object, which was the Market House at the center of the community.

What caused the assault to fail was what in later years would be called "friendly fire" (an experience of Washington at Fort Loyal Hanna). Soldiers in Greene's unit were misdirected by General Adam Stephen (later found to be drunk at the time) and wound up mistaking the infantry of General Anthony Wayne, who were a part of the Sullivan forces, for the enemy. Wayne's men of course fired back. In the chaos that followed somehow the forces of Greene got the impression that they were being hemmed in (General Armstrong later heard that "some officer" had called out, "We are surrounded!") and because ammunition was now almost exhausted, Greene ordered his troops to disengage. At just about the time the Americans were giving up the fight, Cornwallis, with two battalions of British regulars and a Hessian unit arrived from Philadelphia.

And that turned out to be the end of the battle. To his dismay, Washington learned, only after the fighting was over, that the whole battle had been fought without the militia forces. These were the pincers, the troops who were to provide the enveloping movement. Armstrong had followed his route properly, moving down the Manatawny Road to the crossing at Wissahickon Creek, and was right on schedule. Here, as expected, he had encountered some Hessian riflemen, and was able to rout them with the two small cannon he carried. But, according to the reports that came eventually to Washington, the General, who might have launched an infantry charge against this Hessian unit, appeared content to engage in some "leisurely shelling." The consequence was a counter attack by the Hessians, which forced a flight of Armstrong's troops a distance of three miles. Inexplicably, Armstrong had taken his force so far from the actual engagement that he could not presume the course of the battle.[11]

And the story for Smallwood and Forman, far to the other side of the Redcoats, was even more disappointing. These militia of Maryland and New Jersey never even arrived at the battle site, or at least not until the fighting was done. The militia, almost one-third of Washington's force, who had been counted on for so much, were not a factor.

Armstrong, in his own version of the battle of Germantown, seems unaware of any failure on his part. On the day after, from the rebel camp near Trappe (General Peter Muhlenberg's birthplace), he supplied a most interesting account in a long letter to Pennsylvania President Thomas Wharton, whose Supreme Executive Council had evacuated Philadelphia for Lancaster at the same time as the Continental Congress. While referring to the fog, the confused firing, and the Chew Mansion, he insists we "fled from victory." It's a pained letter that he writes:

By a forced march of fourteen miles or upward, on Friday night, General Washington attacked about sunrise, yesterday morning, the British & Foreign Troops encamped at Jerman Town, Vandurings & elsewhere toward the York Road. We marched by four different routes—those on the left [Smallwood] did not arrive so soon as the Columnes on the Center & Right. The Continental Troops drove the principal part of the Enemy at Jerman Town full two miles; yet what I shall say a victory almost in full embrace was frustrated, but by what means cannot yet be fully ascertained. I think by a number of casualties, a thick fogg whereby not only our ammunition was expended without an object, but it's thought that our own Troops had been taken in an instance or two for reinforcements of the enemy, whereby a panic and retreat ensued, which the General could not prevent! Thus may it be said, thro' some strange fatality (tho' not the less faulty on our part,) that we fled from victory. Another reason was the time spent about Mr. Chew's house, where a number of the Enemy took sanctuary, & from which a number of our people were killed & wounded. We can tell nothing perfectly of our loss, nor of that of the enemy. General Nashes thigh & the head of Major [James] Witherspoon[12] were, it's said, both taken away by one & the same Cannon Ball. I shou'd be glad to send you a Copy of Our Order of Battle, or attack, but have it not here.

And then he describes the part played by the Pennsylvania militia. He seems to want President Wharton to know that his troops were "the last on the ground":

My destiny [assignment] was against the various Corps of Jermans encamped at Mr. Vanduring's or near the Falls. Their Light Horse discovered our approach a little before sunrise; we canonaded from the heights on each side the Wissihickon, whilst the Riflemen on opposite sides acted on the lower ground. About nine I was called to joine the General, but left a party with the Coll^r Eyers & [James] Dunlap, & one field piece, & afterwards reinforced them, which reinforcement, by the by, however did not joine them, untill after a *brave resistance they were obliged to retreat, but carried off the field piece, the other I was obliged to leave in the Horrenduous hills of the Wissihickon, but ordered her on a safe rout to join Eyeres if he shou'd retreat, as was done accordingly. We proceeded to the left, and above Jermantown some three miles, directed by a slow crossfire of Canon, untill we fell into the Front of a superior body of the Enemy, with whom we engaged about three quarters of an hour, but their grape shot & ball soon intimidated & obliged us to retreat or rather file off. Until then I thought we had a Victory, but to my great disappointment, soon found our army were gone an hour or two before, & we the last on the ground. We brought off every thing but a wounded man or two —lost not quite 20 men on the whole, & hope we killed at least that number, beside diverting the Hessian Strength from the General in the morning.*[13]

In a letter composed almost a week after the battle he reported to General Horatio Gates that because he was under the strong impression that the British were in retreat, that the Patriots were victorious, he "fell in with the rear of the enemy . . . supposing them vanquished . . . and gave them a brush." But, as he reported to Gates, he was himself forced to withdraw because of the effects of the British artillery. In all, Armstrong reported, he suffered "but thirty-nine wounded."

With Greene's forces withdrawing, and Armstrong not in the main action, a general retreat was ordered. The British, buoyed by success, were quick to pursue, and did so, for a distance of some nine miles, almost all the way back to Washington's former camp at Pennebecker's Mill.

The whole battle had lasted but four hours. What made it all so disappointing was that the American forces were so close to success. And it was a costly engagement. The British, Washington learned long afterwards, lost 537 men killed and wounded. Four officers were slain, and thirty were wounded. The Continental Army, as reported by the Board of War, lost even more, 673 men killed and wounded and 400 more captured. Among those lost in the action were fifty-three patriot soldiers who fell on the lawn and at the doorstep of the Chew House in that vain effort. And

Washington lost one of his most gallant and trusted officers, Brigadier General Francis Nash of the North Carolinians.

In his report to the Congress, filed the day after (before the dying of Nash and before the final figures were in), Washington put a better face on the battle than it deserved: "Upon the whole it may be said that the day was rather unfortunate than injurious." He saw the enemy as "nothing better by the event," and his own troops "not in the least dispirited," and profiting from the experience.[14]

The disappointment at Germantown can be blamed on the unfortunate decision to assault the Chew mansion (Armstrong, for example, thought it "an ill-judged delay."), or on the Wayne-Greene confusion, but Henry Knox, while acknowledging the value to the British of possession of "some stone buildings in Germantown," blamed the failure to achieve victory on the terrible fog, "which had arisen about daybreak [and] become so excessively thick from the continued firing that it was impossible to discover an object at twenty yards."[15] General Armstrong, as he confided to General Gates in that letter composed five days after the battle, thought it all very sad. He reported that the "Continental troops attacked with vigour, and drove the British who frequently rallied and were drove again and again about the space of two miles, when some unhappy spirit of information seized our troops almost universally whereby they began to retreat and fled in wild disorder unknown to the General. So that a victory, a glorious victory fought for and eight tenths won, was shamefully but mysteriously lost, for to this moment no one man can or at least will give any good reason for the flight." The popular thing to do was to blame the defeat on the fog and on the confusion. Armstrong does so: "The morning was foggy and so far unfavourable. It's said ours took the mauvres [maneuvers] of part of our own people for large reinforcements of the enemy and thereby took fright at themselves or at one another. Some unhappy officer is said to have called out: 'We are surrounded, we are surrounded.'" He blames also, again, the "ill judged delay" in assaulting the Chew House.

In this letter to Gates, just as he had done in the letter to Wharton, he attributes his withdrawal to Washington's sending for him, and again he remarks that his troops were the last to leave the field.. "I follered a slow cannonade several miles but found him not, fell in with the rear of the enemy, still supposing them a vanquished party and that we had a victory tho' the firing was then countered. We gave them a brush, but their artillery, so well directed, soon obliged us to file off, near two hours after our troops had left the field." [16]

On the same day that he wrote to Gates, Armstrong wrote another long letter to President Wharton. He repeated his impression that "Seldome was victory more nearly won, nor strangely lost, as on Saturday last" and reported the British barricading of Germantown, the evacuation of Billingsport, and the impression that "as soon as Howe has fortified he is to seek us in the field, to which we have no objection." [17] And T. Will Heth, a Continental officer, writing to Colonel John Lamb from the Camp on the Perkiomen, Oct. 12, expressed the same surprise and disappointment that characterized the accounts of others: "Before this reaches you, the news of our late action at German Town, no doubt will have come to hand. It was a grand enterprize, an inimitable plan, which nothing but its God-like author could equal. Had the execution of it been equal to its formation, it must have been attended with the most happy success . . . the assault nearly completed the total ruin of the British army. In fact we had gained a victory had we known it." [18]

But whatever it was blamed on, it was indeed a lost battle for the Cause, and a costly one. There now stood nothing between the British and the occupation of Philadelphia, which a few weeks ago had been the young nation's capital city. Only the wise Ben Franklin could find any consolation. When he was advised of the American defeats at the Brandywine and at Germantown, and told that now Howe had Philadelphia, he is supposed to have replied, "Does General Howe have Philadelphia, or does Philadelphia have him?"

XXIII

WHITEMARSH

Armstrong was promptly in receipt of the Germantown aftermath orders. On the 8th, just four days beyond the battle, Washington ordered him to send General Potter with "600 of your militia across the Schuylkill, with directions to keep himself in such a situation as will be most convenient for interrupting the enemy's intercourse between Philadelphia and Chester." Washington expressed the hope that Potter could thus cut off convoys, intercept dispatches, prevent the Redcoats from getting supplies from the country, and make of himself a considerable nuisance.[1]

On the 14th, one day after his 60th birthday, from the camp at Towamanzen, Armstrong responded to questions from the Supreme Executive Council. He provided an account of the Pennsylvania militia forces, which were much depleted through desertion, and reported that they never did exceed 2973 rank and file. And he regretted that "no true report of the quantity of spirits given to any particular Battalion can possibly be made." But the big news he had to report was that of General Gates's rout of the army of Burgoyne, "the particulars [of which] you will more fully hear from Congress."[2] Four days later, now in camp at Worcester, he remarked again on Gates's victory: "This is a blessing not only far exceeding America's merit, but even our most sanguine expectations, yet not too high for the God of Americans, the author of justice & beneficence to bestow." He reported, too, that "The General has just now asked me to repair to you in order to concert measures to draw out the strength of this State to aid him in suppressing the arch tyrants now in Philad[a]. I cannot refuse the journey, and shall, I suppose set out in the morning." And, as he regularly does, he urges that his wife be informed: "Please by some direct & early means to forward that to my wife, as in it an early foundation is laid for the people of Cumberland." [3]

As bad weather drew ever closer, the impatient General Anthony Wayne once again proposed an attack on Philadelphia. And, as was his wont when he took hold of something, he put all the force of his personality behind it. Washington himself, not surprisingly, was determined to wrest the city back from Howe. He envisioned a surprise attack, and had even drawn up a rather elaborate and detailed plan, including instructions for all elements of the army, including the Pennsylvania Militia. In this scheme Armstrong's militiamen, including the troops of General James Irvine, would march "to form a junction with Lord Stirling the Moment our lodgment is made; and in the meanwhile, to move towards Matsons ford for that purpose, or for covering our retreat, or securing our Camp, in case of disaster or disappointment." [4]

But when Washington, at some time before November 23, put the plan before the assembled officers, only four, perhaps five, including Lord Stirling and, naturally, the impetuous Wayne, favored an assault. Ten generals, and Armstrong was one, voted against the proposal.[5]

In a letter of the 23rd Armstrong reported to Wharton, "On the subject of a visit to Philad[a], a full Council has been held, resolv'd in the negative . . . . What is to follow must be the result of further deliberation, which may heaven direct." On this same day, in a long letter written from the Artillery Park at Whitemarsh, Henry Knox responded to Washington's query by voicing the same strong opposition.

Armstrong's formal opinion for Washington was expressed on the 25th. He has, obviously, done some thinking about an assault. From the camp at Whitemarsh he wrote to His Excellency:

Without such an acquaintance of the Enemies lines as wou'd discover to you, where they are more or less accessible, I cannot well approve of an attack upon them, nor can I conceive the opposite numbers at Philad^d under six thousand or upward —And question whether an attack can be successful if the lines are not penetrated in so short a space of time (perhaps some seven or at most ten minutes) as will render it impossible for the party thrown into the City shou'd the first attempt on the lines fail, to contribute any effectual influence. The principle upon which that part of the disposition is formed is perfectly just, but the numbers too few, and the contingencies various.

Armstrong instead proposed "carrying the Army over Scuilkill & making tryal of any advantages that yet may be derived from a possession of the Islands &c. &c., by which means either the Enemy may be drawn out or the Scuilkill pass'd to advantage on the Ice." But he will support whatever decision is reached: "At the same time I am totally submissive to your Excellency's commands, begging leave only to add that whether the attack is made or not, but especially if it is, the far greater part of your force in Jersey may suddenly be recalled and join the Army." [6]

With that opinion and the verdict of Knox, and having observed for himself the fortifications of the city, and knowing that Cornwallis with substantial troops had by now moved back into the city, Washington concluded that an assault was simply out of the question. He persevered in his hope that the British would come out. Armstrong summarized all of this for Wharton and the Executive Council:

At the time when Ld Cornwallis was in the Jersey, G^l Washington was much disposed to attack the Enemy's Redoubts and attempt a passage into the city. The thing was deliberated in council and additional methods taken to reconnoitre & examine the lines—for this purpose the Gen., went into Chester County, & from the heights of Scuilkill had a fair view of their left, which was found so strong & well finished, that even the most sanguine for the attack [Wayne] *gave it up as inelligible. At any rate we cou'd not have* made the effort until the 29th, and on the 27th, at four in the afternoon, Cornwallis crossed over to Town with his troops, so that the measure appears to be at an end.[7]

Armstrong had orders, too, from the Council of Safety, ever alert to the Tory activity. One such order arrived on December 1, 1777, when he was asked by the Council, now of course meeting in Lancaster, to make an arrest: "Sir, Information being given to Council, that Doctor Shannon, who is said to have conducted the enemy through Philadelphia County, and to have been with them in the city, is now in the county, and goes at large. This is to empower and direct you to seize his person, and send him forthwith under proper guard to this Council."[8] This duty being promptly accomplished, the Council at its meeting Dec. 15, took it from there.[9]

And the war continued. For three weeks the Continental Army, 11,000 strong, continued in its encampment at Whitemarsh, thirteen miles northwest of the city. With Fort Mifflin on the Delaware, defended courageously by the Carlisle-born Lt. Colonel Samuel Smith,[10] but under siege and heavy bombardment for weeks, Washington was made to appreciate that the river was likely to be opened to British shipping and that an engagement with Howe would be then even more likely. As early as November 29, Armstrong had advised Pennsylvania President Thomas Wharton that "Every intelligence agrees that General Howe, no doubt with his whole force, is immediately to take the field in quest of this army."[11]

The Commander-in-Chief had made Colonel Louis du Portail responsible for the fortifications and for a general defense strategy in the Whitemarsh area, and the Colonel had been hard at work since late October. He had selected three distinct hills, known now as Fort Hill, Militia Hill, and Camp Hill, for the principal fortifications. As these hills not only supplied a desirable elevation, but were so thickly wooded as to provide also excellent cover, they seemed ideal for a defense posture.

The main fortification was erected at the top of Fort Hill, just east of the road leading to Bethlehem. Washington, together with Lafayette, established his headquarters at the home of the recently deceased George Emlen, a very popular and wealthy Quaker wine merchant. Emlen's house, the site today designated by an historical marker, had been built at the foot of Camp Hill, very close to a stream affectionately labeled Sandy Run.[12]

Washington's informers have assured him that a British attack is coming. Washington hopes so. He is pretty well dug in high in the heavily wooded hills, and has fifty-two pieces of artillery. The troops are suffering some from the inclement weather, and are not all that well provisioned, but the General hopes their anger will be taken out on the British, who, he now believes, are on their way.

In fact, they are coming. They are marching in stealth, undetected they think. But Washington has taken his information seriously, and is prepared. His army has been bolstered by the arrival of Captain Daniel Morgan's riflemen, who have been detached from the victorious army of General Gates. With the militia troops, the Continental Army can now boast a force of nearly 13,000 men.

At midnight on December 4, General William Howe gives the command to march. With almost his entire army, 12,000 troops (including the Queen's Rangers of Major John Simcoe, who are specialists in this kind of action), he emerges—he marches out of Philadelphia. Each man has drawn six days' rations. They march in secret, so they think.

Unbeknownst to Howe, he is being observed by one of Washington's most reliable and vigilant scouts, Captain Allen McLane,[13] whom Washington is using to keep Philadelphia under surveillance. McLane is keeping Washington informed. The British are advancing along the Skippack and Manatawny (Ridge) Roads. McLane, who has the command of 100 very select horsemen, attacks the heads of both columns, and puts Howe's troops into such disorder that they change their course. But despite McLane's harassment, the Redcoats proceed, and by 3:00 in the morning, long before the first gleams of light over Philadelphia, find themselves at Chestnut Hill, three miles short of the Rebel encampment. Here they camp until the battle can be joined.

Washington, alerted and prepared, has ordered the building of hundreds of campfires, to give the illusion that his force is stronger than it really is, though in fact he welcomes an engagement. Armstrong, whose Pennsylvania forces are encamped on Militia Hill, on the right wing of the army, is up early on this morning, in time even to get a note off to President Wharton: "'Tis now five in the morning, and as my Division are on their march to meet the Enemy, as, I presume, are the whole army, I can only add that the advanced guard of the Enemy are said to be on this side Jermantown. . . . This may be an important day." [14]

The action begins at eleven o'clock with Washington's order to Armstrong's militia, six hundred troops under Brigadier General James Irvine,[15] to feel out the enemy. Immediately upon receiving the order, Irvine moved out from his position on Militia Hill to intercept the Redcoats. That mission resulted in an engagement with the British 2nd Battalion of light infantry, under Colonel Abercrombie, and some advanced parties, including Hessian grenadiers, in the region of Chestnut Hill. The action proved to be short, but was very fierce, with extremely heavy fire and casualties on both sides. It ended with the capture of the wounded General Irvine, who, stunned by a musket ball that had grazed his head, had fallen from his horse, and thereafter to another musket ball lost three fingers from his left hand and suffered damage to his shoulders and neck. Not much to their credit, the panicky militia abandoned their wounded general, and fled the field in wild disorder.

From this time on the battle resembles that of two boxers moving about the ring feinting for advantage. The British simply maneuver up and down the line of the American positions, rarely approaching closer than one mile, searching for a weakness to exploit. The patriot forces respond of course by shifting their troops to match the heavier British forces. This kind of action continues for three days. Howe's soldiers accomplish little beyond the outrages committed against the civilian population of the region. They burn every house they come close to, despoil property wherever they find it, and create as much a sense of desolation as they can.

On the fourth day, December 8, Howe, disdaining an all-out assault on the American positions, withdraws from the field (but only after the wanton destruction of private property) and marches his army back to Philadelphia. Washington is, of course, much disappointed, for he had had every confidence that his force could win a major engagement.

From his camp at the battle site, at night on the 7th, Armstrong, in the way in which Washington regularly reported to the Congress, had dutifully penned a complete account of the engagement so far to the Executive Council: "The Enemy, in full Force, has now been three days on Chestnut Hill, their left near the Wissaheckin & the right extending to the head of Jermantown, this position guarded on both wings was not thought so elligible as cou'd be wished for an attack on our part."

Unlike the battle of the Brandywine, and unlike the battle of Germantown, the Pennsylvania militia here were much involved. Indeed, they were the first involved. The disposition of his militia force, Armstrong, for Wharton and the Council, described in great detail:

On Friday last [Dec. 5], *none of the Army (except the Horse) moved, but the Militia only attended to annoy them on the march, for this purpose General Potter, with part of his Brigade, by way of Barren Hill Church marched for the Enemies Left. Genl Irwin* [James Irvine], *with six hundred of his, went on a different direction, only to send them out in small partys & give some instructions, but before he had thought proper to disperse his men they fell in with a body of the Enemy, & a warm Scirmish ensued for the space of twenty minutes, a few of ours behaved pritty well, killed & wounded some of the Enemy, amongst the latter was a Baron Knight, whos*[e] *name the informer cou'd not give, but we have lost the use of our good officer & friend Gl. Irwin, three of his fingers being shot off* [as] *he fell from his Horse, and none of his men gave him the least assistance, being at that time broke and running, as did the greater part of them very early. Some of Potters had a short Scirmish, soon repulsed, but killed one* [officer] *& brought off his Sword. The lines manned almost day & night—The bag*[g]*age, &c., being hastily sent off, some hundred of the troops have followed it under the pretext of getting necessarys.*

At the very time he is writing his letter Armstrong is

expecting an attack, if not this night, then in the morning: "At 12 last night [the 6th] the Enemy moved toward our left & the York road, & this afternoon the general attack was expected. Gen'l Potter, with his whole Brigade & the best of our militia was order'd to a certain woods—a part of the Enemies rear who first discover'd ours, attacked & soon dispersed them, they say by falling into bad ground—five came in wounded, & some few, I presume, are prisoners—part of Morgans light troops were also engaged & repulsed by superior numbers. Tomorrow morning, most probably, the general affair comes on, if not this night."

Here Armstrong broke off, delaying his Express until he could report the end of the engagement. He resumed the letter on the next day (the 8th), reporting that, contrary to expectations, this day got passed over without an attack,

the Enemy frequently moveing, & sometimes on different directions from left to right of our lines—Morgans Corps, strengthened by five men from each Continental Batt^n, was this afternoon to have harrassed the Enemies Wings, but at dark we had no intelligence of the effect—at five, we were informed that one of their Columns were in march toward Jermantown, whether retreating or repairing to that Village to avoid rain is yet uncertain. Since they left town we had a considerable number of prisoners & deserters. The Enemy had several waggons employed in carrying off their wounded, on Scirmish of Saturday. . . . Yesterday, General Read [Joseph Reed], *leading on some of our Militia with whom he fell in when reconnoitering, had his Horse Shot thro' the head lost one of his Pistols, Saddle & Bridle, which he was obliged to leave with the dead Horse, himself having a narrow escape.*

A close call indeed. While Reed lay quite helpless on the field, Colonel John Cadwalader drew his sword and was preparing to defend him against the Hessians of General "No-Flint" Charles Grey, who were advancing with fixed bayonets, when McLane and his mounted men came riding up, just in time to panic the would-be murderers.

Armstrong closes out his letter on the 9th, after all is done. In summing up he expresses his contempt for the British and does some "What if" speculating and second guessing:

Last night the Enemy thought proper to retreat [!] to Philad^a, having burnt the new Rising Sun Inn, on their way—whilst they lay on Chestnut Hill they Burnt some good Houses & Barns, and have it's said, left several familys little more than empty walls. As not the least doubt was entertain'd but that they wou'd attack us in our Encampment, the General thought it might have been imprudent in him to have left his Chosen ground to have attacked them on the high grounds which they occupied, as had he been unfortunate, no doubt wou'd in that instance incurred blame: indeed, the attack on the part of Gen'l Howe cou'd not well be doubted with the force & apparatus with which he approached & his knowledge of General Washington's situation, before he left the City, nearly equal to what it cou'd be afterwards—at any rate, had he stayed but one day longer, Gen'l Washington wou'd probably have decamped and risqued the great event on new ground—this was on the Carpet.

So for the Pennsylvania militia forces and the Army of Washington disappointment attends the battle of Whitemarsh. What could have been a major engagement, even, conceivably, bringing a successful end to the rebellion, ended in a stalemate that advanced the war not one way or the other.

This second of his two letters to the Council Armstrong appended with two concerns. One is for the loss of General Irvine to this State, and to himself personally; the other is the urgent need now to arrange a "disspossission of this Army for the Winter." [16]

Wharton's reply to Armstrong's two letters (dated Lancaster, December 12) included the attitude of victory and the expression of confidence in the Continental Army but great concern over the conduct of the Pennsylvania militia: "The precipitate retreat of the enemy, after so much Gasconading, is a convincing proof that their army is not so formidable as they would wish us to believe." They expected us to flee "from hill to hill," he writes, and they found "no want of bravery." But he was made unhappy by Armstrong's account of the militia: "The Conduct of our militia gives me real pain, Council is informed by various hands that they have behaved very infamously. The loss of our worthy General

Irwin [Irvine], I have been informed, was owing entirely to their base behaviour." [17]

XXIV

THE VALLEY FORGE WINTER

As early as the first week of December Washington had been circulating to his officers the question of what to do for winter quarters. But even before the battle of Whitemarsh, on December 1, Armstrong had registered his opinion. In a letter to the Commander-in-Chief, he advised:

> ... with respect to Winter Quarters for the Army—the longer I consider the measure pointed out in the back Villages of this State, the more inadmissable that step appears to be, as by the large lattitude thereby given the enemy thro' the winter & early part of the spring, every doleful & pernitious consequence must be expected . . . . I'm therefore of the Opinion that in proper time, part of your Army take possession of Wilmington, and the Residue form a Chain from thence to Downingtown & perhaps to White Horse on the Lancaster road, as [in] these two some Cover may be had, & Hutts with some use of Houses in the intermediate space—these are the best outlines that appear to me, which may be corrected and better determined when the Army is on that Side.[1]

Three days later, at the very moment Howe was mustering his troops to come out of the city, Armstrong provided some more of his thinking. His opinion now was that the army would do better to be camped in the field rather than in a village. His reasons were that villages were crowded, that "Discipline . . . will be better maintained in the field, that in the field the army would enjoy opportunities for annoying the enemy," and that an in-the-field position would have a discouraging effect upon the "cruel and haughty intruders."

Now at mid-December Washington was compelled to select a site for the winter encampment of the Continental Army. A council of his officers produced a number of nominations, but little agreement. Wilmington had been proposed, and was a popular recommendation, urged by Joseph Reed, Nathanael Greene, Lafayette, and John Cadwalader. When a site at Valley Forge was put forward, General de Kalb passionately expressed his opposition, declaring, "The idea of wintering in this desert can only have been put into the head of the commanding general by an interested speculator or a disaffected man." But Anthony Wayne was very strongly for it and argued persuasively. And of course the Pennsylvania Council of Safety, whose chief concern at this time was Philadelphia, favored the site. And Armstrong, whatever was decided, was very strongly for a site close to the army of Howe. Not two weeks ago he had written to President Wharton, "General Washington must now without loss of time take some new Position relative to the winter, the Safety & support of his army, and such as may appear the best calculated to receive, debate with or occasionally annoy the Enemy. As an individual I am at present in favor of the other side of the Scuilkill, & sincerely wish the Army were now there." [2] In the end, Washington, noting that the Valley Forge site would be partially protected by the Schuylkill River, reached a decision, and Valley Forge it was.

On the 17th of December, which was a Wednesday, the Commander-in-Chief prepared the soldiers to march the four to six miles from Gulph Mills, where the main army had been encamped since the 13th, to the newly selected winter quarters. The day was made memorable not only by this movement but by the address that Washington delivered to the troops.

As historians have described it, Washington congratulated the soldiers upon the campaign just concluded, noting the accomplishments, and then proceeded to praise the officers for their heroism and the foot soldiers for their endurance, counseling all to continue in both fortitude and patience. Then he acknowledged that he had made some mistakes and that failures had occurred. And then he made it plain what it was they were fighting for, noting that "upon the whole, heaven had smiled upon their army and crowned them with success; that the end of their warfare was Independence, Liberty, and Peace, and that the hope of securing these blessings for themselves and their posterity demanded a continuance of the struggle at every hazard." [3]

But the Pennsylvania militia would not be going to Valley Forge. Just two days before, from his camp on the North Wales Road (close to Spring Tavern) Armstrong had advised President Wharton of the rout of the Pennsylvania militia forces under General Potter on the 11th by a foraging body of the enemy. And then, after informing Wharton of Washington's plan for the winter for the Continental Army, he advises that "I am for the present left here to attempt covering a large country with about one thousand of our Militia; a task perhaps impossible fully to effect by, nor was it effected by the whole army—true the good General does not mean that this or several other branches of his instructions can by any such handful of men be wholly complied with, but only to do what we can with reasonable safety to the whole."

He declares that "I am willing for a few days to risk anything I can," and then, prophetically, suggests that "if Gen. Howe does not attack our army in one week, I think he will not this winter, but only send detachments to Forrage & plunder where it may be done with the least impunity." He advises, too, that General Potter will not be able to serve through the winter, and "With regard to myself, the language of nature, & common sense sufficiently argues against a Winter Campaign of this sort, not perhaps two nights in one place, and altho' my determination was not to relax a single day whilst anything important was in view, or during the active part of the Campaign, yet did I fully expect it would have been closed more than a month ago." In short, the Pennsylvania Militia will need some new generals.[4]

During this time Washington was depending upon Armstrong, who remained on the east side of the Schuylkill, in what was called the Forge or Valley Hill, to address a baffling array of problems, including the procurement of leather, wheat, and powder. Of course his chief responsibility during this time was to interfere with the British supply lines. A station of sentinels had been fixed for each of the nine "Capitol Roads," and the men so posted were expected to stop marketers from entering the city with produce and by their patrols to make it difficult for the British to send out forage missions.[5] That Armstrong was doing a good job in that way Washington recognized and commended him for it.[6]

From his camp at Spring Tavern, on December 16, Armstrong penned a very long response to President Wharton's inquiring letter of the 12th. As always, he has high praise for Washington: "The precipitate retreat of the Enemy from Chestnut Hill was not owing to the want of strength but prudence. General Washington's well chosen ground & respectable Army presented to them a formidable front, which, had they attacked, must to them have been fatal.—They dare not risque a Circuitous march to manuvre behind us or attack in rear, as had they been unfortunate, their retreat to Philad[a] must have been cut off. At the same time it must be allowed that taking in the consideration of their previous boasts, the retreat has vailed the glitter of their Arms, nor are they less disgraced by their low Cruelty & plundering spirit."

But he had mixed feelings about the Pennsylvania militia. He was naturally much disturbed by the seeming cowardice of many of the men at the capture of General Irvine: "No man can more deeply resent the infamous conduct of such of the Militia as were in reach of General Irwin [Irvine] when he fell from his horse than I do . . . Many, too many of the militia, are a Scandle to the military profession, a nuisance in service & a dead weight on the publick." At the same time he had a great deal for which to commend his men, and, in sum, was quite proud of them: "Yet, is it equally true, that taken as a body, they have render'd that Service that neither the State nor the Army cou'd have dispenced with." He cites their many contributions: "They have constantly mounted guards, form'd many & distant Pickquets, perfom'd many occasional pieces of labour—Patroled the Roads leading to the

Enemy by day & by night, & that more than their proportion—they have taken a number of prisoners, brought in deserters, suppressed Tories, prevented much intercourse betwixt the disaffected & the Enemy—Met and Scirmished with the Enemy as early & as often as others, and, except the Battle of Brandiwine, of which their Station little fell in their way, have had a proportional Share of Success, hazard & loss of blood."

He advised Wharton that Washington, with his whole army "has now taken his Winter Position in the County of Chester," the other side of the Schuylkill, which Armstrong had favored for a long time. And he then described what he is doing to harass the enemy. He closed by expressing approval of the plan to phase out the militia, by "filling up the Quotas of the several States with Continental Troops." [7]

Six days later, he reported that "General Washington has requested me to write to the Council that the same number of Militia may be kept up throughout the Winter as are at present in the field." The number he takes to be about 1600, plus the four or five hundred under General Potter. Unfortunately, as Armstrong pointed out, the terms are up for a large number of the men. He expresses great concern for the eastern sections of the State, but again applauded Washington's plans for the winter, which have his militia forces patrolling the roads leading into Philadelphia. But most important in this communication is Armstrong's "resignation." He lamented that "the various movements & lodgings are already too hard for me, and severer weather must be at hand." He reminds the Council of General Potter's insistence that he "can by no means tarry the Winter." The Pennsylvania Militia, he insisted must have some Head "very suddenly, else all will go to confusion. I had . . . flattered myself that from my letter [carried] by Doctor Duffield, a new appointment would have been made, and the person ready for duty. A notice of this sort I hope soon to be favour'd with, & think it already on the road." [8]

Indeed, command of the Pennsylvania militia was somewhat scattered and confused during the campaign of late 1777. Among the important figures was Lt. Colonel John Lacey of Bucks County. He had served as a captain under Colonel Anthony Wayne in the ill-fated invasion of Quebec and had enjoyed close associations there with Carlisle's General William Thompson and Colonel William Irvine, as well as with John Sullivan and Arthur St. Clair. For Anthony Wayne, who had him arrested on vague charges, including disobeying orders, he had no use at all. Wayne, he noted in his memoirs "had become my Personal and Bitter Enemy." [9] An exasperated Lacey resigned from the Continental Army after one year and "went home."

    He returned to service as Lieutenant Colonel in command of the Bucks County Regiment of Militia in time to fight at Germantown and Matson's Ford. Because of the great courage he exhibited and because of the military skill with which he performed on the field, he was made a Brigadier General by the Supreme Executive Council on January 9, 1778, thus becoming, at age twenty-three, the youngest general in the Revolutionary forces.

    With the British closeted in Philadelphia, Lacey found himself responsible for the patrol of the entire area between the Schuylkill and the Delaware—with a company of no more than seventy men. His first association with Armstrong occurred when he marched his force into Armstrong's camp near Bartholomews. With General Armstrong he was much impressed: "He was now an Old Man, but stood high as a Friend to the Independence and Liberty of his Country, and in private life of unblemished Character." [10]

    He promptly had orders from Washington via Armstrong, "to proceed to the Cross Roads on the old York Road near the Neshameny Creek, and take Post there." [11] It was very cold, and his men were much unprovisioned and very tired. But action was immediate, and for Lacey intermittent skirmishing would continue until May of the succeeding spring, climaxing with the ugly affair at Crooked Billet.

    A most distressing moment for Lacey and the Pennsylvania Militia occurred with the ignominious retreat from the enemy, noted above. In consequence, General Potter, in command of this force, ordered a General Court Martial, appointing Lacey Judge Advocate "for the tryal of those men who had thrown away their arms in the late retreat." Although Lacey's own men were not guilty, for those who were Potter ordered "fifteen to thirty lashes." When the sentence was carried out, it occasioned "much murmuring," and had the men so much disturbed that Lacey feared a mutiny. "But the Brigade being Ordered to join the other part of the Militia, under the Command of Genl. Armstrong at North Wales—the men became tranquil and passifyed."[12]

When Lacey later complained to Armstrong about the severity of the sentence, the General, now at home in Carlisle, responded with an impression of the effect on the people, and did a lot of equivocating:

The Bearers time will only admit me to tell you that a great deal of heat and publick clamour hath gone abroad against Genl. Potter and the Members of a Certain Court Martial held by his Orders, the sentence of which they say was to punish with whiping & also paying for the Arms thrown away, which they consider as a double Punishment for one offence. In this piece of discipline its [sic] *like some persons where Whiped who in other respects had been well behaved, and when at home are Creditable People I am persuaded on the other hand that the whole matter is not fairly stated, and* [am] *really concerned that the thing happened, which is still the more disagreeable as there is not a full oppertunity of obviating the Peoples objections, they being so far detached from one another—That instance of discipline was no doubt too high; but, however some of them might have fully deserved it, a necessary policy was against it, and it grieves me that an Officer possessed of many good qualities as Genl Potter is, should have such a Clamour raised against him on this occasion. As it is chiefly Western People who have been offended, theres no mention made of you, so that I suppose you will escape the Censure.*[13]

On the state of the Pennsylvania militia Brigadier General John Lacey kept in constant touch with Armstrong through the spring of 1778, lamenting a loss of cattle, and the late arrival of new troops, and reporting on the catastrophe at Crooked Billet. He reported on April 9 that he had 158 men "present, fit for duty." On April 20 he reported a figure of 250; by April 28 he had 53 (!) only.[14]

While the search for a Head for the Pennsylvania Militia continued, a candidate appeared in the figure of Colonel John

Bull,[15] who as a captain had commanded a company under Armstrong on the Forbes Expedition. When General Irvine was captured at Whitemarsh, Colonel Bull succeeded to the command of the Second Brigade of Armstrong's Pennsylvania Militia. On Christmas Eve he led 2000 militia troops on a daring "excursion" into Fourth Street in Howe's Philadelphia. Once in the city he ordered the firing of the three heavy guns he had carried in, the effect of which was a big disturbance about the old Christ Church. Satisfied to alarm the city, the Colonel beat a hasty retreat, and reported to Armstrong without the loss of a single man.[16]

But no new commander for the Pennsylvania militia was to be appointed for quite a while yet. Armstrong was still appealing for replacement on Dec. 30th. On this day he reported to Wharton that while at present he had 2000 men, eight battalions would soon be free through expired enlistments. However, a force of 1000 he feels will prove sufficient to do the job Washington has asked, and he advises Wharton that he will be immediately proposing the same to the Commander-in-Chief. (Washington on the 1st of the year advised Wharton that he agreed with Armstrong.) But he has had enough: "I am now about settleing some of the last things that appear necessary here, and shall, God willing, in two or three days begin my journey to the westward, being already half frozen in this frigid zoan." He has been expecting General Potter, and even before he is able to complete this letter, indeed just as he is reporting the theft of his "nice young horse . . . from the General's door," Potter showed up, prepared to assume command for "some ten or twelve days." [17]

This letter crossed in delivery with the notice sent by the Council from Lancaster December 30 to the General. The Council, while appreciative of Armstrong's service, noted how very difficult it was to find a replacement. The only kind of resignation it is inclined to accept is a temporary one: "The Council see the necessity of some relaxation [!] from the severe duty of a Winters campaign, to a Gentleman of your advanced age, and therefore important as your services have been, cannot do less than to leave this matter wholly to your own feelings, and Judgment, and have only to lament that your health and Vigour are not more equal to your inclination and other abilities to serve your country, in so trying and difficult a situation." [18]

At the same time the Council notified General Potter of Armstrong's retirement from the field and of its desire that Potter might "stay longer." Council advised Potter that Armstrong on his way home would be stopping in Lancaster to confer on the subject, and that relief for him too might be forthcoming. But within a week both Armstrong and Potter, whose wife was quite ill, were permitted to go home, and Lacey was made administrator of the militia.[19]

So General John Armstrong, on the last day of this fateful year, at this most critical juncture of the war, because of the weight of years and uncertain health, withdrew from the field. He was anxious about Pennsylvania, but the great faith he had early placed in Washington remained unshaken, and he was very confident that the rebellion would soon come to a happy end. Although he had an uncanny talent for ascertaining the future, never could he have allowed that the war would drag on for almost six more years. Possibly he did understand that after twenty-two years of commanding soldiers in the field, in fighting the French, and Indians, and now the Redcoats of King George, he was saying farewell forever to military activity.

Armstrong thus returned to Carlisle for the remainder of this Valley Forge winter. But he followed the fortunes of Washington's army closely. Indeed, he had not been home a month before he complained to Thomas Wharton that he has been forgotten. He has not had a word from the Congress, now meeting in nearby York. The "universal silence & inactivity" bothers him no end, and he fears the resources of the State must be soon exhausted. From Lancaster the Council replied promptly, and in great respect. Armstrong was informed of Washington's plans, which included lowering the State's quota of Continental Army soldiers to ten battalions. In response to Armstrong's expressed concern, the Council advised: "Pennsylvania must suffer. It is not to be avoided. It only remains to make the suffering as light as possible." [20]

On the 23rd of February, concerned, as indeed Washington was himself, about the continuing scarcity of lead for ammunition, Armstrong urged Wharton to use his influence with the Assembly to bring together the Board of War and Assemblyman Harman Husbands, who "has some knowledge of a Lead Mine, situate in a certain Tract of Land not far from Franks Town." This letter had the happy result Armstrong hoped for. Though it took some time, General Daniel Roberdeau was commissioned by the Continental Congress to take possession of the land Armstrong had described, and to make secure the region of the reputed lead deposits.

Roberdeau, a wealthy Philadelphia merchant who would serve in the Continental Congress with Armstrong and who was now a Brigadier General in the Pennsylvania militia, early in April set out from Carlisle, with Armstrong's blessing, at the head of a small task force. The land he was heading for was a parcel of some 16,000 acres in a V-shaped valley called Sinking Valley, near present-day Tyrone, Altoona, and Water Street. The land had been surveyed for the Penns by George Wood of the Bedford region, and was still unsold. The General had no trouble locating the site, which was in a narrow strip of land embraced by the heavily forested slopes of Brush Mountain.

General Roberdeau promptly built a stockade around and over the galena ore deposits, and constructed a rude but functional smelting furnace within the fort. In no time at all he had the mining underway, and the smelting keeping pace. The slugs of metal, horseshoe-shaped and called "pigs," were then transported by horseback to the tiny settlement at Water Street, and floated by flatboat down the river to the Susquehanna and on to the ammunition-producing plants. Satisfied that all was going well, Roberdeau shortly turned the operation over to Captain Robert Cluggage, who was able to produce by war's end only 1500 pounds. But, such as it was, it was a help, and more could have been provided if necessary. The stockade was first known as Leadmine Fort and later as Fort Roberdeau.

Later that year, on September 22, after the mine had been operating some time, Armstrong, concerned for its protection, and noting that lead was still in critically short supply, sent a letter directly to the Board of War and Ordnance. His letter was referred from the Board to Congress, where it was assigned to a committee for study. On October 10, the committee reported to Congress: "The committee . . . beg leave to report, That the Importance of the

Lead Mines upon the Frontiers of Pennsylvania requires a competent Force to be kept up on the Frontiers for their Defence. That therefore the Executive Authority of the State of Pennsylvania be requested to call out 100 Men of the Militia of the States to be stationed at or near the said Lead Mines and the Mills appurtenant there to near Standing Stone till further orders, and that Congress will defray the Expence of the Said Detachment." [21]

But Armstrong was involved in the Sinking Spring Valley in another way altogether at this very time. Persuaded by the British that it was in their interest to come over to the side of the King, a motley band of "ignorant" frontiersmen in this region agreed to join a British-Indian force of 300 which was scheduled to lay waste to the settlements in the spring of 1778. The tory band, led by a bold and lawless man named John Weston, and composed largely of settlers from the Frankstown area, held its meetings at Sinking Spring through February and March.

This company was joined about April 1 by a man named McKee from Carlisle, and on April 10, in a secluded glen of the Sinking Spring Valley forest, it held its last meeting. The next morning the band, now thirty-one in all, set out to join the British at Kittanning. They had not gone far when they were ambushed by a party of some 100 Iroquois frightful in their vivid war paint. As these Indians had nothing to do with the British plan and were bent on mischief of their own, they fired at the Tories, instantly killing Weston, and then vanished as abruptly as they had appeared. The terrified settlers by this event were totally discouraged and promptly abandoned their enterprise. Some perished from hunger before they could reach home; others were captured by the aroused frontiersmen and confined to the jail at Bedford.

The brother of John Weston, though pleading innocence, was arrested by a number of workers on their way to the lead mines. Although Weston escaped from the prison in Carlisle, those who remained in prison at Bedford were by order of the Supreme Executive Council placed on trial for capital treason. Presiding over the trial, which required two sessions in the fall of 1778 and in the spring of 1779 was General John Armstrong. As the principals in the affair were either dead or vanished, not a single man was convicted. According to one historian, it seemed to the court that the few who were brought to court were "sufficiently punished by their imprisonment and the contempt of their neighbors." Thus ended this incident of the War.[22]

Earlier, on March 10, Armstrong from Carlisle had addressed a letter to Washington in which he commented on the Tory activity in York and Cumberland counties, and in which he made some conjecture about the designs of General William Howe, and in which he recommended to the Commander-in-Chief, "Wou'd not a device to employ the Army by detail, or in the piecem[e]al way next Campaign be worthy of Consideration—and a particular plan of that Sort concerted." Acutely conscious of the miseries of the encampment, he appreciates the danger of despair: "I am dear General exceedingly at a loss how to write you, knowing your reflexion to be an hundredfold more than mine, yet by the bye hope you have also Some more Sleep, having greater need of it—Our affairs complexly taken, are as they are, and altho' I have often been Obliged to decline the intricate Survey, yet blessed be [to] god, have at no time thought them desperate. One Consolation Still remains, that in a Cause like ours 'tis not presumption to hope that when things are got to such a Crisis as to be beyond the reach of human remedy, the interposition of God will then be more conspicuous and men better disposed to give him the glory." [23]

During the winter and the ensuing spring of 1778, Armstrong was kept regularly informed by John Lacey, in command of the brigade of Pennsylvania militia, which was kept constantly active in patrolling the roads into Philadelphia, and in harassing Howe's foraging expeditions. Communicating from various locales, like Crooked Billet, Camp Doylestown, and the Camp at North Wales, Lacey simply repeated for Armstrong the reports he was making to Washington. Because of expired enlistments and desertion they showed, as before noted, a great fluctuation in the number of men "present and fit for duty." [24]

Meanwhile, back at Valley Forge, as the incredibly cold winter was beginning to show signs of fatigue, the soldiers on May 5, had some very good news. It was the news that France was with them for the duration of the rebellion. It was the news that on February 6 France had formally entered into an alliance with the colonies, with Pennsylvania's Benjamin Franklin signing for the

United States, and the Congress just yesterday ratifying the document. The report occasioned wild celebration, and an ecstatic Washington noted the need "to set apart a day for gratefully acknowledging the divine Goodness." Just how much joy was occasioned in the Commander-in-Chief can be realized from the fact that he promptly pardoned two soldiers who had been condemned to execution, and returned them to their companies. And that night General Washington entertained his officers at the Potts House with the kind of elegant dinner he so much enjoyed.

And in York and in Carlisle the event was of course exciting the same kind of joyous celebration.

But the winter was ending, and it was time to plan another campaign. Washington had been at work for some time organizing a war council. He had, of course, been constantly monitoring the activity of the British army. General William Howe had been recalled to England in March, and Sir Henry Clinton now had the command in Philadelphia. Reports which came to him suggested that the British had a mammoth springtime movement in mind.

Washington was feeling much better now about his army than he had been in the dark hours of January, in fact so good that he could actually consider a significant action. Accordingly, for May 8, he convened a council of war. Invited were the Major Generals Nathanael Greene, Lord Stirling, Thomas Mifflin, Henry Knox, Horatio Gates, Lafayette, De Kalb, and Chief Engineer Louis Duportail. To this council John Armstrong, although he was not now an officer, had been invited as early as April 24: "A council will be held here [Head Quarters, Valley Forge] as speedily as possible to settle a plan of operations for the ensuing campaign which I should be glad, you could make it convenient to attend .... As it is a business of great importance and requires dispatch, if it will suit you to be present, you will be pleased to repair immediately to Head Quarters." [25]

According to the Washington historian Jared Sparks, "The commander-in-chief laid before the council the state of the enemy's forces, which he estimated at 16,000 men; of these about 10,000 were in Philadelphia, 4000 in New York, and about 2000 in Rhode Island. Of the Continental troops there were at Valley Forge about 11,800 men, including the sick; and the other detachments at

Wilmington and upon the Hudson River, with reinforcements that might normally be counted upon, would swell the number of effective troops to 20,000." With these figures before them, the members of the Council were asked for suggestions on what measures might be pursued.[26]

The generals at this point, with the news that Howe had been called back to England, entered into an agitated, but well reasoned discussion of options. The opinion led steadily to a "watch and wait" posture. The generals were unanimous in the view that to take Philadelphia by storm was unthinkable, and that even to effect a blockade of the city would require not fewer than 30,000 men. Armstrong, who was asked about militia strength, offered the impression that the additional force that might be supplied by militia would result still in an inadequate army. Consequently, though there is reason to believe that Washington himself was for doing something, the council produced the decision to wait for some development that would invite action.[27]

And for that, the Continental Army would not have long to wait.

All through the spring and summer of 1778, General Armstrong made himself a part of the war activity. He followed closely the conduct of Washington's army, which included the harassment of Clinton's army on its march to New Jersey, and the battle of Monmouth, in which his Carlisle friend General William Irvine, whose parole had expired, acquitted himself so well. He was constantly directing letters to the Congress, and most of these were relayed to the Board of War.

In his letters of February 5 and March 10, Armstrong had inquired of Washington concerning the possibility of his returning to the army. Washington replied from Valley Forge on March 27, "When the Weather is such that you think you can take the field without injury to your health I shall be glad to see you with the army, as I am, with sincere Regard. . . ."[28] That Armstrong fully intended to return to service in the field is plain from his letter of

April 13, in which he noted for Wharton that while he could not wish for any laborious or distant charge, he would while the action is in Pennsylvania hope "to be at Camp about the latter end of May, there to act as necessity or expedience may point out." [29]

Washington might have pressed the old warrior into service to address a crisis that appeared in the time following Valley Forge and Monmouth. In July of 1777, the Iroquois nation of Indians, including the fierce Senecas, after months of wooing from the British, took up the hatchet on the side of King George. Led by their war-chiefs Joseph Brant (a Mohawk) and the half-breed Cornplanter (a Seneca), they had been assaulting settlements all along the frontier of New York and Pennsylvania for the past year.

A letter of Colonel James Potter, dated May 17, 1778, from the Upper Fort in Penns Valley, and directed to Major General John Armstrong in Carlisle, brings to mind the atrocities after Braddock and during the Pontiac wars. It is a letter of despair. "Dear Sir, " Potter writes, "Our Savige Enemys contenue to murder and Scalp and Captavet. I am informed by Col. [Moses] Long that on the Eleventh Instant there was a few famleys Coming to Locomon [Lycoming], ascorted by a party under the Command of Col. [Peter?] Holsterman, the[y] were attacked by 12 Indians who Killed six of them and six more was a missing about the same time, there was three men Killed at Loyalsack."

And there is more: "He furder Informs that some time ago there was twenty persons Killed on the North Branch [of the Susquehanna], and one Taken presner who has made his escape, and says, that the Indians are detarmined to Clear the two Branches of Susquehanna this moon. If there [is] not something dun to put a stop to these murders soon, this Cuntrey will be entirely given up to the saviges." He reminds Armstrong that the settlers have two forts in the Penns Valley, but "we are too few in number to make a stand." He advises Armstrong that the bearer of the letter, a Major Myles, is going to continue in Cumberland County in an effort to raise men. "If he Cannot obtain them, he will go to the Councal, Requesting a suply of men for this pleace, the sercumstances of his Countrey is truely Lementable, I want for words to Describe it to you, the people are many of them Very pore, and Bread at such a high price, god Knows what the Consequances will be." [30]

By June, the atrocities had so much increased in frequency that pioneer families in central Pennsylvania were fleeing in the all too familiar panic to the forts and returning to the east, to Shippensburg and Carlisle and Lancaster, in what has been called another Great Runaway.

General Armstrong, now that the Iroquois are in the war, feels duty-bound to provide his informed counsel. Appalled and much distressed by the continuing increase in the number of Indian depredations, on the 23rd of June, he got off long letters to George Bryan, Vice-President of the State of Pennsylvania, and to the Continental Congress. Bryan, an Ireland-born Presbyterian, was a good friend.[31] In the letters to both he detailed atrocities and called for action. There is nothing to be gained by a defensive posture, he insisted. "From the great extent of our frontier, and the Indian mode of war, nothing truly salutary nor permanent can be expected from our acting on the defensive." Indeed, what he had in mind was clearly a Kittanning-like expedition. "I cannot yet learn with certainty," he writes, "whether there is any Indian Town in reasonable reach, on either Branch of the Susquehannah, but think it probable there must [be], if so, such Town or Towns might be readily destroyed, without much previous preparation; and one or at most Two hundred Men sufficient for any of these. Shingaclamoose [present-day Clearfield, on the West Branch] (if now inhabited) is but a few days march above the great Island."

In the letter to Bryan he does admit that the harvest season is so near as to make such an expedition at this time impractical, but he urges at least the arming of the settlers, and the providing of patrols. In the letter to Congress he insists that "an immediate attack on their several towns is the only method under God of bringing to an early period this desolating and barbarous War, and not less than three different bodies of men should march at once or near the same time, upon the occasion, one from Shamokin , to proceed up the Susquehannah to a certain small town, the name of which I have not yet learned, but where the perpetrators of some of the late murders are said to reside. Two from Fort Pitt of greater force each than the former, to proceed against such of the Towns beyond the Allegany river as may be thought most proper."

And from his own experience he advises that "The Indians

may evacuate their towns & suddenly flee off, this they have in their power as well as to fight or let it alone at pleasure, but their huts and corn fields must remain, the destruction of whereof greatly affects their old men, their women, and their children, whose complaints on these alarming occasions has a native tendency to bate the ferocity of the Warriors, and reduce them to terms of better behaviour." He knows that many have been urging an assault on Fort Detroit, but he does not himself think that to be the thing to do. For command of the militia and Continental forces required he recommends General Lachlan McIntosh. He meant to supply in his letter to the Congress a list of the towns within reach of Fort Pitt, but found that he had mislaid it.[32]

Most awful of the massacres for which the New York Iroquois (with John Butler's Rangers) were responsible occurred at Wyoming the first week of July, 1778. Historians have so far been unable to find adequate words to account for the horrors of the night of July 3.

Armstrong was mortified by the news, and the moment he had it he shot off a letter to Bryan to chastize "the savage villains of the north" and to remind Council that now at harvest time there is great need to protect the reapers.[33] It was good advice. In the aftermath of the massacre, the Indians, and particularly the Iroquois, and most especially the Mohawk and the Seneca, continued extremely active all along the Pennsylvania frontier. During the spring and summer leading up to Wyoming, and during the months immediately succeeding, the raids continued in an appallingly regular pattern, that is, with steadily increasing frequency. In fact, all of the years from this time to a time long beyond the end of the Revolution would be scarred by the terrors of the Border Wars.

In a response to Bryan's reply, Armstrong even more plaintively lamented the frontier situation, "the painful flight of the populace, Roads & Rivers crowded with miserable objects who have left behind not only part of their effects, but their Harvests." He even declared that if the efforts of McIntosh and Brodhead and Potter fail to put down the savages of the north, "I shall, God willing, ascend these mountains with as many as will follow under the very sensible frailty of nature at this intemperate season, and the still more sensible want of many necessarys."[34]

But in almost every communication during these months, General Armstrong throws cold water on the plans to attack Detroit, which is considered the source of the Indian trouble. On July 22, in a very long letter to the Congress, now headed by Henry Laurens of South Carolina, and meeting again in Philadelphia's State House, he specifies seven well considered reasons for abandoning any such thought. He concludes his letter by insisting that "The first and most natural Excursion wou'd appear to be up the Susquehannah or on a northern Direction, in Order to return the Visit of Mr. [John] Butler & his Friends [the assault on Wyoming]." [35]

And only two days later, in another extremely long letter to Bryan from his home in Carlisle, he provides a great deal of information on the situation as he knows it, some counsel on anti-Indian strategy, and some impressions of the commanders in the field. His letter closes: "It will be intolerable, I fear, to spend the Fall season on the defensive. It is the best season to annoy the Indians." [36]

The Armstrong-Executive Council correspondence of course has but a little distance to travel, that is, between the General's home in Carlisle and Lancaster, where the Council has been meeting since last October 1. Armstrong had most appreciative letters from the Council on both the 23rd and 25th of July, and again on the 29th and the 30th. In his letters to the Council during these two weeks he repeated his insistence (and noted General Gates' similar opinion) that organized expeditions against the "Seneca Towns & others Northward ought to be the first mark." He even detailed the make-up of the force, urging Oneidas for guides. "There must also be an excursion from Ft. Pitt," he writes, noting that there is "time & strength enough for it." He expects that General McIntosh will get the command for the Western body and "some other person for the Northern attack." What he hoped for the whole was a junction of forces at Wyoming, or still higher on the Susquehannah, perhaps at Tioga, "thence to proceed by the most direct rout[e] to the Seneca Towns as the first mark. . . . For this great purpose, together with the notice to be taken of some whites who have lately done us much injury [the Butlers], not less than three thousand men, under a good commander, ought to penetrate that country." [37]

~ *The Valley Forge Winter* ~ 453

    Not surprisingly, what Armstrong has been recommending is exactly what did eventually occur. But it would be a year yet before it happened.
    All in all, the spring and early summer of 1778 proved to be too much for the American colonials. Pennsylvania had had enough. New York State had had enough. Certainly Washington had had enough. It was time to punish the Indians for Wyoming and for scores of other atrocities, like the unspeakable murders occurring at Lycoming in June. Pennsylvania and the Commander-in-Chief were compelled to avenge the barbarities and to make the settlements along the frontier "safe." And thus the general anxiety and apprehension that these frequent atrocities had caused among the settlers led in the fall of 1778 to organized retribution. Because of a torrent of letters pleading for protection, Armstrong's among them, the Supreme Executive Council of Pennsylvania finally appreciated the necessity of providing once again a military defense of the frontier. On August 6 of 1778 Armstrong recommended to Bryan a two-pronged expedition against the Seneca towns. He said that he was "for leaving inferior tribes to be subdued by traverse marches," and his prediction for the destruction of the towns was "peace," at least as far as the Indians were concerned.[38]
    Not long after Armstrong's letter, anti-Indian action was organized. In accord with one arm of his recommendation, and at Bryan's urging, Colonel Thomas Hartley, who had been at the Three Rivers fiasco in Quebec, was ordered by Washington to move his Continental regiment to Sunbury. Pennsylvania ordered 1000 militiamen to join him there. However, when Hartley arrived at Sunbury on August 1, he was disappointed to find but a fraction of the Pennsylvanians he had hoped for. Understanding that with his limited force he could not begin to protect the frontier, he resolved on an aggressive action. But it was not until September 21 that he was ready to proceed. Operating out of Fort Muncy, his force was able to negotiate the deep gorge of Lycoming Creek and make its way north to Tioga, experiencing only one minor skirmish. As predicted by Armstrong, Hartley found the Indians fled. He set fire to Queen Esther's town, and other towns he came upon, including one, unfortunately, which was completely innocent. After burning the Indian villages in the region of Tioga, and confiscating a great

deal of plunder stolen by the Indians from Wyoming, he returned toward Sunbury, almost without incident.

His force had been assaulted only once (September 29), this at Wyalusing (Browntown Mountain). The battle, reported by Hartley as a "sharp skirmish," cost the expedition four soldiers killed and ten wounded.[39]

Apart from his concern with the expeditions, which he regretted to find hanging in suspense, Armstrong was briefly returned to magistrate duties, the Council appointing him, with several others, to conduct a trial of "disloyal parties" in Bedford County, as above noted. Just how highly Armstrong was regarded at this time is apparent in Council's plea: "From your disinterested patriotism and love of justice, rather than from any reward which can be with propriety offered to you, the Council are induced to hope and expect that you will cheerfully render this necessary service to your country."[40] And not long after, Council, fearful of another invasion of Pennsylvania, ordered Armstrong to Philadelphia, where he could expect to have the command of a number of officers who will be organizing a defense of the city.[41]

It was a rough fall and winter for Armstrong, at home in Carlisle. His health was a constant concern, and the pain that attends physical idleness was most annoying. Besides, the war reports were not all that good. Armstrong, like all patriots, was much distressed by news of the massacre at Tappan, near the Hackensack River, when on September 28, the "bayonet butchers" of General "No Flint" Charles Grey put to death by cold steel the sleeping soldiers of Colonel George Baylor, who were quartered in six different barns.

And the report of another Indian massacre was almost more than he could bear. It was Cherry Valley. Hartley's campaign, not surprisingly, had apparently inflamed the naturally vengeful disposition of the Senecas and inspired a fierce attack on the helpless village of Cherry Valley, some fifty miles northwest of Albany, birthplace of the Dutch father of the Seneca war-chief Cornplanter. The settlement was ill prepared for the rapacious horde, led by the Mohawk Joseph Brant and the Tory Walter Butler, that fell upon it November 11. Armstrong was hearing that the massacre was even more horrible than what had happened at

Wyoming. The Indians and Butler's Rangers numbered 700. The defenders under the command of the courageous Ichabod Alden, totaled at best 250, and of these seventy were killed.

On top of this came the news of the rebel surrender of the port of Savannah, Georgia.

Besides, the General had been stewing for months now about the failure to follow up on the Hartley campaign. He was most impatient to see the villages of the hostile Senecas burned and put out of business. The news from Cherry Valley did not make him feel any better about the Indian presence in the war. But it was not until the middle of April, 1779, that his hopes were elevated some. His fellow surveyor, fellow officer, and good friend Colonel Daniel Brodhead, who had been lately in Carlisle, addressed to him a letter from the Colonel's Headquarters at Fort Pitt, where he was serving as Head of the Western Department. From this letter, Armstrong learned that Brodhead quite agreed with him that, while General McIntosh was all for it, an attack on Fort Detroit was unthinkable. And at the same time he noted that, despite the poor condition of his force at Fort Pitt, he has been campaigning for a punitive expedition into the Indian country: "I hope my frequent letters during the course of last winter to a number of Gentlemen in high offices will in some measure be productive of an early campaign to cover this bleeding part of the country." He has resolved on a letter to Washington.[42]

Earlier, in March of 1779, Washington, now convinced that he simply had to address the Indian hostilities, determined on two expeditions into the Indian country. The locations of the Indian villages along the North Branch of the Susquehanna and across the New York finger lake country west to the Genesee were now well known. He began to search among his generals for a man to destroy their towns. Did he consider returning General John Armstrong to the service? He very likely did, as the expedition he had in mind was precisely the expedition that Armstrong had commanded to Kittanning. And Armstrong, probably more surely than any of his present officers, excepting perhaps General Edward Hand, had tons of anti-Indian experience to draw upon. However, General Armstrong, at this time was sixty-one years old, not in the best of health, and was a member of the Continental Congress. So, if his

John Sullivan

name occurred to Washington, it could not have given him pause for long.

And, besides, Armstrong himself, when he heard of the plans, recommended to Washington that Daniel Brodhead be detached from his service at Fort Pitt to command the expedition.[43]

After consulting with General Hand (who had been Commandant of the Western Department and headquartered at Fort

Pitt), Colonel Zebulon Butler (who had had the command at Wyoming on that awful night), and the surveyor and one-time captive of the Indians, Lieutenant John Jenkins, Washington seemed to fix on Horatio Gates. But apparently he rather hoped Gates would decline, and he so worded his appointment letter as to make it easy for him. When in fact he did decline, Washington turned to John Sullivan.[44]

As it turned out, Sullivan was a good choice. Though he, like Armstrong, was not in the best of health, he was not yet forty; and he had proved himself through the first four years of the war. And, as it turned out, the expedition did in fact achieve success. Helped out by the companion expeditions of Colonel Daniel Brodhead up the Allegheny and by General James Clinton, yoked to Sullivan, the mission destroyed at least thirty Indian villages (Sullivan claimed "forty.") and had a most discouraging effect upon Indian depredations. They did not cease, of course, but they were much diminished, and Cornplanter was before long put out of business altogether.

XXV

THE CONTINENTAL CONGRESS

The First Continental Congress, meeting in Philadelphia, concluded its deliberations on October 26, 1774. The Second Continental Congress was convened on May 10, 1775, three weeks after Lexington-Concord It included in its first sessions seventy-four delegates off and on, representing the thirteen colonies. These delegates were appointed by the state legislative bodies. General John Armstrong served two one-year terms in the Continental Congress. He was elected by the Pennsylvania Assembly to the Second Continental Congress on November 20, 1778, "for the ensuing year," elections being for one year, unless otherwise specified. The credentials for the Pennsylvania delegates elected with him were read before the General Assembly on Friday, November 25. The Gentlemen chosen, besides Armstrong, were Daniel Roberdeau, William Clingan, Edward Biddle, William Shippen, the elder, Samuel Atlee, and James Searle. The certificate of election was signed by the Clerk of the General Assembly, John Morris.[1] Delegates who were added later were James McClene (spelled variously), Frederick

Muhlenberg, and Judge Henry Wynkoop of Northampton.

Armstrong's active service did not begin until Friday, February 26, 1779, when the Congress convened in the State House (now Independence Hall) in Philadelphia ("Mr J Armstrong, a delegate from Pennsylvania, attended and took his seat in Congress."). It appears that he was absent from the Congress for a week or ten days in July of that summer, as there is no record of his presence between July 12 and 22. It is known that he requested and was granted a leave of absence on October 11, and his last recorded vote is that for October 13. His letter of October 15 indicates that he is leaving.

He was elected again, on November 12 of that year, for an unspecified term, which means one year; and he attended sessions from May 30 to August 25 of 1780.

Records of the proceedings of the Congress for the years of his membership show that he was among the most active and most conscientious of the delegates. He served on a number of important committees, was responsible for many resolutions, and regularly presented nominations. His most absorbing interests were (1) the financial situation of the country and of the separate states; (2) the condition of the Continental Army, and (3) the conduct and progress of the war. Naturally enough, he seemed from the beginning of his membership to consider himself the principal liaison figure between Washington and the Board of War. Just about everything that came to the Congress from the Board of War occasioned a committee of three, or five, of course, and Armstrong was regularly appointed.

He still very much loved to write letters, and during his tenure in the Congress he unleashed a steady barrage of official, semi-official, and personal communications. His favorite correspondents were, besides Washington of course, President Joseph Reed of Pennsylvania, General Horatio Gates, for whom his son was serving, his close Carlisle friend General William Irvine, James Wilson, Edward Shippen, James Burd, and John Lukens.

He would receive a lot of letters from Washington during his tenure in the Congress. Indeed, early in the 1779 session he had a private message from him. Washington was lamenting the fact that he was not being kept informed by Congress. He had already written to Edmund Randolph to complain of the "cloud of darkness [which] can only be groped at." To Armstrong on May 18, from Middlebrook, in a long "confidential" letter, he repeated the complaint, declaring that he felt left out, so much uninformed by "the great national council," as to suppose himself an alien. It was high time, Washington insisted, that "every Man (especially those in office) should with one hand and one heart pull the same way, and with their whole strength." [2]

To Armstrong the Commander-in-Chief confided the great pessimism that had come over him:

I am much mistaken if the resolve of Congress hath not an eye to something far beyond our abilities; they are not, I conceive, sufficiently acquainted with the state and strength of the Army, of our resources, and how they are to be drawn out. The powers given may be beneficial, but do not let Congress deceive themselves by false expectations founded on a superficial view of the situation and circumstances of things in general and their own Troops in particular; for in a word, I give it to you as my opinion, that if the reinforcement expected by the enemy should arrive, and no effectual measures be taken to compleat our Battalions, and stop further depreciation of our Money I do not see upon what ground we are able or mean to continue the contest.[3]

Armstrong never forgot this grievance, and during his years in Congress he did the very best he could to keep his General apprised of what was going on in the council chambers.

On March 18, and again on April 10, he was appointed to a committee to "take into consideration the circumstances of the southern states," particularly South Carolina and Georgia, and the manner of their defense. And on May 4, he was made a member of the Committee on Indian Affairs.

When on February 3, 1779, charges were preferred by Pennsylvania's Executive Council against General Benedict Arnold, who was presiding over the recovery of Philadelphia, a real tempest ensued. Washington requested of Congress an investigation, and when Arnold was convicted on two of the charges, Congress required Washington to deliver a public reprimand. Henry Knox and many others felt the charges unfair, and likely there were a great many who charged the fuss up to a private quarrel between Joseph Reed ("Governor") of Pennsylvania) and Arnold. Armstrong, in a letter to General Gates, April 3, 1779, opined that "half a dozen of polite or wise words [on the part of Arnold] or a short, plain and candid answer to the Supreme Council would have saved the whole time lost in argument over his case." [4]

He served the summer and fall of 1779, with William Carmichael, Cyrus Griffin, Nathaniel Scudder, and Henry Wynkoop, on the Treasury Board, which had many troubles to address; and it was this activity that got him into economics so deeply that the financial status of the nation became an absorbing concern. On April 22 he had replaced Francis Lightfoot Lee of Virginia on the Committee to Supervise the Commissary, which, likewise, had a very big job to do. Through the rest of April and all of May Armstrong was occupied with the provisioning of the army. Washington wrote to the Board of War on May 27 to describe the distress of the army, which was so much in want of meat that mutiny was threatened. The Commissary Committee at this time was composed of James Duane, of New York, Oliver Ellsworth, of Connecticut, and William Ellery of Rhode Island.

Duane for the Congress replied on May 30: "My dear General, Congress are [so] much affected at the Wants and Distresses of the Army [that] another Committee [Commissary] is appointed on your Excellencys late Representation to the Board of War, and a letter from Commissary Blane. It is now found that the Supplies already demanded from the states are incompetent and in some Instances anticipated. It is to be lamented that we are not furnished with better Estimates at first; but we must endeavour to correct the Error; and to face every Difficulty with firmness; and to remedy it as speedily and effectively as possible . . . ." On the very next day Armstrong replaced Ellery on the Committee.

This new committee met on Wednesday afternoon, May 31, at one o'clock, and promptly composed a letter to the President of Pennsylvania, Joseph Reed: "Sir, we beg leave to inform your Excellency that Congress have appointed a Committee to confer with a Committee of the Supreme Executive Council of the Commonwealth of Pennsylvania on a letter just received from the

Commander in Chief of the Army of these United States respecting Recruits and Supplies. The Committee of Congress are ready to confer at such time and place as the Committee of the Council and Assembly shall appoint." The letter was signed by Ellsworth, Armstrong, and Duane. As both the Congress and the Pennsylvania Assembly were meeting in Philadelphia, the meeting was easily convened. Washington's letter of May 27 was read, and the Committee presented the situation and its difficulties.[5] Such was the work Armstrong was into now.

One of Armstrong's early letters was to General Gates. It is dated April 3. In it he speaks of the lamentable depreciation of the currency, and then, for its failure to tackle problems with zest, he rips into the Congress, noting that pride, ambition, and intrigue have resulted in animosities, division, and destruction. "Compared to Congress, in it's [sic] present attitude," he writes, "I call the Army a Bed of ease, a Pillow of Down." He speaks then of the Benedict Arnold affairs, referring to the questionable activity of the General in his command of the recovery of Philadelphia. And, finally, he has some staggering news: "Congress have passed a resolve to raise and emansipate three thousand negroes in S. Carolina and Georgia, pay feed, and cloath them during the war. The proprietors to have from Congress1000 dollars for each Negroe." This news doubtless meant a lot to Gates, for after the war, from his estates in Virginia (now West Virginia), he freed all of his slaves. Armstrong applauds the appointment of the twenty-five-year-old John Laurens as "the first Lt. Coll of the blacks which I consider as a noble proposal in that young Gentleman."[6]

Armstrong was early into his correspondence with Washington, even to the point of giving advice. He laments the necessity to meet the enemy on so many fronts, one of which is of course the newly arisen Indian problem. "Neccesarily . . . now you must be led to consider the various distributions of your Army, I mean the Seneca or Northern Expedition." And, as with Gates, he complains (1) about the Congress, its "infatuated manner of doing business," which results in costly, perhaps fatal, delay; and (2) the present state of the currency.[7]

For Gates, who had refused the command, on the 22nd of May, Armstrong explained the Sullivan Expedition: "Neither

Niagara nor Detroit are in contemplation, the Seneca Indians and their connexions whether Tories or others, are I presume the only present Object of our Arms to the North . . . . Sullivan has asked of Congress two Extra Aids De Camp for the Campaign, not yet granted nor ought they to be." [8]

All through the summer of 1779, Congress received a steady stream of letters from Washington, headquartered at New Windsor and at West Point. Many of these were turned over for attention to a committee, whose membership more often than not, included Armstrong.

On June 25, in a very long letter to Washington, Congressman Armstrong touched on a number of very important matters, some of which Washington has been asking about. He reported the slowing of the depreciation of the currency; and on foreign affairs he remarked chiefly on the fisheries. He lamented the condition of the army and declared that he very much favors Washington's recommendation for half-pay for life for each soldier. Armstrong was one of only two members to vote for the measure when Washington first proposed it. This, he said, is "the best compound of justice and gratuity to our Soldiery." But he fears great opposition from the Congress. The bill was, however, finally approved, on October 21, 1780, though Armstrong was not present.

In this same letter he reported the prevailing opinion that Britain will be unable to send more troops to America this season. And with some pride he relayed the news that "A great majority of the Irish were in love with the American Cause and much opposed to the late Speeches of the King." [9]

One event he did not mention to Washington was the completion of a fort at the destroyed town of Kittanning. Lt. Colonel Stephen Bayard had erected on the site, actually some two miles downriver from the locale of the Indian town, a stockade, which he was proud to name Fort Armstrong. It had served as a way station for the expedition of Colonel Brodhead and his 650 men.[10] The fort enjoyed but a short life. For lack of provisions, it was, along with Fort Crawford, abandoned in November of that same year. It was not to be an enduring monument to the Old General.

June was also taken up with commissary affairs. On the

16th, after an urgent letter of Baron von Steuben was referred to the Board of War, a June 11 letter from Washington was referred to a committee of Elbridge Gerry, John Armstrong, and Henry Laurens, of South Carolina. This committee delivered to Congress on June 16 the following resolution, in which Armstrong's hand is clear:

> *Whereas the enemy availing themselves of the delays that have happened in the filling up the Continental Battalions, have taken post on each side of the North River, and are fortifying the same; and whereas it is represented to Congress by General Washington, that the advantages of their holding the said posts will be important to the enemy, and the inconveniences on our side great; that it is a step to further their operations against the defences of the river; that our communication by King's ferry is at an end; that the extent and difficulty of land transportation is constantly increased; that a new resort and sanctuary is afforded to the disaffected in that part of the country, and that a new door is opened to draw supplies, and distress and corrupt the inhabitants.*

As this situation required action, the Committee insisted to Congress that it recommend to the several States, "by the most decisive and vigorous effort, forthwith to fill up their respective Battalions agreeable to a resolution in Congress [earlier passed] that the present favourable opportunity may be improved for annoying and dislodging the enemy." [11]

But the Washington-Armstrong correspondence during this time was not confined to the progress of the war. In one letter Armstrong inquired into the possibility that Washington might be able to provide his son, Dr. James Armstrong, some acreage in the area of the warm springs. From West Point Washington expressed his regrets: "I wish it was in my power to accommodate the Doctor with a piece of Land in Berkeley . . . . But several years ago I leased every foot I had in that Country and wish with all my heart he had happened to have been one of the Lessees, as I let them for Cash on very moderate terms for lives, which under the present depreciated state of the currency, is not worth collecting." [12]

And in a letter to Jamey himself a few days later Armstrong noted the landing of British troops in Connecticut and the distress that would follow, stressed the American resolve, lamented the financial situation, remarked the difficulties of recruitment, expressed a fear that Gates may not be able to hold Rhode Island, and observed that militia forces, rather than regular Continental Army soldiers, should be used for the Sullivan campaign. He was keeping in touch with the war.[13]

One of Armstrong's early letters to Washington, now lost, was composed on July 7. In a postscript he expressed an incorrect opinion on Charleston, which was at that time being defended by William Moultrie and General Benjamin Lincoln: "This afternoon came Genl. Lincolns dispatches into Congress which you will soon enough see for all they contain. The best I can at present infer from them is that Charleston is in no immediate danger—and the Worst, that the Enemy may get away if they please." [14]

On July 12, in a letter to General Gates, a much distressed Armstrong expressed himself on the deplorable financial state of the country. At this time he was tackling these problems with Henry Marchant, of Rhode Island, and Samuel Huntington, of Connecticut, and was becoming more and more discouraged.[15]

But great good news came to the Congress at mid-July. It was reported to the unbridled joy of every Congressman that General Wayne, in a surprise nighttime assault with light infantry, had captured the British garrison at Stony Point. According to the report, 600 soldiers were captured, with all their stores, guns, tents, and baggage. A letter of General Washington of July 21 was read. It included his orders to Wayne (July 10) and the orders issued by Wayne on the 15th, and Wayne's letter of the 17th to Washington, which provided a detailed account of the startling success.

On motion by Gouverneur Morris, second by Henry Laurens, it was resolved unanimously to extend the thanks of Congress to His Excellency General Washington, "for the vigilance, wisdom and magnanimity, with which he hath conducted the military operations of these states, and which are among many other signal instances manifested in his orders for the late glorious enterprize and successful attack on the enemy's fortress on the banks of the Hudson's river."

It was also resolved unanimously that the thanks of Congress "be presented to Brigadier General Wayne, for his brave, prudent, and soldierly Conduct in the spirited and well conducted attack on Stony Point." To handle all of this, and prepare an immediate report, the Congress appointed a committee of three: Gouverneur Morris of New York, John Armstrong of Pennsylvania, and Samuel Huntington of Connecticut.[16]

In one of his letters to Gates, this one dated August 16, Armstrong reported "a flood of good news," including the taking of the British St. Vincent and the Grenadas by the French. He is happy to see harmony finally growing within the Congress. He is barely baptized as a Congressman, but already there appears in his letter a note that will be regularly occurring: "My declining Constitution has had a struggle to keep on foot for a week past but now somewhat better, and if the bow of Congress were fairly shot at a few capital things, I shall God willing take a final leave of the publick stations."[17]

This of course was the summer of the Sullivan anti-Indian expedition, and Congress had its hands full with that. Naturally Armstrong was involved. On the 23rd of August he was appointed to a committee of five, which included John Dickinson, to review Washington's letter of August 15, and the attendant papers. And a week later Armstrong found himself serving on still another committee (three members only) to address the difficulty which had arisen between the Board of War and the Sullivan Expedition. The big problem here was Sullivan's censure of the Board of War.

Through September and early October of this year the Congress was active in reviewing Washington's reports on the progress of the war, and in allotting and raising monies for various expenses, including those for members of the Delaware Indian nation.

All of this inspired an Armstrong-to-Washington letter, dated Philadelphia, October 15. In it Armstrong speaks of the need for subsistence for the General Officers of the Army, one of Washington's abiding concerns. He gets into taxes and the prospect of a foreign loan, and confesses that for finance "I never had any talent." And, not surprisingly, he announces the end of his career as a Congressman: "I am now leaving Congress, having exerted the last dregs of any remaining talent that I had under various impediments."[18]

Armstrong requested and was granted a leave of absence on October 11, but was present on October 12, and again on the 15th (as we know by the letter to Washington); and, according to a letter written to his Carlisle friend Colonel William Irvine on October 30, he did not get home until "about a week ago," that is, October 23. In this letter he responds to Irvine's desire for promotion to Brigadier General, by urging him to write directly to the Congress or to the Board of War.[19]

For the 1779 session of the Continental Congress, it can be found that the Pennsylvania delegate John Armstrong recorded votes119 times, not always siding with the majority. He was responsible for many motions, and many seconds. He was very fussy about wording, and would often provide a judicious rephrasing of somebody else's motion. He recommended names for appointments, like that of James Stevenson for Commissioner, and was especially concerned about the Board of War, for which he nominated Colonel Samuel John Atlee. For his service from April 5 to October 20, the Pennsylvania treasury was directed to pay him, "as a member of Congress for this State," 792 pounds.[20]

Though complaining of the infirmities that his age had visited upon him, and suffering some discouragements, especially in the realms of finance, and declaring to Washington that he had had enough of this life, he seemed to appreciate that his service was worth something. Within a month, his health improving some, he felt himself ready to give it another go.

On November 12 of this year the General Assembly of Pennsylvania proceeded to the choice of five delegates to represent the state in the next session of the Continental Congress. On Saturday, the 13th, the credentials for the delegates elected by ballot were read. John Armstrong was the first named. The others were James Searle, Frederich Muhlenburgh (Frederick A. Muhlenberg), James McClean (McClene), and William Shippen, Senior. The certificate of election was signed by Thomas Paine, Clerk of the General Assembly.[21]

In a letter to Joseph Reed, dated Carlisle, November 27, 1779, Armstrong remarked on the appointments: "The Assembly have done right in fixing on five instead of seven delegates to represent them in Congress, but wrong in not varying this choice in two instances, as dr. Shippen & myself might with equal decency & propriety have been left out thro' infirmity, and this I hope may still be thought of & accomplished at the next sitting of the house, as Integrity alone without a capacity for action & attention to business will not do." But far from dropping Armstrong and Shippen, the Council, on Thursday, June 1, 1780, seated in the Congress two additional Pennsylvania delegates, Jared Ingersoll and Timothy Matlack.

In this same letter, which is a very long one, the "old" General first congratulates Reed: "Dear Sir, Amongst the few newspapers I have seen since my return to this place [Carlisle], happily one fell into my hands which conveyed the agreeable account of your Excellencies re-election to the Presidency of the State, whereby my wishes are naturally excited that your heath and happiness, &c., may at least be commensurate with your progressive administration."

And then he refers to an abiding concern, the paucity of wheat and therefore flour: "When in town we fondly hoped that some quantity of flour might safely have been shipped from this State to foreign market, but on coming into the country was much surprised to find the lightness of our last winters crops, to that degree that many farmers thrash out five dozen of shoks for one Bushel of wheat, whereas one Dozen, or from that to eighteen shaves [sheaves] formerly yielded a Bushel, neither is the w[e]ight what it usually has been." He thinks the trouble owing to frost and mildew, and more prevalent on the west side of the Susquehanna than on the east.

After referring Reed to some other matters, like the distressed condition of the public highways, staff for the militia, winter quarters, pay and clothing for the forces, etc., he closes with his regards to Mrs. Reed and other friends, and adds a postscript concerning the failure of his son James to find friends in Philadelphia.[22]

Now at home in Carlisle, he can worry about his son John, Jr., who is serving with General Gates. For his wealthy merchant friend and fellow Pennsylvania delegate to Congress, James Searle, who has been very ill, he has a lot of questions. These he poses in a letter written December 15. He wants to know whether there is any prospect for appreciation in the money. He is hopeful that something can be done about runaway prices. But the question that he really wants to ask concerns Major John Armstrong, Jr. He has read a letter published in the newspapers on November 9, and then printed again on November 10. This is a letter of General Gates on the Evacuation of the enemy at Newport. He is puzzled, and made angry, by the appearance in the second printing of a paragraph omitted from the first printing of the letter. As the paragraph is flattering to Major Armstrong, he is bothered by the suspicion that some editor deliberately omitted it from the first printing. He wonders whether Searle can throw any light on this curious matter.[23]

From a dark and gloomy Carlisle, early in January of 1780, when Washington was in his second encampment at Morristown, suffering " the harshest winter" his officers and soldiers had ever known, Armstrong wrote to him on his favorite subject, the regulation of prices. Price regulation, insisted the General, is the answer to the woes of the young nation. And he wanders into metaphor again to make his argument: "On the subtile subject of finance my pretensions are truly small, but on the necessity of some different measures from any yet adopted what man can shut his eyes? To say nothing of the various aireal schemes that have been thrown out, one thing is clear, that even such as have been tryed from their shew of more reason and solidity, either from their being inadequate in their nature, or too late in their application have palpably failed of the effect. For some time past we have assembled a Patient far gone in disease, given up by his Physicians and left to the mere efforts of nature."[24]

And not long after, January 24, he dispatches a similar, and similarly long, letter to Joseph Reed. He declares that our main concern must be the *deplorable state of our publick affairs,* meaning the financial situation. He is so moved that he continues the metaphor of the diseased patient. He admits for the umpty umpth time that he is ignorant of these matters, but . . . . "Confessing at the entrance that I neither know, nor profess to know any thing of that Subtile Science of Finances as such—We are as a vessel deserted by her crew" or as "a patient abandoned by his physicians." He insists that "our recovery and deliverance" depend on (1) "a Regulation of Prices by Law"; (2) a "speedy reformation of abuses and retrenchment of Expences in the two great lines of the Civil Staff, and some other appendages of the Army, more immediately under the direction of the Board of War"; and (3) "the laying in of certain Quantitys of Grain into Publick Magazines." And in a letter to General Gates he wrote: "The plain highway or Regulation by Law, appears now by fatal experience and dint of necessity the only rational line of our direction—and however doubtful many have been that such a Law cou'd not be put in execution, the more disinterested people here are lamenting the delay of the measure . . . ."[25]

He *very* much wants a law to regulate prices, and he argues for it at *great* length: "However arduous the Execution of the regulating law may be found to be, I humbly presume the necessity and the expedience of it." [26]

While still in Carlisle through the end of winter and into March he continues to pound away on this subject. Letters to Gates on February 16 and to Reed again on March 15 are particularly passionate. To Reed he indicates that "I have at some length lately wrote my Colleagues in Congress on the propriety and necessity of a limitation of prices by Authority . . . ." Then he proceeds to discuss the objections, and dismisses them. And when in May he arrives in Philadelphia as a Pennsylvania delegate to the Congress he continues to harp on finances, particularly the "manner of paying off the Principal and Interest of our borrowed money," and the need for a study of depreciation.[27]

In a long letter to Reed, from Carlisle, May 12, 1780, after some comment on the tax situation, Armstrong, ever sensitive to the Indian presence, sounds a warning:

Altho' no very late Indian depredations have been committed within this State, yet is the Situation of our inhabitants on the Susquehannah deplorable indeed, and if not Speedily relieved I should not think it at all strange if by next Harvest Carlisle should be a Frontier, nor is their [sic] *One Moment to be lost in Sending Troops into that Country* [the Seneca villages of New York] *however little we are to Expect from measures merely defensive, which . . . is perhaps all that can be promised. The*

Militia is the Only refuge I presume we have . . . and if nothing in the way of State Troops (I mean now to be raised) can be done, may not some of our Regiments in the Line be procured to Strenthen, & lead on the Militia.

And he has a person in mind for the command of the necessary forces: "Let me recommend to y^r Excellencys consideration the bearer of this [letter] Richard Butler, a very capable and well disposed Officer. If he Should be thought of for a Command North or Westward, you will no doubt manage that matter with the Commander in Chief, and Shall only at present Say that of this Gentlemans discretion, & abilities as a military Officer and especially in this back Country where his acquaintance must give him an advantage, I have a very good Opinion; and on an interview or two you will find him a genteel man, as well as an Officer in high repute thro' the State."

Richard Butler

Armstrong, a very good judge of character and ability, knew well the Ireland-born Butler, who with his four brothers and his father had come from Lancaster to Carlisle in 1760 to open a gun shop from which they produced the long rifle. As it turned out, Butler was to enjoy a most impressive career.[28]

Armstrong closes with the notation that he is in a hurry to "get down to Congress," and means to leave for Philadelphia in "eight days." A copy of the letter was handed over to Butler.[29]

As this was the time, too, in which Pennsylvania was leaving its proprietary structure, some confusion was developing over rights to the land. President Reed was appalled by how he had been misunderstood. At some time in this year of 1780 he addressed a letter to General Armstrong, John Montgomery, and Colonel John Davis:

> *Gentlemen, I have understood with no small surprise that some Persons in Carlisle have represented that when the Commissioners were at that Place I intimated in Conversation that the Lots & other Estates formerly belonging to the Proprietaries were open to the occupancy of any Persons who might chuse to locate them, to be paid for here after—And in Consequence a number of Persons have taken Possession of Lots & Lands in & about the Town, And also that the Militia were to be paid for a whole Tour of Duty tho they were not in Service more than half the Time. I totally disclaim such Sentiments as equally false in themselves & injurious to me, & am sure none such fell from me in Conversation or otherwise, my Opinion being totally contrary, and I think upon observing some Intrusions near the Town Spot I mentioned to several Gentlemen my Opinion of them as such.*[30]

He leaves it to Armstrong and the others to put a proper face on the situation.

Armstrong returned to Congress, still meeting in Philadelphia, the last week of May, 1780. ("Mr. John Armstrong, a delegate for Pennsylvania, attended and took his seat in Congress.") And he plunged at once into the two matters which were of most concern to the Congress, the progress of the war, of course, and the cost of the war. First off there was read to the Congress an important letter from Washington, who was encamped at Morristown. The Commander-in-Chief reported a desperate want of food, particularly meat, and reported on a number of annoying developments. As the war dragged its weary length along, naturally fatigue and discouragement settled on the soldiers. Of concern to Washington was an effort on the part of the British to take advantage of this condition by trying to persuade soldiers (with a special appeal to the Irish) to desert. Washington enclosed for the Congress "three New York Gazettes" and a "small printed paper found in our Camp, containing an address to our soldiery by the Enemy to induce them to desert." This "Address to the Soldiers of the Continental Army, 1780," read as follows:

> *The time is at length arrived, when all the artifices, and falsehoods of the Congress and of your commanders can no longer conceal from you, the misery of your situation; you are neither Clothed, Fed, nor Paid; your numbers are wasting away by Sickness, Famine, Nakedness, and rapidly so . . . the period of your stipulated Services, being in general expired, this is then the moment to fly from slavery and fraud. I am happy in acquainting the old country-men, that the affairs of Ireland are fully settled, and that Great-Britain and Ireland are firmly united, as well from interest as from affection: I need not now tell you who are born in America, that you have been cheated and abused; and you are both sensible, that in order to procure your liberty you must quit your leaders, and join your real friends who scorn to impose upon you, and who will receive you with open arms; kindly forgiving all your errors. You are told that you are surrounded by a numerous militia, this is also false—associate them together, make use of your firelocks and join the British Army, where you will be permitted to dispose of yourselves as you please.*[31]

Washington's letter was dated May 27. The British address to the Continental soldiers, which he had enclosed, was read to the Congress on the 31st, and promptly referred to a committee composed of Oliver Ellsworth, James Duane, and John Armstrong.

Armstrong in this session of the Congress was quick to resume his correspondence with General Gates. In a very long letter, June 6, he informs the General that (1) the expected 8000 French troops have not yet arrived, and (2) that the treasury is empty ("our finances, at once in the lowest and most delicate situation"). General Gates of course knows about Benjamin Lincoln's surrender of Charleston to the British under Sir Henry Clinton (May 12), but Armstrong, remembering the gallant defense put up by Colonel Moultrie, almost four years ago, is much moved by this disaster. One thing that he wants General Gates to know is that he has put before Congress a recommendation (in the form of a motion) that Gates be moved to Philadelphia instead of sent south: "Your call to the field may be set down as certain, but the time when and the place where, as uncertain; it may be in a fortnight, and yet may not be until the Fall."

As it turned out, Gates, very shortly after he had Armstrong's letter, was ordered by Congress to take command in the Carolinas. Indeed, Armstrong was among the first (June 15) to congratulate him on the appointment. And he promptly informed the General that he has recommended to Congress (with success) a sufficient support for "your journey." But the letter departs in the familiar way from the big subject. John Armstrong, Jr., still Gate's aide, will, of course be accompanying the General south. "I have more privately pressed the Board of War to send also by the Express, one piece of Linnen, meaning the major part for yourself, and the residue for Major Armstrong. This they thought was a little out of their way [!], but gave me more than half a promise. The Major [who, now but twenty-one years old, has been at home in Carlisle] has not a shilling until he reach you to pay what debt he may be in, beside[s] my keeping him in some pocket money these three months past . . . ."[32]

To his friend Colonel John Davis[33] Armstrong reported on July 8 that "For these few days past this place affords but little news. The Enemy remains at Philips's House on the N side of Hudson River, but have not yet made an attempt toward West Point." But after the fall of Charleston, Governor John Rutledge, together with a number of prominent South Carolinians, and Richard Howly, Governor of Georgia, had come north to Philadelphia. Armstrong is apprehensive about the Carolina situation. He thinks it is "very wrong" that the Governors are here in Philadelphia and hopes that what he has heard, that Rutledge will shortly return south, is true.

In a postscript he complains that "Mrs. Armstrong has wrote me for £150 and I cannot send her one pound, but have referred her to you,"a reference to the ongoing quarrel between Francis Hopkinson, treasurer of loans, and the commissioners of the treasury, Ezekial Forman and John Gibson.[34] On July 29 Congress authorized ten thousand dollars for Armstrong, "for which the said commonwealth [Pennsylvania] is to be accountable."

He continues to follow closely the progress of the war, and is overjoyed at the arrival of the promised French fleet at Rhode

Island. To Davis again he reported, on the 12th of July, that there has appeared the long awaited armada of France, "consisting of seven ships of the line, a Bumketcher and three Frigates with five thousand infantry." And, happily, this is not all. To Davis he confides the "private opinion" that additional reinforcements can be expected.[35]

But bad news is coming too. And it is devastating to the Congress. It is the news that on August 16 General Gates was terribly defeated and most disgracefully routed at Camden by Sir Henry Clinton. It was one of the most disastrous defeats suffered by the Continental forces in the entire war, in stunning contrast to Gates's victory over Burgoyne at Saratoga. And because of the loss of Major General Baron de Kalb, and so many of his gallant soldiers, the battle has to go down as one of the saddest moments of the entire Revolution. The heroic De Kalb, after his horse had been shot from under him, continued to fight on foot, shoulder to shoulder with his loyal troops of the Maryland Second Brigade. Finally he fell, mortally wounded, stricken with three musket balls, and pierced eight times by British bayonets. The General was saved from instant death by his lieutenant Charles Dubuysson. As he was being carried away, he could not believe what he was being told, that for the Americans all was lost.

Armstrong had not yet had this sad news when he penned from Philadelphia a personal letter to his friend Dr. William Irvine.[36] Had he that news, he would have been even more distressed than he is. The letter is dated August 17. "Dear General .... My Health has been in jeopardy of late by excessive heat, business and confinement, in this city where many of late have made a sudden exit from the present world—but if my health is spared until the memorial of the General Officers is carried through ... I intend to retire, before which you will hear from me in a future letter." Without the news of Camden, he looks forward to an historic victory: "I begin to doubt whether the 2d Division of the F[rench] Fleet will arrive in time, but still hope that this Campaign will not pass over without some happy event to these States and laurels in the arms of America." [37]

Armstrong was not present when Gates's report of the battle of Camden was read to the Congress, nor had he heard from

Gates since the battle, but he had most of the details when he sat down to write the General on September 3. He knew, of course, how *very* disappointed was the Board of War and the Congress, and he knew that Gates's ignominious flight from the field had been much remarked on; but he here assured the General that no formal censure should be expected, and he is not about to make any judgment himself. To help pick Gates up, he anticipated the time when the French fleet, breaking the British blockade, will finally arrive. It may not be until spring, but it is going to happen. The war is not lost.

Before he could post this letter, Armstrong did hear from Gates himself, who had written on the 29th of August, not so much to report on Camden, but to disclose the illness of Major Armstrong. Armstrong continued his letter: "I . . . have my apprehensions lest his late illness may terminate in a decay, of which should you discover any Symtoms this Fall, I am persuaded your cordial friendship for him will prompt you to advise and give him such leave of Absence, so you may think proper for the recovery of his health, intimating the same to Congress or the Board of War."

He implored the General to "be not discouraged," and in a postscript announced his retirement one more time: "I shall write my Son by Major Maguill—then intend to retire, my strength, talents and constitutional time in Congress being very near a period." [38]

Among Armstrong's letters of interest, as the 1780 session of the Continental Congress wound down, is still another to William Irvine, who is now, after commendable service at Monmouth, a Brigadier General, and in a year's time would be given the command of the Western Department. It's money, money again: ". . . .as you are now to have but a few hints, the great concern of *an Empty Treasury* with a thousand daily demands, forms the front line of my highest fears and deepest distress."

In this communication he expressed the hope that they may soon have clothing from Holland for the Pennsylvania Line of our Army. And he notes the sad news of General Nathanael Greene's "peremptory Resignation in the business of Q[uartermaster] General." Greene of course, from the time he accepted the appointment in March of 1778, has been rendering an incalculable service to Washington's army in this office. But he had been complaining about the Treasury Board's interference in his administration, and he and the Congress had not been agreeing on how the army should be supplied. Armstrong, who on June 19 had been appointed to a committee for reviewing the Quartermaster Department, notes that his resignation, "at this critical moment, has at once disappointed and thrown Congress into a degree of vexatious distress . . . ." [39]

Another letter of interest is his communication to Reed dated August 30. Armstrong is responding to Reed's inquiry into the August 25 resolution of Congress respecting the relative rank of governors in the field, a subject in which Reed is naturally very much interested. The resolution had actually been formed and presented by Armstrong and by attorney John Henry, a delegate from Maryland, and it had passed with almost no discussion or debate.

But Armstrong takes advantage of this request to notify his President that he is (really, this time) ready to step down. "I hope," he writes, "to be at full liberty to retire, especially as Mr. McClane [McClene] now attends. Three good members at once in the House is sufficient . . . ." [40]

When General Cornwallis at Yorktown on October 19, 1781, surrendered to a massive French-American army-navy force, the success of the rebellion was insured. Washington, assured now of peace, considered what it meant. And he was quick to realize that those who had inspired the revolution, together with those who had brought it to a triumphant end, would now be assuming a *huge* responsibility. His concern was for the future. Five months beyond the surrender of Cornwallis he confided to General Armstrong, "We ought not to look back, unless it is to derive useful lessons from past errors, and for the purpose of profiting by dear bought experience." For Washington, " . . . the victory at Yorktown might better not have happened if it induced a sense of relaxation and supineness, of false security." [41]

And of course the war was not over. While the Americans John Jay, John Adams, and Benjamin Franklin negotiated in Paris the peace terms with the British, the rebellion dragged on.

Washington had still the army of Henry Clinton, which was holed up in New York, to address. And all was not quiet on the western front. It is significant that the last fighting of the war involved Indians, and was long continued on the frontiers of Pennsylvania and Virginia. The last real battle of the Revolution was fought in the Blue Licks region of what is now Kentucky, on Monday, August 19, 1783. On this day a huge British-Indian force, organized by the infamous Simon Girty, in a cunning ambush, completely routed the Kentucky militia, killing one-third of the whole force, including eighteen officers and Israel Boone, the son of Daniel. This victory at Blue Licks, however, did nothing toward the King's advantage. Actually, it inspired a Kittanning-like revenge mission, led by George Rogers Clark at the head of more than one thousand (!) experienced riflemen. This force was able to drive the Shawnee from their villages on the Ohio River north of the Blue Licks battle site, and with his huge army Rogers was able to destroy the Indian village of Chillicothe, as well as a number of lesser towns.

  On November 30, 1782, preliminary peace articles were agreed to in Paris, and almost a year later, on September 3, the War for Independence *finally* came to an end.

  Washington resigned his command of the Continental Army at Annapolis on December 23, and "retired" to his beloved Mount Vernon. Although he had his acquired lands to tend to, and much else to do, he remained concerned about the country's future. Independence meant that a government had to be organized, and government was not possible without a constitution. Dissatisfied with the Articles of Confederation, under which the infant nation had been governed since 1781, he participated in the movement to revise or replace the document. And, indeed, elected unanimously, he presided over the historic Constitutional Convention of 1787, which was convened in May in Philadelphia and continued until September 17.

  And so it was for Armstrong, too. His concern for his country and his intense interest in her affairs of course did not diminish, even in the slightest, with the end of his service as Congressman. In writing to William Irvine on August 16, 1787, from Carlisle, he indulged in some speculation upon the Federal

Convention drawing up the Constitution. "Whatever their system may be," he observed, ". . . in my private opinion it ought not to be scan[n]ed with an eye too critical but with great candor and many allowances, nor should cold water be poured upon it . . . because an indifferent one is better than none." [42]

Of course, whatever the final form of the Constitution, there would clearly be the need for the election of a President. For a long time now the name that was being heard was that of George Washington. The most popular and influential *Pennsylvania Packet* mentioned only Washington whenever it spoke of the "President-to-be." When the big-wigs of Massachusetts celebrated the Commonwealth's adoption of the Constitution, a toast was offered "To General Washington—may his wisdom and virtue preside in the councils of his country." [43] And from his many friends, like Lafayette and Rochambeau, the General had expressions of hope that he would accept the office. One of his oldest friends and fellow officer, General John Armstrong, "wrote as if the hand of the Almighty had been placed in Washington's hand." [44]

Armstrong had written to Washington on March 2, 1787, and again on the 20th of February 1788, to warn his friend that he might have to give up his retirement to Mount Vernon. And of course Armstrong was making it clear that he himself very much hoped that Washington would accept the Presidency of the country. On April 25, 1788, the beleaguered favorite replied from Mount Vernon. It is a long and most interesting letter. It is evident that Washington (1) continues devoted to the country, and (2) feels a responsibility for its direction and welfare.

After first apologizing for his delay in responding, the retired Commander-in-Chief addressed Armstrong's urging that he consider the Presidency:

I well remember the observation you made in your letter to me of last year, that my "domestic retirement must suffer an interruption." This [the drafting of the Constitution] *took place, notwithstanding it was utterly repugnant to my feelings, my interests and my wishes; I sacrificed every private consideration and personal enjoyment to the earnest and pressing solicitations of those who saw and knew the alarming situation of our public concerns, and had no other end in view but to promote the interests of their Country; and conceiving, that under those circumstances, and at so critical a moment, an absolute refusal to act, might, on my part, be construed as a total dereliction of my Country, if imputed to no worse motives. Altho' you say the same motives induce you to think that another tour of duty of this kind will fall to my lot, I cannot but hope that you will be disappointed, for I am so wedded to a state of retirement and find my occupations of a rural life so congenial; with my feelings, that to be drawn into public [life] at my advanced age, could be a sacrifice that would admit of no compensation.*

He then proceeds to the Constitution, which would not be sufficiently ratified until the end of June. It is very important, he agrees with Armstrong, to have a good beginning:

Your remarks on the impressions which will be made on the manners and sentiments of the people by the example of those who are first called to act under the proposed Government are very just; and I have no doubt but (if the proposed Constitution obtains) those persons who are chosen to administer it will have wisdom enough to discern the influence which their example as rulers and legislators may have on the body of the people, and will have virtue enough to pursue that line of conduct which will most conduce to the happiness of their Country; as the first transactions of a nation, like those on an individual upon his first entrance into life, make the deepest impression, and are to form the leading traits in its character, they will undoubtedly pursue those measures which will best tend to the restoration of public and private faith and of consequence promote our national respectability and individual welfare.

To Armstrong Washington expressed the fear that the individual states in their wrangling over "particular interests" may not be able to "extend their ideas to the general welfare of the Union." His impression of the delegates from Armstrong's Pennsylvania is not flattering: "I am very glad to find, that the opposition in your State, however formidable it has been represented, is, generally speaking, composed of such characters, as cannot have an extensive influence; their fort[e] . . . seems to lie in misrepresentation, and a desire to inflame the passions and to alarm the fears by noisy declamation rather than to convince the understanding by sound arguments or fair and impartial statements. Baffled in their attacks upon the constitution they have attempted to vilify and debase the Characters who formed it, but even here I trust they will not succeed."

Washington is confident that the opposition in the end will do more good than harm: "It has called forth, in its defense, abilities which would not perhaps have been otherwise exerted that have thrown new light upon the science of Government, they have given the rights of man a full and fair discussion, and explained them in so clear and forcible a manner, as cannot fail to make a lasting impression . . . . There will be a greater weight of abilities opposed to the system in the convention of this State [Virginia] than there has been in any other, but notwithstanding the unwearied pains which have been taken, and the vigorous efforts which will be made in the Convention to prevent its adoption, I have not the smallest doubt it will obtain here." (Virginia ratified the Constitution on June 25.)

Then Washington, in this very long and character-illuminating letter turns to a different subject altogether. It is education. But even that concern he links to the need for a strong constitution. As Armstrong has complained to him about the difficulties Dickinson College has been experiencing, he writes (including one of the longest sentences ever composed),

I am sorry to hear that the College in your neighborhood is in so declining a state as you represent it, and that it is likely to suffer a further injury by the loss of Dr. [Charles] Nisbet whom you are afraid you shall not be able to support in a proper manner on account of the scarcity of Cash which prevents parents from sending their Children thither. This is one of the numerous evils which arise from the want of a general regulating power, for in a Country like this where equal liberty is enjoyed, where every man may reap his own harvest, which by proper attention will afford him much more than is necessary for his own consumption, and where there is so ample a field for every mercantile and mechanical exertion, if there cannot be money found to answer the common purposes of education . . . it is evident that there is something amiss in the ruling political power which requires a steady, regulating and energetic hand to correct and control . . . . if . . . property was well secured, faith and justice well preserved, a stable government well administered, and confidence restored, the tide of population and wealth would flow to us, from every part of the Globe, and, with a due sense of the blessings, make us the happiest people upon earth.

And this long letter Washington signs, "With sentiments of very great esteem." [45]

On December 29, 1790, General John Armstrong, at home in Carlisle, addressed to the President of the United States an affectionate letter of regard. But in the course of it he intimated that his son John, Jr., would be most happy to have a position in the administration if one could be found. Not until February 6 did President Washington respond to this letter. When he did so, he apologized for his tardiness, noting that it was not because of "diminished regard." And he insisted that "Your friendship receives from me the same grateful and affectionate return which I have ever made to it." And then in the language used ever since by every President in replying to office seekers, he writes: ". . . the multiplied duties of my public Station allow me little or no leizure for the cultivation of private regards. . . . I have the best disposition to serve the person [son John] whom you then recommended, and in what may comport with circumstances and public propriety, I shall be happy to do so. At present I know not what offices may be created, and applicants multiply with every new office . . . . In a word, to a man who has no ends to serve, nor friends to provide for, nominations to office is the most irksome part of the Executive trust." [46]

As President Washington tackled a bewildering array of domestic problems, General Armstrong stayed in close touch. Washington's biggest concern of course was the continuing Indian problem, made very serious by the hostility of the western tribes, who did not want to see a white settler beyond the Ohio. He was required, as President, to take a very different view of the Indian peoples, and he now assumed a moral responsibility for the "savages" he had been fighting for forty years. He felt that he had to accommodate the land's first inhabitants, and to testify to his sincerity and good faith, as well as to clarify what he intended for the Indians, he issued in 1790 a Proclamation remarkably similar to that of King George twenty-seven years earlier. He was forbidding state or private encroachment on all Indian lands "guaranteed by treaty with the United States." And, like the Proclamation of King George, there was never any good chance that it could hold for any amount of time or prove the least bit effective.

At the same time, the continuing belligerence of the Shawnee and the Miami in the Ohio Valley offended him. And though the use of force was distasteful to him, Washington made it clear to the Indians that he would resort to whatever means necessary to put an end to hostile activity.

The Indians were unmoved. They made it equally clear to the young government that force would indeed be necessary.

To the incessant hostility, the President responded as promised. And he promptly suffered two most humiliating defeats. The two expeditions dispatched by the War Department of Henry Knox against the Indians of the Ohio Valley were virtually annihilated. The first, a somewhat modest and largely untrained military force, composed of some Federal troops and militia and backwoodsmen, under the command of General Josiah Harmar on October 20-22, 1790, was ambushed and wiped out by the Miami war-chief Little Turtle at the head of a confederation of tribes in the Maumee Valley, north of the Ohio River.

In the succeeding year, on November 4, the second expedition, led by General Arthur St. Clair, who had tons of Revolutionary War experience, was likewise overwhelmingly defeated, again by Little Turtle, this time on the Wabash River, near present-day Fort Recovery. Washington had warned the General to "beware of surprise" and to be sure "to build fortifications" at every encampment. But the General, on his arrival at the Wabash, did not require fortifications of the weary soldiers, and he went to sleep feeling secure. The attack came at daybreak, St. Clair's troops awakening in the bitter cold to find the encampment completely surrounded by a sea of Indians, one thousand warriors made terrifying by the garish war-paint, and fired to a battle frenzy by the cunning Miami chief Little Turtle and the Shawnee Blue Jacket. What happened during the next three hours has been many times called "the bloodiest battle ever fought against the Indians." In the melee, St. Clair lost 900 soldiers (including almost all of the eighty-six officers), seventy-five per cent of his fighting force, killed or wounded. Besides, there were slaughtered a great many of the soldiers' wives, who had accompanied the expedition; and many children were carried off. The General himself only barely escaped, finding refuge in Fort Jefferson, which lay to the south. The Indians lost 66 (!) warriors.

It was a terrible blow to the young nation. Disappointment and discouragement settled over Washington and General Knox and the Cabinet. General Armstrong, when he had the news, was horrified.

St. Clair filed a report with Washington five days after the battle. And when Armstrong, who knew a little about Indian warfare, was satisfied that he had the details, he got off a letter (December 23) to the President. It bristles with criticism of the order of action, but registers praise too for the heroism of the soldiers:

> *Who could doubt, who knows the abilities of the first officers of that army, that the only successful mode of coping with Indians in a forest had not been preconcerted over and over long before that day. The partial or momentary advantage, gained by the flanking parties only, as I apprehend, with screwed bayonets, would easily discover the error of the former arrangement; but alas, it was then too late, either to devise a new one or change the old for a better. Placing the militia in a body over the brook, permit me to say, was an unwarrantable step, when two or three small pickets would have served a better purpose. It seems probable that too much attachment to regular or military rule, or too great confidence in the artillery (which, it seems, formed part of the lines, and had a tendency to render the troops stationary), must have been the motives which led to the adopted order of action. I call it adopted, because the General does not speak of having*

intended any other, whereby he presented a large and visible object, perhaps in close order, too, to an enemy near enough to destroy, but from their known modes of action comparatively invisible; whereby we may readily infer that five hundred Indians were fully sufficient to do us all the injury we have sustained, nor can I conceive them to have been many more.

We shall not do well against the Indians, he insists, unless we take "a few lessons from them." And we must fight them with their methods if we are to be successful. "Tragical as the event has been," he writes to a melancholy Washington, "we have this consolation: that during the action, our officers and troops, discovered great bravery, and that the loss of a battle is not always the loss of the cause." [47]

It would require another four years almost before the Indian problem was put to rest. It was accomplished by Washington's choice of commanders, General Anthony Wayne, who, with mighty preparation, defeated the Federation at the Battle of Fallen Timbers, and accomplished peace with the historic Treaty of Greenville August 3, 1795. This signal moment in the history of Indian-White relations General John Armstrong would not live to see.

XXVI

DICKINSON COLLEGE

On September 3, 1783, the Treaty of Paris, ending the Revolutionary War, was *finally* concluded. The document, signed by John Jay, John Adams, and its principal architect Benjamin Franklin, recognized the independence and the sovereignty of the world's newest nation, the United States of America. It was one of the most historic moments in the record of nations.

    Lots of great things, like the homecoming of the Continental Army soldiers, some of whom had served the Cause for as much as eight and one-half years, took place in the time shortly thereafter. One event that was of historic significance for the people of Carlisle and for General John Armstrong occurred on September 9, even before the news of peace had made its laborious way across the Atlantic. On this date, by a formal act of the Pennsylvania legislature, a college was incorporated for the community. It had already been named Dickinson College, to honor one of the nation's founders, and with this action of the Assembly (the charter having been drafted by Carlisle's James Wilson) it thus became the first college to be born in the new United States of

America.

Dr. Benjamin Rush is regarded by some historians as the most consequential and influential figure of the Revolution, excepting only Washington and Franklin. Certainly he was a distinguished patriot, as statesman, as Surgeon General in the Continental Army, and as physician. At the age of fifteen, he had graduated from a Presbyterian school, the College of New Jersey (now Princeton). And he was a native-born Pennsylvanian. Surely it was most fitting that this distinguished member of the founding fathers, should preside at the birth of the college to be located in the heart of the Presbyterian Scotch-Irish country, in Carlisle, Pennsylvania, which community had spearheaded the quest for independence and was considered a "Bulwark of Liberty."

It would be a good birth. The institution, though not in its teenage years, would one day rise to prominence and marked distinction among the country's pre-professional liberal arts colleges. And it would be a natural birth. But it would definitely not be an easy birth. Dr. Benjamin Rush, at the first sign of labor pains, would find himself virtually alone. He would have his special skills challenged.

The story of Dickinson College, for its founding and its first fifteen years, can be read in the letters that passed among the prime movers, Dr. Benjamin Rush, Colonel John Montgomery, and General John Armstrong. Indeed, Dr. Rush and Colonel Montgomery, who were friends before a college was ever thought of for Carlisle, became during the struggle to get it accomplished very close friends. It was through the great energy and dedication of these "impassioned zealots" that the college finally became a reality.[1] Of course it was Rush who was largely responsible. The college was his idea, and it was he who paved the way for the charter; it was he who raised the necessary funds; it was he who secured the first Principal for the institution; and it was he who fought off the many difficulties.

The story begins in the summer of 1769, when there came to Carlisle from County Donegal in Ireland a young and very scholarly minister. On November 20 of the next year he purchased the house that stood on the southeast corner of Hanover Street and Locust Alley. Before long he had a "school" in session. As the minister's name was Henry Makinly, the school was known as the Makinly School. It was known by other names as well, because of what could be learned there. It was known as the "Latin School" (although Greek was taught as well), the "Mathematical School," the "English School," and the "Grammar School." But whatever the institution was called, the education it supplied was thought of as preparation for college.

The enrollment varied of course, but Master Makinly normally had close to twenty boys in attendance and sometimes as many as thirty. A number of Makinly's pupils did in fact pursue their studies at the college in Philadelphia, but most enrolled at the College of New Jersey (Princeton). The most distinguished of these was John Armstrong's gifted second son, John Armstrong, Jr., who, not yet eleven years old when Master Makinly arrived in Carlisle, would leave the College of New Jersey at age sixteen to embark on a military career.

On March 3, 1773, there was secured from Thomas and John Penn, the Pennsylvania Proprietors, a deed for a grant of land to be used for the erection of a community grammar school.[2] Nine distinguished citizens of the Carlisle community were selected as patentees. It is worth noting that even though the Reverend Duffield had left the community, there were still active the two Presbyterian churches. Of the nine named in the patent, three were New Side Presbyterians (General John Armstrong, Stephen Duncan, and William Lyon); and the other six were members of Reverend Steel's congregation. One of these was a prominent Carlisle attorney, the Ireland-born Robert Magaw.

Another was Reverend Steel's strongest supporter, Colonel John Montgomery, who had been at Carlisle from its beginnings. Montgomery was some five years younger than Armstrong, but he had come to the region that would be Cumberland County a good bit earlier. It is apparent from his letters that he was not well educated. Indeed, during his military service, though an officer, he had had his letters written for him; and Armstrong during the Forbes expedition is supposed to have observed of him that he was "somewhat wanting in horn, hair, and hoof." But he was a most resourceful Scotch-Irish Presbyterian, gifted with good common sense and unimpeachable integrity, in sum, a very fine man and devoted to the Church. His home, called Happy Retreat, at this time was just west of Carlisle. He had served with Armstrong on the Forbes expedition, and was before that and after a very active member of the Carlisle community, serving as a justice of the peace, and burgess, and as an elder in the church of Reverend John Steel.[3]

Still another gentleman who was named in the deed was General William Irvine, one of only two Carlisle physicians at the time, a good friend and close neighbor to Armstrong, and later one of Washington's most dependable generals. Others named were Robert Miller, George Stevenson, and James Wilson. All of these nine, excepting Miller and Stevenson, would later serve as Trustees of the College. Wilson, who had taught Latin at the College of Philadelphia, and had studied law under John Dickinson, and had practiced law in Carlisle, was of course a natural choice.

The grammar school was opened at the time the site was granted, and it was not long before it was proposed to be made an academy. This was the idea of John Montgomery, who had been

William Irvine

serving as head trustee of the grammar school. When on a trip to Philadelphia, he presented his plan to his good friend Dr. Benjamin Rush, the good doctor was promptly enamored, but his vision was a little more grand. "Why an academy?" he asked. "Why not a college?"

Among his personal friends through the year 1782 Rush floated the idea of a college for Carlisle. Recognizing interest, if not enthusiasm, he began to write letters to those he considered most influential in the Presbyterian community. And he stressed in every communication that this institution would be rigidly Presbyterian. He distributed a leaflet entitled "Hints for Establishing a College at Carlisle in Cumberland County, Pennsylvania."

Benjamin Rush

In this monograph Rush, in his most persuasive manner, cited his reasons for promoting the college. He was addressing Presbyterians. He argued that "Every religious society should endeavor to preserve a representation of itself in government . . . . At present they [the Presbyterians] hold an undue share in the power of the State, and it becomes them to retire a little from offices and to invite other societies to partake of them with them . . . . It becomes them above all things to entrench themselves in schools of learning. These are the true nurseries of power and influence . . . . In the present plenitude of power in the Presbyterians let them obtain a charter for a college at Carlisle in Cumberland County."

Now why Carlisle? Rush noted four advantages: "It will draw the Presbyterians to one common center of union. It will be nearly central to the State . . . . Education will be cheaper in Carlisle . . . . The village of Carlisle is one of the most healthy spots in the State." In fact, according to one historian, Carlisle at this time seemed an almost ideal site for a college. "Carlisle," he allowed, "was indeed a small town, consisting of not more than two thousand inhabitants, with scarcely even a regular line of stages to connect it with the more commercial parts of the country. But it had a high reputation for intelligence and enterprize, and an elevated moral and social character, which were looked upon as indispensable to such an institution." [4]

The first, and seemingly insurmountable, difficulty to Rush's dream was presented by Colonel John Armstrong, not only the most influential citizen of the Carlisle community but a patentee of the grammar school, and a man who could prove to be incredibly stubborn. Armstrong was strongly opposed to the installation of a college in Carlisle. It seemed to him that for the time being anyway the grammar school, as it had operated under Henry Makinly and John Creigh was sufficient. If that could develop into an "academy" that would be fine, but there was no need for a college.

Armstrong pointed out that there was already a college in Philadelphia, and another also in neighboring New Jersey. He saw little need for a third in the immediate area. Hadn't he dispatched one son to Philadelphia and the younger to the College of New Jersey? Moreover, as the College of New Jersey was a Presbyterian institution, he expressed the fear that another such college might widen the already unhealthy breach in the Presbyterian community. Not one to oppose a plan without a recommendation, he suggested waiting for a more opportune time, and (or) selecting a more advantageous location, possibly in the western end of the state, possibly at Pittsburgh.

When it was understood that he was heading up the opposition to Rush's plan, Armstrong promptly heard from a great many people of the same mind, including two very important personages, both with reasons to disapprove anything that Dr. Rush might propose. These were John Ewing, a College of New Jersey graduate and Pastor of the First Presbyterian Church in Philadelphia, who served as Provost to the college in Philadelphia known as the University of the State of Pennsylvania; and George Bryan, Armstrong's friend, and very influential politically in the Presbyterian Church. Ewing thought the idea ridiculous, and derisively referred to it as "the moon-shine project." Both men in letters to Armstrong declared their feeling that the school in Carlisle should continue to function as it had been doing. A great many other people, too, including local Presbyterian ministers Robert Cooper and John Craighead, were opposed to Rush's plan.

Armstrong, in his early correspondence with Rush, particularly in a letter of January 6, 1783, took exactly the position recommended by Bryan and Ewing, arguing for a school providing "moderate academics with not less than two professors" for what he called "the back country." He did allow that times change, and suggested that maybe down the road . . . .[5]

Dr. Benjamin Rush, of course, knew very, very well, that no matter how many friends he could win over, his college was going nowhere without the support of General John Armstrong. Accordingly, and with the encouragement of his very close friend John Montgomery, he got off a carefully thought out and well reasoned, very polite letter to the General. It was just one month prior to the date of a meeting of the Donegal Presbytery, which would be discussing the question of a charter for a college at Carlisle. Dated "Philadelphia, March 19, 1783," this *long* letter opens: "The early respect I was taught to entertain for your character, and the agreeable connection we once had together [in the war], are the only apologies I shall offer for opening a correspondence with you upon the subject of a college at Carlisle." Chiefly in this very long letter, then, he proceeds to cite the advantages of such a college. First he dismisses the university of Philadelphia, noting that no real religion prevails there, and that "without religion . . . learning does real mischief to the morals and principles of mankind." He notes, second, that education in Philadelphia is expensive, and that, moreover, the big city is not likely to preserve or to advance the morality of the students.

He argued, next, that Carlisle was in such a position, geographically, as to accommodate Presbyterians throughout the State, and keep them at home. "A college at Carlisle, by diffusing the light of science and religion more generally through our society, may check [the] spirit of emigration among them. It may teach them to prefer civil, social, and religious advantages, with a small farm and old land, to the loss of them all with extensive tracts of woods and a more fertile soil."

He knows Armstrong as a prosperous landowner, and he is astute (cunning) enough to appreciate the value of the argument that a college in Carlisle would do wonders for real estate values, just as the College of New Jersey had done for that region. At the very end of his letter he makes this argument, and he puts it in such terms as will appeal to a land speculator. He is discreet enough to address the citizens of Carlisle, not just Armstrong: "One fact more I must beg leave to mention which I think ought to have its weight with the citizens of Carlisle. The value of land in the neighborhood of Princeton before the College was erected there was from 30/ - 40/ - an acre. It has risen in the space of five and twenty years to £8-0-0 and £10-0-0 per acre, which is £5-0-0 an acre more than land sells for in the neighborhood of most of the villages in New Jersey."

In his closing, Dr. Rush, knowing that flattery gets you everywhere, writes respectfully, "Thus, sir, have I laid before you a few of the many arguments that might be mentioned in favor of a nursery of religion and learning at Carlisle, and at the same time I have I hope obviated all the objections that have been offered against it. . . . The principal design of this letter is to prevent your ancient and respectable character from being lessened in the smallest degree in the opinion of your friends by opposing an institution that promises such solid and extensive advantages to the Church and State." [6]

The letter did not dissuade Armstrong from his position, but it clearly had a mitigating effect, for at the meeting of the Presbytery in Philadelphia in April, the General, while holding fast to his concern did formally withdraw his opposition. And in a letter to Rush at about the same time he indicated he was no longer to be considered opposed.[7] Moreover, as Montgomery noted for Rush, "We put in the gentleman as a trustee, so that he is no longer the same party." Of course, the "gentleman" is Armstrong, and Montgomery credits Rush for winning the General over. "Your letter has done wonders, and your pen was under the influence and guidance of Providence."[8] And as Dr. Cooper, too, was made a trustee, serious opposition to the college largely disappeared.

One little bump in the road appeared when Rush, who was firmly identified with the plan for the college, somewhat indiscreetly in a letter to Armstrong, dated July 30, 1783, remarked critically of Presbyterians. The letter, when it became public, much offended several influential members of the Church, and among them did no good for any cause sponsored by Dr. Rush. The bothersome line was the doctor's statement that the Presbyterians must reform themselves, "before we are driven beyond the Mountains!" In a letter to the merchant and patriot John Bayard, now the Speaker of the Assembly, Rush wrote: "Herewith you will receive the copy of the letter I promised to send you to our mutual and worthy friend John Armstrong." The letter to Bayard is dated July 2, but that is clearly in error as the enclosed Rush-to-Armstrong letter was written July 30.[9]

But no really serious obstacles appeared, and the Presbytery formally approved the plan, and directed a petition to the General Assembly of the State for a charter. Rush appreciated that when the proposal came up before the Assembly it would be a close call. Noting that "Leave has been obtained to bring in a bill to found a college at Carlisle," he implored Montgomery to attend the meeting of the Assembly in June ("You must attend here at the sitting of the Assembly. I can do nothing without you."). Montgomery did not make that session of the Assembly, but the critical moment would occur in September, and for this session Rush insisted that he be there ("Do come to town immediately.").

Rush noted for Montgomery that everything was in order. The charter had been drafted by James Wilson and carefully reviewed by John Dickinson, who at that time was President of the Supreme Executive Council of the State. But "Everything hangs on the next two weeks." [10] And, as it turned out, it *was* a close call. But on September 9, just six days after the conclusion of the Treaty of Paris, the charter for Dickinson College was approved by the Pennsylvania Assembly. Now it was up to Dr. Rush and the Board of Trustees to create the college.

The charter of the college, as composed by James Wilson, was organized into seven sections, and has remained in force, with only slight changes for two hundred and twenty-seven years. The college could have been named for Dr. Benjamin Rush, its prime mover, or for John Montgomery, whose role was large, or for John Armstrong, whose identity with Carlisle and with the early schooling was indelible. But "In memory of the great and important services rendered to his country by his Excellency,

John Dickinson

John Dickinson, Esquire, President of the Supreme Executive Council, and in commemoration of his very liberal donation to the institution, the said college shall be forever hereafter called and known by the name of Dickinson College."

By the charter the number of trustees was limited to forty, though the Board might consist of fewer. As first constituted the Board of Trustees did include forty, twelve of whom were from Cumberland County; and seven of these twelve, including Reverend Dr. Cooper and John Armstrong, were already "trustees" of the old Grammar School.

As noted, the changes which have been admitted to the governance of the College over the years have been slight. But some are interesting: Now, no more than one-third of the Board of Trustees can be filled by clergymen. In 1834, the discipline of the College was entrusted to the faculty; and in May of 1879, the trustee term was set at four years, with, however, the right to immediate re-election. And the head of the College is now to be named President, rather than Principal.[11]

The very first meeting of the Board of Trustees occurred, as ordered, at the home of John Dickinson in Philadelphia on the "third Monday of September," 1783, which was the 15th. Ten members of the Board were present, and all took the oath of allegiance to the Commonwealth of Pennsylvania and to the College. The election of a President of the Board was the next order of business, and John Dickinson, receiving nine of the ten votes (himself voting for James Ewing), was dutifully elected. The second meeting of the Board was held at the home of Dr. Rush, on Second Street, in the city. The third meeting was held at the State House, in which the Continental Congress regularly met. In each of these last two meetings the chief business had to do with raising the money necessary to create the college, and subscription campaigns were accordingly promptly organized. When a lag in the subscriptions occurred, Dr. Rush got off a letter to Montgomery: "I am impatient for your return to Philadelphia to revive the subscriptions. Pray bring General Armstrong along with you. He will assist us among the Arch Street and Hill congregations. . . . I am preparing some thoughts to lay before the board of trustees upon the subject of education proper for a college in a new republican state.[12] I hope you and General Armstrong will not forget to engage a minister to give us a sermon and prayers suitable to the great and solemn sixth of April next [meeting of the Board of Trustees in Carlisle]." In closing, Dr. Rush urged Montgomery to extend his compliments to General Armstrong.[13]

According to Henry Morgan, an historian of the College, James Wilson, the architect of the charter, while much interested, did never attend a meeting of the Board of Trustees. John Dickinson was present for the first three meetings in Philadelphia and for that first Carlisle meeting in 1784, but for no later meeting. Dr. Rush, though very active in securing the first Principal and in raising money and in building, was present for the first three meetings in Philadelphia and the first and third meetings in Carlisle (April 6, 1784 and August 9, 1785), but for no more.[14]

And, indeed, most of the first-appointed trustees were not very active in the early days of the College, supposing the birth accomplished. Even John Montgomery had almost disappeared. But Rush, whose baby it was, was busy, busy. There was much to be done. There was money to raise, ground to be obtained, buildings to build, and a Headmaster (Principal) and faculty to be appointed. He sent letters out in all directions, a great many of them to his chief lieutenant John Montgomery. About a week after the third meeting of the trustees, Rush wrote to his friend: "I cannot wait on the Messrs. Penn without you. They only wait to be asked for a lot of 15 or 20 acres for our college." And then he launched into his favorite metaphor: "I am afraid you are growing careless of the child you have helped to bring into the world."

Montgomery's reply was prompt and in kind: "I was anxious for our child while in embryo, but since it has come forth and has got such a numerous tribe of godfathers, many of whom . . . are fond of it, and although I still love the brat . . . at present I cannot give it much attention." On the matter of ground for the college, Montgomery thought it better to wait until after the Congress elections to approach the Penns.[15]

While soliciting subscriptions, and with some success, Rush turned to the matter of a Principal for the college. As a young medical student at Edinburgh University in Scotland, Rush had come to know a former student at the University, now a practicing

Presbyterian preacher, named Charles Nisbet. At the time Rush was much impressed by the scholarly bearing and the eloquence of the clergyman, and it was natural that his image would now appear in his memory.

Nisbet at this time was forty-eight years old. He enjoyed a well deserved reputation for effective ministry, and for church scholarship.

Rush had been subtly and discreetly testing the name of Dr. Charles Nisbet of Montrose, Scotland, among his correspondents, including members of the Board of Trustees. He found most quite willing at least to consider Nisbet. But he was apprehensive. He was saying his prayers for the April meeting. After all, he was the only member of the Board who had ever met Dr. Nisbet. Nisbet was strictly his own idea. He was praying that (1) the Board would elect Nisbet, and (2) that Dr. Nisbet would accept. Not content with prayers, he had been doing some hard campaigning. In December he responded to Nisbet's last letter, dated August 5: "The Trustees of Dickinson

Charles Nisbet

College are to meet at Carlisle on the 6th of next April [1784] to choose a principal for the College. I have taken great pains to direct their attention and votes to you. From the situation and other advantages of that College, it must soon be the first [!] in America. It is the key [!] to our western world." [16]

But Armstrong (whom he had written on November 7), while not opposed to Nisbet, replied with a most discouraging letter on the whole prospect of the college. Responding two months later, he repeated the concerns he had expressed earlier: "A prolific imagination may too often flatter a wise man into error.... You will admit the reasonableness and expedience of the design to be a matter of distinct consideration and that in the course of human affairs many common as well as more elevated efforts readily miscarry, or at least lose their lustre, by being unseasonably introduced. Those propositions applied to the object in view hang heavy on my mind, lest at this feeble and embarrassed hour our resources and funds should prove greatly inadequate to the real use and reputation of the college." And again, as is always his wont, not to be critical without recommendation, he makes a suggestion. He repeats the advice that he had given in the beginning, urging (1) one or more colleges (or academies) in the west, and (2) that we wait a bit before building the college. Even with the charter granted and a Board of Trustees appointed, and a substantial amount of money subscribed, the General is throwing cold water on the project.

It must have been with some pain that Dr. Rush read his proposal: "That moderate academies with not less than two professors in each be erected in every [one] of our back counties, these tutors to be well appointed and the schools inspected, from whence a certain number could yet repair to the colleges that do exist.... In the exercise of this mode of education for a few years we should be more equal to the expense of the institution ... and better know where to erect a college, for even the local situation is not so obvious as could be wished, unless another is designed in the west."

Henry Morgan, pointing out that "the first fifty years of its history—one could hardly call it life—show no great need for the College," calls Armstrong's letter "prophetic." [17]

It was six weeks before Rush answered the General's letter, and when he did so he continued to make the case for the College, and for the College *now.* He stressed the generous response to his subscription campaign; and, noting for Armstrong that Dr. Nisbet was a real possibility for Principal, he asked him to consider just how much that would mean. Armstrong, who had not yet accepted his appointment to the Board of Trustees, promptly replied. It is a poignant letter, the musings of a man *very* conscious of his advancing years:

I am at once pleased and surprised at the success you speak of . . . for your first meeting. . . . Such a man [as Dr. Nisbet] *would indeed be an acquisition to the church in this country as well as to the proposed institution . . . . But, dear sir, you are exceedingly out at this time of the day in your expectation from my assistance respecting the College; only consider* [to] *what a low ebb my activity is reduced even in the yet necessary affairs of life, to which you may add what experience has too often bought, that when a man becomes old, inactive and out of employ, he is easily forgot and the attention even of his friends becomes cursory and superficial. At the period nothing but a large estate can give influence in such business as you have in view—that I have not. Indeed, Sir, I have an interesting race to run with the world every day (however little I move abroad) not in collecting it in the pecuniary sense nor in counting its smiles in any sense, but to take my leave of it with as much facility, as of late it appears to do of me. I have not, however, obstinately determined to refuse the honor of a seat in your Board, but be that matter finally as it may, you must not, on reflection you will not, call it desertion.*[18]

Armstrong was betwixt and between. Clearly he felt an obligation to the College, which had been progressed so far, but he was feeling his years too, and he was not so impassioned about the project as were others. He held off on accepting his appointment to the Board. Though close friends, like fellow Carlisle citizens Montgomery and Magaw, had taken the required oath, he had not done so as late as April 6, which was the date of the first meeting in Carlisle. Still, when the Carlisle meeting was convened, he was among the fifteen trustees present.

The meeting went off exactly as scheduled. It was quite an occasion. Rush called it "the great and solemn 6th of April." General Armstrong and Colonel John Montgomery, in accord with Dr. Rush's wishes, and as ordered by the Board, had dutifully engaged "one of the ministers of the Gospel [an Episcopalian] who was a member of the Board of Trustees to prepare a sermon and prayer to be delivered" to open the meeting so that "the day may be observed with a religious solemnity suitable to the occasion." [19]

As described by Morgan, "The fifteen thus met went in procession to the Episcopal Church, where a sermon was delivered by the Rev. John Black suitable to the occasion." Afterwards, at about five o'clock in the afternoon, the company assembled at the home of Colonel Montgomery, and here, before the meeting opened, General Armstrong and two or three others who had not before taken the oath, now did so.[20] And General Armstrong's commitment was confirmed by a subscription of $1,000.[21]

Of the fifteen trustees present, nine were from Cumberland County, and none had traveled much of a distance. Besides General Armstrong, three Colonels of the late war were present: Thomas Hartley, who had survived the early disaster at Three Rivers in Quebec and had commanded the Eleventh Pennsylvania in the 1778 anti-Indian campaign of the Wyoming-Tioga region; the attorney Robert Magaw, who had been captured at Fort Washington; and John Montgomery. Also present, besides Reverend Black, who had delivered the sermon, were the ministers the Reverend John King, Pastor of the Presbyterian church at Upper West Conococheague, near present Mercersburg, who from the beginning was a strong supporter of Rush's project; and Reverend Robert Cooper, now an ardent supporter. Coming the farthest were Dr. Rush and John Dickinson, both from Philadelphia.

President John Dickinson, in remarks calculated to inspire the members of the Board, welcomed them all to "the execution of a plan . . . originating from pure intentions . . . and directed by worthy purposes." He proceeded then to thank "the Supreme Governor of the universe" for the happy conclusion to the war of revolution, and then stressed the inestimable value of education and the worth of what they were now doing:

It would little become me in this audience and after the excellent discourse which we have this day heard to employ many words in recommending the advantages of good education. You, Gentlemen, are acquainted with them and estimate them at their high and just value. As you are sensible of their importance to the character of the man, the citizen and Christian, I am sure your hearts will be ardently engaged in generous attempts to diffuse their salutary influences as extensively as possible. Nor can it be reasonably apprehended that your diligence and perseverance will not be properly aided by your fellow citizens.

After continuing in this wise for a little, he concluded, "My best wishes will constantly attend your laudable exertions and I shall be happy at all times and in any capacity to give you every assistance in my power." [22]

It was a very proper speech, and it doubtless pleased Dr. Rush immensely. It is likely, too, that it much moved the sixty-six-year-old John Armstrong.

After resolving to prepare a seal for the College, and naming a committee (Rush and Dickinson), and some discussion of finances, the members turned to the most important matter, the selection of a Principal for the College. The Board, having already elected Mr. James Ross, who had been serving as head of the Grammar School, to the position of Professor of Languages, now agreed unanimously to invite Dr. Charles Nisbet, of Montrose, Scotland, to the office of Principal of Dickinson College. His annual salary was fixed at £250 sterling, and he was to be provided a house for his family.

It was a most productive session, and not the least of its achievements was the bringing into the College family the "Old General" John Armstrong.

After reporting to Montgomery "an agreeable ride" home, Rush declared: "I had the pleasure of finding all our friends highly pleased with what we had done." He said that he himself thinks constantly of the session "with a satisfaction I cannot describe." Still, there are difficulties. Though the charter has been accepted, he is concerned about the Pennsylvania Assembly, which has yet to approve it. So, as before, he urges Montgomery's presence in

Philadelphia the next month, "not only to obtain private subscriptions but to interest Mr. [George] Clymer in behalf of our petition in the Assembly." Clymer, a Philadelphia merchant and a good friend to Rush, was at this time an influential member of the Assembly.[23]

But the big thing now was Dr. Nisbet. First, he must be persuaded to accept the appointment. In this letter to Montgomery, Rush expressed his intention "to convey notice to Dr. Nisbet next Monday [the 19th] in a short letter of his election."[24] But Rush was not the President of the Board of Trustees. That was John Dickinson. And trouble appeared at once. Dickinson, who had written on April 23, 1784, to notify Dr. Nisbet of his appointment, in one of his later letters to Nisbet advised him not to think of coming to America at this time. Dickinson's concern was (1) that the Assembly is likely to repeal the charter for the college, and (2) the lingering illness of Dr. Nisbet. (Out of the same concern for the view of the Assembly, Dr. Rush had written to Montgomery to urge him to urge General Armstrong to "write to all your members.") But when Rush learned of Dickinson's letter to Nisbet, he became enraged. He called the action a "treachery," and to Montgomery, on November 13, he wrote in such great heat that he most unfairly charged Dickinson with selfish motives:

Herewith I enclose a copy of a private letter . . . written without the knowledge of any of the trustees in Philadelphia by our president [Dickinson] to Dr. Nesbit [sic].[25] *It is big with ruin to our hopes and prospects at Carlisle. I am at a loss to account for this most extraordinary act in Mr. Dickinson. Whether he purchased the vote that lately made him president of the state by this secret act of treachery to the last hopes of the republicans, or whether he wished to annihilate our College and thereby to prevent any future drafts being made upon him for its support [!], or whether he is under Quaker influence as to the future power of the Presbyterians, I know not, but certain it is, he is become the most formidable enemy to our College that ever we have yet known. [!]*

Rush informed Montgomery that he had taken two prompt actions. First, he has consulted with the trustees who are in the neighborhood of Philadelphia and has got them to agree to a private letter to Dr. Nisbet to "*contradict*" the expression of the Dickinson letter. Second, he has arranged for the Board to "pass a vote of disapprobation of the said letter" and to declare to Dr. Nisbet that the charter is secure, and that support for the college is there. Third, as he reports, he has already discussed the matter with Dickinson and has insisted to him that in his letter he has disgraced us in Scotland and damaged his reputation with the trustees—all of this, he admits, to no avail. Dickinson was not about to step back from his letter. In some disgust Rush reported to Montgomery that the two had parted with Dickinson saying that "It becomes us to act with prudence." Rush noted that he retorted "in a warm tone" that "Prudence when *honor* was concerned was a rascally virtue."

Finally, Dr. Rush urged Montgomery to write directly to Dr. Nisbet. And he suggested that Montgomery request General Armstrong and Reverend Cooper to do the same.[26]

Nisbet, Rush knew, had been concerned about his health, and he had been raising questions about the salary. He did not need the kind of discouragement Dickinson was providing. His own letter of Nov. 19 to Nisbet bubbled over with enthusiasm for the appointment, and was most persuasive:

> *I beg leave to congratulate you upon this event! The honor intended you by this appointment will be more highly esteemed when I add that your election was unanimous. No name was set in competition with yours. Indeed, sir, so highly do all the trustees conceive of your character and qualifications, that all their hopes of success in establishing their College now seem to depend upon your accepting of their appointment. And if to live with people of principles congenial to your own in religion and government—is to fill a station the highest and most respectable that a minister of the Presbyterian Church can arrive to in any part of the world—if to form the opinions, morals, and manners of the rising generation of half a state—and above all, to diffuse the blessings of science and religion over a tract of country many hundred miles in extent . . . are allowed to have their proper weight with you, I am sure you will not, you cannot, hesitate in complying with our invitation.*

In this very long, exuberant letter he proceeded next to an account of the Board of Trustees, all "men of learning" and all "Calvinists." Then he described the community: "The town of Carlisle lies 120 miles to the westward of Philadelphia and about 18 miles from the river Susquehannah. It consists of about 300 houses, most of which are built of limestone. It lies in a healthy and fertile plain bounded on the north and south by two high mountains. Within a mile of the town there winds a small river called by the name of Canadoginet [Conodoguinet], which after distributing fertility and wealth by watering meadows and turning a number of mills, empties itself into the Susquehannah."

He described the people of the community, noted the prospect of an immediate increase in salary, and prescribed the duties of the Principal. Remarking the College as yet a "new-born infant," he then in his excitement got carried away:

To you, sir [the College] *lifts up its feeble hands. To you, to you alone (under God), it looks for support and nourishment. Your name is now in everybody's mouth. The Germans attempt to pronounce it in broken English. The natives of Ireland and the descendants of Irishmen have carried it to the western counties. The Juniata and Ohio rivers have borne it on their streams through every township of the state that lies beyond Carlisle. Our saints pray for you as the future apostle of the Church in this part of the world. Our patriots long to thank you for defending the cause of America at a time when and in a place where she had few friends.*

It seems unlikely that anyone, regardless of circumstances, could decline the appointment that was being that way presented.

After some special instructions on furniture, etc., he informed Dr. Nisbet that "We shall look for you with great impatience," and "I have only to offer my house as your house upon your arrival in our city. My dear Mrs. Rush joins in her compliments to Mrs. Nesbit. She will do her utmost to make her happy in Pennsylvania." He enclosed a general account of the charter, and concluded, "To the direction of heaven I commend you. May the Governor of the World and the Great Shepherd of the Church send you in safety to the arms and prayers of thousands!"[27]

But not to worry. The hard work in the end paid off. Dr. Nisbet was persuaded. He reported that he was booking passage for the spring, and he declared that he was looking forward with great excitement to the new position.

And indeed, having sailed from Greenwich April 23, he arrived in Philadelphia on June 9, 1785. After five days of "getting to know him," Dr. Rush was much impressed. On June 14 he dispatched a letter to John Montgomery (or, in his absence, John Armstrong) to commend Nisbet to the Board. In praise for the new Principal, it allows no bounds:

Dr. Nisbet expects to see you on Saturday or Monday next. He is impatient to see the place where he is to end his days. I cannot tell you how many friends he has made in our city. His preaching is sensible and elegant, and his conversation and agreeable manners charm everybody. In a letter which I received by him from one of my correspondents in Scotland, he has these words, "I follow Dr. Nisbet with solicitude across the ocean. Such another man you will not soon be able to select and carry from us. He is a moving library. He is a Greek and Latin scholar to whom we have few to compare. He is still more distinguished for his command of modern languages. His reading is extensive, his memory vigorous, his discernment quick, his judgment sound. In theology he is a sound Calvinist, in politics a thorough whig, in heart —an American.

With this estimate of the man Rush is not about to quarrel: "This I believe is the Doctor's true character. I am so chained down to his company that I regret leaving him for a moment to attend my business. Indeed, my friend, in the arrival of Dr. Nisbet I conceive a new sun is risen upon Pennsylvania. His whole soul is set upon doing good, and his capacity for it has seldom I believe been exceeded by any man's in this country." [28]

With his family and some friends Dr. Nisbet reached Boiling Springs on Independence Day. Here he was met by a large number of the trustees, including John Armstrong and John Montgomery, and a great many well-wishing townspeople. In a most sincere expression of welcome, the reception party then promptly escorted Nisbet and his entourage the six miles to Carlisle. They arrived in the evening to find their excitement in perfect accord with the spirit of celebration that on this Fourth-of-July evening was lighting up the whole community.

On the very next day Dr. Nisbet took the oath of office which made him the first Principal of Dickinson College. But all of this gaiety and excitement was in sharp contrast with the later experience of Nisbet and his family. A later president of the College, Dr. William W. Edel, has described the shock they suffered. It was with dismay that Dr. Nisbet first looked upon his "college." The only building was that which had housed the Grammar School for the past twelve years. The tiny structure, composed of weathered brick, was a two-story house thirty by twenty-three feet in size, "fronting on a narrow and dirty alley" quaintly named Liberty. Classes were conducted in the one small room that, most uncomfortably, might accommodate the school's population, thirty to forty "unruly boys." The faculty was embodied in the school's principal, Professor James Ross, "of whom it was said that he taught nothing but Latin and Greek, 'but taught them better, perhaps, than they have ever been taught on this continent.'"

The village itself, Dr. Edel reminds, "was a frontier trading post and militia headquarters, a staging point on the Great Road to Fort Bedford and Pittsburgh over which passed the never-ending stream of pioneers and settlers moving out to the winning of the Ohio country and the West." [29]

One can imagine with what horror the distinguished scholar and minister looked upon his new world. But one does not have to imagine. Dr. Nisbet was quick to advise Dr. Rush of his impression: "The low state of your funds and the present condition of this country fill me with alarm. . . . I am persuaded that nothing can be done with the boys here while they occupy the present school." [30]

Nisbet and his family for a time took up residence in one of the buildings at the "Public Works," as the military storehouses and shops east of town were sometimes called. Rush had hoped to move the college to quarters here, but the trustees were never able to purchase the property.

By the end of the next year, however, the college was to double its size. This was accomplished through the addition of a section built of native stone; and in advertisements the trustees could boast that the college, now composed of three spacious classrooms, a library, and a science laboratory, was located in "a pleasant part of town." [31] For the succeeding nineteen years this building was Dickinson College.

But because of his Scots temperament and the static, crowded and unpleasant conditions, and serious illness (perhaps malaria) in his family, Dr. Charles Nisbet, Principal of the College, grew steadily more impatient and more unhappy through the late summer of 1785. One of his letters to Dr. Rush was headed "From the Tomb of Dickinson College."

In a letter to John Montgomery, dated June 8, 1785, Rush had written: "After congratulating you from the bottom of my heart upon Dr. Nisbet's safe arrival I beg leave to suggest a few things to you that are calculated to make an agreeable impression upon the Doctor and therefore will have an happy effect upon his future opinions and conduct." [32] After attending the meeting of the Board of Trustees in Carlisle, August 9, and upon his return to Philadelphia, he advised Montgomery that "We were happy in being able to contradict the terrible reports of Dr. Nisbet's illness and the sickliness of Carlisle." And then he expressed a physician's concern for that section of town called "The Works," where, on the east side of Carlisle, were located the military storehouses and shops. This included the building which the Nisbets had been provided for their lodging. Said the good doctor: "It will be your own faults if you do not banish fevers forever from the village. The Works I fear will not be made healthy at all times, unless you can prevail upon Major Wilson to sell his mill dam, and afterwards destroy it. Pray lose no time in draining the meadow near the town." [33]

This meeting of the Board of Trustees, August 9, 1785, was given over to organization. John Armstrong served as President pro tem. Nisbet, by charter, was not entitled to a place on the Board, and apparently the Board felt no need to consult him on any matter whatsoever, which is startling, as curriculum was the chief occupation of the members at this meeting. But even this slight was as nothing to that delivered by Dr. Rush. While in Carlisle for this meeting of the Board (which would be the last he would attend), Dr. Rush, who was accompanied by his wife, was hosted by the Montgomerys. In all of the time they were in town, they never visited the Nisbets. Apparently Rush was becoming weary of Dr. Nisbet's complaints about his health, and had become fearful of the damage that might be done the College. In a letter to Montgomery later that month, in which Rush is complaining about Nisbet's constant homesickness and unhappiness with Carlisle, is heard the first intimation of a distance growing between them.[34]

But for the most part, Rush was in good spirits through this summer. On August 23, he reported to Montgomery from Philadelphia that "All our friends *here* highly approve of our building a college in the town of Carlisle." Moreover, he advised that he was sending an abstract of the plan for education, which could be published in the Carlisle papers.[35]

But all was about to change, abruptly and dramatically. Dr. Nisbet had been in the harness for but a little time only when, at some short time after the conclusion of the Board meeting in August he announced his decision to give up his office and return to Scotland. All efforts to dissuade him, including those by Dr. Rush, had failed.

The resignation, which it was expected the Board would accept in its October meeting, produced in Dr. Rush the most severe disappointment, and inspired a letter of despair to John Montgomery. On September 11 of 1785 he wrote: "All is in vain. After using every possible argument with Dr. Nisbet that friendship, religion, or honor could dictate to prevent his returning to Scotland, I find by his letter of the 4th of this month that he is *inflexible*. He complains of the *heat* and *sickliness* of our climate. But from the extract of the letter I sent to General Armstrong and from the good humor and patience with which he bore the hottest of our weather in Philadelphia, I have reason to think he is actuated by *other* reasons." What these other reasons are he can infer, and in doing so he registers, when his friendship and esteem for the man are recalled, a most surprising disgust: Apparently Rush is appreciating that this failure of the man he so strongly recommended will be laid at his door:

Dismal stories are propagated through our city against us from his family by the people who come from Carlisle. In one of his letters to me he talks much of our "scanty funds," and from good authority I hear of complaints which seem to indicate that his family think him disgraced and ruined by so small a charge. They abuse, I hear, everyone that had any hand in bringing him to America, especially me. In short, my friend, we have made an unfortunate speculation in our principal. With all his endowments for his place, he is a mere machine in the hands of his wife and children. This I am told was the case at Montrose, and to such a degree that many people predicted that they would destroy his usefulness in this country. Poor man! I pity him . . . . It remains now only to convey him back to his native country. He prays to have his passage paid home. This will be hard upon us, but I believe we shall in the end be the richer for it.

He was pleased that John Dickinson shared his feeling, recalling for Montgomery that Dickinson, with an implied reference to Dr. Nisbet's always unhappy wife, had said, "No college can be well governed or flourish under the direction of a man who cannot govern his own family." And he was pleased also to find President Dickinson quite friendly in this time of crisis.

He turned next in his letter to the need to find a replacement, and he mentioned two strong possibilities, Dr. Robert Davidson, who in this last April had been called to Carlisle to serve the Presbyterian Church,[36] and Jonathan Edwards, Jr., son of the President of the College of New Jersey, and a minister of a church in New Haven, Connecticut. And he left Montgomery with this: "The sooner the Doctor sails after October, the better. Keep up your spirits. . . . I still maintain that all *will end well.*" And one last note of bitterness: "Do you recollect the harsh and cruel note I received from Dr. Nisbet at Carlisle? O! My friend, it is nothing compared with a letter I received from his son Tom [Nisbet's eldest son, with the reputation of a no-good drunkard] in answer to a most friendly letter I sent to him to try to reconcile him to Carlisle and our country."[37]

At the October meeting of the Board, Dr. Nisbet's resignation was indeed accepted, but for the very strange reason that he would not sail on any ship but the one on which he had arrived, his departure was put off until spring.

In a later letter to Montgomery, having heard enough of Nisbet's complaints about salary and his laments over his illness, Rush unleashed his bitterness: "Dr. Nisbet had no object in coming to America, and, I believe, has no object in staying but salary. He will make no sacrifices to atone for the injury he has done our College." He proceeds, then, at an even greater heat: "In his first letter I ever got from him after he went to Carlisle . . . before his sickness he complained very indelicately of the low state of our funds . . . . I blush for his littleness and ingratitude in this business and wish only to forget and forgive it . . . . I have advised him to be content with the £300 the first year . . . for this advice he has branded me in the most indecent manner in his letters to his skunk friends in Philadelphia. I have many more things to say . . . but I forbear." [38]

But the Board of Trustees had not been moving very fast to secure a new Principal. Consequently, in the reprieve that his superstition about ships provided him, Dr. Nisbet found his health returned, and by the end of winter he was back teaching classes, and hopeful of re-election!

On February 2, 1786, John Armstrong, who is at this time Acting President of the Board, received a letter from Dr. Nisbet, who was proposing a return to the College:

Sir: Having now, by the Divine Goodness, recovered my health, and retaining the same affection to this country which led me to abandon my native soil, I beg the favor that you would communicate to the trustees this unexpected change in my situation. Could I have hoped for such a thing in October last, this trouble would have been unnecessary, but at that time having nothing but death or incompetency in view, and wishing only to convey my family back to their relations, I was advised to resign my charge, that the trustees might proceed to the election of a successor. As this has not been done, my present situation, their own feelings, and the earnestness with which they invited me formerly, will suggest to them what is fit to be done on this occasion. Begging that you would take the earliest opportunity of communicating this to the trustees . . . . [39]

In his official letter to the trustees, dated Feb. 10, Armstrong dutifully did as requested, leaving no doubt about how *he* feels about Dr. Nisbet's return. He informs the trustees that Dr. Nisbet has recovered his health. "He is now willing to remain with us, and very desirous of pursuing the great object which led him from his native country, provided he is reinstated in his former charge, but apprehends there is an obvious hardship in waiting the long interval until the meeting of our Board, and even then a possibility that he *may not be reelected.*"

Then he reports the action he has so far taken:

In order to remove this difficulty as far as in our power, seven or eight of the trustees being occasionally in town, we had a conference on the subject, which issued in the desire of those present, That the Dr. should commit his wishes to writing, and a request that I should communicate them (as now enclosed) to as many of the Trustees as I possibly could; in order to procure their sentiments as individuals, either for or against his reelection, that the dr. may have some ground of confidence, or line of direction to his conduct, until the meeting of the Board in May next. It is also proper to inform you gentlemen that in the conference mentioned above, there was not a dissenting voice to the reappointment of Dr. Nisbet, but on the contrary, very explicit declarations in his favour, alleging that no principle either of honor, or good policy, could justify a refusal of it. Two of the number then present, it's true, hesitated at giving the former salary, being in their opinion more than our funds would allow, others opposed that idea, referring the matter as it must be to the decision of the Board. On this occasion, Gentlemen, your intimations will be expected, as early as may be convenient.

In a postscript, Armstrong noted: "Dr. Nisbet now frequently visits the College, much to the satisfaction of the professors, students and trustees at this place, and I may warrantably add, every other person of discernment, who have gained any acquaintance of the Doctor, since his recovery." [40]

The conclusion to all this was the reelection of Dr. Nisbet, though with a reduction in salary. Both John Dickinson and Dr. Rush were violently opposed to his reappointment, and so too were the trustees under the influence of Rush, including John Montgomery, who favored Dr. Davidson for the post. But when the Board met on Tuesday, the ninth of May, 1786, the nine members present (Dickinson and Rush are not present) voted unanimously to re-elect Dr. Charles Nisbet Principal of Dickinson College. John Dickinson, President of Pennsylvania, was notified by a committee, the Board having had a letter from him, that "We feel a peculiar satisfaction in observing the perfect [!] correspondence of your sentiment with a measure unanimously adopted by us, that is, the election of Dr. Nisbet to the office of Principal of Dickinson College." [41]

Armstrong had been serving as a mediator between Rush and Nisbet. During the breach he addressed a letter to Rush, though he suffered so from arthritis that he had to employ two fingers of his left hand to steady his right hand and the pen. "With respect to what you apprehend of Dr. Nisbets attempting to injure your Character," Armstrong wrote, "I always thought that difference as illy judged & unnatural as it has but too long been unhappy both to yourselves & yr. Friends . . . I have probably said as much to each of you as your tempers would bear & perhaps thereby for a time have vexed you both . . . which cannot possibly contribute to any good thing, however I wish I could finally convince you that you must labour under some mistake or unfair information in this matter, for were such an attempt practised by the Dr surely the people where he lives & with whom he is chiefly conversant must frequently hear it, which I firmly believe they do not, and am certain that I do not," and so on. It is a very long letter, and on this one subject only.

Of course Dr. Rush came to accept the appointment, though not without amazement. In letters to Montgomery, always his closest Carlisle friend and confidant, he indulged in the familiar, somewhat unkind sarcasm. In June of this year, 1786, lumping together the people for whom he had little affection, he queried Montgomery, "How is it my friend? Is it peculiar to Scotchmen and heads of colleges to be sordid and arbitrary? How melancholy the consideration that Smith and Ewing, Witherspoon[42] and Nisbet should all be so much alike in these *two* qualities!"

Apparently at this stage of the breach between Nisbet and Rush, though there is little hope for a real and lasting reconciliation, Armstrong and Henry Hill (also a good friend to Rush and a charter trustee)[43] are still playing the role of mediator. Rush's letter continues: "In consequence of Dr. Nisbet having applied to Mr. Hill to make up the dispute between us, I have written him a friendly letter in which I have forgiven him all the *unkind*, *unjust*, and *cruel* charges he has brought against me. General Armstrong put one of my private letters to him [Armstrong] into his hands. This (though not a friendly act in the General) has produced a reconciliation between us; the letter contained some harsh epithets of the Doctor. You see from this fact that he can be governed only by treating him as he treats other people. This is the nature of most Scotchmen." [!]

At least Rush and Nisbet are now on speaking (or writing) terms. This letter continues: "I have advised the Doctor to be more cautious in complaining of the trustees and of the "sickly" and "dirty" town of Carlisle in his letters to his friends. "It is a sorry bird that betrays its own nest. He will soon ruin our College, as he has done his own reputation, by such mad and impudent conduct."

Perhaps it is just madness after all, Rush continues. Let us charge it up, he says, to a wayward mind: "His letters which are printed in the English papers give a dismal account of this country. They neither show his gratitude nor good sense, I have endeavored to overset them by informing all his friends in Scotland that he was out of his senses when he wrote them." [44]

Toward the end of July he observes to Montgomery, that he is "glad that Dr. N. Gives so much satisfaction and is so popular among you . . . . His wit gives him pain while it is confined, and everybody pain when it is discharged." And then, while noting that Nisbet's complaints are regularly aired in the Irish newspapers, he declares "If he should live an 100 years, he can never atone for the mischief he has done our College." [45]

Neither Rush nor Nisbet made a very real effort to heal the breach that had separated them. They had a common ground as both were ardent Presbyterians, but both were easily injured and needed to be appreciated more than they sometimes were. And they may have even enjoyed a little the skirmish, exercising their wit and their sarcasm in the exchanges. On the relationship of the two, the editor of Dr. Rush's letters observed that it "would make an entertaining comedy."[46]

In any case, it is a sad commentary on the birth of the college that these two major figures, though they had eighteen years in which to manage it, never ever reached a reconciliation or any kind of cordial relationship. How terribly far the early friendship had deteriorated is painfully plain from the bitterness that appears in Rush's letter to Montgomery, August, 1786. As Rush feels slighted in the proceedings of the trustees, the letter includes some digs at John Armstrong too. And, indeed, since Rush threatens resignation from the Board and disassociation with the College, the letter might more properly have gone to Armstrong, Acting President of the Board. Of Principal Nisbet he writes,

He will know the value of my friendship better when he feels the deficiency of his salary occasioned by his own folly, for as I had no vote in his second appointment, I shall not think myself bound to concur in supporting him. I consider myself as neglected and insulted by all the trustees in Carlisle who have tamely witnessed his abuse and calumnies circulated against me. I have not deserved this from your hands. But I have a remedy in store. If you do not oblige him to contradict in all his letters the falsehoods he has told of me before the next meeting of the Board, I shall certainly send in my resignation, and dissolve all connection with the College forever. You may show this declaration and the whole of this letter to all the Trustees in Carlisle. I have bore and forborne long. But all in vain—his heart cannot be softened by favors, nor subdued by Friendship. To prevent a repetition of his insolence to me (for in his last letter he calls me indirectly a rogue and a traitor), you may inform him that I will receive no letter from him now which you or some of the trustees do not first see. If it is sent to me without this formality, I shall send it back unopened.[47]

But time takes a toll of bitterness. Dr. Rush was not about to abandon the child he had brought into the world. Dr. Nisbet had been back at the head of the College for about six months since his reappointment when on October 21 (1786), Rush directed a letter to the Board of Trustees. It was sent to the care of John Montgomery. Noting that he would not be able to make the November meeting of the Board, he took "the liberty of addressing a few lines" to the Board on the situation of the College. First he urged the Board not to consider a site for the college in the region of the Works (east end of town). "A more convenient and elegant building may be erected a few years hence at the west end of the town, and for one half the money that it would take only to repair the public works." He cited the modest beginnings of the College of New Jersey and the University of Edinburgh and the churches of the Emperor Constantine. "If we have golden professors," he declared, "the frugal size and humble appearance of our College will not prevent its growth or injure its reputation for solid and useful learning."

Next he expresses concern for the discipline of the boys in attendance, having heard tales of "irregular conduct," entered into with impunity. He regrets also that subscription monies have not come up to expectation, and he laments the damage done to income by Nisbet's resignation. He has had a change of heart, however, on the resignation and return of the Principal, now indicating that he will be willing to help out: "I neither consented to Doctor Nesbit's [sic] reappointment nor his present salary (for I then foresaw and predicted our present inability to pay it), yet I will not be deficient in bearing my full proportion of the deficient sum."

Although not able to make meetings of the Board, Dr. Rush continued most attentive to the needs and the welfare of the young college. At the close of this instructive letter, he makes a final recommendation. He is thinking of a kind of advertisement. He requests of the trustees that they publish "in all the newspapers in Pennsylvania, Maryland, and Virginia an account of the present state of the College. . . . In this account I wish to see included the names of our professors, the branches of literature taught by each of them, the amount of our library, a general list of our philosophical apparatus, and a particular account of the price of board and the nature of the accommodations in the village of Carlisle." He was hoping that a notice of this kind might "serve to contradict the calumnies of our enemies . . . and become the means of alluring pupils to the College."

Such a description of the College as Rush was requesting did indeed appear on February 7, 1787, in the Philadelphia newspapers.[48] Though the notice is dated December 19, and is signed by John Armstrong, as President of the Board, *pro tem*, it is not known whether the General is the composer. Rush apparently does not think so, as he refers to the article as "signed" by Armstrong.[49] The good doctor was, however, much pleased by the appearance of the advertisement. If not ecstatic, he was at least very happy. He got off a letter to Montgomery: "The publication signed by General Armstrong has given great pleasure in our city. The account of the library astonished everybody. If Dr. N. will only be prudent and silent upon the subject of our present difficulties, we shall soon fill our College with pupils from every part of the state. The German College [Franklin and Marshall, in Lancaster, strongly supported by Franklin] by exciting emulation and increasing a taste for literature, will serve only to increase the number of our pupils, just as the cultivation of wheat on the Juniata has increased the price of it in Lancaster County." [50]

In the account of the library, which so pleased Rush, Armstrong, or whoever the writer was, noted that "the library already consists of two thousand seven hundred and six volumes, in the Hebrew, Latin, English, French, German, Low Dutch and Italian languages, the donations of gentlemen in England, Scotland, and Philadelphia." [51] Composing by far the largest part are the nearly 2000 books donated by John Dickinson in 1784.

Through the first decade of the charter, the most absorbing business of the Board of Trustees was the building program. In the early going the ever-pessimistic Armstrong had declared that "there never will be any Building erected at Carlisle, these seven years to come." This was his observation in a letter to Rush dated December 13, 1784. Turned out to be prophetic. Armstrong himself would never see it. It was not until 1792 that the Board requested architect plans; and it was not until the acquisition from the Penns of a seven-acre lot near the home of Dr. Nisbet on High Street in the west end of town that the Board authorized ground breaking. It was now the early spring of 1799, the fourteenth year of Dr. Nisbet's presidency. It had been some time in coming, but, as the College librarian Charles Sellers later described it, "New

College, built of Stone, rose slowly above the grass and bushes and outcroppings of the gray native stone." [52]

As President Edel has noted, it was even before the deed to the property had been finalized that the new campus was established. On June 20 of the year in which ground had been broken (1799), "the trustees [John Armstrong no longer among them], professors and students of the College went in procession from the old building to the spot on the present John Dickinson campus where West College now stands, and there the cornerstone of the new edifice of Dickinson College was laid." [53] The honor of laying the first stone might have gone to the "Old General" John Armstrong, had he been living; and it certainly could have gone to Dr. Benjamin Rush. But of course it was altogether fitting and proper that the trowel be handed to that earnest and enthusiastic founding father John Montgomery, at this time seventy-eight years old, and very, very proud.

This new building was destroyed by fire, even before its completion, on the snowy night of Feb. 2, 1803. Its replacement, the most beautiful West College ("Old West"), appeared in 1804, but only after the untimely death of the College's sixty-seven-year-old first Principal.

Throughout its early history the College had operated under the aegis of the Presbyterian Church, and had been governed by a Board of Trustees almost exclusively Presbyterian. Armstrong might have been sorely disappointed to see it pass, in 1833, into the control of the Methodist Church.[54]

John Armstrong served on the Board of Trustees for almost eleven years and as President or President pro tempore for nine years. The Board's first President, John Dickinson, served fifteen years, but in name only. John Montgomery served until his death in 1808. Armstrong's good friend Dr. William Irvine was an active member of the Board from 1788 until his death in July of 1804. Armstrong's son Dr. James Armstrong served for thirty years (!) and was President of the Board for sixteen. He enrolled his own son, John Wilkins Armstrong, at the College. Dr. Nisbet presided over the College for nineteen years, until his death on January 18, 1804. Dr. Nisbet is buried, with "the Old General," in the Old Graveyard of Carlisle.

Today the College enjoys a much deserved reputation as one of the finest small liberal arts colleges of the nation. Among its many most distinguished alumni are the fifteenth President of the United States, James Buchanan, Class of 1809, and Roger Taney, Class of 1795, Chief Justice of the Supreme Court, 1836-64, both of whom completed their studies at age eighteen. Certainly John Armstrong would be very proud of his institution, for its lovely campus, which features buildings of the beautiful gray-white native limestone, for its consistently able and dedicated faculty, and for a select co-ed (What would he think of that?) student body that began admitting women in 1884,[55] and peaked to an enrollment of some 2300 in the early years of the twenty-first century.

XXVII

Last Days

The year is 1794. The Old General will celebrate his seventy-seventh birthday on October 13. He has not sung and danced his way through his years. Indeed, he has been but rarely known to laugh, or even to smile. He has been consistently amiable, but not jovial. He has not been what one could call dour, but, rather, sober, ever conscious of responsibility, of *duty*. He has seemed weighed down. In fact, especially as nothing is known of his early life, it is difficult to think of John Armstrong as ever a young and careless man. And indeed he was older than all of his business and military associates (except the ageless Ben Franklin), twelve years older than John Penn, twenty-eight years older than Dr. Rush, twenty-four years older than Dr. Irvine, fifteen years older than Washington.

Though regularly in a position of authority, John Armstrong preferred to have orders rather than to give them. And he did not operate out of a complex personality. His character was an open book. Of course he was, clearly, a sensitive man, and a proud man. Like his friend Dr. Benjamin Rush, he could become testy if he sensed an injury to his reputation. He was normally stubborn and opinionated, but he could be persuaded by logic, and he was ever genuine in his relationships. He was a man whose friendship was precious. His handclasp was firm.

Most impressive, to everyone, was his piety. He was, first of all, a man of God, a soldier for Christ. Although by some he has been judged a fanatic, that is too strong a term. He was devoted to his God, only more impassioned perhaps than many of his brethren, typical of the Church elder. His faith had been tested many times. It was tested again, in this last year of his life. He did not need any more grief, but it came to him in April with the news of the death of his first grandchild, four-year-old John, son of his son James. On April 12th, from Carlisle, having read the pain-filled letter that Jamey had addressed to his mother, he composed a very long heartfelt and consolatory letter in which he urged his son not to turn from God.[1]

General Armstrong has marched his way through this life. He has marched a long way. He has come from the Old World to the New. He has helped to lay out the town of Carlisle, and has done the surveying for hundreds of the properties lived on by the settlers of the counties of Lancaster and York and Cumberland. He has built roads and forts. He headed up the Kittanning expedition in 1756. In command of all the Pennsylvania forces, he served the Forbes Expedition through the year 1758. He defended the Pennsylvania frontier from the marauding Indians for two decades. He served Cumberland County as magistrate and judge, and served the province as Deputy Surveyor. He was an influential patriot in the rebellion against King George, and most important to the Continental Army as a Brigadier General, and to the Pennsylvania militia as a Major General, commanding troops at the battles of Charleston, the Brandywine, Germantown, and Whitemarsh. He prepared the defenses of the Delaware River. For two terms he represented Pennsylvania in the Continental Congress. He built a Presbyterian church in Carlisle and he helped to found a college for the community.

He has been constantly on horseback, among the frontier plantations, among the frontier forts, among the communities of York, Lancaster, Shippensburg, and Carlisle, and over the 120 miles from Carlisle to Philadelphia.

He has enjoyed the growth of the thirteen colonies to an

independent and sovereign nation of fifteen states or commonwealths. He has seen the installation of a Constitution for the country and the election of his close friend to the Presidency. Whatever the final reckoning, it must be allowed that the life of John Armstrong was not a private one, and not an idle one. It was energetic, generous, and productive. Only for the last five years could it be said that "The General is at home in Carlisle." It has been, indeed, a life of service.

He has seen his two sons rise to positions of prominence and influence. He has seen a lot, he has done a lot, he has *endured* a lot. His mind remains sharp and clear. But he is tired.

It is time for the Old General to say goodbye to this life, to his dear and devoted wife Rebeckah, to sons James and John, Jr., to four grandchildren, to the citizens of Carlisle, his home for half a century.

It is time to compose his will.

General John Armstrong was a man of property, but by the time of his last years he did not hold title to a great deal of land. Over the two decades 1754-74 he was steadily acquiring parcels, but he was a piker compared to his friend Washington. If he did take advantage of his position, as some insist, he did not come to possess nearly the property he might have. He was involved in a number of transactions, but acquired in his time only 3,165 acres, and at the time of his death he held title to only a small house and two lots in Carlisle, the modest fifty-acre farm in Middleton Township which he had acquired September 13, 1766, and the 400 acres of Kittanning land he had been awarded by the Penns.[2]

As it was composed in July of 1794 the will was a fairly simple document. To Rebeccah Turner of Chester County, who was his younger sister and married to James Turner,[3] he bequeathed fifty pounds. And to his brother Andrew of the Kingdom of Ireland he recommended fifty pounds. His property, after debts were paid, he let to his wife Rebeckah and to his two sons James and John to "devise equally & share & share alike," with the proviso that "my

House & Lots . . . my furniture & the said outlots & Plantation in Middleton [very close to Carlisle, at present-day Boiling Springs] . . . are to be enjoyed by my said wife Rebeccah during her natural life time unless she gives her full approbation to the sale thereof." He named as an Executor, besides his wife and two sons, Thomas Duncan of Carlisle, and declared that "my friend William Lyon will be ever ready to aid them in the Execution of the trust reposed in them by his advice Counsel & assistance." [4]

But wait. Some drama would yet attach to these last hours of the Old General's very full life. It was provided by the Whiskey Rebellion. The insurrection inspired by the controversial excise tax levied by Secretary of the Treasury Alexander Hamilton on the production of whiskey, brewing now for five years and fermenting into violence, most notably in the region of Pittsburgh, had finally called forth the militia forces of four states. And President Washington himself had assumed personal command of the soldiers being assembled at Carlisle and at Bedford.

Now here on October 4 of 1794 was John Armstrong's close friend for forty years, his Commander-in-Chief and his President, in Carlisle, his first notable appearance ever in the community that had launched the Forbes Expedition, that for eight long years had fueled the Revolution, that was home to many of the President's war-time officers and government associates.[5] He had come by carriage from Philadelphia by way of Harrisburg and across the broad Susquehanna (holding the reins himself) to see to the organization of the militia forces, and here would be reviewing the troops of Pennsylvania and New Jersey. He would be staying on in Carlisle for a whole week.

How much did General Armstrong see of President Washington during this time? As Washington makes no mention of Armstrong in his diary entries for these days, we can only suppose what their meetings might have been.

The President recalled for his journal that "On the Cumberland side [of the Susquehanna] I found a detachment of the

Philadelphia light horse ready to receive, and escort me to Carlisle 17 miles.... Two miles short of it, I met the Governors of Pennsylvania and New Jersey [Thomas Mifflin and Richard Howell (a very close friend to Washington)] with all the Cavalry that had rendezvouzed at that place drawn up—passed them—and the Infantry of Pennsylvania before I alighted at my quarters." [6] But it was a strange reception that was accorded the General upon his arrival in the village at eleven o'clock that Saturday morning of October 4.

    It must be noted that Carlisle, especially during the month just passed (and particularly on the dates of August 28, and September 8-9) had been the scene of riots and "unseemly behavior." Indeed, it seemed that the "Whiskey Boys" had pretty much seized control of the village. Certainly the "Friends of Liberty" were extremely active in the community. During the night of September 8 there had been erected right in the center of the community, in the public square, a Liberty Pole, adorned with the inscription "Liberty and No Excise, O Whiskey." When offended citizens the next morning promptly destroyed the pole, the rioters reassembled and erected (on September 11) an even greater proclamation of their feeling. And, according to one student of the rebellion, "Peaceable citizens who ventured out were stopped and forced to contribute money for the purchase of whiskey for the crowd." [7]

    Besides the liberty poles, the unrest in Carlisle took the form of protest parades and the burning of effigies, all accompanied by the most nerve-racking catcalls and expressions of defiance, and all of course quite audible to the Armstrongs in their home close to the Square. On top of all of this, according to reliable accounts, from the time Washington's militia began to move, the citizens of the various communities through which the soldiers passed had to witness unnecessarily rude and offensive behavior. Soldiers were described as "swaggering" and "bloodthirsty." Indeed two most unfortunate accidental deaths occurred, one because of a private and one owing to an officer, and both much regretted by Washington. But actual wilful violence was not occurring in Carlisle, except that Colonel Ephraim Blaine, who would be hosting General Washington and was known as a Federalist, was shot at on the night of September 9 while escorting his sister Ellen (Mrs. Samuel Lyon) to her home.[8] And as Carlisle was being asked to accommodate for a week thousands of militiamen, "incidents" were inevitable.

So that, although Washington was received with great pomp and ceremony by the military (the New Jersey and Philadelphia cavalry "headed by a dozen generals," the troops drawn up to honor him, lots of salutes and ringing of bells), it was a much subdued and silently impolite citizenry which lined the streets.[9] Of course the Armstrongs and the Blaines and many others devoted to the government would be members of the crowd, and certainly they would be most respectful and gracious to the President.

But Washington did not reside with the Armstrongs. He and his party had their lodging and headquarters, with "meals and hostelry services," at the home of Ephraim Blaine,[10] formerly the Commissary General in the Continental Army, who had done much to save the Valley Forge soldiers, and who was a very warm and close friend to the President. Colonel Blaine owned two houses in Carlisle, one just constructed that very year at 4 North Hanover Street, and both near the central square.[11] Blaine at this time was a much younger man than Armstrong, at fifty-three younger even than Washington.

By all accounts Washington had nothing to complain about in his hosting. With his staff, which included Alexander Hamilton (acting Secretary of War), he was provided lodging in one of the Blaine homes, and all were received for their meals in the other house. The Colonel's wife at this time was quite ill, in fact an invalid, and thus unable to do much. Her place as hostess was taken by the wife of Blaine's son Robert, who came each day from her home at Cove Farm. "The Colonel's two sons, Robert and James, took charge of the horses and all the outside arrangements." Indeed, nothing was left undone "for Washington's comfort and pleasure."[12]

Almost certainly the Armstrongs were members of the Sunday church service the day after Washington's arrival, which was attended by the President. The services were held in the First Presbyterian Church, the oldest public building in the community, in the town Square at the corner of Hanover and High Streets, very near the homes of both Armstrong and Blaine. The sermon, which Washington described as "a political Sermon, recommendatory of order & good government," was delivered by the Reverend Robert Davidson, who had been in the pulpit of the First Presbyterian Church of Armstrong and Blaine for almost a decade.[13] An "outspoken critic of the [Whiskey] Rebellion," in his sermon of the previous Sunday, the minister had made very plain how he felt about the "sinners" who were defying the government. For his text he had determined on "Righteousness exalteth a nation: but sin is a reproach to any people." Passionately he had declaimed, "But if they will *resist*, and involve themselves in the *guilt* of rebellion, they deserve not to be pitied nor spared." [14]

And there is still another reason to believe that Washington and Armstrong did get together during this week. On his return to Philadelphia, the President found a letter from William Augustine Washington, who had been inquiring of the best college in which to enroll his sons. William, the sixth child of George Washington's older half-brother Augustine, at this time was living in the west, in Westmoreland County. On November 23, Washington replied, noting that as the Congress was now in session he would endeavor to discover from its members what he could about colleges. He already knew a little of the colleges in the country, for as early as 1773, before the war, he had surveyed the possibilities for his stepson Jackie, finally enrolling him at King's College (now Columbia University) in New York City. In his letter to William Augustine he mentions "private academies in Massachusetts"and "the College in that State" (Harvard), and Yale, and Princeton, and "the college at Williamsburg" (William and Mary), and Annapolis. He has heard the college at Williamsburg well spoken of, and "when I was at Carlisle [six weeks ago] I heard a good deal said in favor of the Academy at that place; but it was from those who had an interest in so doing." [15] There can not be much question that the "those" with whom he has been discoursing are, besides Blaine, who was a charter trustee, John Armstrong and John Montgomery and possibly General Irvine, all of whom at this time are feeling proudly parental and in a mood to boast about Dickinson College.

On Monday the President was presented an "Address of

Citizens of Carlisle to President Washington." The document is not signed, but surely Armstrong's hand is in it. These concerned citizens here "deplore the cause" which is responsible for your appearance here. "We have viewed with pain, the great industry, art and misrepresentations which have been practised, to delude our fellow citizens." They recognize that "the Sword of Justice" is in the hands of the President; and they continue with "We bless that Providence which has preserved a life so valuable . . . and we pray that He will continue to direct and prosper the measures adopted by you, for the security of our internal peace and stability of our government, and that after a life of continued usefulness and glory, you may be rewarded with eternal felicity." [16]

Washington, most grateful for their warm expression, and ever gracious, promptly replied: "Let us hope that the delusion cannot be lasting; that reason will speedily regain her empire and the laws their just authority." He asserted his determination to govern the country by the rule of law: "In any case in which it may be indispensable to raise the sword of justice against obstinate offenders, I shall deprecate the necessity of deviating from a favorite aim, to establish the authority of the laws in the affections of all rather than in the fears of any." [17]

The President left Carlisle for Bedford at 7:10 a. m. on Saturday the 11th. He dined at Shippensburg, lodged at Chambersburg, breakfasted at Greencastle, and lodged at Williamsport, Maryland, on the banks of the Potomac. He was at Fort Cumberland on the 16th and at Bedford, "a town of a few houses," by the 19th, and after 2-3 days there, returned to Philadelphia, arriving the 28th.

Most assuredly the Armstrongs were in the throng who saw the President off for Bedford on that Saturday. On Monday next Armstrong's Rebeckah would be reminding the Old General that this day marked his seventy-seventh birthday. He did not need to be told that he would never again see his beloved friend and President.

On the day following his death, which occurred Monday,

March 9, the *Carlisle Telegraph* noted the passing of General John Armstrong, "in an advanced age, resident in this town many years past"; and the *Gazette* on the 10th reported of him that he had "Departed this life . . . in this Borough the 78th year of his age." Next day the *Gazette* printed an extended obituary:

> *It may be truly said of this worthy citizen, that his life was eminently useful and exemplary. There are but few characters in which so many amiable and shining qualities are found united— His easy and engaging manners, his sympathy for the distressed, and above all his unfeigned piety, gained him the love and esteem of all true judges of merit. He was the ever-zealous friend of liberty, learning and religion, the advancement of which in the world seemed to be the grand object of his habitual wishes and prayers. His mind was abundantly stored with useful knowledge, especially of the religious kind. He possessed a very clear and sound judgment, and had acquired the habit of communicating his ideas on every topic, in an easy, flowing and perspicuous manner.*
>
> *Although, as to his body, he experienced great debility, in the last weeks of his life—the powers of his mind seemed to be little, if at all, impaired. His conversation was as usual, mild, candid, and edifying: and his character for real piety consistently supported to the last. Indeed his zeal for the glory of the Redeemer, and delight in the duties and ordinances of religion, formed the fairest traits in his character; as they ever must in every character that will command the lasting admiration of mankind—His talents in the military line, have been abundantly conspicuous; and the world has been long acquainted with his spirited enterprises, against the Savage tribes at an early period of his life; and his exertions and sacrifices in the common cause of American liberty and independence.*
>
> *In few words, it is not the language of compliment but that of truth, to say, that he was a steady friend, a kind husband, a valuable citizen, an able statesman, a tried patriot, and to sum up all a sincere Christian.*[18]

In almost every one of the many recollections of the Old General that were made public there occurred mention of his "unfeigned piety." The impression of the Honorable George Chambers, who knew him well (cited above), was typical: "He was a man of intelligence, of integrity, and of high religious and moral character. He was resolute and brave, and though living habitually in the fear of the Lord, he feared not the face of man." [19]

The Old General was laid to rest in the Old Graveyard of Carlisle. There stands in the Graveyard a statue which was "Erected by the Commonwealth of Pennsylvania in grateful appreciation of the services of these soldiers of the Revolutionary War who lie buried here." Besides Armstrong, there are remembered eighteen officers and non-coms. (including General William Thompson and Colonel Robert Magaw, Captain Robert Callender, and Sergeant John Hays) and forty privates (including Hugh Henry Brackenridge, of Whiskey Rebellion fame). Mary Hays (Molly Pitcher), the Reverend John Steel, and Dickinson College's Dr. Nisbet are also here. Members of the Armstrong and Lyon families include the Old General's wife Rebeckah, and son James; James's wife, Mary Stevenson, and their son Dr. John Wilkins Armstrong and his wife, Mary Shell; the daughter of Dr. John Wilkins Armstrong, Mary, and her husband Christian B. Herman; William Lyon and wife Ann.[20]

Afterword

The United States of America has not erected in the nation's capital a monument to the memory of General John Armstrong. The Commonwealth of Pennsylvania has not in Philadelphia or Harrisburg or Pittsburgh or Kittanning erected a monument to the memory of General John Armstrong. In the historic community of Carlisle there stands no statue, nor has there been installed a marble shaft in the town square to preserve the memory of the town's first citizen. Not even in the Old Cemetery has any special notice been taken of the Old General. Indeed, his much weathered grave-site tablet is difficult to locate and is often smothered in leaves or debris from the overhanging red cedar tree. Happily, though too late for the General to relish it, the Commonwealth of Pennsylvania did elect to name a newly formed county for its distinguished pioneer and patriot.

At last count, the Commonwealth could boast sixty-seven counties. About half are named for distinguished men (One is named for a woman.), and many of these are named for friends, or fellow officers, or associates of General John Armstrong—like the heroic Richard Butler, who was killed by the Indians of the Miami war-chief Little Turtle in the terrible defeat suffered by General Arthur St. Clair on the Wabash River, like General Hugh Mercer, who was a tragic casualty at the battle of Princeton, like President James Monroe, who at age eighteen was wounded in the battle of Trenton, like Thomas Mifflin, first Governor of the Commonwealth, like Benjamin Franklin, Lafayette, Nathanael Greene, Anthony Wayne, John Sullivan, and Armstrong's fellow surveyor William Crawford. His close friend George Washington, while he was yet living, even before the end of the War for Independence, in 1781, was honored in the name of a county in the far west of the state.

Armstrong County was created March 12, 1800, by act of the Pennsylvania Legislature. It was formed from parts of Allegheny, Westmoreland, and Lycoming Counties, and was actually attached to Westmoreland County until 1805. The newly formed county included 556 and one-half acres awarded to Colonel John Armstrong, by virtue of "a proprietary letter to the Provincial Secretary, dated May 29, 1771." The property was surveyed on

November 5, 1774, and the Patent was granted by John Penn, March 22, 1775.[1]

This immense tract of land lay almost entirely north of the "purchase line" of 1768, which means that at the time it was turned over to Colonel Armstrong, in 1775, it still belonged to the Indians. Indeed, this was the case until 1788. But Armstrong's title has held up for all time.[2]

The executors of Armstrong's will, his son James and his friend Thomas Duncan, had been authorized to sell all of his personal and real estate following the payment of his debts and designated legacies. When the establishment of Armstrong County was proposed, Dr. Armstrong donated to the County a portion of the land owned by his father, on condition that he receive one-half the proceeds of the sale of lots.[3] Sales of lots and parcels commenced May 19, 1808, and continued for almost two decades.[4]

At the urging of Dr. James Armstrong, the county seat was by act of Assembly directed to be located at a distance "not greater than five miles from Old Kittanning Town." And by an act of April 4, 1803, the appointed trustees (John Craig, James Sloan, and James Barr) were directed to survey some 150 acres of land, including a part of the land which James and John Armstrong, Jr., had turned over to the County in return for locating the county seat at Kittanning. The trustees were ordered (1) to lay out lots for public buildings, (2) to turn the residue into town- and out-lots, which "are to be sold at public auction for county use," and (3) "to lay out a town to be called *Kittanning*, at the place where Gen. [at the time Colonel] Armstrong defeated the Indians in the autumn of 1756."[5]

General John Armstrong was to have his moments in the county that was named for him, and in the town that appeared at the site of the Delaware Indian village he had destroyed. Friday, May 11, 1917, was a big day in Kittanning. On this day, at two o'clock in the afternoon, the Old General was publicly remembered and enthusiastically acclaimed. Next day the newspaper known as *Simpsons' Daily Leader* carried the story. The account appeared on the front-page under the headline **2000 PRESENT AT UNVEILING OF THE MEMORIAL**. The very full report of the proceedings opened with these lines: "In the presence of a large and distinguished assemblage the beautiful bronze tablet presented to

~ Afterword ~

Armstrong County by the Pennsylvania Historical Commission and the Pennsylvania Daughters of the American Revolution in honor of Gen. Robert [!!!!] Armstrong, hero of Indian fame and for whom the County takes its name was publicly unveiled."

The site was the Armstrong County Court House up the hill on Market Street. Although a strong north wind was gusting constantly, the day was comfortably sunny and warm. Mighty preparations had preceded the event and many very distinguished guests had been invited from all corners of the Commonwealth. Among the several members of the clergy was the Reverend Dr. George P. Donehoo of Coudersport, Secretary of the Pennsylvania Historical Commission, whose vital work *Indian Villages and Place Names in Pennsylvania* would appear before long. Other notables included the Regent and Vice-Regent of the Pittsburg Chapter of the DAR, three past Regents, and five additional members. Many visitors arrived by train and were met at the Kittanning station by the Committee in charge of the ceremony.

Those involved in the services either stood or were seated in the platform area at the height of the steps leading into the Court House. The bronze tablet which was being presented to the county in the name of General John Armstrong had earlier been placed by Bill Yale "at the designated spot on the stone wall," head high and just to the right of the entrance to the main corridor of the Court House. Throughout the ceremonies the plaque was concealed by strips of bunting.

The public schools of Kittanning, as well as the St. Mary's Parochial School, had discharged their students for the occasion. One thousand (!) youngsters marched on the Court House, carrying "hundreds of flags" and presenting "a beautiful sight" as they proceeded through the city streets. The vast crowd, vitalized by the children, was wildly enthusiastic, and during the ceremonies entered into the singing of patriotic selections and loudly applauded the speakers. John H. Schaeffer, responsible for the program, presented Mrs. Joseph W. Marsh of Pittsburg, Vice Regent of the Pittsburg Chapter of the DAR, who thereafter presided. After the invocation, offered by the Reverend William J. Hutchinson, pastor of the First Presbyterian Church, and the singing of "America," the Burgess of Kittanning, John W. Rohrer, delivered a welcome in which he applauded the "heroic service Col. Armstrong had rendered in the early development of this place."

Following some remarks by the Regent of the Pittsburg Chapter of the DAR, Mrs. John Brown Heron, and a selection sung by the First Presbyterian Church Main Quartette, Judge James W. King explained, especially for the children, how the Indian houses once occupied this very ground, and how the battle that was fought between Captain Jacobs and Armstrong's men took place just a "stone's throw of the present Court House." He spoke of the "splendid traditions which General Armstrong and the other patriots in this region have handed down to their posterity," and closed with a "strong appeal that every care be taken to see that those cherished traditions shall be transmitted to future generations untarnished and unsullied."

It was Reverend Donehoo's turn next. Explaining fully the meaning of the Indian name *Kittanning*, he declared that he was very glad to see the Indian place names preserved. He lamented that there were comparatively few instances in which such was the case, and he was critical of the New England school teacher "who almost invariably brought about a substitution of classic names for those of local significance." With his characteristic wit he opined, "I am glad, therefore there were no New England school teachers in Kittanning in the early days."

Donehoo concluded his remarks by reminding the audience of the hardships and dangers experienced by the early settlers, and expressed the hope that their lives might be "an inspiriting example for the willingness to sacrifice for the living today."

It was time to present to Armstrong County the bronze tablet which commemorated the services of General John Armstrong to this region and to the country during the Revolutionary War. The plaque was unveiled by two nine-year-old Kittanning schoolchildren, Thelma Adams and Gertrude Kiser, as directed by Charles F. Schaeffer, librarian at the Court House. The presentation to the County was made by Mrs. Anthony Wayne Cook, Pennsylvania State Regent of the DAR, on behalf of the DAR and the Pennsylvania State Historical Commission.

The beautiful tablet, shaped in the Keystone emblem of the Commonwealth and still in place today, is adorned at its top with the Pennsylvania Commonwealth motto "Virtue, Liberty, and Independence." The inscription reads: "In memory of General John Armstrong a Scottish Covenanter and a Soldier of the American Revolution Lieutenant Colonel 2d. Battalion Provincial Troops 1756 Brigadier General Continental Army 1776 Major General Pennsylvania Militia 1778 to close of war In command of Pennsylvania Militia at Brandywine and Germantown Died 1795 Erected by the Pennsylvania Historical Commission and the Pennsylvania Daughters of the American Revolution to honor the memory of the hero of Kittanning for whom this county is named, 1917."

The newspaper article concluded: "The people of Kittanning will never forget the visit of such distinguished personages and are certainly grateful for the beautiful bronze emblem presented to Armstrong County." [6]

Just short of ten years later, on the occasion of the 170th anniversary of Armstrong's Kittanning raid, a similar ceremony was performed. This time the bronze commemorative tablet was presented to Kittanning and Armstrong County by the Pennsylvania Historical Commission and the Armstrong County Historical Society.

On the day following the activities, Thursday afternoon, September 9, 1926, newspapers carried the story. The *Daily Leader-Times* gave it first-page coverage under the heading **GREAT CROWD AT TABLET UNVEILING, COL. ARMSTRONG AND HIS MEN EXTOLLED HIGHLY.**

Again, on a beautiful autumn day, a very large crowd provided a most enthusiastic audience. Estimates had "several thousand" in attendance. The *Leader-Times* reported that "Water Street for half a square north at Market was closed to vehicular traffic," filled as it was with people who had come a long distance. Again the schools turned loose their youngsters, and the nearby towns were well represented, "some sending large delegations." Present were luminaries from every niche of the Commonwealth, including Butler County's Chester Hale Sipe,[7] whose books *The Indian Chiefs of Pennsylvania* and *The Indian Wars of Pennsylvania* would shortly appear. The speakers and thirty-two honored guests were seated on a specially erected platform. Here were two descendants of General Armstrong: great, great, great granddaughter Miss Marion Armstrong and great, great grandson John Armstrong Herman, Esq., of Harrisburg. Representing the Pennsylvania Historical Commission were Mrs. Frank Black of Somerset, Henry W. Shoemaker, and Dr. Albert Cook Myers. Present also were Senator John S. Fisher of nearby Indiana, Reverend J. M. Yeager of Lewistown, Dr. T. J. Henry of Apollo, Dr. S. B. Hamilton, of Punxsutawney, the Honorable George Criswell of Franklin, Judge James W. King (who had participated in the 1917 ceremony), and many members of the Armstrong County Historical Society.

The ceremonies were conducted in the neatly groomed Riverfront Park at the east riverbank, close to the bridge which crosses the Allegheny. The memorial stone, a huge weather-worn monolith, some eight feet wide and more than ten feet high, had been set off and enclosed with ropes by the Boy Scouts, and the bronze tablet, installed in the awesome boulder, was covered by a linen sheet.

The program was opened by Samuel McCain, President of the Kittanning Borough Council, who extended greetings and expressed warm appreciation for the memorial here erected "to the gallant John Armstrong."

Colonel Henry W. Shoemaker, Chairman of the Pennsylvania Historical Commission, and Judge James King, President of the Armstrong County Historical Society, presided over the ceremonies. Judge King spoke in praise of Armstrong and "his little band of frontiersmen," and expressed gratitude for their service. Shoemaker praised the people of Armstrong County for their great interest and great co-operation in the erection of the marker. He declared that the Commission has "never found it excelled anywhere in the Commonwealth." Representing the Armstrong family, John Armstrong Herman paid tribute to the General's wife Rebeckah, insisting that "to her must be given much of the credit for the accomplishments of her brilliant husband."

Secretary of the Historical Commission, Albert Cook Myers, spoke upon a big subject, "The Delaware Indians in Their Habitat in Southeastern Pennsylvania," and Dwight C. Morgan while paying homage to the stone marker as "the oldest stone in the world," explained how it had been selected, transported and installed.

Principal speaker for the occasion was Senator Fisher, who that fall would be elected Governor of Pennsylvania.[8] In a very long, but most eloquent, address (which the *Leader-Times* printed entire on pages one and four of the September 9 paper), he described the colonial conditions which inspired the Armstrong expedition, and then in great detail followed the course traveled by Armstrong's men. He closed out his address with these words:

> *It is difficult for us to relate the scenes of one hundred and seventy years ago with the ceremonies of this occasion. Then, the wilderness, the trail, the rifle, the tomahawk, the scalping knife, the war whoop, the wild savagery. Now, the broad acres and lowing herds on yonder hills, this great Benjamin Franklin Highway running at our feet from sea to sea, the whirr and rush of passing vehicles, those immense establishments and implements of modern industry, the hum and roar and rush of trade, yon high school and churches, these beautiful homes of comfort and convenience that surround us, and everywhere the visible signs and emblems of our marvelous civilization. And the effect is heightened and the significance of these ceremonies emphasized by the presence here of the blood descendants of Col. John Armstrong and Capt. Jacobs, the redoubtable leaders in the strife of that September day. They help us to span the vast stretches that lay between the then and the now. Surely the chain of friendship that the fanciful orators of the tribes forged in imagination at the peace councils with the white brother in bygone days has been wrought into the golden bond between the Paleface and the Redman which shall never again be broken so long as the sun shines and the rivers flow.*

Conspicuous throughout the program was Chief Strong Wolf of the Ojibway tribe. The *Daily Leader-Times* described how "Garbed in all the accoutrements of his people, Chief Strong Wolf brought the impressive program to a close with an impassioned plea for good comradeship and brotherhood." He urged the white people to "stick together," to take a lesson from the Indians' misfortune. He advised them "never to be afraid to explore your strongest convictions," and noted that there are many kinds of bravery. "It's the easiest thing in the world for a man to be courageous when the band is playing and the crowd is cheering and everyone is with him," he said. "But I tell you it takes real, downright courage for a man to stand alone when everyone is against him and do what he sincerely believes to be right." And he closed with "The greatest joy you can experience is in trying to forget yourself and in trying to do something for others."

It was time for the unveiling of the tablet. At either side of the huge stone stood Chief Strong Wolf and Miss Marion Armstrong, who wore a corsage of American Beauty roses. Close by were many of the principals of the program. Miss Armstrong held one corner of the homespun linen sheet, Chief Strong Wolf the other. At the understood signal the sheet was dropped, and the tablet was revealed.

Designed by the well known architect Paul P. Cret, the bronze plaque commemorated the Armstrong expedition in these words: "Kittanning or Attique Indian Town was located on this river flat. The chief settlement as early as 1727, of the Lenni Lenape or Delaware Indians in their early westward movement from the Susquehanna River. Became the most important Indian center west of the Allegheny Mountains. Destroyed September 8, 1756 by Colonel John Armstrong and his 300 Frontier Troops from the Cumberland Valley. Marked by The Pennsylvania Historical Commission and the Armstrong County Historical Society, 1926." [9]

In addition to these two commemorative plaques which occasioned so much ceremony, a number of historical markers have been erected in the Kittanning area by the Pennsylvania Historical Commission. Three of these were dedicated on November 28, 1946. One, commemorating the short-lived Fort Armstrong, was placed on Route 66, 1.8 miles south of the borough of Kittanning. Sadly, it has disappeared. Its text had read: "Located on the nearby river bank, this outpost was built in June, 1779, and abandoned that autumn. It served the Brodhead expedition against the Senecas and was named for Maj. Gen. John Armstrong."

The second is located on the Butler Road (Business Route 422, which becomes Water Street) on the approach to Kittanning from the south. The text: "The most notable Delaware Indian

~ *Afterword* ~

Village west of the Alleghenies, was situated here from about 1730 until destroyed by Armstrong's expedition 1756. Its name meant 'great river,' applying to the Ohio-Allegheny."

And the third is the roadside marker on U. S. 422, 6.5 miles south and east of Kittanning, which remembers Blanket Hill, as described above.

Still another marker was installed outside the Court House, north end of Market Street in the borough of Kittanning, at the right side of the front entrance. It commemorates the inception of Armstrong County. The text: "Formed March 12, 1800 out of Westmoreland, Allegheny, and Lycoming counties. Named for Gen. John Armstrong, who had destroyed the Indian village at Kittanning, 1756. Here, county seat was laid out, 1803, and 'Dougherty Visible' typewriter invented in 1881."

And there are more! Just a stone's throw downhill from the Court House steps, where the 1917 ceremonies took place, is the spot at which there occurred the highest drama of the Armstrong raid. On September 8, 1934, the 178th anniversary of the fighting, the Armstrong County Historical Society installed a beautiful bronze tablet in the Market Street wall of the Rosebud Mining Company building. The memorial inscription reads: "On or near this spot stood the cabin of the Delaware Indian Chief Captain Jacobs, who here lost his life Sept. 8, 1756, when Colonel Armstrong and his 300 frontiersmen from the Cumberland Valley attacked and destroyed the Indian Town of Kittanning."

On the very same day there was erected a second marker at Blanket Hill. This tablet was installed by the Kittanning Chapter of the DAR. It is just a few feet from the Pennsylvania Historical Commission marker. It describes in some detail how Armstrong here left a party of men under Lieutenant James Hogg to watch the Indians discovered at their campfire, and how the next morning Hogg and a number of his men were killed. The inscription also includes mention of the Indians' capture of Fergus Moorhead and his companion on this hill on March 16, 1777.

Mention must be made also of the sailing ship that was named for the Old General. For the War of 1812 one of the privateering vessels that were outfitted to war against the British fleet was the brigantine *General Armstrong*. It enjoyed but a short life, like the Armstrong Fort on the Allegheny, scuttled as it was in one of the most dramatic naval battles of the war, at the Bay of Horta in the Portuguese Azores. Trapped by three British ships, after a valiant engagement, she was sent to the bottom by her captain, Samuel Chester Reid. All of this while Armstrong's son, John, Jr., was serving in the Madison Cabinet as Secretary of War.

But the Pennsylvania county which bears the General's name has not been scuttled. Today, 216 years after the General's death, some 75,000 people live in the lovely, scenic Armstrong County, on the land that lies west of Armstrong Township in Indiana County along Crooked Creek all the way to the Allegheny. They reside in the communities known as Apollo, Ford City, Kittanning, Rural Valley, Dayton, and Freeport, and in one or another of thirty-one townships. The Delaware Indians are remembered in the name Kittanning, of course, and in Lenape Heights, a community which accommodates a few descendants of the Native Americans of colonial times.

Historian of the County, Robert Walter Smith, has put it well: "As Herschel, by his genius and astronomical discoveries, wrote his name upon a star, so Armstrong, by his skill, prowess, patriotism and military achievements, wrote with his sword his name upon the beautiful and ruggedly varied face of this county." [10]

Appendix

Letter of General John Armstrong (Carlisle, April 12, 1794) to his son James (Dr. James Armstrong) on the death of four-year-old John Armstrong:

Dear James:—I have seen your last to Polly, and see nothing wrong in it, only that it manifests an excess of grief, that for many important reasons ought to be moderated and suppressed; the various duties yet incumbent upon you and especially your own eternal concerns should take the place of that natural and paternal grief, which, in a certain degree, is rather laudabale than sinful, but may readily become so by an undue indulgence and want of proper consideration; we must go to him (that is to the state of the dead,) but he will not return to us; therefore preparation for that solemn event is our principal business.

From the nature and circumstances of this remarkable affliction, you may but too plainly and justly suspect, as I see you do, that God has a controversy with the parents of that child, and perhaps with his grandparents too, for so I desire to take it to myself. Now the immediate business which I most earnestly recommend to you is, with a faithful scrutiny, giving conscience its free course, that you may find out and be convinced of the grounds of this controversy, for examination and reflection (the divine word being still the standard,) are the first steps toward reformation in any man. And to assist you in this duty, take a retrospective view of your practical life from the first of your remembrance, more especially in the following particulars: In infancy you were presented to God in the ordinance of baptism—solemn engagements were therein entered into for your instruction, &c., in the faith and practice of Christianity; these vows and promises were to devolve on yourself at the years of discretion—ask yourself whether you have endeavoured to study the nature of that initiating ordinance, voluntarily taking these solemn obligations upon yourself and beseeching the free mercy of God through Christ, the Mediator, to enable you to perform these vows by giving you the spiritual blessing signified in and by that ordinance. Again, take a general survey of your life, how you have improven or misimproven your time and talents, together with the innumerable privileges, opportunities and admonitions received therein; but especially examine what has been the general and prevailing inclination or disposition of your mind and will, for this indeed is the touchstone of the state of the heart, either towards God or against him. And here, there is great reason to fear, you may find but too much cause for the controversy in question, for if a general shyness, a cold indifference or negligence toward God, the state of the soul, the Mediator, his ordinances and institutions, hath been prevalent and habitual, this fully marks an unrenewed state of the soul, involving in it infidelity, aversion and contempt of the gospel and the revealed will of God, (hence are men in a state of nature called haters of God.) Nor is this spiritual and moral disease to be healed by a better education, a few externals and transient thoughts. It requires the hand of the great Physician, the Lord Jesus by his Holy Spirit, and belief of the truth renewing the state of the mind and disposition of the heart as well, whereby leading the soul from a sense of fear of the wrath of God, the penalty of his broken law, and helpless in itself to flee to the merits of Jesus, that only refuge or foundation that God hath laid in his church, and who was made sin for us, (that is, a sin offering,) that all "believers might be made the righteousness of God by him." And this great salvation, though to be given freely, must be sought by adult persons, and earnestly too, only on the principles of pure mercy, because by nature we have neither title nor merit to procure it; at the pool of ordinances must we lie, if we expect to be saved, to which means, looking for a blessing upon them, I earnestly recommend your most serious attention. I conclude this letter by putting you in mind that although you have always had the call of God in his word, and perhaps often in his providence too, (though unobserved and therefore neglected,) God hath again condescended to add another providential call, much more sensible and alarming to us all, in removing a dear and promising child, but with double force to you, therefore, see that you endeavour to bear and improve it in the true sense in which it is designed, that is comparatively at least, that you weep not for him but for yourself and the rest of your family.

I am your affectionate Father,
John Armstrong[1]

Image Credits

Edward Braddock (p. 32), courtesy Wikipedia. No official oil portrait of General Edward Braddock has ever been discovered. As the General's uniform is that of a latter-day American officer, this portrait is anachronistic.

James Burd (p. 33), portrait by Gilbert Stuart, by permission of HMdb.org.

Shaver's Spring plaque (p. 87), Bookstore, Indiana University of Pennsylvania campus. Author photo.

Historical Marker, Blanket Hill (p. 99). Author photo, 2010.

William Pitt (p. 134), portrait by unknown painter; or by W. Hoare. Courtesy of the National Portrait Gallery, London.

John Forbes (p. 136), original portrait. Oil on canvas, 25" x 30", painted by John Watson in Philadelphia in 1758. The original has been in the collection of Alan M. Scaife of Pittsburgh. Courtesy of Western Pennsylvania Historical Society.

James Abercromby (p. 141), painting by Allan Ramsay, ca. 1759-60. Painting is at Fort Ligonier.

Henry Bouquet (p. 141), portrait by John Wollaston, ca. 1759.

Archibald Montgomerie (p. 142), painting by Joshua Reynolds, 1783-84. Courtesy Wikipedia.

Conestoga Wagon (p. 157), courtesy *Global Anabaptist Mennonite Encyclopedia*.

Jeffrey Amherst (p. 238), portrait by Thomas Gainsborough, ca. 1785. Courtesy of the National Portrait Gallery, London.

Stone at Canasorgu (p. 254). Photo by Tom Betts, 1996.

John Penn (p. 259), etching by Albert Rosenthal, from *The Family of William Penn*, by Howard Malcolm Jenkins.

William Crawford Cabin (p. 321). Author photo, 2005.

Reverend George Duffield (p. 333), portrait, oil on canvas, by Charles Peale Polk, possibly from life, ca.1790. Independence National Historical Park.

Reverend Charles Beatty (p. 336). From *Old Redstone*, by Joseph Smith.

Sir Peter Parker (p. 363), taken from the Freemason's Tontine, of which Parker was Deputy General Master, 1787-1811.

William Moultrie (p. 367), engraving by Edward Scriven after the portrait by John Trumbull, courtesy of South Caroliniana Library, University of South Carolina, Columbia.

Charles Lee (p. 369), engraving from the 18th century. Courtesy of Wikipedia.

Hugh Mercer (p. 394), portrait by W. A. Greaves, ca. 1900, from a sketch by John Trumbull. Courtesy of the Mercersburg Academy, Mercersburg, Pa.. Photo by Robert M. Kurtz, Jr., 2005.

~ Image Credits ~

Horatio Gates (p. 395), portrait by Charles Willson Peale, from life, 1782. Independence National Historical Park.

Joseph Reed (p. 400), courtesy of University of Pennsylvania Archives.

Thomas Wharton, Jr. (p. 403), portrait by Charles Willson Peale, 1781-1805. Courtesy Philadelphia Museum of Art.

Louis Lebègue Duportail (p. 410), portrait, oil on canvas, by Charles Willson Peale, probably from life ca.1781-84.

John Sullivan (p. 456), portrait by A. Tenney, after portrait by Ulysses Dow Tenney, developed from 1790 pencil sketch by John Trumbull. Collections of the State of New Hampshire, Division of Historical Resources.

Richard Butler (p. 472), portrait by John Trumbull. Courtesy Butler County (Pa.) Historical Society.

William Irvine (p. 490), portrait from an oil painting by B. Otis, after one by Robert Edge Pine, an eminent English artist who came to America in 1784. The original was taken in New York City, when Irvine (at age 48) was a member of Congress. Courtesy of Archives and Special Collections, Dickinson College, Carlisle, Pa.

Benjamin Rush (p. 491), finished engraving by David Edwin of Thomas Sully's 1813 portrait of Dr. Benjamin Rush (Pennsylvania Hospital, Philadelphia). Exhibited at the Pennsylvania Academy's annual exhibition in 1814. The engraving was done for a series published as "Delaplaine's Repository of the portraits and lives of the Heroes, Philosophers and Statesmen of America." Charles Willson Peale produced a "portrait after Sully" in 1818. Courtesy of Archives and Special Collections, Dickinson College, Carlisle, Pa.

John Dickinson (p. 496), portrait, oil on canvas, by Charles Willson Peale, from life, 1782-83. Independence National Historical Park.

Charles Nisbet (p. 499), painter unknown, the only extant portrait of Nisbet painted from life. Courtesy of Archives and Special Collections, Dickinson College, Carlisle, Pa.

Captain Jacobs, memorial tablet (p. 539), Rosebud Mining Company Building. Author photo, 2010.

Works Consulted

Abbreviations Used

BP	*The Papers of Henry Bouquet*, ed. S. K. Stevens, Donald Kent, et al.
CR	*Colonial Records*
HSP	Historical Society of Pennsylvania
NYHS	New York Historical Society
LMCC	*Letters of Members of the Continental Congress*, ed. Edmund C. Burnett
PA	*Pennsylvania Archives*
PMHB	*Pennsylvania Magazine of History and Biography*
WF	*Writings of General John Forbes Relating to His Service in North America*, ed. James Alfred Proctor

Primary Materials

Manuscript Collections

Burd-Shippen Papers (bulk of collection, 1754-63) (Phila.: American Philosophical Society).
Conarroe Collection (Harrisburg: Historical Society of Pennsylvania).
Ferdinand Dreer Collection, Collection of the Manuscript Department (Harrisburg: Historical Society of Pennsylvania).
Gates Papers (New York Historical Society, available in microform edition compiled chiefly from holdings of N. Y. Historical Society, but drawn from 70 sources, edited by James Gregory).
Gratz Collection (Harrisburg: Historical Society of Pennsylvania).
Irvine Papers (Harrisburg: Historical Society of Pennsylvania).
John Armstrong Business Papers (Dickinson College Archives).
John Armstrong Herman Papers (Harrisburg, private collection).
John Davis Papers (Peter Force Collection).
Joseph Reed Manuscripts (New York Historical Society).
Joseph Shippen Papers (Phila: American Philosophical Society, and New Jersey Historical Society, Mss Collection).
Lukens Family Papers, Special Collections, University of Delaware.
Mifflin Documents, Pennsylvania State Library, Harrisburg ("Documents of Mifflin's Administration, 1790-1799").
Osgood Papers (1702-1938), Manuscript Division, Library of Congress.

Papers of the Provincial Council (Harrisburg: Pennsylvania Historical and Museum Commission, Division of Archives and Manuscripts).
Penn-Gaskell Family Papers, William L. Clements Library, University of Michigan.
Penn Manuscripts, Official Correspondence (Harrisburg: Historical Society of Pennsylvania).
Richard Peters Papers (Harrisburg: Historical Society of Pennsylvania).
Robert Grant Crist Papers, 1975-81 (Dickinson College Archives).
Rokeby Collection (Barrytown, New York). (includes James K. Armstrong's fourteen handwritten pages on "The Life of John Armstrong").
Shippen Family Papers, 1750-75 (New Jersey Historical Society, Mss. Collection).

Printed Works

American State Papers (Washington, D. C.: Gales and Seaton, 1832-1861), 10 Series, 38 vols. (Indian Affairs, Series II, 2 vols.).
Baurmeister, Carl L., *Revolution in America, Confidential Letters and Journals, 1776-1784 of Adjutant Major General Baurmeister of the Forces*, translated and annotated by Bernhard A. Uhlendorf (New Brunswick: Rutgers University Press, 1957).
Beatty, Charles, *Journals of Charles Beatty, 1762-1769* (University Park, Pa.: Pennsylvania State University Press, 1962).
Beatty, Charles, *The Journal of a Two Months' Tour with a View of Promoting Religion among the Frontier Inhabitants of Pennsylvania and of Introducing Christianity among the Indians* (Edinburgh, Scotland: printed by and for T. MacCleish and Co., 1798).
Bouquet, Henry, *The Papers of Henry Bouquet*, ed. S. K. Stevens, Donald Kent, et al. (Harrisburg: The Pennsylvania Historical and Museum Commission, 1972-78). 5 vols.
Boyd, Julian Parks, ed. *The Susquehanna Company Papers* (Ithaca: Cornell University Press, 1962 ff.). 10 vols. (Last six edited by Robert J. Taylor).
Burnett, Edmund Cody, ed. *Letters of Members of the Continental Congress* (Washington, D.C.: Carnegie Institute of Washington, 1921-36). 8 vols.
Butterfield, L. H., ed. *Letters of Benjamin Rush* (Princeton: Princeton University Press, 1851). 2 vols.
Chase, Philander D., editor-in-chief, *The Papers of George Washington* (Charlottesville, Va.: University of Virginia Press, 1985-2008). 17 vols. (ongoing).

Colonial Records, ed. Samuel Hazard (Harrisburg and Philadelphia, 1838-53), 16 vols. (vols. 1-3 printed in 2 editions, with different paginations).

Continental Congress Papers (microfilm).

Craft, David, *Journals of the Military Expedition of Major General John Sullivan against the Six Nations of the Indians in 1779* (Auburn, N.Y.: Knapp, Peck & Thomson, Printers, 1887).

Darlington, William M., ed. *An Account of the Remarkable Occurrences in the Life and Travels of Col. James Smith during His Captivity with the Indians in the years 1755, '56, '57, '58, and '59* (Cincinnati: The Robert Clarke Co., 1907).

Darlington, William M., ed. *Christopher Gist's Journals* . . . . (Pittsburgh: J. R. Weldin & Co., 1893).

Fitzpatrick, John C., ed. *The Writings of George Washington, from the Original Manuscript Sources 1744-1799* (Washington, D.C.: U.S. Government Printing Office, 1931-1944; rptd. N. Y.: Greenwood Press, 1970). 39 vols.

Forbes Orderly Book (September-November, 1758), in *George Washington Papers*, Series 6 (Military Papers, 1755-1798), Subseries A.

Force, Peter, *American Archives*, Fourth Series, Vol. 5 (Washington, D. C.: M. St. Clair Clarke and Peter Force, April, 1844).

Ford, Worthington Chauncey, ed., et al., *Journals of the Continental Congress, 1774-1789* (Washington, D. C.: Library of Congress, Government Printing Office, 1904-37). 34 vols.

Franklin, Benjamin, *The Papers of Benjamin Franklin*, eds. Leonard W. Labaree, Whitfield J. Bell, et al. (New Haven, Ct.: Yale University Press, 1959-2003). 37 vols.

Gibson, Hugh, "Account of the Captivity of Hugh Gibson, among the Delaware Indians of the Big Beaver and the Muskingum, from the latter part of July, 1756, to the beginning of April, 1759," *Collections of the Massachusetts Historical Society* , 3rd series, VI (1837), 141-153. Also in Archibald Loudon, *A Selection* . . . . II, 181-184.

Hamilton, Stanislaus M., ed. *Letters to Washington, and Accompanying Papers, 1755-75* (Boston: Houghton, Mifflin and Co., 1898-1902). 5 vols.

Jackson, Donald, and Dorothy Twohig, eds. *The Diaries of George Washington* (Charlottesville, Va.: University Press of Virginia, 1976-79). 6 vols.

James, Alfred Proctor, ed. *Writings of General John Forbes Relating to His Service in North America* (Menasha, Wisc.: Collegiate Press, 1938).

Johnson, William, *The Papers of Sir William Johnson*, ed. James Sullivan, et al. (Albany: Division of Archives and History, University of the State of New York, 1931). 14 vols.

Lacey, John, "Memoirs of Brigadier-General John Lacey," *PMHB*, XXV, No. 1 (1901), 1-12, 191-202, 341-354, 498-515; XXVI, No. 1 (1902), 101-111, 265-270.

M'Cullough, John, "A Narrative of the Captivity of John M'Cullough, Esq.," in Archibald Loudon, ed. *A Selection . . .*, I, 252-301.

Minutes of the Presbytery of Donegal (1759-69). (Chester, York, and Lancaster Counties).

Muhlenberg, Henry M., *The Journals of Henry Melchior Muhlenberg*, translated by Theodore G. Teppert and John W. Doberstein (Phila. and Evanston, Indiana: Lutheran Historical Society, 1982). 3 vols.

Muhlenberg, John Peter Gabriel, "Orderly Book," *PMHB*, XXXIII (1909), 257-278, 454, 474; XXXIV (1910), 21-40, 166-189, 336-360, 438-477; and XXXV (1911), 59-89, 156-187, 290-303.

"The Narrative of Marie Le Roy and Barbara Leininger, for Three Years Captives among the Indians," trans. Edmund de Schweinitz, *PMHB*, XXIX, No. 4 (1905), 407-420.

Papers of the Continental Congress, 1774-1789, compiled by John P. Butler (Washington, D.C.: National Archives and Record Services, General Service Administration, 1978. (204 microfilm rolls).

Pennsylvania Archives (Harrisburg and Philadelphia, 1852-1949). Nine series, 138 vols.

Pennsylvania Gazette (Philadelphia: Franklin and Hall, 1729-1815).

Rhodehamel, John, ed. *George Washington, Writings* (New York: The Library of America, 1997).

Sparks, Jared, ed. *Correspondence of the American Revolution . . . .* (Boston: Little, Brown, 1853). 4 vols.

Sparks, Jared, ed. *Writings of George Washington* (Boston: American Stationers Company, 1837). 12 vols.

Stauffer, P. B., "Letter of Col. John Armstrong," *Historical Papers and Addresses of the Lancaster County Historical Society*, II (1897-98), pp.104-105.

Taylor, Robert J., ed. *The Susquehannah Company Papers* (Ithaca, N.Y.: Cornell University Press, 1935-69). 11 vols.

"Votes and Proceedings of the House of Representatives, 1682-1776," in *Pennsylvania Archives*, Eighth Series.

Washington, George, *Papers of George Washington*, ed. W. W. Abbott, et al., Colonial Series, 10 vols.; Revolutionary War Series, 8 vols.; Confederation Series, 6 vols.; Presidential Series, 4 vols.; (Charlottesville: University Press of Virginia, 1983).

Washington, George, *The Diaries of George Washington*, ed. Donald D. Jackson and Dorothy Twohig (Charlottesville: University Press of Virginia, 1976-1979). 6 vols.
Washington, George, *The Journal of Major George Washington, An Account of His First Official Mission, Made as Emissary from the Governor of Virginia to the Commandant of the French Forces on the Ohio, October 1753-January 1754* (Williamsburg, Va.: Colonial Williamsburg facsimile edn., 1959).
Weedon, George, *The Valley Forge Orderly Book of General George Weedon* (N.Y.: Dodd Mead, 1902).
Williams, Edward G., ed. *The Orderly Book of Colonel Henry Bouquet's Expedition against the Ohio Indians, 1764* (Pittsburgh: privately printed for the author by Mayer Press, 1960).

Secondary Materials

A History of the Juniata Valley (Harrisburg: National Historical Association, 1936). 3 vols.
Albert, George Dallas, ed. *History of the County of Westmoreland, Pennsylvania, with Biographical Sketches of Many of the Pioneers and Prominent Men* (Philadelphia: L. H. Everts & Co., 1882).
Ames, William Homer, "History of Carlisle," in Donehoo, *A History of the Cumberland Valley*, pp. 437-470.
Anderson, Fred, *Crucible of War: The Seven Years' War and the Fate of Empire in British North America, 1754-1766* (New York: Alfred A. Knopf, 2000).
Anderson, Niles, "The General Chooses a Road," *The Western Pennsylvania Historical Magazine*, XLII, Nos. 2 and 4 (1959), 110-138, 242-258, 383-401.
Armstrong County, Pennsylvania, Her People, Past and Present (Chicago: J. H. Beers & Co., 1914). 2 vols.
Armstrong, James Lewis, ed. *Chronicles of the Armstrongs* (Jamaica, Queensborough, N.Y.: The Marion Press, 1902).
"Armstrong's Bicentennial Celebration," *The Picket Post*, XXXIII (July, 1956), 39-40.
"A Victory over Indians in Paxtang," in Archibald Loudon, ed. *A Selection . . . .*, II, 187.
Baldwin, Leland D., *Whiskey Rebels* (Pittsburgh: University of Pittsburgh Press, 1939).
Bancroft, George, *History of the United States of America, from the*

Discovery of the Continent (Boston: Little, Brown & Co., 1876). 6 vols.
Bates, Samuel P., et al. *History of Cumberland and Adams Counties, Pennsylvania* (Chicago: Warner, Beers & Co., 1886). 2 vols.
Bean, Theodore W., and Henry Armitt Brown, *Valley Forge Proceedings on the Occasion of the Centennial Celebrations of the Occupation of Valley Forge by the Continental Army under George Washington, June 19, 1878* (Phila.: Lippincott, 1879).
Beetem, C. Gilbert, *Colonial Carlisle: Plans and Maps for the Design of Its Public Square* (Carlisle, Hamilton Library, 1959).
Bell, Raymond Martin, "The Family of John Armstrong, Sr. (1717-1795) of Carlisle, Pennsylvania," *Cumberland County History*, VIII, No. 2 (Winter, 1991), 49-53.
Bell, Raymond Martin, "The Brothers and Sisters of Colonel John Armstrong 1717-1795 and of His Wife Rebecca 1719-1797 of Carlisle, Pennsylvania" (Washington, Pa.: n. pbl., 1790).
Bellamy, Francis Rufus, *The Private Life of George Washington* (N.Y.: Crowell, 1951).
Betts, Thomas, "From Home to Paradise," *Pennsylvania Magazine* (May-June, 1987), pp. 46-52.
Betts, William W., Jr., *Bombardier John Harris and the Rivers of the Revolution* (Westminster, Md.: Heritage Books, 2006).
Blaine, John Ewing, *The Blaine Family, James Blaine, Emigrant, and His Children* (Cincinnati: Ebbert and Richardson Co., 1920).
Bolles, Albert S., *Pennsylvania, Province and State, A History from 1609 to 1790* (Phila. and N.Y.: John Wanamaker, 1899). 2 vols.
Bonomi, Patricia U., *Under the Cope of Heaven, Religion, Society and Politics in Colonial America* (New York: Oxford University Press, 1988).
Boorstin, Daniel J., *The Americans: The Colonial Experience* (N.Y.: Vintage Books, Division of Random House, 1958).
Boucher, John N., *Old and New Westmoreland* (N.Y.: The American Historical Society, 1918). 4 vols.
Brackenridge, Hugh Henry, *Incidents of the Insurrection in the Western Parts of Pennsylvania* (Phila.: Printed and sold by John M'Culloch, 1795). Two parts.
Burnett, Edmund Cody, *The Continental Congress* (N.Y.: W.W. Norton, 1941).
Caldwell, J. A., *History of Indiana County* (Newark, Ohio: J. A. Caldwell, 1880).
Carrington, Henry Beebe, *Battles of the American Revolution* (N.Y.: A. S. Barnes and Co., 1876).

Carlisle *Sentinel*

Champion, Walter T., Jr., "Christian Frederick Post and the Winning of the West," *PMHB*, CIV, No. 3 (July, 1980), 308-325.

Chapman, T. J., *The French in the Allegheny Valley* (Cleveland: W. W. Williams, 1887).

Chidsey, A. D., Jr., *The Penn Patents in the Forks of the Delaware* (Easton, Pa.: Northampton County Historical and Genealogical Society, 1937).

Child, Francis, *English and Scottish Popular Ballads*, Students' Cambridge Edition (Boston, New York and Chicago: Houghton Mifflin and Co., 1904).

Cleland, Hugh, *George Washington in the Ohio Valley* (Pittsburgh: University of Pittsburgh Press, 1955).

Collins, Charles, "Rev. Charles Nisbet, D.D., First President of Dickinson College," *Ladies Repository*, XIII, No. 34 (Dec., 1853), 529-532.

Commager, Henry Steele, and Richard B. Morris, *The Spirit of 'Seventy-Six, The Story of the American Revolution as Told by Participants* (Indianapolis and N. Y.: The Bobbs-Merrill Company, Inc., 1958). 2 vols.

Commins, Saxe, ed., with an introduction and notes, *Basic Writings of George Washington* (N.Y.: Random House, 1948).

Craig, Neville B., *The History of Pittsburgh* (Pittsburgh: J. H. Mellor, 1851; new edition, 1917).

Crist, Robert G., *George Croghan of Pennsboro* (Harrisburg: Dauphin Deposit Trust Co., 1965).

Crist, Robert G., *John Armstrong: Proprietors' Man* (dissertation for The Pennsylvania State University, March, 1981).

Crist, Robert G., *The Land in Cumberland Called Lowther* (Lemoyne, Pa.: Lemoyne Trust Co., 1957).

Cummings, Hubertis M., *Richard Peters: Provincial Secretary and Cleric, 1704-1776* (Phila.: University of Pennsylvania Press, 1944).

Cummings, Hubertis M., *Scots Breed and Susquehanna* (Pittsburgh: University of Pittsburgh Press, 1964).

Dallas, George Mifflin, *Life and Writings of Alexander James Dallas* (Phila.:J. B. Lippincott, 1871).

Darlington, Mary Carson, *Fort Pitt and Letters from the Frontier* (n.p.: Arno Press, 1971).

Darlington, Mary Carson, ed. *History of Colonel Bouquet and the Western Frontiers of Pennsylvania,1747-1764* (n.p., privately printed, 1920).

Darlington, William McCullough, "Major General John Armstrong," *PMHB*, I (1877), pp. 183-187.

Davidson, Robert L. D., *War Comes to Quaker Pennsylvania* (N. Y.:

Columbia University Press, 1957).
Davis, Burke, *George Washington and the American Revolution* (N. Y.: Random House, 1975).
Day, Sherman, *Historical Collections of the State of Pennsylvania* (Phila.: George W. Gorton, 1843).
De Schweinitz, Edmund, *The Life and Times of David Zeisberger, the Western Pioneer and Apostle of the Indians* (Phila.: J. B. Lippincott and Co., 1870).
Dickinson College, The Boyd Lee Spahr Lectures in Americana, *Bulwark of Liberty, Early Years at Dickinson* (Carlisle, Pa.: Fleming H. Revell Company, Vol. I (1947-1950).
Dickson, R. J., *Ulster Emigration to Colonial America, 1718-1775* (London: Routledge and Kegan Paul, Ltd., 1966).
Diffenderfer, F. R., "Notices of Col. Armstrong and Colonel Bouquet," *Historical Papers and Addresses of the Lancaster Historical Society*, II (1897-1898), 106-107.
Dillon, John Grace Wolfe, *The Kentucky Rifle* (York, Pa.: George Shamway, 1967).
Donehoo, George P., Editor-in-Chief, *A History of the Cumberland Valley in Pennsylvania* (Harrisburg: Susquehanna History Association, 1930). 2 vols.
Donehoo, George P., *Indian Villages and Place Names in Pennsylvania* (Harrisburg: 1928; rptd., Baltimore: Gateway Press, Inc., 1977).
Donehoo, George P., Editor-in-Chief, *Pennsylvania, A History* (N. Y. and Chicago: Lewis Historical Publishing Company, Inc., 1926). 4 vols.
Drake, Francis Samuel, *Life and Correspondence of Henry Knox* (Boston: Drake, 1873).
Dunaway, Wayland Fuller, *The Scotch-Irish of Colonial Pennsylvania* (Chapel Hill: University of North Carolina Press, 1944).
Dupay, Trevor Nevitt, *The Military Life of George Washington, American Soldier* (N. Y.: Franklin Watts, Inc., 1969).
Edel, William W., "Hugh Brackenridge's Ride: How We Got 'Old West,'" in Dickinson College's *Bulwark of Liberty*, pp. 115-145.
Egle, William Henry, *An Illustrated History of the Commonwealth of Pennsylvania* (Harrisburg: De Witt C. Goodrich and Co., 1876).
Egle, William Henry, *Pennsylvania Genealogies* (Harrisburg: Harrisburg Publishing Co., 1896).
Egle, William Henry, *Pennsylvania in the War of the Revolution, Battalions and Line, 1775-1783*, ed. by John Blair Linn and William Henry Egle (Harrisburg: Lane S. Hart, 1880). 2 vols.
Egle, William Henry, *Pennsylvania Women in the American Revolution* (Harrisburg: Harrisburg Publishing Co., 1898; rptd. 1972 by

Polyanthes, Inc., Cottonport, Louisiana).

Egle, William Henry, "Rebecca Lyon Armstrong," *Notes and Queries, Historical and Genealogical* (1898 annual volume), pp. 126-128.

Ellis, Franklin, and Samuel Evans, *History of Lancaster County, Pennsylvania, with Biographical Sketches of Many of Its Pioneers and Prominent Men* (Phila.: Everts and Peck, 1883).

Emmons, H. H., "John Armstrong and His Descendants," *Papers Read before the Kittochtinny Historical Society, 1915 to April 1922* (Chambersburg, Pa.: Franklin Repository Press, 1923), IX, 289-332.

Fisher, Charles A., *The Snyder County Pioneers* (Selinsgrove, Pa.: n.pbl., 1938).

Fisher John S., The Honorable, "Colonel John Armstrong's Expedition against Kittanning," *PMHB*, LI, No. 1 (1927), 1-14.

Flexner, James Thomas, *George Washington, the Forge of Experience (1732-1775)* (Boston and Toronto: Little, Brown and Co., 1965).

Flower, Lenore Embick, "Townships of Cumberland County, Pa.," in Donehoo, *A History of Cumberland Valley*, I, 533-571.

Flower, Lenore Embick, *Visit of President George Washington to Carlisle,1794* (Carlisle, Pa.: The Hamilton Library and Cumberland County Historical Society, 1932).

Flower, Milton E., *John Armstrong, First Citizen of Carlisle* (Carlisle, Pa.: Cumberland County Historical Society, 1971).

Ford, Worthington Chauncey, "Defenses of Philadelphia in 1777," *PMHB*, XVIII, No.1 (1894), 1-19, 163-184, 329-353, 463-495; XIX, No. 1 (April, 1895), 72-86, 234-250, 359-373, 481-506; XX, No. 1 (April, 1896), 87-115, No. 2, 213-247, 391-404, 520-551; XXI, No. 1 (April, 1897), 51-76.

"Fort Granville Taken," in Archibald Loudon, *A Selection of Some of the Most Interesting Narratives* . . . . II, 185-186.

Franklin, Benjamin, *Autobiography* (N. Y: Heritage Press, 1951).

Freeman, Douglas Southall (completed by John Alexander Carroll and Mary Walls Ashworth), *George Washington, A Biography* (N. Y.: Charles Scribner's Sons, 1948-57). 7 vols.

Froude, James Anthony, *The English in Ireland in the Eighteenth Century* (London: Longmans, Green and Co., 1872). 3 vols.

Garland, Robert, *The Scotch-Irish in Western Pennsylvania* (Pittsburgh: Carnegie Library, 1923).

Gibson, John, ed. *History of York County* (Chicago: F. A. Battey Printing Co., 1886).

Good, Harry G., *Benjamin Rush and His Services to American Education* (Berne, Indiana: Witness Press,1918).

Godcharles, Frederic Antes, *Daily Stories of Pennsylvania* (Milton, Pa.: n.

pbl., 1924).
Godcharles, Frederic Antes, "The First Expedition against the Indians of the Six Nations," in Charles Snyder, ed. *Northumberland County in the American Revolution*, pp. 103-128.
Gordon, Thomas Francis, *The History of Pennsylvania from Its Discovery by Europeans to the Declaration of Independence in 1776* (Phila.: Carey, Lea and Carey, 1829).
Gratz, Simon, "Biography of General Richard Butler," *PMHB*, VII (1883), 7-10.
"Great Cove Destroyed," in Archibald Loudon, *A Selection* . . . .II, 178-180.
Guss, Abraham L., *History of That Part of the Susquehanna and Juniata Valleys, embraced by the Counties of Mifflin, Juniata, Perry, Union, and Snyder* . . . . (Phila.: Everts, Peck and Richards, 1886).
Hanna, Charles A., *The Scotch-Irish or the Scot in North Britain, North Ireland, and North America* (N. Y.: Putnam, 1902). 2 vols.
Hanna, Charles A., *The Wilderness Trail, or the Ventures and Adventures of the Pennsylvania Traders on the Allegheny Path* (N. Y. and London: G. P. Putnam's Sons, 1911). 2 vols.
Hassler, Edgar W., *Old Westmoreland, A History of Western Pennsylvania during the Revolution* (Pittsburgh: J. R. Weldin and Co., 1900).
Hawkins, Charles R., and Houston E. Landis, *York and York County* (York, Pa.: York Daily, 1901).
Headley, Joel Tyler, *Washington and His Generals* (N.Y.: Scribner, Armstrong, and Company, 1875). 2 vols. in one.
Heathcote, Charles Williams, "General John Armstrong—A Capable Pennsylvania Officer and Colleague of Washington," *The Picket Post*, LXVI, No. 36 (Nov., 1959), 3-12.
Higginbotham, Don, ed. *Reconsiderations on the Revolutionary War* (Westport, Ct. and London, England: Greenwood Press, 1978).
Hindle, Brooke, "The March of the Paxton Boys," *William and Mary Quarterly*, Series 3, III (1946), 476-482.
Historical Association of Cumberland County, *Two Hundred Years in Cumberland County* (Carlisle, Pa.: The Hamilton Library and Historical Association of Cumberland County, 1951).
Historical Papers and Addresses of the Lancaster County Historical Society, various editors (Lancaster, Pa.: Lancaster County Historical Society, 1897-1939). 43 vols.
History of Cumberland and Adams Counties, Pennsylvania, ed. Samuel P. Bates, et al. (Chicago: Warner, Beers and Co., 1886).
History of that part of the Susquehanna and Juniata Valleys embraced in the Counties of Mifflin, Juniata, Perry, Union, and Snyder in the

Commonwealth of Pennsylvania (Phila.: Everts, Peck and Richards, 1886). 2 vols.

Hulbert, Archer Butler, *Braddock's Road* (Cleveland: The Arthur H. Clark Co., 1903).

Hunce, Anthony M., "Washington at Whitemarsh," *Bucks County Historical Society Collection of Papers*, IV (1917), 703-724.

Hunter, William A., "Armstrong's Victory at Kittanning," Pennsylvania Historical Leaflet # 17 (Pennsylvania Historical and Museum Commission, 1995).

Hunter, William A., "Edward Armstrong, Hero of Fort Granville," an address given at the Mifflin County Historical Society in 1978. (Unpublished document, Robert Crist Collection).

Hunter, William A., "First Line of Defense, 1755-1756," *Pennsylvania History*, XXII, No. 3 (July, 1955), 229-255.

Hunter, William A., *Forts on the Pennsylvania Frontier, 1753-1758* (Harrisburg: Pennsylvania Historical and Museum Commission, 1960; Wennawoods reprint, 1999).

Hunter, William A., *The Provincial Fort at Carlisle, 1755-1758* (Carlisle, Pa.: Hamilton Library, 1956).

Hunter, William A., "Thomas Barton and the Forbes Expedition," *PMHB*, XCV, No. 4 (October, 1971), 431-483.

Hunter, William A., *Victory at Kittanning* (prepared for the Bicentennial of the Armstrong Expedition, 1756-1956). Rptd. from *Pennsylvania History*, XXIII, No. 3 (July, 1956), 376-407.

Illick, Joseph E., *Colonial Pennsylvania: A History* (N. Y.: Charles Scribner's Sons, 1976).

James, Alfred Proctor, "Fort Ligonier: Additional Light from Unpublished Documents," *Western Pennsylvania Historical Magazine*, XVII, No. 4 (Dec., 1934), 259-285.

Jenkins, Howard Malcolm, Editor-in Chief, *Pennsylvania, Colonial and Federal, A History: 1608-1903* (Phila.: Pennsylvania Historical Publishing Association, 1903). 3 vols.

Jennings, Francis, *Empire of Fortune: Crowns, Colonies, and Tribes in the Seven Years War in America* (N. Y.: Norton, 1988).

Jones, U. J., *History of the Early Settlement of the Juniata Valley* (Phila.: Henry B. Ashmead, 1856).

Kelly, Joseph J., Jr., *Pennsylvania, The Colonial Years, 1681-1776* (Garden City, N. Y.: Doubleday and Co., Inc. 1980).

Kemmerow, Burton K., Christine O'Toole, and R. Scott Stephenson, *Pennsylvania's Forbes Trail, Gateways and Getaways along the Legendary Route from Philadelphia to Pittsburgh*, ed. Laura Fisher (New York and Toronto: Taylor Trade Publishing, 2008).

Kent, Donald H., *The French Invasion of Western Pennsylvania,1753* (Harrisburg: The Pennsylvania Historical and Museum Commission, 1954).

King, J. W., "Colonel John Armstrong, His Place in the History of Southwestern Pennsylvania," *Western Pennsylvania Historical Magazine*, X, No. 3 (July, 1927), 129-145.

Klett, Guy Soulliard, *Journals of Charles Beatty, 1762-1769* (University Park, Pa.: Pennsylvania State University Press, 1962).

Klett, Guy Soulliard, *Presbyterians in Colonial Pennsylvania* (Phila.: University of Pennsylvania Press; London: Humphrey Milford, Oxford University Press, 1937).

Klett, Guy Soulliard, *The Scotch-Irish in Pennsylvania* (Gettysburg: Pennsylvania History Association, 1948).

Kline's Carlisle Weekly Gazette

Knollenberg, Bernhard, "General Amherst and Germ Warfare," *Mississippi Valley Historical Review*, XLI (1954), 491-494.

Knollenbery, Bernhard, *George Washington, the Virginia Period, 1732-1775* (Durham, N. C.: Duke University Press, 1964).

Kohn, Rchard H., "American Generals of the Revolution: Subordination and Restraint," pp.104-124 in Higginbotham's *Reconsiderations*.

Kopperman, Paul E., *Braddock at the Monongahela* (Pittsburgh: University of Pittsburgh Press, 1977).

Leyburn, Jmaes G., *The Scotch-Irish: A Social History* (Chapel Hill: University of North Carolina Press, 1962).

Lossing, John Benson, *The Pictorial Field Book of the Revolution* (N. Y.: Harper and Bros, 1860).

Loudon, Archibald, ed. *A Selection of Some of the Most Interesting Narratives of Outrages Committed by the Indians in Their Wars with the White People* (Carlisle, Pa.: The Press of A. Loudon, 1808 and 1811; rptd. 1888).

Mapes, George E., "Two Famous Military Roads of Pennsylvania," *Kittochtinny Papers*, VI (1920), 93-104.

March, Thomas S., *A History of Pennsylvania* (Stories of the States Series) (Danville, N. Y.: F. A. Owen Publishing Co., 1913).

McConnell Michael N., *A Country Between the Upper Ohio Valley and Its Peoples, 1724-1774* (Lincoln: University of Nebraska Press, 1992).

McGuire, Thomas J., *The Surprise of Germantown, or the Battle of Cliveden, October 4, 1777* (Phila.: Cliveden of the National Trust for Historic Preservations, and Thomas Publications, 1994).

McIlnay, Dennis P., *Juniata, River of Sorrows* (Hollidaysburg, Pa.: Live Oaks Press, 2003).

Meginness, John Franklin, *Otzinachson, or a History of the West Branch*

Valley of the Susquehanna (Phila.: Henry B. Ashmead, 1857).

Miner, Charles, *History of Wyoming in a Series of Letters from Charles Miner to his Son William Penn Miner, Esq.* (Phila.: J. Crissy, 1845).

Montgomery, Thomas L., ed. Report of the Commission to Locate the Site of the Frontier Forts of Pennsylvania, *Frontier Forts of Pennsylvania* (Harrisburg: State Printing Office, 1st edn., 1896; 2nd edn.,1916).

Murray, Joseph Alexander, *A Contribution to the History of the Presbyterian Churches, Carlisle, Pa.* (an historical address, Jan. 12, 1883) (Carlisle, Pa.: Common Press, 1981).

Myers, James P., Jr., "Pennsylvania's Awakening: The Kittanning Raid of 1756," *Pennsylvania History*, LXVI, No. 3 (Summer, 1999), 399-420.

Nester, William R., *"Haughty Conquerors," Amherst and the Great Indian Uprising of 1763* (Westport, Ct.: Praeger, 2000).

Nevin, Alfred, *Churches of the Valley* (Phila.: Joseph M. Wilson, 1852).

Nevin, Alfred, *Men of Mark of Cumberland Valley, Pa., 1776-1876* (Phila.: Fulton Publishing Company, 1876).

Nixon, Lily Lee, "Colonel James Burd in the Braddock Campaign," *Western Pennsylvania Historical Magazine*, XVII, No. 4 (Dec., 1934), 235-246.

Nixon, Lily Lee, *James Burd: Frontier Defender* (Phila.: University of Pennsylvania Press, 1941).

Nolan, J. Bennett, *General Benjamin Franklin* (Phila.: University of Pennsylvania Press, 1936; London: H. Milford, Oxford University Press, 1936).

Osgood, Herbert L., *The American Colonies in the Eighteenth Century* (Gloucester, Mass.: Peter Smith, 1958). 4 vols.

Parkinson, Sarah Woods, *Memories of Carlisle's Old Graveyard* (Carlisle: Mary Kirtley Lamberton, 1930).

Parkman, Francis, *Montcalm and Wolfe* (N.Y.: Collier Books, 1962).

Parkman, Francis, *The Conspiracy of Pontiac*, 10th edn. (N. Y.: Collier Books, 1962).

Peck, George, *Wyoming; Its History, Stirring Incidents and Romantic Adventures* (N. Y.: Harper and Bros., Publishers, 1858).

Peckham, Howard H., *Pontiac and the Indian Uprising* (Princeton: Princeton University Press, 1947).

Pennsylvania Gazette (Phila.: Franklin and Hall, 1729-1815).

Perkins, Elizabeth A, *Border Life: Experience and Memory in the Revolutionary Ohio Valley* (Chapel Hill: University of N. C. Press, 1998).

Phillips, James W., "The Sources of the Original Dickinson College Library," in *Bulwark of Liberty*, pp. 102-114.

Pickering, Octavius, and Charles W. Upham, *The Life of Timothy Pickering* (Boston: Little, Brown, 1867-1873). 4 vols.

Pleasants, Henry J., "The Battle of Paoli," *PMHB*, LXXII (1948), 44-53.

Preston, David L., *The Texture of Contact* (Lincoln, Nebraska, and London, England: University of Nebraska Press, 2009).

Prowell, George R., *History of York County* (Chicago: J. H. Beers and Co., 1907).

Reeve, J. C., "Henry Bouquet and His Indian Campaign," *Ohio Archaeological and Historical Publication*, XXVI (Oct., 1917), 489-505.

Ritchie, Carson, ed. *General Braddock's Expedition* (London: The Woolwich Polytechnic, 1963).

Robison, Robert, "Col. J. Armstrong's Attack on the Kittanning," in Archibald Loudon, ed. *A Selection* .... II, 160-171.

Rowe, G. S., "The Frederick Stump Affair, 1768, and Its Challenge to Legal Historians of Early Pennsylvania," *Pennsylvania History*, XLIX, No. 4 (Oct., 1982), 259-288.

Rowe, James W., "Did Captain Jacobs Die at the Battle of Kittanning?" *Western Pennsylvania Historical Magazine*, XVII, No. 2 (June, 1934), 121-123.

Rupp, Israel D., *Early History of Western Pennsylvania and of the West and of Western Expeditions and Campaigns from 1754 to 1833* (Pittsburg, Pa.: A. P. Ingram, 1848; Harrisburg: W. O. Hickok, 1848).

Rupp, Israel D., *History of York County* (York, Pa.: A. J. Glossbrenner, 1834).

Rupp, Israel D., *The History and Topography of Dauphin, Cumberland, Franklin, Bedford, Adams, and Perry Counties* (Lancaster City, Pa.: Gilbert Hills, 1846).

Scott, Kenneth, *Abstracts from Ben Franklin's Pennsylvania Gazette, 1728-1748* (Baltimore: Genealogical Publishing Co., Inc., 1975).

Seaver, James E., *A Narrative of the Life of Mrs. Mary Jemison* (Canandaigua, N. Y.: J. D. Bemis, 1824; rptd. N. Y.: Corinth, 1961).

Sellers, Charles Coleman, *Dickinson College, A History* (Middletown, Ct.: Wesleyan University Press, 1973).

Simpson's Daily Leader.

Simpson's Daily Leader-Times.

Sipe, Chester Hale, *Fort Ligonier and Its Times* (Harrisburg: The Telegraph Press, 1932).

Skeen, Carl, E., *John Armstrong, Jr., 1758-1843: A Biography* (Syracuse: Syracuse University Press, 1982).

Slaughter, Thomas P., *The Whiskey Rebellion, Frontier Epilogue to the American Revolution* (New York and Oxford: Oxford University

Press, 1986).

Smith, Colonel James, "An Account of the Remarkable Occurrences in the Life and Travels of Col. James Smith," in Archibald Loudon, ed. *A Selection . . . . .*, I, 119-251.

Smith, Joseph, *Old Redstone; or Historical Sketches of western Presbyterianism, its early ministers, its perilous times, and its first records* (Phila.: Lippincott, Grambo and Co., 1854).

Smith, Robert Walter, *History of Armstrong County, Pennsylvania* (Chicago: Waterman, Watkins, and Company,1883).

Smith, William, *An Historical Account of the Expedition Against the Ohio Indians in the year MDCCLXIV under the command of Henry Bouquet, Esq., Colonel of Foot and now Brigadier General in America* (Phila.:William Bradford, 1765; London: rptd. for T. Jefferies at Charing Cross, 1766; Cincinnati: The Robert Clarke Co., 1868).

Smith, William Henry, *The St. Clair Papers* (Cincinnati: Robert Clarke and Co., 1882).

Snyder, Charles F., *Northumberland County in the American Revolution* (Sunbury, Pa.: Northumberland County Historical Society, 1976).

Spahr, Boyd Lee, "Charles Nisbet, Portrait in Miniature," in *Bulwark of Liberty*, pp. 55-73.

Stevens, Sylvester K., *Pennsylvania, Birthplace of a Nation* (N. Y.: Random House, 1964).

Stevens, Sylvester K., and Donald H. Kent, eds. *Wilderness Chronicles of Northwestern Pennsylvania* (Harrisburg: Pennsylvania Historical Commission, 1941).

Stone, William Leete, *The Poetry and History of Wyoming* (Albany; J. Munsell, 1864).

Stotz, Charles M., *Outposts of the War for Empire: The French and English in Western Pennsylvania: Their Armies, Their Forts, Their People, 1779-1784* (Pittsburgh: University of Pittsburgh Press, 1985).

Stuart, Charles, "The Captivity of Charles Stuart, 1755-57," ed. Beverley W. Bond, Jr., *Mississippi Valley Historical Review*, XIII (1926-27), 58-81.

Thayer, Theodore, *Pennsylvania Politics and the Growth of Democracy, 1740-1776* (Harrisburg: Pennsylvania Historical and Museum Commission, 1953).

Thernstrom, Stephan, ed. Harvard Encyclopedia of American Ethnic Groups (Cambridge, Mass. And London, England: Belknap Press of Harvard University Press, 1980).

Thompson, Ray, *Washington at Whitemarsh: Prelude to Valley Forge* (Fort Washington, Pa.: The Bicentennial Press, 1968; 2nd edition,

1974).

Thwaites, Reuben Gold, ed. *Early Western Travels* . . . . (Cleveland: Arthur H. Clark, 1904-07). 32 vols.

Thwaites, Reuben Gold, and Louise P. Kellogg, eds. *The Revolution on the Upper Ohio, 1775-1777* (Madison, Wisc.: Wisconsin Historical Society, Draper Series, 1908).

Tousey, Thomas G., *Military History of Carlisle and Carlisle Barracks* (Richmond: Dietz Press, 1939).

Tower, Charlemagne, *The Marquis de La Fayette in the American Revolution*, second edition (N. Y.: De Capo Press, 1770). 2 vols.

Treese, Lorett, *The Storm Gathering, The Penn Family and the American Revolution* (University Park, Pa.: The Pennsylvania State University Press, 1992).

Trussell, John B. B., Jr., and Harold L. Myers, *The Battle of Wyoming and Hartley's Expedition*, Historic Pennsylvania Leaflet # 40 (Harrisburg: Pennsylvania Historical and Museum Commission, 1976).

Two Hundred Years in Cumberland County, ed. D. W. Thompson, et al. (Carlisle, Pa.: Cumberland County Historical Society, 1951).

Volwiler, Albert T., *George Croghan and the Westward Movement, 1741-1782* (Cleveland: The Arthur H. Clark Co., 1926).

Waddell, Louis M., *The French and Indian War in Pennsylvania: Fortification and Struggle During the War for Empire* (Harrisburg: Pennsylvania Historical and Museum Commission, 1996).

Wainwright, Nicholas B., "Governor William Denny in Pennsylvania," *PMHB*, LXXXI, No. 2 (April, 1957), 170-198.

Wainwright, Nicholas B., *George Croghan, Wilderness Diplomat* (Chapel Hill: University of North Carolina Press, 1959).

Wall, Charles Cecil, *George Washington, Citizen-Soldier* (Charlottesville: University Press of Virginia, 1980).

Wallace, Paul A. W., *Indian Paths of Pennsylvania* (Harrisburg: The Pennsylvania Historical and Museum Commission, 1965).

Wallace, Paul A. W., ed. *Thirty Thousand Miles with John Heckewelder* (Pittsburgh: University of Pittsburgh Press, 1958).

Wallower, Lucille, *Colonial Pennsylvania* (n.p.: Thomas Nelson and Sons, 1969).

Walton, Joseph S., *Conrad Weiser and the Indian Policy of Colonial Pennsylvania* (Phila.: George W. Jacobs and Co., 1900).

Ward, Christopher, *The War of the Revolution*, ed. John Richard Alden (N. Y.: Macmillan Co., 1952). 2 vols.

Warden, G. P., "The Proprietary Group in Pennsylvania," *William and Mary Quarterly*, XXI, No. 3(July, 1964), 367-389.

Watts, Irma H., "Colonel James Burd, Defender of the Frontier," *PMHB*,

L., No. 1(1929-37).
Webster, Eleanor M., "Insurrection at Fort Loudon in 1765," *Western Pennsylvania Historical Magazine*, XLVII, No. 2 (1964), 129-141.
Webster, Rev. Richard, *A History of the Presbyterian Church in America* (Phila.: Joseph M. Wilson, 1857).
Weslager, Clinton A., *The Delaware Indian Westward Migration* (Wallingford, Pa.: Middle Atlantic Press, 1978).
Westcott, Thompson, "Original Letters of Major André: Anecdotes Concerning Him," *Notes and Queries*, X (July, 1854), 77-81.
Wheeler, Richard, *Voices of 1776* (N. Y.: Thomas Y. Crowell Co., 1972).
Williams, Edward G., *Bouquet's March to the Ohio, the Forbes Road* (Pittsburgh: The Historical Society of Western Pennsylvania, 1975).
Williamson, Peter, "Sufferings of Peter Williamson, one of the Settlers in the Back Part of Pennsylvania," in Archibald Loudon, ed. *A Selection . . . .*, I, 74-87.
Wing, Conway Phelps, *A History of the First Presbyterian Church of Carlisle, Pa.* (Carlisle, Pa.: Valley Sentinel Office, 1877).
Wing, Conway, Phelps, et al., *History of Cumberland County, Pennsylvania* (Phila.: James D. Scott, 1879).
Wood, Jerome H., Jr., *Conestoga Crossroads: Lancaster, Pennsylvania, 1730-1790* (Harrisburg: Pennsylvania Historical and Museum Commission, 1979).
Wright, J. E., Elisabeth M. Sellers, and Jeanette C. Shirk, *With Rifle and Plow, Stories of the Western Pennsylvania Frontier* (Pittsburgh: University of Pittsburgh Press, 1938).
Young, Henry James, "The Spirit of 1775: a Letter of Robert Magaw, Major of the Continental Riflemen, to the Gentlemen of Correspondence in the Town of Carlisle, 13 August, 1775, *John and Mary's Journal*, I (March, 1975), 6-60. Magaw's letter is the property of Dickinson College.

Notes

Chapter I: The Scotch-Irish

1. For a fine account of Irish emigration, see Dunaway, pp. 28-65.
2. Thernstrom, p. 898.
3. Dunaway, p. 33; Froude, I, 392.
4. Thernstrom, p. 896.
5. Stevens, *Pennsylvania, Birthplace of a Nation*, p. 66. It is thought that probably one of every thirty Americans living today can claim Scotch-Irish descent (Thernstrom, p. 895). For a fine understanding of the Scotch-Irish of Ulster and their place in America, see James G. Leyburn, *The Scotch-Irish: A Social History* (Chapel Hill: Univ. of N.C. Press, 1962).
6. Stevens, *Birthplace* . . . , p. 66.
7. Idem.
8. Dunaway, p. 148.
9. Quoted by Dunaway, p. 148. See p. 148n.
10. Stevens, *Birthplace* . . ., p. 68.

Chapter II: The Armstrongs

1. In the confused genealogy, the date is sometimes given as 1720 or 1725.
2. John Armstrong's father, James, "was buried at Agahvea, where the inscription upon the monument erected to his memory may still [1900] be easily discerned. Upon this slab is the complete and correct coat-of-arms of the family. The boy Gentle James [son of John Armstrong's brother and therefore John's nephew] became heir to Terwinney; Mrs. Graydon, his aunt, became his guardian, and she and her husband moved to Terwinney. When Gentle James became of age he came into full possession of Terwinney, and Lieutenant and Mrs. Graydon moved away soon afterwards. They are also buried in Agahvea, where the graves and the monument with its inscription may still [1900] be seen." (James Lewis Armstrong, *Chronicles of the Armstrongs*, p. 328).
3. Siward's daughter by his first wife was married to King Duncan.
4. See May 10, 1809, letter of Mrs. Anne Buchannon of Newton-Butler, Ireland, to John Armstrong's son Dr. James Armstrong of Carlisle

(*Chronicles of the Armstrongs*, p. 387).
5. See the will of John Lyon, probated in Carlisle, May 12, 1781 (Book D, p. 38). This will mentions Margaret and eight children, one of whom is William Lyon, thus John Armstrong's nephew (Crist, *Proprietor's Man*, p. 233). According to William Egle's *Pennsylvania Genealogies*, John Lyon, who was the son of William, emigrated from Enniskillen in the year 1763, and purchased property in Milford Twp. (Present Juniata County, near Mifflintown). He had married John Armstrong's sister Margaret in Ireland. He died in 1780, wife Margaret in 1793. They are buried next each other in Tuscarora (Egle, *Pa. Genealogies*, p. 383).
6. *Chronicles of the Armstrongs*, and Bell, pp. 49-53.
7. Bell, p. 1.
8. *Chronicles of the Armstrongs*, p. 370. Warrant in Pennsylvania State Archives, Pennsylvania Historical and Museum Commission, 350 North Street, Harrisburg, Pa. A copy of this deed is with the present author. See Bell, "The Family of John Armstrong, Sr.," p. 50.
9. This Captain John Armstrong, a trader, had property on the Susquehanna "above Peter's Mountain." His brothers James and Alexander also lived in the region. (Godcharles, *Daily Stories*, p. 254).
10. Crist, citing the three biographical sketches composed by Armstrong's grandson James Kosciuszko Armstrong, which can be found in the Rokeby Collection, says, "He seems to have come between 1744 and 1746." (*Proprietors' Man*, pp. 7-9 and 7n) And genealogist Raymond Bell ("The Brothers and Sisters," p. 2) has him leaving Ireland in 1746 and arriving in Pennsylvania "about 1747."
11. *Pennsylvania Archives* (hereafter *PA*), Second Series, II, 18; Bell ("The Family of John Armstrong, Sr.," p. 51) has Archibald Armstrong coming to Pennsylvania in 1740.
12. New Castle County Will Book, K, 228. The will was probated May 18, 1775. A copy of this will was secured by Robert Crist, and is among his papers. Copy is also available from the present author.
13. Hunter, "Edward Armstrong, Hero of Fort Granville."
14. *PA*, Second Series, XVIII, 28-29.
15. 1773 letter in Rokeby Collection. See also Rebeckah's letter to her "Dear Sisters" in New Castle County, Dec. 19, 1795 (Hamilton Collection, Cumberland County Historical Society; Crist, p. 8).
16. Rebecca is spelled variously, Rebeccah, Rebecka, and Rebeckah. Armstrong himself spelled it both "Rebecka" and "Rebekah." Rebeckah's father, Archibald, in his will used the spelling "Rebeckah." That is the spelling that will be used herein.

17. Marsh Creek is a tributary of the Monacacy River, which it joins, with Rock Creek, just below the Gettysburg battlefield.
18. Rupp, *History of York County*, p. 197, and Prowell, p. 122.
19. *PA*, Third Series, I, 336.
20. Bell, p. 2; *PA*, Third Series, I, 146; Crist, *Proprietors' Man*, p. 14. Armstrong, with Hermanus Alricks (Alrichs), was chosen October 15, 1750, to represent Cumberland County. He served at least through 1753 and into 1754. His cousin Joseph also represented Cumberland County. The Land Records show that John Armstrong's brothers James and William, as well as cousin Joseph, also acquired land in Pennsboro Twp., which is the Carlisle area, at the extreme eastern end of the newly formed county along the western banks of the Susquehanna.

Chapter III: The Cumberland Valley

1. On Shamokin, see Donehoo, *Indian Villages*, pp. 186-190.
2. The name for the river Juniata appears in a great variety of spellings. "Tschochpiade" was the name employed by the Iroquois in 1752 (Ibid., p. 77).
3. Donehoo notes that because there was no large river actually within the valley it was unlikely there was ever the site of a permanent Indian town (*History of the Cumberland Valley*, p. 28).
4. Davidson, pp. 68-69.
5. Donehoo, *History of Cumberland Valley*, I, 32, and Dunaway, p. 61. For the history of this region of Pennsylvania see the work of Davidson, and that of Wing, as well as Sylvester Stevens, *Pennsylvania, Birthplace of a Nation*.
6. Donehoo, *History of Cumberland Valley*, I, 33.
7. Dunaway, pp. 60-61.
8. Ibid., pp. 62-63.
9. Donehoo, *History of Cumberland Valley*, I, 39.
10. Croghan was a native of Ireland, and had arrived in America in 1741, barely twenty years old. He settled, first, five miles to the west of Harris's Ferry, now Harrisburg. He was engaged in the Indian trade from the time of his arrival, and by 1748 had established a trading post at Logstown, near present Pittsburgh, and afterwards at many Indian towns. With his trading business imperiled by the wars, he eventually became a Deputy Superintendent of Indian Affairs under Sir William Johnson (Mary C. Darlington, *History of Bouquet*, pp. 55-76).

11. Bell, p. 1.
12. For the geology of the Cumberland Valley, see George H. Ashley's account in Donehoo, *History of Cumberland Valley*, I, 17-23.

Chapter IV: Carlisle

1. See R. W. Smith's *History of Armstrong County*, p. 16.
2. Donehoo, *History of Cumberland Valley*, I, 34.
3. Wing, *History of Cumberland County*, p. 33.
4. On buying the properties necessary for the proposed County Town, see the letter from Thomas Cookson to Thomas Penn (1752), pp. 20-22, in *Two Hundred Years in Cumberland County*. For the letter itself see, *PMHB*, XXIX (1905), 479-482.
5. William Homer Ames, "History of Carlisle," in Donehoo, *History of Cumberland Valley*, I, 437. See also *Two Hundred Years in Cumberland County*, pp. 18-19, 132-133.
6. Wing, *History of Cumberland County*, p. 230.
7. Other springs within twelve or thirteen miles of the borough are Papertown, Perry, Warren Springs, Carlisle Sulphur Springs, and Doubling Gap Springs.
8. Donehoo, *History of Cumberland Valley*, I, 219-220.
9. Crist, *Proprietors' Man*, p. 13.
10. William Lyon, the first born of John and Margaret Armstrong Lyon, was born March 17, 1729, in Ireland, and died in Carlisle, Feb. 7, 1809. He preceded his father to the province, arriving probably in 1748, aged nineteen. He early attained the position of assistant surveyor to his uncle. Commissioned as a lieutenant, he served the Forbes Campaign. He rose to great prominence in Carlisle and in Pennsylvania. He was appointed a magistrate by John Penn in 1764, received appointment to the Supreme Executive Council, was made a member of the Committee of Safety in October of 1776, became Prothonotary for Cumberland County, clerk of the Orphan's Court, and Register and Recorder (Egle, *Pennsylvania Genealogies*, pp. 383-385).
11. Warden, p. 384.
12. Crist, *Proprietors' Man*, pp. 180-181.
13. Donehoo, *History of Cumberland Valley*, I, 257.
14. Rupp, *History and Topography*, pp. 389 ff.
15. Armstrong was a very active member of the Assembly, serving on a number of committees with Benjamin Franklin (See *Votes and Proceedings of the House of Representatives, 1752-1753*, in *PA,*

Eighth Series).
16. Penn Family, Official Correspondence, VI, 133.
17. *Colonial Records* (Hereafter *CR),* IV, 87; *PA,* First Series, I, 549-552; Davidson, p. 73.
18. *CR,* V, 681.
19. *Papers of Benjamin Franklin,* V, 84-107.
20. Franklin, *Autobiography,* pp. 191-193.
21. The name "Wyoming" is a corruption of the Indian term Maughwauwanna or M'cheuomi, meaning large or great (maughwau) plains or flats (wame or wami). See Peck, p. 9, and Donehoo, *Indian Place Names,* p. 259.
22. Boyd, I, 58.
23. *CR,* VI, 259-261.
24. Ibid., p. 261.
25. Armstrong, disappointed in the conduct of John, Jr., although the blame for the awful things that happened could be laid at several doors, expressed regret that his son had ever got involved in the dispute. It was such a mess he felt that "not even the wisdom of Solomon could solve the issue to the satisfaction of all." (Letter of Armstrong, Sr., to John, Jr., August 10, 1784, Rokeby Collection) On the young Armstrong's conduct and the Pennamite Wars generally, see Skeen, pp. 22-26; Peck, pp. 19-31, 63-67, 217-219, and 412-414; Crist, *Proprietors' Man,* pp. 16-24; Miner, pp. 146-179 and ff., and especially for Armstrong, pp. 349, 354, 356-361, and 366-367.

Chapter V: The Braddock Expedition

1. Donehoo, *History of Cumberland Valley,* I, 710-715.
2. Stevens, *Pennsylvania, Birthplace* . . . , p. 52.
3. Idem.
4. Donehoo, *History of Cumberland Valley,* I, 717.
5. On James Burd, see Nixon, pp. 235-246, and Watts, pp. 29-37.
6. Volwiler, p. 92.
7. Wing, *History of Cumberland County,* p. 43.
8. *CR,* VI, 337.
9. Ibid., pp. 323-324.
10. Kelly, p. 323.
11. Letter of the Commissioners to Morris, April 16, 1755 *(PA,* Eighth Series, V, 4082-4083). See Volwiler, p. 92; Kelly, p. 323.
12. *CR,* VI, 368-369; Volwiler, p. 93; Kelly, p. 323; Donehoo, *History of Cumberland Valley,* p. 719.

13. Report of the Commissioners, *CR*, VI, 368-370; Volwiler, p. 94.
14. Cummings, p. 179.
15. Idem.
16. Rupp, *History and Topography*, 424-425.
17. *CR*, VI, 378-379; Cummings, pp. 180-181.
18. *CR*, VI, 378-379, 401-402.
19. Cummings, p. 190.
20. Godcharles, *Daily Stories*, p. 320.
21. Cummings, p. 185; Godcharles, *Daily Stories*, p. 320.
22. Godcharles, *Daily Stories*, p. 320. See, for all of this, Armstrong's letter to Governor Morris, May 18 (*CR*, VI, 401-402).
23. Cummings, p. 190; Godcharles, *Daily Stories*, p. 321.
24. Godcharles, *Daily Stories*, p. 320.
25. Morris to Peters, Richard Peters Manuscripts, IV, 23; see Hunt, p. 458.
26. *CR*, VI, 486. For a list of the officers present and those killed and wounded, see *CR*, VI, 489 ff. For accounts of the action, see *CR*, VI, 480, 513-519.

Chapter VI: Defending the Frontier

1. Stevens, *Pennsylvania, Birthplace* . . . ., p. 44.
2. Ames, p. 438.
3. Hunter, *Forts*, pp. 430-431.
4. Godcharles, *Daily Stories*, p. 721.
5. *CR*, VI, 647-648.
6. Godcharles, *Daily Stories*, p. 722.
7. Ibid., p. 723.
8. Weslager, p. 227. For a good account of the Delaware Indians during the period between the Braddock and the Forbes Expeditions, see Weslager's Chapter 11, "The Warriors Shed Their Petticoats," and Jennings' *Empire of Fortune*.
9. *CR*, VI, 615.
10. Egle, *History of the Commonwealth*, pp. 764-767.
11. Robert W. Smith, p. 20.
12. Donehoo, *History of Cumberland Valley*, I, 330.
13. Ibid., p. 252.
14. Hunter, *Forts*, p. 177.
15. For the narrative of Charles Stuart, see Bond, pp. 58-81.
16. Stuart was taken to Sandusky, then to the French post at Detroit, then to Montreal, then to England (!), and finally released in New York

City.
17. Hunter, *Forts*, p. 177.
18. Godcharles, *Daily Stories*, pp. 760-761. For accounts of the Great Cove murders, see *CR*, VI, 672-677.
19. *CR*, VI, 676; Rupp, *History and Topography*, p. 392.
20. Rupp, *History and Topography*, p. 393. See also Hanna, *The Scotch-Irish*, I, 235.
21. Rupp, *Topography*, p. 392.
22. *CR*, VI, 706-707.
23. Hunter, *Forts*, pp. 178-179, 561. This "fort" at McDowell's was garrisoned by Provincial forces for a short time, March-December, 1756.
24. See Adam Hoops to Governor Morris, Nov. 3 and 6, 1755 (*PA*, First Series, II, 462-463; and "Minutes of the Provincial Council," Nov. 3, 5, 1755, *CR*, VI, 670-679).
25. Weslager, p. 228.
26. Dillin, p. 154.
27. Ibid., p. 155.
28. *PA*, First Series, II, 643.
29. *Pennsylvania Gazette*, Jan. 1, 1756. The seven hundred dollar reward offered in Philadelphia was in April substantially increased by Virginia.
30. Fred Anderson, p. 162.
31. For an account of the council held at Carlisle, see Thwaites, pp. 84-87.
32. At this time, and generally, there were some forty houses, accommodating perhaps 120 warriors in the town. George Washington and his guide Christopher Gist, on their mission to the French at Le Boeuf, were guests here for almost five days in December of 1753.
33. R. W. Smith, p. 20.
34. Vorwiler notes, however, that Morris never seemed to have a high regard for Croghan and his appraisals, observing that Croghan "never procured me any [intelligence] that was very material."
35. *PA*, First Series, II, 575.
36. Donehoo, *History of Cumberland Valley*, I, 160.
37. Robison, in Loudon, II, 160. Ann McCord was one of the prisoners recovered at Kittanning.
38. Donehoo, *History of Cumberland Valley*, I, 161. He supplies the names of those killed or wounded.
39. *PA*, First Series, II, 623.
40. Davidson, p. 174.

41. *CR*, VII, 83-90.
42. John S. Fisher, p. 6.
43. *CR*, VII,103,114,142; Davidson, p. 177; Egle, *History of the Commonwealth*, p. 93.
44. Egle, *History of the Commonwealth*, p. 93.
45. Gratz Collection, 39; Davidson, pp. 174-175. For all of this see issues of the *Pennsylvania Gazette* for March 18, April 8, and April 30, 1756. See Hunter, *Forts*, p. 368.
46. Ibid., p. 431.
47. *PA*, First Series, II, 716-717; also *Pennsylvania Gazette*, July 29, 1756.
48. Hunter, *Forts*, p. 124.
49. *Papers of Benjamin Franklin*, VI, 455-456.
50. Pomfret Castle, scheduled for a site ten miles up Mahantango Creek, from where the stream enters the Susquehanna, never was built.
51. *CR*, VII, 153-163.
52. *Pennsylvania Gazette*, August 5, 1756; Hunter, *Forts*, p. 368.
53. Donehoo, *History of Cumberland Valley*, I, 775.

Chapter VII: Fort Granville

1. Donehoo, *History of Cumberland Valley*, I, 161. For a good account of the fall of Fort Granville, especially of the French connection, see pp. 161-165.
2. Hunter, *Forts*, p. 385.
3. Shippen Family Papers, II, 21; Hunter, *Forts*, pp. 385-386.
4. Shippen Family Papers, II, 31; Hunter, *Forts*, p. 386.
5. *PA*, First Series, II, 611; McIlnay, p. 149.
6. *PA*, First Series, II, 631-632; Rupp, *History and Topography*, pp. 393-394.
7. McIlnay, p. 148.
8. Hunter, *Forts*, p. 383.
9. For a long time it was supposed that Edward Armstrong was John Armstrong's brother Edward, but in fact John's brother Edward never did come to America. William Hunt was the first to note the error. Edward was commissioned Lieutenant May 10, 1756.
10. McIlnay, p. 149.
11. Hunter, *Forts*, p. 389.
12. *PA*, Fifth Series, I, 64-65.
13. Jones, p. 91.
14. Montgomery, *Frontier Forts of Pennsylvania*, I, 606-607; Jones, p.

92; McIlnay, p. 144.
15. Jones, p. 93.
16. *Pennsylvania Gazette*, August 5, 1756.
17. Jones, p. 3.
18. The French account of the battle has Captain Ward returning to Carlisle to collect pay for the garrison.
19. Donehoo, *History of Cumberland Valley*, I, 165.
20. Godcharles, *Daily Stories*, pp. 526-527.
21. Turner had sold out his improvement to John Harris in 1755.
22. Godcharles, *Daily Stories*, p. 526.
23. Montgomery *Frontier Forts*, I, 608; McIlnay, p. 156.
24. McIlnay, p. 156; Godcharles, *Daily Stories*, pp. 164-165. The torture described by Woods will remind those who have read of it of the torture-death of Lieutenant Thomas Boyd, who was captured by the Senecas toward the end of the Sullivan Expedition in 1779.
25. John S. Fisher, p. 7
26. *PA*, First Series, II, 744.
27. *Pennsylvania Gazette*, August 19, 1756.
28. Hunter, *Forts*, p. 393.
29. Ibid., p. 392.
30. For Walker, see *CR*, VII, 716; for Rodmon, see *PA*, First Series, II, 765; for Hogan, see *CR*, VII, 561-562; for Street, see *CR*, VII, 716; for the two soldiers, see *Pennsylvania Gazette*, Oct. 6, 1757 (Hunter's note, *Forts*, p. 392).
31. McIlnay, p. 154.
32. Armstrong's brother George was commissioned a Captain in the Colonel's battalion on May 22, 1756, and re-commissioned December 12, 1757. He accompanied brother John on the Kittanning mission. For the Forbes Expedition he was made a Major in Colonel Mercer's new Third Battalion, and he was promoted to Lt. Colonel on April 13, 1760. For his services he was awarded five tracts of land in the West Branch Officers' Survey. According to Pennsylvania's Land Records, he acquired 236.5 acres of land in Middleton Twp., January 27, 1763. *Kline's Carlisle Gazette* noted in 1789 that his brother John was his "heir at law" (*Chronicles of the Armstrongs*, pp. 369-370).
33. *CR*, II, 232; Jones, pp. 94-95.
34. Jones, p. 96.
35. Armstrong had been appointed Oct. 9, 1756, for Cumberland and York Counties.
36. Montgomery, *Frontier Forts*, I, 609-610.
37. Donehoo, *History of Cumberland Valley*, I, 162.

38. *PA*, First Series, II, 756.

Chapter VIII: The Kittanning Expedition

1. The report is reprinted in *PA*, First Series, II, 767-775, and in *CR*, VII, 257-283; and in Sherman Day's *Historical Collections of Pennsylvania*; and in T. J. Chapman's *The French in the Allegheny Valley*; and in many other places.
2. Loudon, II, 160-171.
3. *Massachusetts Historical Society Collections*, II, (1837).
4. *PMHB*, XXIX (1905), 407-420.
5. Long regarded as the best and most exhaustive account of the expedition is that by William Hunter, "Victory at Kittanning," *Pennsylvania History*, XXIII (July 1956), 376-407, which was reprinted for the Bicentennial of the Armstrong Expedition. Another fine account is that by John Fisher, Governor-Elect of Pennsylvania, who, on September 8, 1926, the 220th anniversary of the raid, delivered a beautifully moving and broadly informative dedicatory address at the unveiling of a weather-worn stone and bronze marker at Kittanning. Francis Parkman's history of the Pontiac Wars includes an account. Still another fine description is provided by Dennis McIlnay, in his *Juniata, River of Sorrows*, which, by the way, is a beautiful book. For an evaluation of the Kittanning affair, see James Myers' 1999 essay "Pennsylvania's Awakening," in *Pennsylvania History*, LXVI, 399-420.
6. The Indian town known as Kittanning was at this time at least three decades old. "Jonah Davenport, an Indian trader, in his examination of an affidavit, taken before Lieut. Gov. [Patrick] Gordon, at Philadelphia, October 20, 1731, says: 'Last spring was four years . . . a French Gentleman in appearance, with five or six Attendants, came down the River to a settlement of the Delaware Indians, called Kittanning, with an Intention, as this Exami' believes, to inquire into the number of English traders in those parts, and to sound the minds of the Indians' etc. James Le Tort's examination taken at the same time, gives the name of that French gentleman as M. Cavalier. A list of Delaware and other Indians on the Connumach [Conemaugh] and Kittanning Rivers and elsewhere is attached to those examinations, in which appears this item: 'Kithenning River—Mostly Delawares. Fam, 50; men, 150. Dist, 50.' The last probably means the distance from Fort Du Quesne." (Smith, *History of Armstrong County*, p. 20).
7. McIlnay, p. 168. For a photo of the map, see Hunter, "Victory at

Kittanning," p. 384, or McIlnay, p. 169.
8. Hunter, "Victory at Kittanning," p. 5; McIlnay, pp.168-169.
9. CR, VI, pp. 230-231.
10. McIlnay, p. 170.
11. Jones, p. 121.
12. Chapman, p.75.
13. For a detailed route of the Frankstown Path, see Paul Wallace, *Indian Paths of Pennsylvania*, pp. 49-54. Wallace in his book traces 131 Indian paths!
14. Denny, born in England in September of 1718, was well educated and in high favor at court. He served as Lieutenant-Governor of Pennsylvania from August, 1756, to October, 1759. On his return to England he settled into retirement on an annuity from the Crown. He died before the Revolution. See Wainwright, pp. 170-198.
15. CR, VI, 230-234; Rupp, *History and Topography*, pp. 116-117. Armstrong apparently wrote a second letter to Morris on the 29th, but it has not survived. See Hunter, "Victory at Kittanning," p. 381.
16. But, according to Jones's history of the Juniata Valley (pp. 324-325), "the name Frankstown comes from an old German Indian trader named Stephen Franks . . . a great friend of the Indians."
17. Hanna, *Wilderness Trail*, I, 259-260.
18. Hunter, "Victory at Kittanning," p. 382.
19. In this year, 1759, Beatty did serve as chaplain on an expedition headed by Benjamin Franklin, "for the protection of the north-western frontier of Pennsylvania." See Guy S. Klett's introduction to the 1962 edition of Beatty's Journal, pp. xiv-xvii.
20. Crist, *Proprietor's Man*, p. 69.
21. The present village of some 520 people takes its name from a huge wild cherry tree which once presided over the junction of the river and a small stream known as Cush Cushion Creek. See Thomas Betts, "From Home to Paradise," p. 47.
22. "Today, in place of that immense cherry tree (which was uprooted by the flood of 1838), a tall granite monument stands." An impressive memorial, the pillar bears the names of the three Pennsylvania counties which meet here, and "above the base, features the carving of a canoe." (Ibid., pp. 47-48).
23. "This tract was later warranted, July 23, 1773, to Samuel Caldwell, a settler, and was situate on the road leading from Frankstown to Kittanning, at the Forks of the Road." (Hanna, *Wilderness Trail*, I, 262).
24. Ibid., I, 262-263.
25. The University's Student Union building sits on Shaver's Spring. A

memorial plaque in the book store notes that fact. The plaque reads: "Shaver Spring, Troops camped here Sept. 6, 1756. Led by Lt. Col. John Armstrong. Erected by James Le Tort Chapter Daughters of American Colonists 1963."

26. Donehoo, *Indian Villages*, pp. 157, 199; and see Caldwell, p. 132.
27. *CR*, VII, 258.
28. McIlnay, p. 171.
29. Although the descriptions are essentially the same in all important details, McIlnay is followed here.
30. It was called both "Ohio" and "Allegheny" as early as 1748 (R. W. Smith's note, p. 20).
31. The Indian village at Ponks-utenik (present Punxsutawney), on Mahoning Creek, was so densely inundated by these tiny gnats that relief could be experienced "only by kindling fires . . . and sitting in the smoke." (Thomas Betts, p. 51).
32. Robison's narrative, in Archibald Loudon, II, 162-163.
33. In present-day Kittanning, the site of the house of Captain Jacobs is on the north side of Market Street, not far above McKean Street, on Jacobs' Hill, "in the rear of the site at the northern end of the stone wall in the garden, on which Dr. John Gilpin built, in 1834-35," and which in 1883 accommodated a "large two-story brick mansion . . . owned and occupied by Alexander Reynolds." (R. W. Smith, *History of Armstrong County*, p. 22) It is said that the bones of Jacobs were dug up when Gilpin's cellar was being excavated. (Day, p. 97).
34. Robison's narrative in Archibald Loudon, II, 163; McIlnay, p.172.
35. Loudon, II, 164.
36. For all of this, see Robison, pp. 162-163, *CR*, VI, 259-260, Wallace, *Indian Paths*, p. 144, and McIlnay, p. 173.
37. Wright, p. 100.
38. Robison, in Loudon, II, 163.
39. James Smith, in Loudon, I, 161.
40. Myers, p. 408 and 408n.
41. For a long time it was thought by some that Jacobs had not been killed here (See Rowe, pp. 121-123), but of course he never did reappear.
42. R. W. Smith, *History of Armstrong County*, p. 22.
43. Robison, in Archibald Loudon, II, 163.
44. R. W. Smith, *History of Armstrong County*, p. 22. According to William Hunter, a French officer by name De Normanville, who had come to the town the day before with a few soldiers, figured in the defense of the village.
45. Godcharles, *Daily Stories*, p. 621.

46. Idem.
47. Robison, in Archibald Loudon, II, 165. Armstrong reported that Chambers was killed at Allegheny Hill (*PA*, First Series, III, 148).
48. In Armstrong's report Scott and Burke were both listed as "missing." Scott was killed, most likely by the Indian who had pursued him and Burke.
49. Robison, in Archibald Loudon, II, 164-165. Hunter, concerned about the validity of Robison's report, insists that Mercer's company could not have lost twenty men at Blanket Hill; and he notes, further, that Mercer actually got to Lyttleton in "half the time allowed by Robison," that is, in two weeks rather than four. He also notes that the Cherokee saviors are unlikely, as they were not known to be in the region of Fort Lyttleton until May of 1757 (See Armstrong letter below.). (Hunter, "Victory at Kittanning," pp. 397-398, 401).
50. Sipe, pp. 315-316; McIlnay, p. 175.
51. *Pennsylvania Gazette*, Sept. 30, 1756. Quoted by Hunter, "Victory at Kittanning," p. 400.
52. R. W. Smith, *History of Armstrong County*, p. 23; Jones, p. 127.
53. Robison, in Archibald Loudon, II, 162.
54. *CR*, VI, 262; McIlnay, p. 175.
55. The site is on the farm which in 1883 belonged to Philip Dunmire. It is in Kittanning Township, on Route 422 between Elderton and Kittanning. (Wallace, *Indian Paths*, p. 148; Robison, in Loudon, II, 165; *CR*, VI, 261; Hunter, "Victory at Kittanning, p. 13; McIlnay, p. 175). The historical marker was dedicated Nov. 28, 1946.
56. For the names of missing, killed and wounded, see Armstrong's report (*CR*, VII, 257-283). See also McIlnay, p. 176.
57. McIlnay, p. 173.
58. Joseph Armstrong, Sr., had come to America from northern Ireland, according to *Chronicles of the Armstrongs* (pp. 378-379), "about 1731," in what was to become Hamilton Twp., Franklin County. According to the *Chronicles*, he served as Provincial Agent in the building of the Great Road from Fort Loudoun to Fort Pitt, and represented Cumberland County in the Assembly 1756-1758. He died at his residence in January, 1761, "leaving a wife Jennet and children as follows: John, to whom he left his plantation in Orange County, North Carolina; Joseph, Jr.; James; William; Catherine ; and Margaret."
59. Of those first listed as "missing," three showed up at Fort Cumberland on the 17th, one appeared at Fort Augusta on the 19th, and of course Captain Mercer came to Fort Lyttleton September 22.
60. Hunter, "Victory at Kittanning," pp. 392-393.

61. McIlnay, p. 180.
62. But Jones (p. 132) insists that the reported death of The Sunfish is a mistake, for "he was a hale old chief in 1781."
63. R. W. Smith, *History of Armstrong County*, p. 24; McIlnay, p. 177.
64. It was later found that the captives had been carried to less vulnerable Delaware towns, including Shenango (present Sharon), Saukunk (present Beaver), and Kuskusky (present New Castle), which soon became the largest of the Delaware communities, composed as it was of four distinct villages accommodating ninety huts housing 200 warriors and their families. (Weslager, p. 232).
65. "An Account of the Captivity of Hugh Gibson," in Loudon, II, 182. Gibson, at age fourteen, was taken captive from Robison's Fort in Sherman's Valley in July of 1756. A captive of the Delawares for five years and four months, before he escaped to Fort Pitt, he had some gruesome stories to relate. This torture is also described by the captives Marie Le Roy and Barbara Leininger ("Narrative of Marie Le Roy and Barbara Leininger," pp. 410-411). See also McIlnay, p. 177.
66. McIlnay, p. 178; Waddell and Bomberger, p. 15; Kelly, p. 357; "Narrative of Marie Le Roy and Barbara Leininger, pp. 410-411; and Loudon, II, 74-83.
67. The little pamphlet is with the Historical Society of Pennsylvania. Composed in German, it has been translated by the Right Reverend Edmund de Schweinitz, and published in the *PMHB*, XXIX, No. 4 (1905), 407-420.
68. *CR*, VII, 257-263.
69. Penn Manuscripts, Official Correspondence, VIII, 239; Myers, p. 410.
70. The "Victory" tract was a long time coming to Armstrong. See note 79, below.
71. *Pennsylvania Gazette*, Sept. 30, Oct. 7, 1756. Quoted by Hunter, "Victory at Kittanning," p. 404. The payment for scalps and prisoners returned was not made to Armstrong until October 29, when the expedition received 271 pounds, 17 shillings, and sixpence.
72. R. W. Smith, *History of Armstrong County*, p. 25; Rupp, *History and Topography*, pp. 396-397.
73. It has been pointed out that the portrayal of the attack is confused, as Armstrong's men, advancing on the town from the south, would have the river on their left (Hunter, "Victory at Kittanning," p. 405).
74. *PA*, First Series, III, 48-49, 54-56.
75. Kelly, p. 380.
76. *Papers of Benjamin Franklin*, VI, 103-104.

77. Ibid., VI, 104n.
78. Kelly, p. 370.
79. Hunter, "Victory at Kittanning," pp. 404-405. The original of the patent, dated March 22, 1775, is, as Crist notes (*Proprietors' Man*, p. 76), at Rokesby, and a copy may be read at the Department of Community Affairs, Land Bureau, Harrisburg. These acres (556.5) were that land north of the present intersection of S. Water Street and Highway 422 and south of Cowanshannock Creek. Armstrong was provided a May 29, 1771, survey of the land on November 5, 1794, shortly before his death.
80. See Internet websites of Lane Savage and Mike Slease. See also *The Battle of Kittanning*, published by the Armstrong County Community Foundation, and *The Attack on Kit-Han-Ne*, by artist Larry Smail. These items, as well as a forty-minute DVD film of the re-enacted battle, are available from the Armstrong County Tourist Bureau.
81. Donehoo, *History of Cumberland Valley*, I, 169.
82. Fred Anderson, *Crucible of War*, p.163.
83. According to Hunter ("Victory at Kittanning," p. 406), just one week after the return of Armstrong's men, on September 20, "the house and mill of George Brown were burned at Conococheague." And "Brown himself was killed and a woman and two children were taken prisoner."
84. Davidson, p. 185.

Chapter IX: Fort Loudoun

1. McIlnay, p 142.
2. Hunter, *Forts*, p. 207. This is the best work on the subject.
3. Ibid., p. 436.
4. Idem.
5. *CR*, VII, 233; Montgomery, p. 6.
6. *PA*, First Series, III, 192-193. See also Hunter, *Forts*, p. 447 and 447n, and Montgomery, p. 46. But this was not the beginning of Carlisle's Presbyterian Church, which was not actually commenced before 1769. On all of this confusion, see Murray, pp. 43-50.
7. Montgomery, p. 6.
8. *PA*, First Series, III, 79; Hunter, *Forts*, p. 445.
9. Montgomery, p. 10.
10. Hunter, *Forts*, p. 394.
11. *PA*, First Series, III, 40.
12. Ibid., p. 58.

13. Donehoo, *History of Cumberland Valley*, I, 253.
14. Ibid., p. 334.
15. *PA*, First Series, III, 105.
16. John Campbell, a Scottish nobleman, was born May 5, 1705. At age twenty-six, upon the death of his father, he became the 4th Earl of Loudoun. During the Jacobite uprising of 1745 he commanded troops, "rather unimpressively," at Prestonpans and at Inverness. In February of 1756, he was named "Captain-General and Governor-in-Chief of Virginia," and in March he was made Commander-in-Chief of the British Forces in North America. In the winter of 1757, before Forbes's march on Duquesne, he was recalled to England, and replaced by James Abercrombie. The British war against the French in the Americas was carried on then by Jeffrey Amherst. Loudoun died in 1782.
17. Donehoo, *History of Cumberland Valley*, I, 253.
18. In 1915, amid dedicatory exercises which included an address by Dr. Cyrus Cort, three historical markers were erected. Within the village of Fort Loudon (about a mile from the actual site of the fort), by the Pennsylvania Historical Commission, the Enoch Brown Association, and "the citizens of this place," was placed a great boulder, seven feet in height and three and one-half feet in width. On the bronze plaque, which is shaped like the keystone emblem is inscribed "Erected by Col. John Armstrong in the winter of 1756, and there follows a detailed history of the fort. Another boulder, six feet high, is located at the actual site of the fort. And a marker bearing the inscription "To Fort Loudon site" was placed at the eastern end of a private road.
19. For the history of Fort Loudoun, see Hunter, *Forts*, pp. 363-473.
20. *PA*, First Series, III, 105.
21. Hunter, Forts, pp. 458-459.
22. Ibid., pp. 356-357.
23. *PA*, First Series, III, 239-241.
24. Idem.
25. Stanwix, coincidentally, had represented the city of Carlisle in England in the British Parliament. He had served England as Deputy Quartermaster-General in 1754. He would build Fort Stanwix, in New York, and would return to Pennsylvania in 1759, to take charge of operations and to build Fort Pitt. On June 19, 1759, he would be promoted to Major-General, and would be succeeded as Commandant of the Southern District by General Richard Monckton on May 4, 1760.
26. Hunter, *Forts*, p. 446. For references to these actions see *PA*, First Series, III, 187, 189, 213-214, 240, 281, 301, and *CR*, VII, 630.

27. *PA*, First Series, III, 173; Rupp, *History and Topography*, p. 398.
28. *CR*, VII, 395; Hunter, *Forts*, p. 417.
29. *CR*, VII, 562.
30. *PA*, First Series, III, 147-147; Rupp, *History and Topography*, pp. 397-398.
31. *CR*, VII, 534-535, 548, 552-558; Hunter, *Forts*, p. 468.
32. *PA*, First Series, III, 187-188.
33. *PA*, Second Series, VI, 527-532; *CR*, VII, 601; Hunter, Forts, p. 418.
34. *PA*, First Series, III, 187-189; Hamilton, II, 100.
35. *PA*, First Series, III, 189.
36. *PMHB*, XXXVI, 438.
37. This letter is unsigned. Peters notes that it is "from Lieut Coll Armstrong." It is in the handwriting of Robert Callender. Printed in *PA*, First Series, III, 201-202. See also Hunter, *Forts*, p. 419. A similar letter was addressed to George Armstrong by George Croghan (*CR*, VII, 630-632).
38. *PA*, First Series, II, 452; Hunter, *Forts*, p. 180.
39. Hunter, *Forts*, p. 508.
40. Davidson, p. 184.
41. *CR*, VII, 744.
42. *Pennsylvania Gazette*, Oct. 13, 1757.
43. Hunter, *Forts*, p. 491.
44. For the organization of Pennsylvania's military forces, see Hunter, *Forts*, pp. 204-205.
45. Later on, Teedyuskung claimed to have won over eight more nations.
46. *CR*, VII, 630, 682.
47. Weslager, p. 234.
48. Ibid., p. 239.
49. Hanna, *Wilderness Trail*, II, 159.
50. Ibid., p. 160.
51. *PA*, First Series, III, 290, 296-297.
52. Ibid., pp. 303-304.

Chapter X: The Forbes Expedition

1. Pitt was succeeding William Cavendish and was governing with the Duke of Newcastle. His first ministry (1757-61) is regarded as much more successful than his second (1766-68). Pitt is remembered in the name of Pennsylvania's second largest city (Pittsborough, now Pittsburgh); in Fort Pitt; in Pittsylvania County, Virginia; in Pittsburgh, New Hampshire; in Pittsburg, Kansas; in Chatham

University in Pittsburgh; and in Chatham, New Jersey.
2. Egle, *Illustrative History of Cumberland*, p. 97.
3. James Abercromby (1706-81) would in 1758 succeed Loudoun as Commander-in-Chief of the British Forces in North America. But because of his shocking defeat at Ticonderoga he was recalled to England on Nov. 9, 1758, and was succeeded by Jeffrey (Geoffrey) Amherst, who had just accepted the surrender of Louisbourg.
4. There is confusion in the reference works, some giving Forbes's birth date as 1707, some 1710.
5. Edward Braddock was also with Cumberland in the pursuit of Charles in the winter of 1745-46.
6. *CR*, VIII, 26-29.
7. James, *Writings of Forbes* (hereafter *WF*), p. 38.
8. *PA*, First Series, III, 365.
9. Idem.
10. *CR*, VIII, 60; *WF*, pp. 58-59.
11. Hunter, *Forts*, pp. 460-461 and 461n.
12. Mary (Indian name Dehgewanus), who was fifteen at the time, was turned over to two Seneca women in Pittsburgh, would marry two different warriors and live among the Senecas for seventy-five years. There has been erected a memorial statue at her grave site on the Council Grounds in the Letchworth State Park in Livingston County, New York. For the story of Mary Jemison see her narrative account, in Seaver.
13. Donehoo, *Pennsylvania, A History*, II, 814.
14. Byrd had been made Colonel of Virginia's 2nd Regiment (900 men) at age thirty. He had served as a volunteer aide to Lord Loudoun.
15. Bouquet, thirty-nine years old at the time of the campaign, was born of a noble French family in Rolle, on the shores of Lake Geneva in Switzerland. He was fluent in the three languages of Switzerland, French, German, and English, and many of his letters to Forbes and Armstrong are in French. He had *lots* of military experience in the Netherlands and in the service of the King of Sardinia, fighting against the armies of France and Spain. After the wars on the Continent, he entered the service of the Prince of Orange as a Lieutenant Colonel and as Captain Commandant in the Swiss Guards. After studies at the University of Leyden, he returned to the military, enlisting in the British Army when King George II issued a call for professional soldiers to serve in the colonies. He was a "natural" for the military as he was a most able organizer and a brilliant strategist. His greatest single triumph was in the miraculous victory over the Indians at Bushy Run in 1763. After his campaign to relieve Fort Pitt

and after his defeat of the Ohio Indians, he was promoted to Brigadier General and placed in command of the Southern District of North America. In time, he became a landowner in Maryland and a naturalized citizen of Pennsylvania. He died in Florida of yellow fever, ten years before Lexington and Concord (See *Bouquet Papers*, hereafter *BP*, passim, and Williams, *Bouquet's Orderly Book*.).

16. *BP*, II, iii, 55.
17. Montgomerie had been a soldier from age seventeen, and very early raised a Highland Battalion. In 1760, after the success of the Forbes expedition, he was placed in command of a mission against the Cherokee in South Carolina. When he finally returned to his native Scotland he became known as the 11th Earl of Eglinton.
18. *PA*, Fifth Series, I, 62, 70, 128.
19. Donehoo, *Pennsylvania, A History*, II, 175.
20. Stanwix, a professional soldier, entered the army in 1706, and was commissioned Colonel Commandant in the British Army in America, Jan. 1, 1756. During 1757 his headquarters were at Carlisle; and on Dec. 27 of that year he was commissioned Brigadier General. He had gone into winter quarters at Lancaster on Nov. 30, 1757, and was encamped by Dec. 22. He was in command in Pennsylvania in 1757 and again in 1759.
21. Haldimand, who on Feb. 4, 1756, had been commissioned Lt. Colonel in the British Army in America, left Carlisle on Nov. 14 with five companies of Royal Americans for Annapolis.
22. *WF*, p. 65.
23. Ibid., pp. 65, 81, 87.
24. Hance Hamilton (1721-1772) was one of the early settlers and the first sheriff of York County. As a captain he had the command at Fort Lyttleton; and he had been a member of Armstrong's Kittanning force.
25. *Chronicles of the Armstrongs* (p. 370) has William coming to Pennsylvania with brother John and locating "on a tract of two hundred acres of land west of the Susquehanna on the 13th of February, 1737." Pennsylvania's Land Records show him acquiring land in Peters Twp. and Pennsboro, etc. from 1752-1762. He was a lieutenant in his brother's battalion as of May 10, 1756, and was promoted to Captain on Dec. 24, 1757, to replace his cousin Joseph Armstrong (*PA*, Fifth Series, I, 44, 91). His chief service during the Forbes expedition was as commander of a troop of light horse (*BP*, II, 2n, 58). He served later on Bouquet's Ohio mission, having been promoted to Major on July 4, 1764. And he participated, for a short time, in the Revolution and was taken prisoner in the battle of New

York with the surrender of Fort Washington, commanded by Carlisle's Colonel Robert Magaw (*PA*, Second Series, XV, 769, and Williams, *Bouquet's March*, p. 48n). William had lived at 100 E. Pomfret Street in Carlisle in a one and one-half story house, built in the summer of 1759 by Stephen Foulk (Records show that workmen were paid eight gallons of whiskey for digging the cellar.). But he died, probably in 1780, on his farm in Middleton Twp., leaving a wife, Jean, and children John, William, Susannah, Charity, Elizabeth, and Alexander (records of John Armstrong Herman, Harrisburg).

26. Lyon, twelve years younger than Armstrong, had been commissioned Lieutenant Dec. 6, 1757. Bouquet appointed him commissary for the stores at Juniata Camp on June 21, 1758, and through the summer he served as Commissary and Paymaster at Juniata Camp and at Raystown. He resigned March 17, 1759.

27. Thompson would enter the Revolution as a Colonel. He was commissioned Brigadier General in November of 1775, and at the Battle of Three Rivers during the patriot invasion of Quebec, together with Colonel William Irvine of Carlisle, would be captured by the British in the patriot invasion of Quebec. After four years (!) of parole he was finally exchanged for Baron von Riedesel. He died in the very next year at his home near Carlisle.

28. The Scotland-born Burd was a prominent and very important figure in colonial Pennsylvania. A survivor of the Culloden massacre, he came to America at the age of twenty-one, at just about the time Armstrong arrived. He was commissioned Captain in the Pennsylvania Regiment, Jan. 17, 1756; promoted to Major in the Third Battalion (Clapham's) April 24, the same year; promoted to Lt. Colonel in the Second Battalion, Jan. 2, 1758. In the reorganization of the Regiment, when the Third Battalion became the Second, Burd was promoted to Colonel Commandant, May 28, 1758. He had constructed Burd's Road, the supply road for Braddock, which runs from present-day Bedford to Brownsville. In 1756 he commanded the frontier post at present Sunbury, Fort Augusta. He built Fort Morris in Shippensburg. In 1759, to serve Fort Cumberland and Fort Pitt, he built at the mouth of Redstone Creek a supply depot, which came to be known as Fort Burd. He was given the command of Fort Pitt in 1760, and served as a King's Magistrate and later as a Lancaster County judge. He married the eldest child of Edward Shippen, Esq., for whom Shippensburg is named. Burd's wife Sarah was a sister to Edward, Jr., who became Chief Justice, and whose daughter "Peggy" married Benedict Arnold. The couple eventually moved to Shippensburg, but James Burd lived his last years on a farm east of

the Susquehanna. Built in 1767, his home was known as "Tinian." The old homestead is still standing, amid what remains of his property, three acres, on an elevated flat looking out over the Susquehanna, near present Highspire in Dauphin County. It is identified by an historical marker. Both James and wife Sarah are buried in Middletown, Pa., at the entrance to the Old Presbyterian Cemetery.

29. Work died in 1790. (*PA*, Fifth Series, I, 62, 70, 128; *BP*, I, 349; Watts, pp. 29-37; Cleland, p. 163).
30. For names of the officers of the three battalions, see *PA*, Fifth Series, I, 178-185.
31. Parliament had authorized on June 20, 1756, the raising of four battalions in America to be known as the Royal American Regiment. On June 28, Governor Robert Hunter Morris issued a warrant for the recruiting of volunteers in Pennsylvania for service in the Royal American Regiment.
32. *WF*, p. 114.
33. *BP*, II, 36.
34. Raystown is spelled variously—Reas town, Reastown, etc. The name derives from the Raystown branch of the Juniata, which was named for John Ray (Rae or Wray), an early Indian trader of this region, who had hoped to have a plantation here.
35. The so-called Raystown Path actually leads from the present-day Harrisburg area west to the Ohio. It was the path followed regularly by the Shawnee and Delaware westward migrations.
36. Donehoo, *Pennsylvania, A History*, II, 180.
37. Idem. Quotation on exhibit at Fort Ligonier.
38. The road that was cut was known for a long time as the Forbes Road. It became the Lincoln Highway, and in the west corresponds closely to Route 30. According to Donehoo (*Pennsylvania, A History*, II, 823), "The course of the road is exactly that of the old Indian trail through Raystown to the road taken by the Delawares when they continued to migrate westward to the Ohio from the Delaware and the Susquehanna in the early years of the eighteenth century."
39. Donehoo, *Pennsylvania, A History*, II, 826.
40. *Pennsylvania Gazette*, May 11, 1758; *WF*, pp. 88-89.
41. Editor's note in *Papers of Benjamin Franklin*, p. 107.
42. *Papers of Benjamin Franklin*, p. 107.
43. Donehoo, *Pennsylvania, A History*, II, 801, 804.
44. *Historical Papers and Addresses of the Lancaster County Historical Society*, pp. 104-105. This letter has been in the possession of P. B. Stouffer, of St. Clair, Pa.

45. *WF*, p. 108.
46. *BP*, II, 39.
47. Ibid., pp. 73-74.
48. This procedure has been conjectured by Douglas Freeman, II, 360n.
49. *BP*, II, 112.
50. *WF*, p. 124.
51. *BP*, II, 145.
52. Editor James in *WF*, p. xi
53. For Bedford, see Montgomery, pp. 476-489. The fort at Bedford was named by Forbes to honor the 4th Duke of Bedford, a leading British statesman of the day, and a member of the Crown's Ministry during the Seven Years' War. The present community at the site is called Bedford.
54. Forbes Marching Journal. See Donehoo, *Pennsylvania, A History*, II, 831-832, for precise detail through to present-day Pittsburgh. Donehoo twice walked the Braddock Road from Fort Cumberland to Pittsburgh. He very much approved of Forbes' decision on the route. Historical markers have been installed all along the Forbes Road. For an account of these, see Stotz.
55. Ibid., pp. 179-182; and Cleland, p. 172.
56. *WF*, pp. 145-147.
57. On Barton's role, see Hunter, "Thomas Barton and the Forbes Expedition," pp. 431-483.
58. *PA*, First Series, III, 483; Fitzpatrick, *Writings of Washington*, II, 243n.
59. "Conestoga Wagon," *Columbia Encyclopedia* and *Encyclopedia Britannica*.
60. *WF*, p. 149, 154.
61. Ibid., pp. 156-157.
62. Ibid., pp. 154, 161, 163, 166, 169.
63. Ibid., p. 179.
64. Ibid., pp. 199-202.
65. Ibid., p. 171.
66. Kickenapauling was the site of a former Indian town named for a Delaware chief. It was on the crossing of the Quemahoning Creek (now inundated by the waters of Quemahoning Reservoir), present-day Somerset County. It lay precisely on the route finally adopted by Forbes.
67. Cleland, p. 177; and see Hanna, *Wilderness Trail*, I, 283.
68. *BP*, II, 277-278; Cleland, pp. 176-177.
69. *BP*, II, 290-293; Cleland, p. 178.
70. Fitzpatrick, *Writings of Washington*, II, 252-253; Cleland, pp. 180-

183.
71. Fitzpatrick, II, 260; Cleland, pp. 183-184; Jenkins, II, 48. For his continued criticism of Forbes's choice of roads, Colonel Washington received a harsh dressing down from the General in a meeting at Shippensburg. Armstrong, in a letter to Secretary Peters, Oct. 3, 1758, included a less than happy comment on Washington's protesting: "Colonel Washington has been a good deal sanguine and obstinate." (*PA*, Series 5, III, 552).
72. *BP*, II, 312.
73. Ibid., p. 356.
74. Ibid., pp. 372-373.
75. Ibid., pp. 377-378.
76. Ibid., p. 380.
77. Ibid., p. 398; and Cleland, p. 190.
78. *BP*, II, 396-397.
79. The redoubt known as Fort Dewart, located at the summit of Allegheny Mountain, was built to protect a depot of supplies and the line of communication. It is the only military structure on the Forbes Road for which evidence remains. Where the two-feet high mounds are visible, and at the center of what had been a sixty-square-feet enclosure, the Pennsylvania Historical and Museum Commission has placed a monument. The large stone presents a bronze plate, by which Fort Dewart is identified. The construction engineer for the fort, Captain Harry Gordon, had a low opinion of the site, thought it not a position for effectively commanding the gap. One-half mile to the southwest, at the head of Coal Run or Dark Shade Creek, was Col. Armstrong's encampment. (Williams, *Bouquet's March*, p. 89).
80. *BP*, II, 408.
81. Ibid., p. 442.
82. Ibid., pp. 449-451.
83. In Bouquet's view Callender, who had been with Armstrong on the Kittanning mission, was the man most familiar with the roads and with the wilderness.
84. *BP*, II, 458. George Armstrong served as Field Officer at the Raystown Camp from August 17 to the middle of September.
85. *BP*, II, 450-451.
86. Extant are perhaps a thousand letters to and from Armstrong, but unfortunately very few of the personal letters to his dear Rebeckah and his two sons. He is rarely descriptive, though producing from time to time a telling metaphor; and he rarely indulged in philosophical musing.
87. *BP*, II, 463-464.

88. There is a Forbes Road historical marker at the Clear Fields, which is between present-day Bedford and Ligonier (Somerset County). Troops were encamped just north of there (at Tomahawk Camp) from time to time, and the fortification installed here was known as Fort Dudgeon.
89. *BP*, II, 466-467.
90. *WF*, pp. 202-206.
91. Grant later participated in the American Revolution as a General in the forces of King George. He was promoted to Lt. General in 1782 and further promoted in 1796. He died "very old" at his home in Ballindalloch, near Elgin, May 13, 1806.
92. The Courthouse is at the western extremity of Grant's Hill. The hill itself, once a very pretty, almost charming, elevation, has disappeared, long ago graded down as it was developed. (Mary C. Darlington, *Fort Pitt and Letters*, p. 197).
93. For accounts of Grant's blunder, see Donehoo, *Pennsylvania, A History*, II, 826-829; Perkins, pp. 58-59; Montgomery, *Frontier Forts of Pennsylvania*, pp. 80-83, 197, 262; William Darlington, *An Account of the Remarkable Occurrences* (Col. James Smith's account), pp. 103-106; and Grant's own report, in Mary Darlington, *Fort Pitt and Letters*, pp. 63-71.
94. Smith, at age eighteen, was captured by two Delaware warriors and a Conafatauga, while a member of a road gang cutting Braddock's road to Turkey Foot in 1755. After five years a prisoner, he returned home from Montreal, to Conococheague.
95. Smith's narrative in Loudoun, I, 202-204. See also William Darlington, *An Account of the Remarkable Occurrences*.
96. Grant's report may be found in Mary Darlington's *Fort Pitt and Letters from the Frontier*, pp. 63-71. See also Cleland, pp. 202-208.
97. William Darlington, *An Account of the Remarkable Occurrences*, p. 106; and James Smith, in Loudon, I, 204.
98. *WF*, pp. 218-221; *BP*, II, 538. This letter is printed in Mary Darlington, *Fort Pitt and Letters*, p. 71.
99. Major Andrew Lewis (1720-81) was a Virginia frontiersman and soldier, who had served with Washington in the Braddock campaign. He participated in the Revolution as a Brigadier General.
100. *WF*, p. 225.
101. *BP*, II, 510-511.
102. *WF*, pp. 37, 40.
103. Editor James, in *WF*, p. xi. The young George Washington, in the early stages of the Braddock expedition, had also suffered a severe attack of the dysentery.

104. *WF*, pp. 212-213; *BP*, II, 538.
105. *BP*, II, 522-523; *WF*, p. 214.
106. *BP*, II, 524-525.
107. *BP*, II, 538; Mary Darlington, *Fort Pitt and Letters*, p. 71.
108. *BP*, II, 542.
109. Barton preached two Sundays of every six in Carlisle from 1755 to 1759 (Crist, *Proprietors' Man*, p. 108).
110. *PA*, First Series, III, 446-448.
111. Ibid., p. 483.
112. Ibid., p. 551.
113. Letter of John Armstrong to Richard Peters, Oct. 3, 1758 (*PA*, First Series, III, 551-552).
114. Forbes would change the name of the fort to Fort Ligonier, after Sir John Ligonier, Commander-in-Chief of land forces in Great Britain. For the eight years of its existence as a garrisoned fort, Ligonier was never surrendered to the enemy. It withstood two attacks by the warriors in the time immediately preceding Bouquet's victory at Bushy Run. In March of 1766, it was decommissioned and never returned to active service. In a postscript to his report to Governor Denny on the fall of Fort Duquesne, Forbes urged "the building of [a] Block House and Saw Mill upon the Kisskaminities, near Loyal Hannon, as a thing of the utmost Consequence to their [the Pennsylvanians'] Province, if they have any intention of profiting by this Acquisition [Duquesne]."
115. Figures vary. The account accompanying the John Buxton painting of the assault (which is on exhibit at the fort in Ligonier) has the force composed of "440 marines and Canadian militia, in addition to 150 native warriors."
116. William Darlington, *An Account of the Remarkable Occurrences*, p. 105.
117. *Pennsylvania Gazette*, Nov. 30, 1758. For descriptions of the assault see Donehoo, *Pennsylvania, A History*, II, 828-829; Montgomery, II, 199-204; *PA*, First Series, XII, 389-394.
118. *WF*, pp. 231-233.
119. *CR*, VII, 308-338.
120. On his two missions into the Indian country Post was extremely successful with the Delaware Indians. Indeed, historian George Donehoo insists that had it not been for Post the Forbes campaign would have come to a very different conclusion. For Post's journal account of these heroic missions, see *PA*, First Series, III, 250-504. See also Thwaites, *Early Western Travels*, I, 234-291.
121. Donehoo, *Pennsylvania, A History*, II, 807-808.

122. *WF*, pp. 251-252; *CR*, VII, 175-223; Cleland, pp. 216-217; Craig, *Olden Times*, I, 161.
123. Craig, *Olden Times*, I, 162.
124. *PA*, Second Series, VI, 427.
125. *BP*, II, 600.
126. *Pennsylvania Gazette*, Nov. 30, 1758.
127. *Scribner's Magazine*, May, 1893; Fitzpatrick, *Writings of Washington*, XXIX, 43-48; Montgomery, pp. 206-208; Donehoo, *Pennsylvania, A History*, II, 829-830.
128. *WF*, p. 255.
129. Donehoo, *Pennsylvania, A History*, II, 831.
130. Freeman, pp. 323n, 360-361.
131. Hamilton, III, 128-129; *WF*, p. 254.
132. Fitzpatrick, *Writings of Washington*, II, 303-304.
133. Ibid., p. 306; and Donehoo, *Pennsylvania, A History*, II, 831.
134. *Pennsylvania Gazette*, Nov. 30, 1758.
135. Forbes' Orderly Book, Nov. 21; Freeman, p. 362.
136. Forbes' Orderly Book, Nov. 24.
137. *Pennsylvania Gazette*, Nov. 30, 1758; Donehoo, *Pennsylvania, A History*, II, 831; Godcharles, *Daily Stories*, p. 828.
138. Godcharles, *Daily Stories*, p. 828.
139. Quoted from Freeman, who notes that the details are much the same in the most reliable accounts.
140. Armstrong's grandson, almost 100 years later, suggested that General (then Colonel) Armstrong had been given the privilege as "a punishment" to Washington, who had lost fourteen of his men to friendly fire in the confused fighting near Loyalhanna ("Life of John Armstrong," Rokeby Collection).
141. Bancroft, *History of the United States*, II, 495.
142. Donehoo, *Pennsylvania, A History*, II, p. 835.
143 Godcharles, *Daily Stories*, p. 829.
144. Albert, p. 31.
145. Cleland, pp. 225-226.
146. Letter to Nancy Willing, Nov. 25, 1758, Shippen Papers. Quoted by Freeman, p. 366.
147. *BP*, II, 610-611; Freeman, p. 366. William Allen was a friend and a powerful member of the Pennsylvania Assembly.
148. *CR*, VIII, 232-233.
149. In dating this letter Forbes used the spelling "Pittsborough." That spelling, or some corruption of it, remained in effect until Dec. 23, 1891, when the United States Board on Geographic Names recommended a spelling change to "Pittsburg." That decision was

reversed on July 19, 1911, and the "h" restored for the now current spelling "Pittsburgh."
150. *WF*, 267-269; Cleland, pp. 220-221.
151. For the report made by the Delaware Chief Custaloga (or Packankie), whose principal residence was on French Creek, about twelve miles up from its mouth, to M. De Ligneris on January 4, see Stevens and Kent, *Wilderness Chronicles of Western Pennsylvania*, or *BP*, II, 624-626.
152. Donehoo, *Pennsylvania, A History*, II, 811; Vorwiler, pp. 140-141.
153. *WF*, p. 279.
154. Ibid., pp. 282-283.
155. Ibid., p. 300.
156. Post was born in 1710 in Conitz, East Prussia. He came to America at about the same time as John Armstrong, in 1742. He worked very energetically as a missionary for the Moravian and Anglican churches. He died in Germantown in 1785 and is buried there, in Hood's Cemetery.
157. Donehoo, *Pennsylvania, A History*, pp. 812-813. There are varying estimates of Post's influence among the Indians, historians Donehoo, Sipe, and Champion insisting that his was a major role in keeping the Delaware and the Shawnee quiet, while some, like Francis Jennings, feel that the role played by Post has been much exaggerated.

Chapter XI: Colonel Bouquet and the Roads West

1. *BP*, II, 631.
2. Ibid., pp. 646-647.
3. *BP*, II, 648; *WF*, pp. 271-272.
4. *WF*, p. 272.
5. *BP*, III, 3-4.
6. Ibid., pp. 16-19.
7. Ibid., p. 18.
8. John Armstrong, Jr., was indeed "promising." He became an officer in the Continental Army, a U. S. Senator, Minister to France, and, finally, Secretary of War in the administration of President James Madison.
9. *BP*, III, 85-87.
10. Jameson, whose name is spelled variously, was two years older than Armstrong, and was commissioned Captain in the Pennsylvania Regiment on May 19, 1756. He was made Brevet Major of the Second Battalion on April 24, 1758, for the Forbes expedition.

Major Jameson built the redoubt on the Forbes Road known as Belle Air. Like Hugh Mercer, he was born in Scotland and was a physician. His home was in York, where he practiced medicine, and he became an ardent supporter of the Revolutionary cause.

11. *BP*, III, 85-86.
12. Ibid., pp. 184-185.
13. Colonel Hugh Mercer was to remain in command at Fort Pitt through 1759, when he was succeeded by General John Stanwix. From 1781 through 1783 another physician had the command. This was Brigadier General William Irvine, Armstrong's Carlisle neighbor and friend.
14. *BP*, III, 249-250.
15. Armstrong had been appointed a Judge of the Court of Common Pleas in October of 1757. The commission is at Rokeby (See Bates, p. 141; Crist, *Proprietor's Man*, p. 104).
16. Peters (1704-1776) was the Pennsylvania Provincial Secretary from 1742 to 1762. He was both a clergyman and an attorney. As Secretary he proved an earnest and staunch defender of the proprietary political position. He served also as a provincial councillor and as an agent to the Indians (*BP*, III, 514).
17. *PA*, First Series, III, 621-622.
18. Benjamin Chew (1722-1810), Attorney General of Pennsylvania, 1755-1769, and a member of the Provincial Council, 1755-1775. It was the Chew mansion in Germantown that distracted Washington in that battle.
19. *BP*, III, 514.
20. George Armstrong would command at Bedford from April 26 to May 4.
21. *BP*, III, 259-261; *WF*, pp. 140-141. This letter also appears in *Two Hundred Years in Cumberland County*, pp. 27-28.
22. *BP*, III, 268-269.
23. Montgomery, pp. 476-489.
24. *BP*, III, 297-298.
25. Ibid., pp. 333-335.
26. Ibid., pp. 335-338.
27. Letter of Edward Shippen to Bouquet, *BP*, III, 342.
28. *BP*, III, 356-357.
29. *CR*, VIII, 268; Weslager, p. 238.
30. *BP*, IV, 66-67.
31. Ibid., pp. 67-68.
32. Ibid., p. 71.
33. Ibid., pp. 73-74.

~ Notes ~

34. Morton in a letter to Bouquet from Ligonier, Sept. 15, notes that he had received the wagons from Armstrong (*BP*, IV, 100).
35. *BP*, IV, 114.
36. *BP*, IV, 89, 94-95. Armstrong's brother James lived near Patterson's Fort, and he served in 1758 in the militia company commanded by Captain James Patterson. According to Raymond Bell, his wife and two of his children were taken by Indians on Jan. 27, 1756, his wife being returned to Fort Augusta "a year later." (Bell, pp. 49 and 53 (note 5). James was commissioned Captain, May 13, 1759, in the new Third Battalion. He was replaced in the command at Carlisle by brother William. Pennsylvania's Land Records show a James Armstrong holding lands on John Penn Creek in 1752 (200 acres), and on Tuscarora Creek (150 acres) in 1762. James died by drowning in Juniata County, 1774 (Bell, p .49).
37. *BP*, IV, 89, 93, 95.
38. Ibid., pp. 93-95.
39. Ibid., p. 106
40. Ibid., pp. 120-122.
41. Ibid., pp. 136-137.
42. Ibid., p. 151.
43. Ibid., pp. 161-162.
44. Ibid., p. 182.
45. Ibid., p. 183.
46. Philip de Haas had been an ensign in Captain Robert Callender's company of Armstrong's First Battalion. He was appointed Battalion Adjutant April 30, 1758. He rose to rank of Brigadier General during the Revolution.
47. *BP*, IV, 277-278.
48. Ibid., p. 302.
49. Ibid., p. 308.
50. Ibid., pp. 384-385.
51. Ibid., pp 395, 422.
52. Ibid., p. 465.
53. Ibid., p. 488.
54. Hanna, *The Wilderness Trail*, II, 25-26.
55. Richard Peters Papers, Thomas Penn Letterbook, VI, f. 172.
56. This estate is described in the grant Sharpe to Bouquet, dated June 9, 1760 (Richard Peters Papers, Thomas Penn Letterbook, VI, 503).
57. *BP*, IV, 564-565.
58. For Bouquet's journal account of this expedition, see *BP*, IV, 603-713.
59. Donehoo, *Pennsylvania, A History*, II, 857.

60. On this event see Kelly, p. 444.
61. Donehoo, *Pennsylvania, A History*, II, 861.

Chapter XII: Pontiac's War

1. Rupp, *History and Topography*, p. 400.
2. Mary Darlington, *History of Colonel Bouquet*, pp. 157-158.
3. *PA*, First Series, IV, 197.
4. Ibid., pp. 108-109.
5. Donehoo, *Pennsylvania, A History*, II, 871.
6. *PA*, First Series, IV, 112.
7. *Papers of Benjamin Franklin*, X, 293-294. Issues of the *Pennsylvania Gazette* for June 9, 16, and 30, 1763, carried reports of Indian depredations in the west.
8. Donehoo, *Pennsylvania, A History*, II, 188; Rupp, *History and Topography*, p. 400.
9. Godcharles, *Daily Stories*, p. 547.
10. Donehoo, *Pennsylvania, A History*, II, 874. As Donehoo acknowledges, "Francis Parkman has pictured the scenes in Carlisle at this time as no other writer has ever been able to picture them."
11. The story of these three forts is a sad one. The garrisons of all three were massacred, the forts having been taken by great duplicity, a fate that Detroit escaped by a hair's breadth. There is some confusion over the date of the Indian raid on Venango. The William Johnson Papers report (IV, 165) that the fort "was attacked June 18 by a large body of Senecas." But in another place the Johnson Papers report that "Venango probably fell June 16." June 16 is the commonly accepted date. Venango was the name of the old Delaware/Munsee Indian village. The stockade first built there was constructed by the French and called Machault. When this fort was utterly destroyed, the British built a new one (in 1760) and called it Fort Venango. After it was burned by the Senecas, under most probably Kayahsotha, in 1763, it was rebuilt by the Americans as a military post. It was constructed by Captain (later Major) Jonathan Heart (or Hart), who had widened the Indian path (always known as the Venango Trail) in order to bring in materials. The new fort, known as Fort Franklin, was located on the south bank of French Creek, and maintained a garrison, sometimes as large as 100, but normally much smaller, until 1796. Nothing remains now.
12. See the Johnson Papers, MS, Historical Collections of Pennsylvania, and see *The Papers of William Johnson*, published by the Division of

Archives and History (Albany, N.Y.), IV, 165n, 169, 171, 182; X, 767-769.
13. *CR*, IX, 35.
14. *PA*, First Series, IV, 114-115.
15. Letter of Bouquet to Amherst, July 13, 1763. See Nester, p. 117, note 28 in Chapter "Counterattacks," and Bouquet Collection, microfilm, A-1065.
16. Donehoo, *Pennsylvania, A History*, II, 874.
17. Nester, p. 117.
18. Ibid., p. 118, note 42 in Chapter "Counterattacks."
19. Ibid., p. 119.
20. Donehoo, *Pennsylvania, A History*, II, 874.
21. *BP*, VI, 227. This letter appears in *Two Hundred Years in Cumberland County*, pp. 31-32.
22. William Smith, *Expedition Against the Ohio Indians*, pp. 10-11.
23. Donehoo, *Pennsylvania, A History*, II, 875.
24. William Smith, *Expedition Against the Ohio Indians*, pp. 10-11.
25. Letter of Captain Ourry to Bouquet, June 20, 1763 (*BP*, VI, 268-269); Nester, p. 113.
26. Letter of Lt. Blane to Bouquet, June 28, 1763 (*BP*, VI, 268-269).
27. Peckham, p. 211. Some historians have Bouquet leaving his wagons and his oxen at Bedford.
28. Kayahsotha's Indian name, which translates as "It sets up a cross," has been rendered over the years in some thirty spellings. Among these are Kiashuta (the spelling used by the first historians), Guyasuta (the name the Shawnees knew him by, popular in the Pittsburgh region), Guyasutha, Guyasotha, Kiasutha, Kishuta, Guyassotha, Keyashuta, and Kiasota.
29. Reeve, p. 499.
30. Donehoo, *Pennsylvania, A History*, II, 189. For a map of the terrain of the battle, see William Smith, *Expedition Against the Ohio Indians*, pp. xiv-xv. For a good account of the battle, see Donehoo, II, 874-880. See also Peckham, pp. 212-213. The Bushy Run battlefield site has been purchased and preserved by the Bushy Run Battlefield Memorial Association in cooperation with the Pennsylvania Historical and Museum Commission. Its 213 acres (ninety of which are wooded) include a Visitors' Center and a monument; and on the grounds, for many years now, re-enactments are staged. The Bushy Run Battlefield site, near Harrison City, is the only historic site in the country that recalls exclusively the Pontiac War.
31. Reeve, p. 500.
32. Simon Ecuyer to Henry Bouquet, June 16, 1763 (*BP*, VI, 228-233);

Ecuyer to Bouquet, June 26, 1763 (*BP*, VI, 258-260); Nester, p. 112.
33. Ecuyer to Bouquet, June 26, 1763 (*BP*, VI, 258-260); Nester, p. 112.
34. *BP*, VI, 261-263. See also Knollenberg, p. 491. The smallpox killed hundreds of Indians that summer and fall.
35. Nester, p.114, note 28, in Chapter "Counterattacks."
36. Peckham, pp. 211-212.
37. Mary Darlington, *History of Colonel Bouquet*, pp. 197-199.
38. Stevens, *Pennsylvania, Birthplace*...., p. 57.
39. *PA*, First Series, IV, 175-176.
40. See "Narrative of John McCullough" and "Narrative of Richard Bard," both in Perkins's *Border Life*.
41. Donehoo, *History of Cumberland Valley*, I, 336.
42. *PA*, First Series, IV, 203-204.
43. For a day-by-day description, see William Smith, *An Historical Account of the Expedition Against the Ohio Indians*.
44. Reeve, pp. 502-503.
45. *Armstrong County of Pennsylvania*, p. 549.
46. *CR*, IV, 481-483.

Chapter XIII: The Susquehanna Expedition

1. On July 4, 1776, a "Declaration of Independence" was signed here by the Fair Play Men, who had "squatted" on the Indian land in 1773. An historical marker identifies the site of the tree, which is no longer standing.
2. The author has himself discovered 2,617 spear points, arrowheads, celts, knives, drills and scrapers (and one gouge!) in the plowed fields of Great Island and the areas of Avis, Jersey Shore, and Lock Haven. Some of these artifacts date from as long ago as ten thousand years.
3. Letter of William Clapham to Governor William Denny, Nov. 8, 1756. (*PA*, First Series, III, 42-43).
4. Letter of William Clapham to Governor William Denny, n.d., 1756 (*PA*, First Series, III, 65). See also Myers, p. 414, and Godcharles, *Daily Stories*, pp. 770-771.
5. Peckham, p. 337.
6. March, pp. 119-120.
7. Letter of Plumsted to Bouquet, Oct. 2, 1763 (*BP*, VI, 425).
8. *Pennsylvania Gazette*, Nos. 1816-1818; Parkman, pp. 337-338.
9. William Darlington, *An Account of the Remarkable Occurrences in the Life and Travels of Col. James Smith*, pp. 108-109.
10. Northampton County at this time was immense, including as it did all

of the present counties of Northampton, Luzerne, Lackawanna, Lehigh, Monroe, Pike, Wayne, Sullivan, Wyoming, Susquehanna, and sections of Bradford, Columbia, and Schuylkill.
11. Nester, p. 156.
12. Clayton, from Lancaster County, was commissioned (at age sixteen !) Lieutenant of the Third Pennsylvania Battalion, May 24, 1756. As Captain and Quartermaster of the Second Battalion, he marched with the Forbes Expedition, and was wounded at Grant's defeat.
13. Donehoo, *Pennsylvania, A History*, II, 187.
14. Gordon, p. 624.
15. John Penn was born in London, July 14, 1729 (Some reference works give the date 1725.). He came to Pennsylvania shortly before the time of the Braddock Expedition, and on February 6, 1753, assumed the most important position in the Provincial Council. After a return to England for some eight years, he came back to Pennsylvania to take office as Lieutenant Governor. On May 4, 1771, leaving the government of the province to the Council, he returned to England because of the death of his father. In August of 1773, just as the revolutionary ardor was appearing, he returned to the Pennsylvania office of Governor. Although he was hardly a Tory, expressing sympathy for the rebel cause and celebrating the repeal of the Stamp Act, he was imprisoned (exiled) in New Jersey for a brief time in the early part of the War. With the end of proprietary role in Pennsylvania, and the installation of the Supreme Executive Council, the Penns were deprived of all properties excepting their manors and estates and whatever may have been purchased from private parties. By this Divestment Act of 1779 the Penns were also awarded a compensation of £130,000. With his one-fourth John Penn was able to live comfortably with his wife Anne, eldest daughter of Chief Justice William Allen of Philadelphia, whom he had married on May 31, 1766. Their country estate, on the Schuylkill, was known as Lansdowne. John Penn died on February 9, 1795. His body was interred under the floor of Christ Church on North American Street in Philadelphia, not far from General John Forbes, but was later removed to England.
16. *PA*, First Series, IV, 135.
17. Ibid., pp. 136-137.
18. Letter of Dec. 2, 1763 (*BP*, VI, 251).
19. *PA*, First Series, IV, 146-147.

Chapter XIV: The Conestoga Massacre

1. Parkman, p. 348.
2. Rupp, *History and Topography*, p. 43.
3. Parkman, pp. 348-349.
4. Ibid., p. 350.
5. Godcharles, *Daily Stories*, p. 912.
6. Smith's account was published in the *Lancaster Intelligencer* in 1843, eighty years after the event. See Parkman, p. 352.
7. One historian has the figure at 100; another at precisely fifty-seven; some say 50-60; one witness reports 25-30. See March, p. 121, and Rupp, *History and Topography*, pp. 171-172.
8. Parkman, pp. 351-352.
9. Rupp, *History and Topography*, p. 166.
10. Reverend Elder, born in Scotland, was a well educated graduate of the University of Edinburgh. He was a passionate Presbyterian pastor in the Paxton Church region, but because of the frontier situation was forced to become a soldier and had become known as the fighting parson. But he was also friendly with the Christian Indians and often visited them at Conestoga and at the Great Island. Elder died at age eighty-six, in 1792, on his farm close to Harris's Ferry.
11. Rupp, *History and Topography*, pp. 163-164.
12. Parkman, pp. 352-353.
13. Rupp, *History of York and Lancaster Counties*, p. 358; Parkman, p. 354.
14. Parkman, p. 354.
15. Ibid., pp. 355-356. For the murder of the Conestoga Indians at Lancaster, see *PA*, First Series, IX, 148-149.
16. Gordon, p. 405.
17. For the activity at this time of Richard Peters, Reverend Elder, and John Penn, see Cummings, pp. 259-269.
18. Parkman, p. 356.
19. Rupp, *History and Topography*, pp. 164-165.
20. Franklin's essay was reprinted, together with notes, in Franklin Papers, XI, 42-69. For an account less emotional and more straightforward, see John Heckewelder's *Narrative of the Mission . . .*, which is extracted in *Thirty Thousand Miles with John Heckewelder*, ed. Paul A. W. Wallace (re-issued in 1985 as *The Tragedy of John Heckewelder*), chapters six and twelve.
21. Parkman, pp. 354-355n.
22. See Gordon, p. 406, and Rupp, *History and Topography*, p. 168.
23. Rupp, *History and Topography*, p. 171.
24. Rupp, *History and Topography*, p. 169. For the names of those Indians living in Conestoga in January of 1755, see Rupp, p. 169.

For an account of the murders, including the Remonstrance of Smith and Gibson, see Gordon, pp. 404-410.

25. Lazarus Stewart (July 4, 1734 - July 3, 1778), much disappointed in the government of Pennsylvania, finally left the Province. In January of 1770, he led thirty-nine of his Paxton Boys company north to the beautiful Wyoming Valley. There he and his men got into the Pennamite Wars, in which Connecticut settlers contested with those from Pennsylvania for the land. They fought, however, on the side of the Yankees, the Connecticut settlers. Stewart led a successful raid on Fort Durkee in February, but in September, while in flight from the recapture of the fort by the Pennamites under Captain Ogden, he was arrested in the neighborhood of York. But he promptly escaped. On returning to Wyoming he recaptured Fort Durkee on December 18, 1770. One month later, with the fort under siege again by Ogden, Stewart felt obliged to withdraw from the valley. But in July, with Captain Zebulon Butler he laid siege to the new Fort Wyoming, and in three weeks was able to possess it. For the next four years Stewart lived the life of a farmer, and with his wife, Martha Espy, raised seven children. The Pennamite Wars were resumed in August of 1775, with Stewart participating, but the War of the Revolution introduced a new element into the contested Wyoming Valley, the British troops and their allies the Iroquois under Cornplanter and Old Smoke. The assault by the British on the forts of the valley concluded in the Wyoming Massacre (July 3), in which Stewart was a casualty.
26. CR, IX, 133; *Muhlenberg Journals*, II, 19; *Papers of Benjamin Franklin*, XI, 72.
27. Gordon, pp. 406-408.
28. *Papers of Benjamin Franklin*, XI, 72.
29. Estimates on the size of the force range from as few as 250 to as many as 1500! (See March, p. 123).
30. *Muhlenberg Journals*, II, 23, and Thayer, p. 86.
31. The "Remonstrance" is printed in full in CR, IX, 138-142 and in pamphlet form as part of the William Bradford publication (Phila.,1764) under the very long title beginning "Declaration and Remonstrance" (*Papers of Benjamin Franklin*, XI, 80-81).
32. *Papers of Benjamin Franklin*, XI, 83.
33. For these proceedings, see *Papers of Benjamin Franklin*, XI, 83-86.
34. *Papers of Benjamin Franklin*, XI, 87n. One of the Moravian Indian villages in what is now Ohio had a similar name, Gnadenhuetten (Huts of Mercy). For an account of their migration and settlement, see Edmund de Schweinitz, *The Life and Times of David Zeisberger,*

the *Western Pioneer and Apostle of the Indians.*
35. Penn Manuscripts, Official Correspondence, IX, 238; Thayer, p. 87.
36. Thayer, p. 87.
37. *PA*, First Series, IV, 152-153; Rupp, *History and Topography*, pp.163-172. John Penn's Proclamations may be viewed in *CR*, IX, 95 and 107.
38. See, for example, Thayer, p. 88.
39. Wallower, pp. 157-158.
40. Awful as they were, the Conestoga massacres pale nearly out of mind when put against the mallet massacre, which was to occur near the end of the Revolution, in March of 1782. Enraged, like the Paxton Boys, by countless atrocities, the settlers of Washington County, south of Pittsburgh, organized a militia force of ninety men to destroy the Moravian Indian villages of Gnadenhuetten, Salem, and Schoenbrun. These ninety men herded ninety helpless and innocent women, children, and old men, like so many cattle, into the village chapel at Gnadenhuetten, and there murdered them in cold blood, mostly with a mallet. Only eighteen of these ninety militiamen refused to participate. Horrified and incensed, Carlisle's General William Irvine, at the time the commander of the Western Department, vowed to hang those responsible. Is it necessary to report that not one man was punished? Irvine very early discovered that the people of the Fort Pitt region, while not applauding the massacre, were not much offended by it.

Chapter XV: The Black Boys

1. For Governor Penn's accounts of his expedition to Carlisle and his unsuccessful efforts to bring the guilty persons to justice, see his letters to Sir William Johnson, May 23, and to General Gage, June 28, 1765 (Johnson Papers, XI, 746). See also *CR*, IX, 275-277.
2. Letter with Penn Papers.
3. Idem.
4. *Papers of Benjamin Franklin*, XII, 142-143.
5. Letter quoted by Webster, p. 131.
6. Ibid., p. 132.
7. For a good account of the Black Boys' "insurrection," see Webster, pp. 125-139.
8. William Darlington, *An Account of the Remarkable Occurrences in the Life and Travels of Col. James Smith During His Captivity*, pp. 120-132, 182-183. Discussed in *Pennsylvania Gazette*, Sept. 12,

Sept. 28, and Oct. 5, 1769. Smith's narrative is also contained in Loudon's *Most Interesting Narratives*. Smith later served in the Revolutionary War forces with the rank of Colonel, fighting the Iroquois, and with a small party of soldiers captured 200 Hessians in New Jersey. He represented the newly constructed counties of Bedford and Westmoreland at the conventions which met in Philadelphia to install a government. His last days were lived in the region of present-day Kentucky, and after that territory was made a state, he served as a most effective legislator. He died in 1812. The story of the Black Boys' Rebellion was made a novel in 1937. The book, entitled *The First Rebel: Being a Lost Chapter in Our History and a True Narrative of America's First Uprising Against the English Military Authority*, was written by Neil H. Swanson. The novel inspired a movie entitled *Allegheny Uprising*, featuring John Wayne as Captain Jimmy Smith.

Chapter XVI: The Frederick Stump Murders

1. Treese, p. 85.
2. Rupp, *History and Topography*, pp. 172-174. For a brief account of the Stump affair, see Godcharles, *Daily Stories*, pp. 26-28.
3. Rupp, *History and Topography*, p. 174.
4. For these letters, see Rupp, *History and Topography*, pp. 179-180.
5. Kelly, p. 616.
6. Rupp, *History and Topography*, p. 176.
7. *PA*, Second Series, IX, 808.
8. Rupp, *History and Topography*, pp. 176-177.
9. Kelly, p. 617.
10. Rupp, *History and Topography*, pp. 176-177.
11. Idem.
12. Ibid., pp. 180-181.
13. Numbers given in the several accounts vary from forty to ninety.
14. Rupp, *History and Topography*, pp. 181-182.
15. Some versions of the rescue have the ruffians stopping at the blacksmith's shop to have Stump's manacles removed.
16. Rupp, *History and Topography*, pp.185-186.
17. Kelly, p. 618.
18. Rupp, *History and Topography*, pp.186-187.
19. Ibid., p. 189.
20. *CR*, IX, 510.
21. Ibid., p. 511.

22. *CR*, IX, 512-513. This verdict may be found in the Provincial Records, vol. T, pp. 321-322. The depositions involved in the affair continue on file in Harrisburg. For the most complete account, see Rupp, *History and Topography*, pp. 173-192.
23. Thomas Wharton, Jr., born in Chester County into a Quaker family, was a prosperous Philadelphia merchant. A zealous patriot, he steadily became more and more active in politics, and on March 5, 1777, under the new Pennsylvania constitution, was elected Pennsylvania's first President of the Supreme Executive Council. He died in office at age forty-three. His burial site, at Trinity Church in Lancaster, on Duke Street, is identified by an Historical Marker.
24. Kelly, p. 619.
25. *Papers of Benjamin Franklin*, XV, 71-73. See also Kelly, p. 619.
26. *Papers of Benjamin Franklin*, XV, 91. For Armstrong's hearing, see *CR*, IX, 488-490.
27. Treese, pp. 89-90. For a record of the conference, see "Minutes of Conference held at Fort-Pitt in April and May of 1768," in *Early American Imprints*, no. 11301.
28. *PA*, First Series, IV, 395.
29. For an account of this incident, see Crist, *Proprietors' Man*, pp. 189-190.

Chapter XVII: The Surveyor

1. *PA*, Third Series, I, 146, 336. At his death he was in possession of thirteen properties, besides those in Carlisle.
2. Copy in Dickinson College archives.
3. Scull's father, who had emigrated from Ireland to Philadelphia, was one of Pennsylvania's most important surveyors. Nicholas the Second served as an apprentice under Pennsylvania's first Surveyor General, Thomas Holme, and also under Surveyor General Jacob Taylor. Scull accompanied Surveyor General Eastburn in the supervision of the notorious Indian Walk of September 1737. He was sixty-two years old when, on July 14, 1748, he succeeded William Parsons as Surveyor General. He died in 1761, and is buried near Scheet's Mill in White Marsh Township.
4. *PA*, Second Series, VII, 263-264.
5. Armstrong Business Papers, Box I, Folder 06, Dickinson College Archives.
6. Ibid., Box 1, Folder 02.
7. Crist, *Proprietors' Man*, p. 117. For a fine account of Armstrong's

surveying activities, see Crist, pp. 162-182.
8. See Armstrong Business Papers, Dickinson College Archives. The papers are housed in one document box, and are divided into three categories: Business Materials, Correspondence, and Survey Maps. They were donated by Boyd Lee Spahr, and reflect Armstrong's service as a surveyor in Cumberland County from 1755 to 1783.
9. Armstrong Business Papers, Box 1, Folder 01.
10. Ibid., Box 1, Folder 03.
11. Idem.
12. John Lukens was appointed Surveyor-General in 1761 by Proprietors Thomas and Richard Penn. He served in that post both for Pennsylvania and the "Lower Counties" (Delaware) until the Land Office was forced to close down because of the rebellion. He served again, for Pennsylvania only, from 1781 until his death in 1789.
13. Armstrong Business Papers, Box 1, Folder 04.
14. Ibid., Box 1, Folder, 07. Tax records show that a good many of those who settled the Cumberland Valley kept slaves. In 1768, for example, records show ten Carlisle residents were assessed taxes for eighteen Negro slaves. Among these names are those of John Armstrong, with two, and the Reverend John Steel, with two (Bates, II, 221). These Negroes, however, were definitely more like house servants than slaves and were regularly taken in as members of the family.
15. Armstrong Business Papers, Box 1, Folder 04. Armstrong constantly owed Lukens money, even as late as 1783, when we find him attempting to explain his debt of fifty pounds (letter of Armstrong to Lukens, Box 1, Folder 05).
16. *Papers of Benjamin Franklin*, X, 246.
17. Ibid., p. 246.
18. Copies of this kind of correspondence are with both Dickinson College and the Cumberland County Historical Society.
19. *Two Hundred Years in Cumberland County*, p. 46. Original letter is with the Hamilton Library of the Cumberland County Historical Society.
20. This letter is printed in many places. See Rhodehamel, pp. 123-124; Slaughter, p. 82, Bellamy, p. 154, and Fitzpatrick, *Writings of Washington*, II, 467-473.
21. Hamilton, III, 295-301.
22. Fitzpatrick, *Writings of Washington*, II, 471-473.
23. Hamilton, III, 302-306.
24. Slaughter, p. 82.
25. Martha (Patsy) Washington had suffered a number of epileptic

seizures. After one collapse, when she was thirteen years old, she was placed in the care of Dr. Hugh Mercer. She died in a sudden seizure suffered July 19, 1773, at age sixteen.

26. Freeman, pp. 186-190.
27. Fitzpatrick, *Writings of Washington*, II, 521-522.
28. Armstrong, together with other officers, had dispatched the twenty-eight-year-old Thompson down the Ohio to search out lands suitable for the officers to buy.
29. Fitzpatrick, *Writings of Washington*, III, 149-150, 155-156.
30. Letter a gift of Boyd Lee Spahr (1968) to Dickinson College. In Dickinsonian Collection.
31. Rokeby Collection, cited earlier.
32. Hamilton, IV, 290-293.

Chapter XVIII: The Presbyterian Church

1. Wing, *A History of the First Presbyterian Church of Carlisle*, p. 1; Davis, p. 454.
2. Bates, II, 211.
3. Bell, p. 51. The Reverend George Duffield died, aged fifty-seven, on February 2, 1790. For a short biography, see Nevin, *Men of Mark*, pp. 88-91.
4. Wing, *A History of the First Presbyterian Church*, pp. 70-71.
5. Ames, pp. 454-455.
6. Rupp, *History and Topography*, p. 421; Wing, *A History of the First Presbyterian Church*, pp. 71-72.
7. Webster, pp. 672-673.
8. Nevin, *Men of Mark*, p. 90.
9. On this subject, see Bonomi, pp. 139-152.
10. Ibid., p. 88.
11. Minutes of the Presbytery of Donegal (1759-69), II, 186-208.
12. Klett, p. 130.
13. Wing, *A History of the First Presbyterian Church*, p. 137.
14. Duffield eventually (1771) preached at the Old Pine Street Church in Philadelphia (built 1768, rebuilt 1837 and 1857, and standing still at 412 Pine Street, corner of Pine and 4th Streets). During the Revolution Duffield served as Chaplain of the Pennsylvania militia and as co-Chaplain of the Continental Congress.
15. Reverend Steel was interred in the Old Cemetery of Carlisle. For a profile, see Nevin, *Men of Mark*, pp. 71-74.
16. Wing, *A History of the First Presbyterian Church*, p. 107.

17. Born in the County Antrim, Beatty, after coming to America, was licensed by the New Brunswick Presbytery October 13, 1742, was called to the Forks of Neshaminy in May of the next year, and was ordained December 14. The Synod of New York sent him ten years later to Virginia and North Carolina. After missions in Pennsylvania and what is now Ohio, he sailed for the West Indies in the service of the College of New Jersey (now Princeton), but died, at age fifty-seven, after reaching Bridgeton in the Barbadoes.
18. Nolan, p. 65.
19. Beatty and the Reverend John Brainerd had been appointed by the Synod of New York and Pennsylvania, on May 24, 1763, "to preach to the distressed frontier inhabitants and to report their distresses," and to visit the Indian country. Owing to the emerging hostility of the Pontiac Indians, this mission was aborted.
20. Donehoo, *History of Cumberland Valley*, II, 205. See Charles Beatty, *The Journal of a Two Months' Tour*.

Chapter XIX: Rebeckah

1. Egle, *Pennsylvania Women in the Revolution*, p.126.
2. Idem.
3. Ibid., p. 127.
4. Letter of Armstrong to son James, April 29, 1773 (Rokeby Collection), which denotes his intent.
5. Letter is in the Dreer Collection (*Generals of the Revolution*, II, 36). A copy is contained in the Crist Papers at Dickinson College.
6. While he was a student at Dickinson College, Dr. James Wilkins Armstrong studied medicine with his father. He completed his studies at the University of Pennsylvania. He practiced medicine in Duncannon, Liverpool, and Bellefonte before retiring to his father's home in Carlisle (in 1844), and then later in Princeton. He died at Princeton in 1879, and was interred in Carlisle (*History of That Part of the Susquehanna and Juniata Valley*, pp. 918-919).
7. Bell, pp. 2-3.
8. Nevin, *Men of Mark*, pp. 103-105.
9. Of course John, Sr., spent the better part of his life on horseback. He was constantly riding to Shippensburg, York, Lancaster and Philadelphia, and all over Pennsylvania on surveying missions, military duty, and as a member of the Assembly and the Continental Congress. He kept quite a stable of horses, groomed and fed and exercised by Cesar and his fellow handymen. And naturally the boys

took very early to riding, and each had his own animal, and was very proud and possessive of it.
10. Skeen, p. 2.
11. Ibid., p. 227.
12. Bell, p. 52.
13. Skeen, p. 36.
14. Letter of James to John, Jr., Dec. 4, 1797 (Rokeby Collection). See Skeen, p. 36.
15. Letter to Gates, Nov. 13, 1797, Gates Papers, NYHS.
16. Letter in Rokeby Collection.
17. *Kline's Carlisle Weekly Gazette*, November 22, 1797. The *Carlisle Gazette and Western Repository of Knowledge* was published beginning 1785 by George Kline and George Reynolds, and continued with changes in title. Obituary reprinted in Egle, *Pennsylvania Women* in *the Revolution*, p. 127.

Chapter XX: The Siege of Charleston

1. Colonel Magaw remained on parole until October 25, 1780 (!), when he was finally set free of the British prison ships, and exchanged, together with Carlisle's General William Thompson, for Hessian Major General Adolf Baron von Riedesel, who had been captured at Saratoga. For much on Magaw, see Young, pp. 6-60.
2. Blaine, an early trustee of Dickinson College, hosted President Washington for his stay in Carlisle during the Whiskey Rebellion. He was the great grandfather of the famous candidate for President James Blaine of Maine.
3. Armstrong's letter, composed August 22, 1769, is with the HSP Collection (see Crist, *Proprietor's Man*, p. 201). Wilson, before long, did move to Carlisle, and established a residence just two blocks from Armstrong's home.
4. Ames, pp. 439-440. For the minutes of the meeting, see Bates, II, 77-78.
5. Letter with Chapel Hill Rare Books, Carrboro, N. C.
6. *PA*, First Series, IV, 693-694.
7. Rupp, *History and Topography*, pp. 401-405. See also Parkinson, pp. 213-221.
8. Ames, p. 440.
9. Ibid., pp. 440-441. And Rupp, *History and Topography*, pp. 405-406. For letters of André written during his imprisonment, see Westcott, pp. 77-81.

10. Jenkins, III, 350.
11. Thompson's commission was dated June 25, 1775, and was signed by John Hancock.
12. Force, 4th Series, III, col. 244; Fitzpatrick, *Writings of Washington*, III, 461-462; Abbott, I, 390-391.
13. Osgood led a local company of militia at Lexington-Concord and served in the siege of Boston. After leaving the army, he served in the Provincial Congress of Massachusetts and on the Massachusetts Board of War. He became, on September 26, 1789, the very first Postmaster General of the country.
14. Osgood Papers, NYHS; Burnett, *LMCC*, I, 255.
15. Ford, *Journals of the Continental Congress*, III (1775), 257. Frye, who was finally elected (nine colonies to three over Thompson), resigned his commission on March 18, and his resignation was accepted on April 23.
16. Force, Fourth Series, V, col. 105; Fitzpatrick, *Writings of Washington*, IV, 381-383; Abbott, p. 392. Frye had been given by Washington the vacant command at Cambridge.
17. Ford, *Journals of the Continental Congress*, IV (1776), 81; also letter of President of Congress, John Hancock, to Charles Lee, March 1, 1776, Force, Fourth Series, V. 37.
18. Force, Fourth Series, V, col. 43. The same letter was addressed to William Thompson, who was ordered to repair to New York to join the Continental Forces under General Charles Lee.
19. Force, Fourth Series, V, col. 43.
20. Force, Fourth Series, V, col. 83; Fitzpatrick, *Writings of Washington*, IX, 353.
21. Wheeler, pp. 116-117. For a good account of the Battle of Charleston, see Wheeler, pp. 116-123. See also Bancroft, V, 271-285.
22. Bancroft, V, 238.
23. Ibid., p. 239.
24. Force, Fourth Series, V, col. 1219.
25. Wheeler, p. 117.
26. Force, Fourth Series, VI, col. 612.
27. Bancroft, V, 234.
28. Force, Fourth Series, V, col. 1186.
29. Bancroft, V, 272.
30. Commager, II, 1064-1065.
31. Wheeler, p. 118.
32. Force, Fourth Series, V, col. 1187.
33. Idem.

34. Ibid., col. 1188.
35. Idem.
36. Idem.
37. Idem.
38. Ibid., col. 1189.
39. Thompson is not to be confused with Carlisle's General William Thompson, who at this time was a prisoner of the British, having been captured at the Battle of Three Rivers, along with Carlisle's Colonel William Irvine, during the futile invasion of Quebec.
40. Bancroft, V, 276-277.
41. Accounts vary in their figures. Wheeler, for example, has Moultrie's entire force, including Thomson, at 800 (pp. 119-120).
42. Commager, II, 1065. For participants' accounts of the battle, see pp.1062-1072.
43. Wheeler, pp. 119-120.
44. Force, Fourth Series, V, cols. 1189-1190.
45. Ibid., col. 1190.
46. Wheeler, p. 121.
47. Idem.
48. Commager, II, 1070; Wheeler, p. 122.
49. Force, Fourth Series, V, col. 1191.
50. Bancroft, V, p. 282.
51. In the many accounts of the battle the ships' names get confused, and the number of guns carried by the various vessels changes with each reporter.
52. The story of William Jasper is quite a story and a very tragic one. Although after this battle he was offered a commission by President Rutledge, he preferred to continue in the ranks. He became a somewhat notorious spy and was a master of disguise. He was mortally wounded in the battle of Savannah when General Benjamin Lincoln attempted to wrest the city back from the British. Jasper was shot down while attempting once again to plant the colors of the Second South Carolina Regiment within the British lines. He was twenty-nine years old. He was buried in a mass grave at the battle site. Today eight counties in the United States, as well as seven communities, are named for him. And two monuments have been devoted to his memory. The Jasper Monument stands in a public square in Savannah; and in Charleston Sergeant William Jasper can be seen atop a monument erected to the defenders of Sullivan's Island. He is clutching a staff with the brilliant blue flag draped about his shoulders. Inscribed on the statue are the words "shall not fight without our flag."

~ Notes ~

53. Wheeler, p. 123.
54. Force, Fourth Series, V, cols. 1191-1192.
55. Idem.
56. Wheeler, 123.
57. Bancroft, V, 285.
58. Commager, II, 1067.

Chapter XXI: The Brandywine

1. Force, Fifth Series, I, col. 720.
2. Ibid., cols. 904-905.
3. Ibid., col. 924.
4. On November 19 the Congress directed the Treasury to meet the General's traveling expenses, "Amounting to 400 Dollars." And on the 23rd Armstrong was paid $1781 for "pay and rations" and traveling expenses to and from Carolina (Force, Fifth Series, III, cols. 1575 and 1580); Ford, *Journals of the Continental Congress*, VI, 977).
5. Rupp, *History and Topography*, p. 451.
6. Dunaway, p. 162.
7. Stevens, *Pennsylvania, Birthplace* . . . ., p. 69.
8. McCartney, p. 7.
9. Force, Fifth Series, III, cols. 1151-1152.
10. Idem.
11. Force, Fifth Series, III, col. 1201; Fitzpatrick, *Writings of Washington*, VI, 363-364.
12. Force, Fifth Series, III, cols. 1228-1229; Ford, *Journals of the Continental Congress*, VI, 1031.
13. Force, Fifth Series, III, col. 1368.
14. Skeen, p. 3.
15. Idem.
16. *PA*, First Series, V, 164.
17. Ford, *Journals of the Continental Congress*, VI, 119-120.
18. *PA*, First Series, V, 229.
19. Fitzpatrick, *Writings of Washington*, VII, 250.
20. *PA*, First Series, V, 324-325.
21. Bates, II, 95.
22. Idem.
23. For a record of these councils and interchanges of letters, see Ford, "Defences of Philadelphia in 1777," *PMHB*, XVIII, No. 1 (1894), 1-19, 163-184, 329, 353, 463-495; XIX, No. 1 (April, 1895), 72-86,

234-250, 359, 373, 481-506; XX, No. 1 (1896), 87-115; No. 2 (1896), 213-247, 391-404, 520-551; XXI, No. 1 (April, 1897), 511-76.

24. *Journals of Continental Congress*, VII, 280; *Papers of Continental Congress*, No. 147, I, folio 143.
25. Joseph Reed, an ardent patriot, served two terms in the Continental Congress. As President of the Supreme Executive Council he is credited with the abolition of slavery in Pennsylvania.
26. The Ireland-born Stephen Moylan had not come to America until 1768, but he was passionate about the Cause. Although a prosperous shipping merchant, he was quick to join the forming army at Cambridge. He had been recommended to Washington by his good friend John Dickinson. Washington appointed him Muster-Master General and in the next spring he was made one of Washington's aides-de-camp. On June 17 of 1776 he was appointed by Congress to succeed Thomas Mifflin as Quartermaster General, but he was not Quartermaster General at the time of Reed's letter. He fought in the battle of New York, and, with great distinction, at Princeton. He would endure the winter at Valley Forge.
27. Thomas Mifflin was born into the Quakers, but was expelled when he entered the military. He became one of Washington's aides-de-camp in August of 1775 and was promptly appointed Quartermaster General. He won promotions to Colonel, and to Brigadier General, and eventually to Major General. He served on the Board of War for a time and then returned to the army. He served two terms in the Continental Congress. On. Nov. 5, 1788, he was elected President of the Supreme Executive Council, succeeding Benjamin Franklin. He was re-elected the next November, at the time Pennsylvania's State Constitution was written and adopted. Thus on Dec. 21, 1790, he became Pennsylvania's last "President" and her first "Governor." He is buried in Lancaster, at the Trinity Lutheran Church.
28. Sparks, *Writings of George Washington*, I, 389-390.
29. Fitzpatrick, *Writings of Washington*, VIII, 341-342.
30. Armstrong had also tried to get the confinement of Judge Chew lightened. Although Penn did take the new Loyalty Oath, he never returned to the Governor's office, but lived out his life at Lansdowne (Treese, p. 179).
31. *PA*, First Series, V, 561-562.
32. Ibid., pp. 563-564.
33. Ibid., pp. 568-569.
34. Ibid., pp. 572-573.
35. Ibid., p. 587.

36. Ibid., p. 598.
37. Fitzpatrick, *Writings of Washington*, IX, 130; Heathcote, p. 8.
38. Some historians have Armstrong's militia much greater in numbers, as high as 3000. See, for example, Dupuy, p. 96.
39. For a very good account of the Battle of the Brandywine, see John B. B. Trussell, Jr., *Pennsylvania Leaflet No. 37* (Pennsylvania Historical and Museum Commission, 1958); and see Burke Davis Chapter 13 of *George Washington and the American Revolution*.
40. Fitzpatrick, *Writings of Washington*, IX, 207-208; Rhodehamel, p. 274.
41. William Henry Smith, *St. Clair Papers*, pp. 97-98.
42. Fitzpatrick, IX, 215; Carrington, p. 382.
43 The French Colonel Louis Lebègue Duportail, with arrangements made by Benjamin Franklin, came to America in 1777. The thirty-four year-old officer became the Chief Engineer in the Continental Army. He was promoted to Brigadier General on Nov. 17, 1777 and given command over all engineers. He became Major General on Nov. 16, 1781.
43. Fitzpatrick, IX, 220-221.
44. Ford, *Journals of the Continental Congress*, VIII, 754.

Chapter XXII: Germantown

1. Pleasants, p. 51.
2. Fitzpatrick, *Writings of Washington*, IX, 265-266.
3. *PA*, First Series, V, 636-637.
4. Scott, who had been born in Cumberland County, Va., had served under Braddock and in Washington's Virginia Regiment. He had fought at Trenton and at the Brandywine. He would endure Valley Forge, participate in the action at Monmouth, and be captured by the British in the fall of Charleston in 1780. He became Governor of Kentucky, the new nation's fifteenth state.
5. Potter had been born in County Tyrone, Ireland. His father was Sheriff of Pennsylvania's Cumberland County in 1750, at the time Armstrong arrived there. Potter served Washington at Trenton and at Princeton, and commanded forces at the Brandywine. He left the Continental Army at the close of the 1777 campaign when his wife became ill.
6. Fitzpatrick, *Writings of Washington*, IX, 297-298.
7. McDougall had been born in Scotland, and had been with Washington at White Plains. After Benedict Arnold's treachery, he

would succeed to the command at West Point.
8. Octavius Pickering, *Life of Timothy Pickering*, I, 166-167.
9. Weedon's *Valley Forge Orderly Book*, pp. 73-74. See also Fitzpatrick, IX, 307.
10. Ward, I, 361; Baurmeister, p. 21.
11. Burke Davis, p. 235.
12. Witherspoon, of the New Jersey Brigade, was the son of the eminent John Witherspoon, a signer of the Declaration of Independence.
13. *PA*, First Series, V, 645-646.
14. Fitzpatrick, *Writings of Washington*, IX, 310; Heathcote, p. 10.
15. Drake, pp. 52-53.
16. Gates Papers, Box VIII, No. 51. Quoted by Commager, I, 628-629. This letter was sent by mistake to Thomas Wharton.
17. *PA*, First Series, V, 655-657. There occurred lots of correspondence between Armstrong and Wharton right through to the end of the 1777 campaign. Most of these letters are in the Gratz Collection.
18. Commager, I, 629.

Chapter XXIII: Whitemarsh

1. Fitzpatrick, *Writings of Washington*, IX, 337-338.
2. *PA*, First Series, V, 672-674.
3. Ibid., pp. 684-685.
4. Fitzpatrick, *Writings of Washington*, X, 202-204.
5. Ibid., p. 103n.
6. Ford, "Defenses of Philadelphia," *PMHB*, XX, No. 1 (1896), 103.
7. *PA*, First Series, VI, 43.
8. Ibid., p. 53.
9. *CR*, XI, 386.
10. Fort Mifflin was known also as Fort Island Battery and also as Mud Island Fort. The siege lasted five weeks! Lt. Colonel Samuel Smith (1752-1839), though born in Carlisle, became a Marylander. He commanded the 4th Maryland Regiment, and "served throughout the Revolution with distinction." He later (1793-1803) represented Maryland in the Congress. For the years 1803-1815 he served in the Senate. He helped to defend Baltimore during the War of 1812. For details on his life, and the Charles Willson Peale portrait see Thompson, pp. 29-39. It might be noted, too, that Captain Charles Willson Peale had command of a company of Pennsylvania militia at Whitemarsh, its activity apparently chiefly one of scouting. See Thompson, p. 29.

~ Notes ~   611

11. Thompson, p. 47.
12. For fascinating details on the skirmishing at Whitemarsh see Thompson's *Washington at Whitemarsh*.
13. For Allen McLane see Thompson, pp. 42-47.
14. *PA*, First Series, VI, .
15. James Irvine (1735-1819) should not be confused with William Irvine. Both were Pennsylvanians, although William was born in Ireland, and James in Philadelphia, the son of the Irish immigrant George Irvine. Both were in command of Pennsylvania units. Both were captured and served long terms as prisoners or on parole. James was not released until 1781! Both attained the rank of Brigadier General. Both served as trustees of educational institutions, William at Dickinson College, and James at the institution now known as the University of Pennsylvania. Besides, there is an Andrew Irvine, a captain in the Seventh Pennsylvania Regiment at the time it was commanded by Colonel William Irvine.
16. *PA*, First Series, VI, 70-72.
17. Ibid., p. 85.

Chapter XXIV: Valley Forge Winter

1. Ford, *Journals of the Continental Congress*, XX, No. 2, 242-243.
2. *PA*, First Series, VI, 43.
3. Bean and Brown, p. 38.
4. *PA*, First Series, VI, 90-91.
5. Ibid., p. 122; Cummings, p. 237.
6. Letter of Washington to Armstrong, Dec. 28 (Fitzpatrick, *Writings of Washington*, X, 215-216).
7. *PA*, First Series, VI, 100-102.
8. Ibid., pp. 122-123.
9. There is some evidence that a reconciliation between Wayne and Lacey was later effected.
10. John Lacey, "Memoirs of Brigadier-General John Lacey," *PMHB*, XXVI, 104.
11. Ibid., p. 265.
12. Ibid., p. 110.
13. Ibid., pp. 110-111.
14. Chase, *Papers of George Washington*, XIV, 436.
15. Bull enjoyed a most distinguished career as a patriot. He served the Proprietaries as an agent to the Indians, served the Forbes Expedition, and during the years 1778-1779 was kept busy erecting defense for

Philadelphia, commanding for a time the works at Billlingsport. He served as Commissary of Purchase at Philadelphia and later became a member of the First Constitutional Convention. He died August 9, 1824, at the "extreme age of ninety-four years." (Godcharles, *Daily Stories*, pp. 544-546).
16. Godcharles, p. 381.
17. *PA*, First Series, VI, 148-149.
18. Ibid., pp. 149-150.
19. Ibid., p. 151; and Cummings, p. 237.
20. *PA*, First Series, VI, 230-231, 238.
21. The fort at Sinking Spring Valley has been reconstructed, very near the original site.
22. For an account of the Sinking Spring Valley conspiracy, see Godcharles, *Daily Stories*, pp. 258-259; also Hassler, pp. 49-53. On the Bedford trials see *CR*, XI, 581, and *PA*, First Series, VI, 744.
23. Chase, *Papers of George Washington*, XIV, 121.
24. Ibid., pp. 48, 251, 436, 570, 661.
25. Ibid., pp. 612-613. See also Fitzpatrick, *Writings of Washington*, XI, 305.
26. Sparks, *Writings of George Washington*, V, 360n.; Fitzpatrick, *Writings of Washington*, XI, 363-366.
27. Tower, p. 325.
28. Fitzpatrick, *Writings of Washington*, XI, 159; Chase, *Papers of George Washington*, XIV, 326-328.
29. *PA*, First Series, VI, 412-414.
30. Ibid., p. 516.
31. George Bryan, born in Dublin in 1731, had emigrated to Philadelphia in 1752. He was an early and ardent patriot, and an Abolitionist as well. He was elected the State's first Vice President on March 5, 1777, and when Thomas Wharton died in office he assumed the duties of President of the Supreme Executive Council.
32. *PA*, First Series, VI, pp. 612-615.
33. Ibid., pp. 635-636.
34. Idem.
35. Ibid., pp. 657-658.
36. Ibid., pp. 661-664.
37. Ibid., pp. 669-670, 680-681.
38. Ibid., pp. 680-681.
39. For a full account of the Hartley campaign, see Trussell and Myers, pp. 1-4.
40. Letters of Armstrong, August 6 and 26, 1778 (*PA*, First Series, VI, 715-716).

41. *PA*, First Series, VII, 18-19.
42. Ibid., pp. 109-111.
43. Letter of Armstrong to Washington, May 10, 1779 (Fitzpatrick, *Writings of Washington*, XV, 97-99).
44. Fitzpatrick, *Writings of Washington*, XIV, 198-201.

Chapter XXV: The Continental Congress

1. *Journals of the Continental Congress*, XII, 1160-1161.
2. Fitzpatrick, *Writings of Washington*, XV, 97-99; Burnett, *LMCC*, I, 394.
3. Fitzpatrick, *Writings of Washington*, XV, 97-99.
4. Burnett, *LMCC*, IV, 135; Freeman, V, 100-101.
5. *PA*, First Series, VIII, 281, 287. John Laurens may have saved Washington's life at the battle of Germantown. Later he fought a duel against General Charles Lee because of the abuse Lee had showered on Washington. It was Laurens whom Washington assigned to the interrogation of John André at his trial.
6. Gates Papers, XIV, 323; Burnett, *LMCC*, IV, 135-136.
7. Ford, *Journals of the Continental Congress*, "Letters to Washington," XXXII, 253; Burnett, *LMCC*, IV, 204, #260.
8. Gates Papers, XIV, 82. Burnett, *LMCC*, IV, 226-227, # 294.
9. Ford, *Journals of the Continental Congress*, "Letters to Washington," XXXIII, 214; Sparks, *Writings of George Washington*, II, 309. (Letter is dated June 5 in Sparks.); Burnett, *LMCC*, IV, 283-284, # 369.
10. Hassler, p. 96; Thwaites, p. 201. An historical marker (presently missing) was erected at the site (Route 66, 1.8 miles south of Kittanning) and dedicated Nov. 28, 1946. The text reads: "Located on the nearby river bank, this outpost was built in June, 1779, and abandoned that autumn. It served the Brodhead expedition against the Senecas and was named for Maj. Gen. John Armstrong."
11. Ford, *Journals of the Continental Congress*, XIV, 740.
12. Fitzpatrick, *Writings of Washington*, XVI, 70.
13. Letter of July 14, 1779, from Philadelphia, in possession of Chapel Hill Rare Books, Carrboro, N. C.
14. Burnett, *LMCC*, IV, 301.
15. Letter with NYHS, Gates Papers, XVI, 151. See Burnett, *LMCC*, IV, 310-311, Letter #404.
16. *Journals of the Continental Congress*, XIV, 886-887.
17. Burnett, *LMCC*, IV, 376-377, letter # 475.

18. Ford, *Journals of the Continental Congress*, "Letters to Washington," XXXIV, 122; Burnett, *LMCC*, IV, 490-491, # 604.
19. *History Magazine*, VIII, 17; Burnett, *LMCC*, IV, 500, # 623.
20. Letter of the Council's Matthew Smith, October 14, 1779.
21. Ford, *Journals of the Continental Congress*, XV, 1263.
22. *PA*, First Series, VIII, 32.
23. Connaroe Collection, II, 58; Burnett, *LMCC*, IV, 536-537, # 683.
24. Sparks, *Writings of George Washington*, II, 377; Burnett, *LMCC*, IV, p. 425.
25. Armstrong to Gates, in Burnett, *LMCC*, V, p. 38.
26. MSS of Joseph Reed, VI; Burnett, *LMCC*, V, 13-14, # 21.
27. Gates Papers, XVI and XVII; Manuscripts of Joseph Reed, VI; Burnett, *LMCC*, V, pp. 37-39, 76-79, 265-266, # 52, 95, 317.
28. Butler had served the Continental Army at Saratoga and at Monmouth. Washington selected him to receive the surrender sword of Lord Cornwallis at Yorktown, and at the victory dinner held for his officers, Washington toasted "The Butlers and their five sons." By this time Richard Butler, a frontier trader, had already enjoyed negotiating relations with the Indians. Later, in 1784, as U. S. Commissioner, he would negotiate the Treaty of Fort Finney. He became a good friend to the Seneca war-chief Cornplanter, for whom he persuaded Pennsylvania to award a grant of land on the Allegheny River. And he became a *very* good friend of Chief Big Tree, who by Butler's tragic death was reduced to melancholia and became deranged. As Major General, Butler was second in command to Arthur St. Clair on the ill-fated mission against the Ohio Indians in November of 1781. While fighting heroically (Two of his four brothers were also in the battle.), he was struck down by a blow from a tomahawk. Richard Butler is remembered in the names of counties in Ohio, Kentucky, and Pennsylvania; in the city of Butler, Pennsylvania; the General Richard Butler Bridge in Butler, Pa.; and in the name of a street in Pittsburgh. The building which housed the Butler gun shop of colonial Carlisle still stands. It is on Dickinson Avenue (sometimes called "Alley") near the College.
29. *PA*, First Series, VIII, 243-244.
30. Ibid., p. 636.
31. Fitzpatrick, *Writings of Washington*, XVIII, 432 and 432n.
32. Gates Papers, XVI; Burnett, *LMCC*, V, 198-200, 217, # 229 and 250.
33. Davis served in 1776 as Commissary of the 6th Pennsylvania Regiment. In the next year he served as Deputy Quartermaster, headquartered at Carlisle, and on March 23 General Nathanael Greene appointed him "to act as Deputy Quarter Master General of

~ Notes ~ 615

the American Army, on the western Side of the Susquehannah in the State of Pennsylvania." (Chase, *Papers of George Washington*, XIV, 122).
34. Papers of John Davis (Library of Congress); Burnett, *LMCC*, V, 250-251, # 297.
35. Papers of John Davis (Library of Congress); Burnett, *LMCC*, V, 295-296, # 343.
36. Irvine, one of two physicians in the Carlisle region, had been born not far from Armstrong's boyhood home, in the Enniskillen region of County Fermanagh, Ireland. Twenty-four years younger than Armstrong, he was very fond of the General. He named one of his sons Armstrong, and his eighth child Rebecca Armstrong. A grandson was named William Armstrong.
37. *History Magazine*, VIII, 17; Burnett, *LMCC*, V, 333, # 387.
38. Gates Papers, Box 15; Burnett, *LMCC*, V, 356-358, # 415.
39. Irvine Papers, X; *History Magazine*, VIII, 16; Burnett, *LMCC*, V, 307-308, # 357. Armstrong was, however, before long made most happy by the news of Greene's extraordinary military successes against Cornwallis in the Carolinas.
40. Manuscripts of Joseph Reed, VI; Burnett, *LMCC*, V, 348-349, # 406.
41. Wall, p. 172.
42. *History Magazine*, VIII, 18; Burnett, *LMCC*, VIII, p. 64n.
43. Freeman, VI, 145.
44. Idem.
45. Fitzpatrick, *Writings of Washington*, XXIX, 464-467; Rhodehamel, pp. 670-673.
46. Fitzpatrick, XXXI, 210-211.
47. William Henry Smith, *The St. Clair Papers*, pp. 276-277.

Chapter XXVI: Dickinson College

1. On the history of the College, see Sellers, Morgan, and *Bulwark of Liberty*.
2. For an account of the grammar school, see Sellers, pp. 36-50.
3. Later, Montgomery would become a member of Pennsylvania's Council of Safety (1775-76) and would be named one of the commissioners to treat with the Indians at Fort Pitt (July, 1776). He would serve as a member of the Assembly (1781-82), as a delegate to Congress (1782-84, and an Associate Judge of the Court of Cumberland County (1794). See Butterfield, I, 300.
4. Wing, *History of the First Presbyterian Church of Carlisle*, p. 119.

5. Sellers, p. 56.
6. Butterfield, I, 294-297. And see Morgan, pp. 10-12.
7. Armstrong letter to Rush, April 16, 1783 (in Butterfield).
8. Morgan, p. 12.
9. Butterfield, I, 303.
10. Morgan, p. 13.
11. Ibid., pp. 14-15.
12. This address is published in Benjamin Rush's Essays under the title "Of the Mode of Education Proper in a Republic."
13. Letter of Rush to Montgomery, Nov. 15, 1783 (Butterfield, I, 313-314).
14. Morgan, p. 17.
15. Ibid., pp. 19-20.
16. Butterfield, I, 315-316.
17. Morgan, pp. 21-22.
18. Ibid., p. 23.
19. Ibid., pp. 16-17.
20. Morgan, p. 25.
21. Sellers, p. 65.
22. Morgan, pp. 25-26.
23. Clymer, an ardent patriot, had served in the Continental Congress and had signed the Declaration of Independence. He was one of only five men to sign both the Declaration of Independence and the Constitution. The small coal-mining town of Clymer in western Pennsylvania is named for him.
24. Butterfield, I, 319-320.
25. Rush used the spelling "Nesbet" or "Nesbit," just about as often as "Nisbet."
26. Butterfield, I, 342-343.
27. Ibid., pp. 321-325.
28. Ibid., pp. 356-357.
29. Edel, pp. 115-116.
30. Ibid., p. 116.
31. Ibid., p. 117.
32. Butterfield, I, 351-355.
33. Ibid., p. 361.
34. Ibid., p. 363.
35. Ibid., pp. 363-364.
36. At Rush's insistence Davidson was appointed Professor of history, geography, chronology, rhetoric, and belles lettres at the College. Upon the death of Nisbet he assumed the presidency of the College, resigning in 1809. Always a favorite with Montgomery, he married

Montgomery's daughter Margaret in 1807 while Principal of the College. One of his early students, Roger Taney, produced a "delightful sketch" of him (Butterfield, I, 320-321).
37. Butterfield, I, 369-370.
38. Morgan, p. 48.
39. Ibid., pp. 48-49.
40. Armstrong remained high on Nisbet to the very end. In a letter to Dickinson, January 10, 1787, he had great praise for the Principal: "The Doctors assiduity in [the] College is very great, he Lectures and Examines on these Lectures, generally twice a day—Moral philosophy & Criticism, I believe is the present business of his Class." And he was constantly lamenting the inadequacy of his salary, noting that Dr. Nisbet is "too frequently left to his last Shilling."
41. Ibid., p. 50.
42. The Reverend John Witherspoon was born near Edinburgh and was educated there. A Presbyterian pastor, and a signer of the Declaration of Independence, he was the sixth President of the College of New Jersey. Naturally he was not friendly to the idea of a College in Carlisle.
43. Hill was a Philadelphia wine merchant, a member of the Provincial Conference and Convention of 1776, a member of the Pennsylvania Assembly and afterwards of the Supreme Executive Council. He would become an executor of Franklin's will (Butterfield, I, 346).
44. Butterfield, I, 393.
45. Morgan, pp. 51-52.
46. *Bulwark of Liberty*, p. 45.
47. Morgan, p. 52.
48. For the text, see Good, pp. 167-169. Nisbet himself wrote an account, dated Nov. 15, 1786, which, however, did not appear in the newspapers.
49. Butterfield, I, 306-309, and 309n.
50. Letter dated Feb. 17, 1787 (Butterfield, I, 411-412).
51. Phillips in *Bulwark of Liberty*, p. 102. This statement appears on the inside cover of the February 1787 number of the *Columbian Magazine*. For the donors to the library, see Phillips, pp. 103-114. The library at Dickinson, so impressive in its beginnings, is today considered one of the finest college libraries in the country.
52. Sellers, p. 125.
53. Edel, p. 118.
54. Donehoo, *History of Cumberland Valley*, I, 246.
55. The first female student was admitted in 1884. Her name was Zatae

Longsdorff. She entered as a sophomore and graduated in 1887.

Chapter XXVII: Last Days

1. See Appendix for text of this letter.
2. Crist, *Proprietors' Man*, pp. 213-214. The Land Records of the Archives at Harrisburg show another John Armstrong purchase of the same September 13 date, this one of 200 acres in Antrim Twp., Cumberland County. There is also record of a John Armstrong warrant for 100 acres on Lost Creek in Cumberland County (Sept. 10, 1766). In all, a John Armstrong is named warrantee for seventeen land acquisitions in Cumberland County between Jan. 15, 1752, and March 8, 1774.
3. Bell, p. 50.
4. The will was proven July 25, 1797. A copy of the will may be procured from the courthouse in Carlisle or from the Cumberland County Historical Society.
5. From letters written to Henry Knox, to Jefferson and Hamilton during his early years of the Presidency, it is apparent that Washington did use an alternate route through the village of Carlisle occasionally on his journey from Mt. Vernon to Philadelphia.
6. Washington's "Diary Notes," in Chase, *Papers of George Washington*, VII. See the painting of Washington's reception, "Washington in Carlisle," done by Mort Kuntsler.
7. Baldwin, p. 209. See affidavits of Samuel Castlewait, George Rowan, Robert Guthrie, and Ephraim Blaine, September 15,16, 1794, in Mifflin Documents.
8. For accounts of the distressing incidents and the alienating behavior of the soldiers toward the civilian populations, see Brackenridge, Part II, 30-33, and Slaughter, pp. 208-212.
9. Baldwin, p. 225.
10. Freeman, VII, 202, 212n.
11. The Ephraim Blaine house, recently reconstructed according to original specifications, is featured on tours of the historic district of Carlisle. Blaine, whose first wife, like Armstrong's, was named Rebecca, operated a distillery (!) at his farmhouse near Yellow Breeches Creek, some 1.5 miles from Carlisle. (Even Washington operated a distillery.) For good detail on the two Blaine houses, see Lenore Flower, *Visit of George Washington*, pp. 11-12.
12. Vol. VII, p. 202, of Freeman's biography of Washington, completed by Carroll and Ashworth. For more details see Dallas, pp. 35 ff, and

Blaine, pp. 48 ff.
13. Nevin, *Churches of the Valley*, p. 238.
14. Baldwin, p. 226.
15. Fitzpatrick, *Writings of Washington*, XXXIV, 45.
16. *PA*, Second Series, IV, 344-345. To the Whiskey Rebellion the *Pennsylvania Archives* devotes 462 pages in this volume.
17. Ibid., p. 345. And Fitzpatrick, *Writings of Washington*, XXXIV, 519-520.
18. *Kline's Carlisle Weekly Gazette*, March 11, 1795.
19. Nevin, *Men of Mark*, p. 77.
20. See Sarah Woods Parkinson, *Memories of Carlisle's Old Graveyard*.

Afterword

1. Robert Walter Smith, p. 377. For a detailed history of the County, including the Kittanning Expedition, see Smith's *History of Armstrong County*.
2. Ibid., p. 377.
3. Day, p. 97.
4. For the sale of these parcels, see R. W. Smith, pp. 376-380.
5. Rupp, *Early History of Western Pennsylvania*, appendix, p. 341.
6. *Simpson's Daily Leader*, May 12, 1917, pp. 1 and 4.
7. The noted Pennsylvania historian and author Chester Hale Sipe was born, lived and died in the same house in South Buffalo, Butler County, Pa. His little book *Mt. Vernon and the Washington Family* had appeared in 1925. *Indian Chiefs of Pennsylvania* appeared in 1927, *The Indian Wars of Pennsylvania* in 1929, and *Fort Ligonier and Its Times* in 1932. He later served the Pennsylvania State Senate as a Democrat.
8. John S. Fisher was born not far from Kittanning, near present Plumville in Indiana County, in 1867. A graduate of the two-year Normal School in Indiana, and elected to the State Senate at age thirty-three, he became Governor of Pennsylvania in 1927. He died in 1940 in Indiana.
9. *Simpson's Daily Leader-Times*, September 9, 1926, pages 1 and 5.
10. R. W. Smith, p. 26.

Appendix A

1. Nevin, pp. 77-78. General Armstrong this same year lost also his granddaughter Rebecca, who was in her infancy.

Index

Abercromby, Gen. James, 139, 145, 148, 156, 163, 164, 171, 180, 187, 194, 201, 213, 565
Aberdeen University, 80
absentee landlordism, 2
Acteon, 380, 382
Adams County, 12
Adams, John, 335, 358, 479, 487
Adams, John (settler), 102
Adams, Thelma, 534
"Address of Citizens of Carlisle to President Washington," 527
Agahvea, 565
Aghalurgher Parish, 11, 339
Agincourt, 199
Agnew, John, 353, 356
Albany, 29, 455
Alden, Ichabod, 455
Alexander, Gen. James (Lord Stirling) (see Stirling)
Aliquippa, 254
Allegheny County, 533, 541
Allegheny County Courthouse, 177
Allegheny Mountain, 39, 95, 152, 168, 170, 208-209, 538, 586
Allegheny River, 8-9, 71, 78, 93, 179, 199, 207, 213, 615
Allen, Chief Justice William, 200, 278, 289, 291, 296, 401, 590, 596
Allen, John, 306
Allen, Samuel, 172
Allentown, 258, 261, 402
Allison, Col. John, 352
Alricks, Hermanus, 301
Altoona, 85, 443
Amboy, 61
Ambridge, 254
Ames, William, 23, 354, 356

Amherst, Gen. Jeffrey, 139, 201, 203, 213, 238, 241-245, 248, 250, 252-253, 258
Andastes Indians, 267
Anderson, Robert, 149
André, Major John, 357
Annapolis, 324, 480, 527, 582
Anthony Thompson's, 39
Antrim, 1
Apollo, 536, 539
Arch Street, Philadelphia, 497
Armagh, 3
armory, in Carlisle, 357
Armstrong, General John, emigration, 8-12; ancestry, 9-11; blazes Braddock Road, 32-44; raid on Kittanning, 82-121; frontier forts, 119-130; commands Pa. Militia on Forbes expedition, 142-218; relationship to Col. Bouquet, 208-233; Pontiac Wars, 234-260; Susquehanna expedition, 256-261; Conestoga massacre, 265-283; the Black Boys, 280-287; escape of Frederick Stump, 288-315; surveying activity, 312-328; Presbyterian Church, 333-344; commissioned Brigadier General in the Continental Army, 354; siege of Charleston, 351-378; recruiting, 391-397; resigns commission, 399; commissioned Brigadier General and promoted to Major General of Pa. Militia, 399; battle of the Brandywine, 397-411; battle of Germantown, 411-425;

Whitemarsh, 426-435; winter quarters for Continental Army 435-437; Valley Forge winter, 438-446; resigns from Continental Army (Pa. Militia command), 440; lead mine, 446-448; council with Washington, 449-450; terms in Second Continental Congress, 459-483; helps to found Dickinson College, 487-526; writes will, 527-528; Whiskey Rebellion, with Washington in Carlisle, 528-530; death and interment in Carlisle's Old Cemetery, 530-532

Armstrongs: Alexander (son of General John's brother William), 583-622; Alfred, 345; Andrew (Gen. John's brother), 8, 530; Andro (Gen. John's sister), 8; Ann (Gen. John's sister), 8; Archibald, 11; Archibald (grandson of Archibald), 11; Catherine (Gen. John's granddaughter), 345; Catherine (daughter of Gen. John's cousin Joseph), 577; Charity (daughter of Gen. John's brother William), 583; Edward (Gen. John's grandfather), 8; Edward (brother to Gen. John), 8; Edward (son of Archibald), 12, 61, 64-73, 90; Edward (son of John, Jr.), 346; Elizabeth (daughter of Gen. John's brother William), 583; George (grandson of Gen. John), 345; George (brother to Gen. John), 8, 61, 74, 76, 80, 84, 90, 107, 124, 131, 162, 165-167, 173-174, 216, 237, 316, 318; Hannah (daughter of Gen. John's son James), 344; Henry Beekman (son of John, Jr.), 346; Horatio Robert Gates (son of John, Jr.), 346; James of Terwinney (Gen. John's father), 8, 10, 345; James (son of Gen. John), 11, 12, 18, 324-326, 344-346, 355-356, 397, 402, 465, 470, 519, 521, 523, 529, 532, 542-543; James (son of Gen. John's son James), 345; James (brother to Gen. John), 8, 223, 316; James (son of Joseph, Sr.), 345, 577; James Kosciuszko (son of John, Jr.), 10, 345; James (son of Archibald), 11; James (grandson of Archibald), 11; James (son of Gen. John's brother Andrew), 8, 347; Jean (wife to Gen. John's brother William), 577; Jennet (wife to Joseph, Sr.), 577, John of Gilnockie (Johnie), 8; John, Jr. (son of Gen. John), 211, 216, 339, 344-346, 394-395, 397, 469, 475, 483, 489, 523, 532; John (son of Gen. John' son William), 583; John (son of John, Jr.), 346; John (son of Joseph, Sr.), 577; John (son of Archibald), 12; John Wilkins (son of Gen. John's son James), 350, 519, 529; John, the trader, murdered at Jack's Narrows, 10; Joseph, Sr., 577; Joseph, Jr., 577;

~ Index ~   623

Margaret (sister of Gen. John), 8, 10, 309; Margaret (daughter of Archibald), 11-12, 309-310, 322, 354, 358, 359; Margaret (daughter of John, Jr.), 346; Margaret (daughter of Joseph, Sr.), 577; Marion, 535, 538; Mary (daughter of Dr. John Wilkins Armstrong), 529; Mary Ann (daughter of Gen. John's son James), 345; Rebeckah (daughter of Archibald, and Gen. John's wife), 10-12, 66, 198, 211, 310, 311, 324, 331-332, 339, 340-350, 362, 523, 528-529, 537, 566; Rebecca (daughter of Gen. John's son James), 345; Rebecca (Rebeckah) (Gen. John's sister and wife of John Turner), 8, 529; Rebecca (second Rebecca daughter of Gen. John's son James), 345; Robert Livingston (son of John, Jr.), 346; Susannah (daughter of Gen John's brother William), 583; Thomas (of Mangerton), 8; William (brother to Gen. John), 8, 10, 163, 223-224, 229, 232; William (son of Gen. John's brother William), 582; William (Christie's Will), 8; William (son of Archibald), 11-12; William (grandson of Archibald), 11; William (son of Joseph, Sr.), 577
Armstrong County, 9, 532-535, 539
Armstrong County Court House, 533-534
Armstrong County Historical Society, 535-536, 538
Armstrong Township, 539
Armstrong's Oak, 88
Arnold, Gen. Benedict, 461-463, 584
Articles of Confederation, 480
Ashalecoa, 187
Ashley River, 362
Ashville, 85
Assembly of Pennsylvania (see General Assembly)
Assunepachla, 84
Astor, William B., 346
Atkin, Edmund, 147
Atlee, Col. Samuel John, 459, 469
Attique Indian Town (see Kittanning)
Aughwick Creek, 63-64, 112, 115, 259
Avis, 256-257

Baird, John, 212
Baker, John, 79, 81, 90-91, 99, 105, 109
Bald Eagle Creek, 46, 257
Bancroft, George, 199, 360
Baptists, 5
Barber, Robert, 269
Barnhold, 71, 73
Barr, James, 524
Barr's Place, 116, 118
Barr, Thomas, 116
Barren Hill Church, 431
Bartholomews, 440
Barton, Rev. Thomas, 75, 93, 104, 160, 184-185
Baskins, Robert, 68
Bassett, Dr., 163
Bay, Andrew, 184
Bayard, John, 495

Bayard, Col. Stephen, 464
Baylor, Col. George, 453
Beatty, Rev. Charles, 85, 199, 200, 331, 337-340
Beaver, Chief (see King Beaver)
Beaver County, 57
Beaver Creek (Allegheny County), 155, 338
Beaver Creek (Chester County), 404
Beaver Dams, 80, 84-85
beaver pelts, 55
Bedford, 8, 39, 159, 210-240, 246, 251, 259, 261, 264, 284-285, 444
Bedford, a rifleman, 258
Bedford County, 21, 133
Bedford Street, Carlisle, 109
Beech Creek, 257
Belfast, 9
Bell, Raymond, 8, 9, 11
Belle Air, 175, 184, 601
Belleville, 310, 344
Benjamin Franklin Highway, 537
Beringer, 86
Berkeley, Va., 323, 465
Berks County, 21, 50, 217, 241, 277, 398
Bethlehem, 258, 261, 422
bible, 9, 329, 335
Biddle, Edward, 459
Big Cove, 48-49, 59, 116
Big Pool, 124
Big Spring, 17-18, 331
Big Tree, Chief, 615
Billingsport, 359, 402, 425
Black Boys Rebellion, 280-286
Black Dog, Chief, 255
Black, Mrs. Frank, 536
Black, Rev. John, 461
Black Watch (42nd Highland Regiment), 147, 239, 245, 282

Blaine, Ephraim, 297, 351, 356, 389, 398, 525-527
Blaine, James, 526
Blaine, Robert, 526
Blair County, 133
Blair, James, 58
Blair, Dr. John, 149
Blair, Gen. John, 148
Blair, Samuel, 331
Blair, Dr. Thomas, 121
Blane, Captain-Lt. Archibald, 145, 212, 234, 242, 243,
Blanket Hill, 9, 83, 96, 98, 99, 105, 540-541
Bloody Run, 232
Blue Hill, 34
Blue Jacket, 484
Blue Licks, 478
Blue Mountains, 16, 23, 47, 77, 111, 232
Blunston License Book, 18
Blunston, Samuel, 17
Blyth (Blythe), William, 288, 343
Board of Trade, 263
Board of War, 390-401, 414, 421, 444-445, 449, 459, 461, 463, 467, 468-470, 474, 476-477
Boiling Springs, 24, 507, 523
Bolivar, Ohio, 251
Bolton's Landing, 372
Bonnie Prince Charlie, 80, 137
Bonny Brook (Great Beaver Pond), 17
Boone, Daniel, 121, 470
Boone, Israel, 478
Bordentown, 391
Borrowelly, Martin, 75
Boscawen, Admiral Edward, 135
Boston, 281, 341-342, 350-351, 355, 359, 397
Boston Massacre, 281

Boston Tea Parties, 281
bounties, 59-60
Bouquet, Col. Henry (Henri), 109,
  117, on Forbes Expedition,
  139-202; road building, 203-
  233; relief of Fort Pitt, 234-
  248; Ohio Expedition, 249-
  253; 255, 256, 260, 279-280,
  283, 337, 341
Boyd, Lt. Thomas, 575
Boyle, Charles, 206
Boynton, John, 280, 282
Boynton, Wharton, and Morgan,
  280, 282
Brackenridge, Hugh Henry, 529
Braddock, Gen. Edward, 31-41,
  44-48, 54, 58, 63, 77, 82, 85,
  111, 113, 115, 123, 125, 133,
  134, 138, 146-150, 155, 159,
  172, 174-176, 195-197, 231,
  242, 250, 264, 309, 332, 340,
  351, 450
Braddock Road, 31-44, 90, 147,
  156, 162, 197, 318
Bradley, John, 72
Bradstreet, Col. John, 249-251
Brainerd, Rev. John, 606
Brandon, 71
Brandywine, battle of, 404-410,
  411, 414, 416, 423, 431, 522
Brandywine Creek, 404-405
Brant, Chief Joseph, 449, 455
Breastwork Hill, 173
Breckenreach, David, 103
Breeds and Bunker Hills, 358
Brinton's Ford, 407
Bristol, 375, 379-380, 382
Brodhead, Col. Daniel, 452, 455-
  457, 463, 540, 616
Brokenstraw Creek, 209
Brookeborough, 7, 339
Brooklyn, 388

Brown, Enoch, 249, 581
Brown, George, 580
Brown, James, 161
Brown, Joseph, 407
Brown, William, 354
Brownsville, 586
Browntown Mountain, 454
Brush Creek, 155
Brush Mountain, 445
Bryan, George, 450-454, 493, 615
Buchanan, Arthur, 67
Buchanan, President James, 519
Buchanan, William, 38, 45, 49, 65,
  67, 84, 108
Buchannon, Mrs. Anne, 567
Buckaloons, 209
Buckinghamshire, 21
Bucks County, 21, 440, 441
Buffalo Valley, 70
Bull, Col. John, 442-443
Bull Creek, 211
Bullitt, Captain Thomas, 214-215
Bull's Eye, 114
Burd, Col. James, 33-34, 37-39,
  45, 48-49, 51-52, 60, 64-67,
  78, 109-114, 123-128, 138-
  146, 148, 150, 153, 155, 162,
  167, 170, 182, 186-187, 195,
  201, 208, 210-215, 234, 270,
  341, 459
Burgeon's Pass, 85
Burgoyne, Gen. John, 414, 425,
  475
Burke, Thomas, 87, 96
Burnt Cabins, 29
Bushy Run, 244-246, 250-251,
  584, 590
Butler County, 537
Butler, John, 451-453
Butler, General Richard, 6, 471-
  472, 533, 616
Butler, Walter, 453, 455

Butler, Col. Zebulon, 457
Butler's Rangers, 451, 455
Butler Road, Kittanning, 540
Buxton, John, 590
Byers, James, 356
Byers, Capt. John, 213, 228, 300, 354, 356
Byrd, Col. William, 138, 141, 158, 179, 186, 201, 584

Cadwalader, Col. John, 396, 432, 436
Caesar (Ceazar, Cesar), 316
Caldew River, 22
Caldwell, Samuel, 577
Calhoon, Dr. John, 351
Calhoun, Andrew, 300
Callender, Ann, 354
Callender, Captain Robert, 104-105, 145, 150, 169, 351, 354-355, 529
Calvin, John, 328
Camden, S.C., 475-476
Campbell, Francis, 34
Campbell, John (Earl of Loudoun), 117, 135, 581
Campbell, John (Indian), 287-288
Campbell, Major, 245
Campbell, Mary, 8
Campbell, Robert, 241
Camp Doylestown, 447
Camp Hill, 428
Canasorgu, 254-255
Canoe Place, 15, 86, 254
Canton, Ohio, 251
Ca-nu-ks-e-sung (Peggy), 272
Cape Fear, 363, 387
Captain John Peter, 49, 54
Captain Will, 49, 54
Carlisle Conference of 1753, 26-29
Carlisle Conference of 1756, 45-47
Carlisle, England, 335
Carlisle Gazette, 575, 607
Carlisle, Pa., 8, 11-13, 17, 21-31, and passim
Carlisle Telegraph, 528
Carmichael, William, 461
Carroll, Hugh, 69
Carrolltown, 86
Carteret, John (Earl of Granville), 66
Castanea, 255
Castle Dewart, 216
Catawba Indians, 143, 187, 291
Cavendish, William, 583
Cayuga Indians, 234
Cecil Court-House, 404
Cessny's Field, 127
Chadds Ford, 404-409, 415
Chalmers, James, 87
Chambers, Benjamin, 117-118, 315, 352
Chambersburg, 18, 35, 39, 53, 115, 117, 280, 345, 352, 528
Chambers, George, 334
Chambers, George, of Carlisle, 529
Chambers' Mill, 58, 117
Chambers, Samuel, 95-96
Chapel (Locust) Alley, Carlisle, 357
Charles II, 21
Charleston, S. C., siege of, 351-381; 385, 387-388, 397, 407, 465, 474-475, 522
Chartiers Creek, 319
Chee-na-wan (Peggy Smith), 272
Cherokee Indians, 97, 121-122, 131, 138, 143, 163, 187, 190, 201, 578
Cherry Tree, 56, 254, 577
Cherry Valley, 340, 455

Chesapeake 15, 404
Chester, 402, 407-409, 425
Chester County, 8, 21, 264, 275, 411, 427, 439, 523
Chester Valley, 483
Chestnut Hill, 273, 413, 417, 429-432, 439
Chestnut Ridge, 156, 191
Chest Springs, 85
Chew, Judge Benjamin, 211, 274, 294, 301, 401, 593, 611
Chew Mansion, 418-422
Cheyney, Squire Thomas, 407
Chickasaw Indians, 54
Chief Belt, 56
Chief Kitchi, 247
Chief Lappawinsoe, 128-129
Chief Strong Wolf (see Strong Wolf)
Chillicothe, 479
Chinklacamoose, 8, 254-255
Christ Church, 443, 598
Christiana Hundred, 11
Christina River, 404
Chronicles of The Armstrongs, 8, 575, 579, 585
Church Hill, 45, 48
Church of England, 2, 24, 327
Church of Scotland, 328
Clapham, Col. William, 73, 78, 113, 118, 125, 196, 255, 585
Clark, Gen. George Rogers, 478
Clark, Col. Thomas, 375
Clayton, Asher, 258
Clearfield, 254, 502
Clear Fields, 85, 95, 589
Clingan, William, 458
Clinton, Gen. Henry, 362-363, 369, 373-379, 383, 386, 448-449, 474-475
Clinton, Gen. James, 457
Cluggage, Capt. Robert, 445

Clymer, George, 503, 618
Coal Run (Dark Shade Creek), 167, 588
Cobleskill, 340
Coleman's Tavern, 274
Coleridge, Samuel Taylor, 22
College of New Jersey (Princeton), 346, 488-489, 492-494, 511, 516, 605
College of Philadelphia, 490
Colonial Records, 27
Committee of Correspondence, 352-357
Committee of Eleven, 363
Committee of Safety, 356
Committee on Indian Affairs, 460
Committee to Supervise the Commissary, 461
Common Sense, 342
Conafatauga Indian, 589
Condon, John, 50
Conemaugh River, 577
Conestoga, 266, 268, 276
Conestoga Indians, 265-267, 271-272, 277
Conestoga massacre, 263-281
Conestoga Wagon, 155-157
Congress of Deputies, 352
Connecticut, 28-29, 130, 257, 258, 4461, 464-465, 511, 600
Connellsville, Pa., 320
Connemara, 1
Conocheague Creek, 18, 48-49, 51, 57-58, 101, 115, 127, 139-140, 148, 226, 257, 280, 308
Conodoguinet Creek, 18, 22, 83, 330, 505
Conolloway, 49-51
Constantine, 516
Constitution, 480-482, 523
Constitutional Convention, 479,

614
Constitutional Convention (Pa.), 352
Continental Congress, 341, 353, - 357, 360, 363-366, 383, 385, 404, 412, 418-419, 444-445, 450, 456, 458-478, 522
Contrecoeur, Monsieur de, 31
Conway, Gen. Thomas, 398, 414, 417
Cook, John (The White Mingo), 287
Cook, Mrs. Anthony Wayne, 536
Cookport, 86-87
Cookson, Thomas, 23, 570
Cooper, Rev. Robert, 493, 495 487, 502, 505
Cooper River, 363
Cornelius, 288
Cornplanter, Chief, 245, 449, 455, 457, 600, 617
Cornwallis, Gen. Charles, 362, 363, 373, 378, 404, 407, 410-412, 418, 429, 478, 616
Cort, Cyrus, 581
Coshocton, 251
Council at Carlisle (1756), 26-28, 56
Council at Easton (1756), 128-129, 194
Council at Easton (1757), 130, 194, 196
Council at Easton (1758), 130, 195, 250
Council at Fort Loudoun (1758), 194
Council at Lancaster (1757), 194
Council at Philadelphia (1758), 194
County Antrim, 1, 3
County Donegal, 1, 488
Cove Farm, 526

Cove Mountain, 48
Cowan's Gap, 39
Cowanshannock Creek, 580
Cox, John, 72
Craig, John, 493
Craighead, Rev. John, 493
Crawford, Archibald, 213
Crawford, a rifleman, 256
Crawford, Col. William, 318-323
Creigh, John, 354, 492
Cresap family, 37
Cret, Paul P., 540
Crist, Robert, 25
Criswell, George, 538
Croghan, George, 18, 33, 35, 37, 40, 45, 55-57, 60-61, 63, 66, 79, 115, 198-199, 209, 226, 229, 263, 279, 282, 305-306
Crooked Billett, and battle of, 440-441, 447
Crooked Creek, 88, 561
Culbertson, Capt. Alexander, 58
Culloden, battle of, 80, 137-138, 145, 411, 585
Cumberland County, England, 20, 22-23
Cumberland County, Pa., 6, 8-9, 12, 21-25, 35, 37, 46, 53, 64, 67-68, 74-75, 77, 82, 116, 196, 211-213, 236, 238, 243, 260-261, 276-277, 281, 283, 289-291, 298, 300-304, 310-317, 330, 344, 345-354, 357, 398, 414, 426, 445, 489-492, 496, 507, 522
Cumberland County Deed Book, 8
Cumberland Valley, 8, 15-19, 22, 56, 59, 232, 236, 242, 258, 540-541
Cunningham, James, 294-297
Cunningham, John, 317
Cush Cushion Creek, 86-87, 577

Custaloga ((Packankie), Chief, 244

Dagworthy, Captain John, 122-125
Daily Leader-Times, 537-538
Daughters of the American Revolution, 535-537
Davenport, Jonah, 576
Davidson, Rev. Robert, 335, 511, 513, 526
Davis, David, 57
Davis, Colonel John, 296, 472, 475
Dayton, Pa., 541
De Belle Isle, Marshal, 186
De Brahm, John William Gerard, 373-374
Declaration of Independence, 200, 354, 357, 391, 400
Dehgewanus (Mary Jemison) (see Jemison)
De Haas, John Philip, 145, 223-224, 594
De Kalb, Baron Johann, 448, 475-476
Delaware Assembly, 33
Delaware Bay, 16
Delaware George, 26, 54, 209
Delaware Jo (Joe Hickman), 57
Delaware Indians, 18, 26, 43-45, 54, 128, 196, 209, 251, 290, 538, 540-541
Delaware River, 9, 129, 327, 399, 404, 409, 522
Delaware Water Gap, 54
De Lignery, Francois-Marie Le Marchand, 182, 203
Delzel, James, 232
Denmark, 7
Denny, Gov. William, 78, 81, 83, 104-105, 108, 112-131, 139-140, 144, 156, 168, 183-184, 197, 201, 234, 318, 341
De Normanville, 578
Derry, Ireland, 3
Despard, Lt., 353
De Villiers, Capt. Louis Coulon, 69
Dewee's Island, 367, 371
Dickinson Alley, Carlisle, 332
Dickinson College, 482, 487-524, 527, 530
Dickinson, John, 353, 467, 490, 495-497, 502-503, 510, 513, 517-519
Divestment Act of 1779, 598
Doctor John, 227-228
Donaghew, Corporal John, 66
Donegal, 1
Donegal Presbytery, 493
Donehoo, Dr. George P., 9, 140, 195, 201, 236, 535-536
Donolly, Felix, 268
Doubling Gap Springs, 570
Douglas, Andrew, 95
Down, 3
Downingtown, 404, 435
Drayton, William Henry, 364
Duane, James, 461, 469
Dublin Township, 121
Dubuysson, Lt. Charles, 476
Duffield, Edward, 107
Duffield, Rev. George, 11, 323, 329-335, 336-337, 341, 343, 439, 489
Duffield, George (grandson), 335
Duffield, William, 280
Duke of Bedford, 587
Duke of Cumberland, 137
Dunaway, Wayland, 2-3, 5
Dunbar, Colonel Thomas, 41
Duncan, King of Scotland, 7-8
Duncan, Stephen, 489

Duncan, Thomas, 524, 534
Dunlap, Colonel James, 356, 420
Dunmire, Philip, 579
Dunmore, Lord John Murray, 342
Dunn, William, 254
Dunning, James, 156
Dunning's Creek, 156
DuPortail, Col. Louis Lubèque, 409-410, 448

Earl of Eglinton, 584
Eastburn, Benjamin, 10
Easton (see Council of)
Economy, Pa., 57
Ecorse River, 231
Ecuyer, Captain Simeon, 240, 246-247
Edel, Dr. William, 507-508, 518
Eden River, 22
Edge Hill, 244-247
Edge's Mill, 416
Edinburgh University, 498, 516, 599, 619
Edmund's Swamp, 161, 164-165, 166, 168, 171
Edwards, Rev. Jonathan, Jr., 511
Egypt (Schuylkill) Road, 415
Eighteen Mile Run, 88
Eisenhauer, John (Ironcutter), 289, 291-196, 301, 305-306
Elder, Rev. John, 265-266, 268-270, 320, 332, 599
Elizabeth Town, 390
Ellery, William, 461
Elliott, Major Bernard, 380
Ellsworth, Oliver, 461-462, 474
Emerald Isle, 1
Emlen, George, 428
Enniskillen, 568, 617
Enoch Brown Association, 581
Episcopal Christ Church, 200
Erin, 1

Everett, Pa., 149
Ewing, Gen. James, 389, 497
Ewing, John, 493
Experiment, 378, 382
Ex-un-das, 272

Fagg's Manor, 330
Fair Play Men, 597
Fallen Timbers, battle of, 485
Falling Spring, 18
Faulkner, Lt., 68
Ferguson, John, 92
Ferguson Plantation, 296
Fermanagh (Ireland), 7, 8, 11, 339, 617
Fermanagh Township, 95
Finger Lakes, 245, 254
Finley, Samuel, 317
First Carolina Regiment, 375
First Continental Congress, 458
First Presbyterian Church of Carlisle, 333, 351, 526
First Presbyterian Church of Kittanning, 535-536
First Presbyterian Church of Philadelphia, 493
Fisher, Senator John S., 538-539
Fisher, Samuel, 311
Fitch, Thomas, 29-30
Fitzgerald, John, 317
Five Nations, 129, 265
Flour Act, 12
Folke, George, 102
Forbes Campaign medal, 199-200
Forbes Expedition, 121, 128-129, 133-202, 212, 222, 225, 260, 281, 310, 320, 334, 335, 341, 360, 394, 442, 489, 522, 524
Forbes, Gen. John, 128-202, 209, 228, 231, 242
Forbes Road, 146, 200-201, 216, 243-244, 260

Ford City, Pa., 541
Forman, Gen. David, 413, 417, 418, 421
Forman, Ezekial, 475
Forts: Armstrong, 463, 540; Augusta, 73, 77, 117, 125-127, 151, 158, 233-234, 255, 257, 275, 291-292; Bedford, 155, 182, 203-228, 234, 236, 242, 283-284, 508, 528; Bigham's, 60, 112; Burd, 578; Carillon, 135; Carlisle (Lowther), 112-113; Chambers' Mill, 117; Church Hill (Steel's), 48, 49, 332; Crawford, 464; Cumberland, 33, 35, 37, 39, 41, 60, 73, 122-123, 125, 130, 143, 147, 154-155, 158, 162, 164, 520; David Davis, 57; Detroit, 232, 249, 444, 448; Dewart, 166-168, 179; Dudgeon, 179; Duquesne, 31, 32, 40, 48, 56, 57, 61, 75, 82, 94, 95, 104, 117, 121, 124, Expedition to Fort Duquesne, 133-202; 229, 341; Fatland, 413; Finney, 617; Franklin, 595; Frederick, 122, 154, 164; George (see Patterson's); Granville, 8, 11, 12, 58, 60-61, assaulted, 63-76; 77, 79-80, 82, 84, 101, 112, 145; Hill, 428; Hunter, 118, 233; Island, 402; Jefferson, 484; Johnson, 375, 382; Leadmine (Roberdeau), 445; Le Boeuf, 209, 215, 232, 237, 242, 247; Lee, 388; Ligonier (Loyal-Hanna), 146, 167, 173, 183-184, 186, 188, 190, 199, 203, 205, 208-209, 212, 214, 217, 232, 234, 236-237, 243-244, 335, 418; Littleton, 58, 63, 73, 78, 80, 96, 97, 101, 112, 114-116, 121, 123, 127, 143, 149, 152-153, 164, 212, 229, 243; Loudoun, 48, 111, 114-122, 149, 152, 156, 158, 174, 177, 183, 207, 228, 249, 250, 251, 280-281, 283, 308; Louisburg, 138; Machault (see Venango); McCord's, 58-59, 80, 10; McDowell, 48-49, 53, 80, 114, 116-117; Michilimackinack, 232; Mifflin, 428; Morris (Shippensburg), 53, 113, 114, 118, 127, 140, 212; Muncy, 454; Necessity, 31, 69, 133; Niagara, 228, 462; Patterson's (Fort George), 57, 60, 73, 77, 80, 92, 112-113, 134; Pitt, 103, 117, 209-212, 214, 220-225, 228, siege of, 232-248; 251-252, 260, 280, 305, 307-308, 337, 354, 451, 455, 456; Pomfret Castle, 63, 64, 112, 117; Presque Isle, 198, 215, 232, 237, 242, 247; Recovery, 484; Robison, 112; Sandusky, 232; Shirley, 58, 60, 63, 64, 69, 73, 74, 77, 79, 80, 83-84, 95-96, 98, 112, 113, 115, 121, 256; Sullivan's Island, 368-383; Venango, 178, 187, 195, 198, 203, 215, 232, 237, 242, 247; Washington, 352, 354, 388, 406, 502
Forty Mile Lick, 87
Foulk, Stephen, 585
Fourth Street, Philadelphia, 441-442

Fox, Joseph, 56, 61, 108
Franklin and Marshall College, 517
Franklin, Benjamin, 9, 12, 26-28, 40, 59, 61, 68, 73, 79, 108-109, 129-130, 135, 151, 188, 200-201, 235, 239-240, 259, 270-275, 276-277, 282, 303-305, 316-317, 323, 335, 347, 355, 356, 423, 447, 478, 487-488
Franklin County, 22, 39
Frankstown, 69, 83-85, 95, 446, 577
Frankstown Road, 83-84, 576
Fraser, John, 130
Frederick Springs (see Warm Springs)
Freeman, Douglas Southall, 190, 194
Freeport, 541
French Alliance, 143, 447
French and Indian Wars, 125, 133, 319
French Creek, Venango County, 178, 209
French Creek, Chester County, 413
French Margaret's Island, 96
Friedenshuetten, 276
Friends of Liberty, 525
Froude, Anthony, 3
Frye, Col. Joseph, 343, 359, 361, 608
Fulton County, 48, 101, 112, 121

Gabriel, George, 288, 291
Gabriel's Mill, 288
Gabriel's Settlement, 47
Gadsden, Christopher, 374, 377, 380, 382
Gage, General Thomas, 250-251, 308
Galbreath (Galbraith), James, 298, 300
Galloway, Joseph, 259, 274-275, 303-304
Gates, Gen. Horatio, 346, 347, 395, 414, 421-422, 425, 429, 448, 453, 456
Gaysport, 85
General Assembly (Pa.), 6, 12, 13, 16-17, 26, 30, 32, 34, 36, 37, 40-41, 46, 53, 59, 78, 79, 110-111, 126, 128, 149, 151, 201, 211, 225, 228, 237, 240, 241, 248, 250, 274, 275, 292, 303, 305, 325, 334, 341, 353, 355, 385, 399, 444, 458, 462, 468, 487, 495, 503-504, 534
Genesee River, 254, 290, 456
Geneva, 258
George II, 134, 365, 584
George III, 125, 134, 365
Germantown, 273, 274, 277, 410, battle of, 411-425; 431, 440, 522, 537
Gerry, Elbridge, 463
Gettysburg, 12
Gibson, Hugh, 78, 101, 103
Gibson, James, 273-275
Gibson, John, 475
Gibson, Owen, 103
Gilpin, Dr. John, 578
Girty, Simon, 101, 478
Girty, Thomas, 101
Gist, Christopher, 152
Glass, David, 258
Gnadenhuetten, 600-601
Godcharles, Frederic, 9, 46
Gordon, Captain Harry, 180, 182, 588
Gordon, Patrick, 5576
Graham, William, 8

Grant, Lt. Charles, 281-283
Grant, Major James, 166, 173-174, 176-182, 186, 195-196
Grant's Hill, 172, 174, 182, 183, 195, 235
Gray, Hannah, 72
Gray, Jane, 72
Gray, John, 72
Graydon, Lt., 8, 567
Graydon, Mrs., 567
Great Awakening, 332-333
Great Beaver Creek, 337-338
Great Beaver Pond, 17
Great Commoner, 134
Great Cove, 48-51, 53, 112, 258, 280-281
Great Crossings, 40
Great Island, 8, 46, 86, 96, 248, 254-255, 258, 277, 287, 292, 309
Great Island Path, 253
Great Knife, 183
Great Meadows, 41
Great Road, 508, 579
Great Runaway, 75, 233, 339
Great Spirit, 28
Green, Col. Timothy, 265
Greencastle, 249, 280, 353, 528
Greene, Gen. Nathanael, 398, 407, 409, 414, 418, 421, 436, 448, 476, 533, 617
Greensburg, 155, 178
Greenville, treaty of, 485
Greenwich, 506
Greenwood, Joseph, 316-317
Grenadas, 467
Grey, Benjamin, 247
Grey, Gen. Charles, 411, 417, 432, 455
Griffin, Cyrus, 461
Gulph Mills, 393, 436

Hackensack River, 455
Haddrell's Point (Mount Pleasant), 369-373, 378-381, 386
Hagerstown, 227
Haldimand, Frederick, 141, 144, 584
Half King, 69
Halifax, N. C., 387
Halkett, Major Francis, 159-160, 163, 199, 204
Halkett, Sir Peter, 159
Hall, David, 235
Hambright, Capt. John, 222, 255
Hamilton, Alexander, 524, 526
Hamilton, Col. Hanse, 45, 49, 80, 83, 128, 145, 168
Hamilton, Gov. James, 12, 23-24, 26, 56, 234, 294, 311
Hamilton, Dr. S. B., 538
Hancock, John, 361-362, 367, 385-387, 392, 394, 408
Hand, Gen. Edward, 389, 456
Hanna, Charles, 84
Hannastown, 155, 178, 245
Hanover Street, Carlisle, 332, 357, 488, 526
Happy Retreat, 489
Harlem Heights, 387-388
Harmar, Gen. Josiah, 484
Harrisburg, 524, 533
Harris, John (of Carlisle), 298, 341, 351
Harris, John (of Harris's Ferry), 265
Harris's Ferry, 34, 41, 66, 117, 229, 232, 236
Hart, John, 86
Hartley, Col. Thomas, 455-456, 502
Hart's Log (Sleeping Place), 85-86
Harvard College, 527
Haslett, Capt. John, 193

Havana, 242
Hay, Sheriff John, 267, 269
Hays, Mary Ludwig (Molly Pitcher), 340, 530
Hays, Sergeant John, 529
Head of Elk, 404-405
Heart (Hart), Major Jonathan, 595
Heckewelder, Rev. John, 48
Hendricks, Tobias, 17
Henry, John, 477
Henry, Patrick, 398
Henry, Dr. T. J., 538
Henry, William, 271, 314, 341, 363
Herman, Christian B., 530
Herman, John Armstrong, 9, 538, 585
Heron, Mrs. John Brown, 536
Herschel, Friedrich Wilhelm, 541-542
Hessians, 390, 402, 404, 406, 415, 418, 419, 422, 431, 433
Heth, T. Will, 422
Hewes, Joseph, 200
Hickman, Jo ("Delaware Jo"), 57
Hicks, Barbara, 101
Hicks, Gersham, 292
Highlanders, 137, 142, 153, 173-175, 190, 193, 203, 205-206, 236, 242, 249, 271, 282-283
High Street, Carlisle, 24, 113, 518, 526
Hill, Henry, 514
Hily, George, 75
historical markers, 99, 109, 201, 428, 540
Hoaks and Buchanan, 116
Hogan, John, 73-74, 121
Hoge, Jonathan, 289, 300, 352
Hogg, Lt. James, 90, 95-105, 541
Hogg, Peter, 39
Hollidaysburg, 69, 84

Holme, Thomas, 603
Holmes, Sheriff John, 291, 294-295, 297-298, 300
Holsterman, Colonel Peter, 450
Hood, Margaret, 101
Hoops, Adam, 33, 38, 51, 62, 83-84, 108, 119, 120, 235, 317
Hopkinson, Francis, 200, 475
Horry, Col. Peter, 375, 379
Horseshoe Curve, 85
Howe, Lord Richard, 135, 388
Howe, General Robert, 361-362, 368-369, 387
Howe, Gen. William, at Brandywine, 385-410; 412, at Germantown, 413-419; 422, 423, 426, 428-430, 433, 436, 437, 443, 446-448
Howell, Gov. Richard, 524
Howly, Gov. Richard, 475
Hubbard, Capt. Edward, 220-222
Huck, Dr., 199
Hudson (North) River, 362, 398, 448, 465, 475
Hughes, James, 208
Hughes, John, 61
Hunter, Joseph, 296
Hunter, William, 45, 113, 120, 574
Hunter's Mill, 233-234
Huntington, Samuel, 465
Huron Indians, 244
Husbands, Harman, 443
Hutchinson, Rev. William J., 535
Hy-ye-na-es (Little Peter), 272

indentured servant, 2, 79
Independence Bell (Liberty Bell), 406
Independence Day, 507
Indiana (Pa.) borough, 87-88, 538
Indiana County, 86, 541
Indian Run, 404

Ingersoll, Jared, 468
Inverness, 137, 581
Ireland, 1-10, 17, 22-23, 43, 80-81, 328, 339, 344, 352-354, 389, 450, 471-472, 488-489, 506, 523
Irish Sea, 22
Iroquois, 26, 29, 88, 121, 125, 254, 265, 290, 394, 446, 449-452
Ironcutter (see Eisenhauer)
Irvine, Andrew, 613
Irvine, William Armstrong, 617
Irvine, George, 613
Irvine, General James, 399, 403, 414, 430-433, 438, 441, 613
Irvine, Rebecca Armstrong, 617
Irvine, General William, 251, 323, 351, 353-357, 389, 399, 440, 449, 459, 467, 476-479, 490, 519, 521, 527, 585, 613
Island Tract, 315

Jack's Narrows, 10
Jacobites, 137-138
Jacobs' Cabin, 40
Jacobs, Captain (Tewea), 40, 48-50, 54, 56, 57, 60-61, 67, 69-71, 74, 79, death of, 91-94; 95, 100-101, 104, 109, 115, 130, 536, 539, 541
Jacobs Creek, 40
Jacobs' Hill, 578
James Island, 364, 374
Jameson, Major David, 128, 168, 171, 180, 207-208, 593
Jasper, William, 381, 609
Jay, John, 478, 487
Jeannette Pa., 244
Jefferson, Thomas, 621
Jemison, Mary, 12, 140, 583
Jenkins, John, 456
Jenkins Tavern, 416

Jennerstown, 155
Jericho, 95
Jersey Shore, 253-254
Johnson, an Englishman, 188, 190
Johnson, Sir William, 130, 198, 214, 237, 252, 290, 292, 322
Johnston, John, 282-284
Jones (Jonas), 287
Jones, U. J., 67
Jordan's Knob, 39
Jumonville, Joseph Coulon de, 31
Juniata County, 8, 95, 112
Juniata Crossing, 284
Juniata River, 10, 16, 39, 52, 55, 63, 67-68, 84, 112, 124, 149, 155, 165, 235, 255, 290, 315, 317, 334, 337, 465, 517
Juniata Valley, 18, 40, 67, 72, 77, 80, 235, 241, 317

Ka-mi-an-guas (Molly Soc), 272
Ka-ren-do-u-ah, 272
Kantner, 170
Kau-ta-tinchunk, 16
Kayahsotha (Guyasuta), 232, 244, 245, 251, 595
Keats, John, 22
Kekeuscund, 199
Kelly, Sarah, 101
Kent County, 311, 313
Kerry, 1
Kickenapauling's (Old Town), 161, 164, 167
Killarney, 1
Killbuck, 54, 209
King Beaver, 130, 184-185, 209, 229
King Charles II (see Charles II)
King George II (see George II)
King George III (see George III)
King George's War, 133, 135
King Henry V, 195
King, Judge James W., 536-538

King, Reverend John, 502
King's College (Columbia University), 527
King's Proclamation of 1763 (Royal Proclamation), 252, 318-319
King's Highway, 417
King William's War, 133
Kiser, Gertrude, 536
Kishacoquillas Creek, 63
Kishacoquillas Valley, 310, 343-344
Kiskiminetas, 87, 89
Kiskiminetas Path, 86, 88-89
Kitchi, Chief, 247
Kittanning (Attique), 49, 51, 57, 69-74, 109, 254-255, 446, 523, 533-538
Kittanning Expedition, 61, 77-108, 110-115, 121, 125, 126, 128, 130, 139, 143, 145, 151-152, 166, 178, 256, 309, 335, 341, 352, 359, 394, 414, 451, 456, 463, 478, 522
Kittanning medals, 106-108
Kittanning Point (Gap), 85
Kittanning River, 576
Kittanning Trail (Path), 69
Kittatinny Mountain, 52
Kittatinny Trail, 87
Kittatinny Valley, 339
Kittiuskung (and son Wolf), 246
Kittochtinny (Blue Hill), 34
Kline, George, 607
Knox, Gen. Henry, 398, 414, 418, 421, 426, 427, 460, 484
Knox, John, 328
Knyphausen, Gen. Wilhelm, 406-409
Ko-qua-e-un-quas (Molly), 272
Kosciusko, Colonel Thaddeus, 391
Ko-wee-na-see, 272

Kuskuski (present New Castle, Pa.), 151, 209, 228
Kyle, James, 317
Ky-un-que-a-go-ah (Captain John), 272

Lacey, Gen. John, 439-443, 447
Laertes, 324
Lafayette, General Marquis de, 398, 407, 408, 430, 436, 448, 479, 533
Lake Champlain, 357
Lake District, 22
Lake Erie, 130, 198, 209, 227-228
Lake Geneva, 584
Lamb, Col. John, 422
Lancaster, 41, 56, 75, 101, 152-153, 157, 183, 199, 207, 213, 214, 225-226, 229, 255, 264-265, 267-273, 297, 298, 307, 309, 340, 357, 393, 396, 412, 419, 428, 433, 443-444, 450, 472, 517, 522
Lancaster County, 9-12, 21-23, 37, 53, 146, 188, 213, 238, 267, 269, 271, 276, 325, 330, 332, 389, 398, 517, 522
Lancaster County (Va.), 327
Lancaster Road, 435
Land Office, 4, 12, 24, 44, 294, 309, 315-317, 321, 323
Land Records, 10, 569
Lardner, Lynford, 41
Laughlan, a rifleman, 287
Laurel Hills, 149, 155, 158, 161-163
Laurens, Henry, 363, 452, 463, 465
Laurens, Col. John, 418, 462, 615
lead mine, 444-446
Lebanon, 393
Lebègue, Col. Louis, 415
Lee, Gen. Charles, 361, 363, 366,

siege of Charleston, 369-387; 394, 615
Lee, Francis Lightfoot, 461
Lee, Light-Horse Harry, 389
Lee River, 1
Lehighton, 336
Lehigh River, 16
Leininger, Barbara, 78, 102-104
Lenape Heights, 541
Lenni Lenape, 67, 254, 362, 540
Le Roy, Jacob, 47
Le Roy, Mary (Marie), 47, 78, 102, 104
Letchworth State Park, 583
LeTort, James, 17, 88
Letort Spring Run, 24
Letort's Spring, 17-18, 23, 352
Le Torts Town, 88
Levering's Tavern, 416
Lewes on the Delaware, 9
Lewis, General Andrew, 174, 361-362, 590
Lewistown (Old Town), Pa., 67, 112, 538
Lexington and Concord, 21, 281, 353, 358, 364, 389, 458
Liberty Alley, Carlisle, 507
Liberty Pole, 524
Licking Creek, 50
Liffey, 1
Ligonier, 149, 155 (See Fort Ligonier)
Ligonier, Sir John, 199
Limekiln Road, 415
Lincoln, Gen. Benjamin, 465, 474
Little Cove, 57
Little Meadows, 69
Little Turtle, Chief, 484, 533
Livingston, Alida, 346
Livingston, Gov. William, 401
Lloyd, Col. Thomas, 128, 145, 208
Lock Haven, 253, 597

Locust Alley, Carlisle, 488
Logan, James, 4
Logan, William, 45, 56, 274, 294, 301
Logstown, 57, 337, 569
London, England, 9, 130, 303, 311, 363
Londonderry, 9, 80
Long Island, Charleston Bay (Isle of Pines), 369, 370, 375, 378-379, 386
Long Island, N. Y., battle of, 353-354, 388
Long Meadow, 227
Long, Col. Moses, 450
Long Way, Indeed stream, 18
Lost Creek, 621
Loudoun, Lord John Campbell (see Campbell)
Louisburg, 135, 138
Lower County troops, 147, 152, 166, 190
Loyal-hanna, 148-149, 155, 165-167, 172-173, 176-187, 190-192, 199
Loyalhanna Creek, 154-155
Loyalsock Creek, 436
Loyalty Oath, 401, 611
Lukens, John, 313-317, 459
Lycoming County, 450, 533, 541
Lycoming Creek, 453-454
Lyndell, 404
Lyon, Ann(e), 530
Lyon, Ellen (Mrs. Samuel), 525
Lyon, James, 12
Lyon, John, 8, 330
Lyon, Margaret Armstrong, 12
Lyon, Samuel, 525
Lyon, William, the elder, 10
Lyon, William, 12, 24, 145, 213, 294-295, 297, 301, 315, 334, 344, 354, 357, 398, 489, 524, 530

~ Index ~

Lyttleton, Sir George, 121

Macbeth, 7
MacCune, William, 317
Macfarlane, James, 17
MacLean, Sir Allan, 153, 165
Magaw, Col. Robert, 352-355, 406, 489, 501-502, 529, 585, 606
Maguill, Major, 477
Mahantango (Manitango) Creek, 64, 112, 574
Mahoney Creek, 41
Mahoning Creek, 577
Mahoning River, 151
Makemie, Reverend Francis, 328
Makinly, Henry, 488, 492
Makinly School, 488-489
Manatawny Road, 419
Manhattan, 388
Manor of Conestoga, 265
Marchant, Henry, 465
Marion, Captain Francis (Swamp Fox), 376, 381
Markes, 39
Market House, Germantown, 416-418
Market Street, Kittanning, 535, 541, 578
Market Street, Philadelphia, 328
Marsh Creek, 11, 12, 75, 140, 568
Marsh, Mrs. Joseph W., 535
Martin, Josiah, 362
Maryland troops, 161, 164, 169-170, 190, 197
Massenbaugh, Baron Felix Louis, 378
Masters, William, 108
Matlack, Timothy, 468
Matsons Ford, 426
Maumee Valley, 484
Maxwell, Gen. William, 53, 119, 398, 406, 411, 415, 417

McAllister, Alexander, 101
McAllister, wife, 101-102
McCain, Samuel, 538
McClene (McClean, McClane), James, 458, 468, 478
McClintogue, James, 325
McClure, John, 296
McConnell, Neal, 161
McConnellsburg, 48, 280
McCord, Annie, 58, 100-101
McCord, John, 58
McCord, Martha, 58
McCord, Mary, 58
McCord, Thomas, 8
McCormick, Hugh, 354
McCormick, John, 119
McDaniel, Sergeant, 380
McDougall, Gen. Alexander, 413-416
McDowell, Alexander (George), 216-217
McDowell's Mill, 35, 39, 53, 57, 80, 114, 116 (see Fort McDowell)
McElhattan Creek, 254
McGlashan, Sergeant, 281
M'chewamisipu, 15
McIntosh, Gen. Lachlan, 455-456
McKee, of Carlisle, 446
McKee's Rocks, 48
McKenzie, Capt. Alexander, 206-207
McKnight, John, 300, 334
McLane, Capt. Allen, 429-432
McPherson, Robert, 223-224
Meadows, 37, 213
Mecklenberg Declaration, 354
Meeting House Springs, 330
Mercer, Col. George, 187-189
Mercer, Gen. Hugh, 45, 60, 80, 83, 90, 96-98, 100-103, 105, 118, 128, 137-139, 141, 144, 145, 186-191, 195, 201, 203, 209-

211, 215, 221, 228, 325, 343, 346, 359, 394-395, 533
Mercersburg, 502
Meredith, Gen. Samuel, 399
Methodist Church, 518
Metuchen Hill, 417
Meyer, Lt. Elias, 115, 117
Miami Indians, 244, 483-484, 533
Middle Creek, 287-289, 304, 306
Middlebrook, 460
Middleburg, 307
Middle Spring, 18
Middleton Township, 583
Mifflin County, 8, 309, 344
Mifflin, John, 61, 108
Mifflin, Gov. Thomas, 448, 524, 533
Mifflintown, 568
Milford Township, 568
Militia Hill, 428-430
Miller, Jacob, 102
Miller, Robert, 18, 291, 295, 301, 352, 356, 490
Miller's Run, 161
Mingo Indians, 50, 69, 244, 250-251, 287-288, 323
Minnimingo, 18, 24
Mohawk Indians, 184, 340, 449, 452, 455
Mohikan Indians, 244
Monacacy River, 568
Monaghatootha, 52
Monckton, Gen. Richard, 215, 582
Monmouth, battle of, 354, 449, 477
Monongahela River, 34, 39-40, 44, 123, 133, 148, 155, 169, 174, 194, 195, 200, 240, 250, 319-320
Monroe, President, James, 533
Montcalm, General Louis, 186, 220
Montgomerie, Col. Archibald, 139, 142-143, 153-154, 173, 186, 187, 190, 194, 201
Montgomery, John, 334, 350, 353, 356, 472, Dickinson College, 488-519; 527
Montgomery, Gen. Richard, 357-358
Montizambert, Ensign Niverville de, 60
Montour, Andrew, 26, 52, 255
Montour, Henry, 198-199
Montreal, 176, 257
Montrose, Scotland, 498, 503, 510
Moore, Gen. James, 361-362
Moorhead, Fergus, 541
Moravian Indians, 273, 275, 276, 307
Moravians, 6, 48, 103, 275, 276, 336, 592
Morgan, Col. Daniel, 429, 432
Morgan, Dwight C., 538
Morgan, Evan, 61
Morgan, Henry, 497, 500-501
Morgan, Capt. Jacob, 214
Morgan, Dr. John, 324, 344
Morris, Gouverneur, 465
Morris Island, 365
Morris, John, 458
Morris, Gov. Robert Hunter, 29-37, 40-41, 45, 51-53, 56-61, 63, 65-66, 78-83, 111-113, 115, 117, 121, 125, 126, 586
Morris, Robert, 200
Morrison's Cove, 48
Morris's Mill, 413
Morristown, 395, 397-398, 400, 470, 473
Morrow, James, 296
Morrow, John, 296
Morton, George, 218-225
Moschkingo, 103
Mother Cumberland, 15
Motte, Isaac, 376

Moultrie, Col. William, siege of Charleston, 365-383; 465, 474
Mount Airy, 417
Mount Holly Springs, 24
Mount Pleasant, 41
Mount Vernon, 319, 325, 479-480
Moylan, Stephen, 400, 610
Muhlenberg, Frederick, 459, 467
Muhlenberg, Rev. Henry, 273-274
Muhlenberg, Col. John Peter Gabriel, 374-375, 377, 406, 414, 420
Muncy Hill, 255
Muncy (Munsee) Indians, 234, 595
Muncy Valley, 255
Murray, Capt., 249
Murrysville, 155
Musgrave, Col. Thomas, 417-418
Muskingum, 100, 103, 130, 248, 250-251, 337
Musmeelin, 10
Myers, Dr. Albert Cook, 538
Myers, James, 93, 104
Myles, Major, 450
Myonaghquia, 257

Nailer (Nailor), Ralph, 281
Nancy's Pack-saddle, 58
Nash, Gen. Francis, 414-415, 417, 421-422
Neshaminy Creek, 605
Nevin, Alfred, 330
New Castle, Pa., 209
New Castle County, Del., 9-12, 3331, 339, 341
New College (at Dickinson), 518
New Haven, Ct., 29, 511
New Lights (New Side) Presbyterians, 333
Newport, 403, 469
New Windsor, 463
New York City, 138, 141, 383, 390, 397, 527
Nine Mile Run, 173
Nisbet, Dr. Charles, 482, 498-519, 530
Nisbet, Tom, 511
Norris, Isaac, 26
Northampton, 460
Northampton County, 21, 57, 238, 257
North American Street, Philadelphia, 200, 598
North (East) Branch of the Susquehanna, 28, 450, 456
North Carolina troops, with Forbes, 144, 163, 183, 190; at Germantown, 406
North Mountain, 16, 239, 258
North River (see Hudson River)
Northumberland County, 21-22
North Valley, 15, 17-18, 22
North Wales, 437, 441, 447
North Wales Road, 437
Nourse, Joseph, 382
Nova Scotia, 138

Ohio Expedition (Bouquet), 249-252
Ohio River, 31, 57, 164, 229, 245, 254, 478, 484, 506
Ojibway Indians, 173, 539
Old Buttonwood, 328
Old Cemetery (Graveyard), Carlisle, 344, 347, 531, 602, 622
Old Lights (Old Side) Presbyterians, 333
Old Pine Street Church, 334, 605
Old Smoke (Chief Sayenqueraghta), 600
Old Town (see Lewistown)
Old York Road, 416, 440
O'Neal, John, 25
Oneida Indians, 453
Orangeburg, S. C., 375

~ *Index* ~ 641

Orchard Camp, 41
Orndt, Major Jacob, 128, 145
Osgood, Samuel, 359
Ottawa Indians, 173, 231-232, 244, 252
Ourry, Captain-Lieutenant, Lewis, 213-214, 217-218, 221, 226, 235, 243
Oven Run, 168, 171
Owens' Camping Ground, 86-87

Paine, Thomas (Clerk of General Assembly), 468
Paoli, 411-417
Papertown Spring, 570
Paradise, 18
Parker, Sir Peter, 362, 370
Parker, Richard, 17
Parker, Sheriff William, 118
Parkman, Francis, 255, 264, 266-268, 271
Parnell's Knob, 116-117
Parsons, William, 603
Path Valley, 39, 53, 117, 226, 235, 337
Patterson, Captain James, 45, 96, 179, 594
Patterson's, 10 (see Fort Patterson)
Patterson, Capt. William, Jr., 256, 290-292, 296, 298, 300, 304
Patton, Matthew, 49, 116
Paxtang Narrows, 53
Paxtang Township, 10, 118
Paxton, 264-266
Paxton Boys, 264-277
Paxton Boys' Remonstrance, 274-276
Peale, Charles Willson, 613
Peepy, Joseph, 336
Pelham Manor, 417
Pendergrass, Gerard, 123
Penn, Anne Allen, 401
Penn, John, 4, 16, 41, 200, 251, 258-260, 265-306, 309, 321, 401-402
Penn, Richard, 258, 309, 314, 332
Penn, Thomas, 24-25, 36, 60, 104, 107, 227, 282, 309, 314, 332
Penn, William, 16-17, 21, 23, 26, 43, 44, 54, 79, 200, 258, 265, 335
Pennamite Wars, 571, 600
Pennebecker, Samuel, 413
Pennebecker's Mill, 412, 413, 421
Pennington, N. J., 457
Penn's Creek, 46, 102, 288, 291
Penn's Creek Valley, 112, 290
Pennsylvania Assembly (see General Assembly)
Pennsylvania Gazette, 9, 68, 71, 97, 106, 126, 150-151, 188, 193, 196, 200, 235
Pennsylvania Historical Commission, 535, 537-538, 540-541
Pennsylvania Journal, 72
Pennsylvania Packet, 479
Perkiomen Creek, 412, 422
Perry County, 22
Peters, Richard, 12, 26, 34, 36, 40, 41, 56, 60, 181, 211, 226, 232, 269, 330
Peters Township, 53
Peters, William, 79, 315
Petteril River, 22
Philadelphia, passim
Philadelphia County, 264, 428
Philips, Ralph, 208
Pickering, Timothy, 417
Pigot, 376
Pinckney, Col. Charles, 375, 377
Pine Creek, 254-255
Pipe, Chief, 209
Piper, Lt. Johnny, 201, 214
Pisquetomen (see King Beaver)
Pittsburgh, 57, 173, 198-200, 209-219, 222, 224, 226, 229, 234-

235, 323, 492, 508, 524, 533
Pitt Street, Carlisle, 113
Pitt, William, 134, 147, 172, 195, 198, 200, 202
Plum Creek, 88-89
Plumsted, William, 256
Plunket(t), Doctor William, 234
Point Pleasant, battle of, 281
Pollan's (Pawlin's), 280
Pollock, James, 353, 355
Pollock, John, 297
Polonius, 324
Pomfret Castle, 61, 63, 64, 66, 112, 117
Pomfret Street, Carlisle, 332, 585
Pontiac, Chief, 231-252
Pontiac's War, 231-252, 255, 258, 263-265, 279-280, 340, 450
Porter, Andrew, 389
Portrush, 9
Post, Christian Frederick, 103, 151, 184
Potawatamie Indians, 173, 232
Potomac River, 17-18, 75, 122, 235, 254, 325, 528
Potter, Gen. James, 64, 83, 315, 399, 403, 405, 414, 425, 431, 437-445, 449-450, 452, 612
Potter, James, 315
Potter, Sheriff John, 45, 49, 51, 53, 60, 80, 83, 116
Pottsgrove (Pottstown), 412
Potts House, 447
Presbyterianism, 327-338
Presbyterian Church of Philadelphia, 328
Presque Isle (see Fort Presque Isle)
Prevost, Col. James, 227
price regulation, 469-483
Prince of Piedmont, 377, 382
Princeton, 330, 242, 488-489, 494, 527
Princeton, battle of, 346, 394-399,

533
Princess of Wales, 125
Proctor, Col. Thomas, 406-407, 418
Province Island, 273
Public Works, Carlisle, 508, 516
Punxsutawney, 538, 577
Purchase Line, 534
Putnam, Gen. Israel, 391
Pyle's Ford, 406-409

Qua-a-chone, 272
Quakers, 4-6, 16, 26, 37, 43-46, 59, 78-79, 239-240, 264, 269, 273, 275-276, 307, 406, 428, 504
Quebec, 220, 223, 351, 354, 358, 439, 454, 502
Queen Anne's War, 133
Queen Esther's Town, 454
Queen's Rangers, 429
Quemahoning Creek, 588
Quemahoning Reservoir, 588

Raccoon Company, 375
Ralston, Andrew, 17
Ramsey's Run, 87
Ray (Rae, Wray), John, 586
Randolph, Edmund, 460
Rappahannock, 323
Ray's Hill, 58
Raystown (Reastown), 33, 35, 38-39, 50, 83, 120-121, 140, 144, 147-149, 155, 161-162, 164, 167, 170-171, 176-182, 203-204
Raystown Creek, 35
Raystown Path, 83, 147
Reading, Pa., 353
Red Clay Creek, 403
Redstone Creek, 586
Reed, Gov. Joseph, 389, 398, 400, 433, 437, 459, 461, 468-472,

477, 610
Reed, William, 258
Remonstrance (see Paxton Boys)
Reynolds, Alexander, 578
Reynolds, George, 607
Reynolds, John, 58
Rhode Island, 461, 464-465, 475
Richardson, Joseph, 167
Ridge Road (Manatawny), 416
Riedesel, Baron Adolf von, 585, 607
rifle, 54-56, 472
Rights' Ferry, 390
Ring, Benjamin, 406
Rising Sun Inn, 432
Riverfront Park, Kittanning, 538
Roberdeau, Gen. Daniel, 274, 443-445, 458
Robertson, Captain, 269
Robison, James, 58
Robison, Robert, 58, 78, 87, 91-99, 104, 112
Rochambeau, Jean Baptiste, comte de, 479
Rock Creek, 568
Rodmon, Jonathan, 73
Rohr, Charles, 182
Rohrer, John W., 535
Rolle, Switzerland, 584
Rosebud Mining Company Building, 541
Ross, George, 200
Ross, James, 503, 508
Royal Americans, 110, 118-119, 123, 144, 146, 173, 182, 193, 206, 208, 236, 242, 274
Royal Fifteenth Regiment, 379
Royal Proclamation (see King's Proclamation)
rum, 27-28, 67, 130, 209, 221-222, 279, 289, 336, 382, 401
Rupp, Israel, 8, 331
Rural Valley, 541
Rush, Dr. Benjamin, 200,

Dickinson College, 487-519; 521
Russell, Dr., 160
Rutledge, Gov. John, 363-369, 381-383, 475
Ruysel, David, 312

St. Augustine, 366
St. Clair, Gen. Arthur, 408-409, 440, 484, 533
St. Clair, Sir John, 33-38, 139-140, 146, 154, 156, 164, 167-168, 171, 180, 182, 186, 201
St. Mary's Parochial School, Kittanning, 535
St. Vincent, 466
Salem, N. J., 351
salt, 87, 119, 212, 217, 220, 393
Salter, Elisha, 65
Salt Springs, 87
Sanderson, George, 311, 317
Sanderson, John, 317
Sanderson, Robert, 317
Sandusky, 232, 572
Sandy Run, 416, 429
Sa-qui-es-hat-tah (John Smith), 272
Saratoga, 475, 607
Saukunk (present Beaver, Pa.), 579
Savannah, 455
Scarroyady, 125
Schaeffer, Charles F., 536
Schaeffer, John H., 535
Scheet's Mill, 603
Schellsburg, 155
Schoenbrun, 601
Schuylkill River, 273, 393, 409, 411, 415, 425, 436-440
Schuylkill (Egypt) Road, 415
Schweinitz, Rev. Edmund de, 552, 580
Scioto River, 130-131, 249, 323
Scotch-Irish, 1-9, 18, 23-25, 48, 240, 255, 258, 264, 277, 303,

306, 330-334, 351, 357, 375, in the Revolution, 388-392; 414, 488-489
Scotland, 7-8, 22-23, 43, 80, 102, 135, 328, 353, 498, 503-504, 507, 510, 515, 517
Scott, Gen. Charles, 414
Scott, Ensign John, 96-97, 101
Scribner's Magazine, 188-189
Scudder, Nathaniel, 462
Scull, Nicholas, 24-25, 311
Scull, Nicholas II, 310, 603
Searle, James, 458, 468-470
Second Church of Philadelphia, 330
Second Presbyterian Church of Carlisle, 332
Selinsgrove, 47
Sellers, Charles, 518
Seneca George, 56
Seneca Indians, 56, 232, 245, 251, 290, 340, 449, 452-455, 462, 471, 540
Seven Years' War, 133
Shades of Death, 164
Sha-ee-kah (Jacob), 272
Shaheas, 266
Shamokin, 15, 46, 47, 53, 86, 101, 125, 151, 253, 254, 288, 451
Shamokin Path, 151
Shannon, Dr., 429
Shannon River, 1
Sharp, a rifleman, 256
Sharpe, Gov. Horatio, 122, 139, 144, 160, 164, 227
Shaver, Peter, 87
Shaver's Spring, 87-89
Shawana Ben, 293
Shawnee Cabins, 88, 165
Shawnee Indians, 5, 17, 25, 45-50, 54, 57, 69, 82, 84-88, 110, 130-131, 140, 143, 151, 158,

165, 173, 183-184, 201, 228, 232, 241, 244, 247, 250-251, 323, 478, 483-484
Shelby, Captain Evan, 217, 219, 169-170, 191
Shell, Mary, 530
Shelley, Percy Bysshe, 22
Shelocta, 88-89
Shenango, 131, 579
Shenango River, 151
Sherman Creek, 334
Sherman's Valley, 49, 69, 77, 258, 299, 311
Shingas, Chief, 26, 46-57, 60-61, 69, 71, 79, 95, 109-110, 115, 130, 151, 184-185, 199, 209, 244
Shippen, Edward, 45, 56, 73, 114, 213, 214, 269, 459, 467, 586
Shippen, Edward, Jr., 457
Shippen, Col. Joseph, Jr., 123, 234, 269, 306-307
Shippen, William, 123, 467
Shippensburg, 34-38, 41, 45-46, 51-54, 57, 75, 77, 84, 113-114, 116-120, 127, 149, 152, 155, 160, 209, 212, 213, 229, 233, 235, 255, 256, 258, 264, 269, 317, 340, 354, 450, 522, 528
Shirleysburg, 84, 112
Shirley, Gov. William, 115
Shoemaker, Col. Henry W., 538-539
Shooting of Squirrels Act, 12
Shute, Atwood, 106
Sideling Hill, 39, 50, 58, 80, 101, 149, 164, 258, 280-28
Silvers Spring, 18
Simcoe, Major John, 429
Simpsons' Daily Leader, 534
Sinclair, James, 205

Sinking (Spring) Valley, 445-446
Sipe, Chester Hale, 537
Sipuas-hanne (Plum Stream) (see Plum Creek)
Siward, 7-8, 567
Six Nations, 26, 57, 184, 292, 321
Skippack Creek, 412
Skippack Road, 414, 417
Slaughter, Thomas, 322
slavery, 102, 462, 473, 604
Sloan, James, 534
smallpox, 162, 239, 247, 275
Smallman, Thomas, 118, 145
Smallwood, Gen. William, 392, 394, 412-416, 419
Smart, David, 247
Smith, Catherine, 101
Smith, Col. James (Jimmy), 93, 173, 175, 183, 257, 280-284, 602
Smith, John, 49
Smith, John (Indian), 272
Smith, Matthew, 265-275
Smith, Robert Walter, 541
Smith, Lt. Col. Samuel, 428
Smith, Rev. William, 93
Smith, William (engineer), 38
Snider, Jacob, 102
Soc (Sauk), Will, 271-273
Somerset County, 170, 589
South Carolina Assembly, 385
South Bend, 89
Southey, Robert, 22
South Mountain, 12, 16, 24
Sparks, Jared, 448
Spears, Joseph, 282
Sphinx, 381
Springer, Mary, 11
Spring Tavern, 438-439
squatting, 4, 44, 239, 258, 288, 306, 312
Stamp Act, 281, 598

Standing Stone, 445
Stanwix, Gen. John,114, 118-124, 127, 129, 144, 150, 209, 212-222, 232, 330, 340, 582
State House (Independence Hall), 12, 46, 452, 459, 497
Steel, Rev. John, 45, 48-51, 59-60, 80, 252, 284, 295, 299, 331-333, 335, 455, 489, 490, 530, 604
Steenson's Field, 127
Stephen, Gen. Adam, 100, 130, 165, 179, 212-220, 223-224, 292, 406, 414-415, 418, 489
Sterett, Ralph, 161
Steuben, Baron Friedrich Wilhelm von, 463
Stevens, Frank (Francis), 84
Stevenson, George, 146, 207, 490
Stevenson, James, 468
Stevenson, Mary, 341, 530
Stevens, Sylvester, 9, 141
Stewart, Capt. Lazarus, 264, 267-272, 600
Stewart, Martha Espy, 600
Stirling, Gen. William Alexander, 29, 361, 362, 398, 406, 412-415, 426, 448
Stoney Creek, 170, 177, 179-180, 182-183, 216
Stony Point, 464-465
Stoystown, 155, 170
Street, John, 73
Stretell, Robert, 41
Strong Wolf, Chief, 539-540
Stuart, Charles, 50-51
Stuart, Mary, 50
Stuart, William, 50
Stump, Frederick, 287-307
Stump's Run, 307
Sugar Cabins, 39, 112
Sullivan Expedition, 78, 456, 457,

462, 464, 466
Sullivan's Island, 363-383
Sullivan, Gen. John, 398, 406-407, at Germantown, 414-418; 439, 456, 533
Sullivan, Thomas, 411-412
Sulphur Springs, 570
Summer House, 177
Sunbury, 449
Sunfish, 100
Supreme Executive Council (Pa.), 359, 398, 401-402, 419, 425, 440, 446, 453, 461, 475, 496
Susquehanna Company, 29
Susquehanna Expedition, 253-261
Susquehanna River, 10, 15-17, 22-24, 28-30, 45-47, 52-57, 63, 65, 77-78, 86, 110-117, 120, 125-127, 157, 233-234, 238, 248, 251, 253-261, 265, 275, 280, 289, 292, 297, 302, 340, 445, 450-453, 456, 469, 471, 505, 524, 540
Susquehanna Valley, 340
Susquehannock Indians, 16
Sussex County, 311
Swedes (Sweed's) Ford, 271
Sweeny, William, 297
Syren, 381

Taney, Chief Justice Roger, 519, 619
Tappan, 455
Tarentum, 211
Taylor, Jacob, 603
Taylor Run, 404
Tea, Richard, 315
Tecaughretanego, 175
Teedyuskung, 110, 129-130
Ten-Mile Lick, 89
Tennyson, Alfred Lord, 22
Ten-see-daa-qua (Bill Soc), 272

Terwinney, 7-9, 567
Test Act, 2
Thomas, Gen. John, 360
Thompson, Anthony, 39
Thompson, James, 289
Thompson, Col. William, of South Carolina, 370-374
Thompson, Gen. William, of Carlisle, 145, 323, 352, 358-362, 389, 440, 529, 607
Thompson, William (a local at Bedford), 284
Thorn, John, 58
Thorn, Mrs. John, 58
Thorn, Martha, 101
Three Rivers, battle of, 454, 502, 585, 608
Thunder, 379
Tiadaghton, 254
Tiadaghton Elm, 254
Ticonderoga, 135, 603
Tilghman, James, 294, 301
Tinian, 586
Tioga, 453, 454, 502
Tohogases, 88
Tomahawk Camp, 589
Ton-qu-as (Christley), 272
Tonoloway Creek, 49
Towamanzen, 425
Townshend Acts, 281
Trappe, 412, 419
Treasury Board, 461, 477
Treaty of Paris, 487, 495
Tredyffrin, 411
Trent, William, 57
Trenton, 388, 390-391
Trenton, battle of, 345, 392, 396-397, 414, 533, 612
Trenton Falls, 392
Tschochpiade, 569
Tuffts, Captain, 374
Tulpehocken, 270

~ Index ~ 647

Turkey Foot Forks, 35, 38-40
Turner, James, 8, 523
Turner, Corporal John, 70-71, 74
Turner, Joseph, 41
Turtle Creek, 40, 191-192, 244
Tuscarora Creek, 226, 241, 317, 594
Tuscarora Mountains, 15, 112, 149
Tuscarora Path, 226
Tuscarora Valley, 52, 60, 68, 101
Tussey Mountain, 48
Two Licks (Salt Springs), 87
Two Lick Creek, 87
Tyrone, Pa., 445
Tyunayate, 16

Ulster, 2, 3, 7, 9-10, 22, 385
Union Jack, 158, 194
Uniontown, 31

Valley Forge, 391, 402, 416, 435-449, 526
Valley Hill, 438
Valley of Virginia, 23
Valley Run, 404
Vandeering's Mill, 416
Van Hamback, Ensign Frederick, 225
Varnum, Gen. James, 398
Venango, 86, 151, 595(see Fort Venango)
Venango Trail, 595
Vetri, Monsieur, 182, 190
"Victory Tract," 343, 580
Villiers, Joseph, 69
Villiers, Louis (Francois), de, 63, 69
Vinord Creek, 226

Wabash River, 484, 533
Waddell, Major Hugh, 183

Wales, 2
Walker, Peter, 73
Walking Purchase, 26, 128-129
Walpole, Horace, 390
Ward, Gen. Artemus, 359
Ward, Lt. Edward, 64, 66, 74, 80, 84, 145
Warm Springs, 320, 322, 346, 464
Warner, Joseph, 416
War of the Austrian Succession (King George's War), 135
Warren Springs, 570
Washington, Gen. George, 31-32, 40, 48, 52, 69, 97, 123, on Forbes Expedition, 133, 139, 141, 143, 147-148, 152-155, 161-163, 176, 179, 186-195, 201-202; 231, 239, land speculating, 318-324; 325, 352-354, 358-362, 365, 383, 387-398, 400-402, at Brandywine, 405-409; at Germantown, 411-423; at Whitemarsh, 425-434; at Valley Forge, 435-450; 453-456, 459-460, correspondence with Armstrong, 462-477; resigns command, 479; elected President, 480; attitude toward Indians and Indian wars, 481-488; Whiskey Rebellion (Washington in Carlisle), 523-528
Washington, John Augustine, 176
Washington, Martha, 322, 604
Washington, William Augustine, 527
Water Street, Kittanning, 537, 540
Water Street, Pa., 445
Watson, John, 60
Wayne, Gen. Anthony, 398, 406-

409, at Paoli and Germantown, 411-423; 426, 427, 436, 439-440, at Stony Point, 465-466; Fallen Timbers, 485; 533
Weedon, Gen. George, 406, 416
Weiser, Conrad, 26, 56, 59, 83, 85, 118, 127, 184
West Branch (of the Susquehanna), 15, 46, 48, 77, 86, 125, 151, 248, 253-255, 257, 292, 340, 404, 451
West Chester, 404
West College ("Old West"), 518
West, F., 317
West Indies, 134, 242, 323, 605
West Lebanon, 89
Westmoreland County, 527, 533
Weston, John, 446
Weston, John's brother, 446
West Point, 463, 464, 475
Wetterholt, Capt. John, 179, 223
Wharton, Samuel, 282
Wharton, Thomas, Jr., 303, 395, 401-403, 419, 428, 444
Whitemarsh, and battle of, 425, 426, 428, 433, 435, 441, 522
Wheeler, Richard, 380
Whiskey Rebellion, 524-529
White Clay Creek, 11
White Eyes, 229
Whitefield, Rev. George, 333
Whitehill, Robert, 354
White Horse, 328, 412
White Horse Alley, 328
White Marsh Road, 416
White Mingo (John Cook), 287-288
White Plains, 388, 406
White, William, 241, 317
Wilkins, Col. John, 307-308
William and Mary College, 527

Williamsburg, Pa., 48
Williamsburg, Va., 527
Williamson family, 258
Williamson, Peter, 101-102
Williamsport, Md., 18, 226, 528
Willing, Nancy, 592
Willing, Thomas, 274
Will's (Wills, Wills')Creek, 33, 35, 38
Wilmington, Del., 402, 404-405, 435, 436, 448
Wilmington, N. C., 363, 387
Wilson, James, 200, 353, 354, 355, 459, 487, 490, 495-497
Wilson, Thomas, 234, 334
Winchester, Va., 123, 124, 146, 147, 343
Windsor, Ct., 29
Wing, Conway, 330, 335
Wissahickon Creek, 416, 419
Witherow, B. J., 5
Witherspoon, Major James, 420
Witherspoon, Rev. John, 514, 619
Woak-hanne (Crooked Stream), 88
Wolcott, Gov. Roger, 28-29
Wolf, at Edge Hill, 246
Wolf (Ojibway) (see Strong Wolf)
Wolfe, Gen. James, 135, 220, 223
Wolfsburg, 155
Wood, George, 445
Woodford, Gen. William, 408
Woods, George, 72
Woodstock, Va., 375
Worcester, 425
Wordsworth, William, 22
Work, Col. Patrick, 128, 145
Wright, John, 12
Wright, Thomas, 267
Wyalusing, 454
Wyandot Indians, 173, 232, 244
Wynkoop, Judge Henry, 459, 461
Wyoming, 28, 44, 120, 129-130,

228, 257, 272, 340, 451-456,
502, 600

Yale, Bill, 535
Yale College, 527
Yeager, Rev. J. M., 538
Yellow Breeches, 18, 24
Yellow Creek, 48
York, 87, 75, 145, 146, 207, 208,
    216, 255, 340, 390, 396, 416,
    444, 448, 522
York County, 9, 12, 21, 22, 37,
    75, 146, 213, 238, 261, 398,
    446, 522
Yorktown, 478
Youghiogheny River, 33-39, 319
Young Jacob, 100
Young, James, 60-61, 117
Youngstown, Pa., 155
Young, William, 317

Zeisberger, Rev. David, 275

ABOUT THE AUTHOR

William W. ("Bill") Betts is Professor Emeritus of English, Indiana University of Pennsylvania. Among his books are *Lincoln and the Poets*, *The Evergreen Farm*, *Slips That Pass in the Night*, *Bombardier John Harris and the Rivers of the Revolution*, and *The Hatchet and the Plow: The Life and Times of Chief Cornplanter*. With his wife Jane, he is at home in Indiana, Pennsylvania; Nobel, Ontario; and Boynton Beach, Florida.

www.ingramcontent.com/pod-product-compliance
Lightning Source LLC
Chambersburg PA
CBHW071214290426
44108CB00013B/1181